The Constitution and Finance of English, Scottish and Irish Joint-Stock Companies to 1720

(Volume II)
Companies for foreign Trade,
Colonization, Fishing and Mining

William Robert Scott

Alpha Editions

This edition published in 2019

ISBN : 9789354001208

Design and Setting By
Alpha Editions
email - alphaedis@gmail.com

As per information held with us this book is in Public Domain.
This book is a reproduction of an important historical work. Alpha Editions uses the best technology to reproduce historical work in the same manner it was first published to preserve its original nature. Any marks or number seen are left intentionally to preserve its true form.

THE CONSTITUTION AND FINANCE OF ENGLISH, SCOTTISH AND IRISH JOINT-STOCK COMPANIES TO 1720

BY

WILLIAM ROBERT SCOTT, M.A., D.Phil., Litt.D.

LECTURER IN POLITICAL ECONOMY IN THE UNIVERSITY OF ST ANDREWS

VOLUME II

COMPANIES FOR FOREIGN TRADE, COLONIZATION, FISHING AND MINING

Cambridge :
at the University Press
1910

PREFACE.

THROUGH technical reasons, connected with the printing of this book, the second volume, with which Part II. begins, is the first to be issued. The first volume, containing Part I., will record the general development of the joint-stock system in Great Britain and Ireland up to 1720, at the same time bringing it into relation with the chief social, political, industrial and commercial tendencies which influenced it. In this way, it is to be hoped that an account of many uses of capital after the close of the Middle Ages will be provided; and in addition the process will be shown, not merely from the purely commercial standpoint, but in close connection with the methods of finance and the conditions governing accumulation at this period. But, in order to base enquiries such as these on a firm foundation, it is necessary to ascertain the mode of internal organization and financial administration of the companies. This is a fruitful field of enquiry which has been strangely neglected. Though much has been written on the history of early British companies, the subject has, as a rule, been treated rather from the point of view of ulterior results than in relation to the system itself, which made those results possible. Foreign trade led to foreign possessions and the foundation of colonies, and what might be termed the external aspect of this movement has already been ably described by many competent writers. But, in almost all these works, the mechanism, by which the resources required were provided and controlled, is dealt with only incidentally; and yet a very little consideration will show that a knowledge of this side of the movement is essential to a complete understanding of it. Besides, there were many companies, which for various reasons have as yet been little noticed and whose influence in several ways has been of great importance.

Therefore to obtain data for the comparative treatment of the system in Part I., it has been necessary to make an attempt to secure exact particulars of the constitution and finance of the joint-stock companies in existence before 1720, and so many points of difficulty must be treated critically that it seemed best in Part II. to record the progress of each company from these points of view. The discovery of a number of minute-books and official documents has made it possible in a considerable number of cases to reach conclusions as precise as those obtainable about a modern company in the *Official Intelligence* or the *Stock Exchange Year-Book*. The lapse of time has precluded the securing of such valuable information concerning some undertakings, but as a rule facts can be ascertained which at least suggest certain inferences as to the origin and development of these undertakings. Data of this kind, whether complete or partially so, are only of real value when placed in their true perspective. The conditions, affecting the growth of companies in the sixteenth and seventeenth centuries, were very different from those influencing bodies of a similar kind at the present time, and it appeared desirable to elucidate quantitative statements by a reference to the causes to which they were due. And those causes were mainly of two kinds. Some were peculiar to special trades or industries, and it was most convenient to deal with these in Part II., where the companies are treated one by one: others again had a general influence, affecting most of the bodies in existence at any given time, and hence events of this character have been investigated in Part I. By this method much repetition has been avoided and the whole work will be found to be a unity.

The present volume treats of several groups of companies, all of which were related, comprising those formed for foreign trade, colonizing and kindred objects, fishing and the extractive industries. In the next volume the water supply, postal, street-lighting, manufacturing, banking, finance and insurance companies will be similarly described.

While the work has been in progress, I have discussed points of difficulty with those who have made investigations in some special direction which was connected with my own enquiries, and it gives me much pleasure to acknowledge the help I have received, either in the alacrity with which information was given me or in the reading of the proofs. Necessarily, however, I am altogether responsible for the result as printed. I have endeavoured to indicate at various points the nature of my indebtedness to Mr J. S. Barbour, Mr W. Foster, Sir W. S. Prideaux and Mr W. Ware, but there is one to whom I owe much of a more general character, namely, Dr Cunningham of Trinity College, Cambridge, in the form of conversations upon matters of principle and the meaning of wide tendencies. I also beg to thank the Secretary of State for India in Council, the Syndics of the University Press, Cambridge, the University Court of the University of St Andrews and the Carnegie Trust for the Universities of Scotland for providing for the publication of the whole book. I have also to acknowledge the courtesy of the proprietors of the *American Historical Review* and the *Vierteljahrschrift für Social- und Wirtschaftsgeschichte* in permitting me to reprint articles which appeared in these publications. These portions have been revised and extended.

W. R. S.

The University,
 St Andrews,
  April, 1910.

CONTENTS OF VOLUME II.

	PAGE
PREFACE	v

PART II. THE CONSTITUTIONAL AND FINANCIAL HISTORY OF EACH OF THE CHIEF JOINT-STOCK COMPANIES FROM 1553 TO 1720, WITH RECORDS OF THE HIGHEST AND LOWEST PRICES OF THEIR STOCKS OR SHARES, THE AMOUNT OF CAPITAL AND THE DIVIDENDS PAID.

DIVISION I. JOINT-STOCK COMPANIES FORMED FOR FOREIGN TRADE.

SECTION I. The Trade to Africa.

    A. The Company of Merchants Adventurers for Guinie (1553–67), the Adventurers in Hawkins' Voyages (1562–7) . . . 3

    B. The Senegal Adventurers (1588) 10

    C. The Governor and Company of Adventurers of London trading to Gynney and Bynney (1618) 11

    D. The Company of Merchants trading to Guinea (1630) . . 14

    E. The Governor and Company of the Royal Adventurers of England trading into Africa (1662–72) 17

    F. The Royal African Company of England (1672) 20

SECTION II. The Trade to Russia.—The Fellowship of English Merchants for Discovery of New Trades.

    A. From 1553 to 1586 36

    B. From 1586 to 1606 48

    C. From 1607–8 to 1620 52

    D. Arrangements for paying the debts of the Company from 1620 to 1628 57

    E. The Russian Trade from 1620 to the end of the last joint-stock undertaking 65

    F. The Greenland Trade from 1620 to 1673 69

SECTION III. The Adventurers to the North-West for the Discovery of a North-West Passage (1576–83) 76

SECTION IV. The Levant Company (1581–1600) 83

Contents

	PAGE
SECTION V. The East India Trade.	
A. The Governor and Company of Merchants of London trading into the East Indies from 1599 to 1657	89
B. The New General Stock from 1657 to 1709	128
C. The English Company trading to the East Indies (1698–1709)	179
D. The United Company of Merchants of England trading to the East Indies	189
E. The Company of Scotland trading to Africa and the Indies (1695–1707)	207
SECTION VI. The Governor and Company of Adventurers of England trading into Hudson's Bay (1670)	228

DIVISION II. COMPANIES FOR PLANTING (OR COLONIZATION) AND SIMILAR OBJECTS.

SECTION I. Expeditions to found plantations in the sixteenth century by Gilbert, Carlile, Raleigh and others	241
SECTION II. The Treasurer and Company of Adventurers and Planters of the City of London for the First Colony in Virginia and the Governor and Company of the City of London for the Plantation of the Somers Islands.	
A. The First Virginia Company to 1618	246
B. The Somers Islands Company to 1618	259
C. The Virginia and Somers Islands Companies from 1618 to 1625	266
D. The Somers Islands Company from 1625 to 1684	289
SECTION III. The Colonization of the Northern Portion of the Mainland of America.	
A. The Second Virginia Colony (1606–20)	299
B. The Council, established at Plymouth in the county of Devon, for the planting, ruling, ordering and governing of New England in America (1620–35)	301
C. (i) The Adventurers to New Plymouth in New England (1620–6)	306
C. (ii) The Governor and Company of the Massachusetts Bay in America (1628–9)	312
C. (iii) The Company of Adventurers for Laconia (1629)	315
SECTION IV. Attempts to colonize Newfoundland, Nova Scotia and Canada—the Newfoundland Company (1610), the New Scotland Company (1621–32), the Adventurers to Canada (1627–33)	317
SECTION V. Colonization in South America, Central America and the West Indies.	
A. The Governor and Company of Noblemen and Gentlemen of England for the Planting of Guiana (1619)	323
B. The Governor and Company of Adventurers for the Plantation of the Islands of Providence, Henrietta and the adjacent Islands (1629–41)	327

Contents

	PAGE
SECTION VI. Planting in Ireland.	
A. The Society of the Governor and Assistants of London, of the New Plantation in Ulster within the Realm of Ireland (founded in 1609)	338
B. The Adventurers for Lands in Ireland	343
SECTION VII. The Reclamation of Land in England by Drainage.	
A. The Governor, Bailiffs and Comminalty of the Society of Conservators of the Fens in the Counties of Cambridge, Huntingdon, Northampton, Lincoln, Norfolk and Suffolk and the Isle of Ely (1631)	352
B. Other Drainage undertakings in the time of Charles I.	356

DIVISION III. COMPANIES FOR THE DEVELOPMENT OF THE FISHING TRADE.

SECTION I. The Society of the Fishery of Great Britain and Ireland (1632–40)	361
SECTION II. The Companies subsidiary to the Society of the Fishery of Great Britain and Ireland—the Associations of William Noy, Lord Portland and Lord Pembroke	369
SECTION III. The Governor and Company of the Royal Fishery of Great Britain and Ireland (1661)	372
SECTION IV. The Royal Company for the Fishery in Scotland (1670–90)	377
SECTION V. The Company of Merchants of London trading into Greenland (1692)	379

DIVISION IV. COMPANIES ENGAGED IN THE EXTRACTIVE INDUSTRIES.

SECTION I. The Governors, Assistants and Society of the Mines Royal (1561)	383
SECTION II. The Mines Royal of Scotland and Ireland—partnerships for gold mining, founded by Höchstetter (1526), De Vois (1567), Peterson (1576), Roche (1583), Atkinson (after 1600) and the Marquis of Hamilton (1631): partnerships for silver mining, founded by Acheson (1563), Carmichaell (1565), Thomas Foullis (1592), Sir George Hamilton (1612) and Sir W. Alexander (1613)	406
SECTION III. The Governors, Assistants and Society of the Mineral and Battery Works (1565)	413
SECTION IV. The Governor and Company of Copper Miners in England (1691)	430
SECTION V. Other Copper Mining Companies founded from 1692 to 1694—Dockwra's Copper Company (1692), Cornish Copper Company (about 1694), Cumberland and Carolina Royal Mines (about 1694), Derby Copper Company (about 1694), the Governor and Company of the Copper Mines in the Principality of Wales (1694)	436

x   *Contents*

	PAGE
SECTION VI. Lead Mining and Lead Smelting Companies (1692-4) . .	440
SECTION VII. The Governor and Company of the Mine Adventurers of England (1698)	443
SECTION VIII. Companies for Coal mining—partnerships for pits at Lumley (1606-7) and at Bedworth (1622), Coal and Iron Company in the Forest of Dean (1653), Old and New Blythe Companies (about 1694), the Plessey Company (about 1695), the Durham Coal and Salt Company (about 1696) .	459
SECTION IX. Companies for the Smelting of Iron—a partnership (temp. Edward VI.), the Company for smelting under the Patents of Sturtevant and Rovenzon (1612-13), Anstell's Smelting partnership (1627), Dudley Dudley's partnerships (1638 and 1651), an Iron Company near Belfast (1681), the Governor and Company for making Iron with Pit-coal (1693).	463
SECTION X. Companies for the Supply of Salt—the Governor and Commonalty of the Society of Salt-makers at the North and South Shields in the Counties of Northumberland and Durham (1635), the Corporation of Salters in the Salt-works near Great Yarmouth (1639), the Droitwich Salt Works Company (1689), the Rock-salt Company (before 1694). . .	468
SECTION XI. Saltpetre Companies—the Undertakers of the Royal Monopoly for Saltpetre (temp. Charles I.), Sir John Brooke's partnership (1627), Col. Ogle's partnership (1656), the Governor and Company for making Saltpetre in England (1692), Companies formed by Thomas Lechmere (1692) and Henry Longueville (1692)	471
SECTION XII. Companies formed to work Alum and other Mines . .	475

DIVISION V. COMPANIES OWNING OR WORKING PUMPS AND MACHINERY FOR DRAINING MINES AND LANDS AND FOR RECOVERING TREASURE FROM WRECKS.

SECTION I. Companies for pumping and other engines—Mr John Loftingh and Company, proprietors of the Sucking-worm Engine (1689), the Company for Captain Poyntz' Engines (1693), the Company for Tyzach's Night Engine.	479
SECTION II. Companies for the Recovery of Treasure from Wrecks—the Adventurers in the expeditions of William Phipps (1687-8), Companies owning the Diving-Engines, invented by John Williams (1691), Joseph Williams (1691) and John Tyzack (1691), the Governor and Company for recovering Wrecks in England (1691), the Company owning the Diving-Engine, invented by John Overing (1692), the Companies for recovering Treasure from Wrecks off Broadhaven (1691), off Bermuda (1692), and in other places (1692), Houblon and Company (1702)	484
INDEX.	491

MAP.

"A Mapp of the Sommer Islands," engraved by Abraham Goos [? 1622-6], showing the land-dividends made to the Shareholders . . . *between* x—1

A Map of the Somers Islands, showin

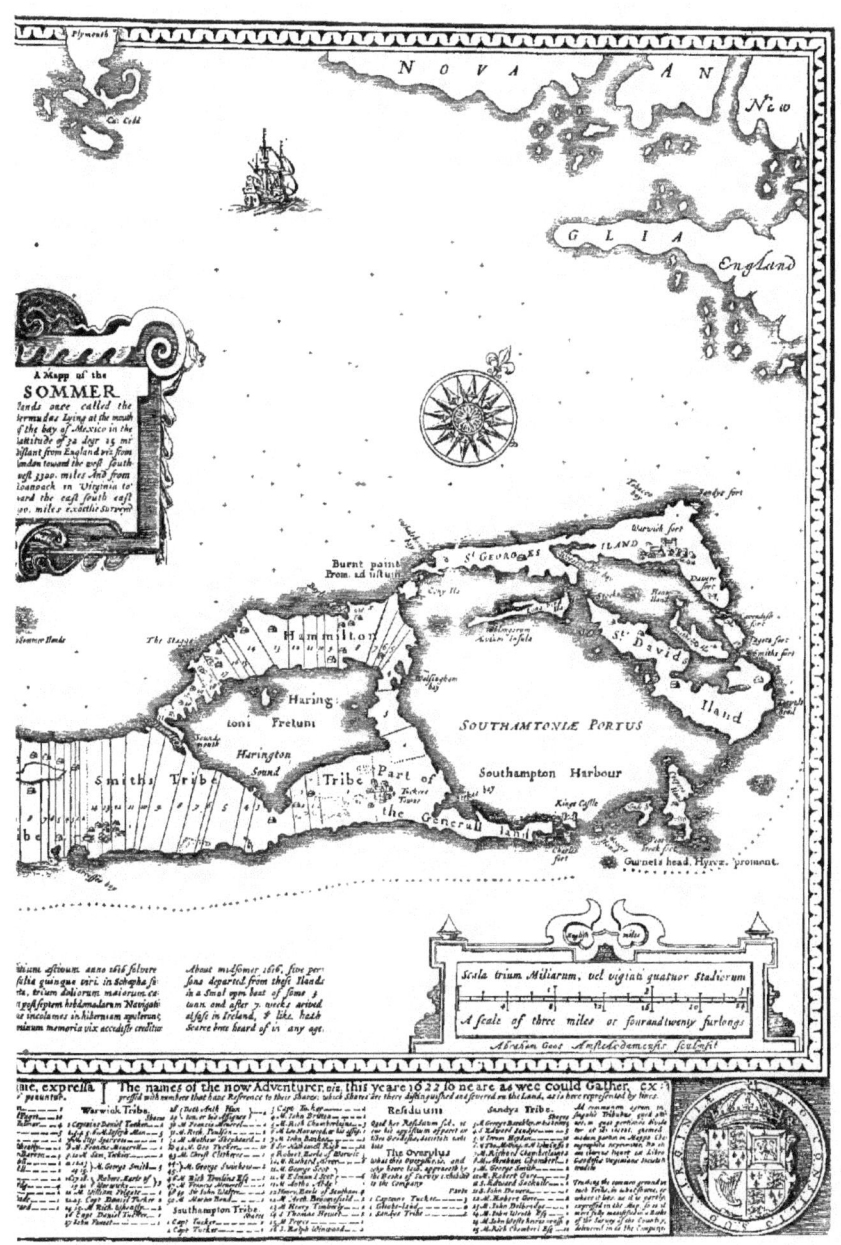

the land divisions to the Shareholders.

PART II.

DIVISION I.
COMPANIES FORMED FOR FOREIGN TRADE.

SECTION I. THE TRADE TO AFRICA.

A. THE COMPANY OF MERCHANTS ADVENTURERS FOR GUINIE, OR THE MERCHANT ADVENTURERS TO THE COASTS OF AFRICA AND ETHIOPIA (1553—1567).

THE ADVENTURERS IN HAWKINS' VOYAGES (1562—1567).

In a communication of the Sieur de Guerchy to the Duc de Praslin, dated February 24th, 1767, the origin of the African company is traced back to 1536[1]. The allusion seems to be to three voyages undertaken by William Hawkins, father of Sir John Hawkins, to Africa and Brazil. William Hawkins armed and fitted out a ship of his own of 250 tons, traded with the natives on the coast of Guinea and sailed thence to Brazil. Ivory and other commodities were obtained and it is expressly recorded that the adventurers were fortunate in obtaining the good-will of the natives. There is no information to show whether these expeditions were at the sole charge of William Hawkins or whether, although he owned the ship, others entered into partnership with him (according to a system to be explained below) for the freight and other expenses[2]. In 1540 divers wealthy merchants of Southampton were engaged in the African trade and this expedition may be taken as the first syndicate or company for this venture[3].

It was not until 1553—the year of the expedition which led to the foundation of the Russia company—that fresh expeditions were made to Africa. There is no doubt that the outlay in this case was borne by a number of adventurers of the city of London acting in partnership. It is interesting to notice that what might be described as the official account of the expedition describes it in almost identical terms to those chosen for the first title of the Russia company, and that, although the

---

[1] *Les Grandes Compagnies de Commerce*, par Pierre Bonnassieux, Paris, 1892, p. 96.

[2] Anderson states that the voyage of 1536 returned 100 lbs. weight of gold, besides ivory and other commodities, *Annals of Commerce*, II. p. 82.

[3] *The Hawkins' Voyages* (Hakluyt Society, 1878), pp. 3, 4.

founders considered they had a right to certain privileges on the ground of discovery, they did not claim a monopoly either of trade or territory. The voyages are recorded as "worthie attempts, so much the greatlier to bee esteemed, as before never enterprised by Englishmen, or at the least so frequented, as at this present they are, and may bee, to the great commoditie of our merchants, if the same be not hindered by the ambition of such, as for the conquering of fortie or fiftie miles here and there, and erecting of certain fortresses, think to be Lordes of halfe the world, envying that other should enjoy the commodities, which they themselves cannot wholly possess. And although such as have been at charges in the discovering and conquering of such landes ought by goode reason to have certain privileges, preheminences, and tributes for the same, yet (to speake under correction) it may seeme somewhat rigorous, and agaynst good reason and conscience, or rather agaynst the charitie that ought to be among Christian men, that such as invade the dominions of other should not permit other friendly to use the trade of merchandise in places nearer, or seldome frequented of them, whereby their trade is not hindered in such places, where they themselves have at their owne election appointed the martes of their traffike[1]."

The expedition consisted of two ships (one of which was the *Primrose*) and a pinnace. Even although there was much difference of opinion amongst the captains as to what commodities should be purchased in addition to gold, it is recorded that the vessels secured 150 lbs. weight of gold and some pepper comparatively early in the voyage[2] and the whole cargoes amounted to more than 400 lbs. of gold, 36 butts of "graines" (*i.e.* chillis) and about 250 elephants' tusks[3]. Obviously such a return, even after payment of wages, left a profit which would be remarkable, especially when it is remembered that the capital would be expressed in a debased currency, whereas the gold obtained was fine. There are no data to make any exact calculation but it may well have been that the profit was some ten times the capital risked. It is almost certain that, judging by analogy, the dividend consisted of a return both of capital and interest, so that, on the completion of the accounts, the stock was wound up and a fresh capital raised for the second voyage which started in 1554.

The expedition of 1554 was equipped by five chief partners whose names are mentioned[4]. It is most note-worthy through the sailors bringing back five natives. Although these are called "slaves," the expeditions of this period did not engage in the slave-trade, being direct

---

[1] *The Principal Navigations, Voyages, Traffiques and Discoveries of the English Nation*, by Richard Hakluyt. Glasgow, 1904, vi. p. 141.

[2] *Ibid.*, pp. 148, 151.   [3] *Ibid.*, p. 163.

[4] *Ibid.*, p. 154.

voyages from and to England. In fact it was the policy of the captains to "use the people gently," partly to induce them to trade and partly to secure early information of the movements of Portuguese ships, since the latter were generally in great strength and the presence of the English was resented by their commanders[1].

In 1555, 1556, 1557 there were three expeditions sent to the African coast. There are no complete details of the cargoes brought home, but since there is frequent mention of large quantities of gold dust being obtained and since the basis of exchange was most favourable to the adventurers—a copper or brass basin was valued at gold worth £30—it may be concluded that these voyages continued to be highly lucrative[2].

It is not certain, although probable, that it was the same group of adventurers which was responsible for the whole series of expeditions. Through the large profits made the original adventurers would have ample funds at their disposal to continue in the trade and naturally would have desired to do so. At the same time they had no monopoly, and the great gains made could scarcely be concealed. It is probably for this reason that in 1561, if not earlier, Queen Elizabeth was taken into partnership. There are exceptionally full details of the voyage of that year. Several of the original adventurers were again interested and the venture was financed in the following manner. Elizabeth provided four ships (one of which was the *Primrose*) and undertook to spend £500 in provisioning them. The other persons interested supplied trade-goods to the value of £5,000 and the profit was divisible into three parts, one of which was to be paid to the Queen and the other two to the merchants[3]. The simplest method of stating the capitalisation of this venture is to regard the £5,000 invested in commodities as the whole capital. Out of the gross profit the adventurers were to pay the sailors' wages and all other expenses, and also, from the balance, the proportion due to the Queen for the hire of the ships. The remainder would then constitute the sum available to repay the capital and to afford profit thereon.

This voyage was not so fortunate as some of the former ones. Soon after leaving England the ships were scattered, some do not appear to have reached Africa, and the Portuguese had notice of the arrival of the others, so that trade was carried on under very great difficulties[4]. Still there was a considerable sum available to divide. The exact amount depends upon the determination of how the Queen's share was dealt with. The agreement between the parties is recorded with more detail

---

[1] Hakluyt, *Voyages, ut supra*, VI. pp. 173, 176.
[2] *Ibid.*, pp. 177–252.   [3] State Papers, Dom., Eliz. XXVI. 45.
[4] Hakluyt, *Voyages, ut supra*, VI. pp. 255–7.

in the case of the next expedition, when the amount paid by Elizabeth for provisioning is to be taken into account " by defalcation out of her third part" of the profits[1]. Therefore, if the same arrangement was made in 1561, the actual payment made to Elizabeth would be less by £500 than one-third of the profits. She received £1,000[2], so that the share of the adventurers was £3,000 on this basis or 60 per cent., and the whole nett returns would be £9,500 as may be seen from the following statement.

	£	£
Return of moneys advanced by Adventurers		5,000
One-third profit (a) including victualling	500	
(b) paid in cash	1,000	1,500
Two-thirds profit for adventurers		3,000
Total returns after paying wages		9,500

If on the other hand Elizabeth's share was not "defalced" the whole returns (nett) would have been £8,000 and the portion of the adventurers 40 per cent. on their outlay. On the former basis there would have been a clear return of £1,000 for the charter of the ships, on the latter, one of £500.

Towards the close of the year 1562 similar arrangements were made for a fresh expedition. The bargain between Elizabeth and the adventurers took the form of an indenture and charter-party under the great seal. In this document it is stated that, her Majesty minding the increase of the wealth and profits of her merchants and subjects and the conservation of the navy and marines of the realm, chartered the *Primrose* and *Minion* to the adventurers to trade to Africa and Ethiopia in any part where the King of Portugal "hath not presentlie dominion, obedience and tribute." The Queen undertook to spend £250 in fitting out the ships and to send gunners, pilots and sailors[3]. The adventurers agreed to find suitable goods to the value of £5,000 as before, and the profits were divisible in the same ratio. The adventurers were bound under security of £1,000 each to furnish the goods and also to pay for any further provisions needed as well as the services of the sailors. Thus, had the expedition proved a failure, there would have been a considerable liability. Further, an audit on behalf of the Queen was provided for, and she forbad any private trade by the members of the expedition[4]. When Elizabeth herself was interested in the venture,

[1] State Papers, Dom., Eliz. xxvi. 44; *Cal.* 1547–80.
[2] *Ibid.*
[3] In the indenture this sum is stated at £500, but in State Papers, Dom., Eliz. xxvi. 45 the amount is reduced to £250, on the ground that there are on this occasion only two ships instead of four.
[4] *Ibid.*, xxvi. 43.

it is not surprising that the Portuguese ambassador did not succeed in obtaining the prohibition of the trading by Englishmen on the Guinea coast for which he asked in June 1562[1].

The ships started in February 1563, but the Portuguese had notice of their arrival on the African coast and the voyage resolved itself into a running fight between the English vessels and some galleys sent to prevent them from trading. In spite of the *Minion* being damaged by a cannon-shot the ships reached home safely on August 6th, bringing with them 166 tusks weighing 1,758 lbs. and 22 butts of "graines." No mention is made of gold, and it would appear that while the native merchants were bringing it to the coast, the Portuguese galleys drove off the English boats[2].

In 1564 some very interesting particulars of a meeting of the adventurers are extant. The expedition was to consist of three ships—the *Minion* belonging to the Queen, the *John Baptist* of London and the *Merlin* of Bristol. At a meeting held on July 11th, 1564, it was agreed to call up 50 per cent. of the sums adventured on account of trade-goods and £29. 10s. 6d. per cent. for the rigging and victualling of the *John Baptist*. The owners of the other vessels would supply this part of the equipment at their own expense. It was also resolved that each of "the chief adventurers" should communicate this call to his partners[3]—a statement showing that, although five members made the arrangements, each had shareholders, as it was later described, "under him." The reason of this method of working was partly legal and partly financial. The adventurers were not a corporation and therefore all contracts were made in their names personally. Besides, each was liable under a penalty of £1,000 for the due performance of the agreement with the Queen and this liability could not have been easily transferred with a sale of shares. To avoid these difficulties, each of the chief adventurers remained nominally responsible for one-fifth of the adventure and was entitled to a two-fifteenth share of the profit, but in reality part of the capital to be provided was supplied by others who again shared rateably.

It is unlikely that this voyage yielded any considerable profit since the *Merlin* had been sunk through an accidental powder explosion[4]; and, when Hawkins last heard of the remaining ships, they had been prevented from trading by the Portuguese, and there were grave doubts whether they could make the voyage home through want of supplies[5]. Fortunately there seems reason to believe that the outcome was less

---

[1] *A Collection of State Papers*, 1571–96, edited by William Murdin, London, 1759, p. 753.
[2] Hakluyt, *Voyages, ut supra*, VI. pp. 260, 261.
[3] *Ibid.*, p. 262.
[4] *Ibid.*, p. 264.
[5] *Ibid.*, p. 265.

unsatisfactory, since there is reference to ships named the *John Baptist* and *Minion* at subsequent dates[1].

Whether this expedition was a comparative or total failure there were other reasons which made it necessary for the English adventurers to withdraw for a time from the trade. The Portuguese had been first on the African coast and they had already established forts and kept armed ships to warn off intruders. Therefore the English traders were forced to fight their way or to avoid the enemy if he was in great force. In such circumstances trade could only be carried on with the good-will of the natives. For a number of years the English and French had treated the people with more consideration than that shown them by the Portuguese. The London Adventurers had not engaged in the slave-trade and it was to this that much of the financial success of the earlier expeditions was due. All this was changed when in 1562 John Hawkins seized 300 negroes and sold them in the West Indies. The effect of these slave-raiding voyages soon became marked. The ships of the London Adventurers were less favourably received, trade was more difficult and information of the movements of the Portuguese galleys was not so easily obtained. All these disadvantageous elements may be clearly noted in the account of the expedition of 1566, which is the last mentioned for a considerable period[2].

The expeditions of Hawkins, though usually described by his name were in reality joint-stock ventures managed in the manner already detailed. Hakluyt mentions five persons, who with others not named, provided the capital for the voyage which started in 1562. The only one of these who can be connected with the co-existent Adventurers to Africa was Sir Thomas Lodge, a governor of the Russia company in 1561, and Lord Mayor the following year. The commencement of the English slave-trade was no after-thought but the original foundation of the venture, since Hawkins formulated his scheme on the basis of negroes being "very good merchandise in Hispaniola." During the cruise off the coast of Africa 300 natives were obtained "partly by the sword, partly by other means." Sales were made in the West Indies on such a profitable scale that Hawkins was able not only to fully load his three ships with hides, ginger and sugar, besides some pearls, but in addition he had to procure two other ships to carry the overplus. The auxiliary vessels were despatched to Spain and were detained there. Some idea of the profits may be gathered from the statement that

---

[1] State Papers, Dom., Eliz. XLIX. 40; cxx. 46; *Cal.* 1547–80, pp. 329, 577. Froude states that, while the *Minion* was sailing with Hawkins, the captain of the former was prepared to join in the "nigger hunt"—*History of England, Reign of Elizabeth*, II. p. 474. The evidence for this statement is not convincing.

[2] Hakluyt, *Voyages, ut supra*, VI. pp. 266–84.

the value of these boats with their cargoes was estimated at 40,000 ducats[1].

The success of the first voyage encouraged many noblemen to adventure in a second which started in 1564 and was described as being profitable to the adventurers besides bringing back "golde, silver, pearles and other jewels greate store[2]." A third expedition left England in 1567. Between 400 and 500 slaves were captured in Africa of which 200 were sold soon after the expedition arrived in the Spanish West Indies. Hawkins found the Spaniards unwilling to trade, and he was eventually attacked by a superior force and with difficulty succeeded in saving a remnant of his ships[3]. It is doubtful if this voyage paid its expenses.

The Hawkins' adventure is interesting from several points of view. It was the first recorded contact of Englishmen with a traffic which became of enormous social importance later. Politically its consequences were momentous. The Spaniards guarded jealously the trade to their Western possessions[4] and more especially the Royal monopoly of importing slaves. Therefore Hawkins' forcing the market open by seizing towns and destroying ships was another cause of complaint against England. Lastly in an indirect manner much light is thrown on the difficult question of the advantages and disadvantages of exclusive grants for foreign trade. At this time there was no monopoly of the African trade and, once Hawkins raided the coast, two sets of Englishmen were working by inconsistent methods. The original adventurers were traders simply, while Hawkins was mainly engaged in capturing slaves. Therefore the presence of the latter, by alarming the natives and destroying the confidence they had previously reposed in Englishmen, destroyed also the chances of the former, while the agents of the adventurers warned the negroes of the coming of Hawkins, and thereby made it more difficult for him to obtain slaves. Therefore from the financial point of view it might fairly have been urged that a monopoly to either kind of traffic would have been more advantageous, while the rival claims of each might have been weighed from the social or political standpoint.

[1] *The Hawkins' Voyages* (Hakluyt Soc., 1878), pp. 5–7.
[2] *Ibid.*, p. 64.   [3] *Ibid.*, pp. 72–81.
[4] *The Genesis of the United States, A Series of Historical Manuscripts now first printed*, edited by Alexander Brown, London, 1890, I. p. 101. The Conde de Lemos, President of the Council of the Indies, is reported to have said "that the Spaniards looked to their Indies with no less watchful eyes than to the government of their wives."

B. The Senegal Adventurers (Chartered 1588).

During a space of about twenty years no voyages to Africa are recorded by Hakluyt[1]. In the years 1567 and 1568 both the mercantile and slave-trading enterprises had been either partial or complete failures as compared with the results of earlier enterprises. Prior to 1588 a group of eight merchants of Exeter and London had sent ships to the district between the Senegal and the Gambia, and it was in all probability recognised that, for reasons such as those already suggested, the revived trade should be protected in some manner. Accordingly in 1588 Elizabeth signed a charter in favour of these adventurers, which set forth "that the adventuring and enterprising of a newe trade cannot be a matter of small charge and hazard to the adventurers in the beginning that...for the better incouragement [of the persons named] to proceede in their saide adventure and trade in the saide countreis shal have the sole use and exercise thereof for a certain time." Therefore a grant is made of the sole right to trade on the Senegal and Gambia and along the coast between them for ten years from the 3rd of May, 1588. This right is assigned not only to the eight persons named but to such other subjects as may be received into the company or society. There is no incorporation clause, but the partners were authorised to meet together and to make laws and orders governing the trade. Such ordinances were to be obeyed by all Englishmen provided they were not contrary to the laws of the realm. The ships and cargoes of any, not members of the company, used in trading within the chartered limits, were subject to forfeiture and the proceeds were to be allocated one-third to the Crown, one-third to the company and the remaining third to the relief of certain Portuguese who had given information to the merchants. Finally, all the privileges granted by the patent were subject to revocation on six months notice either by the Queen or any six members of the Privy Council[2]. There are no details as to the results achieved, but the success of the experiment was considered sufficient to justify the continuance of the monopoly which was now granted to the Earl of Nottingham and others with permission to re-export commodities imported into England from Africa[3].

It is to be remembered that this grant applied to only a small portion of the African coast and therefore English traders were free to resort to any place outside the specified limits. Thus there were two successful expeditions, organised by some London merchants to Benin in the years 1588 and 1590, and in 1592 the privilege of trading to certain places in Guinea was granted to Thomas Gregory of Taunton and other

---

[1] In 1582 a voyage by four ships to Africa and thence to St Thomas was proposed. State Papers, Dom., Eliz. cliv. 24; *Cal.* 1581–90, p. 59.

[2] Hakluyt, *Voyages, ut supra*, vi. pp. 443–50.

[3] State Papers, Dom., Eliz. cclxvi. 34; *Cal.* 1598–1601, p. 16.

merchants associated with him[1]. The commodities brought to Africa were linen and woollen goods, iron work, copper bracelets, glass beads and coral. These were exchanged for pepper, ivory, palm oil, and cotton. It is expressly mentioned that the traders saw neither gold nor silver[2].

Reviewing the African trade at the close of the sixteenth century, it is evident that English merchants suffered from our having no fortified harbours where ships could take refuge and refit in safety. The Portuguese had numerous stations of this kind, and therefore their ships were kept mobile and were able, in many cases, to interrupt the trade of foreigners. As early as 1561 it had been the intention of the Merchants Adventurers to Africa to erect one fort themselves, which could be easily garrisoned, and to induce a native chief to build another[3]. These instructions had been given to John Lok, one of the factors, but he refused to make the voyage. Owing to the unsettled condition of the trade, on the appearance of Hawkins, it is unlikely that any further steps were taken in this direction, indeed it was shown, later, that the first English fort on the African coast was established about 1615[4].

After the foundation of the East India company, the existence of an African company became more important than it had hitherto been. If the English had no foothold on the coast there would be obvious dangers to East-Indiamen on the homeward voyage, and it was for this reason that, during the middle of the sixteenth century, while the then existing African company was unable to hold the forts, the East India company re-built and garrisoned them.

C. THE GOVERNOR AND COMPANY OF ADVENTURERS OF LONDON TRADING TO GYNNEY AND BYNNEY, OR THE GYNNEY AND BYNNEY COMPANY, OR SIR WILLIAM ST JOHN AND CO. (INCORPORATED 1618).

The moving spirit in the formation of the next African company was Sir William St John, who was said to have erected a fort on the coast in 1615. Application was made to James I., and on November 16th, 1618, a charter was signed. The preamble of this instrument sets forth that "divers of our loving subjects have by their long travel and industry and at their great charges and expenses discovered and found out a trade into certain places in Africa." Accordingly some thirty persons named and any others they might assume into partnership, who "joined together and resolved to run one uniform course in the setting up and prosecuting a trade of merchandise" to Guinea and Benin were incorporated as the

[1] *Murdin's State Papers*, 1571–96, p. 799.
[2] Hakluyt, *Voyages, ut supra*, VI. p. 457.   [3] *Ibid.*, pp. 253, 254.
[4] State Papers, Colonial, XI. 15; *Cal. Col.* 1574–1660, p. 339.

Governor and Company of Adventurers of London trading to Gynney and Bynney with perpetual succession and a common seal. The Court was to consist of a governor, a deputy-governor and twelve directors, and the company was granted the exclusive right of trading to Guinea and Benin[1]. It may be noted that this charter differs from the Elizabethan one not only in the more explicit character of the incorporation, but in granting a monopoly of the whole then explored African coast which was south of the limits assigned to the Barbary company. As will be shown below this point was strongly urged in Parliament during the debates of 1624. Even though few voyages had been made by independent merchants to places outside the Senegal grant, much indignation was felt by many who had a more or less definite intention of sailing towards Benin, and it appears that some interlopers did actually trade to Africa with the result of attempted seizures by the company and consequent friction.

The company is reported to have started its career by establishing a factory on the River Gambia[2]. The ship sent to Africa in 1618, in which £1,856. 19s. 2d. was adventured, was lost. In the two following years expeditions were despatched at an outlay of close on £2,000 in each case. The voyage of 1619 only returned £80 from the hides brought back, but that of 1620 was less unfortunate, the returns amounting to £1,386. 12s. 3d., which only sufficed to pay the wages of the sailors. As yet the trade in negroes had not been regularly started and the chief imports of the company consisted of ivory, dyes, spices and hides. No gold had been obtained, and the pepper trade was less lucrative than it had been owing to the competition of the East India company. The following statement will exhibit the disastrous start made by this undertaking:

		£	s.	d.			£	s.	d.
1618	For carrying charges and the setting to sea of the ship *Katharine*	1,856	19	2	1619	The whole adventure lost, the ship being taken and the men slain	0	0	0
1619	For carrying charges and setting out another ship, the *St John*	1,988	6	0	1620	The return was hides which realised	80	0	0
1620	For another voyage in the *Lyon* and the *St John*	1,920	16	8	1621	The returns were hides, teeth, wax, etc.	1,386	12	3
„	Wages and freight at the return of the *Lyon* and *St John*	1,300	18	9		Balance loss to 1621	5,600	8	4
		£7,067	0	7			£7,067	0	7[3]

[1] State Papers, Patent Roll, 16 Jas. I., Pt 6, No. 10.

[2] State Papers, Colonial, xi. 15.

[3] State Papers, Domestic, Jas. I., cxxiv. 115, *Cal.* 1619-23, p. 330.

After 1621, owing partly to the crisis of that year, partly to the losses sustained, great difficulties were experienced in raising fresh capital, and, for the remainder of its existence, this company confined its energies to privateering, and to exacting licences from those traders who were prepared to risk a voyage to the African coast.

During the inquiry into the abuses of patents at this time, a petition to the House of Commons was drawn up by Nicholas Ferrar, whose brother, curiously enough, had been recently elected deputy-director of the tobacco monopoly which was in process of formation in 1622. Ferrar complains that the Guiny patent had been obtained on "untrue suggestions," that the persons interested were the first discoverers of the trade and that its continuance tended to raise the price of materials used by dyers to "a most extreme rate[1]." This petition was referred to the Committee of Grievances, which decided that the patent had been "surreptitiously gotten by false information" laid before the King by the promoters and that the trade had been open previously. This finding was partly true, partly erroneous, since, as shown above, the Senegal grant was in existence up to the date of this patent. The committee further reported that the company had seized and held the ships of interlopers until its agents had received compositions from them and that these operations had enhanced the prices of African commodities. It was resolved by the House that this patent was a grievance[2].

It would appear that in 1626 some steps were taken to revive the company, since there is mention in that year of the King holding shares[3]. In 1627 an African patent was deemed "inconvenient[4]," and in the same year a group of adventurers described as "Sir Thos. Bulton and Co." were engaged in the trade either in spite of the charter or under licence from the company[5]. In the following year Sir Nicholas Crisp, who was the founder of the succeeding company, was an interloper and defied the privileges of the existing undertaking[6]. About 1629, after the strife between the company and independent groups of adventurers had

---

[1] "Petition from the Commons to the King, May 1624, by Nicholas Ferrar"—Ferrar Papers, Magdalene Coll., Cambridge; "Severall Grievances concerning Trade presented to King James I., by Sir R. Heath, May 28, 1624." Harl. MS. No. 2, 244, f. 11; *Journals of the House of Commons*, I. p. 771. For an account of Ferrar's connection with the proposed tobacco-monopoly, *vide infra*, Pt II. Div. II. § 2 c.

[2] *Journals of the House of Commons*, I. p. 793.

[3] State Papers, Dom., Charles I., XXXVI. 79; Charles I., Appendix, Oct. 17, 1626, *Cal.* 1625-6, pp. 439, 576.

[4] *Ibid.*, Charles I., LXX. 45; *Cal.* 1627-8, p. 245.

[5] *Ibid.*, Charles I., LXX. 45; *Cal.* 1627-8, p. 297.

[6] *Ibid.*, CLIV. 42; *Cal.* 1629-31, p. 136.

continued for a number of years—the one endeavouring to enforce their privileges under the charter and the other relying on their "natural rights" as Englishmen and the support of the Commons—both parties found they had made serious losses and each withdrew from the trade what remained of the capital originally adventured[1].

D. THE COMPANY OF MERCHANTS TRADING TO GUINEA, OR SIR NICHOLAS CRISP AND COMPANY (FOUNDED 1630).

Sir Nicholas Crisp, who had broken down the monopoly of the previous company and had himself for a short time withdrawn from the African trade, decided to make a fresh venture in 1629. Accordingly he and several partners sent a ship of 300 tons to the Senegal which was surprised by a French man-of-war and captured in June of the same year. About April 1630 the partners presented a petition in which they alleged that this seizure had been made while they were exercising their accustomed trade and that their loss was £20,000. They asked either for indemnity from certain sequestered French goods or for letters of reprisals[2]. In view of these losses the merchants with certain other persons received a patent, dated June 25th, 1630, and a proclamation was issued in their favour on November 22nd of the following year[3]. These documents prescribe a trading monopoly over even wider limits than those assigned to St John's company. In this case no Englishmen might trade between Cape Blanco in 20° N. and the Cape of Good Hope about 34° S., nor in the adjacent islands. This privilege was granted for 31 years. Moreover none but the patentees might import into England any merchandise which had been produced in Africa. The object of this provision was to protect the company against the indirect importation of such commodities through European countries. In addition to these wide franchises, this undertaking obtained also the right to possess in fee-simple any territory it acquired, and a bombastic clause prohibited the subjects of any other country from entering the limits granted under this patent. The company was bound to bring into England at least £10,000 worth of gold.

By 1631—the year after the charter—the company was in debt and three decrees had been obtained against it in the Court of Wards[4]. It was alleged that this was due to many of the adventurers not having

[1] *Churchill's Voyages*, v. p. 665.
[2] State Papers, Domestic Correspondence, Charles I., CLV. 59.
[3] *Foedera*, XIX. p. 379; State Papers, Proclamations, Charles I., No. 144; *Cal. Domestic*, 1631–3, p. 186; Proclamations Soc. Antiq., Charles I., No. 155.
[4] State Papers, Dom., Charles I., DXL. 82.

paid the calls on their shares, and when a meeting was called, the greatest number and those most concerned failed to appear. The whole debt was returned at £945. 17s. 3d., against which there were outstanding calls or assessments of £78. 16s. 8d. per cent. due by fifteen persons on shares of £1,200, amounting to £946. The shares were of the denomination of £50 each, and ten defaulters only owned one share, three were liable for two each and two for four. It would appear that these calls could not be collected, since in 1635, by order of the Privy Council, a levy of £3 per ton on red-wood, and 4s. per cwt. on ivory was to be made in favour of the creditors; and, when this order was confirmed in 1636, it was estimated that the liabilities would be cleared off in three years[1]. If the company was sufficiently honest to pay its debts, these should have been discharged before the end of the year when a ship returned with gold valued at £30,000 on board[2].

This episode affords a striking instance of the great fluctuations in this trade and accounts for the fascination it possessed for capitalists. From 1631 to 1636 the company was practically bankrupt, yet, in the latter year, one fortunate voyage, as far as can be judged, cleared off the debt and left a surplus. But such results had one disadvantage, for the competition of interlopers began again. In 1637, John Crispe and his partners had fitted out a ship "to take nigers and carry them to foreign parts" which was arrested by order of the Privy Council on the petition of the company[3]. Again in the following year a similar arrest of interlopers was made[4].

For the next ten years there is little information as to the affairs of the company. The trade in negroes was now beginning with the development of the sugar-plantations in the English West Indies. During the Civil War the courtiers who had been included as patentees in the grant were replaced by other adventurers and the trade was carried on; but, owing to the impossibility of enforcing any legal penalty on interlopers, invasions of the patent became increasingly frequent and the Dutch and Danes preyed on the ships of the company and those of the independent traders off the African coast[5]. At the end of the year 1649 the company was called before the Council of State, and at the same time "Samuel Vassell and company"—a group of independent traders—were also summoned[6]. It was alleged that the patent had

[1] State Papers, Colonial, IX. 29; *Cal. Col.* 1574–1660, p. 241.
[2] *Ibid.*, Dom. cccxxxvi., 26,; *Cal. Dom.* 1636–7, p. 204.
[3] Colonial Papers, IX. 75; *Cal.* 1574–1660, pp. 259, 260.
[4] State Papers, Note Book, 1638, May; *Cal. Col.* 1574–1660, p. 273.
[5] *Certain Considerations relating to the Royal African Company of England* (1680), p. 3. State Papers, Domestic, Charles II., cccxiv. 80.
[6] State Papers, Interregnum Entry Book, xci. 373, 401; *Cal. Col.* 1574–1660, p. 331.

been obtained "by procurement of courtiers," but, on behalf of the company, it was urged that they were the first who had established factories, with the exception of one founded by St John's company. The outlay in discovery and trade was returned at £70,000, and the company asked consideration for the losses and disappointments it had sustained through loss of ships[1]. In August 1650 the matter was remitted by the Council of State to the Committee of Trade, with the recommendation that due regard should be paid to the settling of the trade to the best advantage of the Commonwealth, and the due and just encouragement of the company[2]. By April 9th, 1651, the report was approved by the Council and a monopoly of trade was recommended for the next fourteen years within an area extending twenty leagues to the north of the northern factory at Cormantin and twenty leagues to the south of the fort at Sierra Leone. The company was bound to fortify this district and hold it. All the remainder of the coast was to be free to all English traders[3].

After this settlement the company met with several misfortunes. In 1652 a ship and two pinnaces were seized by Prince Rupert and the loss was estimated at £10,000[4]. The following year complaint was made against the Swedes, who had expelled factors of the company from places within the limits assigned to it[5], and in addition to this many captures had been made by the Dutch, so that the aggregate losses of the company and independent traders were estimated at £300,000[6]. It is not clear whether the confiscation of a ship belonging to the Guinea Company of Scotland by the Governor of St Thomas in 1637 was at the instance of the English organisation or not. In any case by 1657 the shareholders in the former undertaking presented a claim for £33,000 for the vessel and cargo, made up as follows:

	£
For 200 lbs. weight of gold	10,000
For the ship and goods	5,000
For interest at 6%, 1637–1657	18,000
	£33,000[7]

---

[1] Colonial Papers, XI. 15; *Cal.* 1574–1660, pp. 339, 340, 389.

[2] State Papers, Interregnum Entry Book, XXXVII. 5; *Cal. Col.* 1574–1660, p. 342.

[3] *Ibid.*, XCIII. 244; *Cal. Col.* 1574–1660, p. 355.

[4] Colonial Papers, XI. No. 56; *Cal. Col.* 1574–1660, p. 383.

[5] State Papers, Interregnum Entry Book, XCVIII. 372; *Cal. Col.* 1574–1660, p. 409.

[6] *The Early Chartered Companies*, by George Cawston and A. H. Keane, London, 1896, p. 231.

[7] State Papers, Interregnum Entry Book, CVI. 419; *Cal. Col.* 1574–1660, p. 462.

By this time it was no longer possible to recover anything from the company which had lost its forts and factories, and the East India company pressed for an arrangement that would afford protection to its ships when passing the African coast. It was eventually agreed that, since the Guinea company was unable to recover the forts, the East India company might do so and garrison them for five years. Accordingly the positions obtained were used as stopping-places on the way to the East. Some English commodities were exchanged there and the gold received in exchange was traded with in India.

There was a double advantage to the India company from this lease of the African forts. It obtained secure anchorages, available if required, and secondly, which was more important, it was able to acquire a supply of precious metals to barter in India, without drawing to a material extent on the stock in England[1]. Thus the company was able to escape unfavourable comment on the exportation of bullion at a critical period in its history. For these reasons, as well as the short term of the lease, the company did not develope the African trade further. The capital it employed there did not exceed £17,400, and, for the Guinea trade proper, other independent traders were licensed by the company.

E. THE GOVERNOR AND COMPANY OF THE ROYAL ADVENTURERS OF ENGLAND TRADING INTO AFRICA (1662–72).

After the Restoration a new company was formed, which was the direct predecessor of the Royal African company. On Jan. 10th, 1662, Charles II. incorporated a number of persons under the title of the "Governor and Company of the Royal Adventurers of England trading into Africa." The charter, besides granting the usual rights of a corporation, conveyed in addition the privilege of exclusive trade from Sallee to the Cape of Good Hope[2]. This company started under distinguished patronage. Prince Rupert was the first governor, and amongst the thirty-six assistants there were several noblemen and merchants of good standing. At first the operations of the company promised to be very successful, but its officials involved it with the Dutch by attacking their forts in Africa. This led to reprisals, and the English forts, ships and goods on the coast of Guinea were seized by the Dutch in 1665. The remainder of the short history of this company is one of

[1] Cf. Thomas Violet, *Mysteries and Secrets of Trade*, 1653, *passim*; *A True Discoverie to the Commons of England how they have been cheated of almost all the Gold and Silver Coin of the Realm*, 1651, p. 46.

[2] Charter of the Royal African Co., Treasury Records (Public Record Office), Royal African Co., No. 1390, f. 3.

financial distress. As in the case of the previous Guinea company attempts were made to farm its privileges to persons who were not members. In 1668 an offer was made of £1,000 a year for seven years for the right to trade to the north coast of Africa[1]. The rents obtainable for the lease of the company's privileges were insufficient to liquidate the debt already contracted; and, in 1672, the charter was surrendered to carry out a scheme of arrangement with the creditors.

The method of satisfying the claims against the company was both drastic and original. To ascertain how the situation was faced it is necessary to examine in some detail the finance of the adventurers. The capital subscribed at the formation of the company amounted to £122,000 in 305 shares of £400 each, divisible into half shares of £200 each. The qualification of the governor was one share, or £400[2]. Out of the £122,000 subscribed, it was agreed that £20,000 should be paid to the representatives of Sir Nicholas Crisp (who had been a prominent member of the previous company) for the forts and factories in Africa. This debt was never discharged by the company of Royal Adventurers and was still owing in 1709[3].

As early as 1664 fresh capital was required and "2 per cent. above the ordinary interest" was offered for loans from the shareholders at par. Subscriptions were invited for £25,000; but, outside the assistants, very little was raised[4]. Later in the same year a fresh endeavour was made to raise capital, and, on this occasion, the bonds were to be issued at a discount. On Nov. 4th, 1665, the King wrote that considering "the greatness of the company's debt and the heavy interest under which the company's stock now labours," all money realized by home-coming ships should be used in paying debts, not in new ventures[5]. At this date loans could only be effected on the personal security of the assistants[6]. In 1667 another attempt was made to float a loan but with small success, though in some cases creditors were induced to accept bonds under the company's seal in satisfaction of their claims[7].

From 1667 to 1671 the position of the company had gone from bad to worse, and at the latter date the undertaking was insolvent. The debts were estimated to amount to £57,000, and beyond the privileges of the charter the assets were of little if any value. The company and

---

[1] Treasury Records, Royal African Co.—Court Book of the Assistants of the Company, 1663–70, f. 82.
[2] Ibid., f. 101.
[3] Journals of the House of Commons, xvi. p. 180.
[4] Court Book, 1663–70, f. 6.
[5] Ibid., f. 37.
[6] Ibid., f. 38. [7] Ibid., f. 59.

its creditors were therefore in the dilemma that there were few if any assets except the charter, and if the charter were to be of any value working capital was required. In the existing state of the company's finances, there being no credit, capital could not be obtained until the creditors had been satisfied. It was therefore to the interest of both shareholders and creditors that the company should be reconstructed even at considerable sacrifice, and in 1671 a scheme was drawn up and accepted which provided for winding up the company and for the formation of a new one while giving some compensation to members and bond-holders. The following was the reconstruction scheme adopted, which provided for the formation of a new company with a capital of £100,000.

TABLE A. *Reconstruction Scheme.*

	£
The existing capital of £122,000 to be written down by 90°/₀	12,200
Creditors for debt of £57,000 to receive two-thirds, or £38,000 in stock of the old company. This £38,000 stock was to be likewise written down by 90°/₀ and exchanged for stock of new company	3,800
Creditors were to receive the remaining third of debt *in cash* out of subscription below.	
Balance of subscription	84,000
Total capital, new company	£100,000

TABLE B. *Allocation of Capital of New Company between Shareholders and Creditors of the Old.*

	£
Stock of new company to shareholders and creditors of the old company	16,000
Cash to creditors of old company	19,000
Cash available as working capital	65,000
	£100,000

TABLE C. *Position of the Creditors on Reconstruction.*

	£	s.	d.
For each debt of £100, there was paid in cash one-third	33	6	8
The remaining two-thirds of the debt converted into stock of old company for the same amount. This was transferred to stock of the new company at 10°/₀ of its nominal value, giving as the equivalent of the remaining £66. 13s. 4d. of the debt £6. 13s. 4d. stock of the new company worth at par	6	13	4
	£40	0	0*

* Conditional on stock selling at par.

In order to carry out this scheme of re-arrangement of capital the charter was surrendered, as otherwise it was held that the new capital to be raised might have been claimed by the creditors of the old company[1]. On the cancellation of the charter, Charles II. incorporated the creditors

[1] Treasury Records, Royal African Co., No. 1390, f. 2.

and shareholders, who assented to the reconstruction scheme, as the "Royal African Company of England" in 1672. As it will be found that two distinct series of events, namely the state of the finances of the company and opposition to the monopoly, were frequently interacting and influencing its fortunes, it will be conducive to a clearer understanding of the transactions of an eventful fifty years to trace the history of each separately.

F. The Royal African Company of England (1672).—Its Privileges.

Under the charter of 1672 the usual privileges of incorporation are granted as well as "the whole entire and only trade" from Sallee to the Cape of Good Hope and the adjacent islands[1]. The company had the right of acquiring lands within these limits (provided such lands were not owned by any Christian prince) "to have and to hold for 1,000 years, subject to the payment of two elephants' teeth," when any member of the royal family landed in Africa[2]. Powers were also given to the company to make peace and war with any non-Christian nation[3]. Amongst other miscellaneous privileges the right of Mine Royal was conveyed to the company on condition that the Crown might claim two-thirds of the gold won, on paying two-thirds of the expenses, the company retaining the remaining third[4].

A considerable portion of the charter is occupied with provisions as to the internal government of the company. The stock-holders were to elect annually one governor, one sub-governor, one deputy-governor and twenty-four assistants[5]. This part of the constitution is similar to that of the East India company at this date, except that the twenty-four officials are here called assistants instead of committees, and that a new office—that of sub-governor—is created. The latter difference is accounted for by the fact that the governorship of the African company was an honorary appointment filled by members of the royal family. The quorum at the court meeting was seven, of whom either the governor, sub-governor or deputy-governor must be one[6]. In 1714 the qualification for an assistant was £2,000. Each £500 of stock commanded one vote up to a maximum of five votes[7]. In 1680 the stock-holders numbered 198[8].

[1] Treasury Records, Royal African Co., No. 1390, f. 15.
[2] Ibid., f. 4.
[3] Ibid., f. 19.
[4] Ibid., f. 20.
[5] Ibid., f. 8.
[6] Ibid., f. 8.
[7] *Proceedings at a General Court Meeting of the Royal African Company*, Feb. 18, 1714. Lond. 1714 (British Museum 8223, e. 4).
[8] Treasury Records, Royal African Co., No. 1741. (Assts. Minute Book under June 17, 1680.)

In addition to the privileges conferred by the charter, the company endeavoured in 1672 to obtain Parliamentary sanction by promoting a bill. This was read a first time in the House of Lords but was "not proceeded with[1]."

For seven years, from its foundation up to 1678, the company was highly successful. In the three years 1676-8, 50 guineas per cent. were paid or nearly 55 per cent.[2] These favourable results engendered hostility in two ways—as with the India company, persons who had suffered for infringement of the monopoly of the company were opposed to it, and secondly those who had lost money from 1662 to 1670 and had failed to take up stock in the new undertaking were jealous of others who had been more fortunate. Writing in June 1679 a member of the company says: "Mr Edward Seymour is very bitter, because in the former stock he lost near £400 and is unconcerned in this. He was a subscriber but never paid his money so he envies us, and I believe we fare never the better at this time by having the Duke of York as our Governor[3]." Later in the year the same writer says that if the King wants money the company was not in a position to lend it, "for that's as poor as a Courtier...we go on paying off our debts that if the company be broke nobody may be sufferers but those that be in it[4]." The pessimistic prognostication of the last sentence was not borne out by events; for in the thirteen years from 1680 to 1692 eight dividends were paid and apparently a substantial reserve fund was formed. In 1691 the amount of each proprietor's stock was quadrupled without payment. This operation, like the doubling of the East India company's shares in 1681, seems to have brought bad luck; for from 1691 to 1697 a series of disasters were encountered partly through the war and partly by disorganisation of trade by persons who infringed the exclusive privileges of the company.

After the India company had passed through the ordeal of an organized attack on its monopoly from 1692 to 1694, the opponents of exclusive grants turned their attention to the Royal African company. The position of the latter both financially and legally was comparatively weak and the assistants with some strategic ability petitioned Parliament in 1694 for leave to bring in a bill to establish the company rather than wait for the expected request for the formation of a regulated company. They alleged that the African trade was impossible unless carried on by a joint-stock company with exclusive privileges. The cost

---

[1] *Report of Royal Commission on Hist. MSS.* IX. Pt II. p. 9.
[2] *Vide infra*, p. 33.
[3] *Report of Royal Commission on Hist. MSS.* VII. p. 472.
[4] *Ibid.*, p. 476.

of the up-keep of the forts was £20,000 a year[1], and a regulated company could not find so large a sum. They also claimed consideration on the ground of the large losses of the company during the war, which were estimated at £400,000[2]. Davenant, who wrote in favour of the company, urged that it was the policy of its opponents to depreciate the value of the forts and factories, so that they should be transferred to the proposed regulated company at a nominal price[3]. Precedent was in favour of a joint-stock company for the African trade, for all other countries managed it on that basis[4] and in no case by a regulated company—the reason being that in dealing with savages, forts and an armed force were necessary and the consequent charges could only be raised equitably from a joint stock. Further in dealing with natives unity of councils and a uniformity of rules were indispensable[5]. A single independent trader, who, for the sake of a quick profit, was prepared to ill-treat the natives had it in his power to injure the trade of other Englishmen by exciting the hostility of the chiefs[6].

As against these arguments some very damaging evidence was adduced against the company at the Parliamentary enquiry which began on March 2nd, 1694. One trader, Richard Holder, swore that he had a capital of £40,000 employed in the Guinea trade under license from the company. On his first expedition he made a profit of 50 per cent., in seven months, after paying 26 per cent. to the company on the value of his cargo. The next year the cost of his license was increased to 40 per cent. and in addition he was compelled to buy his trade-goods from the company, which cost him an extra 3 or 4 per cent. above the market price. He also suffered from being limited to trade only at certain specified places[7]. Besides these and other complaints of the excessive cost of licenses, it was alleged that the company had not complied with the provision in its charter, under which all goods imported were to be sold by "inch of candle," *i.e.*, by public auction. In the case of redwood, sales had been made privately to some three or four favoured persons, with the result that this commodity was engrossed and the price of it was three times what it had been formerly[8].

The first result of the enquiry was that the Parliamentary committee recommended that the trade should be conducted on a joint-stock basis and the company received leave to bring in a bill[9]. This decision

---

[1] *An Historical Account of the Rise and Growth of the West India Colonies and of the Great Advantages they are to England in respect to Trade*, 1690, in *Harl. Miscl.* II. p. 362.

[2] Davenant, *Works*, v. p. 157.

[3] *Ibid.*, p. 126.

[4] *Ibid.*, p. 127.

[5] *Ibid.*, p. 131.

[6] *Ibid.*, p. 137.

[7] *Journals of the House of Commons*, XI. p. 114.

[8] *Ibid.*, XI. pp. 287–90.

[9] *Ibid.*, pp. 542, 592, 622.

DIV. I. § 1 F] *Parliament and Separate Traders 1694-7* 23

gave rise to further opposition and fresh petitions against the company. Finally in 1697 by the Act 9 and 10 Will. III. c. 26 a compromise was effected. The company was continued, but its monopoly was modified so far as to legalize the position of the separate traders, who were to pay the following charges to the company to aid in the maintenance of the forts:

On Outward Voyages.
All goods 10%

Homeward Voyages.
Gold, silver, negroes ... ... nil
Red-wood 5%
Other goods ... ... 10%.[1]

This settlement was to last for thirteen years at least, and the separate traders had the right of establishing factories if they wished to do so. The effect of this arrangement was to render the African trade open to all who would pay the specified charges. The company discharged the duties of a regulated company without the privileges that accompanied them.

Though the separate traders had represented at the enquiry that, failing the formation of a regulated company, they were prepared to pay 5 to 10 per cent. for licenses, they now proceeded to undermine the position of the existing company. After the passing of the act, while the company was raising nearly half a million of nominal capital to equip expeditions, the first ships of the separate traders to reach Africa spread reports that the company was bankrupt and that the assistants were threatened with imprisonment for attempting to sell the forts to the Dutch. They seized several chiefs to ensure larger consignments of slaves for shipment to the plantations. The factors employed by the company were in many instances induced to enter the service of separate traders, and others who did not change masters engaged in private trade[2].

Under such circumstances the trade could not be profitable to the company, and an even greater disadvantage than the hostility of the separate traders arose from the erroneous financial methods of the company which will be explained below[3]. Having issued stock at as low a price as 12 per £100 (nominal) in 1697, further capital was obtained subsequently by the issue of bonds—at first from the public and later by an assessment on stock-holders for which scrip was given. Not only so but out of this money borrowed on bond dividends were paid as an

[1] *Statutes*, VIII. p. 393.
[2] Davenant, *Works*, v. pp. 91, 93.
[3] *Vide infra*, pp. 28-31.

"encouragement" to induce members to make further payments. The result was that the amount borrowed on bond, while only one-fourth of the *nominal* capital, actually exceeded the sums paid for that capital at the average of the various prices of issue[1]. Taking into account the unsatisfactory condition of the trade, the inevitable result of such vicious finance followed in 1708, when interest on the bonds could no longer be paid.

As a last resort application was made to Parliament at first in 1707 and again in 1709. In the latter year, in view of the nearness of the expiration of the thirteen years mentioned in the Act of 9 and 10 William III., the company petitioned for a fresh settlement on the ground that an open trade had depressed the price of English goods in Africa and raised the price of negroes in America[2]. This argument (which was similar to that advanced by the East India company in 1656–7) was supported by the planters, who gave as reasons for the enhancement of the price of negroes, first that there was excessive competition amongst the shippers in Africa and that therefore the cost price at the port was higher and secondly that owing to the want of skill of the new traders the mortality on the voyage was greater, with the result that the price of slaves in the West Indies was double what it had been before the trade was open[3]. The company, with the optimism of a suitor before a Parliamentary committee, stated that the stockholders "were willing to advance more sums on their joint-stock[4]." The other side endeavoured to show that the company, owing to its financial embarrassment, was in no position to maintain the present forts or to raise capital to build new ones[5]. During the season 1709–10 the company's trade was only about one-thirteenth of that of the separate traders, as is shown by the following table.

Comparison of Trade of the Company and Separate Traders[6].

	Number of Ships	Value Cargoes	10 °/₀ thereon
Company	3	£3,944. 2s. 6d.	£394. 8s. 3d.
Separate Traders	44	£50,005. 12s. 6d.	£5,000. 11s. 3d.

Altogether the company's case did not appear to advantage, and on March 31st, 1712, it was resolved by a committee of the House of Commons that: (1) The African trade should be open to all British subjects under the management of a regulated company. (2) The forts were to be maintained and enlarged. (3) The cost of such maintenance should be defrayed by a charge on the trade. (4) The plantations

[1] *Vide infra*, p. 28.
[2] *Journals of the House of Commons*, xvi. p. 64.
[3] *Ibid.*, xvii. p. 636.
[4] *Ibid.*, xvi. p. 64.
[5] *Ibid.*, xvi. p. 235.
[6] *Ibid.*, xvi. p. 552.

should be supplied with negroes at a cheap rate. (5) A considerable stock was needed for carrying on the trade to the best advantage. (6) At least £100,000 value of English goods should be exported annually to Africa[1].

Naturally the company petitioned against these resolutions, which were intended to form the basis of a fresh bill. The assistants urged that the company had a legal right to its forts, and if this right were denied they claimed the same trial at law as any other corporation to defend their freehold[2]. After considerable debate the matter dropped; and, as far as the legal position of the company was concerned, no change was made. An act, however, was passed, December 20th, 1712, to enable the company to make a settlement with its creditors[3], which legalized the arrangement explained below[4]. On April 13th, 1713, the House of Commons again resolved that the trade should be open, subject to charges for the maintenance of forts, and a bill was brought in to give effect to this resolution, which, after passing the Commons, was rejected by the House of Lords[5].

Thus the respective rights of the company and the separate traders remained undetermined. On several occasions Parliament endeavoured to effect some improvement, but without success. In 1750 the joint-stock company was dissolved after many further changes of capital, and in 1752 the forts were transferred from the recently created regulated company to the Crown.

THE ROYAL AFRICAN COMPANY OF ENGLAND (cont.).— ITS FINANCE FROM 1672 TO 1720.

In the foregoing account of the contest against the exclusive privileges of the company it has been necessary to postpone the consideration of the financial operations of the assistants owing to the complicated nature of the capital account. Going back to the formation of the company in 1672, the preamble or prospectus for subscriptions had mentioned £100,000 as the amount of the proposed capital, books for the subscription of which were kept open for nine months so as to give the planters in the West Indies an opportunity of acquiring an interest in the enterprise[6]. By 1676 the total stock issued was £111,100 at

[1] *Journals of the House of Commons*, XVII. p. 164. [2] *Ibid.*, p. 319.
[3] 10 Anne, c. 24. [4] *Vide infra*, p. 31.
[5] MacPherson, *Annals of Commerce*, III. p. 34.
[6] *Certain Considerations relating to the Royal African Company of England, in which the Original, Growth and Natural Advantages of the Guinea Trade are demonstrated, as also that the Trade cannot be carried on but by a Company and Joint Stock*, 1680, p. 4. State Papers, Domestic, Charles II., CCCCXIV. 80.

which figure it remained, during the successful years of the company's history, till 1691, when by order of a General Court held on July 30th it was resolved to give a bonus in stock of 300 per cent. to each stockholder. There is reason to believe that the company had accumulated a considerable reserve out of profits over and above the 10 or 20 guineas per cent. paid annually as dividend[1]. The assistants in speaking of these early years mention "the great and extraordinary success with which the trade had been carried on[2]." Houghton, too, stated in 1683 that "the Guinea company was as safe as the East India company[3]." The wording of the resolution for the bonus addition of capital confirms this view of the company's finances at the time. It is expressed in the following terms: "voted, by reason of the great improvements that have been made on the company's stock of £111,100 that every £100 adventured be made £400 and that the members have credit given them accordingly[4]."

After the date of this resolution the capital stood at £444,400, of which only about £80,000 had been paid in cash—a part of the stock having been reserved for members and creditors of the old company.

The time for quadrupling the stock was ill-chosen, for on the outbreak of the war immediately afterwards the company sustained great losses. In 1693, capital was required to carry on the trade; and, on March 27th, an issue of £180,850 of stock was made at £40 for the share of £100, bringing in £72,340. The issue came at a time when the price of the stock had been falling. In 1692 the quotation had varied from 52 to 44. In the next year, 1693—that of the issue— during the month of January it stood between 47 and 46; in February and March, previous to the new issue, the quotation was 44; afterwards it fell (March 28–30) to 41, so that the issue-price gave a very small bonus to applicants. The price remained at 41 during the months of April and May. With a few temporary recoveries it fell to 36 at the end of September, reaching 32 early in October, the lowest point of the year. Shortly afterwards there was a recovery to 34, which was maintained in November and December.

The evidence of the Parliamentary enquiry of 1694, in combination with other unfavourable circumstances, still further reduced the market value of the stock—the lowest prices of years 1694, 1695, 1696 and 1697 being 20, 18, 17 and 13 respectively. During these years the company had become considerably indebted and, instead of sending ships to

[1] Treasury Records, Royal African Co., No. 1455, ff. 12, 34, No. 1456, f. 1.
[2] *Memorial on Behalf of the Royal African Co.* (British Museum, 816, m. 11).
[3] *A Collection of Letters for the Improvement of Husbandry and Trade*, II. p. 47.
[4] Treasury Records, as above, f. 14.

DIV. I. § 1 F]   *Capital and Assets* 1672–98   27

Africa, it had licensed merchants not free of the company at a high royalty. After the compromise of the act of 1697, which, while not providing a satisfactory settlement of the company's legal position, at least settled matters for some years, an attempt was made to raise funds to discharge the most pressing liabilities and to despatch ships. The governor and assistants decided to make a fresh issue of capital. In 1697 the price of the stock had fallen as low as 13 for cash and 16 for payment in bank-notes. It was resolved on October 7th to double the existing capital of £625,250, the new issue being offered at 12 per £100 stock payable by instalments of £7 "presently," £3 on April 7th, 1698, and £2 on October 7th, 1698. Although the issue-price gave a bonus of nearly 10 per cent. only £475,800 stock was taken up which realized £57,096. Thus the total capital after October 7, 1697, stood at £1,101,050[1].

In 1698, according to a report of the Board of Trade, the balance in favour of the company, including ships, stock and debts due (some of the latter being admittedly not good) after deducting liabilities amounted to £189,913. 5s.[2] It is a somewhat curious coincidence that the middle market price of the year, 16, gave a valuation of £176,168 for the £1,101,050 nominal capital, and the highest price, 17, a valuation of £187,178. 10s.

It will thus be seen that the history of the capitalization of the company is slightly complicated, and from the fact that stock was issued as low as 12 it might be concluded that the shareholders had suffered severely by the reduction of the value of their holdings. It is to be remembered, however, that the total capital of £1,101,050 represented cash payments of £240,536 only (ranking the amount of stock handed over to creditors and shareholders of the old company as cash)[3]. Now taking the four years 1698–1701—being the period intervening between the last issue of share capital and the first floatation of bonds which latter event affected quotations—the mean price was $16\frac{3}{8}$ and, therefore, the valuation of the £1,101,050 stock was £180,297. Therefore, at this price, the total investment of £240,536 was valued at £180,297, the loss being £60,239 or only about 25 per cent., while at the highest price for the four years, 24, the market price showed a profit of nearly 10 per cent. The same facts may be expressed in another form. The original £100 stock was converted into £400 stock, without fresh capital being brought in—in other words by the re-arrangement of 1691 £25 of the original subscription commanded £100 of stock—the issues of 1693

[1] Treasury Records, No. 1459, ff. 1, 134. Also an inset leaf in No. 1458, giving particulars of the various issues of stock.
[2] British Museum, Add. MSS., No. 14,034, f. 104.
[3] *Vide* "Summary of Capital" *infra*, pp. 32, 33.

and 1697 were made at 40 and 12 respectively, so that taking into account the different amounts subscribed the average issue-price of each £100 stock was about 21·85. The following table shows the position of the stock-holder at this average with some representative quotations:

	Average of the High and Low Prices of 4 years	Highest Price, 1698–1701	Lowest Price, 1698–1701	Average of the Highest and the Lowest Price
Stock exchange quotations	16⅜	24	12	18
Average amount paid per £100 stock	21¾	21¾	21¾	21¾
Gain or loss per £100 stock............	−5⅜	+2¼	−9¾	−3¾

In 1702, the company being still in want of money, a new method of finance was adopted. At a General Court held on December 15th it was resolved that a call should be made of £6 per cent. on all stockholders, and bonds were to be given for the amounts paid in response to this assessment. This call represented nearly 50 per cent. of the price paid by persons who had recently purchased stock. Following the same method £7 was called in 1704, £4 in 1707 and £4 in 1708. These calls should have brought in about £230,000, but only £207,098 was paid. By one of the many coincidences in the finance of this company, the total amount of calls (21 per cent.) almost exactly equalled the average issue-price of the stock. Besides these bonds accepted by stockholders under compulsion, there was due to outsiders, also on bond, over £92,000, making the total debt about £300,000. Thus in 1706 the capital of the company was as follows:

   Due on bond, about £300,000
   Stock ... ... £1,056,350[1]

Some of the bonds had been issued at a discount of 20 per cent., so that it is probable the actual amount received in cash for the bonds was but little in excess of the amount of capital actually subscribed, the amounts being approximately as below:

   Amount realized by issues of bonds, say ... £280,000
     ,, ,, ,, capital stock ... £240,536

So far the history of the company had been on the whole unfortunate; it now became little short of dishonest. As an "encouragement" for

---

[1] Treasury Records, Royal African Co., No. 1,488, f. 23. The amount of stock is reduced, owing to forfeitures for non-payment of calls.

shareholders to pay these assessments, dividends were declared, and made out of capital. In this way seven distributions were paid from 1702 to 1707 amounting to $4\frac{1}{2}$ per cent. or about £47,500[1], so that the assessed stock-holders, while receiving back nearly one-quarter of the principal lent (in the form of dividend on their ordinary stock), were being paid interest on the whole of it. Probably the interest on these bonds was also paid out of capital, so that the stock-holders who advanced money were able to rank as preferred creditors for the whole amount of their bonds after, in some cases, half of the amount had been repaid in the form of interest and dividends!

This mode of finance as well as the pressure of loans generally on the company at a critical period of its history was a more serious hindrance to its prosperity than the losses of the war or the competition of the separate traders. If the increment of capital from undivided profits in 1691 was *bona fide* it had confessedly been lost; thus the real capital of the company was actually less than the loans for which it was pledged. In 1710 the company presented a valuation of their assets to Parliament in which its quick stock (including debts due, apparently both good and bad) negroes and stock only amounted to £279,555. It is true that the total was swelled to £517,749 by an exaggerated estimate of the dead stock (forts, etc.) at £238,194[2]; but whatever may have been the value of the latter, it is obvious that the bonds were ill-secured both as to principal and interest. Early in 1708 bonds were sold at 84[3], and later in the year when interest could no longer be paid, according to one account, the price was as low as 30[4]. The embarrassment of the company was reflected in the price of the stock which touched $4\frac{7}{8}$ in 1708 and fell as low as $2\frac{5}{8}$, $2\frac{1}{2}$, $2\frac{1}{8}$, $2\frac{1}{4}$ in the years 1709, 1710, 1711, 1712 respectively—thus at the lowest price the million of capital was valued at no more than £21,500.

Obviously the time for reconstruction had come, indeed the re-arrangement of the capital account had been too long delayed. In January 1709 the governor and assistants had petitioned Parliament for the restoration of the privilege of exclusive trade, and for the next two years this question was under the consideration of the House[5]. At first

---

[1] This is calculated on the amount of stock existing in 1706 which was less than that outstanding in 1697, owing to forfeitures for non-payment of calls (see below, "Summary of Capital," p. 35).

[2] *Journals of the House of Commons*, XVI. pp. 317–19; a description of the situation and condition of the forts about this time is given in *A New and Accurate Description of the Coast of Guinea*, by William Bosman, London, 1721, pp. 12, 13, 16, 17, 23, 27, 42, 45, 46, 49, 51, 56, 59.

[3] British Museum, Add. MSS., No. 14,034, f. 105.

[4] State Papers, Domestic, Petition Entry Book, XII., ff. 109, 110, 132. *Journals of the House of Commons*, XVI. p. 326.

[5] *Ibid.*, p. 64.

there was some difficulty in arranging a reconstruction owing to the necessity of providing fresh capital in a way that would be acceptable to the creditors, who were not willing to take new stock for their debts. The company professed itself ready to raise £500,000 as an additional stock and undertook to write down the existing capital to its present estimated value[1].

According to an estimate made by the company, the capital required was £1,238,194, of which £238,194 represented the previous value of the dead stock, and the remaining £1,000,000 the existing quick stock augmented by the proposed new subscription[2]. Under this scheme the valuation of the existing capital would have been much beyond its market price and therefore both the creditors and new subscribers would have been under a distinct disadvantage. Another scheme, about 1710, proposed the formation of a new or reorganized company, consisting of the members of the old, its creditors and new subscribers. The dead stock was to be valued at £150,000 (little more than half the former estimate), and the other assets were to be taken at the price which they might be expected to fetch in the open market. The total estimated value of all assets on this basis was to be divided equally between the present stock-holders and the creditors[3]. Under this proposal it is probable that the creditors would not have been paid in full even in new stock to the amount of their debts and for this and other reasons no more is heard of this scheme. A further obstacle to an equitable reconstruction arose from the speculation that had grown up in the bonds of the company since the suspension of interest in 1708[4]. There were thus three classes of bond-holders to be considered: (a) those who in the successful years of the trade had purchased bonds as an investment; (b) members of the company who by right of such membership had received bonds either at a discount or who having subscribed at par had received back a part of the sums lent in the form of dividends on their stock; (c) speculators who had bought bonds as low as 30 on the chance of payment being made at par or only a slight discount on reconstruction[5]. Obviously the latter class deserved little sympathy but

---

[1] *A Short and True Account of the Importance and Necessity of Settling the African Trade* (? 1712, British Museum, 816, m. 11 (12)).

[2] *The Royal African Company and the Separate Traders agreed*, etc. (British Museum, 8223, e. 11.)

[3] *A Proposal agreed unto for the more Effectual Support and carrying on the Trade to Africa.* (British Museum, 816, m. 11.)

[4] *Some Queries relating to the Present Dispute about the Trade to Africa.* (British Museum, 816, m. 11.)

[5] A case is recorded when Thomas Albert, Receiver-General for Worcester speculated in these bonds with public funds. State Papers, Domestic, Petition Entry Book, xii. f. 132.

their position was strengthened by the fact that a large proportion of the bonded debt was still held by members of the company, who by their voting rights would exert a large influence on the terms of reconstruction.

Meanwhile the condition of the company's finances had gone from bad to worse. The assistants in 1712 spoke of its difficulties "as being without precedent or parallel[1]." It had in fact come to the end of its resources, having "mortgaged both its stock and credit[2]" and there was no way out of the "labarynth of debt" in which it was involved[3]. Finally in September 1712 a reconstruction scheme was at last agreed to which was sanctioned by Act of Parliament[4]. According to this scheme the capital was to be written down by 90 per cent., thereby reducing it to practically the same amount at which it stood at the formation of the company in 1672. The stock-holders, before receiving stock in the reorganized company, were to pay a call to provide working capital and the money due on bond was to be paid by an issue of new stock to the bond-holders at par[5]. There is some uncertainty as to the amount of new stock distributed amongst the members and the rate of the assessment. In the ten years since 1702 there had been a reduction in the capital from £1,101,050 to £1,009,000 through forfeitures for non-payment of calls. This capital of £1,009,000 was exchangeable for new stock at 10 per cent. of its face value. An assessment of 5 per cent. on the old capital or of 50 per cent. on the new was made and in this way £50,450 working capital was provided. Thus the total amount of new capital available for the old stock-holders was £151,350[6]. The following are the details in tabular form showing the total capital after reorganization:

Capital Reorganization of 1712.

Old capital of £1,009,000 written down by 90% ...	£100,900	
Assessment of 50% thereon	50,450	
New stock allotted to proprietors		£151,350
Stock given in exchange for bonds (about)		300,000
Total capital after reorganization ...		£451,350

Previous to the reconstruction the sum of £240,536 actually subscribed for the nominal capital was, at the middle price of January in 1713,

---

[1] *A Short and True Account of the Necessity of Settling the African Trade.* (British Museum, 816, m. 11.)

[2] *Ibid.*

[3] *The Case of the Royal African Company.* (British Museum, 8223, e. 18.)

[4] 10 Anne, c. 34.

[5] *A Brief Narrative of the Royal African Company's Proceedings with their Creditors*, pp. 1–3. (British Museum, 8223, e. 30.)

[6] Treasury Records, Royal African Co., No. 1489, f. 66.

i.e., $4\frac{1}{18}$, valued at no more than £40,990 or less than 20 per cent. of the total original subscriptions—in other words the £100 of stock, which cost at average issue-prices $21\frac{3}{4}$, could now be purchased at from $4\frac{1}{4}$ to $3\frac{7}{8}$. To compare these quotations with those prevailing after the reconstruction it is necessary to take account of the estimated amount of the assessment, and, making this allowance, the following comparative results are obtained:

Market value of stock prior to reconstruction as above	£40,990	
Assessment paid in cash ...	50,450	Converted into new stock
	£91,440	amounting to £151,350
		which was worth at 60%... 90,810

It therefore follows that the first price quoted after the reconstruction, viz., 60, was practically equivalent to the previous one, taking account of the assessment. The middle price of the year 1713, i.e., $52\frac{3}{4}$, showed a decline and the lowest ($45\frac{1}{4}$) a further decrease. In the next year, 1714, the quotation continued to recede, owing to a further call of 25 per cent., for which neither stock nor bonds was given[1]. At this date the capital had been reduced to £402,950, probably through forfeitures for non-payment of the call at the reorganization. According to a statement made at the court meeting when this call was sanctioned, the assets then stood at £405,519.

From 1715 to 1718 the company continued to be unfortunate. The lowest price of each of the four years was only 15 or 16 for the reduced capital, thus repeating those from 1697 to 1700 for the old. A further instance of the ill-luck of the company came in 1720 when an issue of capital, known as the "engrafted stock," was made at a low price, and within a few months the quotation had risen from $23\frac{1}{2}$ to 185[2].

Summary of the Capital of the Royal African Co., 1672–1712.

	Stock			Cash		
	£	s.	d.	£	s.	d.
1672. In the reconstruction of the old company its members received stock credited as fully paid ... £12,200						
New members paid for remaining stock at par £98,900	111,100	0	0	111,100	0	0
1691, July 30. Bonus addition of 300% without payment	333,300	0	0			
Totals, 1691 ...	£444,400	0	0	£111,100	0	0

[1] *Proceedings at a General Court Meeting of the Royal African Company*, Feb. 18, 1714. Lond. 1714, British Museum (8223, e. 4).

[2] Treasury Records, Royal African Co., No. 1743, f. 2.

DIV. I. § 1 F]   *Capital 1693–1712, Dividends 1676–81*

Summary of the Capital of the Royal African Co., 1672–1712 (cont.).

		Stock £	s.	d.	Cash £	s.	d.
	Brought forward	444,400	0	0	111,100	0	0
1693, Mar. 27.	Issue of £180,850 stock at 40	180,850	0	0	72,340	0	0
	Totals, 1693 ...	625,250	0	0	183,440	0	0
1697, Oct. 7.	Issue of £475,800 stock at 12 ...	475,800	0	0	57,096	0	0
	Totals, 1697 ...	1,101,050	0	0	240,536	0	0
1706, Apr. 9	⎫ Owing to forfeitures for non-	1,052,550	0	0			
,, July 11	⎬ payment of calls total stock	1,055,650	0	0			
,, ,, 15	⎭ was	1,056,350	0	0			
1712, Sept. 25.	At this date total stock was	1,009,000	0	0			
	Old stock written down by 90 °/₀ and exchanged for new stock under reorganization ... £100,900						
	Assessment of 50°/₀ for which stock was given ... 50,450				50,450	0	0
	New stock assigned to creditors (say) 300,000				280,000	0	0
	Total stock after reconstruction £451,350	£451,350	0	0	£570,986	0	0

Dividends and Prices of Stock.

Year	Prices[1]			Dividends[2]
	Date of Highest Price	Highest and Lowest Prices	Date of Lowest Price	
1672 to 1675 1676				{ I 10 guineas °/₀ at 22/- equal 11°/₀ sterling { II 10 do. equal do.
1677				{ III 10 do. at 21/6 equal 10½°/₀ sterling { IV 10 do. do.
1678				V 10 do. at do. equal do.
1679 1680				VI 10 do. equal do.
1681				VII 10 ,,

[1] The prices up to 1703 are taken from Houghton's *Collection for Improvement of Husbandry and Trade*, after that date from the *Postman and Historical Account*, the *Daily Courant* and other newspapers.

[2] Treasury Records, Royal African Co., No. 1455 (Stock Journal), No. 1678 (Minute Book of Assistants).

Dividends and Prices of Stock (cont.).

Year	Date of Highest Price	Highest and Lowest Prices	Date of Lowest Price	Dividends
1682				
1683				
1684				
1685				
1686				From 1682 to 1691 inclusive five dividends were paid [1]
1687				
1688				
1689				
1690				
1691				
1692	Jan.	52—44	May 9, 16	XIII 3 °/₀ on the new capital equal 12°/₀ on the old capital
1693	Jan.	47—32	Oct. 6	
1694	Jan. 12, 19	34—20	Apr. 27, May 3	
1695	Jan. 9, 16, Aug. 21, Nov. 13, Dec. 11	23—18	Dec. 20—31	
1696	Feb. 5	21—17	Apr. 23, May 20, June 24, Dec. 30	
1697	Jan. 6	17 { 16 / 13 [2]	Aug. 25—Dec.	
1698	Aug. 24	17—15	Oct. 5	
1699	Jan. 4, 11, Mar. 28, Apr. 16 to May 10	16—14	Sept. 6	

[1] There are no Stock or Court Books in existence for these years, but the Exchequer accounts to a certain extent supply the gap (*vide infra*, III., "Financial Statements," M, and N). Up to the Revolution the Crown held £3,000 original stock and thereafter £1,000 original stock. The following dividends are recorded as received:

    1685–6. £322. 10s. = 10 guineas per cent. = $10\frac{1}{2}$ per cent. at 21s. 6d.
    1686–7. £322. 10s. = 10   ,,   ,, = $10\frac{1}{2}$,, ,,
    1687–8. £322. 10s. = 10   ,,   ,, = $10\frac{1}{2}$,, ,,
    1691–2. £53. 15s. = 5   ,,   ,, = $5\frac{3}{4}$,, ,,

It may be that one of the payments from 1685 to 1688 includes two separate dividends of 5 guineas per cent. each, or what is more probable that one distribution has not been recorded. In an account of the receipts of the Exchequer for the Calendar year 1687 (State Papers, Domestic, James II., III., 148) the dividend of the Royal African Company is stated as having been £650. This entry may apply to the second and third distributions recorded above or it may relate to one of these and another not included in the Exchequer accounts. Again it may have happened that, if a dividend was made during the confusion of the Revolution, it was not entered in the accounts.

[2] 13 for cash, 16 in "Bank Money."

Dividends and Prices of Stock (cont.).

Year	Date of Highest Price	Highest and Lowest Prices	Date of Lowest Price	Dividends	
1700	Aug. 7	24—15	Jan. 17		
1701	Apr. 16—30	18—12	Dec. 17—24		
1702	Aug. 5, 12	15—11	Feb. 4, 11, Apr. 29 to June 17	I[a]	$\frac{1}{2}$ %
1703	Aug. 25	$22\frac{1}{8}$—12	Feb. 24 to Mar. 17	II[a]	$\frac{1}{2}$,,
1704	Dec. 15	$23\frac{1}{2}$—18	Oct. 30	III[a]	$\frac{1}{2}$,,
1705	Jan. 8, 17	$21\frac{1}{2}$—$14\frac{1}{4}$	Dec. 5		
1706	June 14	$17\frac{3}{4}$—14	Apr. 24	{IV[a] V[a]}	$\frac{3}{4}$,, $\frac{3}{4}$,,
1707	Jan. 8—20	$15\frac{1}{4}$—$7\frac{3}{8}$	Aug. 15—25	{VI[a] VII[a]}	$\frac{3}{4}$,, $\frac{3}{4}$,,
1708	June 7	$8\frac{3}{4}$—$4\frac{7}{8}$	Apr. 14		
1709	June 7	6—$2\frac{5}{8}$	Oct. 7		
1710	Jan. 4	$4\frac{1}{4}$—$2\frac{1}{8}$	Feb. 20		
1711	Oct. 5	$4\frac{1}{2}$—$2\frac{1}{8}$	May 23, July 9—23		
1712	Jan. 11, Feb. 15, 22, March 7	$4\frac{1}{4}$—$2\frac{1}{4}$	May 7		
1713	Jan. 2, 16	$4\frac{1}{4}$—$3\frac{7}{8}$	Jan. 9		

New Stock after Reorganization.

Year	Date of Highest Price	Highest and Lowest Prices	Date of Lowest Price	Dividends
	Feb. 2	60—$45\frac{1}{2}$	Dec. 18	
1714	Jan. 8	46—22	Dec. 10—28	
1715	April 8—27	27—15	July 27—Aug. 22, Sept. 28—Dec. 2	
1716	Oct. 4	30—15	June 18—Aug. 5	
1717	Dec. 6	$22\frac{3}{4}$—16	July 5	
1718	Jan. 3—11	$22\frac{1}{2}$—16	June 3—Aug. 29	
1719	Oct. 23	26—23	Oct. 14	
1720	June 3	185—$23\frac{1}{2}$	Jan. 1—8	

SECTION II. THE TRADE TO RUSSIA.

THE FELLOWSHIP OF ENGLISH MERCHANTS FOR DISCOVERY OF NEW TRADES.

(The Muscovia or Muscovy or Russia Company) including the subsidiary undertaking for whale-fishing at Greenland.

A. FROM 1553 TO 1586.

At the beginning of the second half of the sixteenth century the spirit of maritime adventure had already begun to show itself in England. It had been noticed that the Spaniards and Portuguese had obtained great wealth by opening up a trade with new countries, and in London about 1552 there was a desire to share in the gains obtainable in this way. It seemed that the most hopeful prospect lay in discovering a north-east passage to China, and accordingly a number of London merchants, in consultation with Sebastian Cabot, determined in 1553 to equip a trading expedition. This was the foundation of the first of the great English joint-stock companies for foreign trade. Previously the Regulated companies had been organized so as to enable certain individual traders to prosecute their business, either personally or through their factors, within certain specified limits. Since this expedition was being fitted out to penetrate into countries, either altogether savage or of a low degree of civilization, it was probably felt that the type of company which was adapted to trade with a neighbouring and developed region would be unsuitable in this case; and therefore, while the form of government, in its essentials, was copied from the regulated company it was decided that, instead of each person participating by trading on his own capital, a joint-stock should be established. A contemporary account explains how the stock was raised in the following terms— "whereas many things seemed necessary to bee regarded in this so hard and difficult a matter, they first made choyse of certaine grave and wise persons in maner of a Senate or companie, which should lay their heads together, and give their judgements and provide things requisite and profitable for all occasions: by this companie it was thought expedient that a certaine summe of money should publiquely bee collected to serve for the furnishing of so many shippes. And lest any private man should bee too much oppressed or charged a course was taken, that every man willing to bee of the societie, should disburse the portion of twentie and five pounds a piece: so that in a short time by this means the sume of six thousand pounds being gathered, the three shippes were bought[1]." With this modest capital of £6,000 the enterprise was started in May 1553[2], and soon afterwards a sum of £10,000 had been expended on "this first discovery." The Society at this period was described as "*The mysterie and companie of the Merchants adventurers for the discoverie of regions, dominions, islands and places unknown*[3]." Already a governor had been elected and express instructions were given that no member of the expedition should endeavour to sell or buy to his own advantage in prejudice "of the common stocke of the company[4]." Two of the three ships were frozen in the ice with the loss of all hands, but the third, under the command of Richard Chancellor, succeeded in making land near Archangel. Chancellor, mindful of the object of the expedition, sought an interview with the ruler of the new country he had "discovered." Ivan Vasilowich was disposed to be favourable to the merchant strangers, for Russia, at this period, had no outlet to the Baltic and its goods found their way with difficulty to Europe through Livonia. Accordingly in 1554 the Czar formally authorized the free passage of English ships to Russia "with good assurance on our part to see them harmlesse[5]." It was also promised that a further concession of a free mart in Russia should be drawn up.

On the return of Chancellor, the company believed that there were very good prospects of a profitable trade with Russia, and steps were taken to secure the sole right of the concession for the persons who had undertaken the risk. A charter was sought which was signed on February 6th, 1555. This document is of considerable interest as an early example of the creation of a trading corporation. It incorporates certain persons named "as one bodie and perpetuall fellowship and communaltie" under the lengthy title of "*Marchants adventurers of England for the discovery of lands, territories, isles, dominions and seignories unknown and not before that late adventure or enterprise by sea or navigation commonly frequented.*"

---

[1] *The Principal Navigations, Voyages, Traffiques and Discoveries of the English Nation*, by Richard Hakluyt (Glasgow, 1903), II. p. 240.

[2] State Papers, Domestic, James I., VIII. 59.

[3] Hakluyt, *ut supra*, II. p. 195.

[4] *Ibid.*, p. 201.   [5] *Ibid.*, p. 272.

Sebastian Cabot was nominated governor for life, and after his death "the fellowship or communaltie" might assemble "in places convenient and honest[1]" to elect one or two governors and twenty-eight of "the most sad discreete and honest persons" of the fellowship of whom four were known as "Consuls" and the remaining twenty-four as "Assistants of the governor." These officials remained in office for one year. In the case of a death occurring during the year, the fellowship might elect a person to the vacant office. The quorum consisted of fifteen of whom the governor and at least two consuls must be present; but, should the governor be unable to attend, a quorum might be constituted by three consuls and twelve assistants.

The "fellow-ship and communalty" was endued with perpetual succession and a common seal. It was made "able and capax in law" of holding lands and of suing and being sued under the name previously mentioned. The governor, consuls and assistants were entitled to make ordinances and to inflict penalties provided such were not contrary to existing laws of the land or to treaties with foreign states or to the privileges of the City of London or to the prejudice of any persons either corporate or incorporate who had already received grants from the Crown.

The officials of the fellowship were given power to arrest debtors in every place not franchised, and in places franchised the Mayor was directed, on the receipt of a demand from the governor to render up the insolvent person. Further, the governor, consuls and assistants were authorized to taken possession on behalf of the sovereign of any territory discovered by them or their agents.

The charter concludes with a recapitulation of the privileges already granted by the Czar and confers the sole right of entry into Russia upon the company as well as into any other countries that would be discovered by it in the future and which had not been "commonly frequented" by Englishmen. The company might license persons not free of its privileges to trade within the specified limits, but any persons entering such limits, when not so licensed, were subject to the loss of their ships and cargoes, one half of the forfeiture being payable to the Crown, the other half to the company[2].

About the same date the Czar formally executed a document embodying the concessions conferred upon the company. "The governour, consuls, assistants and communalty of the fellowship" were granted the free right of entry and of buying and selling throughout the dominions of the Czar for ever. The chief factor was authorized to exercise jurisdiction over the

---

[1] Cf. "loco competenti et honesto" in a charter of 1391, *Foedera*, VII. p. 694.

[2] "The Charter of the Russia Company," in Hakluyt, *Voyages, ut supra*, II. pp. 304–16.

agents of the company in Russia. Should any of the subordinates "rebell" against the chief factor, the Russian officials were commanded to assist in capturing the delinquent, and the Czar undertook to lend the chief factor "prisons and instruments of punishment from time to time[1]."

With the grant of the formal Russian concession and the English charter it may be considered that the career of the company really began. At first there were between 200 and 240 members[2]. There is some doubt as to how the capital was provided. Judging from the analogy of the early history of the East India company and other trading expeditions of the period, it might be inferred that the fellowship was financed in a similar manner. In such cases members of the undertaking were at liberty to subscribe capital either for a single voyage or for a group of voyages. Thus under the name of a single company there was in reality a succession of independent but related undertakings. There are apparent indications that this method was followed by the fellowship—as for instance the care with which different expeditions were described as the first, second or third voyage respectively. Then in 1557, the company, writing to its agents in Russia, instructs them "to make in a readinesse about the beginning of June every yeare our whole accompt of the voyage in that yere passed, in such sort that wee may receive the same by our schippes; and that we may plainly perceive what sales are made and what remaineth of the first, second, third and fourth voyage and what charges have been layde out the sayd voyages and what wares bee bought and laden and what they cost and for what voyage every parcell thereof is[3]." Similarly the agent was "in any wise to keepe accompt of every voyage by it self and not mingle one voyage with another at no hand[4]." Further, it is recorded that it was "the usual custom and form" of the company to distinguish the adventures in the different voyages by denominating each by a letter of the alphabet, as for instance Voyage A, Voyage B, and so on[5].

There is however evidence on the other side which is conclusive. It appears that in 1564 the nominal amount of the share had been increased

[1] Hakluyt, *Voyages, ut supra*, II. pp. 297–303.
[2] The figures given by Hakluyt (*i.e.* £6,000 in shares of £25 from each member) would make the number 240. In State Papers, Dom., Mary, Addenda VII. 39, it is stated that in 1555 there were 207 members.
[3] Hakluyt, *Voyages* (ed. 1903), II. p. 386.　　　　[4] *Ibid.*, p. 385.
[5] Record Office—K, R, Exchequer Depositions, 22 James I., Hil. No. 19, "Interrogatories to be administered unto such witnesses as shall be produced on the part and behalf of Hugh Hammersly, Governor of the Company of Muscovia Merchants and the Assistants of the said company defendants against Sir Richard Smith and others complainants." "Depositions of witnesses taken at the Guildhall in the City of London 3rd Dec. 22 James I. by virtue of His Majesty's Commission out of the Court of Exchequer." Though the voyages were arranged alphabetically it is to be noted that the letters did not follow each other in "a precise order."

from £25 to £200, an additional amount of £60 per share having been called in at that time[1]. Thus the following data are obtainable. The original capital in 1553 was £6,000. To equip the voyage of 1555 and the subsequent ones until 1563 additional calls of £115 per share were made, bringing the total capital (subject to forfeitures for non-payment of calls) in 1563 to £33,600[2].

The position may be illustrated by the following tabular statement:

	£
In 1553 call of £25 per share on 240 shares ...	6,000
From 1553 to 1563 calls of £115 per share on 240 shares should have realized	27,600
Total capital 1563	33,600
1564 call of £60 per share on 240 shares should have realized	14,400
Total capital 1564 (subject to deduction for calls not paid)	£48,000

The company exported from Russia train-oil, tallow, furs and felt, and in addition the especially profitable commodities, cordage, masts and wax[3]. At first the hemp was sent to England in a rough state, but the company soon established rope-works in Russia so that ropes could be finished there. Wax, in particular, was esteemed a most profitable item in the trade, since it was anticipated that the making of Archangel the sole outlet from Russia would give the company the monopoly not only of supplying England but also for the whole of Europe[4]. In view of this proposed diversion of Russian trade the company instructed its agents, "seeing the Emperour doth minde that such commodities as bee in his dominions shall not pass to Rie and Revel and Poland as they have done, but bee reserved for us: therefore we must so lay for it, that it may not ly upon their hands that have it to sell[5]."

At this period it certainly was the expectation of the company (which may have been shared by the Czar) that it should be sole exporter of Russian commodities to Europe, and conversely that European commodities could only enter Russia by its agency. At the same time it was not intended that the Russians would be mulcted by excessively high prices since in 1557 the company ordered that "we must procure

[1] State Papers, Domestic, Eliz. xxxv. 20: *Cal. S. P. Colonial East Indies*, 1513 to 1516, p. 4.

[2] Owing to the scanty material available this estimate is based on the assumption that the number of shares was unchanged between 1553 and 1564. The results so arrived at will be found to be confirmed by independent data noticed below.

[3] Hakluyt, *Voyages* (ed. 1903), II. p. 351. [4] *Ibid.*, p. 386.

[5] *Ibid.*, p. 386.

to utter good quantitie of wares, especially the commodities of our realme, although we affoord a good penyworth, to the intent to make other that have traded thither wearie and so to bring our selves and our commodities in estimation[1]." The company believed that it would be recouped by obtaining an European monopoly for the wax trade and in part for that in cordage also. Whether it would have been possible to realize this ambitious scheme is doubtful, and in 1558 an event occurred which forced the company to face serious competition from Englishmen. This was the taking of Narva by the Russians in this year. Thus Russia obtained an outlet on the Baltic and a new route was opened which was certainly shorter than that hitherto used by the company. English traders, who were not members, were eager to take advantage of this opening, and it was contended that, since the charter of 1555 gave the company the monopoly of the trade to the dominions of the Czar as they then existed, Narva, being outside those limits, might be used as a depôt by any English merchant. Accordingly expeditions were despatched to Narva by Alderman Bond of London and by certain merchants at Newcastle-on-Tyne, Hull and Boston. From this time complaints of the damage done to the trade by such invasions of the charter become frequent, and finally in 1566 the company was forced to make application to Parliament. It obtained an act expressly designed to confirm the privileges of the charter. This document is of considerable importance as one of the few cases in which a trading corporation during the Tudor and Stuart periods was able to obtain parliamentary confirmation of the royal charter. The act generally recapitulates and confirms the previous grant, stating that after the fellowship had, "at exceeding great charges," succeeded in bringing to England " divers wares of good estimation," certain persons "utterly to decay the trade of the sayde fellowship, have contrary to the tenor of the same letters patents, in great disorder traded into the dominions of the said mightie prince of Russia[2]." Wherefore it was enacted that no Englishman might legally trade to any country lying Northwards, North-westwards or North-eastwards from the City of London which had not been commonly frequented prior to the first expedition in 1553. In more precise terms the monopoly was described as including all territory then or at any future date under the dominion of the Czar, also "Armenia major and minor, Media, Hyrcania, Persia or the Caspian Sea" or any other country reached from any of these or from the Northern seas and that might be discovered in the future. This grant was subject to the provisos that the company should observe the Navigation Act, and that if, during the time of peace, the society did not trade at St Nicholas Bay or elsewhere on the north of Russia for three years then, for as long as the trade was intermitted, persons not free of the company might trade

[1] Hakluyt, *Voyages* (ed. 1903), II. p. 389.   [2] *Ibid.*, III. pp. 83–91.

to Narva. It was also enacted that any of the merchants residing at Newcastle, Hull or Boston who had "traded the course of merchandize by the space of ten years" might become members if before December 25th, 1567, they "contribute, joine and put in stocke to, with and amongst the said company, such summe and summes of money as any of the said company, which hath throughly continued and contributed to the saide newe trade from the yeare 1552, hath done[1], and before the saide 25th of December 1567 shall do for the furniture of one ordinary, full and intire portion or share." Finally as affecting the internal management of the company it was ordained that, since the title by which it was incorporated in the charter was "long and consisted of very many words," in future "the fellowship, company, society and corporation shall be entitled *The Fellowship of English Merchants for Discovery of New Trades*[2]."

Though this act may have temporarily strengthened the company it failed to stifle dissatisfaction in England and to prevent the trading to Russia by merchants not free of the company. In 1568 there were great complaints of the "greedy covetousness" of the company in England and of the "evil behaviour" of its factors in Russia. It was "brought into the briars and there tied fast as sheep amongst the brambles being of its own country men slandered and belied." In Russia the company was looked upon as a "greedy cormorant" owing to the high prices charged for English commodities there; and other merchants, who offered to supply the Czar at prices one-third less, were able to obtain privileges from him[3]. It was alleged that the factors were badly paid and that some of them embezzled the company's funds, others engaged in private trade, and a few even intrigued with the Dutch or interloping English merchants against the body that employed them[4]. Evidently the unauthorized trade from England had grown, for in 1570 there is mention of a fight at sea near Narva between a fleet of the company's ships and a number of interlopers[5].

It will thus be seen that the attempted European monopoly of imports to, and exports from Russia was subject to various vicissitudes. Losses of ships had been experienced, the Dutch were attempting to enter the country, and by 1570 the trade of English interlopers had become considerable. In Russia the company suffered from the malpractices of its agents and from debts it found difficult to collect from the nobles.

[1] The use of the word "throughly" in this clause has reference to the various calls made. It is probable some of the shareholders may have been in arrear. The meaning then is that the merchants should pay £200 for each share, not less.
[2] Hakluyt, *Voyages* (ed. 1903), III. p. 87.
[3] *Calendar State Papers, Foreign*, 1566–8, p. 463.
[4] *Early Voyages and Travels to Russia and Persia* (Hakluyt Society, 1887), p. cix.
[5] *Reports of Royal Commission on Historical MSS.*, VII. p. 338.

DIV. I. § 2 A] *The Russian and Persian Trades* 1566–81 43

These disadvantages were partly off-set by a successful voyage when the high prices still obtainable in all probability left an important profit. But a more serious element in the prospects of the company at this time was the political situation. The " ambassadors " of the company to the Czar before 1570 were said to have promised him an alliance with Elizabeth. When these expectations remained unfulfilled he held the company responsible, and, in 1570, its privileges in Russia were suspended[1]. In 1571–2 the right of free entry was restored and the grants given to other English merchants revoked[2]. For a number of years, except for the growing competition of foreigners and interloping English merchants, the trade with Russia seems to have been fairly satisfactory until 1583 when the Dutch merchants had obtained a permanent footing in the country. By 1585–6, when the question of the English monopoly was raised, the Czar definitely refused to exclude foreigners, and with this decree the Russian trade proper began finally to fall upon evil days[3].

It thus appears probable that the trade first opened up—that to Russia proper—was one of considerable vicissitudes. Sometimes no doubt when the European-monopoly price could be exacted the returns were large, but there were many adverse factors which in all probability rendered certain voyages altogether profitless. Meanwhile an addition to the company's resources had been discovered with the entry of factors to Persia, whereby a new route had been opened for the conveyance of Oriental commodities to Europe. Although the journey was longer than by the Mediterranean it was in some respects safer, and it would appear that a very profitable trade was established in this way from 1566 to 1581[4]. For instance the "first voyage" obtained goods valued at no less than £40,000, and though some of this was lost by the attacks of Cossacks, the fact that similar losses were not recorded in the case of later expeditions is evidence tending to show that these were successful. To this is to be added contemporary accounts of this trade as the most profitable one carried on by the company[5].

In view of these considerations it is possible to obtain a general idea of the financial results of the trade. It may have been that it was the original intention to wind up the joint stock at the first favourable opportunity and take subscriptions for a new series of expeditions as was done by most other companies of a similar character until a much later

[1] Hakluyt, *Voyages* (ed. 1903), III. p. 176.
[2] *Ibid.*, p. 189; *Russia at the Close of the Sixteenth Century* (Hakluyt Society), p. xxxiv.
[3] *Russia at the Close of the Sixteenth Century*, pp. liii, lx.
[4] *Historical Account of the British Trade over the Caspian Sea*, by Jonas Hanway, p. 8.
[5] Anderson, *Historical and Chronological Deduction of the Origin of Commerce* (ed. 1790), II. p. 171.

period. Several indications tend to show that the early voyages failed to realize expectations and it was probable that some losses had been incurred. These were made good by a call on the shareholders, and by the same means capital was found for the fitting out of a fresh attempt. The company itself stated in 1560 that "of a hard beginning we trust God will send us a good ending[1]." As the fourth voyage started in 1557 this would apply to the first five or six expeditions. According to a statement laid before Parliament at a subsequent period it was stated that, before the trade "could be brought to any good course," the Adventurers had lost much of their principal, all profit allowed, to the extent of £30,000 at the least[2]. In 1564 it was urged in a petition to the Privy Council that such great losses had been sustained it was necessary to call up £60 per share partly to make these good, partly to equip an expedition to Persia. The shareholders were then so discouraged that there was great difficulty in inducing them to pay the amounts due[3]. This was no doubt a powerful argument in favour of the passing of the bill introduced by the company and passed in 1566. Had the previous calls as well as this one been paid in full the capital at this time would have been £48,000, but it is highly improbable that more than £40,000 had been actually received. Indeed in 1568 the company was paying interest on a loan of £4,000 at rates of 12 per cent. and 13 per cent.[4] It may have been that at intervals during the sixteen years the company had been in existence isolated payments on account of profits earned had been made, and so it is possible that a part of the calls might have been provided in this way. However this may have been, the position from 1568 to 1570 appears to have required that, to recoup the losses made in the Russian trade proper, the Persian expedition of 1568–73 should have made a nett profit equal to the whole capital of about £40,000. It shows the great element of chance in ventures of the time that, although two-thirds of the goods were lost, it just succeeded in doing this. The caravans were returning to Russia with goods of great value when on the crossing of the Caspian they were attacked by pirates with a loss of a considerable portion of the freight[5]. An official of the company, writing about 1586, says that except for this mischance this expedition "would have altogether salved and recovered the companies (called the olde companies) great losse, charges and damage[6]." This account of the circumstances appears to be unduly pessimistic. Even on the last so-called "unsuccessful voyage" of

---

[1] Hakluyt, *Voyages* (ed. 1903), II. p. 405.
[2] State Papers, Domestic, James I., VIII. 59.
[3] *Ibid.*, Eliz. xxxv. 20.
[4] *Calendar State Papers, Foreign*, 1566–8, p. 462.
[5] Anderson, *Annals of Commerce*, II. p. 171.
[6] Hakluyt, *Voyages* (ed. 1903), III. p. 335.

1578–81 the shareholders received a division of 106 per cent.[1] It is to be concluded that the previous Persian expeditions yielded large profits, so that the company must have flourished during the period ending in 1581. Thus, even if the loss of the first company had been £30,000 (which is doubtful), it would have been more than recovered by the second joint-stock. The apparent discrepancy between this view of the situation and the account of the official quoted above arises from the latter throwing the burden of the earlier losses on the last Persian voyage, irrespective of the large profits which had to all appearance been made in the four or five previous years.

This represents the fate of the original capital as is shown by the allusion to it in 1586 as that of "the olde company." In order to ascertain the nature of the financial methods adopted subsequently it is necessary to investigate such data as can be recovered relating to the method of procedure in dealing with the monetary resources of the company. As already shown it was the custom to distinguish successive financial statements by different letters of the alphabet. In 1585 the letter used was N. After a dividend had been declared and the remaining property had been transferred to another account, it became necessary, through many debts proving bad, for this latter account to recover these. But that liability was not discharged by N but was carried back to the adventurers in H[2] or I[3]. This shows that, though the voyages were kept separate, there was a continuity of capital from I to N, since if different groups of adventurers had been concerned it would have been unjust to charge those of I with losses on debts guaranteed by different persons interested in N. The question next arises of the date at which H or I began; which, on this supposition, would be that of the subscription of the new stock. It is expressly stated that it was the custom of the company to make out a balance, valuing all the assets, of the account denominated by a single letter, "yearly or in every one or two or three years[4]." The letters ran continuously to H and probably thence to N. Thus there were fourteen separate accounts in over thirty years. These fall naturally into two groups, the one belonging to the first joint-stock which was still in existence in 1564 and may have continued for another eight or nine years. After that time, when the company began to make a fresh start on obtaining a renewal of its concessions, would be the period at which

---

[1] Report of Baron Jaspar Schomberg, incorporated in a despatch of Bernardino Mendoza to Philip II., 15 May, 1582, Simancas MSS.; vide *Calendar of State Papers (Spanish)*, III. (1580–6) pp. 365–9.

[2] K, R., Exchequer Depositions, 22 Jas. I., Hil. No. 19, Hammersley v. Smith, Interrogatories, Item 5.

[3] *Ibid.*, Deposition of Richard Swift, Item 4.

[4] *Ibid.*, Interrogatories, Item 11; Deposition of Richard Swift, Item 11.

a fresh subscription was taken, which, if the foregoing reasoning be sound, would be the beginning of the account denominated H or I. Apart from the date of the commencement of this stock, the amount of nominal capital in existence in 1585 was £28,895[1]. If then from the beginning of the company to 1586 there were two joint-stocks, the capital of the first being close on £50,000 and of the second upwards of £30,000, this interpretation of the information extant is confirmed by the statement made about 1583 that the whole amount of stock employed from the first to that date was £80,000[2].

There is not sufficient evidence to show precisely what profits were made by this company. But it may be concluded from several sources that the Persian trade, on the whole, yielded considerable gains up to 1581[3] when it was given up. A contemporary writer, in 1579, sums up the situation in a rather enigmatical manner as follows—" by unitie small things grow great and great things become small. This may be understood best by the company. The frowardnesse of some few and the evil doings of some unjust factors was the cause of much of the evil successe[4]." The gist of this proverbial philosophy is that the "great thing" (*i.e.* the original Russian trade) had "become small" through the ill-practices of factors, &c., while conversely "the small thing" (*i.e.* the Persian trade) had "become great" through the loyalty of those engaged in it. In 1583, two years after the last Persian expedition of this period, it is recorded that, after long patience and so great a burden of expense, the trade "began to come to some commoditie," but it had again "fallen to very ticklish termes and to as slender likelihood of any further goodnesse as any other trade that may be named[5]."

There can be little doubt that there was a period during the first seventy years of the company's history when large gains were made. In a report to Parliament in 1628 it was stated that for some time " the trade flourished exceedingly[6]," and at a later date an official of the company records that at an early period the profits were " immense[7]."

---

[1] For the means by which this figure is reached, *vide infra*, p. 47.

[2] Hakluyt, *Voyages*, VIII. p. 135.

[3] The division of 106 per cent. on this so-called unsuccessful Persian Voyage was made in October, 1581.

[4] Hakluyt, *Voyages* (ed. 1903), III. p. 335.   [5] *Ibid.*, VIII. p. 135.

[6] *Reports Historical MSS. Commission*, IV. p. 16: *Journals House of Lords*, III. p. 18.

[7] *Historical Account of British Trade over the Caspian Sea*, by Jonas Hanway, p. 9. Hanway gives "De Thou" as his reference. From a subsequent quotation it is evident that the allusion is to a passage in Thuanus, *Hist. sui Temporis* (1732), II. p. 587, which though entered under the year 1572 relates to the results of the trade generally which is described as *eo quæstuosior quod sub Elisabetha per amplissimum illud imperium merces exoticas distrahere solis Anglis concessum fuit.*

If there were ever such a golden age in the company's history it cannot have been before 1564, nor, although early in the seventeenth century considerable profits were made, these were not sufficient to warrant the glowing descriptions quoted. Therefore, if such statements are to be accepted they can only apply to the period of the Persian expeditions from 1566 to 1581[1]. Certainly after the last of these there is an abrupt and significant change in the company's fortunes. On the cessation of the voyages to Persia the company was dependent on its Russian trade, and this had for some years been unprofitable. Probably while attention had been chiefly given to the eastern expeditions the factors in Russia had been even less controlled than formerly, and in 1582-3 they were engaging in private trade and jeopardizing the interests of the company[2]. Soon losses had become so great that ships were sent rarely to Russia and " divers strangers (*i.e.* persons not members)—waiting opportunity of the company's dissolving—sought to thrust themselves in[3]." Many of the contemporary accounts describe the trade at this time as having been decayed, and the valuation of the stock and debts made in December 1585 showed that at that date the whole property after providing for liabilities was estimated, according to the report of the auditors, to be worth £31,461. 19s., showing a profit of £8. 17s. 8d. per cent. on the capital of £28,895. Subsequently as much as £11,508. 13s. of the assets was found to be irrecoverable and the adventurers were compelled to make good the loss, thus the apparent profit of £8. 17s. 8d. per cent. was converted into a loss of as much as 30 per cent.[4]

This part of the history of the Russia Company, comprising the fate of two distinct undertakings, working at different times under the same charter, affords some instructive side-lights on the position of capitalistic associations of the period. Even when the company was undisturbed in the exercise of its monopoly it suffered from a serious element of weakness—not so much in exacting large prices in England and Russia, for the former could have been remedied and the latter is not fully proved—but in the corruption of its agents. In the Regulated Company, the factor was generally more adequately controlled and it required time to enable the joint-stock type of organization to learn how such control should be exercised. The Russia company, at this period, totally failed in this respect and the laxity of the administration abroad in time affected the conduct of affairs at home.

[1] Hakluyt, *Voyages* (ed. 1903), II. pp. 15-246.
[2] *Russia at the Close of the Sixteenth Century* (Hakluyt Soc.), p. 315.
[3] *Calendar of Cecil MSS.*, Part v. p. 463.
[4] K, R, Exchequer Depositions, 22 Jas. I., Hil. No. 19, Interrogatories, Item 5.

B. FROM 1586 TO 1606.

About this time the trade was spoken of as "decayed[1]" and the number of members had fallen to about 80[2]. "By reason of many burdens, crosses, ill-factors and interruptions borne by so many small adventurers" the stock employed was greatly wasted[3]. Accordingly, a Court Meeting of the company was held at Muscovia House on April 8th, 1586, to consider an agreement made for the disposing of the interest of the existing members in the trade. The offer before the meeting was from a new group of adventurers and there was considerable opposition to the acceptance of it. Finally the court determined that the resolution submitted by the governor and assistants was "good and profitable to be followed by the company[4]." Thus the third company came into existence which consisted originally of only twelve persons.

At first this body, being confined to the Russian trade, experienced the fate of its predecessor from 1583 to 1586. In 1588–9 the trade was characterized as being "decayed" and as being in "a desperate state ready to be overthrown[5]." In spite of the negotiations of Fletcher in 1589 and of Horsley in 1590–1[6], the Dutch continued to obtain an increased hold upon the industry. The trade being so depressed it would appear that the new adventurers formed a distinct stock, known as O, which was audited in January 1588. The accounts showed a profit of 11 per cent., and it is noted that the stock and gains were divided and "the remains" transferred to the undertaking P. The matter was far from being ended, for in July 1590 the adventurers were assessed to the extent of $14\frac{1}{2}$ per cent., but conversely they obtained credit for £2,288. 10s. 5d., so that they gained some profit on their investment[7]. P was another distinct stock in which "the principal and gains were divided" in December 1588 at a valuation of $28\frac{1}{2}$ per cent. profit. The adventurers in Q who bought the debts of P obtained a rebate which meant an assessment of £19. 7s. 10d. per cent. on those in P, reducing the profit of the latter to £9. 2s. 2d. per cent. Q may have been the beginning of a new joint-stock, since its whole property was transported to the account R in January 1589 at a valuation of 30 per cent. profit, almost all of which disappeared through losses not known when the accounts

---

[1] *Russia at the Close of the Sixteenth Century*, p. lxxv.
[2] *Calendar of Cecil MSS.*, Part v. p. 463.
[3] Ibid.
[4] "Copy of an Act of Court of the Muscovia Company"—Lands MSS. (Brit. Mus.), 48, f. 80.
[5] *Russia at the Close of the Sixteenth Century* (Hakluyt Society), pp. lxxvii, 327.
[6] Ibid., pp. lxxvii, xcviii.
[7] K, R, Exchequer Depositions, 22 Jas. I., Hil. No. 19, Interrogatories, Items 6, 9.

were audited, leaving a nett gain of only 7s. 8d. per cent.[1] By 1593-4 it was recognized that unless some new outlet were found there was little hope for the future of the company, and in that year a new subscription was made, under the management of Sir John Hart. This was known as A of a new series and appears to have been the beginning of a joint-stock which continued for some time, perhaps to 1607[2]. In the past attempts had been made to extend the sphere of operations by (in the language of the title) "discovering new trades." Such discoveries were sought either to the south-east or the north. The former had resulted in the Persian trade. This having been given up for some years, there remained only the north as a new field. Already the company in existence before 1585 had licensed Frobisher's expeditions from 1577 and that of Gilbert in 1583. Either this group of adventurers or that succeding them had fitted out the voyages of John Davis to discover a north-west passage from 1585 to 1587[3]. When Sir Francis Cherry was governor of the company further discoveries were attempted and the expeditions to Cherry Island began. The first of these was in 1603, when there were expectations of finding lead mines. Though these hopes were not fulfilled, the next voyage in 1604 brought hopes of making profit from the walrus that resorted there, and, in 1605, 11 tuns of train-oil were obtained, a quantity which was doubled in 1606[4]. It was thought that a considerable revenue might in the future be obtained from this source. Since it was a "new trade," discovered within the limits assigned to the company, it was claimed with considerable show of reason as being included within the original monopoly, but it was alleged subsequently that as early as 1598 some Hull merchants had already entered on the industry[5]. This competition, at first of a temporary character, was destined to become very serious later. As yet however the cultivation of this branch of the business was tentative. Further, in 1601, the East India company pressed the older society either to license it or join with it in an attempt to discover a north-west passage, and on representations being made by the Privy Council the Russia company consented to equip an united expedition, some or all of the capital for which was raised by a

---

[1] K, R, Exchequer Depositions, 22 Jas. I., Hil. No. 19, Depositions, Richard Swift, Items 7, 8.

[2] *Ibid.*, Item 11.

[3] A Brief Narration of the Discoverie of the Northern Seas and Countries of those Parts as it was first begun and continued by the singular Industrie and Charge of the Companie of Muscovy Merchants of London. Add. MSS. Brit. Mus. Nos. 33, 837, ff. 72-7.

[4] *Hakluytus Posthumus or Purchas His Pilgrims*, by Samuel Purchas (1906), xiii. pp. 260, 270, 276, 293.

[5] "Statistics Relative to the Northern Whale Fisheries," by Henry Munro in *Reports of the British Association*, 1853, p. 109.

further subscription of 5 per cent. of the amount subscribed to the first "Voyage" by the East India Adventurers[1].

Meanwhile the company was still engaged in carrying on the trade to and from Russia, principally in cordage. Although for several reasons this branch of its operations was less promising than it had been, there was a steady market in England arising out of the great activity in shipping at this period. In this connection an unexpected difficulty was encountered. The Crown was a large purchaser and it only paid long after the goods had been supplied. In 1595 a considerable sum had been due for some time[2], and in the following year the debt was £9,912. 19s. 8d.[3] This sum represented the greater part of the working capital of the company, since Cherry, in petitioning for an early payment stated that the use of this stock could not be forborne and that "they had been forced to strain themselves to the uttermost of their credits to pay freights." A year later the amount due was returned at £13,922. 15s. 2d.[4] In 1602 the trade had fallen off so much that in that year only two ships were sent to Russia (although the number of Dutch vessels had increased) whereas in 1586–7 "a store of goodly ships" had made the voyage[5]. While this comparison shows the decline of enterprize in Cherry's company, the falling off was more apparent than real, since twenty years before (*i.e.* in 1582) the difficulties of the former company had reduced their fleet to the smallest dimensions.

The strain of financial difficulties almost forced the company to exact high prices in England. It had not now the capital to follow the principles established early in its history of endeavouring "to give a good penniworth." Thus it was ill-prepared to resist the wave of indignation against exclusive grants which found expression in the parliamentary agitation of 1604. It was charged with being "a monopoly within a monopoly" because the directors, who then numbered fifteen of the 80 shareholders, "had made one purse and stock of all" and thus "become as one man." This was only a charge against the joint-stock system as such, but it was further alleged that the company had raised the price of cordage in recent years by using their monopoly to create an artificial scarcity[6]. With reference to the monopoly itself, as apart from the manner it was exercised, the report continues—"The Muscovie company, by reason of the chargeable invention of the trade fifty-two years since and their often great losses, was established by Act of Parlia-

---

[1] *Vide infra*, Div. I. § 5 A.
[2] *Calendar Cecil MSS.*, Part v. p. 463.   [3] *Ibid.*, Part vi. p. 511.
[4] *Ibid.*, Part vii. p. 484.
[5] "Observations touching Trade and Commerce with the Hollands, 1601," in McCullough, *Tracts on Commerce* (1859), pp. 15–17.
[6] *Journals of the House of Commons*, I. p. 220.

ment in the reign of Queen Elizabeth. The chargeable invention had been a reason thirty or forty years ago, when the inventors were still living and their charge not recompensed by countervailing gain; which sithence it hath been their loss hath been their own fault in employing one factor who hath abused them all[1]." Considering the social and political reasons that had aroused a bitter feeling against monopolies, this is a well-judged statement of the position. In principle there were two main grounds for exclusive grants to trading companies, first a large capital outlay in establishing a new trade, through payments for the concession or losses of ships and goods in preliminary expeditions, and secondly a similar expenditure on forts and the maintenance of an armed force. The second reason does not apply in the case of this company, and the first is admittedly subject to the proviso that the founders of the undertaking should recoup themselves within a reasonable time. Further, if, as with this company, the privileges were given without a limit being fixed, and it could be shown that profits might have been made save for bad management, then some period should be set for the revocation of the monopoly. This also was not an unfair contention, but the report is silent as to the offer of any compensation to the company. Had Parliament been able to agree on the matter and to induce the sovereign to revoke the charter, the adventurers who subscribed capital in 1593[2] had an equitable claim to compensation, for the authorization of the undertaking which they purchased was one conveying a perpetual monopoly. Finally, the charge that the company was itself to blame for the series of years in which profits were rare is largely true. Up to this date the "fellowship" had had two valuable monopolies, namely, the trades to Russia and Persia. The former had yielded poor results through the abuses of the factors and internal dissensions; the latter apparently succeeded, but only for a time, owing to causes in a large measure outside the control of the company. But, underlying the embezzlements of the factors, there was an even more serious weakness, namely, the dissensions and even dishonesties of the members amongst themselves. This, as will be shown below, led to the loss of the third great monopoly the company possessed.

An instance of want of harmony amongst the members happened at the time the position of the company was under the consideration of Parliament. Since Cherry had been one of the founders of the present company much of the business passed through his hands. In 1605 the other adventurers seem to have been of opinion that there would be difficulty in obtaining the sums belonging to the company, and a reckoning was demanded. It was found that there was a considerable

[1] *Journals of the House of Commons*, I. p. 221.
[2] That is on the assumption that the stock of 1593 was still in existence in 1604.

difference between what Cherry admitted he owed and what the company claimed. The first account was made up to 1604, and it starts with a balance against Cherry of £1,268. 10s. 11d., which he owed on November 30th, 1603; other items are now added, some of which dated back for four years, amounting to £1,767. 14s., making a total of £3,036. 4s. 11d. This was subject to certain allowances made, and payments on account of the company, which came to £697. 13s. 9d., leaving a balance due of £2,338. 11s. 2d. A further investigation in November 1605 brought the total debt to £7,242. 16s. 6d., from which there was deducted £1,149. 10s. 9d., making the nett balance at this date, on account of sums received in Russia and England, £6,093. 5s. 9d. In addition the company claimed £15,600 as payment for the private trade of Cherry, or a total of upwards of £22,000. Cherry, in his reply to "the demands of the right worthy company," only admitted a liability of £7,565. 11s. 11d. There was thus a sum of over £14,000 in dispute, most of which arose out of the bill for "private trade[1]."

There is no information as to the final settlement, but it is reasonable to suppose that this enquiry resulted in a change of governor, an office which was filled by Sir Thomas Smythe from 1607. This was not the only alteration since at the same time a new joint-stock was formed.

C. FROM 1607–8 TO 1620.

It is recorded that in 1607 a contract or bargain of sale was made between the former adventurers and a new group[2]. This venture was denominated A of the third series[3]. It was followed by B, C, D, E, F, G, the latter being in existence in 1617, at which date the stock or shares of the adventurers amounted to £64,687[4]. It appears further, that, since during the currency of G a penalty was exacted from the shareholders which was levied on the adventurers in A, that there was a continuous capital from 1607–8 to 1617, certainly it was described as a joint-stock, this term no doubt being used, as in the East India company, to describe the resources used in a series of years[5].

[1] Add. MSS. Brit. Mus., No. 12,503, ff. 318–31.

[2] K, R, Exchequer Depositions, 22 Jas. I., Hil. No. 19; Deposition of Richard Swift, Item 11. Since most of the accounts were audited in January it is possible the true date of the beginning of this stock was January 1608.

[3] Court Book of the East India company, IV., March 26, 1618.

[4] K, R, Exchequer Depositions, 22 Jas. I., Hil. No. 19; Interrogatories, Items 13, 15.

[5] Ibid., Deposition of Richard Swift, Items 4, 13. Swift refers to "the two last joint-stocks, wherein he was an adventurer."

Owing to the disturbances in Russia the trade there was contracted and Smythe with his fellow-adventurers were anxious to press on with the ventures in the Northern Seas[1]. A further expedition was sent to Cherry Island in 1608, but, though 31 tuns of oil were obtained, this voyage resulted in a loss of £1,000, owing, it was alleged, to a ship sent by Duppa, a brewer of London, and another from Hull "having glutted the place[2]." The dividend for 1608 had been 40 per cent. profit, and that for 1609 was 30 per cent.[3] The voyage to Cherry Island in 1609 resulted in a loss of £500. That in the following year is remarkable through "the great store of whales" observed from the ships. Those in charge of this expedition were censured by the company for having brought home blubber instead of oil, and the dividend paid for 1610 was 20 per cent. Train-oil being used for the manufacture of soap was in constant demand and the company at once decided to enter on the whaling industry for which an expedition was sent out in 1611. It was only in the following year that the venture was successful and for both periods two dividends of 90 per cent. profit each were declared. The Dutch had also entered on the trade[4] and there were isolated English ships sent to hunt walrus from time to time. Accordingly, the company determined to apply to James I. for a monopoly of "this new trade of whale-fishing." It was urged that the industry would be highly beneficial to the country since every £100 adventured brought trade estimated at £500. Therefore in view of the right of first discovery and the advantageous character of the occupation it was asked that English subjects, not free of the company, should be forbidden to capture whales within certain limits[5]. This petition was accepted and a grant embodying the views of the company was made on March 13th, 1613[6]. Further, by a proclamation of September 11th, 1614, the importation of whale-fins by any persons, save those employed on behalf of the existing joint-stock of the company, was prohibited under severe penalties[7]. This grant was expected to warn off other English vessels, and foreigners were provided against by sending out heavily armed ships to protect the whalers.

[1] "The Humble Petition and Remonstrance of the English Merchants for New Trades," Lands MSS. No. 142, f. 301.
[2] "A Commission for Thomas Edge our...factor in the Ship called the Mary Margaret" in Purchas, *Pilgrims*, xiv. p. 30; cf. xiii. pp. 275-6.
[3] Court Book, East India company, March 28, 1618. These dividends relate to the year of account, they were not actually declared until some time afterwards.
[4] For the proceedings of the Dutch vide *Early Dutch and English Voyages to Spitsbergen*, edited by Sir W. Martin Conway (Hakluyt Society, 1904).
[5] "The Humble Petition and Remonstrance of the English Merchants for the Discovery of New Trades," Lands MSS. No. 142, f. 301.
[6] State Papers, Sign Manual, xiii. 10.
[7] Procl. Coll. Soc. Antiq., James I., No. 40.

The success of the voyage for whaling of 1612 together with the grant of the monopoly of this industry encouraged the company to endeavour to develop its various enterprizes. It provided an increased whaling equipment in 1613 and efforts were made to re-organize the business in Russia. It was now over thirty years since the last expedition to Persia, and some attempt was now made to re-open this route. With special reference to the position of affairs in Russia an embassy was sent to represent that, owing to the recent tumults there " the privileges of the company had sustained great prejudice and impeachment" and to ask for redress[1].

The Dutch were far from acquiescing in the claims of the Russia company to the monopoly of the whaling grounds, for in 1614 they sent fourteen vessels protected by four war-ships. These were met by the company's fleet of thirteen armed whalers, and, owing to the strength of the Dutch, the latter made good their position for this year[2]. Without the assistance of royalties from foreigners licensed to enter the whaling ground, the dividend was reduced to only 11 per cent.[3] The management had become inefficient and, in spite of the profits still being made, it was necessary to borrow money. A loan was provided by the East India company in 1614, and another of £5,000 in the following year[4]. At this period the position of the joint-stock appeared exceedingly favourable. On January 18th, 1617, the account known as G was audited, and it gave total assets of £82,800, yielding a profit of 28 per cent. on the capital of £64,687[5]. Thus in eight years' trading on this stock, in addition to the sums provided by the adventurers, there were profits of 339 per cent. or over 42 per cent. per annum. The chief element of weakness was the need of further resources, and on April 26th, 1616, it had been ordered that all those who were shareholders during the first year of G should double their holdings under a penalty of 20 per cent. At the Court meeting on January 18th, 1617, it was resolved that books should be sent abroad amongst the freemen for the subscription of a new stock, which was to be paid up during the ensuing four years, and those who failed to take up stock were to be excluded during that time.

This financial weakness was accentuated by continued bickerings with

[1] Rymer, *Fœdera*, xvi. p. 747.
[2] Purchas, *His Pilgrims* (1906), xiii. p. 16; Anderson, *Annals, ut supra*, ii. p. 346.
[3] The dividend had been 30 per cent. in 1613.—East India company's Court Book, iv., under March 26, 1618.
[4] *Ibid.*, iii., under Sept. 13, 1614, Nov. 3, 1615.
[5] K, R, Exchequer Depositions, 22 Jas. I., Hil. No. 19, Interrogatories, Items 13, 15. The dividend of 28 per cent. declared on January 18, 1617, was reduced to 24 per cent. on January 21, but at a further meeting in February it was restored to the original amount " for the better procuring of adventures."

the Dutch whalers and it left the company ill-prepared to face the most serious attack yet made on its privileges. This came directly from James I., who, by letters patent under the great seal of Scotland, incorporated Sir James Cunningham and a number of other adventurers as a Scottish East India and Greenland company with privileges similar to those of the existing English companies. Thus both the Russia and East India undertakings would suffer from the foundation of a Scottish rival. It was the former which was first attacked, but the other recognized that it, too, was menaced indirectly, since it would be possible (though not within the strict letter of the Scottish charter) for English interlopers to trade to India under a license from Cunningham and his partners. Thus the situation was serious for the two companies affected, and the matter became urgent when Cunningham commenced to fit out a whaling expedition.

It began to appear that the affair was one in which a compromise might be effected. Though the Scottish charter was signed, it was questionable whether James had been strictly fair to his English subjects[1], so that he was not unwilling it should be recalled, provided Cunningham was compensated and the trade prosecuted vigorously. The Russia company's finances were not sufficiently flourishing to make any very large outlay, and therefore the East India company came to its rescue. In addition to previous loans it now undertook to lend the Russia company 100,000 roubles required by the Czar on condition that the Greenland trade should be a separate joint-undertaking for eight years[2]. Accordingly on March 20th, 1618, it was proposed that a committee of management should be appointed, and that a capital of £30,000 should be raised each year[3]. The joint-undertaking was to be liable for the compensation to Cunningham which was fixed at £924. 10s.[4] It was not easy for the Russia company in its present position to raise its share of the capital required. Some was found by loans made by persons not free of the company—as for instance those about this time from Mrs Mary Brocas and Mrs Overton—and the rest by means of an additional subscription from the members. The loans occasioned no little litigation within a few years and the members were very dilatory in paying in their contributions. Even in 1619 there were many of the calls still in arrear, and on April 27th of that year it was necessary for the East India company "to name a peremptory day" for payment to be made[5].

[1] *Vide* under the East India company, *infra*, Div. I. § 5 A.
[2] State Papers, Domestic, James I., xcviii. 2, 9; *Calendar*, 1611–18, pp. 532, 533.
[3] Court Book, East India company, iv., March 20, 1618.
[4] *Reports Royal Com. on Hist. MSS.*, iii. p. 24.
[5] Court Book, East India company, iv., March 19, 23, April 27, 1619.

It thus appears that the whole amount of the capital proposed had not been paid in 1618, when the first joint-expedition sailed. This consisted of thirteen ships. They were attacked and dispersed by the Zealanders and most of them returned home empty[1], and, in order to assist the company, a proclamation was issued in its favour, confirming the grant of 1613, and, in addition, prohibiting any save adventurers in this body from purchasing whale-fins forfeited through invasion of the monopoly[2]. In 1619 nine ships and two pinnaces were equipped—again on the joint-account—and this expedition was a complete failure[3], and all the capital employed during two years of the joint-stock begun in 1617 (which was known as H) was lost[4]. The united undertaking now ceased and steps were at once taken to wind it up by disposing of such stores as remained on hand.

One of the conditions of the union for whaling was that the abuses in the Russia company at home and abroad should be amended[5]. Although there were Court Books it was alleged that about this time no Courts were kept. An apologist for the administration could not make out a better case than to contend that the affairs were "usually governed by the generality and major part of the company[6]." The East India company complained that it had not been fairly treated in the joint-adventure since the Russia company had drawn it into a more extensive undertaking than had been proposed, and that there had been a failure in paying up the proportion of the capital promised[7]. Thus by 1619 the condition of the Russia company was deplorable. It had lost the greater part of the capital invested in the joint-undertaking, and after taking credit for the sale of stores remaining on this account the deficiency appears to have been about £11,000. Then it was stated the Dutch had burned some of the warehouses in Russia, whereby goods valued at £22,000 had been destroyed, and this amount was made a claim against the Dutch[8]. In 1620 it was resolved that the company

---

[1] State Papers, Domestic, James I., xcviii., docket 44, xcix. 40, printed in *Early Dutch and English Voyages to Spitsbergen*, by Sir W. M. Conway, pp. 42–65; Anderson, *Annals*, II. p. 360.

[2] Coll. Proclamations Soc. Antiq., James I. 122, dated May 18th, 1619.

[3] *Ibid.*, p. 367.

[4] K, R, Exchequer Depositions, 22 Jas. I., Hil. No. 19, Interrogatories, Item 21.

[5] Court Book, East India company, IV., March 31, 1618.

[6] Special Commissions and Depositions (Record Office), Exch. Q. B., London, 2 Charles 1. C. 5 Feb., 22 Jas. I., D. 16 Feb., Jas. I., East. 4. Sir Richard Smith and others *v.* Hugh Hammersley and others.

[7] East India Court Book, IV., under Jan. 24, 1620.

[8] *Ibid.*, under Dec. 29, 1619.

should cease to adventure in the Russian trade which is now spoken of as being "totally deserted[1]."

Unless the company was to be finally wound up it had become necessary that there should be fresh capital brought in, and, accordingly in 1620 a new undertaking was formed which took over the assets and liabilities of the old on paying the members a sum of £12,000[2]. This payment secured the transfer of the various privileges and the claim against the Dutch for damage which had been returned at £22,000 in 1619 and at £20,000 in 1622. Against this there were many debts on bond and outstanding claims, so that the essence of the financial situation depended upon whether any part of the sum due by the Dutch could be recovered. If this were so Smythe's company in spite of its difficulties in 1619 was solvent. It was decided—wisely as it turned out—to leave the prosecution of this matter to the new company, so that the position in 1620 was that the undertaking, that was now being wound up, had received back its capital with very substantial additions to it by 1614, and the amount payable by the new company of £12,000 exceeded the loss on the joint-adventure with the East India company. This, however, was not the final conclusion of the matter, for when the legacy of debt left by Smythe's company came to be investigated by the Privy Council and the House of Lords, it was found that there were many bad debts due to the company, and it was ordered that these should be made good to the new undertaking by those who had incurred them[3], while the second moiety of the £12,000 (*i.e.* £6,000) was arrested and diverted to the payment of certain liabilities which, it was contended, had not been disclosed at the time of the transfer[4]. Even allowing for these reductions Smythe's company, as an investment, had proved satisfactory to those interested in it, but the real element of importance was how the new company succeeded in realizing the very speculative property it had purchased.

D. Arrangements for paying the debts of the Company from 1620 to 1628.

The new company began its career by a serious error in finance. It started with assets which were of doubtful value, since if the claim against the Dutch could be collected it would be able to pay nearly

[1] State Papers, Domestic, Correspondence, Jas. I., Addenda (Calendar S. P. East Indies, 1617-21, p. 448).
[2] House of Lords MSS., June 19, 1628. Accounts of the Muscovie Co.—Ralph Freeman's Account; K, R, Exchequer Depositions, 22 Jas. I., Hil. No. 19. Hammersley *v.* Smith, Deposition of Richard Swift, Item 11.
[3] State Papers, Domestic, James I., cxxxiv. p. 50; *Calendar*, 1619-23, p. 322.
[4] *Vide* Ralph Freeman's account, *ut supra*.

or altogether 20s. in the £ without a new subscription. But even on the most favourable possibility, time would be required, and meanwhile there were certain obligations incurred many of which bore interest at 8 per cent. Therefore it would only have been common prudence to have raised enough capital to fit out expeditions and to pay off at least a part of the debt. It is likely that many of the new adventurers had been members of Smythe's company and the unfavourable result of the joint-undertaking of 1618–19 made them disinclined to risk more than the minimum amount. Therefore only enough capital was subscribed to equip ships for a voyage to Russia. When these vessels returned, interest on the loans had fallen into arrear and other creditors became clamorous. Threats were made of seizure of the goods, and the company obtained an Order of Council on October 19th, 1621, which guaranteed them immunity from arrest for debt in order to prevent the "decay of the trade[1]." On December 17th of the same year it was ascertained that the debts amounted to £24,000 and it was ordained that a portion of this amount should be paid by the former company. It was decreed that all the adventurers who had continued in the joint-stock since the second year of G (1616) up to 1620 should provide this sum, which was raised by an assessment fixed at £35. 9s. 11d. per cent. on the capital of G[2]. On the other hand the charges of the embassy sent to Russia in 1620, as well as the remainder of the debt, was to be discharged partly by a levy on the stock of the members, partly by an *ad valorem* charge on the commodities imported from Russia[3]. This order took no account of the claim against the Dutch and since this, if paid, would have more than balanced the whole indebtedness, the company took no steps pending the result of attempts to collect a part of it.

In 1622 an arrangement was made in connection with the whaling part of the trade which was severely commented upon two years later. At a thinly attended Court meeting the Greenland trade was put up to auction ("sold by inch of candle") subject to the payment of £520 a year towards the debt of the company[4]. The purchasers formed a separate undertaking from this date known as the "Greenland Adventurers[5]." This sale, though not strictly in accordance with the orders of

[1] State Papers, Domestic, James I., cxxiii. 41, *Calendar*, 1619–23, p. 300.

[2] K, R, Exchequer Depositions, 22 Jas. I., Hil. No. 19, Interrogatories, Item 19. Those adventurers in G who refused to pay the call of 1616 were exempt from this assessment.

[3] State Papers, Domestic, James I., cxxiv. p. 50, *Calendar*, 1619–23, p. 322.

[4] *Report Royal Com. Hist. MSS.*, iv. p. 18; *Journals of the House of Lords*, iii. p. 18.

[5] In 1620 Ralph Freeman had offered £1,100 for the "implements and merchandize" of the Greenland adventure which was accepted (*Cal. State Papers East Indies*, 1618–21, p. 346). In his account in 1628 he acknowledges having received from the Greenland company £526. 11s. 2d. "for ye parte of ye Implements."

1621, was not unfair as regards the creditors. What appears to have been done was to attempt to provide for the interest by dividing the whole undertaking into two moieties and charging half of the interest upon each. The total debt was returned in 1621 at £24,000, of which the former undertaking was held liable for about £11,000. Averaging the interest on the remaining £13,000 at 8 per cent., the amount due annually on the whole outstanding debt, for which the present company was responsible, would come to £1,040. Half of which was £520 or exactly the sum charged against the separate undertaking for Greenland.

Further, an assessment on the stock was made in 1623, but it would appear that the money so raised, together with other amounts collected, instead of going to the creditors was diverted to the Russian trade to make good the deficiency of working capital[1]. There were disputes as to how much of the debt should be assigned to the old company and how much to the new. A suit was instituted by Sir Richard Smythe (a brother of the former governor) on behalf of himself and other members of the former undertaking against Hammersly, who was now governor. This case began in 1624 and continued for several years. Smythe contended that the former adventurers had been assessed with more than their due proportion of the debt and claimed release[2].

In view of these varied difficulties, financial and legal, it is not surprising that by 1624 interest on the company's bonds was in arrear, and steps were taken by some of the bondholders to obtain redress. On April 29th Mary Overton stated in a petition that she had lent the company £1,300 and had as yet only been repaid £500[3]. The case of Mary Brocas was worse. She held the company's bond for £1,000 at 8 per cent. from January 3rd, 1617. "For a time" the interest had been paid, but afterwards neither principal nor interest. The Committee for Petitions summoned the governor, and the debt was admitted, but attention was drawn to the difficulty of deciding whether this particular claim was payable by the old or the new company—it being one of those in dispute in the case at present in progress in the courts. The Committee then ordered that the last assessment (or "leviation") should at once be paid in by the members of the present company, and from the proceeds Mrs Brocas should be paid her capital with interest since the last payment at 5 per cent. before the other creditors. Smythe and others in the same position were to pay in their assessments to the Court of the Exchequer, and if they won their cause they should receive

---

[1] House of Lords MSS., under 19th June, 1628, Accounts of the Muscovie Co.—Freeman's Account.

[2] Special Commissions and Depositions, Exch. Q. B., *ut supra*.

[3] *Journals of the House of Lords*, III. p. 31.

back their deposits without payment of fees, but if the assessment were sustained the deposits were to go to the creditors[1].

This order was carried out in part. Mary Brocas received £700 for interest and on account of the principal, but the creditors experienced great difficulty in obtaining the money, and all the assessments did not find their way to the object for which they had been designed. The Greenland Adventurers had not yet paid their annual contribution under the agreement for purchase, and they endeavoured to evade the obligation by contending that they had "no common stock[2]." The creditors found it necessary to again present a petition on March 9th, 1625, and a further investigation was made in April 1626. It was then found that the accounts presented to the House "showed gross juggling to defraud the creditors," and an order was made that 5 per cent. interest was to be paid on outstanding debts, that "all that have the common seal" (*i.e.* creditors on bond) should be paid out of the leviation, that all arrears of the assessment must be paid in by May 1st, and that a legacy of Sir Thomas Smythe of £500 was to be added to the funds available for the creditors[3].

Again in 1628 this protracted liquidation was before the House of Lords. Mary Brocas was still "unsatisfied." A group of creditors alleged that no part of the order of 1626 had been performed, and two of them complained that some of the directions in that order "had been slighted and some of them neglected by neglecting all manner of prosecutions which should have been for gathering in of monies, by denying to bring forth their books of accompts, afterwards by not meeting to agree to those accompts, sometimes wilfully hindering, other times diverting the petitioners' proceedings so that no one penny of about £5,000 due to the petitioners by these undue courses has ever been paid[4]."

The Lords called the governor and other leading adventurers before them and "told them they deserved to be punished for their contempts," whereupon it was asked that, since the accounts were complained of, they should be audited. The audit showed that some of the charges were frivolous but that there were grounds for others. The Smythe case was still undecided and therefore it was impossible to present a final account. It would appear also that there was no foundation for the suggestion that this action was a blind to delay the liquidation, for there is every reason to believe that there was much

---

[1] House of Lords MSS., 27th May, 1624. *Journals of the House of Lords*, III. p. 412.

[2] *Reports Com. on Hist. MSS.*, IV. p. 18; State Papers, Domestic, James I., CLXXXI. pp. 33, 34, *Calendar*, 1623–5, p. 442.

[3] *Journals of the House of Lords*, III. p. 569.

[4] *Ibid.*, III. p. 866.

bad feeling between the prominent members of the old company and the administration of the new one. It is recorded that some of the former adventurers were "violently opposed" to the latter, and induced the Czar not to allow the goods of the new undertakers to enter his dominions customs free[1]. As to Mary Brocas it was quite clear that she herself was to blame for her condition of want of satisfaction. The company had ear-marked certain funds for the payment of her debt, and on the money being tendered—there was still £461. 8s. 6d. due to her—she demanded a larger sum. Since there was a greater amount to the credit of this account than was required for this particular debt, the balance remained locked up[2]. The Lords ordered that the £461. 8s. 6d. should be paid her "and that she cease to trouble the Lords Committees or the Court of Chancery or any other person[3]."

The charges relating to the falsification of accounts present some difficulty. It was impossible for the company to frame a final account pending a verdict in the action. Besides some of the creditors (e.g. Mary Brocas) were in fault in delaying the settlement. But when full allowance has been made for these and other considerations in favour of the company there is no doubt that there were some serious malpractices. It is possible to trace these through the accounts filed in 1628 having been preserved. They are not complete since a previous series had evidently been audited in 1624 and passed. Thus the figures of 1628 represent balances of leviations due before 1624 but not then paid, the sums collected since 1624 and some accounts of an earlier date that had not been completed previously. There were six different persons or bodies involved—such as the representatives of the old company, of the Greenland company, two successive treasurers, the treasurer of the leviations, and the governor. The account relating to the old company shows that many of the debts had been cleared off in 1620 and others up to 1624. Some of the accounts were passed without alteration, others were subjected to severe criticism, through money collected for the creditors being diverted to pay the private charges of some members of the company. The whole amount with which all the persons who were acting as trustees were charged was £12,776. 18s. Out of this payments had been made (including the sum held for Mrs Brocas) of £9,192. 18s. 8d., so that there should have been a balance available for the creditors of £3,583. 19s. 4d. But several of the persons responsible presented very heavy contra-accounts, which absorbed over two-thirds of this sum. These claims were some of them frivolous and others dishonest. Expenses in private

[1] *Journals of the House of Lords*, IV. p. 19.
[2] House of Lords MSS., June 19, 1628, Account of Rowland Healyn "Treasurer of the Leviations."
[3] *Journals of the House of Lords*, III. p. 866.

trade in Russia were entered as due on the company's account[1]. The total was swelled by an imaginary fee of £150 to an imaginary governor[2]. In one case interest on a supposed advance was asked at £10 per cent., when, if interest for the use of the company's money had been charged, it would have come to four times as much. Even "a standing cup" presented to "a particular friend" went in to swell the bill[3]. As a detailed illustration of the methods adopted the account of Clement Harbye (printed on the next page) is remarkable. His books showed him indebted to the creditors to the extent of £268. 19s. 9d. He counter-claimed £828. 5s. 8d., which would have left him a creditor of the creditors. When his counter-claim was investigated only £38. 2s. of it was allowed! The other contra-accounts were dealt with similarly though the reductions made were not so great, and of the £2,445. 3s. 10d. demanded only £212. 5s. 9d. was allowed, consisting chiefly of legal and personal expenses[4].

Thus the account was presented to the Lords and then modified as follows:

	£	s.	d.
Sums to be accounted for by the various treasurers	12,776	18	0
Payments made by them and not challenged	9,192	18	8
Balance	3,583	19	4
Claims made by various treasurers	2,445	3	10
Leaving as balance offered to creditors ...	1,138	15	6
Out of £2,445. 3s. 10d. claimed there was disallowed	2,232	18	1
Making cash immediately available for creditors	3,371	13	7

In addition to this sum there was the amount dependent on the result of the action, and this, the Lords ordered, was to be prosecuted vigorously; there were still some leviations to be collected, and for any deficiency remaining the company was directed "to continue the impositions and consulages on the Muscovy and Greenland trades" until a complete settlement had been effected[5].

[1] House of Lords MSS., June 19, 1628, Account of Joab Harbye.
[2] Account of Clement Harbye, *infra*, p. 63.
[3] Account of Freeman.
[4] A fee paid to the Attorney General was £3; to the Solicitor General for two consultations, £3 for one and £2 for the other. Three days' coach-hire and personal expenses came to £7. 1s. 6d.
[5] *Journals of the House of Lords*, III. p. 866. As late as 1631 Sir Wm. Russell, Treasurer of the Navy, stated in a petition that being dissatisfied with the management of the company he sold his stock at great loss and that, being sued for a proportion of the debt, he draws attention to the order for payment of " a great part of it by the former adventurers," State Papers, Domestic, Charles I., CLXXXII. 32.

DIV. I. § 2 D]   C. *Harbye's "Juggled Account"* 1628   63

THE ACCOUNT OF CLEMENT HARBYE (MSS. House of Lords, 19th June, 1628).

The Original Account.

Mr. Clement Harby is Charged with these somes ffg. vizt—

	£	s.	d.
For divers Imposiĉons laid upon him 1625 and 1626 ...	112	0	11
For Imposiĉons Rece^d by him of divers persones 1625, 1626	558	12	9
	670	13	8
Out of wch is to be deducted wch he paid out when he was Treasurer, wch is to be Awdited by the Comp.	401	13	11
There resteth owinge by him by this Accompt somes	268	19	9

He demandeth allowance for these ffg. vizt—

Remarks of the Committee of the House of Lords.

		£	s.	d.
He was T^{rer} as his brother before him and is to have noe allowance for ye reasons above.[1]	For his allowance beinge Treasurer.	060	0	0
If any such error be, Swift & Merrick are to make satisfaccon and not the moneyes due to the Creditors whome ther recoveringe doe not concerne.	For an Eror pretended in Rich. Swifts Sir Jno. Merricks Acco^t.	022	16	4
This allowed him by the second accompt upon y^r Lo^{ps} opinions.	For charges demanded for 5 greekes into the straights.	030	0	0
This was his overhastie sending before the trade setled and was the same with his brother whoe trusted to ther private factor and soe evrie man ranu his own adventure.	For 624 robles imposed on him for Custome in Muskve.	456	0	0
This not paid the Lord Maior,[2] nor consented unto by the company and Sr John Merrick the nowe Govenor hath noe fee.	which he maketh paid to Mr. Alderman Hamersly For his gov^{nors} fee Anno 1626 in wch yeare Sr Jno. Merrick and not Mr. Alderman Hamersly was goveuor.	150	0	0
This messenger is the same in his brothers accompt and was sent for [t]her & ther partners private & not for the Companyes Service nor is there any order in ther owne Court for any such messenger or his allowance.	wch he maketh paid for the charges of Peter Boysell a messenger sent into muscovia: but it is objected that the said messenger was sent for the said Mr. Harbyes private buisiness and not for the Companyes. Which demands of his we humby leave to y^r honours grand judgements.	109	9	4
		828	05	8

Soe that 30^{li} for the Greeks charge & 8^{li} 2^s for an error in his imposicons beinge deducted [from £268. 19s. 9d.] ther is due from him the some of ... ... 230^{li}. 17. 9.

W. DEVONSHIR.

[1] From the remarks on a previous account it appears no allowance was payable to the treasurer.
[2] Hammersly was Lord Mayor in 1628.

This arrangement is of exceptional interest, partly as showing how such an operation was effected at an early period, partly in its relation to the general commercial outlook of the time. The liquidation of the debts of the Russia company was carried on contemporaneously with the beginning of the second joint-stock of the East India company. The severe handling of the older undertaking constituted a warning which was taken to heart by the other corporation in the sense that the former paid dividends instead of providing for the payment of its debts and "had smarted for it[1]." Indeed the same cause had produced the comparative failure of the second joint-stock of the East India company and the financial troubles of the Russia company, namely, the active competition of the Dutch and their successful attacks by force of arms on the English merchants. Two circumstances differentiate the cases. The Russia company had been in possession of the whaling grounds (in so far as possession was possible) and were attacked by the Dutch, whereas the East India company was striving to establish itself in India. In the second place, the Russia company met its monetary difficulties by dishonest devices, whereas the other body escaped the temptation of similar tricks. Underlying the troubles of both was a fundamental weakness of the joint-stock company of the period, namely, the constant payment of the profits earned in dividends without providing a reserve fund. This weakness again was inherent in the popular idea that, even though an undertaking had perpetual powers, the finance must consist of comparatively short-lived independent undertakings. Thus there was no incentive to set aside profits to meet unforeseen contingencies, even though trade to remote places, having certain elements of privateering, was subject to sudden vicissitudes. It may indeed be said that members of the Russia company of 1608 to 1620 had little to complain of since, though they were reprimanded by the Lords and assessed, they had, after allowing for deductions, received back their capital and handsome profits for the risk they ran. But while the individual members may not have suffered the trade as a whole did. The profits were withdrawn as they were made, and when the original capital was lost no prudent person would subscribe more until the foreign situation improved. Yet a trading corporation with perpetual powers had obligations in equity to discharge in relation to the trade as a continuous one, and the idea of terminable capitals rendered it impossible to fulfil such functions satis-

[1] Court Book, East India company, vi., April 30, 1624. The assessments of the Russia company occasioned a very heated debate at a meeting of the Virginia company where various opinions were advanced as to whether private men's estates were liable for the debts contracted by the joint-stock in its corporate capacity. *The Records of the Virginia Company of London*, edited by S. M. Kingsbury, Washington, 1906, II. pp. 165, 205.

factorily, since, as has been shown, there was no reason for the establishing of a strong permanent reserve fund. Therefore the early history of joint-stock companies consisted of the painful learning of a fact that appears now to be almost axiomatic—namely, that just as a corporation *legally* has "perpetual succession," so *financially* it should endeavour to safeguard its capital to be capable of continuous existence.

E. THE RUSSIAN TRADE FROM 1620 TO THE END OF THE LAST JOINT-STOCK UNDERTAKING.

The intricate nature of the rehabilitation of the finances of the company has necessitated the temporary postponement of the tracing of the other sides of the history of the undertaking formed about 1620. As already shown, the right to adventure in expeditions to Greenland was now assigned to a distinct body, the career of which will be dealt with separately. There remained then, as the assets of the new company formed to continue the trade with Russia, the privileges relating to that country and the property connected with it, as well as a claim against the Dutch, which had eventually grown to £50,000, but which turned out to be a bad debt[1].

Owing to the unsettled condition of Russia at this time, and the partial cessation of trade, owing to the difficulties of the old company and other causes, the first step was to re-establish the privileges of the adventurers in Russia. Accordingly commissions were prepared in 1620 for two ambassadors, Sir John Merrick and Sir Dudley Digges[2], and in 1623 a treaty was made which had several clauses relating to the company. The previous grants to English merchants by the Czar were confirmed, always provided that such privileges were confined to members of the company[3]. The claim for exemption from customs in Russia was allowed, but at the same time the Czar bargained that he should have the right of pre-emption of any goods needed for his own use at the price at which such goods were commonly sold in England, without allowing any profit to the company[4]. In 1630 a further embassy was sent to Russia, Fabian Smith being the Ambassador[5].

In spite of the disturbance of business occasioned by the investigations into the company's affairs by the House of Lords, the trade appears to have been prosperous until about 1635. The complaints of the company during this period relate exclusively to the claim against the Dutch,

[1] State Papers, Domestic, Charles I., XLIV. 32; *Calendar*, 1625–6, p. 523.
[2] *Fœdera*, XVII. p. 256; Anderson, *Annals*, II. p. 379.
[3] *Fœdera*, XVII. p. 498.
[4] *A Collection of the State Papers of John Thurloe*, London, 1742, III. p. 375.
[5] *Fœdera*, XIX. p. 168.

and there is no mention of the trade to Russia being either "decayed" or "deserted." It was explicitly asserted by the Russian chancellor that the members of this company carried out the provisions of the treaty of 1623, and that they "grew very rich and got great estates[1]." As time went on it appears that this undertaking was wound up, or that most of the shares changed hands. Thus a new company, or, at least, a new administration, came into being, which brought fewer commodities into Russia. These were higher in price than those offered by the Dutch, and the clause in the treaty establishing the Czar's right of pre-emption at cost price was no longer observed[2]. By 1638 it was again necessary for a leviation to be made to pay the debts of the undertaking then in existence[3], and the late governor had been assessed with the other members, and, on his refusal to pay, he was imprisoned[4]. Once more this undertaking became the stock example of bad finance; and in 1639 the East India Adventurers were warned that if they did not reduce the debt, it would consume the company and bring them to a "Muscovia reckoning[5]." Again in 1644 the then governor, Sir H. Garraway, was discharged from this office and was ordered to be imprisoned during the pleasure of the House of Commons[6]. Probably the state of home politics was beginning to be felt in the internal affairs of the company, for in 1646 Luke Nightingale was prohibited from going to Russia "on the petition of the Muscovy Merchants[7]." In the same year the concessions of the company in Russia were altogether annulled, and the members and their factors expelled from the country.

There are several explanations of this act of the Czar. His representative alleged that, since the company that had followed the one in existence when the treaty was made had broken the provisions of this instrument, "the taking away of the privileges came from themselves[8]." When Cromwell was in power the company stated that the edict of banishment had been obtained at the instance of Lord Culpepper, who was the Royalist agent at the Russian court[9]. Yet another version was that after the death of Charles I., the Dutch represented to the Czar the iniquities of a nation that "had murdered its king," and that it was at their instigation that the edict was issued. The Dutch merchants

[1] Thurloe, *State Papers, ut supra*, III. p. 375.   [2] *Ibid.*
[3] State Papers, Domestic, Charles I., cccovii. 94; *Calendar*, 1638-9, p. 245.
[4] *Ibid.*, DXXXVIII. 65; *Calendar,* 1625-49, p. 600.
[5] Court Book of the East India Company, XVII., July 12, 1639.
[6] *Journals of the House of Commons*, III. p. 514.
[7] *Journals of the House of Lords*, VIII. p. 493. Nightingale was a Royalist agent. He is said to have arrived in Russia and to have conveyed a request from Charles I. to the Czar to abolish the privileges of the company. Anderson, *Annals*, II. p. 542.
[8] Thurloe, *State Papers, ut supra*, III. p. 575.
[9] *Ibid.*, III. p. 50.

appealed not only to the idea of "the right divine" of kings, but also to the more mundane considerations of profit, offering to pay 15 per cent. customs duty from Archangel on the banishment of the English factors[1].

When Cromwell was firmly established, as a part of his vigorous foreign policy, he endeavoured to obtain a re-instatement of the trade. An expedition was fitted out in 1654, and with it went William Prideaux, as ambassador. On arriving at Archangel, permission was asked to trade, and a license was granted that the ships might dispose of their goods at Archangel, Prideaux might travel to Moscow to confer with the Czar, but no factors were to accompany him. All goods landed in the country were subjected to the same customs paid by foreign nations[2].

In this condition the trade remained until the Restoration, when another attempt was made to obtain the renewal of the former preference given to English merchants of the company. Lord Carlisle was the ambassador, but his mission was foredoomed to failure, for, according to the account of the Russians, they had been much less favourably treated by the company during the ten or fifteen years before the expulsion than by the Dutch. Not only were the Dutch firmly established in the trade, but they had agreed to pay 15 per cent. customs on all cargoes landed at Archangel. Thus, to restore the former preference to the company, would involve a loss of revenue and the probability of higher prices of commodities in Russia[3]. For these and other reasons the best answer that Carlisle could obtain was that English merchants might trade to Russia on the same terms as the Dutch. After the return of the embassy in 1669 the last joint-stock was wound up, and the trade continued by a regulated company. For a number of years afterwards this body complained to the Council of Trade of the new customs it had to pay (1676), and that, though (in November 1679) its privileges were described as "broken," it did not consider the present a fit time to move in prosecuting the trade more vigorously[4].

It is an interesting inversion, this change from a joint-stock company back to the regulated type, for the latter was the earlier form of organization. The explanation of the change, both in this case and in that of

---

[1] Harris, *Collection of Voyages*, II. p. 223.

[2] Thurloe, *State Papers, ut supra*, II. p. 562. Some idea of the importance of the previous exemption from Russian customs may be gathered from the epigram of Sir Thomas Roe who, speaking of high foreign taxes in 1641, said that for this reason "the Eastland company could not exist and *without them the Muscovy company*," i.e. that the success of the latter depended on the exemption—"Cause of Decay of Coin and Trade" in *Harl. Misc.* IV. p. 412.

[3] Anderson, *Annals, ut supra*, II. pp. 542–3.

[4] State Papers, Board of Trade Commercial Series, II., vol. 691.

the Royal African company, was that all through the seventeenth and the earlier part of the eighteenth centuries, there was a keen rivalry between the two kinds of companies. When a trade had been for some time unsuccessful as a joint-stock company, there was a tendency to give the regulated type a trial. In the special case of the Russian trade there was no longer the same need for a considerable capital, for English merchants ceased to be responsible to the Czar in the same sense as they had been when they had a preference over other foreigners in the country. At that period a joint-stock was almost a necessity, since the private gain of an individual, in defiance of the treaty of 1623, might have led to the revocation of the privileges. That the trade was not thrown altogether open was due to the idea that commerce with distant countries required some kind of governance. Since this was to be no longer by a joint-stock company, there only remained the regulated one.

The history of the Russia company as a regulated company, falls outside the limits of the present work. But there are several events between 1669 and 1699 that should be mentioned from their bearing on the general controversy between the regulated and joint-stock companies. It appears that one reason for the establishing of the trade about 1669 as a regulated company was to make it more of a monopoly rather than, as might have been expected, to have it more open. It was not long before the fine for admission became £50, and such admission was confined to "regular" or "legitimate" merchants, *i.e.* those who had served an apprenticeship in that particular trade[1].

In 1694, on a petition from a number of London merchants, complaining of the administration of the company, a parliamentary enquiry was ordered. It appears that about this time the company, although a regulated one, was again in debt[2], and a bye-law had been passed not to admit any person to the freedom of the company on any terms whatever[3]. The number of members, after having been 50 in 1654[4], had fallen to between 12 and 14, thus almost exactly repeating the membership of the beginning of Cherry's company more than a century before. It was deposed in evidence that a trader had to pay from £50 to £60 a year to land at Narva but that he might not touch at Archangel. The proceeds of licenses to Narva paid the whole charges of the company, while the freemen reserved to themselves the monopoly of the Archangel trade. On the side of the Adventurers it was argued that although there was a

---

[1] *Journals of the House of Commons*, XI. p. 631.

[2] *The Case of the Company of Merchant Adventurers for the Discovery of New Trades.*

[3] *The Charge of Companies of Merchants more equally born by imposition on Trade than by fines for Admission.*

[4] State Papers, Domestic, Inter., LXV. 60; *Calendar*, 1653–4, p. 377.

bye-law confining admission to those who had served an apprenticeship, at the same time anyone might receive the freedom who paid a fine of £60. But it does not appear that actual admissions had been made on the latter basis. It was resolved by the Committee to bring in a bill settling the terms for admission on terms similar to those obtaining in the other two important regulated companies, the Eastland and Hamburg ones[1]. This measure was rejected on February 16th, 1694, but a similar bill was introduced in 1698, which became law. It enacted that, since "ease of admission would tend to increase the trade for the public good," any subject of the realm should have the right to become a freeman on his paying a fine of £5[2]. With this event the main history of the company ends. It continued to exist as a trading body till the end of the eighteenth century, and as late as 1865 furnished a return to Parliament of certain dues it collected. In the middle of the nineteenth century its dinners were important social functions; and it has been stated in 1891 that "the company still exists for social purposes[3]," while the address of its office still appears in the London directory.

F. THE GREENLAND TRADE FROM 1620 TO 1673.

Either about the same time as, or very soon after, the formation of the Russia joint-stock of 1620, the privileges for whaling were separated from the rest of the trade and sold to an independent undertaking, on terms already mentioned, the members of which must be members of the Russia company, but not necessarily conversely. This undertaking took over the remaining stores of the expeditions financed jointly by the Russia and East India companies, which had come to an end in 1619.

It is stated that at first there were only four members of the Russia company engaged in this venture. Their voyage in 1620 consisted of seven ships, which returned half-laden, bringing 700 tuns of oil. In the following year the fleet of whalers consisted of the same number of vessels, in addition to which another was sent for discovery. The proceeds of this expedition were 1,100 tuns, which "gave the adventurers good encouragement." In 1622 the number of ships was the same, and the yield 1,300 tuns[4]. A fourth voyage was sent out in 1623, but the available information points to its having been unsuccessful[5]. Anderson says that 1623 was "the last year of their union[6]," but it does not appear

[1] *Journals of the House of Commons*, xi. p. 631.
[2] 10 Will. III., c. 6; *Statutes of the Realm*, vii. p. 463.
[3] *The Historic Note Book*, 1891.
[4] Purchas, *His Pilgrims* (1906), xiii. pp. 24–6.
[5] *Ibid.*, xiv. pp. 103–8.
[6] Anderson, *Annals*, ii. p. 381.

whether this partnership was dissolved or became the basis of the Greenland company that appeared before the Houses of Parliament at frequent intervals for many years. It seems to have been about 1622 or 1623 that the new whale-fishing company was formed which endeavoured to escape payment of its contribution to the debt of the Russia company[1]. This undertaking could not free itself from the bad traditions of the parent company. Although the allegations of an unfair sale made in 1628 were exaggerated, there were several disputes amongst the stockholders. For instance, even when the investigation in the House of Lords was proceeding, a new cause of complaint arose, through the Court having credited a share-holder with a smaller amount of stock than that to which he held he was entitled[2]. At the same date (1626) the representatives of Sir James Cunningham were still unpaid the compensation-money for the recalling of the patent, for which this company was liable[3].

The great difficulty that this undertaking had to contend with was the invasion of its whaling grounds by other English ships. The shipowners of Hull had been very early in this trade, and in 1618 they had received a royal license to fish for whales off Trinity Island[4]. In 1626 N. Edwards and his partners received a license from Charles I., as King of Scotland, for whaling. This repeated the Cunningham episode and, as before, the matter was adjusted by the revocation of the permission granted to Edwards on the condition that he should be compensated. He and his partners failed for a time to obtain what was due to them and in 1635 the company was ordered to admit them as members[5]. The controversy with the Hull merchants was more permanent. In 1626 the company complained that, the latter having arrived at Bell Sound, had destroyed all the materials they found there[6]. The following year, at the instance of the Privy Council, the company was forced to assign one-fifth of 3,000 tons of shipping, judged sufficient for that year, to the merchants of York and Hull[7], and the following year a similar arrangement was made.

In 1628 the company obtained an Order of Council (to encourage them, "since in that year they had made a very hard voyage of it"), prohibiting the importation of whale-oil or whale-fins by any persons

---

[1] House of Lords MSS., June 19, 1628, a/cs Muscovy Co.
[2] *Reports Com. Hist. MSS.*, IV. p. 8.   [3] *Ibid.*, p. 5.
[4] Anderson, *Annals*, II. p. 366.
[5] State Papers, Domestic, Charles I., XXXII. 52; LIX. 28; CCLXXXIV. 67; *Calendars*, 1625-6, p. 386; 1627-8, p. 125; 1634-5, p. 577.
[6] *Ibid.*, XXXIX. 67, printed in *Early Voyages to Spitsbergen*, by Sir W. M. Conway, p. 175.
[7] *Ibid.*, LVIII. 56; *Calendar*, 1627-8, p. 113; *Journals of the House of Commons*, I. p. 905.

DIV. I. § 2 F] *Disputes with Interlopers 1626–31* 71

except the company[1]. While the undertaking had been able to enlist the sympathies of the Privy Council, the other English whalers had appealed to Parliament, and, in the same year, the position of the company was referred to the Committee of Grievances of the House of Commons. The Court, in its answer to the petition of the merchants of Hull, relied on the original charter of Mary and the Act of Elizabeth, reinforced by the patent for whale fishing of 1613. Evidently there was considerable doubt amongst the Committee since Coke records that nothing was resolved, but he "was inclined to think" that the original charter and act "did not extend to this[2]." In view of that decision the company continued to exercise its former powers over non-licensed whalers, and in 1632 a bond for £1,000, given by a person previously an invader of the Spitzbergen district, was forfeited on a renewal of the offence[3]. Two years later the ships of the company encounter two vessels sent from Yarmouth at Horn Sound, the one flaunting the commission granted to Edwards, and the other that of the Privy Council; where, during an affray between the rival factions, one man was shot[4].

The persistence with which outsiders endeavoured to obtain a footing in the trade is indirect evidence that occasionally large profits were made. Not only were licenses difficult to obtain, but obstacles were placed in the way of purchasers of the stock. Edwards had to obtain an order to be admitted, and even members of the Russia company sometimes failed to have their subscriptions accepted. In 1631 N. Wright, who was not only a share-holder in the Russia company, but who had already been an adventurer and a director of a company for whaling, was at first refused permission to subscribe[5].

Meanwhile the company had become involved in the controversy relating to the soap business. The importance of the contest between the old and new soaps for this undertaking turned on the fact that the latter was intended to substitute other materials for the whale-oil which had hitherto been used in the manufacturing process. Therefore the Greenland monopoly was arrayed against the new-soap monopoly, and in 1634 the former complained that the non-success of the new process was a most serious burden to its trade[6]. On the failure of the "corporation" established to test the supposed improved method, the whaling company obtained compensation in 1636 by a proclamation prohibiting

[1] State Papers, Domestic, 175, Charles I., xci. 53; *Calendar*, 1627–8, p. 529.
[2] *Journals of the House of Commons*, I. p. 889.
[3] State Papers, Domestic, Charles I., ccxiv. 60; *Calendar*, 1631–3, p. 293.
[4] *Ibid.*, cclxxv. 30, ccccxcix. 47, printed in *Early Voyages to Spitsbergen*, by Sir W. M. Conway, pp. 176–9.
[5] *Ibid.*, cxcv. 19; *Calendar*, 1631–3, p. 92.
[6] *Ibid.*, cclxix. 72; *Calendar*, 1634–5, p. 392.

all persons from invading the limits assigned the company, which, in its joint-stock capacity, was confirmed in the monopoly of catching whales[1].

The independent traders remained undeterred by this proclamation, and in 1641 they petitioned the House of Lords. The latter ordered the company to appear before them, and rashly undertook "to compose the differences" of the antagonistic interests[2]. Four years later (1645) the company obtained another order confirming its monopoly, on this occasion from the Navy Committee[3]. As a result of this acknowledgement of its powers, the Court endeavoured to make good its sole right to the fishing grounds, but in 1650 the Attorney-General condemned its proceedings against Thomas Anderson and Richard Gatcombe of Hull as oppressive[4]. In 1652 the dispute was still in progress, and the company and the Fishing Adventurers were directed "to agree" until Parliament could consider the matter[5].

In 1654 the allegations on both sides were fully investigated. The company in its petition stated that, in spite of the original charter of the Russia company and the act of Parliament (under which new trades discovered were vested in the adventurers, and that whaling had been first practised by them, while these privileges, in so far as they related to whaling, had been transferred to the present Greenland company, which had also been encouraged by proclamations, orders of the Navy Committee and the Council of Trade) the business of the petitioning undertaking had been greatly molested by the independent adventurers, who had invaded the whaling area in defiance of the company's monopoly. It was further urged that through the irregularity of the interlopers, the Greenland company had already lost most of their stock-in-trade. Owing to the necessity for landing to boil down the blubber, if there were different competing bodies, armed conflicts were likely to occur. It was therefore contended that, to prevent disorders of this and other kinds, the only way the trade could be conducted satisfactorily was by a single joint-stock company. The existing body had subscribed £20,000, and this large sum would not have been adventured unless the business were carried on by a joint-stock. The company further drew attention to the evidence given in 1650, when it had been proposed that Bell Sound and Horn Sound should be reserved to its ships, while the independent adventurers might fish off Greenland, managing their voyages on a joint-stock of their own[6].

---

[1] *Fœdera*, xx. p. 16.   [2] *Journals of the House of Lords*, iv. p. 258.

[3] State Papers, Domestic, Inter., lxv. 33; *Calendar*, 1653–4, p. 362.

[4] State Papers, Domestic, Order Book Council of State, 123, p. 385; *Calendar*, 1650, p. 237.

[5] *Ibid.*, 66, p. 553; *Calendar*, 1651–2, p. 178.

[6] State Papers, Domestic, Inter., lxv. 60–70; *Proceedings at the Council of Trade*

DIV. I. § 2 F] *Disputes with Interlopers* 1641–54   73

It was contended by the other side that the company now consisted of about 50 members, and that its shipping was only equal to the aggregate sent by the independent adventurers. The company did not import a sufficient quantity of oil, and the price was thus higher than it would otherwise have been. If the trade were open twice as much shipping would be sent for whaling expeditions. Further, with special reference to the proposed division of whaling grounds, it was replied that Bell Sound and Horn Sound were the most advantageous trying grounds (owing to the presence of ice elsewhere), and that both together would accommodate twice as much shipping as had visited these parts in recent years. Therefore the proposal of the company in effect was to reserve the best districts for its own use and leave the less desirable places to its opponents.

It is a little difficult to decide the merits of this controversy. At first sight it would appear that right lay on the side of the independent adventurers, who were opposed by a comparatively wealthy corporation. But a closer investigation of the facts shows that this was not a case of an aggregation of capital against single individuals. The independent adventurers found it advantageous to pose as distinct individuals, but as a matter of fact, they acted in small companies or partnerships—this was so well known that one group was described officially as "Edward Bushnell & Co.[1]" The argument that the trade was "monopolised" because there were only some 50 or 55 members of the Greenland company falls to the ground, since altogether the separate adventurers of Hull numbered no more than eighteen persons[2]. Similarly the idea that with an open trade the shipping sent to the north would be doubled, is illusory. There is fair evidence that 3,000 tons was a reasonable provision, and at this date the independent adventurers, on their own showing, provided 1,100 tons or over one-third. They had sent 500 tons out of the same amount in 1627–8, so that in the interval they had increased their proportion from one-sixth to over one-third. Some weight should be given to the company's plea that the whaling grounds should be treated as a single area or else be divided into separate districts. It was necessary to protect English ships against foreign aggression, and therefore a fleet owned by one body acting together would have been much stronger than the same tonnage belonging to different owners, whose ships would

between the Muscovia Company...and other adventurers $\left(\text{Brit. Mus. } \frac{518.1.13}{13}\right)$; *Calendar State Papers, Domestic,* 1653–4, pp. 377–8; *English Trade and Finance, chiefly in the Seventeenth Century,* by W. A. S. Hewins, pp. 40–2.

[1] State Papers, Domestic, Order Book Council of State [Jan. 20, 1652, March 12, 1652], 97, p. 70, 66, p. 453; *Calendar,* 1651–2, pp. 111, 178.

[2] State Papers, Domestic, Inter., LXVI. 68; *Calendar,* 1653–4, p. 421.

tend to separate. Besides, the captains at the whaling grounds were removed from home control, and so fights between the crews were not infrequent. This risk would have been minimised by assigning to each owner a distinct area.

Parliament eventually proposed to effect a compromise by giving the regulation of the trade to a committee chosen from amongst the different owners of whalers. It was at first proposed that the 3,000 tons of shipping should be divided as follows:

The company	1,600 tons
The Adventurers of Hull and York	400 ,,
Whitwell and partners	300 ,,
Horth and partners	500 ,,
Battson and partners	200 ,,
	3,000 tons[1]

It was finally decided that the company and the Hull adventurers should have two-thirds of the shipping, and the others the remaining third, while the committee was constituted by assigning 10 members to the company as against 14 to the remaining interests[2].

The company did not acquiesce in this settlement, for in 1657 (or only three years later) it again petitioned for the monopoly of the fishing at Bell Sound and Horn Sound[3], and in the following year its request was granted[4].

It seems that for some years the undertaking had experienced evil fortune, and it is probable that the last joint-stock was wound up not long after the Restoration. During the thirty years from 1620 to 1650 there are various grounds for concluding that, subject to the necessarily speculative nature of the trade, the company had been at least moderately successful. In 1654 it was stated that most of the capital had been lost[5], owing to the fishing in that year, of both the chartered and the independent companies, having been such a complete failure that the country was threatened with a famine of train-oil[6]. A fresh subscription was made soon afterwards, and by 1657 this had also been lost. Hence the company stated at this time that "*two*" stocks had been risked up to that date and had disappeared[7].

For several years before 1672 " the trade had been quite decayed and

---

[1] State Papers, Domestic, Inter., LXVI. 68; *Calendar*, 1653–4, p. 421.

[2] *Ibid.*, LXVII. 42, LXX. 98; *Calendar*, 1654, pp. 16, 136.

[3] *Ibid.*, CLVII. 57; *Calendar*, 1657–8, p. 141.

[4] State Papers, Domestic, Council of State [Jan. 7, 1658], 78, pp. 393–5; *Calendar*, 1657–8, p. 257.

[5] State Papers, Domestic, Inter., LXV. 33; *Calendar*, 1653–4, p. 362.

[6] *The Diary of Thomas Burton*, London, 1828, I. xlix.

[7] State Papers, Domestic, Inter., CLVII. 57; *Calendar*, 1657–8, p. 141.

lost," and in that year a Committee of the House of Commons was appointed to enquire into the matter[1]. An act was passed which, after stating that "whale-fishing had been a profitable trade, giving employment to great numbers of sea-men and shipping, and that neighbouring nations do yearly make great advantage thereby, not only supplying themselves with oil and fins, but vending into other parts great quantities thereof, and particularly into this kingdom," proceeded to enact that in future all English subjects might freely resort to Greenland for whaling, and might import oil and whale-fins that had resulted from the captures taken by British ships[2].

This act opened the trade, and it is interesting to note that it resulted not from the attacks on the privileged company by the independent whalers, but from the common failure of both. But the period of open trade, which lasted from 1672 to 1692, was no more satisfactory than that from 1650 to 1672. In 1681 a partnership, formed by Sir Thomas Allen and others, was engaged in the trade. Notwithstanding a large duty on foreign oil, this company felt the stress of competition so severely that it was stated that, if such importation continued, the revived industry would be destroyed, which had been recently "set up by this company at its great cost[3]." Early in the reign of William III. a new company was formed, which was granted a monopoly[4]. Since this undertaking, which was incorporated as "*the Governor and Company of the Merchants of London trading into Greenland*," was a new foundation and quite distinct from the Russia company, an account of it will be found under the general heading of the Fishery companies[5].

[1] *Journals of the House of Commons*, IX. p. 252.
[2] Statutes, v. 792.
[3] State Papers, Domestic, Charles II., ccccxv. 19, 20.
[4] 4 Will. and Mary, c. 17.
[5] *Vide* Div. III. § 5.

SECTION III. "THE ADVENTURERS TO THE NORTH-WEST FOR THE DISCOVERY OF A NORTH-WEST PASSAGE," OR "THE COMPANY OF KATHAI."

FROBISHER'S VOYAGES (1576–83).

The First Voyage (1576).

ALTHOUGH the charter and act of the Russia company had granted to that body the exclusive right of trade with all countries discovered by it to the north, north-east or north-west of London, no expedition had been sent by this organization to discover a north-west passage to China during the first twenty years of its existence. The vicissitudes of the trade to Russia had fully occupied the energies and resources of the adventurers, and the only record of any attempted additional discovery, beyond the route to Archangel, was the extension of that route as far as the river Obi, by Stephen Burroughs, in 1556[1]. Although the Russia company was content to trust to the eventual finding of a north-east passage, the project of navigating one by the north-west was not forgotten. About 1569 Martin Frobisher "began first with himself to devise and then with his friends to conferre, and layd a plaine platte unto them that that voyage was not only possible by the northwest, but also, as he coulde prove, easie to be performed[2]." At first he applied to the merchants, but without result, and, being himself without means, the idea remained unrealized until he secured the support of Ambrose Dudley, Earl of Warwick. At this early stage a difficulty arose, for the proposed expedition was contrary to the privileges of the Russia company. In 1574 Frobisher brought a letter from the Privy Council to the company, urging it either to attempt the discovery or to license others to do so. At a court-meeting convened to consider the matter it was held that the supporters of the proposal showed "no good evidence" of its feasibility, and the company "suspected some other matter to be meant by the parties." The Russia company therefore replied that it had at great expense already discovered one-half of the north-eastern passage, and

[1] A Brief Narration of the Discoverie of the Northern Seas...as it was first begun and continued by the singular Industry of the Companye of Muscovy (Brit. Mus. Add. MSS., No. 33837, p. 72).

[2] "A True Discourse of the late Voyages of Discoverie...of Martin Frobisher," in *The Three Voyages of Martin Frobisher* (Hakluyt Society, 1867), p. 70.

"proposed to do the rest as soon as they might have good advice." The Council interpreted this reply as an excuse for delay, and in a further communication it ordered the company either to attempt the westward voyage immediately or to allow others to do so. "Wherefore for dyvers consyderations then moving the Cumpany" (which may be interpreted as the unsettled outlook in Russia at the time) Frobisher and any partners, who might venture with him, were granted a license in February 1574-5[1].

At first there was still a difficulty in raising capital, and it was only by the assistance of Michael Lok that funds were eventually procured in 1576. It is owing to the methodical habits of Lok, and also to the fact of certain later legal proceedings, that exceptionally full particulars of the financial operations of this venture have been preserved, which are of great value as showing the methods by which capital was dealt with in very early English joint-stock undertakings.

There were altogether 18 adventurers, of whom four (namely Lok himself, Sir Thomas Gresham, William Bond, the "interloper" in the Russian trade, and a William Burde) subscribed £100 each, five for £50 each, and the remainder for £25 each[2]. In this way the modest capital of £875 was collected, which was expended in the equipping of two small vessels and a pinnace. On June 15th, 1576, the expedition sailed. Frobisher succeeded in penetrating as far as Hudson's Straits and touched at Baffin Land, which he named "Meta Incognita." He had given orders that the landing party should "bring him whatsoever thing they could first find, whether it were living or dead, stocke or stone, in token of Christian possession[3]." Amongst the various things brought to the ship was a piece of stone or mineral, which had a remarkable effect on the future expeditions. It is thus described in a contemporary account:—"One [of the landing party] brought a peece of blacke stone much lyke to a seacole in coloure, whiche by waight seemed to be some kinde of metall or mynerall. This was a thinge of no accompt in the judgement of the captain at the first sight. And yet for novelty it was kept, in respect of the place from whence it came. After his arrival in London, being demanded of sundrie his friends what thing he had brought them home, he had nothing left to present them withall but a peece of this black stone. And it fortuned a gentlewoman, one of ye adventurers wives, to have a peece thereof, which by chance she threw and burned in the fire, so long, that at the length being taken forth and quenched in a little vinegre, it glistered with a bright marquesset of golde. Whereupon the matter being called in some question, it was brought to certain gold finders in London to make assaye therof,

---

[1] *The Three Voyages of Martin Frobisher, ut supra*, p. 89.
[2] *Ibid.*, pp. 164-5. [3] *Ibid.*, p. 75.

who indeed found it to hold gold, and that very ritchly for the quantity[1]."

Thus it happened that the first expedition, which returned on October 9th, had not discovered any country whose inhabitants would become purchasers of English commodities; but on the other hand, it appeared that a very rich mining district had been found. This made the original adventurers anxious to join in a second voyage, and many who had heard rumours of the rich find were also prepared to contribute. As matters stood at the end of 1576 the adventurers of the first voyage had expended their capital of £875, and there was due for wages, &c., in addition, the sum of £738. 19s. 3d., which was temporarily advanced by Lok[2]. Against this there were the discoverers' rights in what was believed to be an exceptionally valuable mine, and accordingly it was agreed that the liabilities and assets of the first voyage should be transferred to the second expedition on certain conditions, thus making one undertaking of both.

The Second Voyage (1577).

In view of the great results anticipated from the second voyage, it was judged expedient to establish the company in a more formal manner than had been done hitherto, and "articles of grant" from the Queen were drawn up, which provided for the incorporation of the former and the new adventurers as "a companye and corporation for ever" under the title of the "*Companye of Kathai*," with power to assemble together and hold courts. The quorum at a meeting was to consist of 15 persons, who might at the first court, elect one governor, two consuls and twelve assistants, who were to continue in office for three years. At the next meeting, and thereafter every three years, two governors, four consuls and twenty-four assistants were to be elected. As it was intended that each joint-stock should run for three years, the continuance of the officials and of the stock would be concurrent. The company was to obtain the exclusive right to trade north-westwards and southward in so far as such grant would not be contrary to the previous privileges of the Russia company. On all goods exported no higher customs should be paid than those in force at the date of the grant, and on imports half-customs were to be remitted for twenty years; and afterwards in no case should the duties exceed five per cent. Frobisher and Lok were each to receive one per cent. on all goods imported by the company, in consideration of their "industry, good order and great travayll in the first voyage[3]."

---

[1] *The Three Voyages of Martin Frobisher, ut supra*, p. 75.
[2] *Ibid.*, p. 116.   [3] *Ibid.*, pp. 111–13.

This grant was supplemented by a number of "Articles consented and fully agreede by the Companye of Kathaye." The sum of £100 was to be accounted "one single parte or share in stok of the company." No one was allowed to own more than "five single partes," except the original adventurers, who might "put in stock doble number of single partes of any other." After the expiration of three years from the beginning of a given stock, accounts of it were to be clearly made up and furnished, and "divydent" made to the venturers according to "the rate of their stok therein put." New venturers for the second voyage were to pay £30 towards the losses on the first expedition of discovery. At the end of three years no one was to be admitted to the freedom except on payment of £200. Fines for admission were subject to the limitations that Frobisher and Lok had the right of nominating five persons each without payment, heirs male of freemen were also admitted without fine and similarly a freeman dying without heirs male might bequeath his freedom by will[1].

Meanwhile the stores and vessels returned from the first voyage had been sold yielding £813 19 3
and, as the debt was previously 738 19 3
there remained a balance of £75 0 0

which represented the amount actually available against the original investment of £875.

New capital began to come in comparatively freely. By March 30th, 1577, £3,225 was subscribed[2], of which only £2,500 was paid in May[3]. In July stock subscribed was returned at £3,500, of which £3,000 was then paid[4]. Since the equipment of the fleet, which had sailed on May 26th, 1577, came to £4,328. 17s. 6d., further subscriptions were received, and eventually the whole amount, adventured by 41 persons, came to £4,275[5]. The capital of the two voyages was made up as follows:

	£	£
Capital Voyage I not transferred to Voyage II	275	
,, ,, transferred to Voyage II	600	600
Total capital Voyage I	875	
New capital subscribed for Voyage II		4,275
Total capital Voyage II		4,875
Add capital Voyage I not transferred		275
Total capital Voyages I and II		£5,150

When Frobisher returned in September 1577 he brought great quantities of ore with him. The capital subscribed had been employed in

[1] *The Three Voyages of Martin Frobisher, ut supra*, pp. 114–15.
[2] *Ibid.*, pp. 164–5.
[3] MSS. Brit. Mus., Otho VIII., f. 45; *Cal. State Papers, Colonial*, 1513–1616, p. 22.
[4] State Papers, Domestic, Eliz., cxix. 34; *Cal. State Papers, Colonial*, p. 23.
[5] Frobisher, *Three Voyages, ut supra*, pp. 114–15.

paying off the debts incurred in fitting out the expedition, and there were no funds available to pay the sailors' wages amounting to about £1,000. Accordingly an order was made for a cessement or levy of 20 per cent., which was exacted from all the adventurers whether they had transferred their stock to the second voyage or not, and in this way, when the whole amount was paid, £1,030 (*i.e.* 20 per cent. on £5,150) was receivable[1]. Further, although the ore was believed to be almost fabulously rich in gold, there were no means of refining it. The only existing appliances, on a large scale, appear to have been owned by the Society of the Mines Royal, whose operations were conducted at places distant from London[2]. It was therefore decided that the Kathai company should erect its own furnaces at Dartford, and for this additional funds were required so that another cessement of about the same rate was made. This brought in £1,105, so that of £7,285 so far obtained, it had been necessary to find £2,135 by cessement, or a levy of about 40 per cent. on the capital[3]. As against this outlay the venturers had certain ships and stores as well as a great quantity of ore, which was reputed to be very rich.

The affairs of the company were in this state when the time came at which a third expedition should be despatched. In February 1678 a trial had been made of the ore, and it was asserted that the yield gave a value to the ton of £67. 1*s.* 8*d.* for one assay, and £53. 10*s.* 3*d.* for another[4]. Estimating the value of the ore at only £30 a ton, and that 2,000 tons could be obtained, would mean a gross profit of £60,000. The expenses of ships, wages and freight were expected to amount to £20,836. 13*s.* 4*d.*, leaving a profit of £39,163. 6*s.* 8*d.* or £20 nett per ton[5]. In view of such optimistic anticipations this third voyage would have returned not only its capital outlay, but would have made good the expenditure on the two previous expeditions, without taking account of the ore already landed. Thus there was small difficulty in securing a considerable subscription from the venturers, and the third voyage started on May 31st, 1578, returning on September 25th, 1578.

The Third Voyage (1578).

It appears that the total subscription for this expedition was £6,952. 10*s.*, which, added to the £7,285 already called up and carried forward[6], would make a total of £14,237. 10*s.* on which dividends would

[1] *The Three Voyages of Martin Frobisher*, pp. 162–4.

[2] *Vide infra*, Div. IV. § 1.

[3] State Papers, Domestic, Eliz., cxxvi. 34, "All the stok of the Venturers in all the iii voyages," vide *The Three Voyages of Martin Frobisher*, p. 358.

[4] State Papers, Domestic, Eliz., cxxII. 52; *Cal. State Papers, Colonial*, 1513–1616, p. 32.

[5] *Ibid.*, cxxIV. 1; *Cal. State Papers, Colonial*, 1513–1616, p. 33.

[6] "All the stok of the Venturers," *ut supra*.

be paid; so that, if the estimate already quoted were borne out by events, the return should have been nearly 300 per cent. But even if such hopes were to be realized in the end, it was discovered on the return of the expedition that more capital was required, since Frobisher had brought twice the quantity of ore expected. The venturers (some of whom had not yet paid up their subscriptions to this voyage) were dilatory in providing fresh funds, and authority was given to Michael Lok to collect £6,000 additional by a levy, and, if necessary, to call upon the Lord Mayor "to perswade them[1]." Nearly the whole of this sum was collected in two separate assessments, so that the whole ventures and levies thereon in the three voyages amounted at the end of the year to £20,160, this sum being made up as to £12,102. 10s. of original subscriptions, and the remaining £8,057. 10s. of cessements[2]. In a later revised account, dated May 1581 covering the same period, the total was slightly increased to £20,345[3].

It will thus be seen that the whole fate of the company depended on the results yielded by the ore. If these even approached the estimate, the whole capital, so far expended, would be returned with increase. Unfortunately, although Lok believed in the value of the ore, the results of the assay were most disappointing, for the only precious metal recovered was only just large enough to ornament a few drops of sealing-wax on the report embodying this finding.

The Fourth Voyage (1582).

The adventurers were thus in a position that over £20,000 had been paid out or due, and there was nothing as yet to show for it. To give up the whole venture would have been to admit the loss as beyond remedy, and it was not long before a fourth voyage was contemplated. At first this expedition also was to be under the charge of Frobisher, but before sailing Edward Fenton was placed in command. There had been so much dissatisfaction amongst the venturers in the two previous voyages at the cessements needed to pay charges on the return, that it was arranged that out of the gains of the expedition (after the payment of charges) there should be set aside one-third for wages and allowances to captains, factors, &c. The remaining two-thirds were to go to the adventurers[4].

The instructions for this voyage contained a clause—that the ships were not to pass to China by the north-eastward, "so will the traffick be better made, and the reason of this charge...is least perhaps he

---

[1] State Papers, Domestic, Eliz., ccxxvi. 20; *The Three Voyages of Martin Frobisher*, pp. 319-20.   [2] "All the Stok of the Venturers," *ut supra*.

[3] State Papers, Domestic, Eliz., cxlix. 42; *Cal. State Papers, Colonial,* 1513-1616, p. 64.

[4] Brit. Mus. MSS. Otho VIII. f. 228; *Cal. State Papers, Colonial, East Indies,* 1513-1616, p. 72.

[*i.e.* Frobisher] should have some desire to search out his formerly pretended passage that way, and so hinder this voyage which is only for trade¹." A total capital of about £11,600 was subscribed², and the fleet sailed on May 1st, 1582³.

It was intended that this expedition should follow one of the known routes to the East, either by the Cape of Good Hope or by the Straits of Magellan. The ships touched at the Cape de Verde Islands and afterwards on the African coast near Sierra Leone. After considerable discussion it was decided not to attempt the route by the Cape of Good Hope, and sail was made for South America. In January 1583 the expedition arrived at Brazil, and a brisk trade was opened, when suddenly three strongly armed Spanish ships appeared, and a hot fight ensued. Although the Spanish vice-admiral was sunk, the English ships were forced to put to sea, and they reached England in June of the same year⁴. If any reliance can be placed on the estimate formed by Fenton that, if it had not been for this encounter, he would have brought home " in honest trade about £40,000 or £50,000 " worth of goods⁵, it shows how one successful expedition at this period would not only have extinguished the previous losses, but would also have left a considerable margin of profit on the whole series of ventures. As matters actually turned out, each voyage had resulted in loss, and with the return of this expedition, the company ceased to attempt to recoup itself, and was eventually wound up⁶.

Summary of Capital of the Company of Kathai.

		£	s.	d.	£	s.	d.
1576.	The first voyage				875	0	0
1577.	The second voyage				4,275	0	0
	Total capital first and second voyages				5,150	0	0
	20% cessement thereon to pay wages, &c.	1,030	0	0			
	Further cessement to provide smelting plant, &c.	1,105	0	0			
					2,135	0	0
	Total capital and cessements first and second voyages				7,285	0	0
1578.	The third voyage, capital subscribed	6,952	10	0			
	First cessement thereon £3,347 10 0						
	Second ,, ,, £2,575 0 0						
		5,922	10	0			
	Total capital raised for third voyage and cessements	12,875	0	0	12,875	0	0
	Capital and cessements all three voyages				20,160	0	0
1582.	Fourth voyage, capital subscribed				11,600	0	0

¹ Brit. Mus. MSS. Otho VIII., f. 85.   ² *Ibid.*, f. 104.   ³ *Ibid.*, f. 179
⁴ *Calendar State Papers, Colonial, East Indies*, 1513–1616, pp. 85–9.
⁵ *Ibid.*, p. 89.
⁶ For some account of the Colleagues of the Fellowship for the Discovery of the North-West Passage and the North-West Passage company *vide infra*, p. 100.

SECTION IV. THE LEVANT COMPANY.

THE GOVERNOUR AND COMPANIE OF MARCHANTES OF THE LEVANT.

(From the foundation until the adoption of the regulated type of organization early in the sixteenth century.)

THE Levant company had its origin in the commerce between England and Italy. As far back as 1412 it is recorded that certain citizens of London had ventured a cargo to the Mediterranean[1], and again in 1437 there is mention of the trade there, while in 1486 the merchants trading to Italy received the privilege of electing "a consul and president[2]." Hakluyt notices a trade extending into the Levant as early as 1511[3], which was carried on at intervals until the middle of the sixteenth century. The first mention of a company of Levant merchants occurs in 1567, when "the governors," William Gerrard and Rowland Hayward, issued instructions to their agents in that year[4]. Evidently this undertaking soon came to an end, for in 1575 the trade had been abandoned for a number of years[5]. Accordingly, Sir Edward Osborne sent an agent overland through Poland to procure a trading-concession from the Sultan, which had been obtained by 1578. Steps were taken to procure further franchises and also to obtain a charter in England. At this period Spanish emissaries were endeavouring to check English trade wherever their influence could reach. It was recognized that wealth was strengthening England, or as Mendoza, the Spanish Ambassador in London, expressed it, "profit to them was like nutriment to savage beasts[6]." These intrigues were especially successful in Venice, and the position of the English merchants there was rendered very difficult,

---

[1] *Fœdera*, VIII. pp. 717, 773. [2] *Ibid.*, XIII. p. 314.
[3] *Voyages*, v. p. 62.
[4] British Museum MSS., Nero B. XI. In 1566 there is mention of traffic from England to the Levant Seas, *Calendar Salisbury MSS.*, I. p. 341.
[5] Hakluyt, *Voyages*, v. p. 168.
[6] *Calendar of State Papers...in the Archives of Simancas*, 1580-6, p. 72.

through increased differential taxes, and also by the monopoly of the exporting of currants from the Mediterranean having been granted by the Syndics to a fellow-countryman of their own[1]. Under these circumstances it was felt that it would have been a hardship to exclude the Italian merchants from the Levant trade, and therefore both the survivors of the old company of Italian merchants and the new adventurers to the Levant joined in a petition for incorporation, with exclusive privileges[2], and on September 11th, 1581, a charter was signed[3]. This instrument has not express incorporating clauses. It simply sets out that the discoverers, together with those they desired to admit as partners, not exceeding twenty in all, should be a society of which Osborne was to be governor. No other Englishmen were to enter the dominions of the Sultan under the usual penalties. These privileges were granted for seven years. Apparently an experimental voyage was undertaken, and when this proved fortunate, preparations were made to extend the trade. The account of the steps taken is given by Mendoza, as follows: "They are trying here to raise a large capital to sustain this Levant negotiation, and not only have the richest merchants and companies contributed largely, but the Councillors and the Queen herself. £80,000 has already been got together[4]." Elizabeth either invested or lent as much as £40,000 of this amount, and her contribution came out of the treasure taken from the Spaniards by Drake, a portion of which had been given to the Crown[5].

It is generally assumed that the Levant company all through its history was organized as a "regulated" undertaking, like the Merchant Adventurers. However, the evidence is quite conclusive that, until nearly the end of the sixteenth century, the trade was conducted on a joint-stock basis. For instance, the references to the membership in the charter of 1581, as consisting of partners is sufficiently clear. Then, when prior to 1591, the company petitioned for a new charter, Burghley made a note on the document asking whether the reorganized company was to be conducted by a society or by every merchant independently[6], and the petitioners replied that the business was to be carried on by one joint-stock as under the former patent[7]. The letters of the company to

[1] State Papers, Domestic, Elizabeth, CXLIX. 58; CLXV. 58; *Calendar*, 1580–90, pp. 21, 148. [2] *Ibid.*, CLI. 34; *Calendar*, p. 37.
[3] Printed in Hakluyt, *Voyages*, v. pp. 192–202.
[4] *Calendar of State Papers...in the Archives of Simancas*, 1580–6, p. 432. The use of the word "capital" is interesting but it does not occur in the original—"Tratan aquí de hacer una gran *bolsa para* entretener esta negociacion de Levante." In a Dictionary in *Spanish and English*, by John Minsheu, London, 1599, the word "capital" does not occur. [5] *Vide supra*, Part I., Chapter IV.
[6] State Papers, Domestic, Elizabeth, CCXXXIX. 140; *Calendar*, 1591–4, pp. 88, 89.
[7] *Ibid.*, CCXLI. 12, 13; *Calendar*, 1591–4, pp. 169–70.

the factors in 1599 show that at that time all goods were consigned on account of the company, and the agents in Turkey had express instructions to confiscate anything sent in the company's ships and owned by an individual[1]. In 1604 in the debate on the position of the companies in Parliament, it was mentioned that this body had been a joint-stock until recently[2].

After the formation of the company in 1581 the profits for some time were very large—the goods imported into England sold at about three times as much as those that had been exchanged for them in Turkey[3]. Both the Venetians and the Spaniards were jealous of the progress made by the English in this trade, which Mendoza described in 1582 as being "extremely profitable[4]." Still there were reverses to be met; the danger from pirates was very great, and the agents of the Spanish government were intriguing against the company in Turkey. By 1586 a scheme had been prepared for closing the Straits of Gibraltar against English shipping[5], and the Venetians were making as many difficulties as they could[6].

The charter of 1581 was due to lapse in 1588, and it was possibly the excitement of repelling the Armada that occasioned some delay in the execution of a new grant. Besides there were some points to be adjusted. Under the charter of 1581 there were only twenty members. It is probable that this limitation had already been relaxed, but a claim was made by merchants who had traded in the western part of the Mediterranean, that, since their trade was gone, owing to the war with Spain, they should be admitted into the company on their paying their share of the charges already incurred[7]. Another reason for extending the membership was the continued opposition of the Venetians to the entrance of English merchants into the Adriatic. It seems that many of the company of Venetian merchants had not entered the Levant undertaking in 1581, and it was now considered advisable to provide for these. In a petition from the company it was stated that the cost of establishing the trade had been £40,000, and that there had been spent about £10,000 in the Venetian republic, which area it was now proposed to include within that over which this organization had trading privileges[8]. Therefore the

[1] *The Dawn of British Trade to the East Indies*, edited by Henry Stevens, London, 1886, p. 276.

[2] *Journals of the House of Commons*, I. p. 220.

[3] Anderson, *Annals, ut supra*, II. p. 299.

[4] *Calendar of State Papers...in the Archives of Simancas*, 1580-6, p. 366.

[5] *Ibid.*, p. 652.

[6] *Calendar State Papers, Venetian*, 1581-90, pp. 329, 408.

[7] State Papers, Domestic, Elizabeth, ccxxxix. 41-3; *Calendar*, 1591-4, p. 58. It was also urged in these petitions that many of the members were not merchants, vide Part I., Chapter VI.

[8] *Ibid.*, ccxxxix. 44; *Calendar*, p. 59 (printed in *The Early History of the Levant Company*, by M. Epstein [1908], pp. 258-61).

situation resolved itself into the formation of a new joint-stock, which purchased from the previous one the concessions it had obtained. This unproductive outlay was divided into shares of £130 each, and subsequently calls were made to provide working capital[1]. When this arrangement was effected, the way was clear for the completion of the charter which was signed on January 2nd, 1592. In this document the undertaking was formally incorporated as the *Governor and Company of Merchants of the Levant*, with powers to choose annually one governor and twelve assistants. The area over which the monopoly extended was now made to include not only Turkey, but, in addition, the State of Venice. This, with the other privileges granted, was to end in twelve years, but Elizabeth reserved to herself and the Privy Council a right of revoking the whole or any part of the charter. In one respect this instrument differs from other similar grants, in so far as it was designed as a retaliatory measure against Venice. For over ten years the government there had paid no attention to Elizabeth's requests for the removal of the restraints on English commerce, and now the Queen decided to prohibit all importation of currants or the "wine of Candia" by Venetians. Since none of her subjects, save the company, might exercise this trade, such a clause in the charter strengthened the monopoly of the Levant merchants[2]. The general argument for extensive privileges in Turkey was formulated by the company at a later date, in the following terms: "The Turkish government being essentially different from any other in Europe, perfectly despotic in its nature, and approached only like that of all Oriental people ancient and modern, through the medium of presents and particular influence, no intercourse can be carried on with the natives with any security unless under certain regulations called capitulations, agreed upon by the respective courts. By the terms of their capitulations, all causes of dispute in which a Frank is concerned, must be determined by the interference of the Ambassador or Consul of the nation by which he is protected, and to support their consequence and to protect their persons, and carry on their correspondence with the authorities of the country, subordinate officers such as dragomen, janissaries, &c., are indispensably requisite." Now as it was the policy of the government of England to throw the whole weight of paying those officers and establishments on the Levant company, it was but reasonable to confer on them the appointment and management of those whom they had to support, and it is clear that this power would be nugatory, unless the British subjects resident in Turkey were made amenable in a certain degree to their authority. It was to this end that the charters and acts

---

[1] Hakluyt, *Voyages*, VI. p. 88.
[2] "The charter of the English merchants for the Levant" in Hakluyt, *Voyages*, VI. pp. 73–92.

DIV. I. § 4] *Monopoly of Currant Trade* 87

restricted the trade to controlable numbers of the company, permitted them to make laws for its regulation, enabled them to resist avanias, by which British subjects might be involved in disputes hazardous to their lives and property, authorized them to levy duties to pay the expenses of the protecting establishments and finally empowered them to send refractory persons out of the country to England, and so prevent the mischief that would certainly arise if they refused to obey the *only* authorities, which by the terms of their capitulations, could restrain them from doing evil[1]." In the time of Elizabeth there was an additional reason for a more far-reaching monopoly, since, by an Oriental fiction, all the goods sent from England, were supposed to be received in Turkey as the personal venture of the foreign sovereign, and therefore, through thus "colouring" the commodities of her subjects Elizabeth incurred a certain personal responsibility for their conduct[2].

The currant trade, as might be expected under the absolute nature of the monopoly, was highly profitable. Mention is made in 1592 of the gain from this source alone, being £11,500 a year[3]; but the whole of this profit did not find its way to the company, since the monopoly was burdened by an exceedingly high customs-duty. Under such circumstances the cost to the consumer was great and attention was drawn to it in Parliament[4]. The company was able to obtain considerable profit after paying the impost, and about 1599 an offer was made of a still larger payment to the Crown on condition that the monopoly should be transferred[5]. The company relied on its charter, which had still a few years to run, whereupon the Privy Council exercised its discretion and suspended it[6]. Under such pressure the undertaking was greatly disturbed and distracted, and the governor was in much doubt as to whether it could continue to trade[7]. Eventually an offer was made and accepted that the company should undertake to pay £4,000 a year as a lump sum in lieu of customs, and the trade was reorganized. This settlement was only of short duration, and the monopoly was again suspended, the company trading in competition with a rival body of adventurers[8]. Under these circumstances the customs-composition of £4,000 was no longer

---

[1] *Account of the Levant Company with some notices of the Benefits conferred upon Society by its officers, in promoting the cause of humanity and the fine Arts;* cf. *Observations on the Religion...of the Turks, to which is added the State of the Turkey Trade, from its origin to the present time,* London, 1771, pp. 357–65.

[2] State Papers, Domestic, Elizabeth, CCLVI. 18; *Calendar,* 1595–7, p. 162.

[3] *Ibid.,* CCXLII. 36; *Calendar,* 1591–4, p. 227.

[4] *Vide supra,* Part I., Chapter VI.

[5] Stevens, *Dawn of British Trade in the East Indies, ut supra,* p. 280.

[6] State Papers, Domestic, Elizabeth, CCLXXV. 27; *Calendar,* 1598–1601, p. 450.

[7] Stevens, *Dawn of British Trade in the East Indies, ut supra,* p. 280.

[8] *Journals of the House of Commons,* I. p. 220.

paid, but this brought no gain to the consumers of currants, since in 1603 the Privy Council authorized the Lord Treasurer to impose such duties as would make good the loss of revenue to the Crown[1]. It was during these struggles that the original joint-stock company was either transformed into, or replaced by a regulated one. In March 1599 the trade was on a joint-stock basis[2], but in June 1600 a list was drawn up of the names of the members of the company, which shows that it was then a regulated body. There were 83 "freemen" (one of whom was a woman) who had 189 servants or factors[3]. The facts that this list records the names of servants who had died abroad, and also that there is mention of there having been *two* companies until recently[4], make it probable that, while the trade was disorganized, a regulated company had been formed in spite of the charter, which made good its position against the older foundation receiving a new incorporation in 1605.

[1] State Papers, Domestic, James I., IV. 46; *Calendar*, 1603–10, p. 51.
[2] *Vide supra*, p. 85.
[3] *Calendar Salisbury MSS.*, x. pp. 214–17. [4] *Ibid.*, p. 249.

SECTION V. THE EAST INDIA TRADE.

THE GOVERNOR AND COMPANY OF MERCHANTS OF LONDON TRADING INTO THE EAST INDIES.

A. THE TERMINABLE STOCKS FROM 1599 TO 1657.

The development of English joint-stock enterprize in foreign trade during the sixteenth century is dominated by the conditions governing the importation of commodities produced in the tropics—indeed, if the African companies be excepted, it was related, as to each new starting point, to the commerce with the Orient. The original aim of the Russia company had been the discovery of a north-east passage, and this enterprize was most successful during the years that the route it had opened overland remained available. The same idea was the incentive in the first three expeditions of the "Company of Cathay" better known as Frobisher's Voyages, though in this case the passage sought was that by the north-west. In the last quarter of the century a number of causes contributed towards the making of fresh efforts in order to secure a share in a branch of commerce which was believed to be exceedingly profitable. Thomas Stephens is said to have been the first Englishman who lived in India, and the communications he sent home revealed some of the secrets that had been hitherto jealously guarded by the Portuguese. Up to 1580 the project of a direct trade with India had been regarded as a promising scheme, but in that year the absorption of Portugal by Spain made the problem an urgent one, since the Dutch were prohibited by Philip II. from trading with Portugal, and just at this time the advisers of Elizabeth no doubt feared that the state of tension between England and Spain would result in a similar exclusion as against this country. Steps were at once taken towards obtaining spices independently of the market at Lisbon. The Levant company was established, thereby starting a new trading-route to the East. The company of Cathay fitted out its last voyage in 1582 which was intended to penetrate to India by the Cape of Good Hope, while in 1583 Ralph Fitch was sent on a mission to Eastern potentates[1].

[1] Hakluyt, *Voyages*, v. pp. 465–505.

A fresh incentive to the movement was given by the capture of the *San Filipe* in 1587, the cargo of which presented in concrete form the immense value of the commodities that could be shipped from the Indies[1]. No sooner had the alarm occasioned by the Armada subsided than application was made to the Crown by a group of merchants for a license which would authorize them to send three ships and two or three pinnaces to India[2]. This was in October 1589 and the adventurers spent two years on the preparations, the expedition sailing in 1591 under the command of Captain James Lancaster. It succeeded in reaching Indian waters by the Cape; and, though at one period the prospects were promising, through one fatality after another, most of the ships were lost, and Lancaster returned almost alone in 1594[3]. Meanwhile Fitch had arrived in England after an absence of eight years, and his reports pictured India as an almost inexhaustible treasure-house. Further evidence was obtained from the capture of the notable intercepted register of the government of the East Indies in the *Madre de Dios* in 1592[4]. In the same year Linschoten had returned to Holland, his native country, and English merchants were able to learn that his experience confirmed that of Fitch. Two years later John Watts, one of the leading venturers in privateering expeditions and afterwards a governor of the East India company, organized a company which fitted out three ships intended to intercept Spanish vessels. Lancaster, who was in command, having learnt that the cargo of a richly-laden Spanish carrack from the East Indies had been stored at Pernambuco, determined to take the town. With the assistance of Captain Venner and some Dutch ships this object was attained, and the quantity of spices secured gave "great comfort" to those concerned in the voyage[5].

By 1595–6, both in Holland and England, syndicates were employed in preparing vessels for India. The Dutch venture which sailed in 1595 was more fortunate than the English one of the following year. The latter was financed by a company in which Sir Robert Dudley was a chief adventurer. News was received in 1598 that two rich Portuguese ships had been taken[6], but many members of the expedition perished through

---

[1] *The Naval Tracts of Sir William Monson*, edited by M. Oppenheim (Navy Records Society, 1902), II. p. 150.

[2] State Papers, East Indies, I. 8.

[3] *The Voyages of Sir James Lancaster to the East Indies*, edited by Clements R. Markham, London (Hakluyt Society, 1877), pp. 1–34; *Annals of the Honorable East India Company*, by John Bruce, London, 1810, I. p. 109.

[4] "Certayne Reasons why the English Marchants may trade with the East Indies" [1600] in Bruce, *Annals of the East India Company*, I. p. 119.

[5] *Voyages of Sir James Lancaster*, pp. 38, 39, 43.

[6] State Papers, East Indies, I. 11. From the mention of the names of Richard Allen and Thomas Broomfield in this commission it has been sometimes taken that

disease, and the vessels were lost[1]. While this misfortune depressed the English merchants and made them unwilling to attempt another voyage, the Dutch expeditions had been remarkably successful. Naturally the great profits obtained in Holland aroused a fresh desire in the citizens of London to participate in the new trade, and further inducements were not wanting. In 1599 the Levant company had fallen into difficulties[2], and the Dutch seized the opportunity, afforded them by a scarcity of spices in England, of raising the price of pepper from 3s. 5d. to 6s. and even 8s. per lb.[3] It became clear that the time had come to make a fresh effort to open a direct trade to the Indies by the Cape of Good Hope, and in the latter half of the year preparations were so far advanced that on September 24th (1599) 101 persons had undertaken to adventure £30,133. 6s. 8d. in the intended voyage[4]. Of these as many as twenty-three can be identified as members of the Levant company[5], which number might be considerably increased if account were taken of those whose names were added subsequently, amongst the latter being Thomas Smythe, who filled the position of governor in both bodies.

The first recorded meeting was held on September 24th (1599), when there were present 57 of the adventurers. Fifteen of the subscribers were elected to serve as "committees or directors," and it was resolved that neither ships nor goods should be accepted in payment of the amounts adventured. It was also decided that the minimum subscription should be £200, and that an immediate call of 1s. per cent. was to be made[6]. The committees at once applied to the Privy Council for a charter of incorporation since the trade to India was so remote that it could not be carried on but in a joint and united stock[7]. Just at this time a proposed peace with Spain was under consideration, and the Council feared that the sending out of the expedition might lead to a failure in the negotiations[8]. Though Elizabeth had expressed her "gracious acceptance" of the voyage[9] it is just possible that, quite apart from the exigencies of the diplomatic situation, she would not have been sorry that it should be delayed. The Crown had obtained

they were shareholders in the expedition. From the form of the document it seems more probable they were the factors or agents.

[1] Purchas, *His Pilgrims*, II. pp. 288-97.   [2] *Vide supra*, p. 87.
[3] *The History of British India*, by Sir W. W. Hunter, London, 1899, I. p. 279.
[4] Court Book of the East India Company (at the India Office), vol. I. The first volume has been printed under the title *The Dawn of British Trade to the East Indies as recorded in the Court Minutes of the East India Company*, 1599-1603, edited by Henry Stevens, London, 1886, pp. 1-4.
[5] Cf. List of Members of the Levant Company, *Salisbury MSS.*, Part x. pp. 214-16.
[6] Court Book, I., Sept. 24, 1599, Stevens, pp. 4-7.
[7] Court Book, I., Sept. 25, 1599, Stevens, p. 8.
[8] Court Book, I., October 16, 1599, Stevens, p. 11.   [9] *Ibid.*

from prizes captured in the "Island Voyage" of 1597 East Indian drugs sufficient to last the country for many years, and it may have been considered worth while in 1599 to maintain the monopoly until the stock was exhausted[1]. In view of these various considerations the adventurers decided to proceed no further with the actual fitting out of an expedition until the obstacles had been removed.

Just a year after the first meeting the adventurers again assembled. Though no entry had been made in the minute-book from October 16th, 1599, to September 23rd, 1600, much had been accomplished in the interval. An undertaking from the Privy Council had been secured under which it was provided that the voyage would not be stayed[2], while amongst the merchants of the City increased support had been gained. In view of these considerations it was proposed that preparations should now be made for the expedition, and this motion was carried, the vote being taken by a show of hands. As a result of the period of reflection from October 1599 to September 1600 it was seen that a larger capital would be required than that originally proposed, and on October 13th the committees decided not to refuse any adventure of £200 until the whole sum had reached £55,000, it being supposed that some who had set down their contributions would withdraw their names[3]. Calls had already been made of which the second was payable on October 28th, and at a meeting held on that day it was announced that the charter was drawn up and was now in the hands of the Attorney-General. Since it was proposed in this instrument that the management of the company was to consist of a governor and twenty-four committees, Thomas Smythe was elected to the former office, and additional adventurers were nominated for the latter posts in order to complete the number[4]. The charter was signed on December 31st, 1600. It incorporates 218 persons, whose names are given, as *the Governor and Company of Merchants of London trading into the East Indies* with the usual privileges of a corporation including the right to have a common seal, which "from tyme to tyme, att their will and pleasuer to breake, chandge and to make new or alter as to them shall seeme expedient." Membership was confined to those mentioned in the charter, their sons at the age of twenty-one, their factors and apprentices, as well as to such as were subsequently admitted to the freedom. The management was to be in the hands of a governor and twenty-four committees. The

---

[1] *Vide infra*, Part II., Div. xv.
[2] Court Book, I., Sept. 23, 1600, Stevens, pp. 11, 12.
[3] Court Book, I., Oct. 13, 1600, Stevens, p. 45.
[4] Court Book, I., Oct. 28, 1600, Stevens, p. 62. The number of committees had been increased from the original 15 to 17 by October 30, 1630, so that only seven names were to be added on this occasion.

first officials were named in the charter, and they were to hold office to July. Subsequently in that month the members were to meet "in any convenient place" to elect persons for these offices for the ensuing year. At any court-meeting a member of the company might be chosen as "deputy to the governor." Full powers were given to the freemen to meet as often as necessary to make "reasonable laws, constitutions, orders, and ordinances...necessary and convenient for the good government of the company." Breaches of such bye-laws were punishable both "by imprisonment of body and by fines and amerciaments."

Special privileges were conferred on the company subject to certain limitations. It was granted "the whole entire and only trade and traffic" in all places where trade was possible from the Cape of Good Hope to the Straits of Magellan, provided that such trade should not be prosecuted in any district already in the "lawful and actual possession" of any friendly Christian prince without first obtaining his permission. The first four voyages were exempted from customs outwards. In each voyage the company was allowed to export all the foreign silver it had brought into the country, provided that such export should not exceed £30,000 in any one voyage, and that £6,000 of it had been first coined at the mint. Licenses might be issued to non-freemen to trade within the specified limits. All Englishmen, save freemen or licensees, are forbidden to trade in the area assigned to the company under penalty of the Queen's indignation and the forfeiture of the ships and cargoes (half the value of these falling to the Crown, the other half to the company). Further, offenders were subject to imprisonment till they had executed a bond of £1,000 as security against a repetition of the offence. It was further provided that freemen, who failed to pay their adventures prior to the sailing of the first voyage were subject to disfranchisement. All these privileges were granted for a period of fifteen years from Christmas 1600, renewable for a like term upon condition that the trade "be not hurtful, but shall be shown profitable" to the realm. On the other hand should the company be found hurtful, its privileges might be recalled or modified on two years' notice[1].

The augmentation of the number of adventurers shows that the scheme had grown in favour since its inception, but it was one thing to obtain signatures to the roll of subscribers and quite another to collect the instalments from them when these became due. Times were bad and capital was scarce, indeed it is not improbable that the greater part that was paid promptly consisted of funds temporarily diverted from the Levant trade where it could not be profitably utilized. When

---

[1] *Charters granted to the East India Company from* 1601, *also the Treaties and Grants made with, or obtained from, the Princes and Powers in India from the year* 1756 *to* 1772, I. pp. 1–26.

the second call was due at the end of October many of the members had not paid it, and a considerable number were in arrear with the first[1]. Similar complaints were again made in November and December 1600[2]. At a general court held on January 1st, 1601, it was reported that the capital promised for the expedition, which was soon to start, was less than the amount required by £4,000 to £5,000 and the adventurers were in arrear by £4,000, so that altogether £8,000 or £9,000 was necessary before the ships could sail. This difficulty was met by a resolution which compelled each shareholder to add a further 10 per cent. to his adventure, thus bringing the minimum holding, which came to be regarded as the share, to £220. It was provided that if additional "voluntary" applications for stock or shares were received, and if the defaulters made good the arrears due by them, this assessment would be treated as a loan, repayable when funds were received under these two heads[3]. Five days later an order had been procured from the Privy Council commanding those in arrear to pay under threat of imprisonment[4]. Even these drastic measures did not suffice to bring in the arrears; and, inasmuch as there was a penalty under which members, who did not pay the assessment of 10 per cent., were liable to have the amount they had previously furnished diminished by a like sum, it was resolved on February 10th, 1601, that those adventurers, who having already paid in both their original adventure and the assessment thereon and who in addition added a further 10 per cent. on the sum first subscribed, should be credited not only with the payments they had made, but there would be given them as a bonus from the penalty, exacted from the defaulters, a quantity of stock equal to their last payment. That is, in fact, in a concrete case, an adventurer who had paid £220 on one share and who added £20 would receive a credit in stock for £260, so that it is interesting and important to notice that this device was tantamount to the issuing of stock or shares at a discount[5]. Finally it was only with considerable difficulty that the voyage started on February 13th, 1601[6], and the governor and committees were pursued by the clamour of such as were owed money by the company[7]. In spite of the assessment and the proposed bonus the debt remained at £9,000, against which there was as much as £7,000 due by adventurers on their shares[8]. By this time it had been recognized that there was

[1] Court Book, I., Oct. 28, 1600, Stevens, p. 62.
[2] Court Book, I., Nov. 21, Dec. 8, 1600, Stevens, pp. 84, 85, 93.
[3] Court Book, I., Jan. 9, 1601, Stevens, p. 110.
[4] Court Book, I., Jan. 14, 1601, Stevens, p. 112.
[5] Court Book, I., Feb. 10, 1601, Stevens, p. 138.
[6] *Voyages of Sir James Lancaster*, p. 58.
[7] Court Book, I., March 2, 1601, Stevens, p. 156.
[8] Court Book, I., March 6, 1601, Stevens, p. 156.

little prospect of collecting the whole of the arrears, and it was resolved to make another assessment of 10 per cent. with "the encouragement" that the penalty of this amount deducted from such as failed to pay it would be divided amongst those who responded promptly[1]. It follows that the minimum subscription was now £240, while the shareholder who had duly paid his assessments was credited with stock considerably in excess of that amount. There were certain minor peculiarities in the capital account of this voyage. It was usual to pay the sailors their wages on the return of the ships; hence in the case of a successful expedition this charge was defrayed out of the proceeds, in an unsuccessful one by a levy on the adventurers. The governor of the East India company introduced a co-operative element by arranging that each mariner should be rated as the owner of an adventure to the extent of two months' wages[2]. A similar arrangement was made in the engagement of the factors, so that a certain proportion of the stock of the voyage was assigned to those who were members of the expedition. Again there was the effect of the financing of an attempt to discover a north-west passage to be taken account of. The funds necessary were raised by a further levy on the stock already subscribed, on this occasion at the rate of 5 per cent., and it was agreed that the capital so provided should rank as if it had been contributed for the voyage to India[3]. In this way a member of the company who adventured in the voyage to discover the north-west passage had a double chance of a profit on his investment, since, besides any gains from the expedition, he was entitled to share *pro rata* in the returns from that sent out *via* the Cape of Good Hope in 1601. It is only after all these various adjustments are made that the nominal capital of "the voyage of 1601" is arrived at, which was returned at £68,373[4].

The immense difficulty experienced in obtaining sufficient capital, as shown by the various inducements offered to secure the later payments, is vital towards the understanding of the early history of the company. It explains for instance the failure of the attempt to float a stock for a second voyage to India in September and October 1601. It had been intended to form a separate stock for this expedition, and it was proposed in September 1601 that the minimum subscription should be £100, and

---

[1] Court Book, I., April 1, 1601, Stevens, pp. 160–1.

[2] Court Book, I., Nov. 6, 1600, Stevens, p. 70. Since the mariners were advanced two months' wages it is not clear whether they were required to pay this against their adventures or whether the latter was intended to be additional to the usual pay.

[3] Court Book, I., March 29, 1602, Stevens, p. 207. This expedition is described in Hunter, *British India*, pp. 266–9.

[4] Jeremy Sambrooke's "Report on the Progress of the East India Trade," MSS. at the India Office, Home Miscellaneous, XL. p. 33.

that no adventurer should be assessed beyond the amount he had undertaken to provide[1]. It required some courage for a member to join the new stock, since the market price of an interest in the first voyage was below par. Thus on July 24th an adventure of £200 paid (which was subject to the assessments of £40) realized £180 or a discount of 10 per cent.[2], while again on November 5th another of £220 paid (and subject to one assessment of £20) was sold for £204. 10s., a discount of about 7 per cent.[3] Accordingly it was not surprising that by October 13th only £11,000 had been promised, which was characterized as "noe convenient proportion to sett out any voyage at all[4]." The adventurers however as a body were determined to await the outcome of the expedition they had provided before risking more, and the governor and committees, in the face of pressure from the Privy Council, were compelled to give way to the general feeling of the members of the company. Pending the return of the ships from India, an effort was made to discover an alternative route to the East by the north-west passage; and, even for this expedition for which only £3,000 was asked, there was, as has been shown, no little difficulty in obtaining capital, which was only procured by the offer of exceptional inducements[5]. From September 1601 till news was received in June 1603 that one of the vessels of the first voyage might shortly be expected with a good cargo, the company devoted itself mainly to the perfecting of its internal organization. Its characteristics have frequently been noted, especially those that contain elements of old-world picturesqueness, such as the march of the beadle carrying the subscription-book or to summon the adventurers to a court, the "feasts" of the freemen, the disciplinary rules by which they were fined for absence from a meeting, late appearance, or a neglect of the courtesies of debate[6]. It is perhaps not unnatural that in these accounts attention should be drawn to certain points of contact between this body and the contemporary type of regulated company, such as the limitation of the freedom and the system of terminable stocks. Care however must be taken not to press the analogy too far, and there is the danger of drawing inferences from the isolated case of this company, and assuming these to represent the general development of the system as a whole. It seems symmetrical to take the terminable stocks of this company as a transition between the regulated and the joint-stock

[1] Court Book, I., Sept. 13, 1601, Stevens, p. 186.
[2] Court Book, I., July 24, 1601, Stevens, p. 181.
[3] Court Book, I., Nov. 5, 1601, Stevens, p. 193.
[4] Court Book, I., Oct. 13, 1601, Stevens, p. 189.
[5] Court Book, I., Aug. 1, 1601, Stevens, p. 184.
[6] Cf. Hunter, *British India*, I. pp. 255–65; "Collections for a History of the East India Company," by James Pulham, Brit. Mus. Add. MS. 24934, ff. 100, 104, 140–4.

company. It is necessary to note however that other and earlier undertakings, such as the Russia company, the Mines Royal and the Mineral and Battery Works, had each of them capitals which were relatively permanent. It follows that the terminable stocks of this undertaking are to be ascribed to something exceptional in its position. The explanation is to be found partly in the state of feeling at the time of its incorporation, partly to certain personal characteristics of the adventurers. Attention has already been directed to the important part played by the Levant company in the foundation of the younger society, and just about 1600 there was much division of opinion amongst the members as to whether the former body should be still conducted on a joint-stock basis or should be reorganized as a regulated enterprize. Traces of this point of view are to be found in the East India charter, which, while intended primarily for a joint-stock body, has many expressions that would be more appropriate to a regulated one. Instances of this tendency are to be found in the importance given to the freedom and in the stipulations describing the monopoly as granted to the members and their factors. In the second place the groups from which the adventurers were drawn is deserving of attention. A few were members of the Russia company and of other companies with a comparatively permanent capital. There was a large body, amongst whom the most prominent was Watts, which had been accustomed to the privateering syndicates of the period, in which it was convenient to treat each separate cruise as, financially, a distinct enterprize. Again the influx of the Levant merchants was due to the lack of opportunity for profit in their own business. This was regarded as temporary, and these merchants no doubt contemplated withdrawing their resources from the Indian trade when the outlook in the Mediterranean became less overcast. For these special reasons the East India company was somewhat exceptional in adopting the system of terminable stocks. Nevertheless there were countertendencies which prevented the forces indicated from exerting their full influence during the earliest years of the company's history. Just when the ships of the first voyage reached England the country was being decimated by the plague, which was raging most fiercely in August and September 1603 and continued to claim victims till the close of the year[1]. Business was almost at a standstill till the end of the year, and it was found impossible to realize the cargoes of the ships. The sending out of the second voyage (which should have sailed in 1602) was urgent, and the only method by which the expedition could be set forth in the

---

[1] "London's Lord Have Mercy upon Us, A true Relation of the Seven Modern Plagues or Visitations in London, 1665," in Somers' *Tracts*, VII. p. 54. The deaths from plague in the out-parishes exceeded 2000 a week from August 11 to Sept. 22, the highest return being for the week ending Sept. 1, when the deaths were 3034.

spring of 1604 was by applying all the resources that could be realized to the supplying of the fleet. This involved the continuance of the joint-stock, and therefore the accounts of the first and second voyages were amalgamated, and the divisions applied to both. According to the statement of the company the capital of the second voyage was £60,450[1], which was added to that of the first, and dividends were paid on the total of £128,823[2]. The question arises as to how this operation was carried through, and it is unfortunate that the minute-book covering this period is missing[3], since it would have shown whether a new capital of £60,450 was subscribed and paid in or whether the adventurers in the former voyage were given the option of transferring their stock from the first to the second expedition, and having it doubled. The reasons in support of the guess that the second alternative may have been adopted are drawn from the financial condition of the company at this time. It was only able to send out in 1604 goods and bullion to the value of £12,302, the rest of the resources being required for the repair of the ships. Now the first voyage had given good returns, and, after paying expenses, there should have been a certain amount realized before the fleet sailed again or very shortly afterwards. That sum would have been available in addition to a further subscription of fresh capital, if there had been one, and it would have been folly to have sent the vessels with such a meagre lading had there been any possibility of increasing it.

Not only was the company confronted with financial distress in 1604, but in the same year its legal position was seriously endangered by attacks made upon it both by the Crown and in Parliament. The latter may be best understood in relation to the general position of foreign trading companies, and it has already been dealt with from this point of view[4]. The other assault on the company's status arose through a license granted by James I. to Sir Edward Michelborne, who had been one of those named in the charter, and who asked employment as a principal commander in the first expedition. Being disappointed, he failed to pay his adventure, and was solemnly disfranchised in 1601[5]. Through the favour of the King he was able to obtain a permission, dated June 18th, 1604, in favour of himself and his associates to trade to China and other places in the East notwithstanding any grant or charter to the contrary[6]. On the strength of this instrument Michel-

[1] Sambrooke's Report, *ut supra*.
[2] *Vide* "Summary of Capital," *infra*, p. 123.
[3] The Court Book now marked vol. I. ends on June 28, 1603, that known as vol. II. begins Dec. 31, 1606.
[4] *Vide supra*, Part I. Chapter VI.
[5] Court Book, I., July 6, 1601, Stevens, p. 178.
[6] *Fœdera*, XVI. p. 582.

borne's syndicate sent out an expedition which is said "to have made the English name abhorred in the Eastern seas" by reason of the number of its piracies[1]. While Michelborne's ships escaped with a part of their plunder, the company was left to bear the odium of their misdeeds, and the ill-effects of this visit were experienced for some years to come. To these anxieties at home and abroad there were added fears as to the safety of the ships of the second voyage, which became considerably overdue. At one time many of the adventurers had become so discouraged that they were inclined to abandon the whole enterprize[2]. At length in 1606 the expedition returned, and it was known that a considerable profit had been obtained. Steps were taken to begin the winding up of the stock by clearing accounts and making divisions (on account of principal and profit) to the members. It was only in 1609[3] that the liquidation was completed, and the total divisions came to 195 per cent.[4] This result is to be understood in relation to the methods by which the capital had been obtained since it relates to the nominal amount, and it has been shown that those adventurers who paid their instalments at the dates they were due received a substantial bonus in stock, and it may have been a very large one[5]. Moreover some of the distributions were made in commodities which were rated at the wholesale price or below it, and it follows that the adventurer who accepted such a division had the opportunity of making a further profit on the realization of it.

The success of the first and second voyages had the important result of establishing the trade, and the company at once began to take subscriptions for a third voyage which sailed in 1607, and from this date onwards for a long period vessels were sent to India each year. The whole capital raised was £53,500, out of which £6,000 was paid to the former stock for certain assets purchased from it[6]. As early as May 13th plans were under consideration for the preparation of another voyage which was to be ready early in 1608. It was proposed that a new stock should be subscribed for the fourth and fifth voyages, which was to consist of shares (or minima subscriptions) of £500 each, and the adventurers were authorized to take in others under them. The sum required was fixed at £50,000, and it was announced that if the whole amount

---

[1] Hunter, *Hist. of British India*, I. p. 284.

[2] *History of the European Commerce with India*, by David Macpherson, London, 1812, p. 84.

[3] Cf. Court Book, II., Feb. 7, 1609, Sept. 9, 1607. The Court Books are summarised in the *Calendars of State Papers, Colonial Series, East Indies.*

[4] *Vide infra,* "Summary of Capital," p. 123.

[5] *Vide supra,* pp. 94, 98.

[6] Court Book, II., Sept. 9, 1607.

were not provided by the freemen of the company by June 20th any of the King's subjects would be admitted to subscribe[1].

The measure of success obtained in 1606 was not without its penalty, for on January 9th, 1607, Richard Penkevell and his associates obtained a grant, under the title of "*the Colleagues for the Discovery of a Northern Passage to China, Cathay, and other parts of the East Indies.*" This patent was for a period of seven years, and conferred the absolute possession of all lands, not previously occupied by any Christian power, discovered by the agents of "the Colleagues," on their society[2]. While this instrument was less injurious to the company than the license to Michelborne in 1604, the two in conjunction were sufficient to show that James I. could not be relied upon not to modify the charter of Elizabeth. When a favourable opportunity presented itself a new charter was obtained, in which James I. binds himself and his successors "not to grant any licence contrary to the tenour of this present patent." The new grant, dated May 31st, 1609, expressly states that "the whole entire and only trade" to the East Indies within the specified limits was conferred on the company "for ever hereafter," subject to a revocation clause on three years notice[3]. In order to meet the objection that the company was hindering the progress of geographical discovery, it joined with the Russia undertaking and a number of independent adventurers in the following year to finance Henry Hudson's expedition in search of the north-west passage, and on July 26th, 1612, the shareholders in this venture were incorporated as "*the Governor and Company of the Merchants of London, Discoverers of the North-West Passage*[4]."

Meanwhile the trade with India had been subject to considerable fluctuations. The third voyage of 1607 left before all the money necessary had been paid by the adventurers[5]. Those who had promised to support the next two expeditions refused to provide capital for more than one[6], and accordingly the fourth voyage of 1608 was set out with a stock of its own of £33,000. In June 1608 there was a debt on both these voyages, and it was proposed to unite them in one company[7], but this scheme was frustrated by the loss of the ships belonging to the fourth voyage. This misfortune diminished subscriptions for the fifth

---

[1] Court Book, II., May 13, Sept. 1, 1607. The minimum subscription was subsequently increased to £550.

[2] *Fœdera*, XVI. p. 660.

[3] *Charters granted to the East India Company*, I. pp. 27–53.

[4] State Papers, Domestic, James I., Sign Manuals, II. 30; *The Genesis of the United States...A Series of Historical Manuscripts*, collected by Alexander Brown, London, 1890, II. pp. 573, 574; *Calendar State Papers, Colonial, East Indies*, 1513–1616, pp. 238–41.

[5] Court Book, II., Feb. 27, 1607.   [6] *Ibid.*, II., Sept. 1, 1607.

[7] *Ibid.*, II., June 14, 21, 1608.

expedition, which was due to sail in 1609. Though efforts were made to secure the support of adventurers, the total obtained was only £13,700, and it was decided to amalgamate this capital with that of the third voyage, and to continue to trade upon the united stock of both. When the accounts were finally made up there were assets available for distribution which enabled a distribution of 334 per cent. to be paid, yielding a profit of 234 per cent., which was the largest in the history of the early terminable stocks of the company[1]. Beginning with 1610 there were seven independent voyages, each with a separate capital, and which were sent out up to January 1613. The largest stock was that of the sixth, for which £80,163 had been paid in, while the smallest belonged to the twelfth, which had only £7,142. The most profitable was the eleventh (1612), which gave its shareholders divisions of 320 per cent. Even the sixth, which was the least successful, returned divisions of 221⅔ per cent.[2]

These results were considered very favourable, and it is recorded that they put new life into the trade. It was recognized that the co-existence of separate stocks was disadvantageous, and it was decided in 1613 to make a fresh subscription on the basis that the capital adventured would be used for four successive voyages. The proposal was well received, and as much as £400,000 was underwritten in a fortnight[3], while the whole amount paid in was £418,691[4]. It was to be provided in annual instalments of equal amounts which were to be employed in dispatching a succession of voyages for four years. The idea of a series of expeditions with one capital was a natural development of the previous interrelation of two voyages and it is possible that the change of title may have been thought desirable to avoid the associations that might be connected with the name of a "thirteenth voyage." Whatever may have been the reason, instead of "thirteenth voyage," the term joint-stock was used, and so the whole series of expeditions was described as the "First Joint-Stock."

At this time, as in 1604 and 1607, the degree of success obtained by the company induced fresh opposition which manifested itself in 1615 on the appearance of a book entitled *The Trade's Increase*. This tract was occasioned primarily by the movement in favour of the fishing industry; and, in support of his contention, the writer surveyed the commerce of

[1] Cf. "Summary of Capital," *infra*, p. 123.
[2] *Ibid.*
[3] State Papers, Domestic, James I., LXXV. 28.
[4] *Vide* "Summary of Capital," *infra*, p. 123. This is based on Sambrooke's Report. Sir William Hunter, on the authority of the MS. Marine Records of the company, gives the capital of the First Joint-Stock as £429,000, *History of British India*, I. p. 306, II. p. 177.

his time, urging that this trade was most adapted to the fostering of the mercantile marine. In adopting this line of argument he was conscious that many of his readers would instance the recently established commerce with India as a case where shipping had been greatly increased. To meet a reply of this character, the East India company, in certain of its aspects, was severely criticized. It was alleged that out of twenty-one ships used by it, four had been totally lost, and the remainder returned home "crazed and broken." The mortality amongst the crews was said to have been lamentably great. The whole number of men that had sailed from England in the service of the company was given as 3,000, two-thirds of whom were missing. "David," the author continues, "refused to drink of the well of Bethlehem, when he thirsted and longed, because it was the price of blood. This trade, their commodities are at a far dearer rate being bought with so many men's lives." Moreover the company was described as resembling the "enemies of Christendom for they carried away the treasure of Europe to inrich the heathen" by the purchase of unnecessary commodities. Finally it was boldly claimed that no subjects of the Crown should be debarred "from trading equally in all places[1]."

The company was highly indignant at the attack upon it. Perhaps the title of the tract caused more offence than the contents, since the writer had enforced his views on the waste of shipping and the spoil of woods by naming his work after the great East Indiaman, of which the adventurers were justly proud, and which had been burned by the natives at Bantam in 1613. Application was made to the Archbishop of Canterbury for the suppression of the offending publication as treasonable and dangerous, but on further reflection Sir Dudley Digges was able to convince his fellow-adventurers that the case was one for a reply in defence of the East India trade rather than any penal measures[2]. The answer to *The Trade's Increase* appeared soon afterwards under the name of Digges, who was able to dispose of many of the exaggerations of his opponent. He points out that, considering the length and danger of the voyage, a loss of only four ships was not excessive in fifteen years. The large cost of repairs was shown to be a temporary, not a permanent condition of the trade. It arose from the fact that the vessels first used were purchased from others, and had not been designed for use in the tropics, and it was claimed that now the company had begun to build its own ships the expenditure under this head had been greatly reduced. As to the export of treasure, Digges was able to show that from Michaelmas 1613 to Michaelmas 1614 pepper had been exported to the

[1] "The Trade's Increase," by J. R., London, 1615, in *Harleian Miscellany*, IV. pp. 207-11, 219, 220.

[2] Court Book, III., Feb. 17, 22, 1615.

value of £209,623. 14s., while the reduction in the price of spices that had been effected since the company had imported them to England saved the consumers of that country £69,666. 13s. 4d. annually[1]. The appearance of another tract, which was designed to show that India was an "earthly paradise" from which great wealth could be drawn, was no doubt intended as a further reply to the aspersions of *The Trade's Increase*[2].

The period up to 1620 was one of very considerable prosperity for the company. It had established itself against the opposition of the Portuguese. A foothold in the Moluccas or Spice Islands had been secured, and, as early as 1613, a factory and a valuable trading concession on the mainland at Surat had been procured. In 1614 and 1615 there were negotiations with the Dutch company which it was expected would establish a working agreement between the two undertakings. It is significant that in 1614 Dutch merchants became adventurers for £3,000 to £4,000 in the First Joint-Stock[3]. In 1615, in spite of the attack made on the company, its shares sold at $141\frac{1}{2}$ to $144\frac{1}{2}$, and it is of interest to note that the governor and committees had directed some of these adventures to be disposed of by auction in order that members might better know the worth of their holdings, and, as it was said, "to give a good reputation to the voyage" if a satisfactory price were realized[4]. In the next year there were numerous transactions varying between 208 and 218. The first two voyages of this stock had yielded considerable profits; and, when it was due to terminate in 1616, there were most favourable expectations formed of the prospects of the company. Some of the increased prosperity was attributed to the substitution of a capital extending over several years for the previous annual voyages. In fact the company was being forced to adopt some degree of continuity, almost against its will. It had been found advisable, in order to wind up each voyage, to transfer certain unrealized property belonging to it to a later undertaking. Thus "the remains" of the first and second voyages were purchased at a valuation by the third, and those of the ninth voyage by the First Joint-Stock[5]. Similarly the latter, on its expiry, sold its assets both "in esse and posse" to the

---

[1] *The Defence of Trade in a Letter to Sir Thomas Smith Kt. Governour of the East India Company,* from one of that Society [Sir D. Digges], London, 1615.

[2] "An Exact and Curious Survey of the East Indies even to Canton: All duly performed by land by Monsieur de Monsart," 1615, in Somers' *Tracts,* IX. p. 165.

[3] Court Book, III., July 27, Oct. 1, 1614. As aliens a large fine (£400—£600) was required from these adventurers.

[4] *Ibid.,* III., Oct. 13, 1615. The adventures sold were purchased by persons who were not free of the company. This shows that outsiders could attend the Court of Sales.

[5] Court Book, II., Sept. 5, 1607, III., Sept. 8, 1615.

next group of adventurers whose capital was known as the "Second Joint-Stock." This undertaking was in course of formation during the closing months of 1616. Everything seemed to be favourable, and when the books were closed in January 1617 as much as £1,629,040 had been subscribed by 954 persons, some of whom adventured from £10,000 to £14,000. It appears to have been laid down in the preamble that the sums subscribed would be called up in eight equal instalments of 12½ per cent. each, and by 1620 at least one-half of the whole amount had been actually paid in[1].

The Second Joint-Stock during the first months of its existence was fated to experience the misfortune that had followed each previous manifestation of the progress of the company. No doubt those who had adventured in 1616–17 did so largely on the faith of the charter of 1609, by which James I. had bound himself and his successors not to issue any licenses or other patents contrary to that grant. Some of the rapacious courtiers by whom he was surrounded found a method by which, while the letter of this engagement was observed, its spirit was broken. This device consisted in the grant of a royal license covering the limits assigned to the company, but issued under the great seal of Scotland. Accordingly on May 24th, 1617, Sir James Cunningham, his heirs and associates, constituting *the Scottish East India Company*, were authorized to trade to the East Indies, the Levant, Greenland, Muscovy, and all other countries and islands in north, north-west and north-eastern seas[2]. This grant in reality invaded the charters of the East India, Levant and Russia companies. It was the latter which was chiefly affected, since it was to whaling that the new company proposed to direct its energies in the first instance. Accordingly the East India company assisted the Russia undertaking, and eventually the license to Cunningham's company was purchased from him[3].

From 1617 to 1620 as much as £1,600,000 had been expended by the Second Joint-Stock[4]. A considerable portion of this amount had been provided by the calls on adventurers, some of it consisted of profits made on the first and second expeditions of this series and again reinvested, while the remainder was borrowed. A change of fortune began with the crisis of 1620, which assumed a form which vitally affected the company. It was the prevalent opinion that the distress was due to the exportation of bullion, and it was natural, while such views were accepted, that the East India company should be regarded as a prime offender. In the House of Commons, during the Parliament of 1621,

[1] Court Book, vi., Oct. 22, 1623.
[2] State Papers, East Indies, i. 65; partly printed by Bruce, *Annals of the East India Company*, i. pp. 193–4.
[3] *Vide supra*, p. 55. [4] Bruce, *Annals*, i. p. 194.

frequent complaints were made concerning "this grievance¹." As in 1615, the governor and committees viewed such criticisms with apprehension, and Thomas Mun (who had been a candidate for the post of deputy-governor in July 1621, and who subsequently filled this office) and Edward Misselden, an adventurer, stated the case on behalf of the company. Mun laid emphasis on the fact that the strength of his case was based on the greater cheapness of the route by the Cape of Good Hope as compared with that *via* the Mediterranean. Hence Oriental commodities were cheaper since the company had been founded. Moreover this change had been effected without permanent injury to the Levant company; for, at the date he wrote, there was a large re-exportation of spices, much of which was carried to the Levant. It followed that such re-exportation was a good answer to the charges that the East India company diminished the nation's store of the precious metals, for the spices shipped abroad and sold there "have their finall end in money which might bee brought into the realme in that kind, if our other trades did not divert the same." As he expresses it elsewhere, "Let no man doubt but that money doth attend merchandize, for money is the prize of wares and wares are the proper use of money; so that their co-herence is unseparable²." Mun's *Treatise* appeared in 1621, and in the following year, during the controversy between Malynes and Misselden, there are several references to the East India company. Though these two writers differed on many points, they agreed on the whole that the company was deserving of support. Misselden, in tracing out the explanations of the prevailing want of money, mentions as "a special remote cause" the large amount of capital employed in India which had not as yet been returned to England in the tangible form of divisions to the adventurers³. He takes note of the contention of those that "presse, or rather oppresse that plea of equity, that is that all subjects should bee alike free to be merchants in all trades," to which he replies it is against public utility that all should be merchants adding that it had ever been the policy of the State "to reduce trades to corps and societies⁴." He points out that the East India trade is far beyond any other⁵, and that to carry it on without government is "like men making holes in the bottom of a ship in which they are passengers⁶."

[1] *Proceedings and Debates of the House of Commons*, 1620 *and* 1621, Oxford, 1766, I. pp. 17, 259.
[2] "A Discourse of Trade from England unto the East Indies; Answering to divers Objections which are usually made against the same," by T. M., 1621, in McCullough, *A Select Collection of Early English Tracts on Commerce*, 1856, pp. 1–47; Purchas, *Pilgrims*, 1905, v. pp. 262–301.
[3] *Free Trade or the Means to make Trade florish, wherein are discovered the Causes of the Decay of Trade in this Kingdom* [by E. Misselden], 1622, pp. 13, 27–9.
[4] *Ibid.*, pp. 65, 66.   [5] *Ibid.*, p. 78.   [6] *Ibid.*, p. 84.

Malynes too supports the company though in more guarded terms. While he approves of the reduction it had effected in the prices of spices[1], he claims that he is not one to flatter it or any other body when "they deal unadvisedly[2]." He instances some defects in the companies of his time. In certain cases a society may become a monopoly (and be subject to the defects assigned to such sole trading) when "a few merchants have the managing of a trade to the hurt of the commonwealth[3]." In another direction the small number of those who were at the head of some companies did not suffice for efficiency[4], while the choice of the higher officials from amongst persons resident in London tended to make the capital rich and to keep the rest of the country poor, besides in certain cases involving needless expense of carriage[5]. The progress of the discussion had been such that by 1624 the governor, Morris Abbot, was able to inform the adventurers that, of the various charges made against the company for almost ten years, all " were already blown away" with the exception of the allegation that it wasted the treasure of the country[6]. In the spring of 1624 a further attack on this trade was made in the House of Commons, which was debated with considerable violence[7]. Much that was pressed against the company had already been disproved, but the temper of the House was such that reasoned arguments were heard with impatience. It was the misfortune of this enterprize to be involved to some extent in the hostility to grants depending on the prerogative, and to be still more affected by the great quarrel between Sir Thomas Smythe and Sir Edwin Sandys in the Virginia and Somers Islands companies[8]. Just at the time that Sandys began his open campaign against Smythe in the Virginia company, he pursued the same tactics at an East India Court in July 1619 where he introduced his now celebrated ballot-box. This new method of recording votes was almost unanimously rejected, Smythe was reappointed governor (and he continued in this office till he retired voluntarily in 1621) while Sandys secured election as one of the committees[9]. Though Smythe and his friends maintained their position in the East India company, Sandys and his following had arranged to obtain control of the two plantation undertakings. But at the beginning of 1624 Smythe was exercising the functions of governor of the Somers Islands company, and the Commission for which he had agitated in relation to the administration of Virginia, had condemned Sandys. It was only to be expected that the latter would use his influence in the House of Commons where he

[1] *The Maintenance of Free Trade*, by Gerard Malynes, 1622, p. 27.
[2] *Ibid.*, p. 68.   [3] *Ibid.*, p. 69.
[4] *Ibid.*, p. 51.   [5] *Ibid.*, p. 52.
[6] Court Book, vi., April 16, 1624.   [7] *Ibid.*, vi., March 8, 1624.
[8] *Vide infra*, Div. ii. § 2 c.   [9] Court Book, iv., July 2, 1619.

had a number of supporters to exact reprisals from Smythe. Thus the company complained that its deputations met with "very coarse usage" from a Committee of the House by which it had been treated with reproach and scandal[1].

In quite another direction the company suffered from the crisis of 1620. At that time it was trading to a considerable extent on borrowed money, and the lenders began to press for repayment. As early as November 1621 it was reported that it was temporarily unable to pay its debts[2], and through the enterprizing competition of the Dutch and the dishonesty of many of the factors the governor stated that "their affairs in India lye a bleeding[3]." These events reacted on the First Joint-Stock, which was now being finally wound up. Though the first two voyages of this undertaking had been successful, a combination of unfavourable circumstances made the remaining expeditions less profitable, so that the divisions on the whole series amounted to no more than $187\frac{1}{2}$ per cent. This result involved considerable losses to those who had purchased stock (after some dividends had already been paid) in 1618 at between 214 and $218\frac{1}{2}$. This fact coupled with the depression at home made it difficult to exact the instalments from the adventurers in the Second Joint-Stock, and in 1623 calls to the extent of £92,000 were in arrear[4]. It was not long before the financial stringency became so great that the factors were complaining that they were hampered through want of resources to purchase commodities for shipment to England[5]. It was at this time that the adventurers, when asked to anticipate the date at which the next instalment was due in order to reduce the debt, which was about £200,000, replied that their expectation was for "thicker dividends" rather than more payments[6]. To meet their demand in 1624 a substantial distribution was made which brought the whole amount divided up to half the total capital, the last call having been recently paid in. When the financial state of the company was under consideration the significant motion was made that no further dividends should be paid till the debt had been reduced, since it was noted that the Russia company had failed to show prudence in its finance and "had smarted" for its neglect[7].

Just when the company was endeavouring to rehabilitate its finances

[1] Court Book, vi., May 19, 1624.
[2] State Papers, Domestic, Correspondence, James I., cxxiii. 100.
[3] Court Book, v., Nov. 12, 1621. [4] *Ibid.*, vi., Oct. 22, 1623.
[5] *The English Factories in India*, 1618–1621, *A Calendar of Documents*, edited by W. Foster, Oxford, 1906, pp. 229, 343.
[6] Court Book, vi., Sept. 24, 1623. At this time six divisions of $6\frac{1}{4}$ per cent. each had been made.
[7] *Ibid.*, vi., April 30, 1624.

and to avoid giving offence to a hostile House of Commons it received news of the massacre of Amboyna, which had happened in 1623, but was known in England in May 1624[1]. At first the adventurers were buoyed up by expectations of obtaining reparation. It was not long before they began to realize that, though James I. might threaten the Dutch, redress would not be gained through his intervention. The Courts of the company were scenes of deep depression. Many of the members complained of the injuries the company had sustained through false friends abroad and obloquy at home[2], and they expressed the opinion that the best course would be to wind up the stock and retire from the trade, unless the enterprize was supported by the State. At this juncture James I. offered to become an adventurer, and to send out the company's ships under the royal standard[3], but the governor and committees discreetly replied that it was found, on taking the opinion of counsel, that the effect of the proposed arrangement would be that the whole undertaking would revert to the Crown, since there could be no partnership with the King[4].

The financial difficulties of the company had now become acute. It was said in July 1624 that no man's adventure "was now worth money[5]," and those members who were in arrear to the extent of £80,000 flatly refused to meet their engagements[6]. Meanwhile the greater part of the existing stock was lost, or at least not recoverable without further expenditure. When many of the adventurers declined to provide more capital the problem confronting the governor and committees became a very difficult one, and their troubles were not lessened by the different views taken by groups of the stockholders. Even before news of the massacre had been received there had been dissensions within the company, though of a temporary nature. Thus in 1623 there had been a scene at a Court-meeting when Sir Randall Cranfield had demanded the return of the money he had invested in the Second Joint-Stock[7]. There were also charges of corruption in the administration, which were prosecuted with great heat[8]. From 1625 the contentions, that had previously been rare, became frequent. The smaller adventurers would have been content to recover what they could, provided they were not required to furnish more capital. There were others

---

[1] A very full account of the struggle between the Dutch and English in the Spice Islands culminating in the massacre is given by Hunter, *British India*, I. Chapters IX., X.

[2] Court Book, VI., June 16, 1624.   [3] *Ibid.*, VII., July 16, 1624.

[4] *Ibid.*, XI., July 2, 1628.   [5] *Ibid.*, VII., July 20, 1624.

[6] *Ibid.*, VII., Dec. 3, 1624, X., Sept. 19, 1627; State Papers, Domestic, Correspondence, James I., CLXX. 52.

[7] Court Book, VI., July 30, Oct. 22, Dec. 8, 1623.

[8] *Ibid.*, VI., Nov. 11, 1623.

who were more courageous, and a number of schemes were devised for the continuance of the trade. A prolongation of the existing stock was proposed by means of an assessment of 6¼ per cent.[1] Simultaneously it was suggested that subscriptions for a Third Joint-Stock should be taken, but by June 25th, 1628, only between £12,000 and £13,000 had been adventured[2]. Finally, it was only when the outlook was judged too uncertain to justify the investment of capital for a term of years that the governor and committees reluctantly decided to revert to the system of independent voyages which had been abandoned since 1612, and in 1628 £125,000 had been adventured for a new separate stock known as the "First Persian Voyage." It was only as a last resource to keep the charter alive and to recover the remaining assets of the Second Joint-Stock that this method of trading was adopted. It was fully recognized by the more experienced adventurers that the co-existence of separate stocks involved endless confusion, indeed it was stated that the disputes between the agents of the different bodies had been almost as bad as those with the Dutch[3]. During the protracted discussions which ended in the formation of the Persian Voyage an adventurer, named Thomas Smerthwicke, proved himself a fruitful source of trouble to the governor and committees. He was almost invariably in opposition, and he occasionally obtained some sympathy and support from a few of his fellow-shareholders. In 1628 he was accused of circulating "libels" affecting the position of the company. It appears these took the form of long draft motions which contained criticisms of the existing management—as, for instance, in one of these dated February 19th, 1628, it is said to be "very strange that the old stocke (so great and so long employed) should produce so dismall a reckoning as it doth[4]." In the summer of the same year he combined with Mellinge and Spruson, who had been active supporters of Sandys during the disputes in the Virginia company, to demand a commission to enquire into the management of the East India undertaking. This petition suggested that the distress of the company was due to maladministration, and it effectually prevented the subscription of the Third Joint-Stock that had been proposed. By July events revealed what was behind Smerthwicke's agitation, namely a scheme to admit Charles I. as adventurer for one-fifth of the whole stock and profits, without payment on his part, in return for taking the

[1] Court Book, x., June 25, 1628. The terms of the proposal were "the supply of half a capitall on the old joint stock." From the divisions made it appears that the capital was computed at ⅛ of the whole subscription.

[2] *The English Factories in India*, 1624–1629, *A Calendar of Documents*, edited by W. Foster, Oxford, 1909, p. xxxiii.

[3] Court Book, x., June 25, 1628.

[4] *A Motion to the East India Company*, by Thomas Smerthwicke, Feb. 19, 1628; Coll. Broadsides, Soc. Antiq., No. 294.

company under the royal protection[1]. This unauthorized proposal was much resented by the whole body of shareholders, and eventually Smerthwicke was forced to make "a submission" to the governor[2].

Another fruitful source of dispute was the form in which divisions should be made once it was found possible to resume such distributions. In 1627 it was calculated that the assets, then remaining, were only worth £100,000, which had increased four years later to upwards of £800,000[3]. The practice of dividing commodities produced a considerable amount of friction. Persons who were not in trade, whose dividend consisted of pepper or calico, found a difficulty in disposing of it to advantage, while, on the other hand, merchants obtained, in addition to the nominal return on their capital expressed in terms of the price at which the commodities were rated, a further profit in retailing them. In 1629 there was a long discussion, lasting three hours, as to whether the dividend it was then proposed to declare should be paid in calicoes or cash; it was eventually decided, "in order to give contentment to the gentry," that the distribution should be made in money[4]. Another proposal that also occasioned discussion and difference of opinion was the transference of a dividend to the First Persian Voyage, that is, the division was sanctioned, but instead of its being paid to the adventurers in the Second Joint-Stock, the amount of it was subscribed to the Voyage, and thus the shareholders entitled to this payment received it in stock in the latter undertaking.

No sooner had the Persian Voyage been started, than pressure was brought to bear on the governor and committees to wind up the Second Joint-Stock. According to one of the adventurers, widows and orphans were crying out for a liquidation of this stock, and executors had been advised that they could only consent to its continuance at their own peril[5]. Sandys brought forward "a religious and conscionable motion" that, as a man on his death-bed desires to pass away with the least pain, so this "dying stock" should be ended with as little loss as was possible[6]. Such a consummation was precluded by the large amount of debt (being between £250,000 and £300,000) which must be paid off before the accounts could be closed, and therefore it was necessary to defer the liquidation. Meanwhile a Second Persian Voyage was floated in 1629, with a capital of £150,000, and a third in the following year. In 1632 it was judged that the time was ripe for the formation of a Third Joint-Stock, so that in 1633 there were no less than five distinct separate undertakings in existence, namely the three Persian Voyages and the

---

[1] Court Book, xi., July 2, 1628. [2] Ibid., xi., Feb. 11, 1629.
[3] State Papers, East Indies, iv. 97.
[4] Court Book, xi., Jan. 19, 1629; cf. State Papers, East Indies, iv. B 39, 39 (i).
[5] Court Book, xi., March 2, 1629. [6] Ibid., xi., Feb. 20, 1629.

Persian Voyages and Third Joint-Stock

two joint-stocks. Now that the outlook was more favourable many of the adventurers were desirous of reducing all these to one joint-stock. The Second Joint-Stock presented little difficulty. The shareholders in it had at length received back the capital they had paid in, and they had long been anxious to dispose of "the remains." It was decided that all such assets should be transferred to the Third Joint-Stock, the adventurers in the second being credited with stock in the new undertaking to the extent of $12\frac{1}{2}$ per cent. of their former holdings. Taking such stock at par, the shareholders in the Second Joint-Stock received a division of $112\frac{1}{2}$ per cent.

The arrangement with the Persian Voyages presented greater difficulties. The first of these had not many assets remaining in 1633-4, but much of the property of the third had still to be realized. It was accordingly agreed in 1634 that the Third Joint-Stock should purchase "the remains" of all the Voyages, paying 20 per cent. of the amount of their nominal capital to the adventurers in the first, 30 per cent. to those in the second, and 40 per cent. to those in the third, such payment to be taken in the form of adventures in the Third Joint-Stock[1]. When this transaction had been completed, if the stock exchanged against the remains of the Voyages be taken at par, the adventurers in the first received divisions of 160 per cent., those in the second 180 per cent., and those in the third 140 per cent. The amalgamation of the separate undertakings with the Third Joint-Stock had been accomplished only just in time. For on the arrival of ships from India bringing goods consigned to all three Voyages, the confusion of accounts was such that it would have been impossible to make a fair division. Hence, in the words of the governor, merchants on the Exchange declared that it was doubtless "the finger of God" that pointed the way to the reconcilement of the jarring interests[2]. On the other side there was before long a minority within the company which complained that the terms had been too favourable to the Voyages[3]. From the nature of the absorption of the previous undertakings by the Third Joint-Stock, it follows that of the total nominal capital of £420,700 of this enterprize only a part had been subscribed in cash by the adventurers, the remainder representing the allocations made to the Second Joint-Stock and to the Voyages. Therefore at first the Third Stock had an insufficient amount of liquid resources and large loans had to be made to carry on the trade. In 1635 there was owing £400,000, and the governor and com-

---

[1] Court Book, xv., Oct. 3, 1634. [2] Ibid., xv., Nov. 21, 1634.
[3] Ibid., xv., Feb. 6, 1635. The *Calendars, East Indies and Persia* end at Dec. 31, 1634. From Jan. 1, 1635 to Dec. 30, 1639 the Court Books and other documents are calendared in *The Court Minutes of the East India Company, 1635-1639*, by E. B. Sainsbury, Oxford, 1907.

mittees were forced to take the extreme measure of concealing the amount of the liabilities from the generality[1]. This policy placed the management in the difficulty that it had to withdraw the privilege, which had previously existed, of permitting adventurers to anticipate future dividends and to reject a motion in 1635 for a division, without being able to give satisfactory reasons in either case[2]. This method of finance might have been justified if the company had been able to maintain its credit, and, as far as the trade itself was concerned, the future seemed to be most encouraging. The danger, that ultimately became a serious one, was to come from a different quarter, namely the relation of the company to the Crown.

Between 1627 and 1629 Charles I. had several causes of complaint against the governor and committees. They had refused to lend him £10,000 when required, nor would they admit him as an adventurer *gratis*. Moreover an appeal had been made to Parliament in 1628, in which Mun, who drew it up, recapitulated the arguments of 1621, and a strongly worded protest was added against the lack of support the company had received when it was confronted by the aggression of the Dutch[3]. Charles I., being thus unfavourably disposed towards the East India adventurers, would be prepared to support any attack on their privileges, especially if those organizing it could promise any direct advantages to the Royal Exchequer, which at this time was greatly depleted. In the early part of 1635 Endymion Porter, a prominent courtier, obtained a license to fit out two ships as privateers. The funds necessary were obtained by taking certain London merchants into partnership, amongst whom were Thomas Kynaston and Samuel Bonnell, the latter being closely connected with Sir William Courten, one of the prominent capitalists of the period. The vessels sailed in April 1635 and were intended to take the ships of any power not in amity with the King of England as prizes, and they proposed to cruise in the Red Sea. So far this venture resembled that of Michelborne, and, though the consequences to the company would have been sufficiently serious, a combination of circumstances soon made the outlook still more grave. The convention of Goa came into force by which English subjects might trade in Portuguese India. Under the charters of the company such commerce was reserved to it, but Sir William Courten was astute enough to see that if Charles I. could be induced to license an expedition, financed outside the company, the results were likely to be highly

[1] Court Book, xv., Feb. 18, June 12, Sept. 9, 1635.

[2] *Ibid.*, xv., June 12, Sept. 9, 1635.

[3] *The Petition and Remonstrance of the Governor and Company of Merchants of London trading to the East Indies, exhibited to the Honorable House of Commons*, 1628 [Brit. Mus. 1029.c.30]. Mun's book, *England's Treasure by Forraign Trade*, was written soon afterwards but not printed till 1664.

profitable. With a considerable amount of secrecy a syndicate or company was formed. Charles I. was to be credited with stock to the extent of £10,000, without payment, but when the profits came to be divided interest and insurance were to be deducted from the division on this amount[1]. Similarly Windebank, the Secretary of State, was to be an adventurer for £1,000 on exactly the same conditions[2]. After the King's share had been determined the remaining profits were divisible as to one-quarter to Porter, one-sixteenth to Kynaston; the commanders of the ships were to have a division in proportion to their adventures, and the remainder, amounting probably to five-eighths, was to be at the disposition of Courten[3]. But Courten did not provide the capital required himself. According to one account the outlay was £120,000[4], of which John, Earl of Shrewsbury, adventured £2,500[5], and Sir Paul Pyndar as much as £35,000[6], or £36,000[7]. The preparation of six ships did not escape the notice of the East India company, and in January 1636 the governor was aware of the proposed expedition. A strongly-worded remonstrance was compiled which pointed out that some of the adventurers had taken alarm, and asked for a declaration from the King which would allay their fears[8]. Though Charles I. pledged his word that nothing was intended against the company[9], it is evident that his assurances were received with some suspicion since it is recorded that in future all outgoing ships were to sail "sufficiently furnished," such furnishing consisting of larger crews and heavier ordnance[10]. By December 1636 news had been received by the company of seizures of native junks effected by the first expedition sent out by Porter in April 1635[11]; and, as had happened before in similar cases, the company was

[1] State Papers, East Indies, IV. B, 19; *Court Minutes*, 1635–9, p. 188.

[2] *Ibid.*, East Indies, IV. B, 8; *Court Minutes*, 1635–9, p. 124.

[3] *I.e.* Porter $\frac{1}{4}$, Kynaston $\frac{1}{16}$, Commanders (say) $\frac{1}{16}$, Courten $\frac{5}{8}$. State Papers, East Indies, IV. B, 21.

[4] State Papers, East Indies, IV. B, 43. It is stated that Courten adventured on "his particular account" £150,000, but this is no doubt an exaggeration. *Strange News from th' Indies, or East India Passages further discovered*, by J. D[arrell], 1652 [Brit. Mus. 1029.g.20], p. 5.

[5] *Lex Talionis: or the Law of Marque or Reprisals*, 1682 $\left[\text{Brit. Mus.} \ \frac{712 \cdot \text{g} \cdot 18}{2} \right]$, Dedication.

[6] *Ibid.*, p. 19.

[7] *A brief Narrative of the Cases of Sir W. Courten and Sir Paul Pyndar*, by E. Graves, 1679 $\left[\text{Brit. Mus.} \ \frac{515 \cdot \text{k} \cdot 21}{5} \right]$, p. 3, *A Brief Remonstrance of the grand Grievances suffered by Sir Paul Pyndar*, by Thomas Brown, 1680, p. 3.

[8] State Papers, East Indies, IV. B, 16.

[9] Court Book, XVI., Feb. 17, 1636.

[10] *Ibid.*, XVI., March 4, 1636.

[11] *Ibid.*, XVI., Dec. 23, 1636.

held responsible by the Governments in India, its goods being seized and the factors at Surat imprisoned. The surviving ship of this privateering venture reached England in May 1637, having made "a reasonably good voyage," yielding £20 as a single share of prize-money to each of the sailors[1]. One result of this success was that the shareholders in the syndicate that had sent out the second voyage were able to make out a plausible case for the grant of such privileges as would place their undertaking on a more permanent basis. In response to this request Charles I. on June 1st, 1637, authorized *the Adventurers to Goa and other parts*[2] to trade to all places in India where the company had not settled factories prior to December 12th, 1635, and this license was to last for five years from Lady-day, 1637[3].

When it is remembered that the East India company had been in a position of financial difficulty before the rival association had been established by Courten, it may be readily guessed how much its credit suffered under the exceptional disadvantages it had now to face. In 1637 it was found impossible to pay £770 of dividends on the Persian voyages, which had long been due, for want of money[4], and the treasurer was forced to report that unless he was supplied with cash "there would be no keeping open the Treasury door[5]." Indeed, even after the goods brought from India by the ships that had arrived recently had been sold, the company was in debt to the extent of £100,000, and was without any immediate prospect of meeting this liability[6]. In 1635 the stock had been sold at 80, and this was before the extent of the opposition was known.

The reason of this great depression is not to be found so much in the threatened competition as in the attitude of Charles I. to the company. When the governor, on discovering that Kynaston and Bonnell were interested in the Red Sea voyage, had instituted a suit at law, the King had protected them, and in addition he had burdened the imports of the Third Joint-Stock with increased customs, the rise in the duty on pepper being, it was said, as much as 70 per cent.[7] There was deep depression amongst the members of the company, and many of them were determined to wind up the current stock and abandon the trade. These were the smaller adventurers; but, taken as a body, they were in a

[1] State Papers, Domestic, Charles I., ccclv. 142.
[2] This is the title in the grant, but this company was generally described as *Courten's Association*, and later as *the Assada Merchants*.
[3] *Fœdera*, xx. p. 146.
[4] Court Book, xvi., Feb. 1, 1637.
[5] *Ibid.*, xvi., March 24, 1637.
[6] *Ibid.*, xvi., Jan. 13, 1637.
[7] *Ibid.*, xvi., Dec. 9, 1636. This increase arose through an addition to the rateable price of the goods due to the new "book of rates."

DIV. I. § 5 A] *Financial Proposals 1636–9* 115

majority, since each individual who had the minimum amount of stock possessed one vote[1]. Once more there was considerable friction in the courts. Some of the discontented adventurers asserted that one or more of the committees were shareholders in Courten's Association[2]. Smerthwicke took a prominent part in the disputes, and at one meeting the governor was forced to order the beadle "to carry or thrust him out[3]." One method of freeing the company from some of its troubles, namely, by the purchase of Courten's privileges and immunities, was impossible for financial reasons. As early as June 1636, after the death of Sir William Courten, when his son, finding the estate was in debt, endeavoured to borrow, some of those consulted in the matter suggested the sale of the whole East India adventure to the company[4]. At this time the expedition sent out by Courten and his partners was at sea. It acquired rich cargoes, but eventually all the ships were either taken or destroyed by the Dutch[5], and in 1638 further overtures were made to the company to buy up the license[6]. Just at this time there was a third proposition for the formation of a new company, independent both of the existing one and of Courten's Association, which was to be financed in Holland, for which an initial capital of £160,000 to £200,000 was proposed[7]. The fact that such negotiations were seriously undertaken shows that the majority of the company were at this time firmly resolved to wind up the stock as soon as possible, and to retire from the trade. Further evidence in the same direction is afforded by a proposal to constitute a regulated company for the East Indies[8].

In 1639 the outlook became somewhat more favourable. It was known that not only had the voyage of Courten's Association miscarried, but that there was no immediate prospect of another being fitted out. On December 10th, 1639, after a report by a committee of the Privy Council, Charles I. ordered the shareholders in Courten's Association to desist from the trade after allowing them a sufficient time to collect their effects in India[9]. A week later the committees of the company were considering the best means of inviting a new and ample subscription[10]. It is significant that some adventurers were in favour of the proposed new stock being current for a longer period than seven or eight years, and

[1] State Papers, East Indies, IV. B, 39.
[2] Court Book, XVI., March 9, 1636.
[3] *Ibid.*, XVII., October 25, 1639.
[4] State Papers, East Indies, IV. B, 13.
[5] *Strange News from th' Indies*, by J. D[arrell], 1652, p. 596. *A Brief Narrative... of the...Cases of Sir W. Courten and Sir Paul Pyndar*, by E. Graves, 1679, pp. 3, 4.
[6] State Papers, East Indies, IV. B, 52.
[7] *Ibid.*, IV. B, 57, 57 (i). [8] *Ibid.*, IV. B, 56.
[9] *Ibid.*, IV. B, 71.
[10] Court Book, XVII., Dec. 18, 1639.

that small subscribers should have no votes in the courts, these having been found by experience to have been "the most turbulent and clamorous." The lists for town were to close on March 25th, 1640, and for the country on May 25th. It was clearly provided that the completion of the new stock was conditional on Charles I. making good his promises of a new charter[1]. Unfortunately these engagements were not fulfilled, and the subscription was not continued.

The withdrawal of the proposed new joint-stock left the company in considerable financial embarrassment, especially as arrangements had been made for winding up the Third Joint-Stock, which had been due to terminate in 1636. On January 5th, 1640, it was announced that the liquidation was to be begun as soon as possible. It was believed that there would be a considerable surplus in excess of the liabilities, and a dividend of 25 per cent. was declared with the stipulation that there should be no further distributions till the debt had been discharged[2]. In June adventures on which 50 per cent. had been divided were sold at 90[3], and soon afterwards it was computed that there was a balance over and above the debts of 168 per cent.[4] Then came an event which produced a great change in the financial position of this stock. Owing to the bankruptcy of the personal administration of Charles I., he was exceedingly hard pressed for money, and he compelled the company to sell him its stock of pepper for which payment was to be made over the ensuing two years, on the security of the farmers of the Customs[5]. Charles I. contracted to pay the company £63,283. 11s. 1d., and to obtain ready money he threw the spices on the market, selling them at a loss[6]. As the political situation became more depressed there was great doubt as to whether the money due could be obtained. The difficulties of the Crown were well known in the City, and merchants had become sceptical of the value of the protestations of the King that he would meet his engagements, even though he spoke of selling himself to his very shirt to pay his creditors[7]. The East India company too received ample promises, but the adventurers still waited in vain for the redemption of these in cash[8].

[1] Court Book, XVII., Dec. 24, 1639.
[2] Ibid., XVII., Jan. 5, 1640, ff. 63, 64.
[3] Ibid., XVII., June 26, 1640, ff. 105-8.
[4] Ibid., XVII., Aug. 15, 1640, f. 131.
[5] State Papers, Domestic, Charles I., CCCCLXV. 64.
[6] Ibid., CCCCLXXIII. 83; Bruce, *Annals of the East India Company*, I. p. 371. Mr W. Foster has placed at my disposal the MS. of his introduction to "the Calendar of the Court Minutes of the East India Company" (1640 to 1643), where the amount realized is given as £50,626. 17s. 1d.
[7] State Papers, Domestic, Charles I., CCCCLXIX. 2.
[8] Ibid., CCCCLXXXVIII. 86.

DIV. I. § 5 A]   *The First General Voyage* 1641   117

The expectation of so great a loss was prejudicial to the existing joint-stock. It was necessary to withhold a dividend of 30 per cent. that had been proposed, and the price of the stock fell heavily[1]. On March 19th, 1641, it was resolved to expedite the collection of the remaining assets with a view to the distribution of the property that remained amongst the adventurers. Meanwhile the failure of the Crown to pay the balance due for the pepper delayed the liquidation, and it was decided in the meantime to fit out an expedition with a separate capital of its own which was known as the *First Particular Voyage* or the *First General Voyage*. The proposed stock was £120,000, of which £80,450 was actually subscribed. The adventurers were urged to take this risk by the emergence of Courten's Association from the state of quiescence in which it had remained since it had fitted out the expedition of 1636. At this time a new voyage of that Association was dispatched largely on funds raised by borrowing, by William Courten[2]. On the renewal of opposition an attempt was made to consolidate the interests of the East India adventurers by amalgamating the Third Joint-Stock and the Particular Voyage, but this scheme was rejected[3].

When the revival of Courten's Association took place the company determined to appeal to Parliament, and the petition of 1628 was revised and reprinted[4]. At this time there was a considerable body of opinion in favour of the company. It was held "absolutely necessary to maintain the trade[5]." Lewes Roberts draws attention to "the fetters and encroachments of late years on this enterprise," and declares that "the bad point and low passe," in which it was at this time is to be attributed to the action of the Crown. He was of opinion that the best type of organization for commerce with India was by means of a joint-stock company with extensive privileges, since, though some fortunate adventurers, trading independently, might make larger profits than those generally obtained by a company, the probability was that single merchants or even a few in partnership ran exceptional risks, and the result of failure was their total ruin[6]—a conclusion obviously drawn

---

[1] Court Book, xvii., ff. 143, 157.
[2] *Lex Talionis*, 1682, p. 19.
[3] Court Book, xviii., f. 111.
[4] *The Petition and Remonstrance of the Governour and Company of the Merchants of London trading to the East Indies, exhibited to the Right Honourable the Lords and Commons in Parliament Assembled*, 1641 [Brit. Mus. 1029. c. 31].
[5] *Sir Thomas Roe's Speech in Parliament*, 1641, in Harl. Misc. iv. p. 413.
[6] *The Treasure of Traffike or A Discourse of Forraigne Trade*, by Lewes Roberts, 1641, in McCullough's *Early English Tracts on Commerce*, pp. 86, 105, 106. Roberts, it may be noted, was a shareholder in the company—*The Merchants' Mappe of Commerce*, 1638, p. 236.

from the fate of Courten's first voyage[1], and which, as will be seen below, applied also to the second. Similarly another writer concurred in stating that the purses of "private men cannot extend to making such long, adventurous, and costly voyages" as those to India[2].

Had the company pressed its petition to Parliament it is not improbable that it would have received some measure of support as against Courten's Association. Charles I., in an interview with the governor, explained that he himself was interested in the latter venture, and this was a fact which he was desirous of concealing from the House of Commons[3]. Such a revelation would have proved a most valuable argument in favour of the company's petition, but the adventurers had to take account of the outstanding balance of "the pepper loan," and it was necessary to avoid injuring the cause of the King, which was in effect their sole security. Accordingly it was deemed advisable to withdraw the petition.

Thus for a time the company was compelled to adopt an attitude of expectancy pending the outcome of the civil struggle. Meanwhile the liquidation of the Third Joint-Stock was continued, and in October 1642 a new valuation was made, according to which the adventurers were entitled, in addition to 110 per cent. divided up to this time, to a further 25 per cent., which could be taken in cash or transferred to the Fourth Joint-Stock which was at length being floated[4]. Times were bad, and the total subscriptions only amounted to £105,000.

In 1643 the investment in the First General Voyage began to yield a return to the adventurers in it, and by July 10th, 1644, total divisions of 125 per cent. had been made[5]. Further encouragement was derived from the total failure of the expedition of Courten's Association sent out in 1641, and Courten himself was proclaimed a bankrupt both in England and Holland[6]. It might have been expected that this enterprize was now defunct. It had been founded on acts difficult to distinguish from piracy, and its two trading expeditions had resulted in the insolvency of the chief shareholders. There remained one resource, though the least reputable of all. The Association had established a station on the island of Assada near Madagascar, and there base money was coined which was circulated in India. Under the concessions made to the

---

[1] Sir William Courten's estate showed a deficiency of £146,000—*A Brief Narrative of the...cases of Sir W. Courten*, by E. Graves, 1679, p. 2.

[2] *A Discourse consisting of Motives for the Enlargement and Freedom of Trade*, 1645 $\left[\text{Brit. Mus. } \frac{1102 \cdot h \cdot 1}{3}\right]$.

[3] Hunter, *Hist. of British India*, II. pp. 40, 41.

[4] Court Book, XVIII., Oct. 14, 1642, ff. 109, 114.

[5] *Ibid.*, XIX., Aug. 18, 1643, July 10, 1644, ff. 12, 98.

[6] *Navigantium atque Itinerantium Bibliotheca*, by John Harris, 1744, I. p. 896.

DIV. I. § 5 A]   *The Fourth Joint-Stock* 1642   119

company, it was responsible to the native powers for the delinquencies of all English subjects, and therefore, as long as it maintained its factories, it had to make good the damages claimed against Courten's Association.

On the whole, the time was not unfavourable for an application to Parliament which would strengthen the hands of the company in obtaining redress for itself against the rival association. Porter's connection with it was known, and he had shown himself one of the most energetic supporters of Charles I.[1], while the royal favour this body had received would inevitably prejudice the Long Parliament against it. Moreover the company could urge some special claims for consideration. In 1643 the Committee of the Navy had asked for a loan of £10,000, promising that in return Parliament would be ready to give all fitting encouragement for the advantage of trade[2]. Therefore, after negotiations with the committee, the company was authorized to draw up an ordinance "for the hindering of enterlopers," and it was resolved to lend the State £5,000 or £6,000. The money was raised after considerable delay, and with either real or alleged difficulty[3], and in 1646 it was urged that on the Ordinance being passed a new stock would be raised, special inducements being offered to members of the House of Commons who would adventure[4]. Though this measure passed the Lower House it was rejected by the Lords, and the proposed subscription was postponed. At first it was suggested that not only should the Fourth Joint-Stock be wound up, but that also the factors in India should be brought home[5]. At Swally the servants of the company were reduced to great straits, the credit of the station being so impaired that on one occasion even 100 rupees could not be raised at Surat[6]. In 1645 it had been reported that this stock "was much lessened by disaster." The loss of two ships involved the writing off of £66,000, added to which as much as £35,000 had been paid in interest. Altogether the debt was £120,000 more than there were assets in Europe towards meeting it. On the other hand there was an estimated surplus in India of £178,000 or £188,000, leaving a nett balance in favour of this stock of about £60,000 against the subscribed capital of £105,000[7]. Eventually it was decided to endeavour to continue the trade by making a subscrip-

[1] *Life and Letters of Mr Endymion Porter*, by Dorothea Townsend, London, 1897, pp. 187–226.
[2] Court Book, xix., Nov. 27, 1643.
[3] *Ibid.*, Feb. 14, Aug. 2, Sept. 6, 1644.
[4] Bruce, *Annals of the East India Company*, I. p. 423.
[5] Court Book, xx., March 19, 1647.
[6] Letters from Swally Marine to the Company, March 31, 1645. *O.C.* xix., No. 1922.
[7] Court Book, Aug. 28, 1645.

tion for a Second General Voyage. In the beginning of 1648 £194,600 had been adventured, on which at this date 75 per cent. was called up. Some of the subscriptions were withdrawn, and several of the instalments were in arrear, so that there was actually available £141,200[1].

Some encouragement was derived from the fact that, considering the times, the First General Voyage had been moderately successful, having been able to make divisions by October 17th, 1648, of at least 221 per cent.[2], while in 1647 the Fourth Joint-Stock was able to begin to make dividends, the great majority of these dividends being made in commodities such as pepper, indigo, cinnamon, and calicoes. On the other hand the company was threatened by those who had purchased the shares in Courten's Association, who petitioned Parliament for encouragement to plant Assada. The original undertaking, having lent the Government £4,000[3], appealed to the Council of State on October 28th, 1649[4]. The view taken by this body was that, whatever may have been the irregularities of the Assada adventurers, the latter had been in existence for a considerable period, and that it lay with the rival associations to come to terms. The company proposed that a new stock should be subscribed to last for five years by the members of both undertakings. The Assada adventurers made a counter proposal, some of the clauses of which were accepted. It was mutually agreed that there should be a new subscription, which was later known as the *United Stock*, of £300,000 payable in four years, in which no one who adventured less than £500 was to be entitled to vote. The Assada adventurers endeavoured to carry stipulations that planters in Assada might trade to India, and that any members of this society after the union might trade to places in India to which no ships had yet been sent. The company stoutly refused to grant these terms, and eventually on November 21st, 1649, an agreement between the two bodies was signed[5]. Application was made to Parliament for the promised encouragement, and on January 31st, 1650, it was resolved by the House that " the trade to the East Indies should be carried on by one joint-stock."

The flotation of the stock of 1650 was not a success. By January 2nd, 1650, only £30,200 had been subscribed[6]. Information is wanting as to the total amount taken up, but it is certain that the sum of £300,000 mentioned in the preamble was not reached, indeed there appears reason to believe that there may not have been more than £125,000

[1] Court Book, xxii., f. 36.
[2] *Ibid.*, xix., ff. 12, 98, 235, xx., ff. 48, 69, 141.
[3] *Ibid.*, xx., f. 79.
[4] "Petition of the East India Company to the Council of State," Bruce, *Annals of the East India Company*, i. pp. 434, 435.
[5] *Ibid.*, i. pp. 436–9.
[6] Court Book, xx., f. 255.

adventured[1]. In 1652 it was proposed that the property of the Fourth Joint-Stock should be purchased by the existing undertaking[2], which received the name of the United Joint-Stock on the double ground of uniting the East India adventurers and the Assada merchants, and also as amalgamating the Fourth Joint-Stock and the General Voyages. The latter part of the proposal was not carried out, and the Fourth Joint-Stock and the Second General Voyage continued to exist as distinct enterprizes.

The United Joint-Stock began its career by pressing vigorously for a settlement of the claims of the company against the Dutch, and these, which were now stated at over two millions, constituted one of the pretexts for war against the Dutch. Though an attempt had been made in 1650 to develope the trade with vigour, in 1651 the company found itself beset with difficulties. Some of those who traded under the license to the Assada merchants had not joined the United Stock and were proposing to fit out ships for India. On the company appealing to Cromwell for assistance in suppressing these interlopers, he replied that he "had so much public business that he neither could nor would attend to private matters[3]." This was in 1651, and in the same year it was decided that no ships should be sent to India for that season. During the Dutch war prompt measures were taken towards reducing expenses, both at home and in India. On the death of the treasurer in 1653 a successor was not appointed, on the ground that the stock had no trade[4], and the factors were earnestly pressed to diminish the charge to as small a proportion as possible[5]. When peace was made with Holland in 1654 and the company soon afterwards obtained £85,000 in cash as compensation, together with a promise of the restoration of Pulo Run, it would appear that the time was ripe for a revival of the operations of the United Stock on a large scale. But one important element of uncertainty remained. Beginning in 1651 the governor and committees had adopted an attitude of great caution, and they had reduced the trade to very small dimensions. It was easy for opponents of the company to claim that the trade to India was deserted; and, as early as 1652, application was made to the Council of State for a license authorizing a single voyage. The company itself met this new attack by granting similar permissions to its own members. When this order was repealed in 1654 there was considerable dissatisfaction amongst a group of the adven-

[1] According to a balance-sheet dated September 1, 1655 (printed by Bruce, *Annals*, I. p. 507) at that date the surplus was £156,317. 7s. 8d. As far as can be gathered from this time divisions of 125 per cent. were made. This would give £120,000 as the amount of the stock.
[2] Bruce, *Annals*, I. p. 469.
[3] Collections for a History of the East India company, by James Pulham, Brit. Mus. Add. MS. 24,934, f. 176.
[4] *Ibid.*, f. 176.
[5] Letter of Company to Surat, 12 Sept., 1653, Letter Book, I., f. 221.

turers[1]. At this time the United Stock might have been determined and a new subscription made. There were several reasons which induced the company to defer the taking of this step. It was not known how much the Dutch indemnity would amount to, and when the sum total had been fixed a new difficulty arose in determining the proportions receivable by the different financially distinct undertakings which were entitled to participate. Much of the damage for which compensation had been claimed had been done during the currency of the First Joint-Stock. That enterprize had sold its remains "both in esse and in posse" to the Second Stock, which in like manner had handed over its assets to the Third Stock. At this point the continuity ends. The Fourth Stock did not acquire all the assets of the Third, and therefore each of these, as well as the United Stock, had claims on the indemnity. It was desirable that these should be settled and the liquidation of the earlier undertakings far advanced before a new stock was subscribed. It was found necessary to submit the claims of the different stocks to arbitration, and in the meantime £50,000 of the money in dispute was lent to the State. Another and a more serious tendency towards delaying a new subscription was the increase in the number of licenses, which was considered so great a discouragement by the committees that in 1655 the factors were directed to take steps towards winding up the company's affairs in India[2]. There was a minority of the adventurers which did not acquiesce in this decision. This body wished to continue an East India company, but to revert to the system of independent voyages or alternatively to carry on the trade by means of a regulated company[3]. Thus at the end of 1654 there were at least four distinct views as to the future of the trade. Some wished it to be completely open under license from the State, others asked that a regulated company should be established, others again favoured a company such as had existed from 1600 to 1612, while finally the governor and committees with the older adventurers, remembering the numerous evils of over-lapping separate undertakings, were emphatic in their adherence to the single joint-stock type, as had been recommended by Parliament in 1650. The varying arguments were remitted to the consideration of a committee of the Council of State, which reported on December 18th, 1656. The company, dreading further delay, announced on January 14th, 1657, that unless a decision had been reached within a month it would offer its whole property for sale to any natives of the commonwealth. The Council of State held a meeting for the consideration of the whole matter, as a result of which it was resolved that the trade "should be managed by a united joint-stock exclusive of all others," and on February 10th, 1657, a committee

[1] Court Book, xxiii., f. 176.
[2] Letter of Company to Surat, 31 Jan., 1655, Letter Book, i.
[3] Bruce, *Annals*, i. pp. 492–4.

of the Council was appointed to draw up a charter, which was sealed on October 19th.

The resolution of the Council of State involved the winding up of the existing separate undertakings. The Second General Voyage had come to an end in 1653, yielding divisions of at least 148½ per cent.[1] Though the Fourth Joint-Stock had been begun earlier it was still awaiting its share of the Dutch indemnity, and it was only in 1663 that the liquidation was completed, the divisions being at least 180 per cent. The United Joint-Stock was wound up about the same time or rather earlier, and though it had been in existence during two wars and the period of licensed trade, the total divisions were the largest of any of the early joint-stocks (that is as apart from the separate undertakings of distinct voyages), being 205 per cent.

Summary of Capital, Divisions and Prices of Adventures.

The First Voyage (1601—February).

Capital[2] £68,373

Divisions. The stock of this Voyage was not wound up but was transferred to the account of the second Voyage.

Prices of adventures (£100 paid):
July 24, 1601, 90 (subject to call of 20°/₀[3]).
Nov. 9, 1601, 93 (,, ,, 10°/₀[4]).

---

[1] Vide "Summary of Capital," *infra*, p. 128.

[2] The divisions on the Voyages and early Joint-Stocks are based on Jeremy Sambrooke's "Report on the Progress of the East India Trade," MSS. at the India Office, Home Miscellaneous, XL. p. 33. The capital is arrived at from this document and another, entitled "An Abstract of the Stock and Trade ventured by the Governour and Company of Merchants of London traidinge to East India" (Home Miscellaneous, XL. p. 23, printed in *List of Marine Records of the late East India Company*, 1896, p. ix.). Sambrooke's "Report" is not complete, while the "Abstract" records the total amount adventured during the company's financial year which was the calendar year, *old style*. Mr Foster of the India Office has very kindly given me the benefit of his researches into the dates of the sailings of the early voyages, so that these documents can be used to supplement each other. With this clue, the apparent great differences can be completely reconciled, subject to the trifling exception that in a few cases the "Abstract" records in round numbers the next thousand or hundred to that given by Sambrooke, *e.g.* according to the former the capital adventured in "1609" (*i.e.* 1609–10) was £82,000, while the latter gives that of the Sixth Voyage as £80,163, or again the former has the venture of "1612" as £7,200, while Sambrooke places it at £7,142 for the Twelfth Voyage. To preserve the basis of these results I have added after the year of the Voyage the month in which the ships sailed according to Mr Foster's list. I have also to thank Mr Foster for reading the proofs of Division I. and making many valuable suggestions.

[3] *The Dawn of British Trade to the East Indies as recorded in the Court Minutes of the East India Company*, 1599–1603, edited by Henry Stevens, London, 1886, p. 181.

[4] *Ibid.*, p. 193.

The Second Voyage (1604—? March).

Capital.	Subscription of First Voyage brought down	£68,373
	,, Second Voyage	60,450
		£128,823
Divisions (on £128,823) ...		195 °/₀

The Third Voyage (1607—April).

Capital ... £53,500

Divisions. The accounts of this Voyage (which was very profitable) were merged in those of the Fifth, the divisions being made applicable to both.

The Fourth Voyage (1608—March).

Capital ... £33,000

This Voyage resulted in loss of the capital owing to the wreck of the two ships employed.

The Fifth Voyage (1609—April).

Capital.	Subscription of Third Voyage brought down	£53,500
	,, Fifth Voyage ...	13,700
	United Capital of Third and Fifth Voyages	£67,200
Divisions (on £67,200) ...		334 °/₀

The Sixth Voyage (1610—? April).

Capital ...	£80,163
Divisions ...	221⅔ °/₀
Price of an adventure, sold "by inch of candle," July 22, 1614 ...	216⅔ [1]

The Seventh Voyage (1611—February).

Capital ...	£15,634
Divisions ...	318 °/₀

---

[1] *Calendar State Papers, East Indies,* 1513–1616, p. 307. In this and subsequent quotations the price is given as that of an adventure of £100 paid, thus in this case the actual transaction was a sale of an adventure of £60 for £130.

DIV. I. § 5 A]   *Summary of Capital &c.* 1604–13   125

The Eighth Voyage (1611—April).

Capital	£55,947
Divisions	311 %.[1]

The Ninth Voyage (1612—February).

Capital	£19,614
Divisions	260 %
Prices of adventures, sold "by inch of candle," Dec. 30, 1614	192–194[2]

The Tenth Voyage (1612—February).

Capital	£46,092
Divisions	248 %

The Eleventh Voyage (1612—February).

Capital provided by a supply of 25 per cent. from the adventurers in the Third Voyage, which should have amounted to £13,375, but it seems that there was actually paid up	£10,669[3]
Divisions	320 %

The Twelfth Voyage (1613—January).

Capital	£7,142
Divisions	$233\tfrac{11}{12}$ %

The First Joint-Stock (1613).

Capital	£418,691
Divisions	$187\tfrac{1}{2}$ %
Prices of adventures in 1615	$141\tfrac{1}{2}$–$144\tfrac{1}{2}$[4]
1617	208–218[5]
1618	214–218[6]

[1] This is the first opportunity for checking Sambrooke's figures by the Court Books, the entry in the latter being "11 per cent. to be divided to the adventurers in the Eighth Voyage who have taken out three capitals." *Calendar State Papers, East Indies,* 1617–21, p. 65.

[2] *Ibid.*, 1513–1616, p. 363. The sale in this case consisted of an adventure of £1,000 in lots of £100 each.

[3] This amount is not explicitly stated in either of the documents referred to in note 2, p. 123. According to the "Abstract" the sum ventured in the financial year "1611" was £76,375, which was allocated to the Ninth, Tenth and Eleventh Voyages. When the stocks of the Ninth and Tenth Voyages, as given by Sambrooke, are deducted the remainder will be that of the Eleventh Voyage.

[4] *Calendar State Papers, East Indies,* 1513–1616, pp. 434, 437.

[5] *Ibid.*, 1617–21, pp. 56, 64, 65, 79.

[6] *Ibid.*, 1617–21, pp. 133, 145. The adventure was sold subject to three half-capitals having been taken out—as to the meaning of which see Part I., Chapter VIII.

The Second Joint-Stock (1617).

Capital subscribed ...	£1,629,040[1]
Divisions ...	112½ °/₀
Prices of adventures in 1617	115–115¼[2]
1618	110–116¼[3]
1624	80[4]
1626	80[5]
1627	80[6]
1628	70–80[7]
1633 (ex divisions of 100 °/₀)	£10. 12s.[8]

The First Persian Voyage (1628).

Capital. In March 1629 £125,000 had been subscribed, of which £44,000 was paid up to date. The remainder was subsequently called ... £125,000[9]

Divisions ...	160 °/₀[10]
Prices of adventures in 1632 (ex divisions of 100 °/₀) ...	41[11]
1633 ,, ,, ...	60[12]

The Second Persian Voyage (1629).

Capital ...	£140,000 to 150,000[13]
Divisions ...	180 °/₀[14]
Price of an adventure in 1633 (cum all divisions) ...	134 °/₀[15]

The Third Persian Voyage (1630).

Capital. On September 17th, 1630, the estimates of the governor provided for the employment of £100,000 on account of this stock[16] ... ? £100,000

Divisions ... 140 °/₀[17]

---

[1] The whole amount subscribed for this stock was not paid up.
[2] *Calendar State Papers, East Indies,* 1617–21, pp. 79, 85.
[3] *Ibid.*, pp. 145, 194, 198. [4] *Ibid.*, 1622–4, p. 255.
[5] *Ibid.*, 1625–9, p. 179. [6] *Ibid.*, p. 398.
[7] *Ibid.*, p. 538. [8] *Ibid.*, 1630–4, p. 429.
[9] *Ibid.*, 1625–9, p. 638.
[10] *Ibid.*, 1630–4, pp. 572, 573. Up to September 1634 the adventurers had received 140 per cent. "The remains" were transferred to the Third Joint-Stock at a valuation of 20 per cent. on the capital of the First Persian Voyage.
[11] *Ibid.*, p. 314. [12] *Ibid.*, p. 429.
[13] *Ibid.*, p. 456.
[14] *Ibid.*, pp. 572–3. Up to September 1634 150 per cent. had been divided. "The remains" were handed over to the Third Joint-Stock at a valuation of 30 per cent. on the capital of the Second Persian Voyage.
[15] *Ibid.*, p. 429. [16] *Ibid.*, p. 45.
[17] *Ibid.*, pp. 572–3. Up to September 1634 100 per cent. had been divided. "The remains" were handed over to the Third Joint-Stock at a valuation of 40 per cent. on the capital of the Third Persian Voyage. In May 1631 subscriptions were taken for a Fourth Persian Voyage, but, there being only £11,000 promised, this undertaking was not proceeded with. *Ibid.*, pp. 157, 161.

DIV. I. § 5 A] *Summary of Capital &c.* 1617–42

The Third Joint-Stock (1632).

Capital	£420,700[1]
Divisions	135 °/₀[2]
Prices of adventures in 1634	80[3]
1635	80[4]
1636	90[5]
1639	72[6]
1640 (ex divisions of 50 °/₀)	91–95½[7]

The First Particular or General Voyage (1641).

Capital. The amount to be subscribed was fixed at £120,000, of this £80,450 had been taken up at first, and it was resolved on October 15th, 1641, that the "subscription must be increased" ... ... £80,450[8]

Divisions ... ... 221 °/₀[9]

The Fourth Joint-Stock (1642).

Capital	£105,000[10]
Divisions	180 °/₀[11]

[1] In a statement prepared by the company in 1637 the capital was given in round numbers at £425,000. *A Calendar of the Court Minutes of the East India Company, 1635–9*, p. 284.

[2] This is Sambrooke's figure, but it seems highly probable that his return was made before the Dutch indemnity on account of Amboyna was received. The Third Joint-Stock participated in the division of it (Court Book, xxi., October 24, 1655, April 10, 1656), and therefore the total division would be larger than that stated above.   [3] Court Book, xv., f. 132.

[4] *A Calendar of the Court Minutes of the East India Company*, 1635–9, p. 16.

[5] *Ibid.*, p. 156.   [6] *Ibid.*, p. 351.

[7] Court Book, xvii., ff. 105–8. Hunter, *Hist. of Brit. India*, ii. p. 40, notices a transaction at 60 in this year.

[8] Court Book, xviii., ff. 8, 21, 26, 28.

[9] Without the aid of Sambrooke's Report there is considerable difficulty in determining the total capital paid up and more particularly the amount of the divisions. Fortunately in some cases the total sum divided up to a given date is recorded. Thus in the case of the First General Voyage it is noted that up to July 10, 1644, the total divisions had been 125 per cent. (Court Book, xix., f. 98), and again, that up to October 17, 1648, 207 per cent. in all had been paid, to which another of 14 per cent., presumably the final one, was added (Court Book, xx., f. 141).

[10] This stock was begun in November or December 1642. Up to December 19, 1642, only £68,000 had been subscribed and it was proposed to borrow £30,000 or £40,000 (Court Book, xviii., f. 133). On August 28, 1645, the governor stated that the whole amount found by the adventurers had been £105,000 (*Ibid.*, xix., f. 159).

[11] The total amount of the divisions is uncertain. On Oct. 14, 1647, there is mention of a division of indigo (*Ibid.*, xx., f. 79). On June 19, 1650, and again on Aug. 26, 1650, 50 per cent. in pepper on each occasion was distributed (*Ibid.*, xx., f. 271, xxi., f. 8). Then follows a series of money-divisions: 20 per cent. (Oct. 3, 1655), 10 per cent. (May 20, 1656), 10 per cent. (9 July, 1656), 10 per cent. (Oct. 2, 1657), 10 per cent. (May 23, 1663), *Ibid.*, xxi., ff. 139, 146, 149, 155, 162.

The Second General Voyage (1648).

Capital. There was subscribed £194,600		
Of which there was withdrawn 1,800		
Leaving a total subscribed of		£192,800
Three calls aggregating 75 %, were made, and on July 26, 1649, a further call was ordered[1].		
Divisions		148½ %.[2]

The United Joint-Stock (1650).

Capital. The capital proposed was £300,000[3], but on January 2nd, 1650, only £30,200 had been subscribed[4].

Divisions ... ... 205 %.[5]

B. "THE NEW GENERAL STOCK" (1657–1709).

The charter granted by Cromwell to the East India company cannot now be discovered[6], but its main provisions may be traced from various scattered references. The privilege of exclusive trade was granted within the same limits as before, and the company was endowed with the powers it had previously enjoyed of making laws to govern the trade and bye-laws for the regulation of its members. The committees desired a clause empowering the company to exercise martial law, but this was omitted in the charter, and the granting of this power was to be dealt

---

[1] Court Book, xxii., ff. 36, 45.

[2] Divisions were ordered as follows: 25 per cent. in money (Dec. 26, 1649, Court Book, xxii., f. 66), 25 per cent. in money (Feb. 1, 1650, *Ibid.*, xx., f. 236), 25 per cent. in pepper (Aug. 28, 1650, *Ibid.*, xxi., f. 7), 12½ per cent. in money (Oct. 2, 1650, *Ibid.* xxi., f. 12), 25 per cent. in money (Jan. 24, 1651, *Ibid.*, xxiii., f. 15), 15 per cent. (Aug. 6, 1651, *Ibid.*, xxi., f. 61), 12½ per cent. in money (Jan. 21, 1652, *Ibid.*, xxi., f. 80), and 8½ per cent. in money (Jan. 28, 1653, *Ibid.*, xxi., f. 109).

[3] Bruce, *Annals of the East India Company*, i. p. 436.

[4] Court Book, xx., f. 225.

[5] On March 9th, 1658, it is recorded that 170 per cent. had already been divided and that it was expected further distributions of 35 per cent. would be made, *Ibid.*, xxiii., f. 316. Up to this date there are particulars of the following payments: 25 per cent. in pepper (Dec. 9, 1653, *Ibid.* xxiii., f. 155), 15¼ per cent. in money (March 8, 1653, *Ibid.*, xxiii., f. 173), 10 per cent. in money (April 27, 1655, *Ibid.*, xxiii., f. 207), 30 per cent. in money (*Ibid.*, xxiii., f. 232), 10 per cent. in money (June 20, 1656, *Ibid.*, xxiii., f. 260), 20 per cent. in money (Sept. 19, 1656, *Ibid.*, xxiii., f. 269), 10 per cent. in money (March 11, 1657, *Ibid.*, xxiii., f. 282), 10 per cent. in money (July 24, 1657, *Ibid.*, xxiii., f. 290), 10 per cent. in money (Nov. 17, 1657, *Ibid.*, xxiii., f. 310). After March 9th, 1658, the following divisions are noted, 10 per cent. in money (Sept. 28, 1658, *Ibid.*, xxiii., f. 323), 10 per cent. in money (June 23, 1659, *Ibid.*, xxiii., f. 334), 10 per cent. in money (June 21, 1660, *Ibid.*, xxiii., f. 344).

[6] Sir W. Hunter traced out each copy mentioned in contemporary documents and made extensive enquiries, not only in London, but also at the Hague and Batavia.

with by special commission. The claim for immunity from customs was postponed at the meeting of the Council of State when the clauses were settled. Finally Cromwell reserved the power of recalling the charter if he saw due cause for such action[1].

On the charter being sealed, steps were at once taken to obtain capital, and a preamble for subscriptions was drawn up and advertised by October 22nd, 1657[2]. Vellum books were provided for the subscriptions, which were to close on November 10th for London and the district within a 20 mile radius, and on the 25th for the country. The minimum subscription was £100, but it required £500 to qualify for a vote and £1,000 for membership of the committee. Calls were payable as follows:

1st payment of	$12\frac{1}{2}$ %	on	December 1, 1657
2nd	,,	$12\frac{1}{2}$	,,	March 1, 1658
3rd	,,	$18\frac{3}{4}$	,,	September 1, 1658
4th	,,	$18\frac{3}{4}$	,,	March 1, 1659
5th	,,	$18\frac{3}{4}$	,,	September 1, 1659
6th	,,	$18\frac{3}{4}$	,,	March 1, 1660

It was further provided that at the expiration of seven years the assets should be valued, and thereafter at the end of each third year, and, on the basis of such valuation, any stockholder should be entitled to receive the estimated equivalent of his original subscription, his place being taken by another who wished to join the company. New members who purchased stock were to pay £5 for their freedom[3].

In some respects it was unfortunate that it was necessary to procure capital at an unfavourable time, when trade was very depressed. Had the outlook been brighter adventurers would have come forward more readily. As it was, even by relaxing the conditions as to the minimum subscription, the whole amount taken up was £739,782. 10s.[4] Arrangements had already been made to secure the property acquired by the "United Stock." The sum of £20,000 was to be paid by the "New General Stock" to the former adventurers for the forts and franchises in India, while the shipping, goods and bullion were to be transferred from the old to the new stock at a valuation. Though every effort was made to prosecute the trade vigorously[5], it was soon found necessary to modify the clause in the preamble relating to the payment of calls. The combined effects of the financial difficulties of the Protectorate, bad

[1] State Papers, Domestic, Order Book of the Council of State (Oct. 1, 1657), I. pp. 189, 190; *Calendar*, 1657, pp. 115, 116, cf. authorities cited by Hunter, *Hist. of British India*, II. pp. 132, 133.

[2] In *Mercurius Politicus*, October 22–9, 1657.

[3] "The Preamble"—MSS. India Office—Home Miscellaneous, XL., ff. 76–9.

[4] *Journals of the House of Commons*, XII. p. 311.

[5] *A Treatise touching the East India Trade*, 1664 [India Office Tracts, vol. 268], p. 10.

trade and political unrest had produced a great strain on mercantile credit. In 1659 business in the city was so poor that some merchants visited it only rarely; while, through want of employment, a great number of poor families were in danger of perishing, and the burden of relieving them in some wards was found almost insupportable[1]. Under these circumstances it was deemed advisable to call up only 50 per cent. (instead of 100 per cent.) on the stock, so that the company, as re-established, made a fresh start with a subscribed capital, paid up, of only £369,891. 5s. Its working resources were larger than this amount, since by June 1659 £40,000 had been borrowed. It was at this juncture, when there was only £1,900 in cash in the coffers of the company, that the Council of State sent an order to the committees demanding a loan of £30,000. The security proposed, in view of the political situation, namely that of the monthly assessments, was not satisfactory, and it was decided that the future customs payable on the goods of the adventurers must be substituted. On this change being made, the generality took a vote by ballot whether the sum to be lent should be £30,000 or £15,000, with the result that the majority of votes was cast in favour of the smaller amount[2]. The providing of this loan, as well as the capital needed for the trade at a time when it was difficult to borrow, precluded the payment of dividends; and, for several years after the formation of the "General" Stock, no distributions were made.

In some respects the Restoration was far from being an unmixed gain to the company. Indeed the mere fact that it had succeeded in making terms with Cromwell was not unlikely to prejudice it with the advisers of Charles II. However there can be little doubt that the adventurers, in their capacity of East India merchants, viewed the change with satisfaction, since, within a short period after the signature of the charter of 1657 by Cromwell, his son Richard had licensed a ship owned by persons who were not members of the company, thereby contravening not only this instrument but the whole series of principles upon which the grant of it had been based[3]. It was decided to suppress the Cromwellian charter, and the company was one of the first bodies to offer its address to Charles II., at the same time presenting him with a service of plate worth £3,000 and the Duke of York with £1,000 in cash. This action was followed up on November 27th, 1660, by a petition to the Council of Trade, which reported on January 3rd, 1661, recom-

---

[1] "Mercurius Redivivus," Add. MS. (Brit. Mus.), 10,117, ff. 20, 170.

[2] Court Book, xxiv., June 22, June 24, June 27, 1659.

[3] *Annals of the Honourable East India Company*, by John Bruce, London, 1810, I. p. 537. That it was found necessary for the company to make "a gratification" to some persons at Whitehall may be connected with this episode. Court Book, xxiv. (March 16, 1658).

mending the company "to the royal protection[1]." Accordingly on April 3rd, 1661, a charter was signed by Charles II. This instrument repeats almost word for word the grant of James I. The privilege of sole trade is granted "for ever hereafter," subject to revocation should the company be found unprofitable, on three years' notice being given. The clauses relating to the internal management of the organization are similar to those of the patent of half a century earlier save that the date of the court-meeting for the choice of a governor and committees is changed from the first ten days of July to a day between April 10th and 30th in each year. For the first time the voting qualification, announced in the preambles of 1650 and 1657, was incorporated in the charter, and it was provided that stockholders who owned less than the specified £500 might join their respective holdings, for purposes of the poll, and "vote jointly for the same." At the beginning of the latter half of the seventeenth century a qualification of £500 as the minimum for a vote may seem to have been too high, but it is to be remembered that at this period only 50 per cent. was paid up, so that, at the date of this charter, a cash payment of £250 would have secured a vote. How rudimentary was the conception of the representation of members of the joint-stock company at this time is shown by the fact that the stock issued was not an exact multiple of the minimum voting qualification. The total number of possible votes was 1,479, and there remained a balance of £282. 10s. stock which could not be represented. In one respect the charter of 1661 was wider than that of 1657, since under the former the company obtained the right of making war with any non-Christian prince within the limits assigned to it[2].

When the Crown had performed its part in recognizing the legal status of the company, it was expected that the body so established would make a suitable return for the royal favour shown to it; and, in May 1662, Charles II. asked for a loan of £20,000 or £30,000 at 6 per cent.[3], and in June the company responded by lending £10,000[4]. In the same month the first dividend on this stock was actually paid (though it had been declared in September 1661) amounting to 20 per cent. About this time the stock was selling from 90 to 94 for £100 paid up, that is at 10 per cent. to 6 per cent. discount[5]. In declaring the dividend of 1661-2, the governor and committees outlined the principle that in future these distributions would consist of profits earned, not "divisions"

[1] "Proceedings of the Council of Trade," Add. MSS. (Brit. Mus.) 25,115, ff. 39, 91: cf. *Growth of English Industry and Commerce in Modern Times*, by W. Cunningham, Cambridge, 1903, p. 916.

[2] *Charters Granted to the East India Company*, I. pp. 58, 75, 76, 78.

[3] State Papers, Domestic, Charles II., LIV. 33; *Calendar*, 1661-2, p. 366.

[4] Court Book, XXIV., June 25.

[5] *Vide infra*, "Summary of Prices and Dividends," p. 177.

(without distinction between capital and income) as had been the case in the past. In fact, owing to the relatively small amount of the capital subscribed in 1657 and to only one-half of this being paid up, it became necessary for the company to devote all the profit earned during the first four years to the development of the trade, and in addition loans had to be provided both for the Protectorate and for the Crown. Though the stock was below par, this course had strengthened the credit of the company, and it was able to obtain additional funds by borrowing on its bonds, sometimes, it is said, at from 4 per cent. to 5 per cent.[1] Evidently the management considered that by 1662 sufficient working capital had been acquired, and, once the payment of dividends had been begun, it was continued—20 per cent. being divided in 1663 and again in 1664, making 60 per cent. in the first seven years of this stock. The time had now come, when under the terms of the preamble, adventurers might withdraw from the company without selling their stock in the market. Accordingly it was resolved on October 13th, 1664, that a general valuation should be made of all the assets[2], and on December 12th this account was presented, which showed that the nett value of the property (after allowing for liabilities) was £495,735. 6s.[3] Therefore in addition to the dividends paid of 60 per cent., there was undivided profit of 30 per cent., so that the whole gain for the seven years may be taken at 90 per cent. or an annual average of about 13 per cent. Few if any of the proprietors availed themselves of the privilege of being bought out, indeed the fact that transfers of stock occur occasionally amongst the subjects discussed at the meetings of the committees shows that there was a sufficiently free market in the shares to render a provision of this kind unnecessary[4]. That it was announced at all marks a step in the transition from the terminable to a permanent capital. Had it been impossible for adventurers to sell their stock, the septennial and triennial valuations would have remedied the defect. At this date the stock was well distributed, since it is recorded that the largest holding was only £4,000[5].

The disclosure of the financial state of the company in 1664 had one unfortunate result, in so far as it became necessary to divide the reserved profits of 30 per cent. In fact more than this was done, as a dividend of 40 per cent. was paid in 1665. On the supposition that 10 per cent. was from profits made after the valuation, this would leave assets of the par-value of the stock, but on the outbreak of the Dutch War there

---

[1] State Papers, Domestic, Charles II., cxxxiii. 4; *Calendar*, 1664–5, p. 565.
[2] Court Book, xxiv. (Oct. 13, 1664).
[3] *Ibid.* (Dec. 12, 1664), Add. MS. (Brit. Mus.) 17,476, f. 194; Harl. MS. 7,310, f. 17.
[4] Cf. Court Book, xxiv. (Dec. 12, 1664).
[5] "A Regulated Company more National than a Joint-Stock Company in the East India Trade," Harl. MS. 7,310, f. 1.

were several losses to be met, and during the depression in London the stock sold at 70, subsequently falling to 60. There can be little doubt that this low price was occasioned in part by the action of the committees, who, in the early part of 1666, announced two dividends amounting to 50 per cent. payable in the following year. The ostensible cause of this policy was alleged to be the impossibility of employing the capital of the company in trade owing to the war, and there can be little doubt that, in the prevailing scarcity of ready money in London at the time, the adventurers pressed for large distributions. But behind the ostensible reason for these divisions there were certain obscure events or foreshadowings of future possible events, which made it desirable that for some years to come the Court should not have at its disposal any large liquid assets. As the war progressed the finances of the Crown became seriously embarrassed[1], and no doubt the committees feared that the company might be compelled to make very large loans to meet the emergency. Moreover there was another source of anxiety. One of the schemes for the "improvement of the revenue" was based on the recovery from the company of £100,000 which was alleged to be due to the State under the charter granted by Cromwell[2]. Doubtless as long as there were large resources in the possession of the company other pretexts would be adduced for drawing on them for the relief of the Crown, and it was judged wise to make considerable returns to the stockholders. This course however did not preclude demands being made upon it for financial assistance, and it was forced to lend £50,000 in 1666 and £70,000 in 1667[3].

The management would have been well-advised to have invited further subscriptions of capital on the restoration of peace. With prospects of extensive trading operations before it, the company suffered from a depleted capital account. If, at the end of 1664, its nett assets were worth almost £500,000, of that amount more than £330,000 had been paid away in dividends from July 1665 to February 1667, while a further £120,000 was locked up temporarily in advances to the Crown. Making allowance for the nett profit (in excess of losses) during the war, it is clear that the available capital in 1667 was very small and that it was necessary to supplement it by borrowing, which could only be entered

---

[1] *Vide supra*, Part I., Chapter XIV.
[2] State Papers, Domestic, Charles II., CLXXXVI. 83. No details are given of the ground of this claim, but in *Two Letters concerning the East India Company*, 1676 [Brit. Mus. 1029.g.22 (1)], it is stated that under the statute 21 Jac. cap. 3 the company is liable to pay treble damages "to all whom they have abused, hindered, grieved or disturbed in their trades to the Indies," and it is added that "perhaps such damages may amount to £100,000 at least."
[3] Court Books, XXV. (April), XXVI. (July and December).

on, at that time, at onerous rates, since capital was in great demand, partly through the re-building of London after the Great Fire, partly too through the activity of trade. Therefore it again became necessary to set aside all earnings during the three years 1668, 1669, 1670 to provide funds for the carrying on of the business. In 1671 the stockholders pressed for some return on their investments, and in declaring a dividend of 10 per cent. the committees " acquainted them that the stock had been reduced to a low level by the great dividends made in the year 1666 (through there being little opportunity to trade by reason of the Dutch War). Therefore the Court had not been capable of making any since that time, it having been found necessary not only to employ all the stock and the profit that hath arisen therefrom, but also to take up great sums of money at interest to carry on the trade, and having now by the blessing of God supplied this trade with a convenient stock and observing that the adventurers do generally desire to have something divided as soon as may be, the Court have resolved on a dividend of 10 per cent.[1]" A balance-sheet of this date shows that the financial position was satisfactory. It contains the following items:

	£	s.	d.
Debts due to the company	136,735	19	0
Value of 8 ships	17,709	18	3
Balance at Surat and subordinate factories	170,586	8	10
,, St Helena			
,, Bantam and cost of cargoes	129,213	8	6
Balances elsewhere in the East	235,709	11	0
Goods in England	313,255	11	6
Cash	3,902	16	3
Profit on cargoes in transit			
Desperate debts £65,542. 17s. 2d.			
Total assets brought into account	£1,007,113	13	9
Liabilities to be deducted:			
Debts due at home and abroad, April 30, 1671 £361,286. 11s. 6d.			
Dividend of 10°/₀ £36,989. 2s. 6d.	398,275	14	0
Balance, being nett assets	£608,837	19	9[2]

It is a striking testimony to the general return of confidence that, while during the three years 1665–7 (when large dividends were paid) the stock was below par, from 1668–70 (while there were no distributions at all) the quotations are at least 108, and on some occasions 130 may have been recorded. The combined effect of the crisis in London and the second Dutch War produced a fall in the stock which appears to have been about 80 in 1672–3. At this time, judging by the dividends paid—namely 40 per cent. in 1672, 20 per cent. in 1673, and

[1] Court Book, xxvii. (May 5, 1671).
[2] MSS. at the India Office, Home Miscellaneous, iv. p. 12.

20 per cent. in 1674—the trade was prosperous. But in the next two years (1675 and 1676), owing to the losses arising out of the defence of the factories in India, it was impossible to make any distribution. Indeed it was stated that this war had cost the company £400,000 besides very great damages from the interruption of trade[1]. In the following year (1677) however 40 per cent. was paid. Thus from 1668 to 1677 (inclusive) altogether 130 per cent. was divided; a satisfactory record when it is remembered that this period embraced both an European and an Indian war.

At the same time there were signs that might be construed as ominous for the future, for such success in itself constituted a possible element of danger. Since its foundation the East India company had to face a considerable amount of adverse criticism as representing an innovation on the traditional ideas of English trade. In two respects especially its progress became capable of being considered prejudicial to accepted economic beliefs, namely in so far as it exported bullion and also imported goods which competed or appeared to compete with the cloth trade. Thus there were arrayed against the company the clothiers, the merchants engaged in the English silk industry as well as all the bullionists. These interests were supported by the interlopers who had suffered from the confiscation of either ships or goods. The opposition to the company might have failed to produce any marked effect for a considerable period, since it consisted of persons of different trades who were not in the habit of acting in concert. Moreover any attempt to take concerted steps would have revealed the irreconcilable opposition in the ideas of the different groups which were endeavouring to work together. For instance, the woollen industry was hostile to the company because the former wished the Indian trade to be kept within the narrowest possible limits, while conversely the interlopers were equally against the existing chartered body, but with the object, as they alleged, of extending commerce with the East. It is clear then, that ultimately, the enemies of the company would disagree, but in the meantime all their energies could be temporarily co-ordinated in supporting the Levant company in its campaign against the East India undertaking. The former body first moved in 1670[2], and its attacks were continued intermittently until 1676. Thus, in the first instance, the struggle was not between individual traders and a monopolistic corporation, but between two chartered companies. The Levant company had fallen upon evil days.

---

[1] *A Brief Account of the Great Oppressions and Injuries which the Managers of the East India Company have acted on the Lives, Liberties and Estates of their Fellow Subjects* [?1698], Bod. Lib. Pamphlets θ, 658 (24), cited by Sir W. Hunter, *History of British India*, II. p. 279.

[2] Anderson, *Annals of Commerce, ut supra*, III. p. 77.

Its internal management suffered from fraud and the abuses of the factors abroad; while, as the East India company began to succeed, the former organization had suffered from the competition of the latter. Both brought oriental commodities to England, but the trade-route of each was protected from the competition of the other or of independent merchants by their respective charters. Though the distance to be traversed by the East India company was much longer, it proved to be more economical, and therefore the rival organization endeavoured to recapture the ground it had lost by initiating a campaign against the younger corporation in Parliament. Public opinion would have paid scant attention to the disputes of the two bodies of merchants had the Levant company not been astute enough to see how it could secure the support of the woollen industry and of the bullionists. The form of argument which united these diverse interests, when stripped of irrelevancies was reducible to the following statement. Each company supplied England with similar foreign commodities, and, in normal circumstances, the competition of the two bodies might even be beneficial. But, according to the contention of the Levant company, the situation was abnormal. Attention must be paid not only to the nature of the imports, but also to that of the exports. Now, the complainants exported woollen goods, whereas the East India company shipped a very much smaller quantity of these. Therefore from the point of view of the clothiers, the encouragement of the Levant enterprize would tend to increase the demand for their products. Further the allegation, that the deficiency in the amount of cloth exported by the East India company in order to pay for its purchases in India was made up by shipments of bullion, added to the opposition all those who felt keenly on the maintaining of a favourable balance of trade with each country individually.

As time went on the woollen trade began to experience a check to the great prosperity it had enjoyed for a considerable number of years. Employment was becoming less, and the demand for wool and all kinds of appliances was also less than it had been during the ten years following the Restoration. An instance of the beginning of the decline is afforded by the rental of a mill which had been built during the boom in this trade early in the reign of James I., and which then yielded a rent of £240 a year. After the Civil Wars the tenant paid from £40 to £80, but after 1673 all that could then be obtained did not suffice to pay one-sixth of the repairs and taxes[1]. Spurred on by the decline of the cloth trade, the opponents of the East India company renewed their attack in 1676 in a *Letter from a Country Gentleman to a Barrister of the Inner Temple*. The points, already discussed, were again brought forward and were reinforced by a number of new arguments, some of

[1] *England's Improvements*, 1675, p. 33.

DIV. I. § 5 B]   *Attacks on the Company* 1670–6   137

which relate to the legal status and the organization of the company. It was urged that the whole monopoly of trade was liable to be abolished, since the undertaking depended solely on its royal charters, which had not been confirmed by Parliament. For this reason the author endeavoured to dissuade his friends from investing in the bonds of the company. Moreover he criticised the joint-stock type of organization, which he alleged was inferior to the regulated[1].

The issue involved was of very great importance to the company, and a considerable amount of information was furnished which throws light on the position of the trade at this period. The bullion exported annually amounted to a large sum as is shown by the following account:

	£	s.	d.
1667–8	128,605	17	5
1668–9	162,394	9	10
1669–70	187,458	3	8
1670–1	186,149	10	11
1671–2	186,420	8	3
1672–3	131,300	5	11
1673–4	182,983	0	6[2]

This account may be supplemented by another, showing the shipments of cloth about the same period:

		£
Broad-cloth and other woollens 1676		48,684
1677		52,445
1678		24,764
1679		32,913
1680		51,666
Total cloth and woollens 1676–80		210,472
Other goods, stores, &c. ,,		194,646
Total		405,118
Cloth and woollens ... 1681		94,855
1682		42,630
1683		24,448
1684		47,827
1685		48,414
Total cloth and woollens 1681–5		258,174
Other goods, stores, &c. ,,		187,440
Total		445,614[3]

It is clear from these figures that the company was unable to afford a convincing reply to the attacks upon it by the clothiers and the

[1] *Two Letters concerning the East India Company*, 1676 (Brit. Mus. 1029. g. 22), pp. 2, 3.
[2] Bruce, *Annals, ut supra*, II. p. 353.
[3] State Papers, Domestic, James II., v. 104.

bullionists. Indeed its case suffered by its supporters over-stating the amount of bullion exported in 1674–5, which was returned at £320,000[1]. At the same time, while no attempt was made to minimise the shipment of silver to the East or to inflate that of cloth, the company had an ingenious answer to the arguments against it under these heads, namely, that of its imports from India about £200,000 in value was re-exported annually and that the proceeds were remitted to England in bullion. Therefore, much, if not the whole, of the precious metals taken out of the country was returned eventually by this indirect trade[2]. The general advantage of the commerce with India was shown by the statement that the gross profit was 100 per cent. The working expenses (including salaries, outlay on garrisons, and presents to the native princes) were moderate, being about 15 per cent. of the profit, while customs in England came to a further 8 per cent.[3] In reply to the alleged merits of the regulated type of organization it was said that at least a million "was engaged in the necessary defence of the trade[4]," whereof £300,000 had been spent in the fortifying of Bombay (which had been granted to the company by Charles II. in 1668), and that so large a sum could not be raised by a regulated company[5]. The sense in which this statement is to be interpreted can be gathered from a balance-sheet of the company in 1678, where the "dead stock" was valued at £216,483. The following are the details:

"Dead stock"—fortifications, &c.[6]	£216,483
Quick stock—ships and goods	£1,511,619
Total	£1,728,102[7]

It follows that the expression—"defence of the trade"—is to be understood as including not only fortifications and payments for the right of entry into the native states but also the cost of large armed ships.

Before the points in dispute between the company and its adversaries had been thoroughly discussed, the Crown intervened by granting a fresh charter, dated October 15th, 1677, which sets forth that "diverse transactions having happened, where the proceedings of the governor and

[1] *The East India Trade a Most Profitable Trade to this Kingdom, and best secured and improved in a Company and a Joint-stock*, 1677 [written under the direction of T. Papillon], Brit. Mus. 1029. g. 24, p. 7.

[2] *Ibid.*, p. 9.

[3] *Ibid.*, p. 11. These charges are given in the form of the ratio to the whole profit, since, as shown above, the figures in this work are over-stated.

[4] Cf. *An Answer to two Letters concerning the East India Company*, 1676 [Brit. Mus. 1029. g. 22 (2)].

[5] *Ibid.*, p. 18.

[6] In 1685 the dead stock was valued at £719,464. 16s. Add. MS. [Brit. Mus.] 22,185.

[7] Court Book, xxxi. (Aug. 12, 1678).

company may be liable to some question, how far they are warranted, by the strict letter of the said charters and the charters themselves may be in danger of being impeached as forfeited for some misuser or non-user of rights," wherefore all the previous grants were explicitly ratified and confirmed in the most ample manner[1]. On this occasion the charter was both preceded and followed by a loan from the company to Charles II., £40,000 having been advanced in 1676 and £50,000 in 1678[2].

On the defeat of the opposition to the company the price of the stock advanced, being quoted at 245 in 1677. That year, after a temporary cessation of dividends in 1675–6, there was divided 40 per cent. In 1678 a distribution, rated at ½ per cent., was made in damaged calico which could not be sold. The following year 40 per cent. was divided, and in 1680 the dividend was increased to 50 per cent., relapsing to 20 per cent. in 1681. Thus in seven years from 1675 to 1681, 150½ per cent. had been paid, or an average of more than 20 per cent. per annum. This was not a large return for the times, and the yield, on this basis, at the price at which the stock stood was under 6 per cent., though, should 50 per cent. dividends be maintainable, it would have been about 12½ per cent. According to the statistics of the gross profits and expenses the gain should have been higher, and the discrepancy is accounted for by the fact that a considerable amount of the profits earned had been withheld to develope the trade. According to the valuation of 1678 the assets amounted to over 1¾ millions. At this time the loans taken up by the company were about half a million[3], leaving nett assets of 1¼ millions. In view of the depleted condition of the capital of the company in 1667 probably upwards of a million had been obtained from undivided profits; and, as the stock provided partly in this way, partly by borrowing, became adequate for the business to be done, it became possible to increase the rate of the dividend.

Meanwhile the opposition to the company, which had been temporarily suppressed by the grant of the charter of 1677, was renewed in 1680. The Levant company appealed to the Privy Council, and counsel representing both bodies were heard on August 27th[4]. The arguments already summarized were repeated, and, in addition, the criticism of the joint-stock system was further developed. Many of the contentions of the Levant company were founded on the idea of maintaining the privileges of the mercantile class as such, as for instance when stress was laid on the plea that the rival body "did not breed up East India mer-

---

[1] *Charters granted to the East India Company*, I. pp. 108–15.
[2] Court Book, xxx. (August, 1676, January and October, 1678).
[3] Add. MS. (Brit. Mus.) 17,476, f. 193; *The History and Proceedings of the House of Commons* (printed by R. Chandler), Lond. 1742, I. p. 411.
[4] *A Brief Historical Relation of State Affairs*, by Narcissus Luttrell, Oxford, 1857, I. p. 119.

chants since anyone may purchase a share of their trade and joint-stock," whence it followed that not one-fifth of the proprietors were merchants. It was further objected that the stock had not been wound up after the expiration of the first seven years, as it was alleged had been promised in the preamble for subscriptions in 1657, with the result that there was no opportunity for young merchants to come in on a new issue of capital. The continuance of the general stock had the further consequence that it had become engrossed so that some forty persons obtained more than half the aggregate amount distributed in dividends. Attention was also drawn to the existence of "private trade." Under this system it was said that the more influential members sent home the choicest goods on their private accounts to the injury of the remaining adventurers. Further, clamour was raised against the financial methods of the company, especially in respect to the large amount of its borrowings, which were stated to amount to £700,000. It was urged that the lenders of this sum, who received only 3 per cent., "clearly ventured the hazard of their principal," while the company obtained 50 per cent. profit on the capital lent it "without any hazard at all[1]." On November 9th of the same year (1680) a debate was initiated in the House of Commons on the status of the company when a petition from the weavers had been read. The speeches were all in favour of the woollen industry, and they are marked by a considerable amount of exaggeration and of animus against the company. One speaker said that the East India trade would "in the end be the destruction of the manufactury trade...because the people in India are such slaves as to work for less than a penny a day; whereas ours will not work under a shilling; and they have all materials also very reasonable and are thereby enabled to make their goods so cheap as it will be impossible for our people to contend with them." As another member expressed the same fear—"the East India company have been very industrious to promote their own trade, but therein have given a great blow to the trade of the nation." Every effort was made to excite prejudice by over-stating the ratio of the company's imports to the total trade of the country, by asserting that the exports of bullion were £500,000 to £600,000 a year and "may increase to millions," or by drawing attention to the large dividends received by individuals, one man [Sir Josia Child] obtaining £20,000, others £10,000 each[2].

Many of the arguments used against the company were exaggerations,

[1] *The allegations of the Turky Company and others against the East India Company, relating to the management of that Trade* [1681], Brit. Mus. $\frac{522.1.5}{8}$. *A Discourse concerning the East India Trade; wherein is shewed by arguments taken from a treatise written by Sir Josiah Child, that the said Trade may be carried on by a Regulated Company to much greater Advantage of the Publick, than by a Company with a Joint-Stock.* Somers' Tracts, x. pp. 634–47.

[2] *Hist. and Proceedings of the House of Commons, ut supra,* I. pp. 409–11.

others were mutually destructive. If the advantages of the organization of the regulated company be insisted on, it was inconsistent to censure the East India company for its departure from the conception of the joint-stock type and its approximation to the former in so far as it admitted private trade. Moreover the assertion that the stock was to be wound up after seven years was not well-founded, and as a matter of fact the terms of the preamble had been strictly carried out. That there were larger holdings of stock than in 1664 was a proof that sales had been numerous. These purchases could only have been made by persons who, like Child, had faith in the prospects of the undertaking even when quotations were low and who had the courage to take the risk of buying largely. Now that their courage had been justified by events and the stock commanded a premium of 200 per cent. purchases could still be made (as was indeed admitted during the debate in Parliament), but the "young merchants" objected to the payment of the premium, and they were searching for some device by which they could obtain stock at par and at the same time secure a proportion of the undivided profit that belonged to the existing stockholders. Mention of a proposed new subscription—even as early as 1680 it was suggested that the capital should be augmented to two or three millions[1]—reveals the inevitable cleavage amongst the opponents of the company, some desired to impose terms on it to limit, others to increase the trade. The further contention that the loans contracted by the committees were prejudicial to the prosperity of the country was in effect no more than a testimony to the superiority of the joint-stock to the regulated type of organization. The former, by means of the combination of the capital resources of individuals, was able to extend its credit, and it was asserted that, even with interest at 3 per cent., the company was unable to induce its creditors "to take back their money."

As was almost inevitable, the issues in this discussion were greatly confused, and the whole dispute tended to proceed by arguments on either side involving an *ignoratio elenchi*. Apart from the inconsistencies of the attacking party, their views consist in comparing the ideal regulated company with a partly imaginary joint-stock body. Conversely the defenders of the East India undertaking contrast the ideal joint-stock organization with the Levant merchants, as representative of the regulated type. Thus, as the case stood, both companies had about five hundred members, and both had monopolies. Child and other apologists for the joint-stock type were able to show that in reality it

[1] *The Allegations of the Turky Company and others against the East India Company relating to the management of that Trade* [1681] $\left(\text{Brit. Mus. } \frac{522.1.5}{8}\right)$; *Britannia Languens* (1680) in McCullough, *Tracts on Commerce* (1856), pp. 332–41.

was the more comprehensive, since in it "noblemen, gentlemen, shopkeepers, widows, orphans and all other subjects" were able to employ their capital in the trade, whereas in a regulated company only those who could make good their claim as legitimate merchants—that is those who served an apprenticeship to that particular trade—were eligible for membership[1]. For this reason Child contended that existing "barrs and hindrances" should rather be removed from the Levant, than imposed on the East India company.

If it be granted that, in a comparison between the ideal joint-stock and a regulated body, such as the Levant company, the balance of advantage lay with the former, it remains to enquire how far the East India undertaking, as it existed in 1680 and 1681, had reaped the advantages which might be expected to accrue from its constitution on a joint-stock basis. If, as was alleged, the stock was engrossed in the sense that a few persons were able to control the voting, it was obvious that the condition was not satisfactory. This complaint appears to have been based on a misapprehension, due to jealousy of the success of Child's investment. He at this time owned upwards of £17,000 stock or considerably less than 5 per cent. of the whole, and his was much the largest holding[2]. In 1679 there were no less than 223 persons who owned £1,000 or over that amount, and in 1681 there were 181 similarly qualified[3]. It follows that about half the proprietors held less than £1,000 stock, and the remainder that amount or over it. Therefore there should have been nothing in the disposition of the stock or voting rights enabling a small group of individuals to control the company, contrary to the wishes of the remainder.

The immediate effect of the agitation against the company was the reference of the petitions against it to the Grand Committee for Trade of the House of Commons, while it was not long before the inevitable cleavage in the ranks of the adversaries of the chartered body became marked. Hitherto the campaign had proceeded on the assumption that

---

[1] *Answer of the East India Company to the Allegations of the Turky Company* $\left(\text{Brit. Mus. } \dfrac{522.1.5}{8}\right)$. *A Treatise wherein it is demonstrated that the East India Trade is the most National of all foreign trades* [by Sir Josia Child]. Somers' *Tracts*, VI. p. 35. It was said the Jews offered Charles II. £50,000 if he would grant a new charter to the company under which they would be entitled to own stock, *Life and Times of Charles II.*, by R. W. Blencowe, 1843, I. p. 211.

[2] *Treatise, ut supra*, Somers' *Tracts*, VIII. p. 463. Thus on a 50 per cent. dividend being paid Child could not receive more than £4,250, not £20,000 as stated in Parliament. Similarly he was entitled to not more than 34 votes instead of 60.

[3] *A List of their names, who by their Adventures are capable of being chosen committees by the East India Company for the year* 1679. Bod. Library Pamphlets θ, 658 (28). A List...for 1681, State Papers, Domestic, Charles II., CCCCXXI. 104.

trade with India was to be reduced in the interests of home manufactures, and Child was able to answer the arguments against the company on this head with considerable force. "The truth of the case at bottom," he writes, "is this, the importation of better and cheaper raw silk from India may probably touch some Turkey merchants' profit at present, though it doth benefit the kingdom and not hinder the exportation of cloth. What then? Must one trade be interrupted because it works upon another? At that rate there would be nothing but confusion in a nation, *ad infinitum*[1]." After the failure of the Levant company to make an impression on the defence of the company, the leadership in the attack was assumed by those who desired not to contract but to increase the East Indian trade. In 1681 efforts were made to promote a rival joint-stock company. In April 1682 a million of the stock had been taken up, and it was proposed to make the capital up to no less than three millions. It was noted, as a remarkable development, that "tickets were sent through the post to promote subscriptions[2]." Steps were taken to obtain a charter, but the company had already protected itself by taking measures to secure the support of Charles II. In October 1681 Child, on behalf of his fellow-adventurers, had presented the King with a gift of 10,000 guineas[3]. This presentation, which was continued till the Revolution each year[4], was of a nature not uncommon at the time. The Dutch East India company had for some years past given the Prince of Orange £6,000 annually[5], and the Hudson's Bay Adventurers had been in the habit of making a similar donation to Charles II.[6] The effect of this handsome present was to gain the adhesion of the Crown, and the effect of it began to appear when a proclamation was made on November 22nd, 1681, which was designed to strengthen the company against those who infringed its privileges[7]. At the end of May in the following year the petition of the promoters of the proposed rival organization for a charter was refused, and the privileges of the existing body confirmed[8]. In the next year this decision was expressly stated in a further charter, which confirms the previous grants and prescribes penalties against interlopers, at the same time recording the verdict reached up to this time that "the trade can by no means be maintained

---

[1] *Treatise, ut supra,* Somers' *Tracts,* VII. p. 460.
[2] *London Mercury,* No. 5 (April 20, 1682); Luttrell, *Brief Relation, ut supra,* I. p. 178.
[3] Luttrell, *Brief Relation,* I. p. 135.
[4] *Vide infra,* Financial Statements M and N.
[5] *London Gazette,* No. 1470, Dec. 18–22, 1679.
[6] *Vide infra,* Division I. § 6.
[7] Luttrell, *Brief Relation,* I. p. 145.
[8] *Ibid.,* I. p. 184; *Domestic Intelligence,* No. 107, June 1, 1682.

and carried on with such advantage as by a joint-stock and that a loose and general trade will be the ruin of the whole[1]."

In one sense the charter of 1683 represents the close of the controversy which had now continued intermittently for upwards of thirteen years, but in another it meant the beginning of a fresh phase of the dispute. This change of attitude arose not from external pressure, but from the internal history of the company itself. The weak point in its defence had been in certain aspects of its finance, since it is obvious that if the investing public were anxious to subscribe more stock it was highly desirable that their wishes should be met. Both Child and Papillon, the governor and deputy-governor respectively, had expressed themselves in favour of a new subscription "if we can come honestly by it, that is, without injustice to the new adventurers[2]...which notwithstanding is a matter of great difficulty, it being in trade as with trees, great care is to be taken in removing an old one, lest upon removal it die, or at least suffer a shrewd stunt[3]." There was an obvious difficulty in dealing with this question. Those who were most insistent on a fresh issue of capital were anxious that such should rank *pari passu* with that already in existence. Therefore, supposing as had been suggested that a million of new stock were created and offered for subscription at par to persons who were not already members of the company, the effect of this operation would have been to transfer roughly three-quarters of the undivided profits from the old to the new adventurers. Therefore it was clear that the first step was to safeguard the present stockholders. At this date, though the assets were large and capital could be borrowed with ease, there can be little doubt that the free capital was too small. Thus in March 1679 the company owed £216,000 more than all its effects in England and £100,000 of bills on the treasury had to be postponed for payment[4]. Therefore it may be assumed that capital would have been useful. It was first proposed on November 2nd, 1681, that a call of 50 per cent. should be made, which would make the stock fully paid[5]. This method would have provided additional resources, but it would have failed to have safeguarded the interests of the present adventurers should a future public subscription be made. Accordingly in January 1682 it was decided to make a dividend in stock of 100 per cent., in addition to the distribution of 50 per cent. in cash[6]. The effect of this arrangement was that each adventurer, who had

[1] *Charters granted to the East India Company*, I. p. 119.
[2] *i.e.*, the adventurers in the "*new* general stock," that is in fact the existing stockholders.
[3] *Treatise, ut supra*, Somers' *Tracts*, VII. p. 459.
[4] Court Book, XXXI. (March 26, 27, 1679).
[5] *Ibid.*, XXXII. (Nov. 2, 1681).
[6] *Ibid.*, XXXII. (Jan. 14, 1682).

previously owned £100 stock with £50 paid, was entitled to dividends as if payment had been made in full. It follows that, on a public subscription being made at par, the present members would only suffer in so far as the nett assets exceeded £739,782. 10s., this being now the amount of the capital considered as paid up. According to a balance-sheet of the following year, the clear value of the various properties was £1,672,871, after making provision for all liabilities which amounted to £870,185[1]. According to these figures there were undivided profits more than equal to twice the increased capital, and therefore the reserved profits, in excess of the capital, remained rather more than that capital after the stock bonus was included[2]. Possibly however some deductions must be made from this apparent surplus. The account includes upwards of £70,000 of debts that were classed as "desperate," while it was urged that the dead stock was valued not at its worth to the trade, but at the total outlay upon it[3]. On the other hand it is to be noted that no allowance is made for "good-will," which would have been worth a considerable sum. This was adjusted in the market-price of the stock which sold at 300 in 1680, 365 in 1681 and at 460 in 1682, these quotations applying to the security in its original form.

Having made this adjustment, the company had every reason to press on towards the taking of the public subscription, since it was believed that on this widening of the membership an act of parliament could be obtained confirming the charters[4]. There appears reason to believe that just at this time differences of opinion arose within the company, which delayed and finally increased the difficulties in carrying out the proposal. Hitherto the management had been careful to keep out of home politics. But from the time that Child made the New Year's gift of 10,000 guineas to the King, if not earlier, he allied himself to the Court party. Such action was viewed with regret by many adventurers whose sympathies lay in the opposite direction[5].

[1] Add. MS. (Brit. Mus.) 22,185.
[2]
	Nett Assets	£1,672,871
	Capital	£739,782
	Surplus	£933,089

[3] *A Discourse concerning the East India Trade* [in answer to Sir Josia Child], Somers' *Tracts*, x. p. 645. In *A Brief Account of the Great Oppressions, ut supra,* it is stated that the balance-sheets of the company were not accurate.

[4] Child, *Treatise,* Somers' *Tracts,* viii. p. 459.

[5] Cf. Hunter, *Hist. of British India,* ii. pp. 284–8. Hunter lays too much weight on Papillon's support of a new subscription, since Child also admitted he was in favour of it. Nor can it be maintained that the former wished "to reconstitute the company on a broader basis" in the sense of making the monopoly less stringent, since he defended it in his *Treatise* (1677). It is true that from some of his notes on

Prominent amongst these was Thomas Papillon, who had been deputy-governor in 1681. At the next election of the company, in April 1682, the voting was influenced by political considerations, and Papillon failed to secure re-election as deputy-governor, though he was returned to serve as a " committee." His being involved in the disputed election for sheriffs of the City of London in the following June further weakened his position in the company, and eventually his supporters, finding themselves in a minority, sold out their stock and many of them became interlopers. In view of the future developments of the struggle between the company and its opponents it is important to notice that the dissentient stockholders were able to dispose of their holdings at the average price of about 300 for the original stock, which in some cases had been purchased as low as 80. The immediate effect of the purging of the company was to transfer a great accession of strength to its opponents; and further, owing to the delay through these dissensions, a favourable opportunity for the taking of the proposed public subscription in the summer of 1682 was missed. It may have been thought that little would be lost by delay; or again, it may have appeared that the company was now sufficiently secured by the favour of the Crown to be able to neglect the enlarging of its membership. Whatever were the grounds of this decision it was ill-advised, since much of the stock sold had been purchased by those who were already members, so that the proprietary instead of being increased in numbers, as proposed, was contracted. Moreover, there was the distinct danger that the company would be regarded as definitely committed to one of the political parties, and should the latter be defeated it might expect to suffer at the hands of the victors. This actually happened after the Revolution. The immediate consequence of the indefinite postponement of the projected new subscription was to leave the company short of free working capital. Thus when the crisis came towards the end of 1682 the finances were ill-prepared to meet it. The minority stockholders had now become "rich interlopers" who had already fitted, or were fitting out ships for India; this, together "with all the jealousies imaginable raised by them and their friends upon the company, made a great many of the fearful members eagerly sell their stock[1]." It was reported that the fall was as much as 200 per cent. by August 1682[2], but the apparent decline is to be attributed to the comparison of quotations

the petition of the company to the Crown (Nov. 11, 1681) asking for a proclamation against interlopers, he shows that he differed in some respects from the majority of the committees. *Memoirs of Thomas Papillon*, by A. F. W. Papillon, 1887, pp. 80-3.

[1] *Collection of Letters for the Improvement of Husbandry and Trade*, by John Houghton, London, 1681-3, I. pp. 148-9.

[2] *Domestic Intelligence*, No. 131.

DIV. I. § 5 B] *The Suspension of Payment* 1682–3   147

cum stock-bonus with those ex-bonus. Still by the end of the year the price was only 150 for the doubled stock, equal to 300 for the old, as contrasted with 460 for the latter earlier in the year. From January to February the fall reached the lowest point, the quotation being 245 in terms of the original stock or $122\frac{1}{2}$ for the new[1]. The depression of the stock market was far from being the most serious phase of the situation. When the company needed money to equip its out-going fleet, instead of finding lenders anxious to accommodate it, "its creditors ran earnestly on it" to obtain payment of the money due to them, which reduced the management to such straits that, though high rates were offered for loans, it eventually became necessary to suspend payment for three months[2].

The discredit of the company in the winter 1682–3 was doubtless claimed by the critics of its large borrowings as a verification of their prognostications in 1680 and 1681. The true cause of the difficulty is however to be found partly in the indefinite postponement of the new subscription, partly in the political split within the company. In view of the scarcity of working capital and of difficulties to be faced in India no dividends were paid in 1683 and 1684, and the profit made was used for developing the undertaking. According to a balance-sheet, dated September 30th, 1685, the gross assets were close on $3\frac{1}{4}$ millions, the debt was $\frac{3}{4}$ of a million (approximately equal to the nominal capital), leaving nett assets of nearly $2\frac{1}{2}$ millions, consisting roughly of $\frac{3}{4}$ of a million of "dead stock," and the remainder of quick stock[3]. It follows that the dead stock was equal in value to the nominal capital, and that of the liquid assets, amounting to nearly $2\frac{1}{2}$ millions, nearly one-third had been borrowed and the remainder had been provided from undivided profits. From the point of view of the stockholder the statement would have justified a price of $327\frac{1}{2}$ for the new stock, and during the year 1685 it realized from 360 to 500. At this quotation the yield, on a dividend of 25 per cent. (being the rate paid annually from 1685 to 1688), was very low, especially in view of the aggressive attacks made by those who had been formerly members and who had sold their stock after the split of

[1] Houghton, *Collection, ut supra*. He says, speaking of the years 1682 and 1683, the stock "fell from 365 to 245," which I take to mean that the second quotation is stated in terms of original, not new, stock; otherwise it would be inconsistent with other prices in this period.

[2] *Ibid.*, I. p. 149.

[3] Home Miscellaneous, IV., f. 45. Add. MS. (Brit. Mus.), 22,185:

Dead stock	...	...	...	£719,464 16 0
Quick „	...	...	...	£2,487,312 11 3
Gross assets	...	...	...	£3,206,777 7 3
Debt ...	...	...	...	£783,890 5 2
Nett assets	...	...	...	£2,422,887 2 1

1681–2. One of the first signs of the accession of strength to the opponents of the company was the attack on the validity of the charter when, in 1683, the company took proceedings against Thomas Sandys, claiming £1,000 damages from him for trading within its limits without a license. Many of the most eminent pleaders of the day were briefed on the side of the defendant and the company was represented by a strong bar. The case lasted until 1685, and before it had ended James, Duke of York, who had purchased £3,000 of stock in 1684[1], had come to the throne. Since the company based its claim on the privileges given it under the charters, it was inevitable that the nature of these grants should be discussed. This raised the question of the prerogative of the Crown in relation to foreign trade, which was supported or attacked by the citation of a vast array of precedents. There can be no doubt that the defence suffered from a radical inconsistency in the instructions given to its counsel. It was pleaded by them that "the sea shall be open to all manner of merchants to pass with their merchandize where it shall please them." This argument however necessarily would apply to the privileges of the Levant company, and some of its members were interested in the defence. Therefore the problem confronting the counsel for Sandys was to show how, in law, a merchant was entitled to trade in the Indian Ocean without paying for a license or undergoing any other restriction, while he might not enter the Mediterranean save by coming to terms with the Levant company. A solution was attempted by the making of a violent attack on the joint-stock principle and comparing it disadvantageously with the regulated type of organization. "The Turky company...consisted of improvers of trade....They ingross not, they admit every man that will to be free of the company... and none among them...makes unreasonable advantages." "But this invisible East India merchant, the body-politic, covers and countenances some few men among them to ingross, buy and sell at their own rates and that exclude all others for the great and excessive advantages of the few." It was stated too that trading on a joint-stock was an innovation and that "the companies of Turkey, Barbary, Russia, Muscovy and Hamburgh, nor any other, till of late years, did ever trade with a joint-stock[2]." The plaintiff undertaking was able to reply (as in the previous course of the controversy) by showing that the Levant company was only open to legitimate merchants, and it was added that these must be free-men of the City. Moreover, it was admitted that the charges

[1] *Journals of the House of Commons*, x. p. 154.

[2] As a matter of fact the only one of the companies named which had not at some time traded on a joint-stock was the Hamburg company. The Turkey or Levant company had promoted a joint-stock for the Morea trade which had been in existence twenty years before this date.

involved in the general management of the Turkey trade (such as those for ambassadors and presents) were raised by an imposition on the goods exported there. Whence it appeared not unreasonable, that in the case of India, where a much larger outlay was involved, payment for a license should be made by the man who wished to manage his own venture, or alternatively the capitalist pure and simple should purchase stock. This aspect of the case was summed up by Jeffries in the following terms: "It is very well known, that had it not been for a joint-stock the trade would never have been so beneficial as it is, and Mr Sandys would not have had such a desire to trade, for it would not have been so well settled and fixed...Mr Sandys and his partners are very zealous now to reap the fruits of the company's labours. But suppose this question should be asked—'Will you be contented to come in and pay your proportion of all the charge these people have been at, to put the trade into this capacity it is in?' But, is it fair, after they have reduced it into so good a condition, at a vast expense and trouble, for other particular persons to come and say, 'let us have the benefit of it that have had nothing of the burden and charge[1]?'" This contention had weight against many of the interlopers who were endeavouring to obtain the benefit of the reserved profits of the company in some form, as for instance by using facilities for trade it had secured at large outlay or by endeavouring to procure a new subscription for capital which would rank *pari passu* with the old. On the other hand, its force was weakened when applied to those who had been members of the company and who found themselves unable to agree with Child. Doubtless the best solution would have been to have kept the company out of politics altogether. Once however it was decided to take sides, it was likely, as actually happened, that the active support of the Crown would result in the privileges of the company being pressed to the fullest possible extent.

Probably at any period the restricted issue placed before the Court in this trial would have ensured a verdict for the East India company— just at this time one was certain. This was followed by a new charter dated April 12th, 1686[2], in spite of further petitions of the Levant company[3]. It is interesting to notice that in the following year James II. acquired £7,000 of East India stock[4].

[1] Cobbett, *Complete Collection of State Trials*, London, 1811, x. pp. 372–554.
[2] *Charters granted to the East India Company*, 1. pp. 125–40.
[3] State Papers, Domestic, James II., v. Answer of East India company to the Turkey company (May 5, 1685); Petition of Turkey company against East India company (March 16, 1686).
[4] *Journals of the House of Commons*, x. p. 154. The Exchequer accounts, Financial Statements P and Q, do not show that this acquisition was paid for by James II., but it is possible that the money required (supposing it were not a gift) would have

In 1688-9 the company experienced two disasters of the greatest magnitude. In India, friction with Aurangzeb resulted in its servants being driven out of Bengal, while at home the Revolution shattered the influence that Child had been building up during the previous seven or eight years. The position of the company had been made to depend upon the favour of a sovereign, now in exile, and all the deposed committee-men, like Papillon and Bernardison, and many of the interlopers were exceedingly powerful in the convention Parliament. As early as April 18th, 1689, petitions were presented from interlopers whose goods had been seized and who had failed (before or after the Sandys case) to obtain redress. The Skinner incident, which was upwards of thirty years old and which had already produced something of the nature of a constitutional crisis between the Lords and Commons, was revived. Charles Price and company complained of the seizure of the *Andalusia* in 1684 and 1686[1]. Samuel White declared he had lost £40,000[2], and Jeffrey stated he had suffered to the extent of £30,000[3]. Though the report of the committee, to whom it had been remitted to consider these petitions, was referred back to it "as being only a narrative of evidence without stating a case[4]," it was rumoured in the City as early as June 16th, 1689, that the company was likely to be dissolved[5]. Though nothing was effected in this session, the prospects of the opposition to the existing body were considered so hopeful that, by January 16th, 1690, £100,000 had been subscribed to be used as a campaign-fund[6], and soon afterwards £180,000 was raised[7]. Three courses were open to this syndicate. If it could secure the support of Parliament, it might force the company to take a new subscription; or failing this, in some respects the line of least resistance, it might obtain authorization for a new company which might either be constituted on the regulated or the joint-stock basis. A new subscription would fail to meet the views of the syndicate unless the company could be forced to accept a sliding scale of votes, under which it would be

been provided by an assignment on the customs or some other branch of the revenue.

[1] State Papers, Domestic, Will. and Mary, I. 56; *Journals of the House of Commons*, x. p. 92.

[2] State Papers, Domestic, James II., III. 140, IV. 60; *The Answer of the East India Company to S. White* [1689], Brit. Mus. $\frac{522.1.5}{5}$, *Reflections on...the Answer of the East India Company*, 8223.g.2.

[3] *Journals of the House of Commons*, x. p. 167.   [4] *Ibid.*

[5] *Diary of John Evelyn*, London (1859), II. p. 310.

[6] Luttrell, *Brief Relation, ut supra*, II. pp. 7, 8. Luttrell was a subscriber to the New East India company in 1698.

[7] Bruce, *Annals, ut supra*, III. p. 83.

possible to oust Child from his position of dominance. Though the claims of the regulated type of organization were still advanced, the only alternative seriously considered was a new monopolistic joint-stock company, which would have involved the dissolution of the Elizabethan foundation. On the whole the scheme for compelling the existing body to create fresh capital, with its constitution amended to suit its adversaries, was the policy which was accepted by the syndicate, but it was necessary to profess that the establishing of a new company was the object aimed at; since otherwise it would have appeared plainly that the money subscribed was intended to be used for the acquisition of votes in the Commons and of interest at Court. Thus elaborate pretensions were made with the object of showing that the financial position of the old company was thoroughly unsound. It was alleged early in 1690 that an account lately presented to Parliament was "a dark, general and unmercantile" one, intended not to reveal but to conceal the actual position. The assets, owing to losses in India and through the war, were now valued at only £700,000, but the goods in England were said to be worth about £400,000, not £635,155. 11s. 10d. as stated. It was alleged moreover that, when the dividend of 50 per cent. was declared and paid, there had not been sufficient money in hand to make the distribution and that funds were only provided by borrowing[1]. Everything that was possible was done to injure the credit of the company, and its misfortunes in India were alleged to be wholly due to its own mal-administration. Events too played into the hands of the syndicate, since owing to the depredations of French men-of-war and privateers, to its losses in India were now to be added those of ships on the high seas. In 1690 only two vessels reached home as against fourteen belonging to the Dutch company[2], and no dividend could be paid. When it was announced towards the end of the year that peace had been made with Aurangzeb, the syndicate was careful to point out that the summary published by the company had translated what was a somewhat ignominious defeat into a glowing victory. Further, the campaign against the company was carried from Parliament to the stock market. All unfavourable intelligence was magnified and a succession of raids was made upon the stock in order to depress the price. The losses were insisted on, and a great amount of ingenuity was expended in the effort to prove that there were not nett assets of a value equal to the nominal capital. This development of the contest forced the management to adopt the policy of supporting the market in

[1] *Reasons against Grafting or Splicing, and for dissolving this present East India Company or Joint-stock, and erecting and establishing a new Joint-stock Company*, Jan. 3, 16$\frac{89}{90}$, Bod. Lib., fol. θ, 658 (69).
[2] Luttrell, *Brief Relation*, II. p. 114.

the stock, and with this end in view a dividend of 50 per cent. was paid early in 1691. This policy was temporarily successful, and in September the price was over 200, having been as low as 158 early in the year. The object, in depressing the price, on behalf of the opposition was to show that a new subscription should be taken on the basis of valuing the existing stock at no more than par, but it was obvious that the company had a good answer to this demand as long as the price was twice the nominal amount and, so far, Child had been able to defeat this phase of the attack.

In October 1691 the syndicate again endeavoured to bring parliamentary pressure to bear on the company, and a petition to the House of Commons, presented in the name of the London merchants, on October 28th, stated that the trade to India had hitherto been managed for private gain, not for the public good, and that it was likely to be utterly lost "unless by some better regulation on a new joint-stock[1]." The company replied by pointing out that previous parliaments had on many occasions taken notice of their charters without any disallowance thereunto but "on the contrary rather implicitly approved thereof." Attention was drawn to the discouragement sustained by the attacks of interlopers and an act was asked which would ratify the charters. This request by the company constituted the opportunity of the opposition. It was proposed to submit to the committees a series of conditions, acceptance of which was to precede the introduction of the act that had been asked for. These included the writing down of the assets to £744,000 and taking a new subscription which would at least bring the capital up to a million and a half, and in certain circumstances to two millions. Steps moreover were taken, which it was hoped would enable the members of the syndicate to obtain complete control[2]. When details came to be discussed, the personal animosities, which had arisen out of the long and bitter struggle, prevented an agreement being reached, and the opposition seized what it believed to be its opportunity, and on February 6th, 1692, addressed the King praying him to dissolve the company and to incorporate a new one[3]. William III. replied that the matter was of great importance and that he would take time to consider it. The whole question was remitted to the Privy Council and the King used his influence towards the making of an accommodation between the company and some of the interlopers. About half the whole number came to terms with the company on

---

[1] *Journals of the House of Commons*, x. p. 451.

[2] *Abstract of Proceedings in the House of Commons in Relation to the East India Company and Trade*, 1691.

[3] *An Account of some Transactions in the Honourable House of Commons and before the...Privy Council, relating to the East India Company*, 1693, Somers' *Tracts*, x. p. 618.

DIV. I. § 5 B] *The Terms of the Syndicate 1692–3* 153

the basis of receiving a bonus of 25 per cent. on their respective expenditure and half the profits. One, named Godfrey, and some others stood out for 30 per cent. bonus and refused to take part in the accommodation[1]. The company paid some handsome commissions to persons who negotiated the agreement.

By this means a wedge had been driven into the ranks of the opposition, but, though half the members of it and perhaps half the capital had been brought to terms with the company, those that remained had very considerable influence in Parliament, and they had funds at their disposal which could be used in gaining votes. They were able too to impress their views on the Privy Council and, at the hearings of both sides in the spring of 1692, many of their conditions were accepted as those to be imposed on the company by the Crown[2]. First of all it was arranged that the capital should be in future not less than £1,500,000, nor more than £2,000,000. The present stock was to rank as a part of this sum up to its nominal amount of £744,000, subject to two conditions. On the one hand, security must be given that there were nett assets of that value; while on the other hand, if this sum were exceeded the surplus was divisible amongst the proprietors. A subscription was to be taken for the remainder of the capital authorized and allotments were to be made *pro rata*. But it was further provided that no member might own stock, whether under his name (not being in trust) or under the name of another, exceeding £10,000. The effect of this stipulation would have been that, while nominally the allotment of the new issue was to be made *pro rata*, none of the influential members of the committee could apply, and further they would be compelled to sell any stock owned in excess of £10,000, not at the market price (which was then about 150) but at par. Further, it was determined that while £500 stock commanded one vote, as before, it required £4,000 stock to secure two votes, and thereafter a further vote for each £2,000, nominally making a maximum of five votes. Therefore instead of Child having some sixty votes as was alleged, though this was probably a great exaggeration, he would be reduced to one-twelfth of that number[3]. In this way it was calculated that the syndicate and its supporters would obtain and keep control of the company as reorganized[4].

The regulations proposed were of a more drastic nature than Child and his friends had expected them to be. He saw clearly that the

---

[1] *A Collection of the Debates and Proceedings in Parliament in 1694 and 1695 upon the Inquiry into the Late Briberies*, London, 1695, p. 11.
[2] State Papers, Domestic, Will. and Mary, IV. 24; *Calendar*, 1691-2, p. 222.
[3] *A Regulated Company more National than a Joint-stock in the East India Trade*.
[4] Somers' *Tracts, ut supra*, x. pp. 619–20.

acceptance of them would prove his own downfall in the committee, and that he would be ousted from the management as Papillon and others had been ten years before. Therefore, the committees, at his instigation, took up the challenge of their opponents and returned a "humble answer" to the proposed regulations, which was in effect a defiance of the Privy Council. It is true that the company stopped short of a downright refusal to accept the modifications suggested, but it is plainly stated that these arose out of the self-seeking of a small group of individuals and that, where the regulations were not framed by malice, they were the fruit of ignorance. The whole agitation, it was contended, had been organized by "interlopers, their adherents and such as had sold their stock at high rates who cried down the company to fright the adventurers and come in again at low rates[1]." In so far as the syndicate had shown itself vengeful, the company was able to expose the indirect nature of some regulations. The committees, in a document evidently drawn up by Child, "recommending their righteous cause to God and his Majesty's known and famous justice in the whole course of his happy life—say, that the value of every thing is what it will sell for, and their stock, under all the calumnies and persecutions of their adversaries, now currently sells for 150 per hundred and they know and can prove it to be intrinsically more worth than the current price: but they know no law or reason why they should be dispossessed of their estates at any less value than they are really worth in ready money, by all the measures any thing is valued in any part of the world[2]." "Without any restraint, cramping, or taking care of rotations or changes in the East India company, the whole stock, without such forced political restrictment or limitation is in a kindly, natural and continual changing motion; in so much that the value of the stock, once in two years or thereabout, changes owners; and there is not now in the present committee three men that were of the committee above twenty years past...If it be thought by any that envy the company's good fortune, that some few of the company are too rich and powerful in the committee, the company answer that to cure that, if it be a fault, there needs be no new laws nor articles in any charter; for a very few years will cure that without such preternatural force; for that the sons of such men were never known to succeed their fathers in the painful fatigue of the company's affairs; but did always settle themselves upon an easier course of life by a revenue in land. If there be some of the present adventurers that had courage enough to keep their stock, and never sold any part thereof during all those violent and unreasonable attempts that have been made against the company, whether such

---

[1] Somers' *Tracts, ut supra*, x. p. 626.   [2] *Ibid.*, p. 621.

persons do not rather deserve the thanks which the Roman Senate gave Terentius Varro, *Quod non desperâsset de republica*, than any blame[1]." Against the limitations of holdings the protest is couched in equally vigorous terms. "Trade," it was said, "is a free agent and must not be limited or bounded—if it be so it will never prosper. It is against the laws and customs of England and all nations on the face of the earth that any man that buys a commodity and pays for it in ready money, should be compelled to swear it is his own money[2]." Similarly the sliding-scale for voting (which was at this stage the crux of the whole question) was characterized as "a hysteron proteron, never known before in any part of the world in merchants' affairs, wherein as far as the sun shines, all men vote according to their proper shares in shipping, or as they are interested, and not otherwise[3]." The opponents of the company had laid themselves open to adverse criticism by making it one of the regulations that, at the expiration of twenty-one years the present stock was to be wound up and a new subscription taken. "This," Child retorted, "is so strange that, if it should be admitted, would make the company ridiculous all the world over; and is as much as to say a man should be obliged to plant a great orchard and remove his trees, or depart from his possessions at the end of twenty-one years, or to build a famous mansion house, a town or a city, on such terms. The Dutch company have spent within thirty or forty years past above £700,000 upon Ceylon and have not yet seen their principal by about £400,000 to this day; this company have been building and fortifying at Bencolen about ten or eleven years and they must proceed in building and fortifying there for twenty or thirty years to come; and in that chargeable and dangerous work they have spent near £250,000 to £300,000 sterling...The company by the true rules of policy ought never to alter nor any man be forced to sell his stock, any more than he can be forced to buy a stock that has none; or any gentleman that has an over-grown estate in land in any country can be forced to sell part to make way for some purchasers that pretend they will buy land in that country[4]."

For the next year (May 1692 to May 1693) it appeared that everything favoured the opponents of the company. The criticism by the committees of the proposed regulations was construed as a deliberate flouting of the House of Commons from which they had emanated. When, on November 14th, William III. replied to the address of the previous February, which had asked for the dissolution of the company, that this could only be effected on giving three years' notice, which course would, he feared, be prejudicial to the trade, he added that, since

[1] Somers' *Tracts, ut supra*, x. pp. 626, 627. [2] *Ibid.*, p. 622.
[3] *Ibid.*, p. 623. [4] *Ibid.*, p. 625.

the company would not accept such modifications as were acceptable to the House, the best method on which to proceed was by the drafting of a bill which would settle the questions at issue. It was felt, no doubt, that the opposition to the company would only remain harmonious as long as its work was destructive not constructive, and therefore the Commons returned a further address praying that notice of a dissolution, on three years' warning, should be given to the company[1]. William III. hesitated to take this extreme course, since he may have heard, as was reported in the following year, that any action on his part against the existing undertaking would be construed as at the instigation of some persons in Holland who wished to possess the trade on the winding up of the English body[2].

Then in March 1693 came the dramatic incident when, under the Act 4 & 5 *Will. & Mary*, xv. § 10, the company failed to pay, by the last available date, the first quarter of the tax of 5 per cent. on the value of its stock, and, according to the letter of the law, its charters were subject to forfeiture. News of this misfortune affected the price of the stock, which had been over 140 before the mistake was made and was as low as 90 in July. Thus one object of the opposition, namely the depressing of the stock below par, had been achieved. Then after considerable negotiation[3] on October 7th, 1693, a charter was signed binding the company to accept all such alterations as should be imposed on it by the Crown, and on this condition all its former privileges were restored to it[4]. What may be termed the regulating charter was signed on November 11th of the same year, and it was popularly considered to embody all that had been contended for by the chief opponents of the company.

This was the external aspect of the situation, but the inner history of the fifteen months, May 1692 to November 1693, was such that the apparent victory of the adversaries of the company was valueless to them and became in reality a conditional triumph for Child. From November 1692 both sides had been bribing freely[5], but success lay with the agents of the established company. It was even hoped that sufficient support could be obtained in this way to obtain an act of

[1] Somers' *Tracts, ut supra*, x. pp. 627, 628.
[2] State Papers, Domestic, King William's Chest, xv. 55; *Calendar*, 1694–5, p. 273.
[3] Luttrell, *Brief Relation, ut supra*, III. pp. 190–5.
[4] *Charters granted to the East India Company*, I. pp. 141–51.
[5] It was shown, by the same evidence on which suspicion was directed to the Duke of Leeds, that the agent of the company, who offered £2,000 or £3,000, was informed that more had been promised "by the other side." The latter bribe was discovered to have been £5,000, whereupon the company promised 5,000 guineas. *Collection of Debates in* 1694 *and* 1695 *upon the Inquiry into the Late Briberies*, p. 41.

DIV. I. § 5 B] *The Voidance of the Charters* 1693 157

Parliament confirming all the privileges that were regarded as of chief importance, and large sums were promised towards the end of 1692 and payments made on account expressly towards this end[1]. At the same time the New Year's gift of 10,000 guineas that had been paid to Charles II. and James II. was begun again in favour of William III. Therefore, while at the beginning of 1693 it appeared that success was likely to crown the efforts of the opposition, the company was strengthening its position by every means in its power. Then at the end of March there came the apparent collapse of the defence of the company, since the failure on its part to pay the instalment then due on the 5 per cent. tax on joint-stocks meant that, if its privileges were renewed, it would be necessary to accept all the regulations that had been contemptuously refused a year before. There are two accounts of the reasons which led to the technical forfeiture of the charters—the one being carelessness on the part of the company and the other, that of the committees, which was to the effect that an official actually attended to make the necessary payment at the Exchequer, but found that the day was kept as a holiday[2]. When it is remembered that the long duel between the opposing interests in the East India trade was the most absorbing subject in the City, it is almost inconceivable that such an oversight could have been committed either through inadvertence or ignorance of government holidays. It would have been a desperate expedient for the company of its own accord to vacate its charters knowingly, but it is to be noted that this course had already been adopted at the Restoration. There can be little doubt that the status of the undertaking was endangered by its having no confirmation whatever of the pre-Revolution grants. It is just possible that owing to negotiations in the winter 1692-3, the inner circle of committees may have had reason to believe that, if the Crown were in such a position that either the company ceased to exist or else that a new charter must be granted, the latter course would be adopted and the instrument, so obtained, would be without the most obnoxious of the regulations which had been proposed in 1692. Moreover, the financial position of the company was such, that a new subscription had become desirable. In December 1692 it was alleged that no funds were available to equip twelve ships it was proposed to send to India in the following January. Indeed, it was stated that the debt at Surat was so great that the agents of the company there had been imprisoned[3]. About this time it was

[1] *Collection of Debates in* 1694 *and* 1695 *upon the Inquiry into the Late Briberies,* p. 22.
[2] *Journals of the House of Commons,* XIII. p. 132.
[3] *Reasons for the East India Company's sending out Twelve Ships to India about the 15th of January next,* Dec. 7, 1692. Bod. Lib. Pamphlets θ, 658 (37). The debt at Surat was £230,000 in 1695. Brit. Mus. Add. MS. 5540, f. 111.

proposed that the capital should be increased to a million and that the new stock should be offered for public subscription, the government receiving the par-value, while the company retained the premium[1]. In May 1693 the committees resolved to invite the adventurers to lend any sums, not exceeding 50 per cent. of their respective holdings, and in this way £325,565. 0s. 4d. was raised[2].

In any case, whether the charters were designedly forfeited or not, that obtained in November 1693 was most ingeniously drawn; so that, while apparently complying with the regulations of 1692, it in reality prevented the opposition from obtaining control of the company. Though this instrument seems to contain all that was asked by the House of Commons and did perhaps contain all that could be reasonably asked, a few of the clauses are so dexterously worded that there could be no certainty that the new subscribers would be able to secure any large representation on the committee, much less expel Child and his associates. It is true that a sliding-scale of votes was introduced on the basis of one vote for £1,000 up to £10,000. Thus the maximum was ten votes, not five as suggested in the previous year. The various stipulations as to a new subscription for £744,000, to be wound up in twenty-one years, for the export of a specified amount of cloth and the supply of powder to the State on certain conditions, were all incorporated, but the regulation that no one should *hold* more than £10,000 stock in his own right and must sell the overplus, was replaced by a clause that no one might *subscribe* more than that sum to the new issue of stock[3]. Thus it was unlikely that for some years to come the new members could obtain a majority of votes.

By these modifications in the original regulations, Child and his party had secured the continuance of the existing composition of the committee, but it remained to be seen whether it would be possible to procure the continuance of the company itself. The committees were sanguine—too sanguine as events proved—that partly by judicious expenditure in the House of Commons, partly too since the instructions given could be now said to have been accepted, an act ratifying this charter could be obtained and very large sums were promised to its supporters[4]. But, long before this stage was reached, it was necessary that the subscription for the new stock, which was to be

---

[1] *Proposals for the Sale of £260,000 of the East India Stock*, Bod. Lib. Pamphlets θ, 658 (25). The existing stock was taken at £740,000, to which £260,000 was to be added, making £1,000,000.

[2] *Journals of the House of Commons*, XII. p. 312.

[3] *Charters granted to the East India Company*, I. pp. 153–68.

[4] *Collection of Debates in 1694 and 1695 upon the Inquiry into the Late Briberies*, pp. 30, 31, 44.

DIV. I. § 5 B] *The New Subscription of Capital* 1693 159

opened before November 17th, should be a success[1], since it was recognized that had there been no considerable number of new adventurers, the next step would have been the constituting of a new company[2]. Under ordinary circumstances this issue would have presented no difficulties, but just at this time, under the continued attacks of the syndicate (which met daily to concert measures against the company) and the non-arrival of the ships from India, the stock already in existence was below par, being quoted from 94 (at the beginning of November) to 92 during the time the lists remained open. It was conceivable that those who were already adventurers might take up the new stock to protect their original investment, but it is clear that persons outside the company would have found it cheaper to have purchased the old stock in the market rather than to have taken up the new. For some time it appeared that the issue might be a failure, and it was decided that the company should embark on a species of underwriting by which favoured persons, who subscribed, were guaranteed against loss either on the whole or a part of the stock allotted them[3]. By this device there were total applications for £1,220,341. 13s. 5d., coming as to one-half from new adventurers and the remainder from those who were already members[4]. As the quantity of stock to be offered was £744,000 the applications were in excess of the amount to be issued and allotments were made *pro rata* according to the terms of the charter. The cost of underwriting this subscription fell very heavily on the company in 1694. The stock continued to fall and the committees under their contracts with some of the new adventurers were bound to purchase their holdings at 100, while only 75 was obtainable in the market.

Almost before this difficulty had been surmounted, a new misfortune, largely due to the mistake of the committees themselves, was experienced. On the signature of the charter, without waiting for the act which was hoped for later, the management took proceedings against certain merchants on the ground that they were interlopers, with the result that on December 7th, 1693, fresh petitions were presented against the company, which asked that an altogether new organization should be erected. Finally the House of Commons resolved that "all the subjects of England have equal right to trade to the East Indies, unless prohibited

[1] *At a General Court of the Adventurers for the general Joint-stock to the East Indies, holden...November* 11, 1693, Brit. Mus. $\frac{816.m.11}{80}$.

[2] State Papers, Domestic, King William's Chest, xiv. 42; *Calendar*, 1693, p. 323.

[3] *Collection of Debates in* 1694 *and* 1695 *upon the Inquiry into the Late Briberies*, pp. 35, 45, 70, 71, 78.

[4] *Journals of the House of Commons*, xii. p. 312. Pollexfen stated that only £372,000 of the whole amount was taken up. *Discourse on Trade*, 1696 (India Office Tracts, 53. A. 11), p. 49.

by act of Parliament[1]." The direct effect of this explicit denial of the privileges of the charter was to prevent seizures of interlopers' ships in England, but it produced no distinctive effects on the policy of the servants of the company in India. On the other hand, it became obvious that the legal position had become intolerable, inasmuch as powers confirmed by the Crown in November 1693 were denied by Parliament less than two months later. The effect of this continued tension, together with the losses sustained by the company during the war, is shown by the fall in the price of the stock, which had touched 94 when it was known that the subscription had been, as far as then appeared, a success, only to fall to 66 in May. From this low level there was a recovery, till 97 was recorded in November. After which there was a relapse, and the quotation at the end of the year was 88. According to a balance-sheet of this period, which is dated January 16th, 1695, there was a considerable depreciation in the nett assets, which were valued at a million and a quarter, against an issued capital of about a million and a half[2].

Meanwhile the syndicate, not content with the resolution of the House of Commons which implicitly denied the privileges of the charter, determined to initiate a campaign for the complete overthrow of the company. Having been outbid by the agents of Child, the members of the former were able to form a shrewd guess as to how much it had cost to obtain the charter and to fill the subscription list. Accordingly, on March 7th, 1695, a Committee of the House of Commons was appointed to inspect the books of the company, and suspicion was soon attracted to the disbursements of "secret service money," to certain sales of saltpetre, and to options on the stock. The total outlay was very large, perhaps upwards of £200,000, and sufficient evidence was obtained to imprison Cooke, who was now governor, and to impeach the Duke of Leeds[3]. Opinion in the City regarded this enquiry as no more damaging than the pamphlet attacks, which had now become too common to be taken seriously, and it is remarkable, that, despite the disclosures, the stock varied only from 80 to 88 and back again to 80 from February to May—this period covering the deliberations of the Committee as well

[1] Cobbett, *Parliamentary History of England*, v. p. 828.
[2]

Assets ...	...	...	...	£2,336,483. 10s. 1d.
Liabilities	...	...	...	£1,110,981. 9s. 0d.
Balance	...	...	...	£1,225,502. 1s. 1d.

Harl. MS. (Brit. Mus.) 7,310; *Journals of the House of Commons*, xi. p. 507. Or according to another account at £864,875, the liabilities being stated at £1,663,400, Add. MS. 5,540, f. 111.

[3] *The Examinations and Informations upon Oath of Sir Thomas Cooke*, India Office Tracts, vol. 268; *Collection of Debates* in 1694 and 1695 *upon the Inquiry into the Late Briberies*, pp. 24–61.

DIV. I. § 5 B] *Bribery.—The Darien Company* 1695   161

as the month before and that after. A much more serious blow came in October, when subscriptions were taken in London for the Darien company which was established by an act of the Scottish Parliament[1]. Under the original form of the scheme this enterprize was intended to foster trade between Scotland and Africa or India, and it was at once seen that interlopers could protect themselves by holding stock, and nominally sailing from a Scottish port, while in reality they found the chief market for the goods they brought back in England[2]. These apprehensions were sufficient to depress the stock of the English company from 80 to 50.

It will be shown elsewhere[3] that Parliament intervened to suppress the subscription of capital for the Scottish company. Such intervention however was not obtained without another great struggle with the representatives of the interlopers, the scene of which was the House of Lords. The East India company had contended that the action of the Scottish Parliament constituted a precedent in its favour, and renewed application was made for an act to confirm its privileges. Its opponents, though some of them had been censured for holding stock in the Scottish company, appeared in force and the arguments which had done duty for the past twenty years on both sides were repeated. On this occasion, however, each party was permitted to submit criticisms in writing on the contentions of its adversaries, and by this method a volume of valuable evidence was collected. The statement of the case for the woollen industry and against the importation of East Indian manufactures is chiefly memorable for the utterance of a maxim by Pollexfen, which has often been repeated since in various forms, namely " companies have bodies, but it is said they have no souls; if no souls, no consciences[4]." The claim that a regulated was more diffusive than a joint-stock company was again urged at considerable length, but without introducing much that was new beyond the argument, against the need of forts, that these were not required, "since the English nation has been treated by the Mogul very kindly[5]," or, alternatively, that if forts were necessary, those owned by the company were not efficient[6]. The disingenuousness of the continued laudation of the regulated type of organization is shown by the very curious relation of several of the petitioners (prominent amongst whom were Gilbert Heathcote and John Cary) to the Russia company at this time. An attempt had

[1] *Vide infra,* Div. I. § 5 E.
[2] *Some Considerations on the Late Act of the Parliament of Scotland for Constituting an India Company,* London, 1695 (Pamphlets, Advocates' Library).
[3] *Vide infra,* Div. I. § 5 E.
[4] *The Manuscripts of the House of Lords,* 1695–7, II. p. 11.
[5] *Ibid.,* p. 8. [6] *Ibid.,* pp. 32–8.

S. C. II.   11

been made to reduce the fine for admission in 1694 (which was then £60) and to obtain a relaxation of the test for membership of candidates being "mere merchants[1]." Though the bill did not pass, some time afterwards a joint-stock company was formed, consisting (in 1698) of seventy persons, who by lending £12,000 to the Czar had secured from him a monopoly of importing tobacco into Russia, and who described themselves as *the Contractors with the Czar of Muscovy for the importation of tobacco into his dominions*. A new phenomenon had now come into existence, namely the relation of such a body to the existing regulated company. "The Contractors" wished to pay a minimum fine, and the company offered to license their joint-stock trade in tobacco at £500 a year. "The Contractors" refused this offer and claimed the right to export from Russia any commodities they chose to purchase. When it is remembered that many of the members of this body, who were fighting a regulated company in 1698 were upholding this type as the ideal one in 1696, the hollowness of their arguments may be recognized[2]. It is still more remarkable that the expeditions of the interlopers were organized as joint-stock companies, the capital in which was provided by voluntary subscription, and a constitution was drawn up providing for voting rights and the election of managers. It is noted too that these bodies consisted of "all degrees of persons" of whom "not one-third were merchants[3]."

On January 28th, 1696, it was resolved by 46 votes to 24 that the trade to India should be carried on by a joint-stock. Subsequently it was decided that a public subscription was to be taken which was to be at least one million and might be three millions. The capital of the existing company was to be taken as a part of the proposed amount at a valuation acceptable to the Lords. Rules were to be embodied in the proposed bill of the nature of those framed by Nottingham in 1692[4].

While the position of the present stock to that to be formed was under discussion, the adversaries of the company used every argument in their power to depreciate the value of the former. It was said to be impaired by stock-jobbing[5], and when the committees produced a valua-

---

[1] *Journals of the House of Commons*, XI. p. 631.

[2] *The Manuscripts of the House of Lords*, 1697-9, III. pp. 219-21, 296, 297. Of sixteen persons who signed the petition of "the Contractors" more than half were subscribers of stock in the New East India company in 1698.

[3] *A Letter to A Friend concerning the East India Trade*, 1696 [India Office Tracts], p. 5.

[4] *The Manuscripts of the House of Lords*, 1695-7, II. pp. 8-10.

[5] *Ibid.*, p. 33; *The Naked Truth in an Essay upon Trade*, London, 1696 [Brit. Mus. $\frac{1102.\text{h}.1}{17}$], p. 5.

tion showing nett assets of a little over a million and a quarter[1], exception was taken to almost every item, until the total was reduced to only £217,721. 1s.[2] Some of these reductions were of an exceedingly drastic nature, as for instance in the case of the dead stock, valued by the company at £637,193, and which, though it included properties in India yielding a considerable rental, was rated in the reduced estimate at only £50,000[3]. Little progress had been made in the adjusting of the proportion to be allowed for the property of the company in the proposed subscription and Parliament adjourned before any decision had been reached.

By 1698 the burden of the war expenditure had become so great that it began to be thought the best method of dealing with the conflicting claims was to offer the monopoly of the East India trade, under Parliamentary sanction, to any body of capitalists that would contribute most towards relieving the necessities of the State. This phase of the situation constituted the opportunity of the company, had its finances been in a condition to meet the demand likely to be made upon them. By means of its corporate organization it should have been possible for the existing body to have raised a larger amount of capital than could be commanded by its adversaries. During the war, however, there had been great losses[4], and the nett assets were only valued at about half the amount of the nominal capital. No dividend had been paid since the 50 per cent. distributed in 1691, and in 1696 and 1697 the stock had not been quoted above 67 and had fallen as low as 37. During the same period the debt had varied between £746,808 (1696) and £595,896 (1697). It follows then that it was not possible for the company to borrow any large sums. There remained only one alternative, which was suggested by the example of the floatation of the Bank of England, namely to take a new subscription and to lend to the State the funds thus obtained. But it was clear that new subscribers would not come in to take up a stock at par which would rank equally with one which at this time (April—May 1689) realized only 55 to 57. Therefore, according to a proposal made by the governor and committees on May 4th, 1698, it was provided that the present capital of £1,574,608 should be

[1]
Assets ... ... £2,336,483. 10s. 1d.
Liabilities ... ... £1,110,981. 9s. 0d.
Surplus ... ... £1,225,502. 1s. 1d.

The Manuscripts of the House of Lords, II. pp. 56, 57; *vide supra*, p. 160.

[2] *Ibid.*, pp. 58, 59.

[3] According to another estimate the value of the dead stock was given as £417,000. *Ibid.*, pp. 60, 61.

[4] During the season 1695-6 the homeward-bound fleet of five ships was taken by the French. Bruce, *Annals, ut supra*, III. p. 179.

written down by 50 per cent. The original stock would then amount to £787,304. A new subscription would then be taken for £712,696, making the total stock £1,500,000, and out of the funds received the company undertook to lend the government £700,000 at 4 per cent.[1] The attraction of this offer consisted in the very low rate of interest, but its weakness lay in the comparatively small amount of the loan. The opponents of the company, under the pretence of obtaining evidence as to its financial stability, initiated another enquiry into the proceedings of the management, nominally in relation to the subscription taken in 1693–4. A case was laboured to show that those who had come in then were defrauded by the old proprietors, since the loan of May 1693, provided by the latter, was paid out of subscriptions of the former. Though a resolution was passed condemning this transaction, the enquiry had another object. The opposition were prepared to make a counter offer, and as the sum involved was very large, it was necessary to arrange as far as possible that public support would be forthcoming. Therefore, under the pretence of exposing the extravagant dividends paid by the company, these were disclosed in the report of the committee with all the art of the framer of the modern prospectus. Hence this document effected the double object of discrediting the present financial position of the company, while the citation of dividends of $840\frac{1}{2}$ per cent. from 1657 to 1691 on the original stock would make capitalists anxious to participate in such a lucrative venture once it was settled by act of Parliament[2].

The tender of the syndicate and its supporters was held in reserve till the last moment and was put in at a loan of two millions at 8 per cent. This offer provided nearly three times as much capital but the rate of interest was twice that which the company proposed to charge. The necessities of the government were so great that the large loan was more important, even if the terms on which it was obtained were high; and on May 26th a bill was brought into the House of Commons for Ways and Means which contained a series of clauses accepting the offer of the two million loan. On June 10th it passed a first reading by 135 votes to 99. On the 20th the company, after protesting in vain against the establishment of a rival undertaking, produced an amended offer proposing to lend two millions also and giving security for the whole amount, whereas its rivals only bound themselves to furnish one millon in the event of the public subscription being a failure[3]. The effect of

---

[1] *I.e.*, capital of £1,574,608 to be reduced by 50%=£787,304
New subscription £712,696
Total £1,500,000
Journals of the House of Commons, XII. p. 253.

[2] *Journals of the House of Commons*, XII. pp. 311–16.

[3] *Ibid.*, XII. pp. 321–2.

DIV. I. § 5 B] *A New Company established* 1698 165

the report of the Committee of Enquiry was now apparent, the proposal of the company was rejected and the bill passed the Commons on June 26th by 115 votes to 78. In the House of Lords some objection was raised to the settlement of the India trade being included in a money bill, and the second reading was only carried by 65 votes to 48, after a protest by the minority had been recorded[1]. During the course of the proceedings the existing company obtained some concessions, such as the recognition of the clause of its charters that it could only be dissolved on three years' notice and also that corporations might subscribe to the two million loan. Therefore, in any case, it could continue to exist for three years, and, after that date, it was possible that, if it took up two million loan stock in its corporate capacity, it would still persist in order to manage the investment.

The legislation of 1698, entitled an *Act for raising a Sum not exceeding two millions, upon a fund for payment of Annuities after the rate of Eight Pounds per cent. per annum, and for settling a trade to the East Indies*, was an avowed attempt at a compromise between the different ideas that had been debated during the last ten years for the management of this trade. It had been decided that a capital of from one and a half to two millions was required and therefore, by a slight confusion of ideas, the latter amount was fixed on as the sum to be lent to the State. All the subscribers were to be incorporated as the *General Society entitled to the advantages given by an Act of Parliament for advancing a sum not exceeding two millions for the service of the Crown of England*, each member of which was entitled to the same proportion of the trade to India as that which he held in the loan. But it was further provided that any of the members of this General Society, who desired to do so might join their respective rights under the act and unite to trade on a joint-stock, obtaining a charter of incorporation. Thus the scheme of the legislation of 1698 provided for a regulated company with provision for one or more joint-stock bodies connected with it.

Even before the act was passed would-be adventurers were prepared to subscribe; and, as early as May 7th, £700,000 had been offered, and on the 17th the applications had reached £1,200,000, and it is stated that the books were then closed temporarily "in order to make room for the old company to come in, if they please[2]." In view of the scheme of the committees to outbid the syndicate, which was laid before the House of Commons on June 20th, no notice was taken of this suggestion at the present stage. Meanwhile the success of the opposition caused the stock to fall. At the beginning of May the price was 57, but on the

[1] *The History and Proceedings of the House of Lords*, II. pp. 4, 5.
[2] Luttrell, *Brief Relation, ut supra*, IV. pp. 378, 381.

introduction of the bill it was only 43, and when the measure had passed it was further reduced to 33¼—the lowest point touched. This was prior to the opening of the subscription lists for the two million loan which were taken on July 14th, on which day the applications amounted to £500,000. By the 16th the whole sum had been subscribed[1], and when it was known that the company had come in and taken up £315,000 of the stock, the price of its securities advanced somewhat, remaining at 40 or over during the rest of the year.

On the successful floatation of the two million loan it at once became apparent that a vast amount of the capital subscribed was only forthcoming on the understanding that a charter of incorporation as a joint-stock company should be granted. Accordingly on September 5th, 1698, a corporation was established as the *English Company trading to the East Indies*, and from this date, until the amalgamation of the two bodies, it was customary to describe that originally incorporated by Elizabeth as the "Old Company" or "the London Company," while that founded in 1698 was characterized as the "New Company" or "the English Company." The proportion of the two million loan stock divided as between the two companies and such members of "the General Society" as did not join either is instructive as showing how little reliance is to be placed on the arguments for carrying on the trade by a regulated company, or else how much opinion on this question had changed since 1676 and 1685[2]. The following are the details:

Statement showing the different classes of holders of the two million loan stock.

Subscribers who traded on a joint-stock and were incorporated as the English company	£1,662,000
The Old or London Company	£315,000
Total amount employed in joint-stock companies	£1,977,000
Stock held by members of the General Society who did not join either joint-stock company	£23,000
Total	£2,000,000

Thus, though it had been so often contended that the regulated type had many advantages over the joint-stock body, when the experiment was made, only a trifle over 1 per cent. of the whole capital was retained under the General Society and outside the joint-stock organizations.

The success of the subscription of the loan and the incorporation of the New Company appeared to be the final blow to the rival insti-

---

[1] Luttrell, *Brief Relation, ut supra*, IV. pp. 402, 403.

[2] In 1694 the House of Commons condemned the following resolution of the Levant company: "That none ought to be looked upon or esteemed mere merchants but such only as have been so educated from the very beginning, or who have been of another trade and have foreborne the same and followed the trade only of a merchant for seven years." *Journals*, XI. p. 185.

tution which had suffered so many reverses. Indeed on the day the subscription lists were opened William III. gave notice to the Old Company that its privileges would expire on three years' notice, that is on September 29th, 1701[1]. This view, however, only represents a superficial interpretation of the situation, and the close of the year 1698 represents the turning-point in the fortunes of the company. The long Parliamentary war was over and any further legislative action was more likely to strengthen than to weaken its position. The return of peace with France meant the cessation of losses of ships, with a consequent improvement in its finances. It is true that, while hitherto it possessed a monopoly of the trade, it had now to face competition, but the incorporation of the New Company had the effect of concentrating such competition. Thus the committees had to deal with commercial, not political attacks; and, having all the organization and equipment of an established undertaking at their command, the issue of the coming struggle was likely to be in their favour.

No illusions were entertained on either side as to the ultimate outcome of the contest. It was clearly seen that an amalgamation was inevitable. The Old Company had written to its representatives abroad in this strain, even before the subscription had been taken[2], while on November 8th—that is only two months after the charter of the New Company had been signed—Papillon on its behalf proposed "an accomodation" with its rival[3]. The Old Company, finding that delay was wholly in its favour, was sufficiently adroit to seize on the one remaining weak point in its legal position and to use it to obtain an important concession it required. Up to Sept. 29th, 1701, it could trade to any extent it pleased, after that date there was some uncertainty in one respect. The two million loan stock it had subscribed was in the name of its secretary and it was not known whether the company as a corporation could exercise the rights this stock conferred or whether it would be necessary after 1701 to divide it amongst the individual stockholders. Therefore the committees urged with considerable force that they could not consider a union until the company had been continued as a corporation to manage the trade which was reserved to the ownership of £315,000 of the two million loan stock. Application was made to Parliament in 1699, but, though the House appears to have been sympathetic[4], the act did not pass.

[1] Hunter, *History of British India, ut supra*, II. pp. 318, 324.
[2] Letters to Council at Bombay, July 8, to Council in Bengal, Aug. 26. Bruce, *Annals*, III. pp. 256, 257.
[3] *A True Relation of what passed between the English Company trading to the East Indies and the Governor and Company of Merchants of London trading to the East Indies touching an agreement between both companies.*
[4] Luttrell, *Brief Relation, ut supra*, IV. p. 487. On the motion to bring in a bill on Feb. 27, 1699, the voting was 175 in favour and 148 against, and the stock of the New Company fell 2 per cent. next day.

During this year there were several indecisive interchanges of opinion between the rival companies, but the Old Company saw clearly that time was on its side and excuses were made to break off negotiations. In February 1700 an act of Parliament was passed which continued the company as a corporation after 1701 and, in giving the Royal Assent to the bill, William III. urged the company to be ready to enter on an amalgamation. Everything that the skill and knowledge of the committees could suggest was tried to weaken the position of the New Company. Its credit was attacked on the Exchange and its directors found it difficult to obtain funds for prosecuting the trade. Since its establishment, the exports of the Old Company had been very greatly in excess of those of the body lately established, and it began to be seen that though Parliament could confer the right to a certain proportion of the trade, only knowledge could make this profitable. By the end of April 1700 the rise in the stock of the Old Company had been remarkable. From the lowest point of $33\frac{1}{4}$, touched in 1698 when the two million loan act had been passed, it had advanced to upwards of 60 at the end of 1699, and by April 24th, 1700, it had risen to 142—that is the quotation had been more than quadrupled in less than two years[1]. The financial position having been so much strengthened, the company, in May 1701, offered to pay off the whole two million loan and to re-lend the sum to the State at 5 per cent. instead of 8 per cent. as reserved by the act of 1698, provided that the proposed new loan should have similar rights in relation to the India trade[2]. At this time the New Company proposed that their members should sell to the Old Company so much of the two million loan stock as would bring the holding of the latter up to one-third of the whole sum owned by the two companies[3]. This proposal reopened all the points of difficulty in regard to the control of the trade which had occasioned so much dispute in 1692 and, now that the Old Company had made so much progress in re-establishing itself, they could not be entertained. It became clear too that negotiations were not likely to be satisfactory as long as they were conducted between the two courts of the companies. Sir Basil Firebrace, on the promise of a substantial reward, should his efforts result in an amalgamation, became

---

[1] In *England's Almanack, showing how the East India Trade is Prejudiciall to this Kingdom*, 1700, it is stated that in the year 1699 (*i.e.* to March $\frac{1699}{1700}$) the stock of the Old Company increased from 58 to 138.

[2] *A Dialogue between two members of the New and the Old East India Companies*, Bod. Lib. Pamphlets *θ*, 658 (64), *Sam against Shepherd*, *θ*, 658 (62); *A Letter to a Member of Parliament showing the Injustice of the proposal made by the Old East India Company*, 1701. Godw. Pamph. 2086 (5).

[3] *I.e.*, the existing holdings were: Old Company £315,000, New Company £1,662,000. It was now proposed that the proportions should be readjusted as ollows: Old Company £659,000, New Company £1,318,000.

DIV. I. § 5 B] *Working Agreement of the Companies* 1702

the intermediary of committees representing both companies[1]. During the remainder of the year (1701) terms were discussed, and by January 1702 a preliminary agreement was reached and embodied in an Indenture Tripartite, which was executed on July 22nd, 1702[2]. The basis of the settlement now proposed was that the shares of each company in the two million loan stock should be equalised and that neither should trade on its own account for the ensuing seven years. During that period the trade was to be controlled by a committee of management, consisting of an equal number of representatives from each company. At the end of this period the final union was to be effected by the dissolution of the committee of management and the transfer of one-half of the two million loan stock (which was to be held by the Old Company in its corporate capacity in the interval) to the individual members, when, on the dissolution of that company, this stock would rank with, and be in all respects similar to, that owned by the members of the New Company. At this stage there would no longer be any distinction between the members, and it was provided that the English company should become the United company.

The exact division of the two million loan stock between the two companies in 1702 involved some complicated financial adjustments. This arrangement did not affect those subscribers to that loan who were members of the General Society but not of either company. There was thus £1,977,000 loan stock[3] to be equally divided and the transfer was carried out by each member of the New Company selling 40 per cent. of his holding at par, for which he received bonds pending payment by the Old Company[4]. The following statement will show the nature of this operation:

Effect of the Indenture Tripartite on holdings of the two million loan stock.

The stock to be allocated was £1,977,000.

	Old Company £	New Company £
Stock to be held	988,500	988,500
„ already held	315,000	1,662,000
„ to be transferred	+673,500	−673,500[5]

[1] Bruce, *Annals, ut supra*, III. pp. 425, 426.
[2] *Charters granted to the East India Company*, I. pp. 243–344.
[3] *I.e.* Loan stock £2,000,000
             Separate Traders £23,000
             Balance £1,977,000
[4] India Office MSS., General Court Minutes, April 15, 1702—June 21, 1734, f. 3.
[5] It follows that 40 per cent. of £1,662,000 (=£664,800) is less than the £673,500 to be transferred by £8,700.

So far the competing interests were partially equalized but they were not harmonized. It was therefore further provided that the governor and committees should hold the proportion of the two million loan stock, now assigned to it, in trust for the company without transferring any part of it for the space of seven years[1]. During this period the court of each company was to choose twelve persons to represent it on the committee of management of the united trade[2] and neither company was to trade or transact business beyond bringing home its separate estate from India. In this way what might be called the "East India Trading Trust" was established, the court of joint-management regulating the trade and taking all steps for carrying it on. At the expiration of the specified seven years it was expected and intended that both companies should have wound up their separate affairs and have forgotten their previous animosities. As each was on an exact footing of equality there would be no object in continuing the trust and the union would be consummated by the exchange of the two million loan stock for that of the Old Company.

To carry out this scheme of absolute equality some minor provisos were necessary. So far nothing has been said as to the dead stock of the two companies. This had been valued and the amount was accepted by both companies. The valuation of the Old Company's dead stock was £330,000
The New Company's dead stock was 70,000
£400,000[3]

The same method was adopted here as in the case of the loan stock, the dead stock being divided equally between the two companies and the difference paid in cash.

State of account (Dead Stock).

Total dead stock valued at	£400,000	
Half of which is	£200,000	
	Old Company £	New Company £
One-half of dead stock	200,000	200,000
Company's dead stock valued at ...	330,000	70,000
Amount payable	+130,000	−130,000

Therefore the final state of the account under the Indenture Tripartite stood as follows:

	Old Company £	New Company £
Balance £2,000,000 loan	−673,500	+673,500
,, Dead stock	+130,000	−130,000
Balance payable by Old Company ...	−543,500	+543,500

[1] *Charters granted to the East India Company*, I. p. 231.
[2] *Ibid.*, p. 278. [3] *Ibid.*, p. 252.

DIV. I. § 5 B] *The Finance of the Agreement* 171

From the point of view of the capital account this transaction regarding the dead stock received a different treatment from that equalizing the two million loan stock. The latter, as already shown, was treated as original capital, whereas the dead stock, being new capital (from the point of view of the accounts), was dealt with as the nucleus of the additional capital and was vested in the joint management committee, to be held in trust, in equal shares for the two companies, and transferable to each on the termination of the trust.

There is one further complication to be unravelled. The New Company already had an additional stock in existence, known as "the Shares," issued to provide working capital. This, by a special clause in the Indenture, was to be determined as soon as possible, and the surplus, if any, of the company's separate estate, distributed amongst the proprietors of "the Shares[1]."

Capital of the Old and New East India Companies before and after the Indenture Tripartite of 1702.

A. *Before* 1702.

Old Company	New Company
£1,574,608, stock of the proprietors	£1,662,000, loan stock
	£531,700, additional stock

B. *After the Indenture Tripartite.*

Old Company	Court of management Additional stock	New Company
£1,574,608		
£998,500	£400,000	£998,500

on a/c of Old Company £200,000 — on a/c of New Company £200,000

[Under powers to create further additional stock, there was issued *in all* £1,383,900

on a/c of Old Company £691,950 — on a/c of New Company £691,950]

The arrangement for eventual amalgamation gives no information as to how the scheme affected the finances of the Old Company. To acquire the amount, needed to make one-half of the specified stock of the two million loan, required that the Old Company should find £543,500, after allowing for the amount receivable from the New Company on account of the equalization of dead stock.

To find how the capital was raised and the effect of the obtaining of it on the company's finances makes it necessary to glance back at the state of the debt, due on bond. As already mentioned, towards the end

---

[1] *A Collection of Charters, ut supra*, 1. 268.

of 1693 large repayments of bonds were made[1], and on November 18th the debt stood at £256,359. 6s. 11d.[2] Soon after the indebtedness began to increase again, as will be seen by the following figures:

Amount due on Bond.

	£	s.	d.
1693, Ap. 29	451,507	16	10
,, Nov. 18	256,359	6	11
1694, Nov. 30	401,813	8	5
1695 ,, ...	637,296	12	0
1696 ,, ...	746,808	19	6
1697 ,, ...	595,896	19	9
1698, March 31	631,554	19	10

This debt was divided into two classes, first the bonds proper of the company issued to investors at a fixed rate of interest, and secondly, what were known as bottomry bonds. The latter constituted the insurance fund of the company against loss of ships. Bottomry bonds were issued to the stockholders who cared to subscribe, often at a discount, and were repayable only on condition that one or more of certain ships returned within a specified time. Thus the company was provided with cash when its capital was locked up in trade abroad, while, in the event of a disaster to the fleet, part at least of the value of the cargoes was secure and the principal was easily found after the goods had been sold, supposing the ships returned safely. On the other side, the stockholders received interest and the issue of the bonds at a discount offered attractions to those who were speculatively inclined. Thus in 1697 bonds were issued for £294,493. 8s. at 80, bearing interest at 6 per cent. When the company no longer traded on its own account there was no need to issue bottomry bonds, and thus in time a considerable part of the debt was extinguished. Besides the Indenture Tripartite authorized the committees to collect and realize the separate estate of the company, and such assets were available for the further reduction of the debt.

On the other side the amalgamation involved very large liabilities. First there was the cash payment of £543,500 to the New Company to be made. In the second place, as the Indenture Tripartite had enforced the withdrawal of the working capital of both companies from the trade, it rendered each liable for one-half of the capital needed to work the trust. In 1708, this additional capital amounted to 70 per cent. of the £1,977,000 two million loan stock, and therefore each company was under obligation to provide £691,950 or 70 per cent. on £988,500— their respective halves of the two million loan stock. It will be remembered, however, that of the additional capital £200,000 was credited

---

[1] *Vide supra*, p. 164.   [2] *Journals of the House of Commons*, XII. p. 312.

to each company on account of its dead stock, and therefore the amount raised in cash by each company was £491,950. Therefore the total to be raised by the Old Company was as follows:

Difference payable under Indenture Tripartite		£543,500
To be raised for additional stock:		
Additional stock a/c Old Company	£691,950	
Less valuation dead stock	£200,000	
Balance payable in cash	£491,950	£491,950
Total to be raised		£1,035,450

The method of raising this sum was to first pay off the existing debt as the separate estate became available and then borrow on bond upon the security of the additional stock, backed by the company's proportion of the two million loan stock; the two together amounting to £1,680,450. This account of the company's financial methods is confirmed by the fact that on September 29th, 1708, the amount due on bond was as nearly as possible that set out above, namely £1,035,448. 9s. 3d.[1]

On these figures it is obvious that the £1,574,608 stock of the company should not have been quoted above par. Taking the government and additional stocks at par, the £645,002 remaining after discharge of the debt would have justified a price of about 35 for £100 of the company's stock and any higher price depended on the valuation made of the worth of the half-share in the monopoly of the trade. As the stock touched 120¼ in 1702, 134 in 1703, 139½ in 1704, 128½ in 1705, and 123¾ in 1706, either the trading rights were greatly overvalued, or, as is more probable, the extent of the debt of the company was not known.

The state of indebtedness of the Old Company proved an obstacle to the final union of the two undertakings. When the matter was brought forward towards the end of 1706, the Old Company asked that, prior to any union, it should receive bonds for as much of the additional stock as possible to pay its debts, in other words it proposed to exchange bonds of the trust for its own[2]. This proposal was not acceptable to the committee of management, who held that besides the dead stock there should be a considerable amount of quick stock "to be a fund of credit for borrowing on their common seal for carrying on the united trade[3]." A proposal was made to meet the Old Company by dividing

[1] Court Book, XL., f. 209, printed in Bruce's *Annals of East India Company*, III. p. 672; cf. *infra*, p. 175.

[2] Home Miscellaneous at India Office, "Papers Relating to the Union of the Companies," 43 A, ff. 1, 2.

[3] Home Miscellaneous, 43 A, f. 2.

a part of the additional stock to each, but there were many other difficulties. For instance, supposing the additional stock in possession of the Old Company, it might have been divided amongst the members, and, when the stock of the company was merged in that of the proposed United Company, the latter would become liable for the undischarged debts of the Old Company.

For such and other reasons it became necessary that a higher and independent authority, outside the companies, should intervene to adjust such differences. Therefore by an Act of 6 Anne *for assuring to the English Co....on account of the United Stock, a longer time,* &c. all outstanding points in dispute were referred to the arbitration of Lord Godolphin, who, having heard the witnesses and counsel of both parties, delivered his award on September 29th, 1708. He decided that the debts of both companies should be liquidated, so that the United Company should be free from all liabilities incurred by its predecessors[1]. The debts of the London Company abroad were found to exceed its separate estate abroad by £96,615. 4s. 9d., and this sum was to be paid by the Old Company to the New, in trust for the amalgamated or United Company, payable as to one-third on or before October 31st, 1708, one-third by December 31st, and the remaining third on or before February 28th, 1709[2]. He further awards that, inasmuch as the company "is indebted for a considerable sum in England," the committees shall make a call to realize a sufficient sum to discharge all the home debts[3]. To enable them to make the necessary payments, as soon as the company had raised £100,000 by the call, the managers of the joint-committee were authorized to hand over one-third of the additional stock, and upon a second £100,000 being raised, to transfer the second third of the additional stock. When enough had been obtained, together with the remaining third of the additional stock to discharge all the company's liabilities, this final third of the additional stock was to be transferred to the company with the exception of a sum of £70,000, held as a pledge for the carrying out of the legal requirements of the award, such as the surrender of the charters and the assignment of all moneys owing to the company on account of its separate estate and which were not yet collected, to the United Company.

The following is the balance-sheet of the company upon which the foregoing award is based, and dated the same day as the award, September 29th, 1708:

---

[1] "The Earl of Godolphin's Award," in *Charters granted to the East India Company,* I. p. 347.

[2] *Ibid.,* p. 350.

[3] *Ibid.,* pp. 352–3.

The Governor and Company of Merchants of London trading to the East Indies their account current[1].

Dr.		£	s.	d.	Cr.		£	s.	d.
1708. Sept. 29.	To money at interest owing to sundry on the company's seal ...	1,065,448	9	3	By 70% on £988,500 due by United Company	...	691,950	0	0
	To 6 months' interest thereon due to date ...	31,063	9	1	By interest to date ...	...	20,768	10	0
	To "Interest for several bonds that may have been 12 or 18 months due" ...	3,000	0	0	By six months' interest on £988,500 due at Christmas	...	39,540	0	0
	To Almshouse at Poplar, "owing to them" ...	2,700	0	0	By the eighth and twelfth quarter's dividend on same in arrear ...	...	22,364	19	8
	To Customs and to Freight and to several persons for goods sold in private trade ...	9,728	10	9	By money advanced on stock and disbursements for the united trade ...	...	56,329	13	5
	To Customs and to Freight due to United Company	16,312	5	3	By goods remaining in the warehouses ...	...	1,000	0	0
	To dividends on stock (unclaimed) ...	6,918	18	5	By good debts in England ...	...	5,000	0	0
	To Factors' salaries payable in England and cash paid by Factors in India for remittance home (estimated) ...	20,000	0	0	By cash in hand ...	...	24,504	19	4
					By balance ...	...	372,514	11	8
	To interest on bonds due by company more than the interest receivable by company on the 70% Additional Stock will pay to March 1, 1709 ...	5,175	16	7					
	To charges from date to March 1, 1709 ...	7,000	0	0					
	To balance Indian accounts per award ...	96,615	4	9					
		£1,233,962	14	1			£1,233,962	14	1

Second (and revised) account current of same date (condensed)[2].

		£	s.	d.			£	s.	d.
1708. Sept. 29.	To total liabilities	£1,249,807	7	6	By total assets	...	850,011	18	5
					By balance	...	399,795	9	1
							£1,249,807	7	6

[1] Court Book, XL, f. 209.

[2] Ibid., printed in Bruce's *Annals of the East India Company*, III. p. 673. The difference in the totals and balance is accounted for by the fact that in the second account allowance is made for depreciation in market value of £29,100. 10s. stock of the company purchased at a higher price than that quoted at date, the difference amounting to £6,694. 13s. 5d. The revised balance-sheet takes account of the fact that the company paid £6,425. 16s. 7d. more in interest on its bonds than it received on the government and additional stocks. The small amount necessary to reconcile the two balances due is accounted for by a more exact valuation of certain items.

It will be seen that this leaves a balance of £399,795. 9s. 1d. against the company. The call required to raise this amount was 25½ per cent. (which would realize £401,525. 3s. 5d.), and this was duly made, whereupon the additional stock, with the exception of the specified £70,000, was transferred in three parts as specified by the award. The latter sum was also transferred upon the surrender of the charters.

The last stage of these complicated financial transactions was the exchange of the Old Company's stock as against that of the United Company, and this is perhaps the most interesting episode of the whole series, since the exact proportion received per cent. is essential to the forming of a judgment as to how the individual stockholders fared in the amalgamation. Before making the final transfer, the joint-committee of the trust decided on January 5th, 1709, that the sum of £1,200,000 recently lent to the State should be added to the capital divisible amongst the proprietors of the two companies. Thus £600,000 stock approximately was added to the share of the Old Company and the same amount to that of the New Company. There appears to have been a deficiency in the subscription of the £1,200,000 of some £14,000, so that the amount divisible was proportionately reduced. Therefore the amount of capital of the United Company divisible amongst the stockholders of the Old Company was about £1,581,600[1]. Now the capital of the company was slightly less than this amount, being £1,574,608. 10s. 7d., so that the proprietors received very nearly £100·444 stock in the New United Company in exchange for £100 stock in the Old. In other words, £100 old stock exchanged for between £100. 8s. 10½d. and £100. 8s. 10⅔d. united stock. The total amount received by all the old stockholders was £1,581,599. 15s. 7d. stock in the United Company as against their £1,574,608. 10s. 7d. stock in the London Company. Thus the passion for an equal division which dominated the whole procedure led finally to a remarkably toilsome book-keeping adjustment, as well as incidentally to the impossibility of getting a perfectly accurate formula for the transfer. For instance the following were some of the amounts of new stock given for the specified quantities of old:

Old stock £	exchanged for	United stock £	s.	d.
100	,,	100	8	10
100	,,	100	8	10⅔
500	,,	502	4	5
500	,,	502	4	10
1,000	,,	1,004	8	10
7,000	,,	7,031	1	7
12,000	,,	12,053	5	8[2]

[1] Home Miscellaneous, 43 A, f. 79.   [2] *Ibid.*

DIV. I. § 5 B] *Capital* 1657–98, *Dividends* 1658–63

When the distribution of the stock had been accomplished nothing remained but to wind up the company, and the closing scene was not without a certain simple dignity as it is recorded in the last page of the Old Company's Court Book. "The common seal of the company was defaced immediately after the deed of surrender of the company's charters was sealed therewith, as was also the company's larger seal, and both of them brought down to the adventurers, who no longer continued as a general court of the said company[1]."

Capital.

		£	s.	d.
1657.	Stock subscribed £739,782. 10s., 50% called up	369,891	5	0
1682.	Bonus of 100% on paid up capital making stock 100% paid up[2]	369,891	5	0
	Total 1682	739,782	10	0
1682–92.	Stock issued	4,217	10	0
	Total 1692[3]	744,000	0	0
1692.	Stock issued[4]	744,000	0	0
	Total 1693	1,488,000	0	0
1694–8.	Stock issued	86,608	10	7
	Total 1698–1708[5]	1,574,608	10	7

Prices of Stock and the Dividends.

Year	Prices of stock	Dividends		
		Rate %	When declared	When paid
1658				
1659				
1660				
1661	90—94[6]			
1662		20[7]	Sept. 2, 1661	June 8, 1662
1663		10	June 23, 1663	"forthwith"
		10	Sept. 11, 1663	Sept. 25, 1663

[1] Court Book, XL., f. 224 (Tuesday, March 22, 1709).
[2] *Journals of the House of Commons*, XII. p. 311.   [3] *Ibid.*, pp. 312, 313.
[4] *Charters granted to the East India Company*, I. p. 157.
[5] India Office MSS., Home Series, Miscellaneous, III., Alphabet Books 71 [c], 72 [c], 74 [c], 78 [c].
[6] State Papers, Domestic, Charles II., XXXII. 98; Hunter, *History of British India*, II. p. 276.
[7] This and the subsequent dividends are from the Court Books. Those from 1682 onwards till the dissolution of the company are printed in the Report of the Committee of the House of Commons, 1698, *Journals of the House of Commons*, XII. pp. 311–16.

S. C. II.

Year	Prices of stock	Dividends		
		Rate %	When declared	When paid
1664	60—70[1]	20	Aug. 12, 1663	July 25, 1664
1665		40	Aug. 3, 1664	July 3, 1665
1666		40	Feb. 2, 1666	Feb. 20, 1667
1667		10	March 27, 1666	
1668	130[2]			
1669	108—130[3]			
1670	111[4]			
1671		10	May 5, 1671	May 18, 1671
1672	80[5]	20	Apr. 15, 1672	April, 1672
		20	Sept. 11, 1672	Oct. 8, 1672
1673		20	Nov. 24, 1673	forthwith
1674		20	Apr. 6, 1674	Apr. 13, 1674
1675				
1676				
1677	245[6]	20	Mar. 19, 1677	Mar. 19, 1677
		20	Oct. 3, 1677	Oct. 10, 1677
1678		$\frac{1}{2}$[7]	Jan. 25, 1678	
		20	Aug. 20, 1679	
1679		20	Sept. 26, 1679	10% Oct. 1679 / 10% Mar. 1680
1680	300—245[8]	50	Sept. 8, 1680	
1681	365[9]	20	Feb. 14, 1681	
	460[10]	50	Jan. 14, 1682	
1682	Price of the doubled stock 150—260[11]	100	,,	in stock
1683	170—122½[12]			
1684	210[13]			
1685	500—360[14]	25		Oct. 21, 1685
1686		25		Apr. 14, 1686
1687		25		Oct. 12, 1687
1688		25	Apr. 20, 1688	

[1] Add. MS. (Brit. Mus.), 17,476, f. 194; *The East India Trade a Most Profitable Trade*, 1677, p. 17; Anderson, *Annals of Commerce* (1790), II. p. 638, III. pp. 65, 82.

[2] State Papers, Domestic, Entry Book, XXVI., f. 91.

[3] Court Book, XXVI. (Feb. 15, 1669). [4] *Ibid.* (March 30, 1670).

[5] *The Merchant's Dayly Companion*, London, 1684, p. 349.

[6] *The East India Trade a Most Profitable Trade*, 1677, p. 17.

[7] In damaged calico.

[8] Add. MS. 17,476, f. 193. *Hist. and Proceedings of House of Commons*, I. p. 411. Child, *Treatise, ut supra*, VIII. p. 459.

[9] *A Collection for the Improvement of Husbandry and Trade*, by John Houghton, London, 1681-3, I. p. 150.

[10] *Domestic Intelligence*, No. 107.

[11] *Ibid.*, No. 131; Houghton, *Collection, ut supra*, I. pp. 149, 150; *Evelyn's Diary* (Dec. 18, 1682).

[12] Houghton, *ut supra*; *Merchant's Dayly Companion*, p. 349.

[13] Anderson, *Annals*, III. p. 94. [14] *Ibid.*, III. p. 91.

DIV. I. § 5 B] *Dividends, Prices of Stock 1664–1709*

Year	Prices of stock			Dividends		
				Rate %	When declared	When paid
1689				50	Oct. 2, 1689	
1690		300[1]				
1691		200—158[2]		50	Apr. 8, 1691	
1692	Mar. 30	158—131	May 5			
1693	Feb. 8—15	146—90	July 26, Aug. 2, Aug. 24, Sept. 20			
1694	Nov. 14	97—66	May 23			
1695	Sept. 4	93—50	Oct. 23			
1696	May 20	67—38	Nov. 22			
1697	Sept. 29	65—47[3]	Apr. 28—Aug. 25			
1698	July 15	75—33¼	July 6			
1699	Nov. 8—22	59—41	June 28—July 4			
1700	April 24	142—58½	Jan. 3—10	10		
1701	Jan. 1 to Feb. 12	119—75½	Apr. 9	8		
1702	Oct. 21	120¼—77¾	May 6	8		
1703	Sept. 1—15	134—106¾	Apr. 7—14	8		
1704	April 10	139½—117¼	Oct. 30	8		
1705	Jan. 17	128¼—93½	Aug. 1	8		
1706	June 3	123¾—87½	Feb. 8	8		
1707	April 11	115¾—103¾	Nov. 19	8		
1708[4]	March 8	108¾—98¼	April 30			
1709	Feb. 11	105—104½	Jan. 28			

C. THE ENGLISH COMPANY TRADING TO THE EAST INDIES (1698–1709).

The "New Company" or the "English Company."

The history of this company is paradoxical in so far as the chief events, in which it was concerned, took place prior to its incorporation. The varying fortunes of the long struggle extending over twenty years, which resulted in the charter by which this body was incorporated, have already been described[5], as well as many of the incidents in the subsequent contest between the rival organizations for the India trade, with the main conditions of the agreement of 1702, which was the prelude to the complete union of 1709. Necessarily, in the foregoing account of this intricate arrangement, it was desirable that attention should be

---

[1] *Cato's Letters, or Essays on Liberty, Civil and Religious*, London, 1733, III. p. 209.
[2] Luttrell, *Brief Relation, ut supra*, II. p. 282.
[3] This quotation is for Bank-money. Houghton gives prices for cash from Jan. 22 to June 25, during which period the extreme fluctuations (for cash) were from 42–37.
[4] The 8 per cent. dividend was payable half-yearly in April and October. The first payment for 1708 was ordered but was revoked. Court Book, XL., ff. 182, 200.
[5] *Vide supra*, pp. 135–65.

concentrated, as far as possible, on these transactions in their relation to the Old Company, and it remains to glance back at the same phenomena from the point of view of the rival body.

As already shown, on the success of the subscription for the two million loan, adventurers, holding considerably more than four-fifths of the stock, decided to avail themselves of the clause in the act which promised them incorporation. Accordingly, on September 5th, 1698, these persons were incorporated as *The English Company trading to the East Indies*[1], and, as matters turned out, this charter became of great importance, since it was by its authority that the United Company regulated its affairs for a considerable period. The stockholders were granted the usual powers of assembling to hold courts, and they were empowered to elect twenty-four managers or directors of whom, at their meetings, thirteen constituted a quorum[2]. It is remarkable that for the first time there is no mention of a governor or a deputy-governor, as in most, if not all, previous companies. The comments made by the promoters of this body against large individual holdings in the Old Company produced one result, which can scarcely have been satisfactory to several of them. Samuel Shepherd had subscribed as much as £35,000, so that it was clear that all that he and others had said of Child's "engrossing" stock in the older organization was likely to apply to this one also[3]. To meet this objection there was a clause in the charter that each adventurer owning £500 stock was entitled to one vote, but that no person might have more than one[4]. The qualification of a director was the holding of £2,000 stock[5]. Somewhat minute rules were prescribed for the management of the internal affairs of the company—for instance, the charter specifies the forms of oaths and of transfers, and admits of Quakers making a declaration instead of an oath. Arrangements too were made in case of directors becoming incapacitated, and also, in the event of a difference of opinion within the company, that nine members holding each £500 stock or over might summon a court[6].

Though the clauses of this charter which governed the finance of the company were soon modified by the steps taken towards the amalgamation of the rival institutions, a knowledge of their provisions is essential to the understanding of the conditions under which the trade was carried on until 1702. The legal position of the subscribers of the two million loan was somewhat involved. All the adventurers, who

---

[1] *Charters granted to the East India Company*, I. p. 207.
[2] *Ibid.*, I. pp. 213, 221.
[3] Luttrell, *Brief Relation*, IV. p. 403.
[4] *Charters granted to the East India Company*, I. p. 223.
[5] *Ibid.*, I. p. 225.
[6] *Ibid.*, I. p. 228.

contributed, were granted the right to trade to India to an extent each year equal to the amount of that loan which they had taken up. These subscribers were all incorporated on September 3rd, 1698, as the "General Society," which was intended to be a regulated company. But, of the whole two millions, raised by those who *ipso facto* became members of this projected organization, only £23,000 was owned by persons who determined to trade themselves, the remainder being provided by the Old Company and by adventurers who were incorporated as the English Company. On the charter constituting the latter body being completed, the individual holdings in the two million loan were consolidated and the State acknowledged itself indebted to the company, in its corporate capacity, for the whole sum of £1,662,000, while the proportions of loan stock now became the stock of the company[1]. Therefore, when the members had paid up the calls, no funds would have been available for providing trading capital beyond what the directors could borrow on the security of the debt due by the government. To meet this difficulty it was provided that the company might raise an "additional stock," not exceeding the original stock[2]. It very soon appeared that the promoters of the company had made a miscalculation which was likely to be disadvantageous to them up to September 29th, 1701, and still more after that date. The ideas that had governed the drafting of the act had been that the total trade with India was not likely to exceed two millions in any one year. Up to 1701 the Old Company could trade without limitation, but after that date it could only export goods to the value of its subscription in the two million loan, namely £315,000. It followed, when the limiting clauses of the act came into force that, if the Old Company still continued to exist, there was every probability, while this body and the separate traders could export to the full value of their holdings of loan stock, the New Company would not be able to do so, and thus, expressed in terms of its capital commitments, it had paid too much for its privileges. Necessarily this was only one side of the situation. If, as the more sanguine of the subscribers hoped, the Old Company could be ruined, this disadvantage would in time disappear. Such hopes were soon proved to be fallacious, since the Elizabethan foundation proved that it possessed remarkable vitality. Moreover, the circum-

[1] *Charters granted to the East India Company*, I. p. 209. In connection with the payment of the instalments of this loan a curious and interesting technical point was raised. The first call was tendered before the due date, and 1 per cent. was deducted for discount. Therefore it was contended that, since the company had not paid the instalment specified in the act, its charter was void. *A Letter from a Lawyer of the Inner Temple to his Friend in the Country concerning the East India Stock*, 1698 [Tracts at the India Office, vol. 268], p. 12.

[2] *Charters granted to the East India Company*, I. p. 212.

stances, under which the subscription was taken in 1698, were prejudicial to the new venture. The adroit puffing of the prospects of the India trade by means of the report of the Commons' Committee had made it easy to fill the subscription-lists, but, since many adventurers had taken up more stock than they could pay for, it became difficult to obtain the due discharge of the calls, even when discount was offered for prompt payment[1]. It was decided, in order to provide funds for trading, that further calls should be made on each adventurer over and above the 100 per cent. for which he had subscribed. For this additional stock there was called 10 per cent. (on the original capital of £1,662,000) in 1698, a further 15 per cent. up to September 1699, subject to discount for prompt payment, and another 15 per cent. in the same year[2]. The final 5 per cent. was remitted, and therefore "the additional stock for trade" or "the Shares" consisted of total calls of 35 per cent., which were due to realize £581,700[3]. This method of finance had two main consequences, namely that the company had to find altogether £2,243,700; but, to employ less than £600,000 in trade, it was forced to lend nearly thrice that sum to the State. The other result was of more immediate importance. As already shown, would-be adventurers had taken up quite as much of the loan stock as they could pay for, and in 1699 they were confronted with the certainty of being compelled to find £135 for each £100 of the loan they had taken up[4]. Under these circumstances as early as the end of 1698 the stock of the company was weak. When it was known the issue was a success a premium of 2 per cent. was paid, but, by August 6th, this had been converted into a discount of the same amount. In October, when £20 per cent. had been paid in and a further call of a like sum had been ordered, the price of the certificates was £4 less than the payment actually made, that is, where full advantage was taken of the discount for cash, a receipt "for £20 paid in" could be obtained for an actual disbursement of £17, and this sold as low as £14, so that the discount in the stock-market was as much as 30 per cent.[5] This decline was viewed with considerable satisfaction by the committees of the Old Company, since in the same period its

---

[1] Letter (of the Old Company) to the Council at Fort St George. *Annals of the East India Company*, by John Bruce, London, 1810, III. p. 259.

[2] *London Gazette*, Jan. 16, March 27, June 26, Sept. 4, 1699; *Flying Post*, Aug. 26, Sept. 30, 1699.

[3] General Court Minutes, Ap. 5, 1702—June 21, 1704, ff. 5, 9; *Postman*, Oct. 30, 1701.

[4] *I.e.* loan stock   £100
      additional stock   35
                          £135

[5] Bruce, *Annals, ut supra*, III. p. 259; Luttrell, *Brief Relation, ut supra*, IV. p. 428.

stock, instead of falling, had risen from 33¼ to 40. It is evident that the directors of the New Company regarded the situation as being very serious since, according to Luttrell, about October 18th, they had " a project under consideration for keeping their stock alwaies at parr, which is by raising a fund of £100,000 to be as a bank, and to give to any person that will sell within one per cent. of specie and be obliged to sell the same at parr[1]." It was fortunate that this dangerous scheme of supporting the market in the stock was not adopted, since apart from other disadvantages it would have had the effect of diverting funds, urgently required for the development of the India trade, to speculation on the stock-exchange. In 1699, though the pressure of the remaining calls continued to be felt, the discount was not increased, being between 22 and 23 in May and July[2]. Before the end of the year, however, the price reached 100.

There seems reason to believe that the depreciation in the stock of the English Company during the year following its establishment is to be ascribed not only to the difficulty experienced in obtaining capital, but also in some measure to the attacks made upon its credit by the rival body. This, however, was only one aspect of a campaign which extended from the Houses of Parliament and the City to remote places in the East. The Old Company was determined that it would not make the way easy for a rival and possible successor, and every device was used to strengthen its defences before any serious attack could be made upon them. The New Company was subject to several disabilities in this contest. From the declaration of peace in September 1697, the Old Company had upwards of two years before any serious competition was experienced, since the other undertaking had not any considerable trading capital, ready to be employed in India, before the latter part of 1699. Moreover, for the first time in ten years or more, the fruits of this commerce could be enjoyed without being attacked by interlopers, and therefore the profits were large. The difficulty, that confronted the committees, was the depleted state of the company's resources, but extraordinary efforts were made to provide funds and, by the loyal support of the stockholders in lending money to the management to meet the emergency, it was possible to take full advantage of the favourable opportunity. In this way much of the weakness of the financial position was overcome, before the New Company was able to

---

[1] *Brief Relation*, IV. p. 440.

[2]
	Original stock	Additional stock	Total	Price	Discount
Called up May 1699 ...	50	20	70	57	13
,, July ,, ...	70	25	95	74	21

Letters (Old Company) to Council at Bombay, May 5, July 28, 1699. Bruce, *Annals, ut supra*, III. pp. 291, 292.

enter upon any dangerous competition. When this stage had been reached it is plain that, under normal circumstances, there were no longer any grounds for the hopes, that had once been entertained, of forcing the Old Company into liquidation under the pressure of its debts.

Not only was the New Company compelled to see its opponent making large profits before it had capital ready to contest the trade, but when, in 1699, it was able to compete it had a difficulty in organization still to face. It required factories and factors, and the loyalty of the officials of the Old Company was such that the directors of the other body were forced to employ men who had been dismissed from the service of the former, or to take those who had some experience in interloping expeditions. Thus there were many impediments to be overcome and an organization to be built up in the face of an active and enterprizing opponent.

In yet another direction the New Company was failing to gain ground. Those who had promoted it could count on the support of the House of Commons up to the time that the act of 1698 had passed. In 1699 there were several indications that Parliament had become less hostile to the Old Company. The act continuing it as a corporation virtually meant that, though the holdings of the rival institutions in the two million loan were so disproportionate, the amalgamation, that was now recognized as inevitable, would be unlikely to give the New Company more than a half interest in the trade. The directors felt that after their brilliant start matters had of late not been going in their favour and, in order to gain support in Parliament, they rivalled the Old Company in the profusion and variety of their payments for "special services[1]." After the spring of 1700 the strife between the companies entered on its final phase, in which the older body aimed at consolidating and increasing the advantages it had won. Early in February 1701, when the concluding negotiations were in progress, a very ingenious attack was made on the supporters of the New Company, which developed into a run on the Bank of England. There was a certain artistic completeness in this episode, since, after the great split in the Old Company in 1681–2, which might be described as the beginning of the long contest which lasted for twenty years, the dissentient stockholders (who became the promoters of the New Company) had forced the old undertaking into a position in which it was unable to meet its engagements for several months. In 1701, on the eve of the settlement, the Old Company was sufficiently strong financially to be able to collect a large quantity of the notes issued by the banker of the

---

[1] Cf. *The Free-holders Plea against Stock-Jobbing Elections of Parliament Men*, in Defoe's *Tracts* (1703), pp. 170-1.

DIV. I. § 5 C] *Finance of the Union of the Cos.* 1701–2 185

rival organization and to present these simultaneously for payment. The run so engineered resulted in a drawn battle with perhaps some advantage to the Old Company. Shepherd, a private banker and director of the New Company, was forced to suspend payment, but, on the other hand, it is reported that the latter body delivered a counter attack, and the cash-keepers of the Old Company found themselves in a similar predicament[1].

During the latter part of 1701 the superiority of the Old Company began to assert itself. This was shown first in the acceptance of Sir Basil Firebrace, who had been one of the committees, as intermediary between the two courts for the settling of terms of union. When these came to be discussed the effect of the raid made on the stock of the New Company became manifest. Much depended on the price at which the block of £673,500 loan stock should be transferred to the Old Company. In 1700 the so-called stock of the New Company (which consisted of loan stock, together with "the Shares") was quoted at a premium of about 8 per cent.[2] After the attack early in 1701 this had been converted into a discount of nearly 20 per cent.[3] Just at the time the agreement was made the price was about par, and it was at this figure the transfer was carried out, each party paying one-half the expenses. On the other hand, it would appear that the New Company obtained some advantage in the valuation of the dead stock, since, though the sum with which it was credited was comparatively small, this was in reality not inconsiderable, in view of the short time there had been for opportunities either to erect buildings or to obtain privileges in India[4].

On the completion of the agreement, the New Company decided to obtain the funds required to pay for its half of the dead stock by cancelling £15 on each of the £35 shares[5]. It will be remembered that under the Indenture Tripartite, the separate estate in quick stock was to be wound up and that the proceeds, together with £27,000 of arrears of interest on the loan stock, after the payment of debts due, were to be divided amongst the proprietors of "the Shares" or "Additional Stock[6]."

---

[1] *The Villainy of Stock-jobbers Detected, and the Causes of the Late Run on the Banks and Bankers Considered*, 1701, in Defoe's *Tracts* (1703), pp. 255–66 ; Luttrell, *Brief Relation, ut supra*, v. p. 14. If, as suggested below (p. 186), the par of the New Company's "stock" was not 100 but 135, the price realized in March of only 100 represents a considerable depreciation. At the same date the stock of the Old Company was quoted at 76.

[2] *I.e.* £135 paid in quoted at 154.   [3] *I.e.* £135 paid in quoted at 100.

[4] *I.e.* dead stock, Old Company £330,000
  New   ,,   70,000
  ———————
      £400,000

[5] General Court Minutes (June 25, 1702), f. 4.   [6] *Vide supra*, pp. 168–71.

The effect of this resolution was, therefore, that the first assets, realized on behalf of "the Shares" from the quick stock, were used for payment for the dead stock. Since, moreover, the Committee of Management held one-half of the dead stock in trust for this company as the nucleus of "the New Additional Stock," the ultimate consequence of the change was that the sum, written off "the Shares," was converted into the former security, though this was not divisible to the individual stockholders until the determination of the trust for the trade. "The Shares" being now of £20 each, it became necessary to re-adjust the qualification of directors, and it was resolved that in future it should consist of £2,000 original and a proportionate interest in "the stock in trade of the 35 per cent." Subsequently by a motion passed on March 16th, 1703, it was determined that "the proportionate interest" in "the Shares" should be defined as thirty-five, which were now computed at £700[1]. The fact that original stock was over par and that payment was to be made for it at par by the Old Company occasioned some difficulty, but this was overcome by the resolution that each proprietor should part with 40 per cent. of his holding on these terms[2]. A certain loss in making the change was unavoidable, and it was considered that in this way it would be most equitably distributed over the whole body of the adventurers.

Up to the end of June 1702 no distinction appears to have been made between the original and additional stocks, and it seems probable that the quotations up to that date are to be interpreted in the sense that what was called "New East India stock" meant the whole calls of £135 on £100 originally applied for. If this was so, the par for the stock as quoted (not for the loan stock transferred to the Old Company) would be 135. By the Indenture Tripartite all the remaining nett assets became the property of the "Additional Stock" or "the Shares," as they now were commonly called, which were to be gradually paid off by divisions, as these properties were realized. It became necessary therefore that the two classes of securities should be now distinguished and quoted separately. This fact explains an apparent anomaly in the price at this time. On June 24th "the stock" (*i.e.* presumably £135 paid) was quoted at $138\frac{1}{2}$, whereas a week later it stood at only $116\frac{1}{4}$. Just at this time "the Shares" are mentioned as being 28, so that it may be inferred that $116\frac{1}{2}$ was the price of the original stock considered as £100 paid[3].

[1] 35 Shares of £20 each—General Court Minutes, ff. 5, 9, 15.
[2] *Ibid.* (June 25, 1702), f. 3.
[3] Price, June 24, 1702, for £135 paid $138\frac{1}{2}$.

July 1 £100 original stock £100 paid ... ... $116\frac{1}{2}$
"One Share" representing the balance of total calls of £135   28
$144\frac{1}{2}$

The quotation of "the Shares" is of great interest as being a striking commentary on the financial results of the trade of the company, since all the benefits of it were to be distributed to the owners of these securities. At the price of 28 for the £20 share it was evidently expected that there would be a substantial bonus in addition to the return of the principal. Divisions were begun as soon as possible, and it was decided on September 29th, 1702, that a distribution or "allowance" at the rate of £2 per share per annum, payable quarterly, accruing from Midsummer, should be made[1]. These payments were made regularly till June 1707, and thus £10 per share had been returned[2]. That the sums to be divided were regarded as a return of capital is clear from the fact that the price had fallen to about 15. In 1707 and 1708 £11 per share was returned[3], and there still remained some assets to be realized. Under Godolphin's Award, in order to expedite the union of the companies, it was decided that the United Company should take over these claims, paying the proprietors of "the Shares" £66,005. 4s. 1d.[4] This sum was handed over by the managers on October 27th, 1708[5], but there appear to have been some questions still to be settled, and the final payment to the owners of "the Shares" (which was 50s. per share) was not made till 1710. Though the proprietors received considerably more than their principal of £20, if allowance be made for interest during the time the liquidation continued, it may well be doubted whether they obtained enough to cover the latter claim at the rates then ruling on industrial investments.

Apart from the winding up of "the Shares," there were few complications in the capital account of the New Company. When the original stock was reduced to £988,500, the adventurers received £673,000 from the Old Company for that amount of stock transferred to it. This, when divided amongst the members, was available to meet the calls made by the directors, in order to supply funds for the united trade. These were raised in the form of bonds issued by the Committee of Management, and the disposal of these occasioned the only remaining difference of opinion, just before the conclusion of the amalgamation. On November 16th, 1706, the Old Company proposed that it should receive so much of these bonds as consisted with the credit of the united trade, to enable it to pay its debts[6]. In reply, the New Company pointed out, not unreasonably, that, in addition to that part of the

---

[1] General Court Minutes, *ut supra*, f. 12.   [2] *Ibid.*, f. 51.   [3] *Ibid.*, f. 51.
[4] "The Award" in *Charters granted to the East India Company*, I. p. 351.
[5] Court Book, XLIII., f. 211. The company had to pay the Committee of Management £15,200 towards its share of the expenses of the latter. *Ibid.*, f. 407.
[6] India Office MSS. "Papers relating to the Union, 1706-8," 43 A, f. 1.

new additional stock, which represented dead stock (and which was valued in 1702 at £400,000) there should be a considerable amount of quick stock "to be a fund of credit for borrowing on their common seal for carrying on the united trade." Yet, to meet the Old Company, the directors were willing that one-half of the whole new additional stock should be divided between the two companies[1]. Eventually, however, on £1,200,000 being lent to the State in 1708 it was decided that one-half of this sum should be added to the capital of the company[2]. Owing to the discount on this payment the actual sum paid out by the Committee of Management was £1,186,000, so that the members of the New Company were credited with stock of the nominal value of half that sum. Since this security, in the form of the capital of the United Company, realized 114, the adventurers received a satisfactory bonus when the transfer was made to them early in 1709.

Capital.

	£	£	£
1698–9. Subscription of the two million loan which became the original stock of the company ...	1,662,000		
1698–1700. 35°/₀ thereon, which was used for trading and became the "additional stock for trade" or "the Shares"		581,700	
July 1702. Original stock sold at par to the Old Company	673,500		
July 1702. Additional stock paid off (to pay the Old Company for a half-share in the total dead stock) being 15°/₀ on the original stock of £1,662,000, leaving "the Shares" 20°/₀ called up on that stock		249,300	
1702–3. Balances	988,500	332,400	
1702–10. Capital returned on a/c of the remaining additional stock		332,400	
1702–3. Bonds of the Committee of Management on account of dead stock			200,000
1703–9. Bonds of the Committee of Management on account of quick stock			491,950
Total being 70°/₀ on the original stock of £988,500			691,950

[1] India Office MSS. "Papers relating to the Union, 1706–8," 43 A, ff. 2–6; Court Book, XLIII., f. 183.

[2] Court Book, XLIII., f. 365.

Prices of Stocks.

Year	Original stock			Additional stock or "the Shares"		
	Date of highest price	Prices	Date of lowest price	Date of highest price	Prices	Date of lowest price
1698	July 19	2 pr.—4 disc.[1]	Sept. 17			
1699	Feb. 15	$50\frac{3}{4}$[2]—$106\frac{1}{2}$	Dec. 22			
1700	Apr. 24	154—126	Jan. 3			
1701	Dec. 31	$140\frac{1}{2}$—100	March 19			
1702	Dec. 23	161—$125\frac{3}{4}$	May 6	Dec. 22	$37\frac{1}{2}$—28	July 3
1703	Sept.	219—$151\frac{3}{4}$	Feb. 17	Jan. 5, 26	36—$27\frac{1}{2}$	Nov. 15
1704	Apr. 13	260—$202\frac{1}{2}$	Jan. 5–17	Apr. 26	$33\frac{3}{4}$—$23\frac{3}{4}$	Dec. 15
1705	Jan. 18	$258\frac{1}{4}$—234	July 11	Jan. 3	24—$12\frac{3}{4}$	July 27
1706	June 3	260—$238\frac{1}{2}$	Jan. 25, Feb. 1	Sept. 20	$17\frac{1}{4}$—$14\frac{1}{2}$	Jan. 18
1707	Sept. 19–24	272—$254\frac{1}{2}$	Jan. 31	Jan. 8–20	$15\frac{1}{4}$—$7\frac{3}{8}$	Aug. 15–25
1708	March 8	$258\frac{1}{2}$—$240\frac{1}{4}$	Apr. 16	March 8	9—$6\frac{5}{8}$	March 12
1709[3]	Jan. 28 March 12	114—112	Feb. 11	Feb. 11 Apr. 1	$4\frac{7}{8}$—$1\frac{5}{8}$	May 6
1710				March	$2\frac{1}{2}$—2	Jan. 4

D. The United Company of Merchants of England trading to the East Indies.

Though the complete establishment of this company did not take place until the two bodies, which composed it, were finally amalgamated, in one sense its history begins when the Committee of Management for the united trade was constituted in 1702. That committee, composed of equal numbers of representatives of the Old and New Companies, became the embryo from which seven years later the United Company was to emerge, and in the meantime it was the only organization which had direct powers to control the trade. It is possible that some justification for the cumbersome provisions of the Indenture Tripartite is to be found in the need, that doubtless existed, for the keen personal animosities, which had been aroused during the years of struggle, to pass

---

[1] The prices for 1698 are from Luttrell's *Brief Relation of State Affairs*, IV. pp. 403, 409, 411, 417, 420, 426, 428, 460. From 1699 to the end of Sept. 1703 the quotations are from Houghton's *Collections* (cf. *Hist. Agriculture and Prices in England*, by J. E. T. Rogers, VI. pp. 724, 725). For the remainder of the period these are taken from the newspapers (cf. for Original Stock, *Ibid.*, VII., Pt. II. pp. 798–803).

[2] Partly paid. Up to the end of June 1702 the quotation is for £135 paid in, thereafter for £100 of original stock.

[3] January to March only; after the latter month this stock was merged in that of the United Company.

away. Once this deed had been signed, the two companies continued to exist in their corporate capacity, but their powers were confined to providing capital, which was disbursed by the joint-committee. Every precaution had been taken to make their interests absolutely identical, and as time went on the old feelings of antagonism gave way to a sense of solidarity. This happy change was no doubt hastened by the coming of a new generation as committees and directors. Many of those who had been in the thick of the strife had been removed by death[1], and most of those remaining were advanced in years. Thus when all the real causes of friction had been removed, it was only to be expected that the general body of adventurers would desire to hasten, rather than to retard the final amalgamation.

While good progress was being made towards a complete union, the joint-committee found that the situation in India was not only troublesome but threatening. After close on fifty years of a permanent capital, it was necessary to return to the chaos that had marked the financial arrangements of the early voyages. There were three distinct sets of accounts to be kept at every important factory, first those for the united trade and then those of the separate estate of each of the companies which was to be realized and the proceeds brought home. Then there was a further element of confusion in the existence of the separate traders who had not joined the New Company and who were entitled to trade to an extent equal to the amount they had subscribed to the loan of 1698. With the best will in the world it was almost inevitable that there should be friction in India, and the leading officials there had espoused the cause of their employers so thoroughly that enmities had been contracted, which made it impossible that some of those sent out by the Old Company could work with, or even tolerate, others who had been employed by the other body. One effect of the agreement was that, in some cases, one official on the spot took the opportunity of obtaining revenge on the agent of the rival company. Thus Sir William Norris seized at Surat three members of the Old Company's Council and handed them over in irons to the Mughal governor[2]. Moreover, if economies were to be effected by the union, it was necessary that some members of the two staffs in India should be recalled, and the uncertainty, as to who should be retained and who dismissed, added to a state of tension, which was already great. It follows that much of the seven years during which the trade was controlled by the Committee of Management was spent in the endeavour to re-organize the staff abroad.

Another difficulty which this Committee had to face was the situa-

[1] Both Child and Papillon had died in 1699, and Barnardiston followed them the next year.

[2] *A History of British India*, by Sir W. W. Hunter, London, 1900, II. p. 373.

Position of the Separate Traders 1702-9

tion which arose out of the position of the separate traders. The evident intention of the act of 1698 had been that their proceedings should be regulated by the General Society. Since, however, the number of those, who had taken up loan stock, but did not join the New Company was so small, this organization became inoperative, and any control exercised over these merchants was exerted by the Committee of Management. Friction soon arose, partly through some of them claiming that, when they had failed to ship goods up to their quota in any one year, such deficiency should be credited to them in the ensuing season, partly too by their contention that commodities might be taken on board at ports out of the United Kingdom. For instance, in 1707, John Powell wished to complete his quantum by shipments to be made either at Lisbon or Madeira, and the Committee, not being in a position to verify the proposed bills of lading, refused to consent, and eventually he was interdicted from trading, with the result that he was a frequent applicant to Parliament for redress against the company[1]. To end a position which was fast becoming intolerable, the Committee began to purchase the loan stock owned by the separate traders. By the end of 1708 £15,800 had been acquired, leaving only £7,200 outstanding[2]. As much as £5,034 of this sum was reported by the managers as having been secured at one time in November 1708[3]. Large prices had to be given to obtain the stock, in one case 383 per cent. and in another 400 per cent.[4] Powell had been offered 270 per cent. for his holding, but he asked 820 per cent. and refused to sell below 550[5].

Advantage was taken of the act passed in 1708 (6 Anne, c. 17) to obtain a clause which enabled the company, on giving three years' notice after September 29th, 1711, to pay off the remaining loan stock held by separate traders at par, but at that date all this stock had been bought by the company with the exception of £4,200[6]. The legislation of 1708 not only arranged for the completion of the union but it added materially to the privileges of the company. The Committee of Management undertook to lend £1,200,000 to the State, without interest, thereby reducing the charge on the loan made by this company from 8 to 5 per cent. In return, it was enacted that the undertaking should be continued as a corporation until March 25th, 1728, after which date

[1] *Journals of the House of Commons*, XVII. pp. 249, 252, 253, 529; XIX. pp. 23, 119.

[2] This explains the discrepancy in the amounts of this stock mentioned at the foundation of the New Company and in 1708. Hunter, *Hist. Brit. India*, II. p. 379 (note).

[3] Court Book, XLIII., f. 362.

[4] *The Case of John Powell of London*, Brit. Mus., 8223. d. 43.

[5] *Journals of the House of Commons*, XVII. p. 253.

[6] *Ibid.*, XVII. p. 253. Of this amount £3,700 belonged to Powell.

it was determinable on three years' notice and the repayment by the State of the monies advanced to it by the company.

When the United Company was formally constituted in 1709 there was much to be done in organizing its business both at home and abroad. Rules had to be drawn up for the conduct of its affairs and many points remained to be settled, such as fixing the powers of the directors, the rights of the stockholders, as well as the development of the corporate character of the undertaking. In 1709 it was decided that the fee to be paid on a transfer of stock should be in future 5s., and the officials were directed to take special care that those signing the deed, as vendors, should "be the very persons to whom the stock belongs[1]." To prevent any improper use of the common seal, it was to be kept under three locks and only to be used under order of the court of directors[2]. Very elaborate arrangements were made for the recording of votes at the general courts. These were taken by ballot upon a motion, but, for the election of directors, and subsequently for members of committees, the procedure was somewhat complex. Two glass urns were provided for receiving the votes, and these were sealed at six o'clock on the day that the poll closed[3]. It was resolved that the time should be taken from the clock in the court-room, and, on August 18th, 1714, directions were given for the purchase of a new timepiece "which was to go a month," and of which the chairman or deputy-chairman for the time was to keep the keys[4]. It is stated that "the general court of the proprietors took an active part in almost every question, whether connected with the foreign or domestic affairs of the company[5]," and on several occasions general courts were held frequently when there were matters of importance to be considered. Thus, when it was proposed in 1712 to increase the duty on East India goods by 10 per cent., general meetings were held on May 17th, 19th, 20th, 21st and 22nd[6], and the adventurers were urged to use their individual interest with their friends against the proposal. The stockholders exercised a close supervision over the proceedings of the directors. In 1709 it was resolved that no director should receive any fee or reward (over and above the sum allowed by the general court) by reason of any business of the company[7], while he was further bound to disclose his interest in any transaction with the company, in which he was personally concerned in his private capacity[8]. These resolutions were put in force in 1716–17, on a report that 40 bars

---

[1] Court Book, XLIII., ff. 513, 695.   [2] Ibid., f. 695.
[3] Ibid., XLIV., f. 1; XLV. f. 1.   [4] Ibid., XLVI., f. 104.
[5] Draft Memoir of the History of the East India Company. India Office, Home Miscellaneous, XLV., f. 15.
[6] Court Book, XLV., ff. 41, 43, 44, 45, 47.
[7] Ibid., XLIII., f. 596.   [8] Ibid., f. 775.

of silver had been embarked on one of the company's ships to be used in private trade, and that it was supposed that some of the directors were cognisant of the abuse. A full general court was held on March 8th, 1717, when the charges were debated before "a large appearance of the generality." John Hopkins, one of the adventurers, declared that he had communicated the fact of the secret shipment to the company's solicitors and, "though a show of prosecution was made, the question was since stifled." This, he argued, proved a guilty knowledge on the part of the directors. The meeting seems to have taken the view that the charges had not been proved, and finally a resolution was carried which remitted the matter to the directors for enquiry. Afterwards the solicitor appeared and declared that he had not communicated with any of the directors, so that there was no evidence on which to continue the agitation[1]. From the date of the amalgamation the salary of a director had been fixed at £150 a year. On January 18th, 1711, it was determined that this sum should be divided into two portions, one of which, amounting to £100, was regarded as payment for his services on the court and the remainder for attending the committees, especially at the sales[2]. These fees were subject to large deductions in case of irregular attendance. The secretary was authorized to deduct £4 from the first payment to each director. By this means a fund was established out of which those, who attended every meeting, were entitled to divide £12 amongst them, and similarly in the case of all committees[3]. An hour's grace was allowed for an attendance to count for this division, but it was provided that the director must appear "before the clock ceases striking and must also remain to the end[4]." In spite of this wide margin allowed to the members of the board, it was reported in 1711 that some attended irregularly[5], and in 1714 it was decided that, owing to the deposits in certain cases having fallen into arrear, under such circumstances these were to be deducted from the dividend-warrants[6]. For several years all the directors ranked equally as to fees in proportion to their attendances. At first they elected a chairman, but, at the general court held on December 9th, 1713, it was proposed that steps should be taken to obtain an alteration in the charter, empowering the company to choose a governor and deputy-governor. The proposal was referred to a special committee, which reported that no change in the charter was necessary, but, upon further consideration, it was decided that the existing nomenclature was to be continued[7], while, according to

---

[1] Court Book, XLVII., ff. 219, 300, 301, 307.
[2] Ibid., XLIV., f. 300.
[3] Ibid., f. 586.
[4] Ibid., f. 6.
[5] Ibid., f. 327.
[6] Ibid., XLV., f. 673.
[7] Ibid., XLV., ff. 558, 572, 573, 620.

a resolution of June 19th, 1719, the chairman and deputy-chairman were to receive a salary of £200 a year each instead of £150[1]. From time to time some interesting points in procedure arose. Thus in 1711 the directors were instructed to take counsel's opinion as to whether a "feme-covert" could vote, and also at what age a minor was entitled to take part in general courts. The opinion, as to the former query, was in the negative, while it added that the minor could vote "at the age of discretion," which was generally taken to be fourteen or fifteen years of age. If, however, he could show that he understood the nature of an oath, though he was less than the age specified, his vote might be admitted and conversely[2]. The practice of recording votes by ballot gave rise to an interesting discussion in 1716, which was begun by one of the directors, who wished to know whether, on a vote being taken by this method in which he was in a minority, he was entitled to have his dissent entered on the minutes. This motion was twice debated, and finally it was carried that such protest ought not to be recorded[3]. Another curious situation is revealed by the grave arguments, pro and con, on the proposed amendment of the bye-law that no one might buy at the sales "while on the hustings." It was reported that this rule was a prejudice to the company, as it prevented "some gentlemen of figure from coming in person, who used formerly to buy considerable quantities of goods." Evidently the persons of aldermanic proportions were mostly directors of the Bank, the South Sea and East India companies, and an exception was made in their favour under which they might bid from within the hustings "provided they stand up and speak audibly[4]."

There are many matters which were discussed from time to time that might be considered to have been outside the usual business of a trading company. Thus the directors endeavoured to secure the moral welfare of their servants abroad, and they were particularly severe on any cases of intemperance that were brought under their notice[5]. Every assistance was given to the Society for Christian Knowledge in Foreign Parts[6], and in 1716 "it was earnestly recommended to the adventurers to let the Poplar almshouses be partakers of some part of the money they shall at any time be disposed to bestow on charitable uses in their life-time or at their death[7]." The court was always prepared to reward any servants who had performed any exceptional service. Captain Martin, who had made a gallant fight against a French ship, was granted £1,000 and a gold medal[8], and the same spirit is shown in the following resolutions,

---

[1] Court Book, XLVIII., f. 307.
[2] Ibid., XLIV., ff. 393, 405.
[3] Ibid., XLVII., ff. 205, 210, 256.
[4] Ibid., XLVIII., f. 41.
[5] Ibid., XLIV., f. 182.   [6] Ibid., ff. 288, 461.   [7] Ibid., XLVI., f. 455.
[8] Letter to President and Council at Bengal, Feb. 15, 1716 : Letter Book, xv., f. 783.

DIV. I. § 5 D] *Matters discussed at the Courts* 1709–20   195

relating to the conflagration of January 14th, 1715, in which the powder-warehouse at Bear Quay had twice caught fire—" the Court taking into consideration that the present dreadfull fire, which began at Thames St. near Bear Key and has spread itself as far as Tower St. and is not yet fully extinguished, threatens their warehouse in Seething Lane and may extend its fury yet further, did therefore think it necessary to summon their severall warehouse-keepers and surveyors and direct them as follows: 'That they attend constantly all this day and the ensuing night and endeavour to prevent any mischief that may happen to the company's warehouses, that they get such of the company's porters and those usually labouring in their warehouses and, if necessary, any others to assist them in all places and particularly at the warehouse in Seething Lane, which seems most exposed, and that Mr Gilbert, the warehouse-keeper, do gratify them and those who have already been very helpfull in removing part of the goods from thence as he shall think they deserve[1].'"

The most critical situation in the internal affairs of the company, during the years immediately following the union, arose out of the winding up of the assets belonging to the owners of "the Shares" or the old additional stock of the English company. It had been intended that this distribution should have been completed by 1708 but, after dividing £3 per share on April 19th, 1709, it was reported that there still remained "a considerable overplus[2]." Some of the property was of such a nature that it was difficult to realize, and it was therefore suggested that the holders of "the Shares" should dispose of all their rights and claims to the company. The former thereupon brought forward large "pretensions and demands," and finally asked for a final division of £4 per share. The company considered this claim was unreasonable, and at a meeting held on March 24th, 1710, it was resolved that a valuation should be made[3]. The danger of this difference of opinion was that, since "the Shares" were owned by those, who had been members of the New Company, the opposition was likely to revive the friction that had existed up till 1702. It shows how much the stock-holders in the Old Company had secured the predominance since the amalgamation that a series of resolutions was carried adverse to adventurers who held "the Shares." On June 7th, 1710, it was decided that the property in dispute should be acquired by the company and that a fixed sum was to be paid to those who owned "the Shares[4]." Three weeks later this sum was settled as 50s. per Share, payable to each owner who would transfer his holding in Shares to the company[5]. Though this offer was

[1] Court Book, XLVI., ff. 253, 254.
[2] Ibid., XLIII., f. 497.
[3] Ibid., ff. 974, 975.
[4] Ibid., XLIV., f. 39.
[5] Ibid., f. 67.

declined, at a general court held on June 29th, 1710, the proposals of the directors were carried[1]. On reconsideration many of the shareholders accepted these terms, but a year later some still stood out[2], and towards the end of 1711 it was necessary to announce that six months' grace would still be given for the completion of the surrender by those who had not yet assented[3]. From the fact that there is no further mention of the matter it is to be inferred that the final division was accepted by the dissentients in 1712.

Another legacy of trouble from the act of 1698 was the existence of a balance of the separate stock. At the end of 1708 there had been £7,200 of this security outstanding. On December 21st, 1709, £3,000 of this was purchased at 300, leaving £4,200 still in existence[4]. The trade, which could be carried on by the owners of this stock, was characterized by the court as "a pernicious one to the company[5]," and, though at one time the opinion was expressed that Powell was unlikely to perform "any great feats with his stock[6]," the directors found reason to revise their opinion, when they discovered that their servants at Bengal "had given unwarrantable assistance to separate stock ships[7]." Powell's dispute with the company is to be attributed partly to his grievance over the refusal of the officials to accept his bill of lading in 1706, partly to his endeavouring to obtain a very high price for his stock[8]. It is at first sight puzzling that larger prices were given by the company for separate stock than could be obtained on the stock-market for its own securities. The explanation appears to be based on a change in the situation since 1698. At that time it was estimated that the trade with India would amount to about two millions a year, and hence the fixing of the loan stock at this amount[9]. But after the union, the export from England was less than a quarter of this sum, while the owners of separate stock were entitled to ship goods to the nominal amount of their stock. It follows that those who had invested £4,200 as separate traders were able to send out commodities of that value, whereas the company which had lent the State over three millions could only export, in a bad year, goods worth about one-tenth of the latter sum[10]. It appears to have been on this basis that the purchase price of separate

[1] Court Book, XLIV., f. 71.
[2] Ibid., f. 298.
[3] Ibid., f. 588.
[4] Ibid., XLIII., f. 951.
[5] Letter Book, XIII., f. 469.
[6] Ibid., f. 612.
[7] Letter to President and Council at Bengal, Jan. 13, 1714: Letter Book, XV., f. 197.
[8] The Case of John Powell (Home Miscellaneous, India Office), LVIII., passim.
[9] Vide supra, pp. 153, 165.
[10] Cf. "Exports of Bullion to India" in The Trade to India critically and calmly considered, 1720, Appendix. India Office Tracts, $\frac{53 . A . 11}{1}$.

stock was taken at between 300 and 400 up to 1709. As the time drew near when, under the act of 1708, it could be paid off at par, the price declined, and though Powell offered to sell, in 1712, at the same price that had previously been paid, the company refused to accept his terms. He thereupon appealed to the House of Commons, and in 1714 presented a fresh petition and again in 1719. On the last occasion it was resolved that his petition should not be received[1].

Another aspect of the activities of the management was the control over the officials in the East. Long reports were required of all transactions of importance and the duplicate accounts were scrutinized by the directors with great minuteness. For instance, in 1710, it was declared that the annual charge at Fort William required "the utmost care in retrenching it," and it was hinted that secret leaks were suspected[2]. The same demands for economy were almost continually being urged. The expenses at Bencoolen were described as "prodigious[3]," and the staff was warned that "servants guilty of extravagant management or a desire of unjust gain seldom survived[4]." In 1714 the directors wrote that the general charges in Bengal were increasing and had grown to double what they had been a few years before[5]. The reprimand which followed was very severe: "What can the bookkeeper say," the directors wrote, "to these monstrous charges, could they escape his observation, did he not think it his duty to have remonstrated them to the Council, or could any of the Council be so unthinking as not to compute what remittances were annually made to Patna and what value of goods was returned for the same and thereby have entered into the account of the vast charges we were at; in short let us have no more such careless or rather unfaithful management?[6]" Similarly complaint was made of "the intollerable carelessness" of a clerk who copied a consultation book at Bencoolen, "which was writ in such a scrawling, scribbling fashion" as to be illegible in places[7]. A like reprimand was administered when, on a certain account book being required from Surat, it was found that the leaves had been cut out and only the cover left[8]. When strongly-

[1] Home Miscellaneous, India Office, LVIII., *passim*; Journals of the House of Commons, XVII. pp. 253, 529; XIX. p. 23.

[2] Letter Book, XIII., f. 679.

[3] *Ibid.*, f. 761.

[4] Letter to Governor and Council at Bencoolen, March 20, 1713: Letter Book, XV., f. 15.

[5] Letter to President and Council at Bengal, January 13, 1714: Letter Book, XV., f. 213.

[6] Letter to President and Council at Bengal, January 12, 1715: Letter Book, XV., f. 468.

[7] Letter to Governor and Council at Bencoolen, March 20, 1713: Letter Book, XV., f. 30.

[8] Court Book, XLVII., f. 237.

worded letters produced no amendment, the erring officials were dismissed. A particularly bad case happened at Bencoolen in 1710, where $2,000 had been spent on liquor in six months, while timber and other stores were exposed to the weather and allowed to rot[1]. To mark their displeasure, the directors sent out a completely new staff from home[2], but seven years later a fresh remonstrance was required. On February 6th, 1717, the court wrote, "Could we once hear sobriety was become as fashionable on the west coast as hard drinking hath been, we have strong hopes that your new settlement at Marlborough...would give a better reputation to the west coast for health. We have often recommended you to use great care about your water. It is positively affirmed you have good water, if you will be at the pains of fetching what is so[3]." On the other side "an hearty, zealous, and wise management" was always commended and rewarded[4].

The policy of the directors, which they enforced in their dispatches, followed certain well-defined lines. Their representatives were urged "not to despise the day of small things but, as we have begun by easy and gentle methods," so to continue and to aim at making the revenue from customs and rents suffice for the expenses of the settlements[5]. They were "to carry it so civilly and justly to the natives as to beget in them a good esteem of their fair dealing[6]." Instructions were issued drawing attention to the satisfactory results that had followed from the policy of succouring the great men on both sides during a native war, "wherefore, which ever side was victorious considered itself obliged to the company[7]."

The directors were opposed to any great outlay on buildings or fortifications. Such repairs, as were absolutely necessary, were to be executed but nothing more, outlay of this character at Bencoolen "had been made the pretence of squandering away a prodigious deal of money—to hear the very name of it on the west coast is enough to chagrin us[8]." The same insistence on economy in disbursements of this character is repeated again and again. Thus in 1718 the directors wrote: "we should be glad to hear that they [*i.e.* expenses of buildings and fortifications] were once at an end. It is very unhappy to have so many calls

---

[1] Court Book, XLIV., f. 182.　　　　[2] *Ibid.*, f. 188.

[3] Letter to Governor and Council at Bencoolen, Feb. 6, 1717: Letter Book, XVI., f. 153.

[4] Letter Book, XIII., f. 680.　　　　[5] *Ibid.*

[6] Letter to Governor and Council at Bencoolen, March 20, 1713: Letter Book, xv., ff. 23, 24.

[7] Letter to General and Council at Bombay, March 27, 1713: Letter Book, xv., f. 69.

[8] Letter to Governor and Council at Bencoolen, March 20, 1713: Letter Book, xv., f. 28.

for such great sums out of our cash at a time and in all places[1]." They complained of the diversion of the money from investments in trading "which are, as we term it, the very heart blood of the company, for, without the supplies by return of the investments, the company can't survive and by so many drains must of necessity languish[2]."

To some extent these were counsels of perfection and occasionally, especially when the company had suffered from the aggression of its Dutch rival, there is a less pacific spirit in the instructions. In 1709 the directors urged their servants " to make the English interest in India considerable." The Dutch, they add, " are a pregnant instance of the success of this policy and well worth the imitation of other Europeans," through their sparing no pains in strengthening their position. "This made them formidable to all the powers round about their settlements, and, as they by a long series of years have been continually spreading and taking firmer root, we hope all our servants for their own honour and their countrey's, as well as for their employer's benefit, will endeavour to imitate them and evidence that their genius, inclination and diligence are able to keep equall pace with any other Europeans[3]." As early as 1711, it was found that places of strength were required in certain districts in order to secure justice from the native rulers[4], and soon afterwards the directors wrote: " it may be sometimes necessary that the natives should have an apprehension of our power and strength that they may not be tempted to insult or attack us, especially during such times as there have been of late, while the countrey has been unsettled and it remained doubtfull who should acquire the sovereignty of it[5]." Thus the court in London was forced to speak with two voices. It repeatedly ordered, in the most peremptory manner, that outlay on fortifications and buildings should be kept as low as possible. On the other hand, when the company suffered from attacks made upon its servants and was unable to obtain redress, it was forced reluctantly to authorize expenditure for the defence of the settlements.

There was another circumstance, altogether outside the control of the directors, which tended to increase the working expenses. It will be remembered that during the great Parliamentary struggle after the Revolution there was strong opposition to the company by those who

[1] Letter to President and Council at Fort St George, January 8, 1718: Letter Book, XVI., f. 339.
[2] Letter to President and Council at Fort St George, October 17, 1718: Letter Book, XVI., f. 519.
[3] Letter Book, XIII., f. 441.
[4] Letter to the President and Council at Fort St George, December 28, 1711: Letter Book, XIV., f. 401.
[5] Letter to the President and Council at Bengal, January 13, 1714: Letter Book, XV., f. 211.

condemned the India trade as a whole, on the grounds that it failed to find a market for English manufactures. The foundation of a second company and the amalgamation in 1708 only intensified the views of such opponents. Complaints were still made that the cloth exported by the company was only about one-tenth of its whole shipments, while the remainder consisted of bullion. "Specie sent elsewhere," it was said, "returns, but India, like the grave, swallows up all and makes no return; that is the money never returns, what they send us back is nothing, 'tis consumed here and so vanishes and dies away[1]." Or, as it was stated elsewhere, "if the East India trade could be carried on with its full swing, it would ease us of every penny of our money and destroy every manufacture in the kingdom as well as every man in it[2]." To disarm this kind of criticism, as far as was possible, the court endeavoured to press the sale of cloth and frequently gave instructions to that effect[3]. To force cloth on the natives and to open up new markets for the sale of it was urged on the representatives in India in almost every dispatch. This policy involved the locking up of capital until the stock could be realized and paid for, while some factories were unable to dispose of a great part of the bales sent them. These had to be sent elsewhere, so that the expenses, through loss of interest and deterioration, in time became considerable.

There was yet another difficulty arising out of the amalgamation which the directors had to face. This was purely financial. Though the share-capital of the company in 1708 was £3,163,000, none of this was available to be used in carrying on the trade. Working capital had to be provided by borrowing on bonds and the rate of interest, for some years after the union, was 6 per cent. The first dividend paid after the amalgamation was 5 per cent. for the quarter ending Lady-day 1709. For the following six months the rate was increased to 8 per cent. and for the next two years (*i.e.* from Michaelmas 1709 to Michaelmas 1711) 9 per cent. per annum was divided. During the period from 1709 to 1711 the stock fluctuated between 140 and 108, and by this time commerce with India had become of sufficient importance to justify the compilation and printing of a work describing the mechanism of the trade and giving tables of the different native currencies, weights and measures[4]. In the season 1711–12 a combination of misfortunes had been experienced. There had been famine and wars between the native

---

[1] *The Trade to India critically and calmly considered*, 1720, p. 41.
[2] *Cato's Letters* (August 25, 1722), London, 1733, III. p. 213.
[3] Letter Book, XIV, f. 85.
[4] *An Account of the Trade in India, containing rules for good government in Trade, Price Courants and Tables: with descriptions of Fort St George, Acheen, Malacca, Condore, Canton, Anjengo, Muskat, Gombroon, Surat, Goa, Carwar, Telichery, Panola, Calicut, the Cape of Good Hope and St Helena*, by Charles Lockyer, London, 1711.

powers in India[1], as well as losses of homeward bound ships which were taken by French privateers[2]. In the summer of 1711 the financial stringency was considerable and the court was compelled to borrow 12½ per cent. of his holding from each adventurer, or upwards of £400,000, besides obtaining a loan of £120,000 from the Bank of England[3]. In spite of the resources obtained by these means, the shipments of bullion were reduced, being only £206,749. 8s. 6d. in 1711 and £167,585. 4s. 7½d. in 1712, as compared with £346,887. 10s. 10½d. in 1713[4]. Moreover the quality of goods obtainable in India was below the average (for instance several pieces of muslin were found to be full of holes and "rather like rags[5]"), and high prices had to be paid there, while those obtainable in England were low[6]. For these reasons no dividend was paid during the year Michaelmas 1711 to Michaelmas 1712. In the summer of 1712 the situation showed signs of improvement, and bonds amounting to £852,400 were paid off[7], while the committee of the Treasury was directed to use such proper methods from time to time as were necessary for the further raising of the company's credit[8]. A dividend at the rate of 10 per cent. per annum was paid for the nine months from Michaelmas 1712 to Midsummer 1713. Then for the next year it was impossible to make any distribution, since all the available funds were required to take advantage of the better prospects for trading opened up by the declaration of the peace, that had been long and anxiously expected by the directors. The servants in India were informed that the exports sent there would be larger than ever before[9]. The whole shipment of bullion in 1714 had been only £222,465. 4s. 9d., but in 1715 it was £432,868. 9s. 10½d., and in 1716 £440,526. 15s. 3d.[10] According to the statement of the company its total exports (both bullion and goods) were, in 1715–16, £400,000, and in the following season £500,000[11]. In 1717 the bullion sent to India was over £800,000, and it exceeded £500,000 in 1718 and 1719[12]. The return of prosperity was shown by the regular distribution of dividends of 10 per cent. which were taken as accruing due from Midsummer 1714. Payment was now made half-yearly instead of quarterly as had been the previous practice. In announcing the change

[1] Letter Book, xiv., ff. 95, 399, 461.   [2] Ibid., f. 515.
[3] Court Book, xliv., ff. 456, 461.
[4] The Trade to India critically and calmly considered, Appendix.
[5] Letter Book, xiii., f. 629.   [6] Ibid., xiv., f. 640.
[7] Court Book, xlv., f. 113.   [8] Ibid., f. 155.
[9] Letter to President and Council at Fort St George, January 13, 1714: Letter Book, xv., f. 152.
[10] The Trade to India calmly and critically considered, Appendix.
[11] Court Book, xlvi., f. 389, xlvii., f. 61.
[12] The Trade to India calmly and critically considered, Appendix.

the directors stated that quarterly distributions had proved inconvenient by reason of the frequent closing of the books, besides throwing extra work on the accountants at times when they were fully occupied with the accounts of the sales[1]. In 1715 it was thought that the time had come to reduce the interest paid on the bonds from 6 to 5 per cent. but, after a resolution had been passed to this effect, the committee of the Treasury reported on September 20th that " they were apprehensive from the present circumstances of affairs that the demand for paying off the bonds [*i.e.* by those who would refuse to renew at 5 per cent.] may be greater than was expected, and that, by reason of the expected ships not having arrived, the sum arising from the present sale will be much short of what was depended on. They are therefore of opinion that the company's bonds should be continued for some time longer at 6 per cent.[2]" This recommendation was adopted and the reduction of the interest to 5 per cent. did not take effect until June 24th, 1716. Two years later the rate was lowered again and only 4 per cent. was paid[3].

The fact that the company was able to borrow at this rate shows that its financial condition was regarded as highly satisfactory, indeed " its security was considered equal to that of the Dutch" undertaking[4]. There were, however, certain anxieties which troubled the directors considerably. In July 1716 news had been received of the arrival of a ship named the *Victory* in India. This vessel had sailed from Ostend under a commission from the Emperor of Austria but was commanded by an Irishman, and it was shrewdly suspected that she carried investments on behalf of English merchants. The adventurers resolved that "such practices were extremely prejudicial to the company[5]." Within a month a petition had been drawn up which was presented to the Prince of Wales at Hampton Court on October 4th. He promised to issue a proclamation on behalf of the company, at the same time informing the directors "I am glad the measures I have taken for your service have been so acceptable to you and I will alwaies continue to do you all the good I can[6]." On receiving the proclamation, which was dated October 18th and which forbade any British subjects to serve on the Ostend ships[7], the directors repeated their injunctions to their representatives in India commanding them, where they found any Englishman endeavouring to trade under licenses from foreign princes, to seize such

---

[1] Court Book, XLVI., f. 51.   [2] Court Book, XLVI., f. 430.
[3] *Ibid.*, XLVII., ff. 49, 52, 583.
[4] *An Essay on the East India Trade*, 1770, p. 34. India Office Pamphlets, 53.A.11/5.
[5] Court Book, XLVII., f. 75.
[6] *Ibid.*, ff. 97, 136, 139, 148.
[7] Home Miscellaneous, LXXIV.

persons "so as to crush the interloping at the very beginning[1]." The Ostend venture, however, was not a mere isolated expedition but the beginning of a new East India company which, though not incorporated until 1722, soon began to conduct a considerable trade. Thus in 1717 five of its vessels were reported to have reached India[2], and it was necessary for the directors to reiterate their instructions to their servants that no help should be afforded to these ships in anything relating to trade[3]. At first sight it might appear that, since most of the chief mercantile nations had India companies already in existence, the apprehensions, arising out of a further addition to the number, were excessive. Much more it would seem that there was exaggeration in the following description of the various "fatal" effects to the English and Dutch nations, which this new company "was now hatching, and in time like caterpillars in their nest, when ripe, will burst forth and spread themselves far and wide and then mock the wisest counsels taken to destroy and extirpate them." Both nations were urged "to join in the most vigorous and resolute measures to destroy this cockatrice, whilst young, before it comes to maturity to sting the two nations to death[4]."

The disquietude of the directors is to be attributed to their fears that this new Ostend venture would revive some of the most disadvantageous characteristics of the earlier form of the Darien scheme[5]. In 1718 it was asserted that much of the capital, subscribed in Flanders, was in reality owned by British subjects, while cases were recorded of Englishmen who had hoped to escape the proclamation of 1716 by becoming burghers of Ostend[6]. Moreover a vast smuggling trade in East India goods soon grew up. At first large boats, propelled by ten or twelve oars, made the voyage from the Thames to Ostend. The loss to the customs became so serious that an act was passed, which prohibited the use of any boat on the river with more than four oars[7]. Such legislation, however, only increased the difficulties of the smugglers without putting a stop to their trade. India goods were now brought to Ostend, there transhipped into sloops, and these were met at sea by British rowboats from which the goods were conveyed inland and distributed[8]. The

[1] Letter Book, xv., f. 718; xvi., f. 71.   [2] Home Miscellaneous, LXXIV.
[3] Letter to President and Council at Bengal, January 18, 1717: Letter Book, xvi., f. 71.
[4] *The Importance of the Ostend-Company consider'd*, London, 1726, p. 4 [Brit. Mus. 1391.c.23]. Cf. *Lettre à un ami en Hollande au sujet de la Nouvelle Compagnie Imperiale des Indes* [? Brussels, ? 1726, Brit. Mus. $\frac{8245.b.90}{6}$].
[5] *Vide supra*, p. 161, *infra*, Div. I. § 5 E.
[6] Court Book, LVIII., f. 127, *A succinct but compleat History of the rise, progress and suppression of the Imperial Company of the Indies, established at Ostend* in *Navigantium atque Itinerantium Bibliotheca*, ed. John Harris, London, 1744–8, I. p. 966.
[7] 8 George I., c. 18, § 3.
[8] *The Importance of the Ostend-Company consider'd*, 1726, p. 33.

loss of revenue stimulated the government to intervene and energetic representations were made through the British embassies abroad. Certain clauses in various treaties with Austria were relied on, but it was not till 1728 that the charter of the Ostend company was suspended.

Before this result was reached, the East India company had to surmount the crisis of 1720. As early as May 25th there is hint of difficulties already faced. On that date "it was represented to the adventurers that some persons had been employed to solicit the company's affairs in Parliament and that they ought to be considered for their trouble and charges therein[1]." This distribution of secret service money may relate either to the resistance of the plans of the South Sea company for controlling the East India trade[2], or else to the making of interest in the House of Commons to meet certain attempts, which were suggested for the invasion of the privileges of the company[3]. These attacks having been repulsed, the projectors of the period made overtures to the directors with a view of obtaining some sort of license to trade, which would serve for the floatation of a company. On June 17th, proposals were laid before the adventurers with a view to the formation of an undertaking to trade to the south-east coast of Africa on the basis that the promoters would pay £300,000 for such a license for 31 years and in addition a royalty of 10 per cent. on all the goods exported[4]. The company, however, determined that it would be most advantageous to work this trade itself, and it was resolved to give such gratuity to the proposers of the scheme as the directors thought fit, if it was found practicable[5]. The beginning of the subsequent crisis not only precluded the extension of the company's operations but made it difficult to provide for the export of bullion for the coming season. "When we took up in August last," the directors wrote, " the large quantity of shipping before mentioned, it was upon the prospect of our trade being carried on with its usuall currency, but some little time after that a general stagnation of credit overspread all these parts of Europe: Holland, France, Spain and Italy as well as Great Britain have felt the sad effects of it, each country affecting the others in so much that bullion was not to be gotten, tho' we thought we had made a sufficient provision of it. The merchants abroad were afraid of parting with their ready money (for bullion is such). This was heightened by many and very eminent merchants being run upon beyond what they were able to answer, having their effects abroad. The same evil has befallen severall of the most

---

[1] Court Book, XLIX., f. 28. So far as the Court Books show the company had not been extravagant in its outlay on secret service. The only other entry after the union of this nature before 1720 was a payment of £100 in 1709. Court Book, XLIII., f. 612.

[2] Vide infra, Div. x. § 5.　　　　[3] Harris, Bibliotheca, ut supra, I. p. 915.
[4] Court Book, XLIX., f. 42.　　　　[5] Ibid., f. 45.

eminent bankers in this and the neighbouring countries. It is not much to the purpose to give you an account of the first spring of this common calamity, you will hear more or less of it from severall hands. Thanks be to God, people begin to come to themselves, the generall consternation being pretty well over, so that we have reason to hope trade will take another and more advantageous turn and be brought again into its usuall channel. However this evil hath afflicted us very greatly in our last sale, so that we could not raise the ready money we depended on[1]." The scarcity of funds was such that only a limited amount of bullion could be exported. This was not divided *pro rata* amongst the various factories, but used in making full shipments to places in the far East where the competition of the Ostend company was most felt. It was hoped that this policy "would make them [*i.e.* the Ostenders] sick of it[2]."

An even more serious effect of the crisis was the pressure, brought to bear on the directors, to come to the rescue of the South Sea company. On September 15th, 1720, a committee was appointed to treat with representatives of the Bank and of the South Sea company to take such steps as were judged necessary for maintaining the public credit. On December 2nd, a general court was held, which was followed by a further meeting on the 5th. A proposal, made by the ministry, was discussed. This scheme was to the effect that nine millions of the debt, due by the State to the South Sea company, should be purchased from it by the East India Adventurers[3]. It was intended that payment should be made by a creation of India stock, which was to be rated at 120, as against South Sea stock at par. Though this ratio represented the difference in market values at the time the scheme was drafted, the directors of the East India company were of opinion that the fall in South Sea stock had not yet come to an end. Accordingly, they replied that the proposition was unreasonable, since it would reduce the dividend, and a counter proposal was put forward, which provided that a bonus of 20 per cent. on the nine millions should be paid to the company. It was contemplated that this bonus should be dealt with as follows: part of it was to be used in adding 20 per cent. to the holding of every member, while the remainder would be retained for the benefit of the company[4]. Eventually, after a protracted discussion, an act was passed by which nine millions of the debt due to the South Sea company might be engrafted on the East India capital, but since this measure was permissive, not obligatory, the latter company did not put the proposal into practice.

[1] Letter to the President and Council at Bombay, February 24, 1721: Letter Book, xvii., ff. 539, 540.
[2] Court Book, xlix., f. 113. [3] Court Book, xlix., ff. 176, 179.
[4] Court Book, xlix., ff. 183, 192, 199, 200.

Capital up to 1720.

	£	£
Stock owned by the Old Company in loan of 1698 ...	988,500	
Additional stock created under the act of 1708 and transferred to the members of the Old Company	593,000	1,581,500
Stock of New Company (arising out of loan of 1698) ...	988,500	
Additional stock of 1708 transferred to members of the New Company	593,000	1,581,500
Total capital of the United Company 1709		3,163,000
Additions thereto 1709 to 1717		31,080
Total 1718 to 1720		3,194,080

Prices and Dividends.

Year	Prices			Dividends[1]		
	Date of highest price	Prices	Date of lowest price	Extending from	Fraction of a year	Rate % per annum
1709	Aug. 5, Sept. 22	134—113$\frac{1}{2}$	Apr. 15, Aug. 5	Xmas 1708 to Lady-day 1709	$\frac{1}{4}$	5
				Lady-day 1709 to Mich. 1709	$\frac{1}{2}$	8
				Mich. 1709 to Mich. 1710	1	9
1710	Feb. 24, 27, Mar. 20, 24, 25	140—112	Nov. 1	Mich. 1710 to Mich. 1711	1	9
1711	Nov. 19	132—108	Aug. 29			
1712	Dec. 29	127$\frac{1}{4}$—108$\frac{3}{4}$	July 30, Aug. 1	Mich. 1712 to Mids. 1713	$\frac{3}{4}$	10
1713	Sept. 10	128$\frac{3}{4}$—120	Feb. 26			
1714	Sept. 20	141—116$\frac{3}{4}$	Apr. 2	Mids. 1714 to Mids. 1715	1	10
1715	May 11	144$\frac{3}{4}$—126	Oct. 27	Mids. 1715 to Mids. 1716	1	10
1716	Oct. 14	188—131$\frac{1}{4}$	Jan. 24—30	Xmas 1716 to Mids. 1717	$\frac{1}{2}$	10
1717	Dec. 30	210—158$\frac{1}{4}$	March 8	Mids. 1717 to Mids. 1718	1	10
1718	March 10	219$\frac{1}{2}$—183	Oct. 8, 9	Mids. 1718 to Mids. 1719	1	10
1719	Jan. 5, Feb. 9	214—188	Aug. 10	Mids. 1719 to Mids. 1720	1	10
1720	June 23	449—140	Dec. 17	Mids. 1720 to Mids. 1721	1	10

[1] *Report from the Committee of Secrecy to enquire into the state of the East India Company*, IV. p. 73. It is to be noted that the rate per cent. given above is *per annum* not the actual rate paid which was often for periods of $\frac{1}{2}$ and occasionally for $\frac{1}{4}$ year, and once for $\frac{3}{4}$ of a year. Thus the payment of the 5% dividend (on £3,163,000) for $\frac{1}{4}$ year at 5% *per annum* came to £39,540, that for $\frac{3}{4}$ of a year at 10% *per annum* to £237,240, while the next distribution at the same rate being for a whole year amounted to £316,320.

E. The Company of Scotland trading to Africa and the Indies.

The African or Darien Company[1] (1695–1707).

Of all the trading associations mentioned in this volume there is none (with the possible exception of the Old East India company) that has gained so much attention and the history of which has been so fully recorded as that of the ill-fated Darien enterprize. This fact is accounted for not only by the natural interest of Scottish historians in the bid for a colonial empire by their countrymen, but also through the grandeur of the scheme, which, in the words of its founder, aimed at securing "the door of the seas—the key of the universe," the enthusiasm which it inspired in Scotland, and finally the intensity of bitterness against England, which accompanied the awakening of the nation after its disillusionment.

The place of this venture, in Scottish commercial policy, is related to the state of industry in that country in the closing years of the seventeenth century—in fact if Darien were "the key of the universe," a Scottish colonial empire was the key-stone of the Parliamentary legislation since the Restoration[2]. The political aspect of the scheme has also been expounded, often with considerable acrimony and sometimes with no little eloquence, both by the pamphleteers of the seventeenth and the historians of the nineteenth centuries. To complete a picture that combines both tragedy and farce it is necessary to add some details of the internal and financial history of the company which have been either ignored or relegated to a subordinate position[3].

The conception of a trading settlement at Panama was originated by William Paterson, the founder of the Bank of England, and it constituted the dream of his life. He had the genius to see that, from the commercial point of view, the isthmus of Panama possessed unique

---

[1] The classification of this company, according to the method adopted in the present work, presents some difficulty. The scheme *as conceived* was related to foreign trade, but in so far as *it was carried out* it had an affinity to the colonizing enterprizes dealt with in the next division. For various reasons it is more convenient to treat the Darien company in connection with the foreign-trading bodies, even though this course involves the treatment of the colony of New Caledonia, before Nova Scotia, *vide* Division II. § 4.

[2] *Vide infra*, Division IX. § 1.

[3] Since this account was written there have appeared *The Early History of the Scots Darien Company* by Hiram Bingham, in *The Scottish Historical Review*, III. pp. 210, 316, 437; and *A History of William Paterson and the Darien Company*, by James Samuel Barbour, Edinburgh, 1907. I am much indebted to Mr Barbour for the care with which he has read my history of this company, and for several valuable suggestions.

advantages as a possible *entrepôt* for the trade between the East and the West. Oriental products could be conveyed to European markets in almost a straight line from the port at which they were shipped, and, by being unloaded at Panama, could be re-shipped in vessels waiting to convey them to Europe. Voyages would be shortened by more than half, and, by improved facilities for trade, the consumption of home commodities would be more than doubled[1]. While working as a merchant in the West Indies, Paterson had realized the possibility of such a scheme, and on his return home had hoped to realize it. According to one account, he endeavoured to obtain support not only in London but abroad, without being able to attract capital[2]. It was only when Scotland had become desirous of building up a foreign trade that Paterson's opportunity came. Having heard from a friend in London that the Parliament at Edinburgh was prepared to consider favourably schemes for commerce abroad, he drafted certain proposals about May 1695, which were well received in Scotland and an act for establishing the company was soon prepared, which was duly considered and amended on June 15th, 17th, 21st, and again on the 25th, 1695, by the Committee of Trade[3]. It was passed by Parliament on June 26th. The title of the company, thereby incorporated, and also by a patent, was *the Company of Scotland trading to Africa and the Indies*. At least half the capital was to be allotted to Scotsmen, and the minimum subscription was £100 sterling and the maximum £3,000. Provision was also made that stock, allotted to Scotsmen, could only be transferred to Scotsmen resident within the kingdom. The powers, which were common in English patents for similar undertakings, such as the right of possessing absolutely lands not in the possession of a friendly Christian Prince, of making peace and war under similar limitations, were also granted[4]. The company was vested with the exclusive privilege of trading to Africa and the Indies as against all other Scotsmen. The management was in the hands of twenty directors—a number which was subsequently increased to fifty[5].

To retain Paterson's services an agreement had been made by which he was to receive 2 per cent. of the total capital subscribed, as well as a commission of 3 per cent. on the profits made during the first twenty-

[1] "A Proposal to Plant a Colony in Darien," 1701, in *The Writings of William Paterson*, edited by S. Bannister, 1858, i. p. 147; cf. *A History of William Paterson and the Darien Company*, by J. S. Barbour, Edinburgh, 1907, p. 40.

[2] Dalrymple, *Memoirs*, Edinburgh, 1773, ii. p. 95.

[3] Parliamentary Papers, 1695 (General Register House, Edinburgh), "Minutes of the Committee of Trade."

[4] *Acts of the Parliaments of Scotland*, ix. pp. 377-9.

[5] Miscellaneous Collection of MSS. and other Papers relating to the Darien Company (Advocates' Library), i. p. 19.

one years[1]. From some of his correspondence, which has been preserved, it is clear that Paterson was the moving spirit in the undertaking. The first steps presented the extraordinary contrast of being taken in Scotland with the enthusiastic support of the ministry, while in England those interested in the infant company had to act with the secrecy of conspirators. It must be remembered that the East India company under the patent of James II. (which had been ratified by William III.) had the monopoly of the Indian trade, and *all subjects* of the King, except the company, were forbidden to enter the prescribed limits for purposes of commerce[2]. Therefore an Englishman, or a Scotsman resident in England, was necessarily bound by this patent, and his joining the Scottish company rendered him liable to be treated as an interloper. Paterson was fully aware of this danger, and he urged the other founders of the enterprize in Edinburgh to "so act that their principal designs would only be discovered by their executions[3]." Writing again four days later (July 9th, 1695) he says that his supporters in London think "we ought to keep private and close for some months to come that no occasion may be given for the Parliament of England directly or indirectly to take notice of it" (*i.e.* the proceedings of the company)[4]. Accordingly, those who had joined the company in England "bound themselves by oath not to disclose anything that shall be given them in charge by the president of the court to be kept secret[5]," and, the secretary had also sworn not to reveal the names of subscribers or the amounts subscribed[6]. On October 22nd the same declaration was repeated in a more stringent form, namely "that all discourses and transactions of the company were to be inviolably kept secret from all other persons whatsoever[7]."

Meanwhile the amount of capital to be offered for subscription was discussed. At first Paterson proposed that only £360,000 of stock should be issued—half being available for Scotland and the other half for selected persons in England[8]. Under the company's act the sub-

---

[1] "Preamble for Subscriptions," *Journals of the House of Commons*, xi. p. 406.

[2] *Charters granted to the East India Company*, i. p. 127. "The said King did thereby for himself his heirs and successors further grant to the said Governor and Company and their successors that the said East Indies...should not be visited, frequented or haunted by any of the subjects of him his heirs and successors."

[3] *The Darien Papers: being a Selection of Original Letters and Documents relating to the Establishment of a Colony at Darien by the Company of Scotland trading to Africa and the Indies*, 1695–1700 [edited by J. H. Burton], Edinburgh (Bannatyne Club, 1849), p. 1.

[4] *Ibid.*, p. 3.

[5] *Journals of the House of Commons*, xi. p. 401.

[6] *Ibid.*, p. 401.

[7] *Ibid.*, p. 402.

[8] *Darien Papers, ut supra*, p. 1.

scription list was to remain open till August 1st, 1696, unless the whole amount offered was subscribed earlier. Paterson was of opinion that the lists in Scotland should not be opened till "within three or four months of that time." "For," he continues, "if we should lay bookes open in Scotland for six or eight months or a year together we should become ridiculous at home and abroad, and for that we have many instances here in England, where, when the Parliament gives a long day for money, that fund has hardly ever success; and where the dayes are short they seldom ever fail. The Bank of England had but six weekes time from the opening of the bookes and was finished in nine dayes and in all subscriptions here it is always limited to a short day; for if a thing goe not on with the first heat, the raising of a fund seldom or never succeeds, the multitude being commonly ledd more by example than reason. Besides, if we take care to publish our subscriptions and the times of it sufficiently through the kingdom for three or four months, none will have reason to complain, and every man will have time enough to enter, unless it be full sooner. Thus they think, that if good and solid preparations be made, the subscriptions may be time enough begun about the beginning of April next, and then hope it will soon be full[1]." Evidently Paterson's plans involved the maturing of all the preliminary steps of the venture and then opening lists for subscriptions in Scotland, as he says, in April 1696, while an equal amount of stock was likely to be taken up simultaneously in London.

The effect of his advice on the supporters of the scheme in Scotland produced a postponement of the public issue of stock, but in the meantime events in England, by the beginning of September, had altered the position of affairs. On the 3rd of that month Paterson wrote from London that "what was before a reason for us to delay our business for a time, proves now an argument for us to hasten it, because it is now as publick as it can well be[2]." For the next six weeks the members of the company in Edinburgh were urged to send three of those named in the act to London, so that, with ten persons there who were also mentioned in the act, a quorum might be constituted[3]. By the 29th of August, a meeting had been held, directors elected, and in November the court met regularly in London for a brief period.

The result of the need for haste made it imperative that capital should be at the disposal of the company. The opening of the lists in Scotland had been definitely postponed till the following year, so that it fell to the group of English members to subscribe. It was found that more capital than Paterson had originally estimated would be needed, and it was decided to issue £600,000. Half of this sum (*i.e.* £300,000)

---

[1] *Darien Papers*, p. 3.   [2] *Ibid.*, p. 6.   [3] *Ibid.*, pp. 6, 7, 8.

was subscribed for, privately, by October 29th in London; and when the list closed on November 22nd, the applications exceeded the quantity of stock at the disposal of the directors, the whole amount being applied for by about two hundred persons, some of whom were stockholders in the East India company[1]. The "preamble," which corresponds to the modern application-form, is a document of some importance in the development of joint-stock enterprize. It formed a general heading, and applicants for stock "subscribed" or "underwrote" their names, hence the survival of these terms, though the former is disappearing from common use, and the latter has acquired the altered meaning[2].

Preamble:

"Pursuant to an Act of Parliament of the Kingdom of Scotland, intituled, 'An Act for a Company trading to Africa and the Indies,' we, the undersigned, do each of us, for himself, and not for one another, become obliged for the payment of the respective sums by us severally subscribed, subject to the following rules and conditions.

"That the joint-stock or capital fund of the said company do consist of £600,000 sterling, whereof one-quarter part shall be paid at the time of subscription, to two or more of the persons named in the said Act of Parliament, and the remainder thereof, in such parts and proportions, time and manner, as the company shall from time to time direct.

"That if any of the subscribers or proprietors of the said stock or capital-fund shall not pay, or cause to be paid, the remaining part of his, her or their subscription in such time, manner or proportions, as shall from time to time be appointed by the said company, or in case they or any of them shall become indebted to the said company any other ways howsoever; the part or share of stock, in the said fund belonging to such person or persons, shall, from henceforward, be and remain to the use of the said company, to be by them sold and disposed of, for paying and satisfying such debt so become due unto them.

"That in regard Mr William Paterson and others concerned with him have been at great pains and expence in making several considerable discoveries of trade and improvements in both Indies, and likewise in procuring needful powers and privileges for a company of commerce, from several sovereign princes and states; which he and they have contrived, suited and designed for the said company. In consideration whereof it is hereby agreed, that the said William Paterson, his

---

[1] *Journals of the House of Commons,* xi. p. 403; *The Manuscripts of the House of Lords,* 1695–7, ii. p. 15.

[2] A facsimile of a part of the Scottish subscription is given in *Darien Papers,* p. xxiv.

executors, administrators or assigns, shall, out of the first payment, have, and receive two per cent. of the money to be subscribed in the said capital-fund, as also three per cent. of the issues, profits and product of the said fund for the space of twenty-one years, which shall be redeemable for two per cent. more of the said capital-fund any time in five years.

"That the government, management, power and disposition of the said joint-stock or capital-fund, and other matters, things and effects whatsoever, of or belonging to the said company shall in all times hereafter be and remain in a court of directors, consisting of the persons named in the said Act of Parliament together with such others as shall be proprietors of the respective sums of £1,000 sterling or more in the said joint-stock or fund, and who shall likewise be deputed in writing by such other proprietors therein as including such £1,000 sterling or more shall complete the sum of £20,000 sterling thereof; provided that none be admitted to depute more than one person, for one and the same sum or proportion of his stock. And in case the full number of fifteen persons be not deputed by the stock, in one month after one moiety thereof shall be subscribed or if the full number of thirty persons be not deputed one month after the whole shall be subscribed, in either of the said cases the court of directors for the time, may by majority of votes signified by scroll and scrutiny, complete the said numbers or either of them.

"And it is hereby declared and understood that the persons named in the Act of Parliament or the survivors of them, are, were, and ought to be a complete court, until others be added unto them in manner aforesaid; and that the manner of completing the number and continuing the succession, of such fifty directors, appointing the times and places of meeting, the quorum of persons, the constituting and impowering of committees and sub-committees of their own members, fixing of servants, settling of fees and salaries, and all other matters and things relating to the said company, shall be ordered, fixed, and settled, in the constitutions to be made by the said court of directors; and that every director or member of the said court and all others concerned in the said company be concluded by and subject unto such elections, successions, scrutinies, censures, deprivations, disabilities, ordinances and rules as shall be made and contained in such constitutions.

"And the said joint-stock and capital-fund shall be, remain and continue subject unto all further and other rules, conditions and qualifications to be used, governed, ordered and disposed of, as the said company shall, from time to time, direct and appoint[1]."

---

[1] *Journals of the House of Commons*, xi. p. 406.

Effect on the East India Co. 1695

Immediately the capital of £300,000 available for issue, in the terms of this preamble, had been taken up, a great struggle between the English and the Scottish companies began, which was sufficiently serious for the former and a life and death matter for the latter. The East India company had been very successful up to 1691. Dividends of a considerable amount had been paid, and the stock stood at a premium[1]. From 1692 to 1694 losses of ships and difficulties with the home-government had weakened the position of the company. Still, for the first four months of 1695 the price of the stock had fluctuated within narrow limits—from 87 to 80. During May and June a sale had been recorded at 73 (June 12th), and afterwards the market advanced till 93 was reached on September 5th. In the next four weeks a reaction of over £20 had resulted from rumours of the progress of the Scottish company; and, when it was thought, at the end of October, that the floatation of the English branch of that company was likely to be successful there was a further fall of £20 in a week, reducing the price to 50, the lowest in that year. Thus the development of Paterson's scheme had effected a loss of 46 per cent. in the quotation of the stock of the company. The shock to public confidence, which these prices reflected, was on the whole justified. The East India company was in bad odour with the Government and the public. Doubtless many men were of opinion that the English Parliament might be induced to make terms either with the Scottish enterprize or with the proposed rival English companies. It was generally feared that the London interlopers, who had not joined in the settlement of 1693-4, would trade to India under authorization of the Scottish body. Under such circumstances the exemption from taxes granted to this undertaking, under the act of 1695, would have been more serious than the competition. Further, should friction between the two companies arise, as was probable, the Scottish one had been granted full powers for making reprisals, against which the English organization could not legally retaliate[2].

If the condition of the Scottish company be investigated it will be found that, while up to November 1695, it had made remarkable progress, there were very serious dangers to be faced before business could even be started with any hope of success. It had to build up a trade in Africa and the Indies by entering into competition with two long-established English companies, the one enjoying the monopoly of the African and the other that of the Indian trade. The nominal capital of the former at this time was £625,250, some of which however

---

[1] *Vide supra*, pp. 132-5, 138-9, 144, 177-9.

[2] Petition of the East India Company to the House of Lords, December 5, 1695, *The Manuscripts of the House of Lords*, II. p. 14; MS. Parliamentary Proceedings, Home Miscellaneous (India Office), xxx., *passim*.

was made up of stock issued without payment, being made as against undivided profits, and another part was accounted for by an allotment of stock at a discount, so that the total cash payments for the £625,250 stock amounted to no more than £183,440[1]. The East India company's capital now stood at £1,488,000. Taking the middle market price for the first six months of the year[2], as giving some index to the actual worth of the assets against the nominal stock, we reach the total £1,372,540 as the investor's estimate of the property owned by the two companies. Now the Scottish undertaking had ventured to enter into competition with a proposed capital of no more than £600,000, of which at this date £300,000 had been taken up, and on which only £75,000 was called. Therefore, in round numbers, the capital of the Darien company, when all subscribed, would be less than half that of its rivals, and at the date of the struggle with the East India company, the new venture had a capital called up which amounted to the paltry total of but 5 per cent. of the estimated value of that of the African and East India companies. Thus the Scottish enterprize had a hard battle before it, even if it could obtain all the proposed capital of £600,000; but if its opponents could arrange that no funds, except those of Scotland, were available for the prosecution of the scheme (owing to the meagre quantity of capital for investment north of the Tweed), the whole project would collapse for want of the necessary support. Therefore the real fate of the venture was decided on the exchanges of London and Amsterdam, and that too before the subscription in Scotland had been completed and before a single ship had sailed to that golden West from which so much was expected. Paterson was too far-seeing to neglect this aspect of the question, and a few months before the financial battle was fought he clearly outlined the results of defeat to his side. Writing on July 9th, 1695, of the need of a large capital he said, "we may be sure, should we only settle some little colony or plantation and send some ships, they would look upon them as interlopers and all agree to discourage and crush us to pieces[3]"—and it was precisely the object of the East India company that its rival should have resources "only to settle some little colony."

The weak point in the organization of the Scottish company is to be found in the necessity of raising capital outside Scotland. Whatever view may be taken of the respective rights of the rival businesses—the one endowed with a monopoly of the India trade as against all subjects of the King by patent, and the other granted liberty to conduct

---

[1] *Vide supra*, p. 33.

[2] 22 in the case of the Royal African Company, and 83 in that of the East India company.

[3] *Darien Papers, ut supra*, p. 3.

commercial operations within the same limits by act of the Scottish Parliament—it is apparent that the legal position of persons resident in England, who joined the Darien company, was exceedingly doubtful. The East India company seized upon this fact and, by means of its dear-bought Parliamentary influence, brought the matter before the Houses of Lords and Commons in December 1695. An address was presented to the King, which pointed out *inter alia* that, under the act of the Darien company, Scotland "must be the magazine" of eastern and colonial produce to the great detriment of England. To this address the King replied that "I have been ill-served in Scotland, but I hope some remedies may be found to prevent the inconveniencies which may arise from this act[1]." The House of Commons, under the prompting of the East India company, decided to seize the papers of the subscribers to the Scots company resident in England and to impeach the leading members of high crimes and misdemeanours[2]. After such a marked example of the displeasure of Parliament, the stockholders allowed their interests to lapse, through failing to pay the 25 per cent. deposit required in terms of the preamble, and the £300,000 capital subscribed was thus no longer available[3].

At the beginning of the year 1696 the position of the scheme was almost hopeless. It had been incorporated for over six months and was without any capital resources whatever. Not only so, but the area from which funds could be raised was now confined to Scotland, and probably the opponents of the company, relying on the poverty of the latter country, counted that the battle was all but won. If such an expectation had been formed, the enthusiasm of the Scottish people and the magnetism of the personality of Paterson had been overlooked. Being one of those impeached by the English Parliament, Paterson found it advisable to leave England for a time. On his arrival at Edinburgh, according to an account of an opponent, "he had more respect paid him than the King's High Commissioner, and happy was he or she that had a quarter of an hour's conversation with this blessed man. When he appeared in public he looked with a head so full of business and care as if he had Atlas's burthen on his back. If a man had a fancy to be reputed wise, the first step he was to make was to mimic Paterson's phiz[4]." According to the suggestion of Hill Burton, it may have been that the strenuous opposition of England had con-

[1] *Journals of the House of Lords*, xv. p. 615.
[2] *Journals of the House of Commons*, xi. p. 407.
[3] According to Anderson, in cases where the 25 per cent. deposit had been paid, the money was returned. Anderson, *Historical and Chronological Deduction of the Origin of Commerce*, 1790, iii. p. 152.
[4] Quoted in Bannister, *Life of William Paterson*, ii. p. 274.

vinced the Scots of the benefits of the proposal, and therefore the scheme seemed not only advantageous, but a matter of patriotism—"Scotland would now keep to herself the glory and all the other rewards of the great national undertaking[1]." The more reflective investors saw in the scheme the last stake in the great game of making Scotland a manufacturing country, while the enthusiastic had dreams of an important foreign trade and of gold discoveries. The lists for subscriptions of the £300,000 sterling originally intended for Scotland, were opened on February 26th, 1696[2], and, considering the situation, there was a rush to obtain stock, close on £50,000 nominal being subscribed the first day. Popular sentiment was altogether in favour of the enterprize, so that the nobility, the merchants, even public bodies, were anxious to support such a laudable scheme and share in the benefits anticipated from it. According to Dalrymple, "the frenzy of the Scots nation to sign the Solemn League and Covenant never exceeded the rapidity with which they ran to subscribe to the Darien company. The nobility, the gentry, the merchants, the people, the Royal Burghs without the exception of one and most of the other public bodies subscribed. Young women threw their little fortunes into the stock, widows sold their jointures to get command of money for the same purpose[3]." Pamphlets in favour of the scheme were issued and applications for stock were handed in by a vast number of subscribers during the five months the lists remained open. The directors, finding that the issue of capital was so well received, endeavoured to complete the authorized amount of £600,000, by adding £100,000 to the £300,000 already available in Scotland, making it thereby £400,000, while the remaining £200,000 was offered for subscription in Hamburg[4]. The court however discovered that the English company had a long arm and its opposition began to be felt again. The attitude of the Dutch East India company is more obscure. It might either disapprove of a Scots company as a competitor to itself or, on the other hand, it might encourage it so as to plant a rival to the English company at its very door. It would appear that Paterson's enlightened views on freedom of trade alienated Dutch support; and, no doubt, the strongly expressed views of the English resident had considerable weight. Finally the foreign merchants returned the diplomatic reply that they were prepared to support the project, if the company could procure a declaration from the King sanctioning their proceedings abroad. This declaration, for

---

[1] *The History of Scotland*, by John Hill Burton, Edinburgh, 1873, VIII. p. 28.
[2] *Darien Papers, ut supra*, p. 371.
[3] *Memoirs of Great Britain and Ireland, ut supra*, II. p. 96.
[4] Hill Burton, *History of Scotland, ut supra*, VIII. p. 37.

DIV. I. § 5 E] *The Scottish Subscription* 1696   217

reasons to be investigated below, was not forthcoming, and consequently no capital came from the Continent.

Thus the company was forced to rely solely on the capital that could be raised at home. In spite of the favour with which the formation of the enterprize had been received, great difficulty was experienced in inducing people to take up the whole £400,000 of stock. The subscription list was due to be closed on August 1st, and a few days before there was still a balance not taken up. On the 1st of the month two prominent members of the company entered their names for the quantity remaining and the subscriptions were closed. In this case the deposit was returned to the underwriters in 1700[1]. The payment of the deposit of 25 per cent. was fixed for June 1st, 1696; and, to encourage prompt payment, discount at the rate of 3 per cent. per quarter was allowed on all prepayments[2]. It was also arranged that this call should bear interest from August 1st, 1698.

This first call was duly met in most cases. It should have produced £100,000 and actually realized £98,223. 17s. $2\frac{3}{4}d.$[3], and it was with this amount of capital that the operations of the company were started. Immediately calls began to be paid in, it was decided (on June 18th, 1696) to issue bank-notes[4]. Some of these found their way into circulation as loans, made by the company to stockholders on the security of their stock. It is curious to find a company, whose policy was directed by a man like Paterson with sound views on credit, sanctioning such a course, one which was responsible for the failure of Law's Mississippi scheme in 1719 and of the South Sea company in 1720. As shown elsewhere, about this time, there was a movement towards the issue of paper money on insufficient security in Scotland[5], and Paterson may have been overruled by his colleagues; or again it may have seemed necessary to make loans to proprietors who had subscribed for more stock than they could pay the calls on, so as to enable the further payments to be made. The directors, requiring more capital, found that the stockholders were indisposed to honour additional calls till the results of the undertaking had been seen. Therefore those made, after the first, were of a ludicrously small amount, as is shown by the following list.

[1] *Darien Papers, ut supra*, p. xxiv.
[2] Hill Burton (*Ibid.*, p. xxvi.) gives the rate of discount at three per cent. This however represents the allowance for three months, and therefore Mr Barbour states the rate per annum at 12 per cent. *Hist. of W. Paterson and the Darien Company*, p. 26.
[3] *Darien Papers*, p. xxvi.
[4] *Ibid.*, p. 9, *vide infra*, Bank of Scotland, Division x. § 3.
[5] *Vide infra*, Bank of Scotland, Division x. § 3.

Calls made by the Council of the Darien Company[1].

On application 25 per cent. payable on June 1, 1696, bearing interest from August 1, 1698.

1st call, one half of 7½ per cent. payable on November 11, 1698, bearing interest from November 11, 1698.

2nd call, one half of 7½ per cent. payable at Candlemas 1699, bearing interest from Candlemas 1699.

3rd call, 5 per cent. payable on May 15, 1699, bearing interest from May 15, 1699.

4th call, 2½ per cent. payable on November 11, 1699, bearing interest from November 11, 1699.

5th call, 2½ per cent. payable on February 2, 1700, bearing interest from February 2, 1700.

Thus the total calls of 42½ per cent. should have produced £170,000, but in 1707 only £153,631. 7s. 10¾d. had been paid, leaving nearly 10 per cent. outstanding[2]. Thus the company was reduced to a position little better than that which Paterson had seen in 1695 was hopeless, for with a capital of such small amount, even under the most favourable circumstances, nothing more could be achieved than the founding of a small colony which was likely to be treated as a band of interlopers, and this in effect is exactly what happened. The relative disproportion of the resources of the company, as compared with the estimated value of the assets of the East India and African companies, may be seen perhaps more clearly when it is remembered that the paid up capital of the former was very little more than one-tenth of the market valuation of the combined stocks of the latter[3].

The company would have found success all but impossible with such meagre paid up capital, but circumstances, united with bad management, made failure certain. Even with Paterson's local knowledge, it would have been a matter of the greatest difficulty to obtain a temporary appearance of success by one or two successful voyages before the place of the company's operations abroad was known. But as early as 1696, his influence was materially weakened by disputes amongst the directors. Paterson all along had fixed on Darien as the place to be settled, but other members of the court were in favour of sending expeditions to India[4]. Such differences of opinion produced tension, and about 1697 an unfortunate incident happened, which deprived him of influence. To obtain ships and stores for the expedition,

---

[1] *Darien Papers, ut supra*, pp. xxv., xxvi.

[2] Balance Sheet of the Company in Miscellaneous Collection of Papers (Advocates' Library), vol. III., No. 70. This sum is slightly in excess of that given by Hill Burton in *Darien Papers*, p. xxvi., the reason probably being that he quotes from a document made at an earlier date when the amount in arrear was larger.

[3] *Vide supra*, p. 214.

[4] Bannister, *Life of Paterson, ut supra*, I. p. xlviii.

which was being prepared, a large sum of money was entrusted to Paterson to make payments in Holland. He remitted it to a trusted correspondent there, but his agent absconded with a considerable part of the money. Though Paterson was exonerated, he lost weight in the councils of the company and so was forced to sail as a volunteer, without any powers to decide the proceedings of the expedition[1].

The loss of Paterson's experience was the beginning of a series of blunders. The expedition, which started in the latter half of July 1698, was ill-equipped and badly organized[2]. The ships were freighted with manufactured commodities, for many of which there was no demand from the savage population at Darien. It would appear that the greater part of the money provided by payments of the first call was expended on the vessels and their cargoes[3]. The provisioning of the fleet was cut too fine, under the impression that the colony would be able to obtain food from the natives in exchange for the goods it brought to sell. According to Defoe very little cash was available, and it is to this oversight that many of the subsequent hardships of the expedition are to be ascribed[4].

Not only was the equipment imperfect but the organization was faulty. There was no adequate scheme for the direction of the colonists, and the system of government by a council, without any duly appointed chief, led to frequent and unseemly disputes. When this body spent its time in intrigues, the spirit of insubordination spread amongst the colonists. Proper measures for the health and provisioning of the settlement were neglected, and there was much sickness during the rainy season. The directors at home took no measures to support the enterprize by sending fresh supplies and reinforcements, so that there was no prospect of success remaining.

It only needed the opposition of the Spaniards, who claimed the territory occupied by the Scots, to render the position untenable. Though a first Spanish expedition to dislodge the immigrants had been beaten off, a serious blunder was made in the attempt to exact reprisals. A Jamaica sloop, commanded by an Englishman, was seized by the colonists and confiscated by the council, either by mistake or under the supposition that it was owned by Spaniards. The representations of

[1] Bannister, *Life of Paterson, ut supra,* I. pp. l.–lv.
[2] The following account of the expeditions to Darien is condensed from the history of the enterprize given in the following and other works, *Darien Papers, ut supra*; Burton, *History of Scotland*; Anderson, *Annals of Commerce*; Chambers, *Domestic Annals of Scotland*; MacIntosh, *History of Civilization in Scotland*; MacKinnon, *Union of England and Scotland.*
[3] For the details *vide* Barbour, *Hist. of W. Paterson and the Darien Company,* pp. 50–1.
[4] *History, ut supra,* p. 35.

the Spanish Ambassador at the English Court had weight with the King, and a proclamation was issued by the Governor of Jamaica forbidding persons under his jurisdiction to hold any correspondence with the Scots colony. Under these accumulated misfortunes, the settlement was abandoned on March 31st, 1700, by the few emaciated survivors, who found great difficulty in manning the remaining ships.

Meanwhile the directors of the company were making preparations to support the first expedition. During the end of 1698 and the year 1699, 15 per cent. was called up from the proprietors, and as the money was paid in (which should have amounted to £60,000) more ships were purchased. In May and September, successive expeditions were dispatched, but the same causes, that had made the first voyage a failure, rendered these also unsuccessful. There is no little irony in the fact that Edinburgh was illuminated on or about June 20th, 1700, to celebrate the receipt of news of a temporary success against the Spaniards when the colony had been evacuated by the settlers two months earlier. Thus after an active existence of little more than two years the main design of the company had ended in disaster and the loss of the paid up capital.

As often happens, when some enterprize, from a great campaign to a filibustering voyage, has been spoiled by mismanagement, those responsible looked for a scape-goat and were the first to cry "nous sommes trahis." In Scotland, it was almost universally believed that England was responsible for the failure of the expeditions. No doubt the hostility of the East India company had rendered the success of the Scots scheme impossible from the beginning, but this opposition had failed to make the same impression on the popular imagination as the aloofness of the King and the needless severity (as matters turned out) of the Jamaica proclamation. The refusal of succour to starving men has seemed to many a blot on the administration of William III. However the slowness of communication with America at the end of the seventeenth century must be borne in mind, and it is not improbable that the hint on which the proclamation was based was sent from London at a time when there was no expectation that the Darien colonists would have been reduced to the dire distress into which they afterwards fell[1]. In fact Sir William Vernon, who issued the proclamation, wrote on December 14th, 1700, that "he was willing to show the Scots what respect he could and they have owned so much[2]."

It has sometimes been considered that, under existing treaties between

---

[1] The instructions were sent from London in January 1699. As late as May of the same year it was believed in Scotland that the colony was flourishing.

[2] *Darien Papers*, p. 304.

England and Spain, William III. was bound to discourage the Scots colony[1]. But such interpretation of the facts depends upon the supposition that England admitted that the isthmus of Darien was in the possession of the Spanish Crown. No doubt the place was within the sphere of Spanish influence, but it would appear that there had as yet been no effective occupation by any Europeans. As early as September 16th, 1697, that is nearly a year before the first expedition had started for Darien, the English Committee of Trade had reported that this tract of land had never been possessed by the Spaniards[2]. This being so, it would seem at first sight that it was the duty of William III. to support his Scottish subjects, even at the risk of a war with Spain. But there was a higher duty to be considered, namely the security of Great Britain as a whole. In fact, the procuring of a favourable balance of trade for Scotland had to give way to maintaining the balance of power in Europe, upon which, according to the statesmanship of the period, the interests of both England and Scotland were dependent. Any false step by William might have provoked an European war, and it would have been dangerous in the highest degree to have openly encouraged the Darien enterprize[3]. In addition to these reasons against supporting the expedition, there was also the fact, already explained, that from the beginning success was all but impossible, and the English statesmen were sufficiently far-sighted to have recognized the fact. Therefore William was bound to discourage the undertaking, and doubtless he was well aware that he was only hastening a result that would have come to pass in any case.

Reasons such as these could not be appreciated in Scotland at a time when the country was seething with indignation. The harvests had been very bad for some years and the people felt the pinch. The period from 1693 to 1700 was known as "the seven ill years," and a number of parishes in Aberdeenshire and other parts of the country were depopulated[4]. Many investors in the company had subscribed for as much stock as they could pay the deposit money of 25 per cent. on. Therefore the subsequent calls, small as they were, could only be met with the greatest difficulty. Taking the financial condition of the country as a whole, investments had been made beyond the quantity of capital available. The funds subscribed to the Darien company were lost, and, with the failure to establish a colonial trade, many of the

[1] Hill Burton, *History of Scotland*, VIII. p. 48.
[2] Bannister, *Life of William Paterson*, II. p. 261; amongst the signatures to this report is that of J. Locke.
[3] Cf. *The History of the Union*, by James MacKinnon, p. 45.
[4] *On the Price of Wheat at Haddington from 1627 to 1897*, by R. C. Mossman, in *Accountants' Magazine*, 1900.

recently founded manufactures had collapsed. The prolonged efforts of Parliament and the monied classes to inaugurate a new era of extension of commerce had ended in a lamentable disaster, which left not only serious losses but also a widespread condition of indebtedness from which it would take the country years to recover[1].

The source of this state of embarrassment was to be found in the collapse of the Darien company, and it was to the re-establishment of this enterprize that people looked to recover some of their losses. In January, 1701, Parliament considered the business of the African and Indian company. Motions were proposed protesting in the strongest terms against the proceedings of the English Parliament in 1695 as "an undue intermeddling with the affairs of this Kingdom." The memorial presented to the Senate of Hamburg by Sir Peter Rycaut (which prevented foreign subscriptions) was declared "most unwarrantable" and "contrary to the law of nations." The Jamaica proclamation was characterized as "injurious and prejudicial to the rights and liberties of the company and its execution inhuman, barbarous, and contrary to international law." It was also moved that the colony at New Caledonia was a legal and rightful settlement; and again that the seizure of the *Dolphin*, one of the company's ships by the Spaniards, was contrary to existing treaties. The debate was marked by extraordinary scenes of clamour, and a division could only be taken when the members had exhausted both patience and breath[2]. It was at last decided to state the grievances of the company in the form of an Address to the King, in which the petitioners prayed the prevention of "all encroachments for the future, that may be made, either by your Majesty's ministers abroad or any other, to the prejudice of the kingdom and our said company or any other we may lawfully design, and to assure the company protection in their just rights and privileges and reparation for the losses, suffered by the injuries and violence of the Spaniards[3]." William had come to see that the only method to prevent future disputes of the same kind was through a more complete Union of the two countries, and, in February 1700, he recommended the consideration of this problem to the House of Lords. Through the jealousy of what the House of Commons considered undue interference by the Lords, the first named body rejected the proposal, and so for the time the matter

---

[1] The financial distress is clearly shown in many entries in the minutes of the Newmills company from 1701. *The Records of a Scottish Cloth Manufactory at New Mills, Haddingtonshire*, 1681–1703, edited by W. R. Scott (Edin. Scottish Hist. Soc. 1905), pp. 222–356.

[2] "The cry rose again till they were all, as it were, out of breath, and a silence for some time." Hume, *Diary*, p. 54.

[3] *Acts of the Parliaments of Scotland*, x. p. 250.

was dropped[1]. Further negotiations towards a Union in 1702 and 1703 broke down, and the year 1704 was one of very great tension between the two countries.

It seemed fated that the Darien company should be brought into prominence in the adjustment of relations between England and Scotland. Though the capital had been lost, attempts were still made to carry on some sort of foreign trade by means of borrowed money. Such expeditions had to run the gauntlet so as to escape seizure by the two English East India companies, which were now in process of amalgamation[2]. A ship, belonging to the Scots company, had been seized in the Thames, and the latter body retaliated by arresting the captain and crew of a vessel owned by the New English India company, which had put into the Forth. Not only so, but the popular feeling against the English companies was vented on the unfortunate prisoners, who were executed on an unfounded charge of piracy[3].

Circumstances of this kind constitute a sufficient commentary on the proposals made on June 21st, 1706, by the Scottish Commissioners for framing the Union, that "the rights and privileges of the company in Scotland trading to Africa and the Indies do continue in force after the Union." This proposition was impossible for many reasons. The recent execution of English seamen at Edinburgh was an object-lesson as to what might be expected if the Scottish company were to co-exist, not only in competition but in bitter animosity with the English ones. Under the act of the Scottish Parliament, passed on September 16th, 1703, not only were all the privileges of the company confirmed, but also it was authorized to "communicate" them to others, and it was further enacted that "all persons and ships trading to Asia, Africa or America by the commission or permission under the said company's seal and returning to Scotland, in the terms of the said act of Parliament and Letters Patent, are and shall be hereby entitled to and invested with all privileges and immunities contained in the said acts, as fully and freely in all respects as if the absolute property of both ship and cargo did entirely belong to the said company[4]." English trade had been disorganized for over five years by the strife between the "Old" and the "New" East India companies, which had only just been over-

[1] *Journals of the House of Lords*, February 12, 1700.
[2] *Vide supra*, pp. 167-76, 182-8.
[3] Mr Andrew Lang, after investigating the available evidence, has decided that Green (the English captain) had been guilty of piracy off the coast of Malabar, but that the vessel he seized was not the *Speedy Return* belonging to the Darien company, though it was for the "murder" of the crew of the latter that Green and others were condemned. *Historical Mysteries*, London, 1904, pp. 193-213.
[4] *The Proceedings of the Parliament of Scotland begun at Edinburgh, 6th May,* 1703. Printed in the year 1704, p. 46, Appendix VIII.

come by arrangements for an amalgamation that was not yet complete. To have recognized the Scottish company would have involved the revival of a similar state of contest in a more acute form. As the fusion of interests of the two English companies was not consummated till 1708, it would have been possible to have arranged that shareholders in the Darien company could join the United English company. But there was one fatal objection, which prevented such a scheme from being proposed. Quite apart from the unwillingness of the English East India stockholders to admit Scotsmen, the amalgamation of the English companies had been accomplished on the basis of a valuation of their respective assets, and the Scots company not only had lost all its capital but was considerably in debt.

	£	s.	d.
When the accounts were made up, the assets amounted to the small sum of...	1,654	11	0$\frac{3}{4}$
Against which there were debts and interest thereon of ...	14,809	18	11
Leaving a balance against the company of ...	£13,155	7	10$\frac{1}{4}$[1]

Still more important, in spite of the protests of the directors, the public in Scotland had lost faith in their powers to raise more capital. Even when the Union was under discussion and there was a prospect that there would be some compensation paid to the proprietors, the stock was sold at a mere fraction of its nominal value[2]. Defoe, writing at the time, stated "that the interest in the said stock was come to so low an ebb that people valued themselves little or nothing on their shares in it," and were glad to effect a sale so as to be secured against the dread of further calls[3].

For these reasons the company was dead and there was no prospect of its reconstruction after the Union. At the same time England was determined that the company should be wound up finally, and that the friction which had existed over the East India and colonial trade for the last ten years should be ended. The position then was as follows: Scotland had formed a company which was bankrupt, but the privileges granted the undertaking remained. At present these were worthless[4],

---

[1] *Report of the Committee concerning the Indian and African Company*, Edinburgh, 1707.

[2] *Vide infra*, p. 226. Thus Paterson writes, in the debate of the Wednesday Club, January 16, 1706, that "the principal lost together with interest at 6 per cent. should be paid to the proprietors." *An Inquiry into the Reasonableness and Consequences of an Union with Scotland*, London, 1706, p. 94.

[3] *History of the Union*, p. 156.

[4] The privileges were worthless because there was no capital for developing a trade on any large scale. It was said that some English merchants would have given £4,000,000 for the franchises of the company, but, owing to the restrictions as to the holding of stock, these were useless to any but Scotsmen.

but in some unforeseen contingency they might become of value. As long as there was a second company in Britain it was a menace to the English India trade. The Scots had something which, while useless to themselves, was dangerous to England, and therefore, considering the poverty of the one country and the comparative wealth of the other, and the reiterated charges that the failure of the company was due to English jealousy, the case became one for compensation for the Darien proprietors on condition that the company should be wound up.

The only doubtful point that remained was the exact amount that should be offered the stockholders. Although, when it came to the actual bargaining, some proprietors represented the prospects of the company to be even yet so good that "it alone was able to enrich the nation[1]," the low price of the stock showed that the total rights could be bought for a moderate sum. However the English Commissioners were prepared to be generous, and it was at last decided that England should refund the total capital, which had been paid up, with 5 per cent. interest from the respective dates at which the different calls had been received by the company. The payment of the calls had extended from June 1st, 1696, to February 2nd, 1700, and interest was calculated up to May 1st, 1707, or the date when the money was handed over, so that the total interest worked out as extending over a period of more than eight years. It is a coincidence, possibly worthy of mention, that the capital called up was $42\frac{1}{2}$ per cent. of the nominal amount subscribed, while the interest paid on that capital also came to just about the same figure of $42\frac{1}{2}$ per cent.

Several concessions were made in addition to the payment of capital and interest. Under the orders of the company, interest would only have been payable from August 1st, 1698, whereas it now accrued from June 1st, 1696. The debts of the company were paid, and the small balance of its remaining assets was granted to cover the expenses of winding up.

By these concessions England showed that, once the principle of compensation had been admitted, she was prepared to deal generously with the stockholders of the company. The financial condition of Scotland was such that any immediate assistance was desirable. Such assistance was received in the Darien compensation money. England on the other hand was seeking not immediate but deferred benefits, which were obtained to a marked degree in the temporary suppression of the Scottish manufacture of fine cloth[2].

---

[1] Defoe, *History of the Union, ut supra*, p. 87.
[2] *Vide infra*, Division IX. § 1.

Capital, Dividends and Prices of the Stock.

Capital.

The proposed capital was £600,000 sterling. Of this only £400,000 was actually subscribed and 42½ per cent. or £170,000 called up. The cash available for the purposes of the company was less than £170,000, as some of the proprietors had not paid up the calls in full.

Dividends.

By May 1st, 1707, not only had the total paid up capital been lost, but considerable debts had been incurred, which with interest amounted to £14,809. 18s. 11d. The assets at the same date, as against the subscribed capital and indebtedness, were valued at no more than £1,654. 11s. 0⅔d. or about 1 per cent. At the Union of England and Scotland, it was agreed that England should pay, from the "Equivalent," the debts of the company with accrued interest, that the assets should be realized and set aside to discharge the expenses of winding up and, in addition, the money paid by each proprietor should be returned to him with interest at the rate of 5 per cent. from the date of the payment of the respective instalments up to May 1st, 1707, or the day on which the capital was repaid. This charge on the Equivalent for principal and interest came to £229,482. 15s. 1⅝d.

Prices of the Stock.

The only record of the price of the stock is found in Defoe's *History of the Union*. He writes that "the stock was a dead weight upon a great many families, who wanted very much the return of so much money. It had not only long been disbursed, but it was generally speaking abandoned to despair and the money given over for lost, nay so entirely had people given up all hopes that a man might even after this conclusion of the treaty [under June 25, 1706] have bought the stock at 10 pound for a hundred[1]." "Interest in the said stock had fallen so low that people valued themselves little or nothing on their shares in it, and when the first view of the Union came on, and some thought one way of it and others another, they either bought or sold as their opinion of the Union and its prospect of success either increased or decreased; and indeed the publick expectation of the success of the Union ran very low at this time [30th December, 1706], as may be

---

[1] p. 87.

supposed from the value now put on the stock of the African company, which was fallen so low that several people offered to sell their whole interest for 10 per cent. on the original stock though at the same time they saw that, if the Union took place, the whole principal money with interest was to be repaid them[1]."

From this statement it may be concluded that from 1700 till 1705 the stock was unsaleable. On the proposal for the expropriation of the company upon the Union being passed, prices were obtainable, but whether, between June and December, 1706, these were 10 for £100 *stock* or 10 for £100 paid up does not appear. It is more probable that the former is intended, which would be equivalent to a price of $23\frac{1}{2}$ for £100 paid up—the £100 stock being only paid up to the extent of $42\frac{1}{2}$. If this were so the speculators who bought at 10 in the end of 1706 would have received more than £60 from the Equivalent in less than a year or the satisfactory profit of over 600 per cent., which was made at the expense of the original subscribers from whom they purchased.

[1] p. 157.

SECTION VI. THE GOVERNOR AND COMPANY OF ADVENTURERS OF ENGLAND TRADING INTO HUDSON'S BAY[1].

(INCORPORATED 1670.)

THE remote causes, which resulted in the foundation of this company, are to be traced backwards to the voyages of discovery made by English seamen, partly also to the success of the French in developing the Canadian fur trade. With reference to the former tendency, it will be remembered that "the company of Kathai," under which name Frobisher's expeditions were organized, had penetrated to the north of Labrador[2], and in 1607 Henry Hudson discovered the Bay which still bears his name. Interest in England in the fur trade had been aroused in the first quarter of the seventeenth century, as is shown by the establishment of *the Company of Adventurers to Canada* at that period. It was unfortunate that, after this body had driven back the French and obtained large quantities of furs, it was forced by Charles I. to forego the fruits of its successes[3]. Thereafter, for over thirty years, there was, as far as is known, no direct trade on a large scale between England and Canada. But towards the end of this period there were obscure events tending almost accidentally towards the formation of a new venture of some magnitude. The French company, known as *la Compagnie des Cent associés de la Nouvelle France ou du Canada*, which had been the rival of the English undertaking in the time of Charles I., though still in existence, had for a number of years been leasing its privileges to subordinate organizations and in 1663 it resolved to go into liquidation[4].

---

[1] The following account of the company is partly based on data from its Minutes supplied me by Mr W. Ware, the Secretary. The exhaustive histories of Mr Willson and Dr Bryce (*The Great Company*, by Beckles Willson, 1900, and *The History of the Hudson's Bay Company*, by George Bryce, 1900) have rendered it unnecessary to do more than provide a summary of such information as is of specifically constitutional or financial interest.

[2] *Vide supra*, p. 77. [3] *Vide infra*, Division II., § 4.

[4] *Les Grandes Compagnies de Commerce*, par Pierre Bonnassieux, Paris, 1892, pp. 350–3.

During the concluding years of its administration, two fur traders, Groseilliers and Radisson[1], had penetrated by land to Hudson Bay. They returned, believing that great prosperity awaited them, only to find that a new company—*la Compagnie des Indes occidentales ou d'Occident*—had been incorporated and its officials totally refused to countenance the "private trade" the two explorers had been contemplating. They accordingly went to Boston and, failing to obtain support there, subsequently proceeded to Paris. The only measure of success they gained was the securing of an introduction to Prince Rupert, which was followed by an interview in June 1667. The possibility of "a great traffic of beavers" to be got in the region of Hudson Bay was viewed "with great joy" and a small syndicate was formed which fitted out a vessel for trade. This expedition sailed in June 1668. It arrived safely at its destination, built a fortified trading station and, after wintering, opened up a brisk trade with the natives. Leaving a garrison at the fort, the ship set sail for England in June 1669. The shareholders in the syndicate found the prospects and profits so remarkable[2] that they fitted out a second ship in 1669, and, in order to safeguard the fruits of their enterprize, steps were taken to secure a charter through the good offices of Prince Rupert. This grant was signed on May 2nd, 1670, incorporating *the Governor and Company of Adventurers of England trading into Hudson's Bay* and conferring the right of sole trade in all "seas, straights, bays, rivers, lakes, creeks and sounds...that lie within the entrance of the straights, commonly called Hudson's Bay," and the possession of all lands and territories "as aforesaid," not "actually" possessed by other English subjects or those of any Christian Prince. The company was constituted "true and absolute lords and proprietors" of such territories, with full powers of making peace and war with any non-Christian power. The company or "fellowship" received full corporate powers and was granted the privilege of holding general courts and electing a governor and a committee of seven persons, one of whom was to be chosen by the meeting of members as a deputy-governor. At meetings of the committee the governor and three committees constituted a quorum[3].

In 1671 it was decided to make arrangements for the internal

---

[1] Radisson, as will be seen, was one of the pioneers of the Hudson's Bay company, and he seems to link it with the Adventurers to Canada already mentioned. An expedition of the latter in 1627 was led by a Captain David Kirke (*vide infra*, Division II., § 4), and Radisson married the daughter of John Kirke, afterwards Sir John Kirke.

[2] *The Universal Dictionary of Trade and Commerce*, by Malachy Postlethwaite, London, 1774, vol. I., Art.—Hudson's Bay.

[3] The charter is printed in *The Great Company*, 1667–1871, by Beckles Willson, 1900, II. pp. 318–33.

management of the company. There were nineteen members, whose names are mentioned in the charter but very soon afterwards there were thirty-two shareholders[1]. A place of meeting was settled on at Mr John Horth's, "the Excise Office," Broad Street, and rules were framed for the presentation of accounts weekly, so that the adventurers should be acquainted with all the details of the business of the company. At the same meeting the amount of "the gratification" to be made to Prince Rupert[2], in addition to the stock held by him, was settled. A fee for the "committees" was arranged, subject to the stipulation that at the beginning of the meeting an hour-glass should be turned over and anyone arriving after it had run out or who departed without leave of the others was to forfeit his share in the amount distributed that day. As in the case of the Darien company, it was specified how the time was to be taken—"the time aforesaid be determined by the clock in the court-room, which the secretary is to set as he can by the Exchange clock[3]." The trade was so new that there were many points presenting unexpected difficulties and the adventurers endeavoured to aid the "committees" by expressing their views, often at considerable length, and sometimes with no little force. Thus on one occasion the court was much perplexed on comparing two lists of the Indians with whom the company traded. The later document had few names that could be identified with those in the first statement, and Rupert exclaimed—"Gentlemen, these Indians are not our Indians. 'Fore God, out of the nineteen I see only five we have dealt with before," or as another member put it, "these are not men but chameleons[4]."

The profits made were remarkable. In 1676, the merchandize exported did not exceed £650 in value, whereas the furs imported were rated at £19,000[5]. In spite of the payments made towards obtaining the charter, the capital was very small, being, in 1676, only £10,500. Mr Willson takes this as consisting of 34 equal shares of £300 which were reckoned as paid for in cash, while a further share of the same amount was assigned to Prince Rupert and credit was "given him for £300[6]." This may have been so, and there is the analogous case of the Royal Adventurers to Africa, where the share was £400[7]. But if the

---

[1] *A List of the Names and Stocks of the Governor and Company of the Adventurers of England trading into Hudson's Bay* [November 1672-3].

[2] Rupert was followed in the governorship by James, Duke of York, who resigned on succeeding to the throne. After the Revolution, dividends were paid to his representatives down to 1746. William III. became a stockholder and the governor and committees attended at Whitehall and paid the dividend in person, making the pounds, guineas. George II., on Jan. 8th, 1752, by proclamation, appointed a deputy to receive dividends of £653. 8s., due on April 17th, on £2,970 stock.

[3] *The Great Company*, I. p. 241.   [4] *Ibid.*, I. p. 87.

[5] *Ibid.*, I. p. 215.   [6] *Ibid.*, I. p. 70.   [7] *Vide supra*, p. 18.

original nominal value of the former share was £300, transfers must have been comparatively numerous, since, only a few years after the charter was granted, there were great disparities in the holdings, the Earl of Shaftesbury being registered as owning £600 and others only £50[1], while in 1690 the capital was regarded as consisting of 105 shares of £100 each and the voting rights were one vote for every £100[2].

When the capital was so small and the profits great, it is surprising that the first dividend, of which there is any mention, was made in 1679, and then only at a very moderate rate, for the times, of 20 per cent. The reason for the course adopted was in all probability similar to that influencing another very successful enterprize, namely the New River company, based on the principle of providing capital expenditure out of income. In the case of the Hudson's Bay enterprize there may have been also an additional incentive to this course, since there were possibly considerable outlays in connection with the obtaining of the charter. All the indications point to the trade having been very lucrative from 1670 to 1680, yet, as far as can be ascertained, only 20 per cent. was divided. From 1680 to 1690 the company had begun to suffer from the attacks of the French on its forts, yet in that period, which must have been less profitable than the former decade, no less than 275 per cent. was distributed[3]. The losses sustained by French aggression from 1682 to 1688 were estimated at £38,332. 15s., and the company may have derived some consolation from the mention of the attacks made upon it in the Declaration of War against Louis XIV. More substantial sympathy was to be found for it in the recognition of its status by act of Parliament. It appears that there had been some attempt to invade the monopoly of the company, since in 1688 James II. had issued a proclamation prohibiting trade by any of his subjects, save the company, within the limits assigned to it[4]. In 1690 the company appealed to Parliament for support, representing the losses it had sustained and asking confirmation of its charter for a period of seven years. There was some opposition from the Felt-makers' company and other sources. It was objected that the price of beaver skins was high

---

[1] *A List of the Names and Stocks of...the Company, ut supra.*
[2] *Journals of the House of Lords*, XIV. p. 497; *Reports Royal Com. Hist. MSS.*, XIII., Pt. VI. p. 73.
[3] That is taking the dividend of 25 per cent. in 1690 on the trebled stock as equivalent to 75 per cent. on the original stock, *vide infra*, p. 237.
[4] On March 4, 1688, the company petitioned asking for such prohibition, and for power to confiscate beaver skins imported contrary to the Navigation Act. State Papers, Domestic, Entry Book, LXXI., f. 471; *A Proclamation, prohibiting his Majesties subjects to trade within the limits assigned to the Governour and Company of Adventurers of England, trading into Hudson's Bay, except those of the Company* (31 *March*, 1688), Bod. Lib. Ash. H. 23 (362).

and that the company "was a small number of men, with an inconsiderable stock, in no way serviceable to the nation," which had been founded on "a mistaken suggestion that it would discover a new passage to the South Seas[1]." The company was able to answer the objections against it and its act received the Royal Assent on May 20th, 1690, after a clause had been inserted to protect the Felt-makers, which enacted that at least two sales of coat-beaver should be held annually and not more than four. The lots were to be about £100 each in value and not more than £200. Between the sales no beaver might be sold at a higher price than that realized at the last auction[2].

On obtaining its act, the company proceeded to reorganize its capital. The resolutions set forth that it had goods on hand to the value of its original stock. The ships and cargoes for the year amounted to more than this amount and the profit expected to at least an equal sum. Therefore, taking account of the profit not yet received, under these headings, the estimated present value was three times that of the original capital. Further the beaver skins to be received from Port Nelson River "by God's blessing were modestly expected to be worth £20,000." Then there was the value of "the dead stock" which was estimated at "a considerable intrinsic" sum. Lastly there was "the great expectancy" of £100,000 from the French as compensation[3]. So that altogether it was calculated that, apart from the dead stock, the company had real and hypothetical assets worth £151,500 or just fifteen times its original capital. However, all of this amount was not available and it was decided that the stock should be trebled—"each interestent shall (according to his stock) have his credit trebled in the company's books and that, from henceforth, no one shall have a vote in any of the affairs of the company who has less than £300 credit[4]."

The trebling of the stock took place just at a time when the fortunes of the company changed for the worse, through the continued successful aggression of the French; and for the long period of twenty-six years, from 1691 to 1717, no dividends were paid. At the beginning of this period of depression, it could scarcely have been foreseen that it would have been so protracted; and the first records of transactions in the stock show that the prospects were considered promising. The earliest of these is in March 1692 when the price of £100 of the trebled stock was 260, representing a premium of 680 per cent. on the original amount paid in. Early in May the quotation had fallen to 250, and by

---

[1] *Reports Royal Com. Hist. MSS.*, XIII., Pt. VI. p. 73.
[2] *The Great Company, ut supra,* I. p. 184.
[3] These resolutions are printed in *The Great Company, ut supra,* I. p. 185.
[4] That is, the total number of votes remained the same. *Reports from Committees of the House of Commons,* II. p. 261.

the 9th it was no more than 215, repeating this figure till the end of the month. There was a recovery in June to 245, but during the remainder of the year the market was weak, and in January 1693 it stood at 190 and then fell to 180, which was repeated during the whole of February and the first week of March. During the remainder of the latter month there was a temporary recovery to 185, but, by the middle of April, the quotation was 175 and this was continued till the middle of July when the fall recommenced, 150 being recorded on August 18th. This was the lowest point of the year and it represented a fall of 40 from the price of January. The recovery which began at the end of August continued steadily and is to be attributed partly to the news of successes against the French, partly also to the excitement in the stock-market at the time. By the middle of October the whole loss had been recovered and the price was again 190, the next week it was 200 and on the 27th 220, at which it stayed till the end of November, being 205 a month later. The relapse continued during 1694 until the end of February, when 190 was touched, a quotation that was repeated till the end of April. Then the fall began again and each sale was at lower prices, till 150 was recorded, when there was a pause in the decline. After the stock had stood at 150 from May 23rd to June 13th, it again lost ground till 130 was touched from July 4th to 23rd, representing a total fall since January of 75. By August 22nd there had been a recovery to 150 and a month later the price was 185. During the last quarter of the year fluctuations were between this quotation and 170 and, at the end of December, the price was 175. In January 1695, the stock gave way, and, on February 1st, it realized 155, which was repeated till March 1st. Then followed a steady improvement till 230 was touched on June 14th. Thereafter, with one exception, it was 220 till August 16th. Then came a severe and steady fall till 130 was reached at the end of November. In 1696 the quotation opened at the reduced level of 130 and, through the continuance of the struggle in Canada, it gave way almost without any recovery till on June 26th it touched 98. In July it rose to par and then to 105, this price being repeated till the close of the year. Owing to the financial crisis in London at the beginning of 1697 the quotation further relapsed, 80 being recorded for payment in cash or 95 in bank-money during January and February[1]. Till the end of the summer the market was lifeless, but prospects of peace and the lessening of monetary stringency brought an improvement and the stock reached 130 in October. After a slight relapse, this price was repeated on November 24th, and a month later it was 115. It soon began to be recognized that the terms of the Treaty of Ryswick were

[1] This was during the suspension of the Bank of England, when all quotations of stocks and shares were in this form.

far from favourable to the company and it was seen that it would have to re-open its trade under difficulties, so that during 1698, 1699 and 1700 the market was very dead, the extreme fluctuations being from 110 to 100. This represents a heavy fall from the price of 260 which was current in 1692[1].

The short period of peace was regarded by the company as a breathing space to fit itself for a renewal of the struggle, in which it hoped to regain the positions it had lost. During the war which broke out in 1702, the agents of the adventurers re-established themselves at Hudson Bay and their interests were fully safeguarded under the Treaty of Utrecht.

During the twelve years from 1702 to 1713 the company had only been able to trade intermittently, but it endeavoured to make profits by opening up other kinds of business. For instance about 1708 it had started one of the insurance offices which later became popular and which are described elsewhere[2]. The object of this venture was "to raise or increase the stock of such as serve an apprenticeship[3]." When the act of Anne c. 6 § 57 was passed in 1711, the company protested against being compelled to desist from this class of business. It showed that it was in a different position from those offices it was intended to suppress, being a substantial incorporated company. It had given security for £30,000 to the Chamber of London for the due performance of its contracts of insurance and had divided amongst those insured with it, in the three years it had been at work, over £11,000, without any complaint being made against it[4]. Though no new contracts had been made since March 8th, 1711, on February 6th of the following year payments were still being continued to policy-holders and it was then necessary to insert an advertisement offering a reward for the discovery of persons who had made fraudulent claims[5].

[1] After 1700 the newspapers cease to record quotations. This is to be attributed partly to the decline of public interest in the stock-market after the crisis of 1696-7. It is noticeable, however, that John Freke in his *Prices of the Several Annuities and other Publick Securities* does not mention this company. Mr Willson points out that from 1690 to 1700 many of the old proprietors were disposing of their stock (*The Great Company*, I. p. 240) which may account for the active dealings before 1700 and the absence of transactions on the Alley afterwards. In any case, the brisk market in the stock shows that Adam Smith is not correct in treating this undertaking as a partnership, since it fails to conform to his own definition; *Wealth of Nations*, Bk. v., ch. I., Part III., § 1 (ed. Cannan, II. p. 235).

[2] *Vide* "Undertakings for effecting insurances," Division XI., § 3 c.

[3] *Postman*, August 19, 1710.

[4] *Reasons humbly offered on behalf of the Hudson's Bay company that they may be exempted in the clause that will be offered for suppressing the Insurance offices* [Bod. Lib. Bromley's Parliamentary Papers, II., No. 130].

[5] *The Insurance Cyclopaedia*, by Cornelius Walford, I. p. 179.

Necessarily the excursion into insuring was only an episode in the career of the company, which served to fill a gap in its operations until peace was declared. After 1713 it was in a better position than it had been during the past twenty-five years. The sovereign rights conferred by the charter were now confirmed by an international treaty. Further, by refraining from dividing up the liquid assets, that had been saved from its enemies, it was in a fairly strong position to develope its trade. The same prudent policy was continued and, though large profits began to accrue again, no dividend was paid till 1718, and then only 10 per cent., followed by 6 per cent. in the next year.

During the excitement of the years 1719 and 1720 none of the industrious recorders of the erratic movements of the bubbles of the time mentions any transactions in Hudson's Bay stock, indeed it was stated by the company that none of its securities had been bought or sold on the market at this period[1]. At the same time the promotion of new companies with large capitals was so common that it produced some effect on the minds of the committees, and, in August 1720, it was decided to re-arrange the capital. Owing to the system of using earnings as capital, by this time there was a large reserve, and it was estimated that "at a moderate valuation" the quick and dead stocks were worth £94,500[2]. This was thrice the existing capital, and, on August 29th, it was resolved to again treble the stock, bringing it up to exactly that amount. To take advantage of the boom, it was further determined that new stock to the extent of £283,500 should be created and offered to the present members for subscription for cash. The effect of this scheme was to make a new capital three times that with the bonus augmentation of 1720, or, in other words, had the cash-subscription succeeded, the whole stock would have been twelve times what it was in 1719 and thirty-six times that of 1670–89. A lady member of the company—a Mrs Mary Butterfield—though she professed herself unable to understand the details, showed that she had a just appreciation of the position. She wrote in a letter to a friend, "I cannot tell you how it

---

[1] *Reports from Committees of the House of Commons*, II. p. 230.

[2] *Ibid.*, II. p. 261. If the profits for the six years 1714–9 approximated the annual average for the ten years 1739–48, which came to close on £8,000 a year, these, after allowing for the dividends paid, would have more than provided the bonus of 1720. The following are the figures for the period from 1739 to 1748:—

	£	s.	d.
Trading goods	157,432	14	4
Other expenses	36,741	11	5
Total	194,174	5	9
Sales	273,542	14	10
Balance	£79,368	9	1

is to be done, for that passes my wit; but in short the value of our interests is to be trebled without our paying a farthing; and then to be trebled again if the business is to the publick taste and we are told it cannot fail to be[1]." Possibly, had the boom lasted, the advisers of the lady would have been correct in their prognostications, but it was arranged that the first call of 10 per cent. should be paid on September 7th, and thereafter in similar equal instalments at intervals of three months. By October there had been a panic in the stock-market, and only one-third of the new shares were taken up. On these £3,150 was paid, but it was recognized that it would be difficult to exact the remaining calls. Accordingly, on December 23rd, it was resolved to withdraw the new subscription, and at the same time the call paid in was considered as trebled and stock to that amount allotted. This brought the whole capital up to £103,950[2], at which sum it remained for a considerable period. Finally the qualification of the management was fixed or re-arranged, that of the governor being settled at £1,800 stock and that of the deputy-governor or a committee at £900 stock.

In 1720 the company had been in existence for just fifty years, and it is an interesting problem to decide how the representatives of an original adventurer would have stood at the later date. The whole dividends, known to have been paid, amounted to 343 per cent. on the original stock in this period. During the whole half-century interest on a first-class security may be estimated to have averaged a trifle over 6 per cent.[3], so that, as far as the actual distributions were concerned, the return was only a fraction higher than economic interest. There remained the undivided profits, dealt with in 1690 and 1720 by way of a stock-bonus. Thus the original £100 of 1670 was represented by £900 stock in 1720; and, if the latter was worth par, after allowing for interest on the original capital, there would remain a profit of at least £800[4].

[1] Quoted in *The Great Company*, I. pp. 264, 265.
[2] *Vide infra*, p. 237.
[3] *I.e.* 1670–89, 6 per cent., 1690–9, 8 per cent., 1700–4, 5 per cent., 1705–9, 6 per cent., 1710–19, 5 per cent. per annum. It is interesting to notice that, on this basis, the profit on an investment in the East India company and in this one for fifty years, in the one case from 1658 to 1708 and in the other from 1670 to 1720, after allowing for interest, was about the same, being in the first about 750 per cent. and in the second about 800 per cent., *vide supra*, Part I., Chapter XIX.
[4] If compound interest were allowed the profit would have been much larger, since, owing to the bulk of the dividends being made before 1691, on this basis the adventurer would have had more than the interest on the best security.

Capital[1].

Date		Amount of Stock
1676. Oct. 16 ...		£10,500
1690. September.	Bonus in stock ...	21,000
Total after September, 1690 ...		31,500
1720. August 29.	Bonus in stock ...	63,000

At the same time it was proposed that a further £283,500 of stock should be created and issued at par, making the proposed capital £378,000. Had this operation been carried out the stock would have been twelve times as much as it had been at the beginning of the year. Calls were payable 10°/₀ on Sept. 7 and 10°/₀ on Dec. 6, 1720. At the end of the year only £3,150 had been paid on account of these calls, and it was decided by resolution of Dec. 23 that this sum should be trebled, and stock to that amount registered   9,450

£103,950

Prices of Stock and Dividends.

Year	Date of highest price	Prices	Date of lowest price	Dividends, °/₀
1671 to 1678				None known to have been paid[2]
1679				20
1680 to 1682				—
1683				50
1684				50
1685 to 1687				—
1688				50
1689				50
1690				25[3]
1691				—
1692	March to April 18	260—215	May	—
1693	Oct. 27 to Nov. 17	220—150	Aug. 18	—
1694	June 5—12	205—130	July 4—25	—
1695	June 14	230—130	Dec.	—
1696	Jan. 3—17	125— 98	June 26, July 3	—
1697	Oct. 6—13	130— 95[4]	Feb. to Aug.	—
1698	Jan. 6—26, Mar. 16, April 30	110—100	Feb. 10—23	—
1699	(nominal)	110—105		—
1700	,,	110—105		—
1701 to 1717				—
1718				10
1719				6

[1] *Reports from Committees of the House of Commons*, 11. pp. 230-61.

[2] The Minute books are not quite complete during this period. For particulars of the dividends I am much indebted to Mr W. Ware, Secretary of the Company. Some of the early distributions are mentioned by Bryce, *Hist. of the Hudson's Bay Company*, pp. 24, 25.

[3] On the trebled stock = 75 per cent. on the original stock.

[4] This quotation is for Bank-money. The lowest price, for cash, was 80.

DIVISION II.

COMPANIES FOR "PLANTING" (OR COLONIZATION) AND SIMILAR OBJECTS.

SECTION I. EXPEDITIONS TO FOUND PLANTATIONS IN THE SIXTEENTH CENTURY.

PROPOSED EXPEDITION OF HUMPHREY GILBERT (ABOUT 1566).

THE COMPANY FOR CAPT. CARLILE'S INTENDED DISCOVERY AND ATTEMPT IN THE NORTHERN PARTS OF AMERICA (1583).

GILBERT AND OTHER ADVENTURERS FOR THE PLANTING OF AMERICA (1578–83).

THE COLLEGES FOR THE DISCOVERY OF THE NORTH-WEST PASSAGE (? 1583).

RALEIGH'S EXPEDITIONS TO VIRGINIA AND GUIANA.

IT is far from easy to classify the different English maritime expeditions during the second half of the sixteenth century. Some were mainly voyages of discovery, others were intended to open up a foreign trade, as, for instance, the voyages to Russia, to Africa and to India. In certain cases fleets were fitted out with the avowed object of despoiling the Spaniard, and finally, towards the close of the century, expeditions were sent to found or assist plantations. But at such an early period exact specialization of this kind was impossible. Ships were armed and carried merchandize with a view either of trading with foreign countries or establishing settlers there, or again of capturing plate ships, should these be met. Thus whether an expedition became one for foreign trade, or for privateering or for planting, depended to a large degree on circumstances, and the simplest method of treatment is to isolate such expeditions as were mainly intended for colonizing from those that opened up a foreign trade, which have already been dealt with.

One of the earliest proposals of importance for planting is that of Humphrey Gilbert, or Gylberte[1], about 1566. In a memorial to

[1] He was afterwards knighted.

Elizabeth he stated that, although the grants to the Russia company comprised the exclusive rights to new trades discovered to the north-east or north-west of London, as yet no voyages had been sent in the latter direction. Being a member of the company, he was prepared to fit out four expeditions to the north-west and, in consideration of "his great charges and hazard," he asked that he should be allowed the use of two of the Queen's ships, that goods exported to the territories discovered should only be subject to half customs for forty years, and that imports thence might not be taxed at more than 12d. per ton. The additional clause that Gilbert and his heirs were to enjoy the tenth-part of any lands discovered, "by the yearly rent of a knight's fee," shows that this proposal was directed towards colonization as well as trade[1]. The governor of the Russia company protested against any invasion of the privileges of the adventurers, and in particular that body "misliked wholly" the part of Gilbert's petition relating to the possession of one-tenth of the lands discovered. As a result of negotiations between the parties, Gilbert had shown himself "very conformable to surcease his suit in any thing derogatory to the privileges of the company," and the members "very well liked" that, if Gilbert fitted out an expedition, he might be governor of any territory occupied[2]. Some time elapsed before Gilbert's proposal was realized, and for the present his ideas remained without result, except in so far as they inspired the movement which led to the voyages of Frobisher nearly ten years later[3].

Between 1574 and 1583 another scheme was originated by Christopher Carlile, one of the navigators of the period, who was supported by a body of Bristol and London merchants. The proposed expedition was to sail for the "northern parts of America conveying one hundred settlers, who were to remain one year," and, by "friendly entreaty of the people, might enter into a better knowledge of the country[4]." The exceptionally full information as to the internal organization of this company is of interest in throwing light on other contemporary ventures of the same kind. The shareholders elected a governing body, known as the committees. The estimated capital outlay for the first voyage was £4,000. Of this £1,000 had been "very readily offered" by the merchants of Bristol, and it was hoped that the remainder might be raised in London. The Russia company, especially, was supposed to be favourably disposed towards the project, but it is

---

[1] State Papers, Domestic, Eliz., xlii. 23.

[2] *Ibid.*, 5; *Cal. State Papers, Colonial, East Indies*, 1513–1616, pp. 7, 8.

[3] *Vide supra*, pp. 76–82.

[4] State Papers, Domestic, Eliz., xcv. 63; *Cal. State Papers, Colonial*, 1574–1660, p. 1.

probable that, since this company came into existence after 1580, the state of the finances of the other undertaking precluded any contribution being made. The capital of £4,000 was to be divided into shares of three different denominations, described respectively as whole, half and quarter shares, of the nominal amount of £25, £12. 10s. and £6. 5s. each[1]. It was a characteristic of the early colonizing companies that the shares were generally of small nominal value, and that the shareholder was entitled to an allotment of land as a "division" or dividend.

By 1578 it became plain that, although Frobisher's voyages might result in establishing a mining settlement, as yet there were very small prospects of a colony being founded. Accordingly Gilbert again came forward, and on June 11th he obtained a patent "for inhabiting and planting our people in America." This grant invested Gilbert with full powers, during the ensuing six years to settle remote countries, not in the possession of any Christian prince, and to exercise jurisdiction within 200 leagues from the place where he should fix his place of residence[2].

In order to raise the capital necessary, Gilbert assigned the benefit of the patent to those who joined him, and in this way a company was formed[3]. Having secured "the support of a great number of persons," Gilbert determined to plant in Newfoundland. In the summer of 1578, the expedition was ready to sail, when "the majority of the adventurers departed from their agreements and signified their intention of reserving their property for the support of plans concerted among themselves"— probably of a privateering nature[4]. Gilbert sailed almost alone and, after touching at Newfoundland, returned home. Exactly five years after the date of the patent, when it had only one more year to run, on June 11th, 1583, Gilbert sailed from Plymouth, and on August 6th, having landed at St John's, Newfoundland, he read his commission and made certain grants of land. A piece of ore had been found, which, the mining expert on board one of the ships said, contained silver, and Gilbert was confident that he could obtain from Elizabeth a loan of £10,000, on the security of the discovery, to prosecute his colonization. On the voyage home a storm was encountered, and all the ships, except one, were lost[5]. The death of Gilbert ended this venture, but in the same year a similar proposal was brought forward by his brother,

[1] Hakluyt, *Voyages* (ed. 1904), VIII. p. 135, cf. *supra*, p. 47.
[2] Hakluyt, *Voyages* (1904), VIII. p. 17.
[3] State Papers, Domestic, Correspondence, Eliz., CXLVI. 40.
[4] *The History of the Island of Newfoundland*, by Lewis Amadeus Anspach, London, 1827, p. 59.
[5] *Ibid.*, pp. 61-73.

Adrian Gilbert, which may have been a continuation of the scheme for the Newfoundland colony. The persons interested, about 1583, prayed for incorporation as "*the Collegiate of the Fellowship of new Navigations Atlantical and Septentrional*," with powers to "inhabit and enjoy" all places discovered between the equinoctial line and the North Pole[1]. This petition was granted, and the title in the grant was fixed as "*the Colleges for the Discovery of the North-West Passage*[2]."

The history of the expeditions of Raleigh to Virginia and Guiana from 1584 to 1595 is well-known[3]. Two causes rendered these fruitless as permanent settlements, namely the temptations of privateering and the belief that the primary cause of such voyages should be to obtain gold or silver. Thus, when colonists had been established in Virginia, after the voyages of 1584 and 1585, the prospects of capturing Spanish ships in 1586 diverted the expedition from its original purpose in that year. Not only did the passion for the precious metals by capture prevent the settlers from obtaining regular supplies from home, but it caused them to neglect providing themselves with provisions for the winter—for instance, this happened in 1585 in the case of the settlers of Sir R. Granville's voyage.

Although Raleigh is said to have spent £40,000 on these expeditions[4], there is ample evidence that, though associated with his name, the voyages were in reality of the nature of joint-stock undertakings. The patent, which was dated March 25th, 1584, for the settlement in Virginia was in the name of Raleigh, but the ships that sailed on April 7th of that year were fitted out "at the cost of Raleigh and some associates[5]." On March 7th, 1589, like Gilbert before him, he assigned the benefit of the patent to a company of twenty-nine merchants, reserving to himself one-fifth part of the gold and silver ore obtained[6]. The capital raised by this body was described as "considerable[7]," and Raleigh exercised his sovereign rights by incorporating some of the settlers as "the Governor and Assistants of the City of Raleigh in Virginia." There were to be twelve assistants, and this grant is to be

---

[1] State Papers, Domestic, Eliz., Addenda; *Cal. State Papers, Colonial, East Indies*, 1513–1616, p. 93.

[2] State Papers, Domestic, Eliz., cxxx. 20; *Cal. ut supra*; Hakluyt, *Voyages* (ed. 1904), VII. p. 378.

[3] *The Growth of English Industry and Commerce in Modern Times*, by W. Cunningham (1903), p. 125; *The Cambridge Modern History*, VII. pp. 2, 3.

[4] *A Brief Relation of Sir Walter Raleigh's Troubles*, London, 1669, in *Harleian Miscellany*, IV. p. 60 (note).

[5] *The Discovery of the Large, Rich and Beautiful Empire of Guiana by Sir W. Raleigh* (Hakluyt Society, 1848), p. xxvii.

[6] *Historical Collections*, edited by Ebenezer Hazard, Philadelphia, 1792, I. p. 42.

[7] Anderson, *Annals of Commerce* (ed. 1790), II. p. 209.

taken as applying rather to the government of the settlers than of the body of shareholders[1].

Similarly the last ill-fated voyage to Guiana was financed in the same way, and "many merchants both at home and abroad contributed to the adventure[2]." Such contributions are not to be understood as consisting exclusively of money subscribed. It was one of the characteristics of early planting expeditions that capital was subscribed in kind. Thus Sir Robert Cecil proposed to adventure a ship, the hull of which stood at £800, in one of Raleigh's expeditions[3], that is, Cecil would be credited with stock to the extent of £800 in the venture, although that sum was not paid in cash. Another similar case was that of Sir Francis Drake in the fourth voyage of the Kathai company, who subscribed a bark valued at £700[4]. This would apply to a ship ready to sail, but it often happened that the owner was not able to pay for the equipment necessary. Others would then supply the goods or stores required, participating *pro rata* in the benefits of the stock at which the vessel was rated. Under these circumstances the ship as complete would be subscribed at a certain value, for which the owner would be credited by the adventurers with stock or shares. He again would contract with those, who found the capital for equipment, for a proportionate part of his stock. For instance, if the owner of a ship worth £500 (which cost another £500 to equip) joined in an expedition with a capital of £5,000, he would be credited with stock to the value of £1,000, but of the profits on that amount he was bound to pay one-half to those who had provided stores. These persons were known as "adventurers under" the ship-owner.

[1] *Discovery of Guiana, ut supra*, p. xxx.
[2] *Ibid.*, p. 169.   [3] *Ibid.*, p. 153.
[4] Brit. Mus. MSS., Otho VIII., f. 104; *Cal. State Papers, Colonial, East Indies*, 1513–1616, p. 73.

SECTION II. THE TREASURER AND COMPANY OF ADVENTURERS AND PLANTERS OF THE CITY OF LONDON FOR THE FIRST COLONY IN VIRGINIA,

AND

THE GOVERNOR AND COMPANY OF THE CITY OF LONDON FOR THE PLANTATION OF THE SOMERS ISLANDS.

A. THE FIRST VIRGINIA COMPANY TO 1618.

AFTER the failure of Raleigh's efforts to plant a colony in Virginia nothing was effected for some time. In 1602 a syndicate, formed by the Earl of Southampton, sent a ship, under the command of Captain Bartholomew Gosnold, to America; and, at the same time, Raleigh also dispatched a vessel[1]. The former expedition met with considerable success in opening up a trade with the natives, and, in 1605, another syndicate, or small company, fitted out a voyage under the direction of Captain George Weymouth[2]. The results of these and other ventures were sufficiently encouraging to lead to hopes that a plantation might be founded, and application was made to the Crown for a charter. The patent, which was signed on April 10th, 1606[3], granted the adventurers a considerable measure of encouragement, and is perhaps chiefly important as recognizing explicitly that the movement for colonization was a national one. The charter itself is wanting in precision, and is to be construed in close relation to the "Instructions for the Government

---

[1] *The Historie of Travaile into Virginia Britannia*, by William Strachey (Hakluyt Society, 1849), p. 153.

[2] *Rosier's Relation of Weymouth's Voyage to the Coast of Maine*, 1605, edited by H. S. Burrage (Georges Society, 1887), p. 14.

[3] *The History of the First Discovery and Settlement of Virginia*, by William Stith, Williamsburg, 1747, Appendix; *The Genesis of the United States...A Series of Historical Manuscripts now first Printed*, edited by Alexander Brown, London, 1890, I. pp. 52–63; Hazard, *Historical Collections*, I. p. 50.

of the Colonies," which were dated in November of the same year[1]. Inasmuch as the scheme for an American plantation had been developed independently in London and in the western sea-ports, the charter authorized the formation of two distinct colonies. The Atlantic seaboard between 34° and 45° N. latitude was granted for settlement, and the management of the enterprize was committed to a Council of thirteen persons nominated by the Crown and acting under instructions received from the King. The supporters of the venture, who were resident in the vicinity of London, were permitted to establish a plantation anywhere within the eight degrees of latitude between 34° and 41°—this was to be known as the "First Colony" or the "London Colony." The "Second Colony," which was to be supplied from Plymouth and the out-ports, might be settled within the area from 38° to 45°[2]. It will be noted that there was an apparent overlapping in the areas assigned to the two colonies. The whole line of coast that was made available for plantation consisted of 12°, of which 4° were assigned exclusively to the London colony (34°—37°), 4° were similarly allocated to the Plymouth colony (42°—45°), while the intervening 4° (38°—41°) might be settled by either colony, always provided that there must be a space of 100 miles between the first settlements of the two bodies. On the actual establishment of a plantation, the charter grants to the colony, effecting it, all the land 50 miles northward and 50 miles southward, also 100 miles inland, and any islands 100 miles seaward to be held in free and common soccage and not *in capite*. The control of the affairs of the colony, that were peculiar to it, was entrusted to a council, appointed by the Royal Council for both plantations. It is clear from these provisions that there was no express intention of forming joint-stock bodies for the specific purpose of making settlements, indeed, it seems to have been expected that settlers, either singly or in groups, would arrange for their transportation; and, having obtained their respective proportions of land, would be under the government of the council for that colony, this again being controlled by the Royal Council for both colonies. The joint-stock element emerges more clearly in relation to the trade of the first, or

[1] Brown, *Genesis of the United States*, I. pp. 65–75. Owing to the unfortunate disputes in the company at a later date, it has been deemed advisable to give particulars of the headings of the documents on which the following account has been based. Generally speaking the records of the company up to April 1619 reflect the views of Sir Thomas Smythe and his adherents, but after that time those of Sir Edwin Sandys and the Ferrars. Most of the Ferrars Papers show a similar bias, while the Manchester Papers give the views of the members of the Rich family (who were shareholders) as does the *Historye of the Bermudaes*.

[2] The history of the Second Virginia company will be dealt with below in Section III. of this Division.

London colony. For five years from the landing of the first expedition in Virginia there was to be a direct trade both inward and outward. Commodities exported from England for the use of the settlers were to be supplied by those who would join together either in a single joint-stock, or in more than one, but not exceeding three "at the most." When the cargoes arrived they were to be placed in store-houses or "Magazines," which were under the charge of a "cape-merchant" or treasurer, who sold the goods to the settlers and remitted the proceeds to the adventurers in the joint-stock at home.

It is sufficiently obvious that this type of organization was unlikely to succeed. There was little incentive to induce those, who would be disposed to assist in the plantation, to overcome the initial difficulties. Unless the Royal Council, which was to initiate the policy for both colonies, was exceptionally far-seeing and energetic, there was likely to be a hopeless gap between the colonial and the commercial sides of the scheme. Signs of this danger are to be found in the objects of the first expedition, as these were expressed in December 1606. The ships were to remain in Virginia for two months, and this period was to be employed in exploration, particularly in endeavouring to discover a passage to "the other sea." Attention was also to be paid to the discovery of minerals and to opening up a trade with the natives[1]. In July, 1607, news was received in London that a settlement had been established and fortified. High hopes were entertained of discoveries of gold and copper[2], while some consignments of timber and sassafras had been sent from the colony[3]. As far as can be gathered from various statements of contemporary opinion, the danger that was foreseen was the risk of an attack upon the settlement by the Spaniards. At this time the difficulties that were likely to arise from imperfect organization, divided councils in Virginia, and particularly from the adventurers becoming wearied before the colony became self-supporting, had not been anticipated; indeed as early as September 1607 many persons in different parts of England were forming plans for sending out planters to secure land on their behalf[4]. It was not long before there were signs that those, who had provided the capital to fit out the first expeditions, expected an immediate, or at least an early return. The mechanism of

---

[1] Instructions of the Council for Virginia, Dec. 1606: Brown, *Genesis of the United States*, I. pp. 79–85.

[2] Captain Newport to Lord Salisbury, July 29, 1607: Brown, *Genesis of the United States*, I. p. 105.

[3] The Council in Virginia to the Council in England, June 22, 1607: Brown, *Genesis of the United States*, I. p. 107.

[4] Don Pedro de Zuñiga to the King of Spain, September 22, 1607: Brown, *Genesis of the United States*, I. p. 117.

the finance of the period was not sufficiently developed to solve the problem of raising funds for colonization where the period of waiting for concrete results was protracted. It was expected that, if possible, each voyage should pay its expenses, and if it made a serious loss, it was unlikely that capital would be readily forthcoming for a further expedition. The presence of such expectations can be traced in letters sent from London to Virginia in 1608. The local council was warned that hitherto it had fed the adventurers, " but with ifs and ands, hopes and some few proofes," while the settlers were warned that if they could not make some return for the supplies sent them, which had cost between £2,000 and £3,000, " they were like to remain as banished men[1]." By means of such pressure the ship which returned from Virginia in January 1609 brought a number of commodities such as timber, " soap-ashes," pitch, tar and dyes, besides reports of success in the production of glass and iron. It was urged that the fishing had been shown to be as promising as that within the limits assigned to the northern colony, there was " no improbable hope of rich mines," and many reports were favourable to the general fertility of the country[2].

The supporters of the scheme could claim that the way had been prepared towards the establishment of a colony that would ultimately become a flourishing one. But, as yet, it remained to convert the possibilities into actualities. Under the charter of 1606 there were no sufficient incentives towards the development of the main element in the scheme, namely the providing of suitable settlers. This side of the enterprize was to be carried on by the Royal Council, but during the three years the scheme had been in operation, it had advanced rather as a commercial than a colonizing undertaking. The Council had established no organization which would make the emigration of settlers easy. If, then, the plantation was to increase rapidly, such an organization must be created. The simplest method was to place the colonizing and commercial branches under one joint-stock company, which would arrange for the raising of capital, for the transportation of planters, and for the survey and division of lands. The necessary change was effected by the second charter, which had been drafted in February 1609. This grant incorporates a joint-stock company under the title of *the Treasurer and Company of Adventurers and Planters of the City of London for the First Colony in Virginia*. Its government consisted of

---

[1] Letter of Capt. Smith to the Council of Virginia, printed in *The Generall Historie of Virginia, New England and the Summer Islands*, by Captain John Smith, Glasgow, 1907, I. pp. 147–8.

[2] *Ibid.*, I. p. 179; Letter of Chamberlain to Carleton, Jan. 23, 1609, Council of Virginia to the Corporation of Plymouth, 1609, in Brown, *Genesis of the United States*, I. pp. 205, 239.

a council and treasurer nominated in the first instance by the Crown, but the company had power to displace any holder of these offices and to elect their successors. Provision was similarly made for the choice of a deputy-treasurer. The company was given powers to allocate land, and at the same time the area which might be settled in the first colony was increased. It was now defined as consisting of 200 miles north and 200 miles south of Cape Comfort, extending inland from sea to sea and including all the islands within 100 miles of the coast of either ocean[1].

Although the company was first formally constituted by the second charter, a corporate character had been assumed three years earlier, as is shown by the opening of the first court book on January 8th, $160\frac{6}{7}$[2]. Similarly, though Sir Thomas Smythe was only formally nominated as treasurer in 1609, he had been a prominent supporter of the enterprize at an earlier period.

While the charter was under consideration, an opportunity was made to secure a large measure of financial support, and intending adventurers were urged to join the company by the offer that those, who subscribed early, should have their names inserted in the charter. The terms offered were framed to attract both those who would adventure personally or who would provide capital. A man, having a trade, who emigrated was promised 100 acres of land, while persons of condition, who went to Virginia, were to receive a proportionately larger division. For those who adventured their capital, and not their persons, considerable inducements were offered. The share was fixed at £12. 10s. In return for this payment a large division of land was promised, when a survey had been made. In the meantime, for the space of seven years, all produce from the colony was to be collected by the cape-merchant and returned to England on account of the joint-stock, and it was confidently asserted that the profit from this source would ultimately be as large as that from the land-division. The owner of a single share became free of the company, while any alderman of the City who subscribed £50 was given the option of becoming a member of the council of the company[3]. Under the joint influences of the prevailing

---

[1] The Second Charter, printed in Stith, *History of Virginia*, Appendix; Brown, *Genesis of the United States*, I. pp. 208–37. In 1620 an attempt was made to obtain a new charter which would give the chief officer "the more eminent title" of governor: *The Records of the Virginia Company of London*, edited by S. M. Kingsbury, Washington, 1906, I. p. 442.

[2] *Records of the Virginia Company*, edited by S. M. Kingsbury, I. pp. 25, 171.

[3] The Council of the Virginia Company to the Lord Mayor, printed by Brown, *Genesis of the United States*, I. p. 253; *Nova Britannia, offering most excellent Fruits of Planting in Virginia*, London, 1609, in *Tracts and other Papers relating Principally to the Origin, Settlement and Progress of the Colonies in North America from the Discovery of the Country to* 1776, collected by Peter Force, Washington, 1836, I. No. 6.

enthusiasm and the deftly worded promises of a prospectus entitled *Nova Britannia*, the scheme met with extensive support, and when the charter was signed on May 23rd it contained the names of 56 City companies and of 659 individuals. Information is wanting as to how many shares had been taken up at this time. A substantial amount of capital had been required to finance the settlement during the three years since its foundation, and all the contemporary accounts agree in stating that the issue of shares in 1609 was received with enthusiasm. Even had a statement of the sums underwritten by the adventurers been preserved, it would convey little information as to the financial resources at the disposal of the council, since calls were payable in three equal annual instalments[1]. Many of the adventurers, but by no means all of them, punctually met the first demand; and, with the proceeds of it, the expedition of Sir Thomas Gates, consisting of eight ships and 600 men, was dispatched in May 1609. At the end of November news arrived that the results attained had been much less than those expected. The remnant of the fleet returned "laden with nothing but bad reports and letters of discouragement[2]." It is recorded that "when the adventurers saw the expectance of such a preparation come to nothing, how great a dampe of coldnesse it wrought in the hearts of all may easile be deemed[3]," indeed the council was faced by the dilemma of obtaining more capital or abandoning the plantation[4]. But many of the shareholders had counted on the profits of the first instalment to enable them to meet the second; and, when the latter became due, a number of them refused to pay, and still more were in arrear for the third and final instalment on the shares issued in 1609[5]. Even as late as 1620 the amounts due by adventurers on this and subsequent issues were returned at £16,000[6]. To meet the financial exigency, Sir Thomas Smythe, who was one of the leading merchants in the City, was forced to borrow largely on the security of the unpaid calls[7]; and, from the funds raised in this way, the expedition of 1610, under Lord de la Warr, was supplied. Early in 1611 it was recognized that, unless a large amount of capital could be procured, the situation was desperate. It was

[1] Christopher Brooke to Lord Ellesmere, April 28, 1613: Brown, *Genesis of the United States*, II. p. 626.

[2] Brown, *Genesis of the United States*, I. p. 333.

[3] *The New Life of Virginia*, London, 1612, in Force, *Tracts*, I. p. 11.

[4] *A True Declaration of the Estate of the Colonie in Virginia*, London, 1610, in Force, *Tracts*, III. p. 21.

[5] Chamberlain to Carleton, August 1, 1613: Brown, *Genesis of the United States*, II. p. 655.

[6] *Records of the Virginia Company*, edited by S. M. Kingsbury, I. p. 390.

[7] Brooke to Ellesmere, April 28, 1613: Brown, *Genesis of the United States*, II. p. 628.

estimated that £30,000 was required to be paid in two years. Of this sum £18,000 had been promised about March, and strenuous efforts were made to obtain the remainder[1], letters soliciting subscriptions being sent to the chief towns in England and even to the Netherlands[2]. Pressure was directed against the shareholders who were in arrear, and a number of Chancery suits were instituted against some of those who had refused to pay the instalments[3].

Though the reports from Virginia continued to be depressing, some hope was aroused by favourable accounts of the possibilities of the Bermudas as a subsidiary settlement. One of the ships of the expedition of 1609 had been wrecked there, and eventually it was determined to form another company to colonize these islands[4]. The Virginia company sold its rights for £2,000[5], but these were not strictly legal, since the Bermudas lay outside the limits of the charter of 1609. This discovery was made the occasion for an application for extended privileges on behalf of the Virginia company, and a third charter was signed on March 12th, 1612[6]. Its ostensible purpose was to include within the limits, assigned to the company, all the islands 300 leagues from its Atlantic coast-line, but the provisions relating to finance and organization were much more important. With regard to the former, the company was given powers to establish lotteries in London during the Royal pleasure, in order to raise funds for the support of the enterprize. All exports from England for the use of the colony were to be free of duties for the ensuing seven years. As to the organization of the company, regulations were framed for the admission and expulsion of members and for the holding of courts. The latter were divided into two classes. Four great or quarter courts were to be held on the last Wednesday, but one, of each term in which matters of importance might be decided. Other courts could be held as often as required. At these the quorum consisted of five members of the council (of whom the treasurer or deputy-treasurer must be one) and fifteen of the generality.

Advantage was immediately taken of the permission to establish lotteries, and a drawing for prizes was begun on June 29th, 1612, and concluded in the following month. It appears that the company had

---

[1] A Circular Letter by the Council of Virginia: Brown, *Genesis of the United States*, I. p. 463.

[2] Council of Virginia to Sir Ralph Winwood, MSS., Duke of Buccleuch.

[3] State Papers, Chancery Proceedings, James I., Bundle U, Nos. 2/27, 4/17, 2/69.

[4] For the early history of the Bermuda company see this section, B.

[5] The price is given as £1,000 in "The Case of the Bermuda," Bod. Lib. MSS., Clarendon, 102, f. 1.

[6] Stith, *History of Virginia*, Appendix; Brown, *Genesis of the United States*, II. pp. 540–53; Hazard, *Historical Collections*, I. p. 72.

formed too great expectations of the success of this venture since it was necessary to destroy no less than 60,000 blanks. This was done without "abating any one prize," and the drawing "was so plainly carried and honestly performed that it gave full satisfaction to all persons[1]."

A little more than a year later, namely in October 1613, some light can be obtained on the finances of the company. The source of this information was a statement made by Smythe, the treasurer, to the Spanish Ambassador, according to which the outlay on Virginia or on both Virginia and the Somers Islands had been £46,000 from the beginning[2]. Owing to the continuous dread of an attack by the Spaniards on the settlements, it was the obvious policy of the treasurer and council to represent the position in the most gloomy light. It follows that this statement is likely to err on the side of exaggeration, the intention perhaps having been to produce an impression that, through large sums having been spent without a prospect of profit, the adventurers had become wearied out and were ready to abandon the enterprize—indeed in the same document mention is made of a report to this effect. A second uncertainty arises from the doubt whether the estimate, whatever be its value, relates to both colonies or to Virginia only. On the whole it would appear from the context that the former is the correct interpretation. Assuming then that the sum mentioned refers to the two colonies, in view of later data it does not appear unduly large for the outlay from 1606 to 1613. To obtain a more definite result it is necessary first to ascertain how much of the amount is to be allocated to the expenditure of the Somers Islands company. Since it had begun its outlay in 1612, and by the end of 1614 it had spent £20,000[3], the date of Smythe's conversation with the Spanish Ambassador having been midway between these periods, and, taking into consideration the size of the expeditions sent to the Bermudas and the other expenses, it may be estimated that the outlay on this plantation was about £10,000 in October 1613. This would leave a balance of £36,000 as the total cost of establishing the colony in Virginia up to the same date. It must not be hastily assumed that this sum was represented by the calls paid in by the shareholders. It was in fact drawn from four distinct sources. There were first and largest the instalments of the adventurers, next the profits from the lottery, then the loans on the security of the company, and lastly

---

[1] *A History of English Lotteries*, by John Ashton, London, 1893, pp. 28–9; *London and the Kingdom*, by Reginald R. Sharpe, London, 1894, II. pp. 49, 50.

[2] Diego Sarmiento de Acuña to Philip II., October 5, 1613: Brown, *Genesis of the United States*, II. p. 661.

[3] See the account of the Somers Islands company, this section, B.

certain items of miscellaneous revenue, such as the purchase price paid by the Somers Islands company, the proceeds of goods sent from Virginia, and any payments made by individuals for passage-money. The data are so scanty that it becomes hazardous to attempt any allocation of the whole amount between these different headings. It is certain that the most important item consisted of the calls received from shareholders. As already shown, in 1611 promises had been received of £18,000, and every effort was made to increase the amount to £30,000. It is doubtful whether the whole sum asked for was subscribed, since those who were inclined to support the plantation-scheme had the double option soon afterwards of taking an interest in the Bermudas or of purchasing lottery tickets. It may be concluded then that not much was obtained by further sales of shares between the early part of 1611 and 1613. It might possibly be taken as the basis of a rough estimate that the sums paid for shares of the issue of 1611, after £18,000 had been already taken up, would balance such instalments of the £18,000 as remained in arrear in 1613. It follows further that, deducting this amount from the whole expenditure of £36,000, there remains a like amount furnished by the calls paid on shares taken up from 1606 to 1610, by the lottery, from loans and other sources. If the receipts from these latter be estimated at £6,000, this would leave £12,000 as the produce of the shares actually paid for of the issues from 1606 to 1610, or a total of £30,000 provided by the adventurers in all up to 1613.

Apart from the inevitable mistakes in the initial stages of an enterprize of this kind and the difficulties that would certainly arise from the emigration of "unruly gallants" (who, it was significantly said, were sent to Virginia "to escape ill destinies[1]"), as well as the practice of "parents disburdening themselves of lascivious sons, masters of bad servants and wives of ill husbands," making such an "idle creu" as would "rather starve for hunger than lay their hands to honest labour[2]," the financial hindrances to an early success have not been sufficiently recognized. It had often happened that funds could not be obtained when they were most required, and for three years, from 1613 to 1616, the most part of the adventurers abandoned the enterprize, leaving it to a small remnant "of undaunted spirits" to support it. These, under the leadership of Smythe, continued to hold meetings every week and to send such supplies as they could obtain to the plantation[3]. The with-

---

[1] *The Generall Historie of Virginia*, by Captaine John Smith, Glasgow, 1907, I. p. 189.

[2] *A Publication by the Counsell of Virginia touching the Plantation there*, 1610 [Soc. Antiquaries Broadsides, No. 122].

[3] *A Briefe Declaration of the Present State of Things in Virginia* [? 1616], Brown, *Genesis of the United States*, II. p. 776.

drawal of so many of the adventurers meant that the undertaking could not be financed by any considerable further issue of shares, and the chief source from which funds could still be drawn for supplying the colony was the lottery. In 1614 preparations had been made for holding "the great standing lottery," which was drawn in 1615. Some of the conditions are of interest in their bearing on the details of the finances of the company in the future. Anyone who paid in £12. 10s. and who, before the drawing took place, renounced his chance of winning a prize, was entered as the holder of one share. Again special terms were offered to those adventurers who were still in arrear. If they ventured in the lottery twice the sums due by them, they were exempted from all suits for the recovery of such arrears, besides ranking for prizes. But if, further, they remitted any prizes they might obtain, the amount paid in to the lottery would be credited to them in the form of shares in the company[1]. The profit of the lottery enabled the colony to be supplied during a time of great difficulty and anxiety. A new development contributed materially towards saving the situation. In 1613 an experimental consignment of tobacco had been sent from Virginia[2], and it was soon recognized that this crop would enable the plantation to subsist. The treasurer and council were so impressed with "the very good and prosperous condition" of the colony that in the earlier part of 1616 it was announced that a division of lands would be made to those adventurers who applied and conformed to certain regulations. The chief of these was that those, who intended to participate in this dividend, must pay in to the company £12. 10s. for another share to raise money towards meeting the expenses of the survey and allocation. The first instalment of this division was to be 50 acres per share, and the same amount to adventurers of their persons[3]. Ultimately the dividend of land was arranged on the basis of 100 acres per share as a first division. On the adventurer settling the land so obtained, he received another 100 acres, together with an addition of 50 acres for each person he transported to his estate[4]. The working of this principle may best be seen by an illustration expressed in terms of the cost per acre of land in Virginia. The adventurer who took his division of land, but failed to supply it, acquired a title to 100 acres per share and no more. Thus the cost to him was 2s. 6d. per acre. When a supply was

---

[1] *A Declaration for the Certaine Time of Drawing the Great Standing Lottery*, reproduced in Brown, *Genesis of the United States*, II. p. 760*.

[2] Brown, *Genesis of the United States*, II. p. 639.

[3] *A Briefe Declaration of the Present State of Things in Virginia*, Brown, *Genesis of the United States*, II. pp. 775-9.

[4] *Records of the Virginia Company*, edited by S. M. Kingsbury, I. pp. 75, 425.

sent the acreage was increased, but the planter had to find the passage-money and other expenses of the men he sent out to Virginia. This outlay amounted to £20 per head when the emigrants were provisioned from the date of their arrival till they could produce a crop[1]. Suppose, then, a member of the company had subscribed for four shares, his outlay so far would be £50; if he sent out five men to his land he would have to pay £100 for their expenses. Against this £150 he would obtain 1,050 acres, so that his property in Virginia would cost him less than 3s. per acre. If he sent ten men instead of five, the price per acre would be increased to 4s.

The land-division had several important consequences. Prior to 1616, the expenditure on establishing the colony was identical with that of the company. After the land had been divided this was not so, for the adventurers were individually responsible for the outlay on their respective estates. Moreover, up to 1616, all the produce of Virginia exported to England was, at least in theory, the property of the company. Once the land, allocated as dividend to the adventurers, began to yield a crop, such produce was the property of the owner of the land, subject to any arrangement he might make with those who actually worked the estate. This phenomenon introduced the problem of the trade between England and Virginia under the new conditions. As population in the colony increased, more capital would be required for purchasing the commodities in demand in the plantation, exchanging these against tobacco and marketing the latter in England. It was decided to form a subordinate joint-stock company to carry on this part of the undertaking which was entitled *the Society of Particular Adventurers for Traffique with them of Virginia in a joint-stock*, but it was generally described as "the Magazine," "the great Magazine," and later as "the old Magazine[2]." This undertaking began in 1616-17[3] and was under the control of a director and five committees[4]. The capital payable by the adventurers was divided into three portions, to be provided in successive years, and instalments in arrear were charged 20 per cent. interest annually[5]. The total amount paid up reached £7,000[6]. The method of trading was to exchange the commodities from home against tobacco, which was rated at 3s. for the best quality, and for which about 5s. per lb. was obtainable in England[7].

[1] Purchas, *His Pilgrims*, Glasgow, 1906, xix. p. 167.
[2] *Records of the Virginia Company*, i. p. 282.
[3] *Ibid.*, i. pp. 227, 239, 244, ii. p. 305; Brown, *Genesis of the United States*, ii. p. 790; *Generall Historie of Virginia*, by Captain John Smith, i. p. 241; Purchas, *His Pilgrims*, xix. p. 120.
[4] *Records of the Virginia Company*, i. p. 238.
[5] *Ibid.*, i. pp. 329, 552.
[6] *Ibid.*, ii. pp. 297, 315.
[7] *Ibid.*, i. pp. 282, 291; Smith, *Generall Historie*, i. p. 241.

DIV. II. § 2 A]   *The Great Magazine* 1616–17   257

The principle of the association of members of the company in a subordinate joint-stock venture was also applied to the settlement of land, by a number of persons joining together their dividends and arranging that these should be located in the same district. By this method settlers from the same place remained within reach of each other, a large tract of land was gradually developed under one management, and it is possible that the cost of transporting colonists was somewhat lower per head than if these were sent in smaller numbers. The first of the "particular plantations," as they were called, was organized by Smythe in 1618, and was named after him Smythe's Hundred. This undertaking was formed on the model of a joint-stock company with a committee, the proceedings of which were recorded[1]. In the early months of 1619 most of the initial difficulties had been surmounted and the colony had been brought to the threshold of success. At this period the trade of Virginia was said (though doubtless with some exaggeration) to have amounted to £100,000 a year[2].

The measure of success which had been achieved contained the germs of future danger. As the colony progressed the patronage of the chief offices in Virginia became increasingly valuable, and several of the leading adventurers endeavoured to advance the interests of their friends who were candidates. This resulted in a vigorous canvass and finally in serious dissensions, which brought about the retirement of Smythe from the treasurership in April 1619. Subsequent events led to the continuance of the friction, but, since the Somers Islands company was even more deeply involved, it will be necessary to postpone the consideration of these disputes until the early history of the latter undertaking has been dealt with.

The partial defeat of Smythe's party in 1619 makes this date a convenient one for reviewing the finances of the company up to that period. Most of the statements from this time onwards were framed with more regard to the interests of individuals than to the merits of the case. Still, with due consideration to the partisan character of the data, the total outlay on account of the general stock may be determined. Smythe himself returned it as "having been less than £70,000[3]." His successor, Sir Edwin Sandys, at first placed it at 100,000 marks or £66,666[4]. Later, Smythe's opponents alleged that the true amount

---

[1] *Records of the Virginia Company*, I. p. 129. The name was afterwards changed to Southampton Hundred.

[2] *Ibid.*, I. p. 31.

[3] An Answer to a Declaration of the Present State of Virginia: Manchester Papers, Record Office, No. 362. These papers have been summarized in *Rep. Royal Com. Hist. MSS.*, VIII., Pt. II. pp. 31–48.

[4] *Records of the Virginia Company*, I. p. 350.

was greater than this, owing to there being outstanding debts. This account was verbally accurate, while in reality untrue. Smythe resigned, leaving the company in debt to the extent of about £5,000, but it should be added that he handed over cash and stores of approximately an equal value[1]. It follows that, even on the corrected statement of his adversaries, the expenditure during Symthe's administration was approximately £67,000. The sources of this outlay can be traced and are set out below:

Receipts of the Company to April 1619.

Total paid by Adventurers[2]		£36,624
Profits of Lotteries to 1620[3]	£29,000	
,, ,, 1619–20[4]	9,000	
		20,000
Borrowings and debts due (partly estimated)		5,000
Miscellaneous receipts (partly estimated)		5,500
		£67,124

It is not easy to determine whether the results obtained early in 1619 were commensurate to this outlay. To some extent the success of the colony was to be measured by the number of persons planted there at this time. Estimates of the total settlers in Virginia vary according to the bias of those who framed them. One statement places the total of those remaining then as low as 400[5]; according to Sandys it was 600[6], while Smythe made it 800[7]. Even if the latter number were accepted, the whole population could have been sent, adequately equipped, to the plantation at a cost of £16,000. It follows that, since there is to be added to the expenditure of the company that of individual adventurers in supplying their estates, the whole outlay, against which there were few tangible assets, was considerably over £50,000. That there should have been waste from the experimental character of the beginning of the scheme was unavoidable, and it is to be remembered that the founders were hampered by want of knowledge, besides being badly served by many of their agents in Virginia. When the whole circumstances are reviewed, it must be admitted that one of the greatest causes of the delay lay at the door of the adventurers

---

[1] *Records of the Virginia Company*, I. p. 216.

[2] *A Declaration of the State of the Colony and Affaires in Virginia*, 1620, Brit. Mus. 1447.c.11.

[3] *Records of the Virginia Company*, I. p. 556.

[4] *Ibid.*, I. p. 355. The amount received till April 1620 was £7,000, the remainder of the amount in the text is added to cover receipts till the lotteries were suspended.

[5] Answer of the General Assembly in Virginia to the Declaration of the State of the Colony: State Papers, Colonial, II. 20 (ii).

[6] Note of the Men sent to Virginia: Manchester Papers, No. 352.

[7] Notes to show the Real Condition of Virginia: Manchester Papers, No. 340.

DIV. II. § 2 A] *Outlay and Results to April* 1619   259

themselves. Even as late as July 7th, 1620, there remained due as much as £16,000 on the shares taken up[1]. Had this sum been paid at the proper time, the supplies could have been sent more regularly, and progress would have been more rapid. As it was, it required the commercial influence of a man like Smythe to obtain credit to raise the large loans that were necessary when the situation was at its worst. There can be little doubt that, if he had not been able to borrow as much as £8,000 or £9,000[2] at the time when capital was most needed, the whole scheme might have failed through want of the necessary supplies.

B. THE GOVERNOR AND COMPANY OF THE CITY OF LONDON FOR THE PLANTATION OF THE SOMERS ISLANDS.

(THE SOMERS ISLANDS COMPANY OR BERMUDA COMPANY.)

FROM 1612 TO 1618.

The connection of England with the Bermudas began by the wreck of a ship commanded by Sir George Somers, which was a part of the supply sent to Virginia by the company in 1609. The crew and passengers were greatly pleased with the situation and fertility of the islands, and Somers wrote a letter to the company, praising them, which was received in London in September 1610[3]. Two main causes directed attention to the possibilities of the new possession, acquired in this accidental manner. The plantation in Virginia at this time was largely dependent on supplies sent from home, and it was reported that, in an emergency, both hogs and fish could be obtained quickly from the Bermudas. Moreover the strategic importance of their situation began to be recognized as one which, when fortified, would protect Virginia against the attacks of Spain which were believed to be imminent. The effect of these considerations is shown by the rumour that the Virginia company intended, in August 1611, to erect a fort and keep a garrison on the Bermudas[4].

This scheme required capital, and all the resources that could be

[1] *Records of the Virginia Company*, I. p. 390. Adding this amount to £36,624 actually paid, a total of £52,624 is arrived at as the share capital *subscribed*. After the date of the return in 1620 some receipts were presented for money paid on account of shares, not entered in the published list.

[2] *Ibid.*, I. p. 350.

[3] Somers to Salisbury, dated June 15, 1610, printed in Brown, *Genesis of the United States*, I. pp. 400–2.

[4] Dispatch of Don Alonso de Velasco in Brown, *Genesis of the United States*, I. p. 495.

raised by the parent organization were needed for the prosecution of its own enterprize. Accordingly it was decided to form a subsidiary, or "under-company," in January 1612. Some difficulty was experienced in discovering a suitable title for the place to be developed. It was first proposed to name it "Virginiola," but it was eventually decided that the title should be the Somers Islands, partly in commemoration of the discoverer, partly in punning allusion to the temperate climate (Summer Islands)[1]. The company itself was described as "*Undertakers for the Plantation of the Somers Islands*[2]." Sufficient capital was subscribed to send out a ship with 60 persons to begin a separate plantation. Just when the scheme had been translated into practice, a legal difficulty arose. The discovery of the islands had been made by an expedition belonging to the Virginia company, which under its charters was entitled to all islands within 100 miles of the coast. To meet this claim the older body sold its rights, on November 25th, 1612, to the members who were interested in the new scheme, for £2,000[3]. The raising of this sum involved the making of a second issue of shares, and the whole number was fixed at 400 in which 117 persons were interested[4].

The ill-fortune which had dogged the plantation in Virginia did not pursue that in the Somers Islands. The younger enterprize had the benefit of the experience gained since 1607, and there was not the same temptation to divert the energies of the settlers from agriculture to the search for mines. In another respect also this company was fortunate at the beginning of its history. Many of the difficulties that had already been experienced by the Virginia colony were financial, through the shareholders refusing to pay the instalments until they saw some return from the plantation. Such a return was forthcoming from the Somers Islands within a year after the company had been formed, through the discovery of a great quantity of ambergris by the men left on the islands by Sir George Somers, and which was recovered by the local governor, Richard Moore. At this period ambergris was a valuable commodity, being used both in medicine and as a perfume, and

---

[1] Chamberlain to Carleton, Feb. 12, 1612: Brown, *Genesis of the United States*, II. p. 537.

[2] Commission to Richard Moore, April 27, 1612, printed in *Memorials of the Bermudas*, by J. H. Lefroy, 1877, I. pp. 58–63; Force, *Tracts*, III., No. 3, p. 23.

[3] *Records of the Virginia Company*, II. p. 47.

[4] From a MS. note (Manchester Papers, Record Office, No. 273) "the Earl of Warwick, his account of Shares," it appears he obtained one share on the first subscription and another at the second. The remainder of his subsequent holding was acquired by purchase. Colonial Entry Book, XVII. pp. 1–46; Lefroy, *Memorials of the Bermudas*, I. p. 83.

DIV. II. § 2 B] *Success of the Plantation* 1612–13   261

it realized from 75*s.* to 60*s.* per oz.[1] The piece discovered was as large as the body of a giant, which it resembled in shape, save that the head and one arm were wanting. The weight of it was said to have been 160 lbs. to 190 lbs.[2] The finders succeeded in embezzling some at least of this quantity. There is a great variety in the estimates of the sum actually received by the company. Two contemporary accounts make the amount as large as between £9,000 and £11,000[3]. On the other hand, according to the account of the company in 1622, if the whole weight was 160 lbs. only one-third of it was actually received on behalf of the shareholders, which would be worth rather less than £3,000[4]. Like many other statements made during that period of acute controversy from 1619 to 1624, there is reason to believe that this one is inaccurate; indeed it was given as a mere estimate, since the account books were not available. It is known that the ambergris was sent home in three separate consignments, and there is some contemporary information relating to the quantities either received or exposed for sale on behalf of the company. The first consignment was between 20 lbs. and 30 lbs., the second is said to have been 64 lbs.[5] Independently of the third, which was still to arrive, these should have realized from £4,500 to £5,000, so that it is probable the total amount obtained was about double what was admitted by the company in 1622.

The funds derived from the sale of the ambergris, to which were to be added the proceeds of pearls found at the islands, were important in launching the company successfully. Not only did these resources diminish the need for pressing the shareholders to pay up instalments at short notice, but also, when capital was required later, it was readily provided. Operations were pushed on vigorously, first for fortifying the largest island, and then for planting the whole group. In 1613 the prospects of this colony were considered much more promising than those of Virginia, and some of the leading members who held shares in both were prepared to continue to contribute to the support of the

---

[1] Court Book, East India Company, III. p. 184; *Cal. Colonial, East Indies*, 1513–1616, p. 313; Chamberlain to Carleton, Oct. 27, 1613: Brown, *Genesis of the United States*, II. p. 667.

[2] Petition of M. Somers printed in *Records of the Virginia Company*, II. p. 46; *The Historye of the Bermudaes or Summer Islands*, edited by Sir J. H. Lefroy (Hakluyt Society, 1882), p. 21; cf. *A Plaine Description of the Bermudas*, by W. C., London, 1613, in Force, *Tracts*, III., No. 3, p. 13.

[3] Purchas, *His Pilgrims*, Glasgow, 1906, XIX. p. 179; Letter, Molina to Velasco in Brown, *Genesis of the United States*, II. p. 648.

[4] Answer of the Company to Somers' Petition: *Records of the Virginia Company*, II. p. 48.

[5] Chamberlain to Carleton, Aug. 1, 1613; Dispatch of Gondomar, Oct. 5, 1613: Brown, *Genesis of the United States*, II. pp. 655, 661.

Somers Islands, rather than of the older plantation[1]. As a consequence of these high expectations and under the stimulus of the success already achieved, as much as £20,000 had been expended on the Somers Islands at the end of 1614, and the population was 600 persons[2]. This outlay comprised the original purchase-price paid to the Virginia company, the cost of erecting fortifications and of transporting the settlers. Since, however, it was paid for to a considerable extent by the produce of the islands in the form of the ambergris, only the balance constitutes the share capital actually paid in by the members. By the end of 1613 settled rules of procedure in the transaction of business at the meetings of the members had been framed, as is shown by the opening of the first Court Book of the company, which began on December 3rd, 1613[3].

In 1614 matters were so far advanced that a survey of the land was ordered so that divisions might be made. In view of the large expenditure and the favourable prospects, it was decided to make the legal position of the company more secure by obtaining a charter. As a necessary preliminary step, on November 23rd, 1614, the islands were surrendered to the Crown[4]. By the charter, dated June 29th, 1615, those who had contributed the capital for the settlement were incorporated as *the Governor and Company of the City of London for the Plantation of the Somers Islands*, and to this body the Bermudas were formally granted. In this instrument the model of the first Virginia company was abandoned, and the undertaking for the Somers Islands was constituted with a governor and twenty-four assistants, one of the latter being chosen as deputy-governor. Sir Thomas Smythe, who was already head of the Virginia company, and who had been a prominent undertaker from the beginning of this venture, was governor, and William Canning deputy-governor. The company was empowered to make laws conformable to the laws of England and to grant lands[5].

When everything seemed to be promising there were concealed causes which temporarily arrested the progress of the plantation. The

[1] Digby to Carleton, May 22, 1613; Dispatch of de Acũna, March 17, 1614: Brown, *Genesis of the United States*, II. pp. 634, 680, 681.

[2] Brown, *Genesis of the United States*, II. pp. 755–6.

[3] Receipt for the Somers Islands Court Books: Ferrar Papers, Magdalene College, Cambridge. This book continued till Jan. 24, 1621. The second volume began on February 7, 1621, and at the date of this receipt had been continued till February 19, 1623.

[4] Brown, *Genesis of the United States*, II. p. 748. Mr Brown attributes this surrender to "fear of the Spaniards." It was purely formal and was due to legal reasons, since the Crown had granted the Bermudas to the Virginia company *after* the sale of them by that body to the Somers Islands company.

[5] State Papers, Colonial Entry Book, XVII. pp. 1–46, printed in Lefroy, *History of the Bermudas*, I. p. 83 et seq.

fortifications were well advanced, at the end of 1614 some tobacco had been shipped and the survey was begun[1]. But in 1615 the adventurers perceived some obstacle had arisen which delayed the dividend of land. This, they found, was due to the action of the governor of the islands, Richard Moore, who had placed impediments in the way of the surveyor[2]. Accordingly, in the general letters of the company, he was sharply reproved for "his peevishness and presumption," and he determined to return home, though his term was not expired[3]. Then followed a period of disorganization. The local executive consisted of a council, each of whom was to govern in turn for a month. None of the men were fitted to exercise authority, and they neglected the necessary works that should have been carried on, at the same time subsisting on the stores of the company. The adventurers discovered that a "perpetual Christmas" was being kept in the islands, and, through the neglect of those responsible, rats had multiplied to such an extent as to become a serious danger to the crops[4].

The problem of the choice of a new governor was a difficult one, and in the special circumstances there was little time for deliberation. At the Quarter Court, held in February 1616, Daniel Tucker was elected on the ground of his experience in Virginia, and he reached the Bermudas in the following May[5]. There he reformed the administration, continued the erection of fortifications, and opened up a direct trade with the West Indies, which promised to be profitable[6]. The adventurers in 1616 raised the first subsidiary stock for whale-fishing, but, at this time, the results were not satisfactory[7]. Meanwhile the survey of the land was pushed forward, and by 1617 the division to the adventurers was made. Since there were 400 shares, it was resolved that the dividend was to be 25 acres per share, distributed by lot, while the remaining land was reserved as "public," from the profits of which it was expected that the expenses of defence and administration should be defrayed. First of all the 400 shares and 10,000 acres to be divided were arranged in multiples of 50 shares and 1,250 acres, which were known as tribes. Each of these was named after one of the original adventurers of position who held ten shares. These were the Countess of Bedford, Sir Thomas Smythe (the governor), Lord Cavendish (after-

---

[1] *The Historye of the Bermudaes*, pp. 36, 41. [2] *Ibid.*, p. 36.
[3] *Ibid.*, pp. 39, 46.
[4] *Ibid.*, pp. 47–75; *The Generall Historie of Virginia, New England and the Summer Isles*, by John Smith, Glasgow, 1907, I. pp. 355–9.
[5] *The Historye of the Bermudaes*, pp. 69, 70; Brown, *Genesis of the United States*, II. p. 1033; Charles Wolferstone to Sir Robert Rich, May 24, 1617: Manchester Papers, No. 217.
[6] *The Historye of the Bermudaes*, pp. 78, 85.
[7] *Ibid.*, p. 82; Purchas, *His Pilgrims* (1906), XIX. p. 184.

wards Earl of Devonshire), Lord Pagett, the Earl of Pembroke, Sir Robert Mansefield, the Earl of Southampton, Sir Edwin Sandys. By the time the division was made, or soon afterwards, Sir Robert Mansefield has sold his shares, and Robert Rich, who succeeded to the Earldom of Warwick, became the titular head of this tribe, which was known as Warwick tribe. The shares of the Countess of Bedford, "being," it is said, "upon some secrets passed over to the Marquesse Hambleton," this tribe was called Hambleton, or Hamilton tribe. These changes were announced by proclamation in 1620[1]. The naming of the tribes did not imply any voluntary joining together of friends or acquaintances, since the land which fell to the lot of the same adventurer, who had a number of shares, was often situated in different tribes. An inspection of the map[2] will show at a glance how the remaining details of the allocation were arranged.

When the land had been assigned to the adventurers, the plantation entered on a new phase. A few of the members themselves proceeded to occupy and cultivate their property, but the majority sent out settlers who became their tenants, on the basis of retaining half the produce in return for their labour. One of the most difficult stages in the organization of the colony was the arranging for the transportation of people and supplies. This was effected by means of a separate joint-stock, which, as in the Virginia company, was called the Magazine. This subordinate undertaking hired shipping and bought the commodities required by the people on the islands. Any owner of land, who wished to send out tenants or labourers, paid the Magazine the agreed upon sum for passage-money[3], as also the freight on any goods he sent for his friends or dependents, who were already in the Bermudas. In addition, the officials of the Magazine-company purchased goods likely to be in demand, and on the arrival of the ship at the colony these were sold as against tobacco rated at 2s. 6d. per lb. The return cargo comprised this tobacco, together with that consigned by the tenants to the owners of land in England, on which freight was paid to the shareholders in the Magazine.

At first the arrangement of a tenancy on the basis of a half profit-system had been one of several methods of renting the land. By an order of the Court made in 1618 and confirmed on May 29th of that

---

[1] *The Historye of the Bermudaes*, pp. 165, 166; *Relations of Summer Islands*, by Richard Norwood 1625 [Brit. Mus. 679.h.14]; Smith, *Generall Historie* (1907), I. pp. 368–72.

[2] *Vide* the frontispiece of this volume.

[3] The rate for passage, apart from other expenses of supply, was £5 per head: Manchester Papers, No. 243.

DIV. II. § 2 B]   *Rules for Supply of Lands* 1618   265

year, this was ordained as the sole type of tenure¹. As early as the summer of this year the greater part of the acreage, divided to the shareholders, had been occupied, or, as it was termed by the company, "supplied." Some of the adventurers were backward, and, since rats multiplied in the vacant ground, two methods were adopted to stimulate the complete occupation of the islands. At a court meeting held on June 10th it was resolved that, in those cases where adventurers had not begun to occupy the land which had fallen to their lot, unless they gave security by the Quarter Court to be held on June 24th, of "making a supply," such land might be sold by the company, and the defaulting shareholders were to receive only "half the profits"—that is presumably half the sum realized in excess of the amount paid up on their shares. The remaining half of the profit was to be used towards discharging any debts due by the adventurers to the company and the Magazine, also to encourage others to supply the shares². At the Quarter Court of June 24th, the 36 standing orders already made were read, and a new one was added embodying this order, to which there was added the further clause that in the meantime, before the land was supplied, the tenants in the tribe where the vacant share was situated, might work it, paying one-fifth of the tobacco to the owner and dividing the rest rateably amongst them³. For several years a few shares of land remained unsupplied, and it appears that, though the penalty of a compulsory sale was not exacted, such shareholders were precluded from voting at the meetings of the court. At the same time efforts were made to remedy cases of individual hardship. Though the most fertile land was set apart for the division, it was alleged that parts of Warwick and Harrington tribes were barren. The court, while repudiating this statement, admitted that the land in these areas was less fertile than the average, by granting an addition to each of 200 acres from the public or surplus lands⁴.

When Tucker, the local governor, left the Bermudas in December 1618, the state of the plantation was very prosperous. As much as 30,000 lbs. of tobacco had been consigned to England in one cargo, which, it is recorded, "coming to a lucky market, gave the undertakers

---

¹ Proceedings of a Court of Committees of the Somers Islands, May 29, 1618: Manchester Papers, No. 235.
² Court of the Somers Islands, June 10, 1618: Manchester Papers, No. 235.
³ A Quarter Court of the Somers Islands, June 24, 1618: Manchester Papers, No. 235. These were printed with some additions, February 6, 1622, as *Orders and Constitutions partly collected out of his Maiesties Letters Patents and partly by authority and in Virtue of the said Letters Patents* [Brit. Mus. C. 32 . g . 22].
⁴ Court of Committees Somers Islands, June 30, 1618: Manchester Papers, No. 235.

great encouragement and contentment[1]." It is highly significant, in view of the frequency with which shareholders in early companies are recorded to have been in arrear in the payment of calls, that it was stated in 1618 that "few or none" of the Somers Islands adventurers were "indebted for their shares[2]." The reason for this exceptional punctuality in the payment of instalments is to be found in the good price at which the shares cum land-division could be sold. The Rich family had a relative, Robert Rich, in the Bermudas, who wrote about this time forecasting that the next harvest would yield "a great store of more vendible tobacco," and strongly urging the purchase of additional shares[3]. This advice was adopted, and in 1620 Robert Rich, Earl of Warwick, Sir N. Rich and Joseph Mann were the registered owners of 33 shares, while in 1619 as much as £12. 10s. a year (or 10s. per acre) was offered as rent for one of these[4].

C. THE VIRGINIA AND SOMERS ISLANDS COMPANIES FROM 1618 TO 1625.

The period from 1618 to 1625 was one of acute dissensions in the Virginia and Somers Islands companies. The issues involved in this protracted dispute are very complex, but an analysis of them is necessary since the origin of the strife and the manner in which it manifested itself were both conditioned by the methods of management of the internal affairs of the two companies, and, as the struggle progressed, the whole question of the representation of shareholders in influencing the policy of the management became increasingly important.

The beginnings of the tension are to be found in the relations of the local executives in Virginia and the Bermudas on the one side to the adventurers in England, and on the other to the planters in the colonies. An early instance of such difficulties is to be found in the indignation of the Rich family when Tucker, the local governor in the Somers Islands, imprisoned Robert Rich, who was agent for the land obtained in the division by his relatives in 1617[5]. Tucker was supported by Smythe, and a breach thus began between Smythe and the Earl of Warwick.

[1] *The Historye of the Bermudaes*, p. 110.
[2] Court of Somers Islands, June 10, 1618: Manchester Papers, No. 235.
[3] Robert Rich to his brother: Manchester Papers, No. 220.
[4] John Beckweth to Nath. Rich: Manchester Papers, No. 242. This particular share, being in Southampton tribe, did not participate in the bonus divided out of the surplus land in the previous year.
[5] Letter of Robert Rich to N. Rich, March 12, 1618: Manchester Papers, No. 231; *The Historye of the Bermudaes*, pp. 100, 101, 115.

This was intensified in the following year, when it became known that the council of the Virginia company had censured Samuel Argall, who was then deputy-governor and admiral of the colony, for maladministration and for "heaping many unjust accusations against the Magazine[1]." Now there was a close connection between Warwick and Argall, so that this reprimand constituted a further cause of offence to the former. It follows that in 1618 there was a division of opinion amongst the members of both companies as to the conduct of their representatives in the plantations. Warwick and his supporters were opposed to the continuance of Tucker in the Somers Islands, while they advocated the cause of Argall in Virginia. Smythe, and those who thought with him, took the opposite view in both cases. At a court meeting of the Somers Islands in the first half of the year 1618, it had been proposed that the qualifications of a possible successor to Tucker might be discussed "as a preparative" to the election of a new local governor, which was due to take place in 1619. Smythe, who was in favour of the re-election of Tucker, according to the account of an adherent of Warwick, refused peremptorily "and with much heate and passion" to accept this motion[2]. After the lapse of some months Smythe abandoned Tucker and decided to support Captain Southwell, while Warwick fixed on Nathaniel Butler as his candidate. Sir Edwin Sandys, a member of the council of the Virginia company and one of its audit committee, endeavoured to make interest in favour of his cousin George Sandys. During the vigorous canvass which ensued, the members of the Virginia company became involved in the contest, through Sandys' attempt to use his position as auditor to bring pressure to bear upon Smythe. The latter would not give way, and a considerable degree of acrimony was manifested at the meetings. Sandys declined to audit the books of account at Smythe's house, which was used as the office of the company, and Smythe refused to permit them to pass out of his own keeping. On the basis of this refusal, Sandys complained of the state of the accounts, hinting that the resources of the company had been squandered or misapplied[3]. Since Smythe had had a serious illness about 1616 it may have been that the books were not brought up to date, and it is to be noted that, when the list of adventurers was published in 1620, there were several instances of persons, who had paid in moneys on account of shares, whose names were not included[4]. In fairness to Smythe it

[1] Copy of a Letter from the Treasurer and Deputy Treasurer of the Virginia Company to Argall, August 22, 1618, in *Records of the Virginia Company*, II. pp. 51–3.
[2] *The Historye of the Bermudaes*, p. 116.   [3] *Ibid.*, p. 129.
[4] *Records of the Virginia Company*, I. pp. 581, 590, 618, 622; II. 77, 97, 145. In most cases there were peculiar circumstances. Some of the sums omitted being small payments on account of a single share, others being shares taken up from the lottery which were already included in the account of the latter, *vide supra*, p. 258.

should be added that (apart from the insinuations of Sandys) there was no real question of his integrity. On this point the testimony of Captain John Smith, a consistent opponent, may be taken as conclusive, especially when he records that the administration of 1616 "would hold it worse than sacrilege to wrong the company but a shilling[1]."

From innuendoes, Sandys proceeded to more detailed charges, eventually asserting that there could be no complete audit as long as Smythe, whose proceedings were to be examined, remained in "a perpetuall dictatorshyp[2]." Thus the next phase of the campaign involved the deposition of Smythe from the treasurership of the Virginia company. The chances of the campaign initiated by Sandys depended on the formation of groups of adventurers and also upon the method by which votes were taken on a division at the courts. Voting was by show of hands amongst those entitled to be present at the meeting, all of whom might not be shareholders, since a member of council could continue to hold office though he had never subscribed for stock. In the Somers Islands company the great majority of the shareholders were actively interested in the progress of the plantation, but in the Virginia company this was not so. Out of a total membership of close on 1,000 probably more than three-quarters had long considered the scheme to be impracticable, and many of these had not paid up the full amounts due on their shares. In the House of Commons alone there were 49 members who had abandoned their shares[3]. It was amongst this class that, under the existing conditions of voting, Sandys found the basis of his following. When the total poll was about 100 it would be comparatively easy to raise a sufficient following to turn the scale, if the opposing faction were not equally alert. It will be seen then that the strength of Sandys in the coming struggle was potential rather than actual. That of Smythe and Warwick was apparent. The latter was the largest shareholder in the Somers Islands, and he had many friends in both companies. Smythe had the support of James I. and of the leading merchants. Not only was he in close touch with many of the important shareholders, but he was considerably interested in the Magazines of both companies, while he may be taken to have represented the great holdings of the livery companies. Thus from several points of view his influence was great, even when voting was individually, not in proportion to the shares held and when there was no provision for proxies. By one ingenious device Sandys succeeded in diminishing Smythe's prospects of election. At a Preparative Court of the Virginia company, he represented that several of the adventurers could not vote according to their real opinions on a show of hands owing "to their

---

[1] *Generall Historie*, I. p. 233. [2] *The Historye of the Bermudaes*, p. 129.
[3] Manchester Papers, No. 371, printed in Brown, *Genesis of the United States*, II. pp. 802–3.

dependences" upon Smythe, wherefore it was resolved that the coming election should be *by ballot*[1]. The final step was a coalition of the Warwick and Sandys factions upon terms which were arranged at formal meetings between the leaders. Sandys on his part agreed to withdraw his candidate for the local governorship of the Bermudas and to give his influence towards the election of Butler, while Warwick on his side undertook to support Sandys for the chief office in both companies[2].

The outcome of these preparations appeared at the Quarter Court of the Virginia company, held on April 28th, 1619. Smythe, either from a desire to resign the cares of office or knowing the extent of the opposition, declined to seek re-election. Besides Sandys, two of Smythe's supporters were nominated, his son-in-law, Alderman Johnson, and Sir John Wolstenholme[3]. The ballot resulted in 59 votes for Sandys as against 41 divided between the other candidates. John Ferrar secured a slightly larger majority for the post of deputy-treasurer. It shows how far this election had been fought on strictly partisan lines, when it is noted that Ferrar had not either paid up calls nor purchased a share at the time he was nominated, indeed he contented himself with subscribing £12. 10s. for a single share[4] until he obtained four others on the death of his father, Nicholas Ferrar, sen. The holdings of the others were in 1620: Smythe, £145; Sandys, £212. 10s.; Johnson, £185; though these amounts are to be interpreted subject to the qualifications that both Smythe and Johnson were largely interested in the Magazine, while the former is recorded at this time to have sold some of his shares in the general stock and in Smythe's Hundred.

So far the coalition between the Sandys and Warwick factions had been successful. In the following month (May 1619) the final stage of the agreement was reached at the Quarter Court of the Somers Islands company, when Warwick secured the election of Butler as the local governor. Then came a hitch in the carefully planned scheme. Sandys, much to his chagrin, was defeated in his candidature as governor, and Smythe was re-elected, while Johnson was continued as deputy[5]. Thus Sandys and his supporters had failed to obtain a complete victory over Smythe, since the latter remained in control of the Somers Islands

[1] *The Historye of the Bermudaes*, p. 131.   [2] *Ibid.*, p. 130.
[3] *Records of the Virginia Company*, I. p. 212.
[4] A complete List of the Adventurers to Virginia: Manchester Papers, No. 241; Shareholders in the London Company [of Virginia], Colonial Papers, II. 33; *A Declaration of the State of the Colony and Affairs of Virginia*, 1620 [Brit. Mus. 1447. c. 11].
[5] Chamberlain to Carleton, May 8, 1619: State Papers, Domestic Correspondence, James I., CIX. 18; *The Historye of the Bermudaes*, p. 131.

company with the subsidiary joint-stocks of that undertaking, as well as the Magazine of the Virginia company. It was not long before friction showed itself in connection with the enterprize last named. The adventurers in the Magazine elected their director and committees, while most, if not all, of this body were adherents of Smythe. Sandys used the same strategy, that had already served him well, in demanding an account within two months of his own election. On July 7th, 1619, he threatened Johnson that complaint would be made to the Privy Council and a suit instituted. Johnson replied angrily and was censured[1]. The next step was to secure the winding up of the Magazine. This was effected on February 2nd, 1620, when a resolution was passed by the court of the Virginia company declaring the trade to the colony open, and that the Magazine would be dissolved as soon as its affairs could be wound up[2]. The minutes of the meeting are so carefully worded that they convey the impression that a part of the policy of the new administration was the abolition of the restrictions on commerce with the colony, which had been framed in the interests of the merchants who had formerly been in control. A careful scrutiny of the available information shows that the real object was not to abolish magazines, financed by subsidiary joint-stocks, but to manage that the direction of this enterprize should be in the hands of supporters of the party that was now dominant. It is true that the minutes are silent as to the formation of a new Magazine, but it was not long before incidental references begin to appear, which show that a new one had been constituted. Thus in July 1621 there is mention of "the last Magazine adventure[3]," and in the previous May Sir George Yeardley writes directly to the New Magazine company[4]. It appears further that this undertaking was begun immediately after the Magazine company of 1617 had been noticed to dissolve, since in a dispatch, dated September 11th, 1621, the former is described as having been begun "almost two years ago," while, from other references in the same document, it is clear that no steps had been taken in 1619, so that the commencement of this venture may be assigned to the earlier part of 1620[5].

---

[1] Minutes relating to the censure on Alderman Johnson, July 8, 1619; Short draft of censure on Alderman Johnson: Manchester Papers, Nos. 250, 251; *Records of the Virginia Company*, I. pp. 241, 244.

[2] *Ibid.*, I. p. 303.   [3] *Ibid.*, I. p. 519.

[4] Sir G. Y. to the New Magazine Company, May 16, 1621: Ferrar Papers, Magdalene College, Cambridge.

[5] Letter of the Council and Company to the Governor and Council in Virginia, Sept. 11, 1621, MS. Records Virg. Co. (Library of Congress, Washington), III., Part II. pp. 19, 20, printed in *The Virginia Company of London*, by Edward D. Neil, Albany, 1869, p. 242.

Sandys found other difficulties to face, outside the friction with Smythe's supporters in the company. The close connection with the Somers Islands colony was now broken, and, though joint action was often desirable, it had become impossible. An instance of this arose in 1620, which dissolved the alliance between Sandys and Warwick. The latter was either the owner of, or a principal shareholder in the ship *Treasurer*, which had been sent on a voyage which was characterized as piratical by the Spanish Ambassador. The Privy Council took action in the matter, and Sandys found himself in a position of great difficulty. According to the account he gave at a later date, when his rupture with Warwick was complete, the latter had " deterred him by threats of blood " from disclosing the names of the true owners of the vessel[1]. Whether Sandys had permitted himself to be terrorised or not, it is certain that the name of Warwick was erased from the documents that were submitted to the Privy Council[2]. It had happened that the *Treasurer* had returned from her expedition to the Somers Islands, where some negroes, which were Warwick's share of the plunder, were handed over to Butler, the local governor. Sandys took the opportunity of endeavouring to use this incident as the occasion of attacking Smythe, on the ground that the Bermudas had become infested with pirates for whom the inhabitants were said to have "a great likinge," but the court refused to hear him, and he was forced to make the speech at a later meeting of the Virginia company[3].

Two different tendencies had the effect of ultimately making Sandys' control of the Virginia company untenable. Owing to his political views he was out of favour with James I., and in alienating Smythe he had closed many of the sources from which the company had been hitherto financed. During the first year, after the change of treasurers, the general stock was increased by £9,830, £7,000 of which was derived from the profit of the lottery and the remainder from various sources, most of which were unlikely to recur. The expenditure had been £10,431, the excess being accounted for by the old debts discharged being greater than those recovered[4]. Besides the general stock there was the subordinate company of the New Magazine, the paid up capital of which was £1,000[5]. The formation of particular plantations was encouraged, and a number of patents for such were issued. Several persons, who were interested in missionary enterprize, had given money towards starting this work, and the expenditure of these funds was under the control of the treasurer.

---

[1] *Records of the Virginia Company*, II. p. 405.
[2] Statement by Sir N. Rich [? 1620]: Manchester Papers, No. 279.
[3] *Records of the Virginia Company*, I. p. 367.
[4] *Ibid.*, I. p. 355.   [5] *Ibid.*, I. p. 480.

A little consideration will show that the whole financial superstructure rested on the receipts from lotteries, since, the colony not being able to exist without further capital expenditure, this was the sole source of funds for that expenditure. Whether James I. was sufficiently antagonistic to Sandys to show his displeasure in relation to the Virginia company, or whether, as seems likely, he was urged to action by the Smythe party, it was not long before Sandys began to feel the royal displeasure. When the time came for a new election of treasurer, James sent a strongly-worded message forbidding the adventurers to choose Sandys—according to one account his words were "Choose the Devil, if you will, but not Sir Edwin Sandys[1]." As a result of this interference, which was contrary to the charters, Henry Wriothesley, Earl of Southampton, was chosen unanimously as treasurer, at a meeting at which it is said as many as 500 persons were present[2]. He was a large adventurer, but as treasurer took little part in the affairs of the company, Sandys remaining the moving spirit. There were many at Court who were ready to show that the King's wish had been evaded, and the result was that the license to hold lotteries, which was dependent on the royal pleasure and was determinable on six months' notice, was withdrawn in March 1621[3]. If this action was taken on the advice of Smythe and his adherents[4] their conduct in the matter was highly reprehensible. It is true that the Somers Islands company, which they controlled, would be unaffected, and the opposed administration of the Virginia colony would be left with such meagre resources that its failure was inevitable. At the same time there was the danger that, while the Sandys party was becoming discredited, the interests of the colony, thus deprived of the capital urgently needed for its development, would be endangered. Thus the dissensions of the past two years were tending towards disaster in the future.

The outlook was made more serious by the position of the tobacco trade on which the planters depended for a living. In the early part of the year 1619 a patent had been applied for, which aimed at the sole importation of tobacco[5], and a grant of this nature was made on April 10th, 1620[6]. Meanwhile, on December 30th, 1619, the company had

[1] *A Short Collection of the Most Remarkable Passages from the Originall to the Dissolution of the Virginia Company*, London, 1651.
[2] *Memoirs of the Life of Mr Nicholas Ferrar*, by P. Peckard, Cambridge, 1790, p. 95.
[3] State Papers, Colonial Entry Book, LXXXIX. p. 201; *Calendar, Colonial*, 1574–1660, p. 25; Soc. Antiq. Proclamations, James I., No. 164.
[4] Southampton seemed to blame Smythe and his party as having "misled" James I., cf. *Records of the Virginia Company*, II. p. 35.
[5] *Records of the Virginia Company*, I. p. 219.
[6] State Papers, Privy Council Register, James I., IV. p. 475.

Effects of the Tobacco Monopoly 1620

obtained a proclamation forbidding the planting of tobacco in England on condition of paying an extra 6*d.* per lb. in customs[1]. The joint effect of this additional tax and of the monopoly of importation had been unfortunate for the company. The two Magazines were special sufferers, since both companies were compelled to take the tobacco from the planters at the specified rates, while the changed conditions at home prevented the former ratio of profit being realized. The Old Magazine, which had been moderately prosperous in the time of Smythe's treasurership, sustained losses on its remaining assets, so that by 1624 out of £7,000 subscribed only £4,000 had been repaid to the adventurers. The position of the New Magazine was even more endangered, and it appears that the adventurers obtained very little, if any, of the capital they had subscribed, when it was wound up[2]. Feeling between the Virginia and Somers Islands companies had become so embittered that hearty co-operation was impossible. Neither side was satisfied to let past disputes rest. Mention has already been made of the possibility that the Smythe party had influenced James I. against Sandys; while, in the Virginia company, the supporters of the latter showed themselves intolerant to the minority. One by one the more prominent members of the opposition were silenced. Canning, a former deputy-governor of the Somers Islands company, had been censured as "a great disturber of the peace" of the sister-plantation[3], while Woodall, who was said to have characterized an official publication of the company as a libel, was both censured and suspended from attending the courts for three months[4]. A dispute, initiated at the instance of Sir Thomas Wroth, raises a question which is fundamental, in so far as he challenged the accuracy of the minutes of the court as giving a fair representation of the general tenour of the proceedings[5]. A careful inspection of the copy extant shows that, in the report of the meetings, the speeches of members of the Sandys party are recorded at considerable length, while those of the opposition are dealt with in a summary manner. Obviously there are only two fair methods of constructing such documents; either, on the one hand, to include only motions, resolutions and official documents, or, on the other, if the gist of speeches be given, to summarize these with strict impartiality. Now it was admitted that Sandys, but chiefly the two Ferrars—John and Nicholas junior—subjected the draft minutes to a considerable amount of editing[6]. How far this practice extended (or was

---

[1] Soc. Antiq., Proclamations, James I., No. 133.
[2] Letter of the Company to the Governor and Council in Virginia, Sept. 11, 1621, in Neil, *Virginia*, p. 242.
[3] *Records of the Virginia Company*, I. p. 259.
[4] *Ibid.*, I. p. 408.   [5] *Ibid.*, I. p. 366.
[6] *Ibid.*, I. p. 372.

believed to extend) is shown by the subsequent demand of the opposition that what were called the "blurred" minute books should be produced[1]. The complaint in this case was that there would be found important discrepancies, showing that the original record by the secretary had been altered and emended by the Ferrars or others. Much, necessarily, turns on the question whether this editing consisted of the making of merely verbal or essential alterations. Fortunately there exists a document of the Somers Islands company, written at a later date when the Sandys party was in control, which has all the appearance of having been dealt with in manner similar to that described[2]. In this case alterations have been made in the handwriting of John Ferrar tending to improve the arguments of his party, while, when he comes to deal with those of the opposition, these are mutilated; indeed the speech of Richard Edwards is so heavily inked (or blurred) out that only the opening sentences are legible. It is thus clear that the reliability of the extant court books is subject to no little suspicion.

It is not to be concluded that the Sandys party were the sole offenders. Their opponents in the Somers Islands courts exacted reprisals. At the election of a governor in May 1620 (when Smythe was again returned) the celebrated ballot box was sent by the Virginia company and, as was perhaps not unnatural, the dominant party gave expression to their feelings by confiscating it[3]. The Sandys party, who remained in a minority there for another year, complained that the courtesies of debate were not observed. Thus when Southampton, according to the Virginia minutes, went to a Somers Island court to endeavour to settle some outstanding questions concerning the Old Magazine with Johnson, there appears to have been a heated argument which ended in "Mr. Alderman" saying "there was not a word of truth" in "his Lordship's" statements[4].

In July 1620 Sandys discovered a method of exacting retribution from the Somers Islands company, under the guise of performing a disinterested and charitable action. The patentees for the sole importation of tobacco had given notice to the two companies that, during the ensuing year, only 55,000 lbs. of tobacco from the colonies might be imported. Sandys himself proposed that, since the Somers Islands subsisted solely on this crop and stood "in need of all the help which in that kind may be given them," the whole amount specified should be assigned to the smaller company, the Virginia plantation taking its

---

[1] Draft Instructions for the Commissioners for Virginia: Manchester Papers, No. 330.

[2] Proceedings at an Extraordinary Court for the Somers Islands, March 17, 1623: Ferrar Papers, Magdalene College, Cambridge.

[3] *Records of the Virginia Company*, I. p. 368.   [4] *Ibid.*, I. p. 376.

chance of marketing its produce abroad[1]. The ingenuity, and at the same time the irony of this proposal are apparent when it is noted that the English customs on the tobacco of the plantations were at least 6d. per lb., while the Virginia company was able to agree with the town of Middleburg to land theirs there subject only to dues of ½d. per lb.[2]

This incident suggests the necessity of examining somewhat closely another instance of the apparent generosity of the Virginia company to the shareholders in the Somers Islands. Some members of the latter body urged the Quarter Court (held on November 15th, 1620) of the larger plantation to take into consideration the small acreage that it had been found possible to allot the adventurers in the Bermudas, contending that the area had proved much smaller than it was thought to have been at the time of the original sale. It was accordingly resolved that members of the Somers Islands company should rank for a dividend of land in Virginia as if their shares in the Bermudas were transferred to the older colony; in other words, they received an immediate bonus in land of 40,000 acres, subject to the specified scale of augmentation on their supplying it after the division had been made, and in addition 5,000 acres of public land[3]. It is significant that no steps were taken to give effect to this resolution until seven months later[4], when a patent for a part of the grant had been referred to the auditors. A knowledge of the relations between the companies suggests the inference that this bonus is to be construed in relation to the election of a governor of the Somers Islands company in May 1621. Previously Smythe had a small majority, sufficient to secure his election in 1620. Obviously the promise of such an immense bonus would influence the voting, and that all the more since it had not been fulfilled when the vote was taken. Whatever may have been the causes, Southampton was returned as governor and John Ferrar as his deputy, Nicholas Ferrar succeeding him in 1622 as deputy-treasurer of the Virginia company, so that the Sandys party, after two years of effort, was at length in power, not only in both companies, but also in the subsidiary joint-stocks.

More however lay behind. Some of the syndicate, owning the patent for the importation of tobacco, were members of the companies, and both Sandys and Smythe had already formed schemes for a transfer of this lucrative monopoly from the present managers of it[5]. Neither would accept the proposals of the other and therefore, from the point of view of Sandys, it was absolutely necessary that his nominees should hold office in the Somers Islands company. It would appear that this success

---

[1] *Records of the Virginia Company*, I. p. 406.
[2] *Ibid.*, I. pp. 282, 422.
[3] *Ibid.*, I. p. 425.
[4] *Ibid.*, I. p. 493.
[5] *Ibid.*, II. pp. 67, 68.

came too late to allow the companies to tender for the year 1621-2, but Sandys was fully prepared in 1622 and had an elaborate proposition ready which he expounded at a court held on June 5th, 1622[1]. The details of the proposal were frequently modified on subsequent discussion, but the main principles of the scheme remained the same, namely that the companies should be the sole importers of all tobacco, not only from the plantations but also from Spanish possessions, they on their part increasing the revenue of the Crown from this source. Thus the outcome of the situation was that Sandys, the determined critic of exclusive privileges for foreign trade in 1604[2], by 1622 becomes the propounder of a monopoly much more far reaching than any of those he condemned. Whether this inconsistency was real or only apparent can be best discussed later, though it should be noted that, in support of the second alternative, it might be pleaded that the monopoly was already in existence and that it would be less oppressive if administered by persons who were connected with, and vitally interested in the future of the plantations[3]. A partial explanation, on somewhat different grounds, was afforded by Sandys himself, who urged that it was clearly shown by the effects of the currency crisis of 1620 that it was desirable to diminish the exportation of bullion to Spain in payment for commodities, chief amongst which was tobacco, which was imported to England from that country to the extent of £100,000 annually[4].

In another direction the capture of the Somers Islands company by the Sandys party seems to have encouraged it towards increased activity. The want of financial resources had hindered the development of Virginia. The suspension of the lotteries—"the reall and substantiall food" by which the plantation had been nourished[5]—had left the company in debt[6]. The general stock was described as being "clean exhausted[7]," and the shares were selling at from 40s. to 50s. each in May 1621[8]. To carry on the plantation it was clear that a new source of capital must be discovered, and this was sought in an extension of the principle of subsidiary companies, each formed for some specific purpose. In July 1621 a number of these were floated. There was *a Joint-Stock for providing Apparel and other Necessaries*, with a capital of at least £1,800, which took over the remains of the previous one at a valuation[9]. This enterprize was expected to return a good profit to the adventurers

---

[1] *Records of the Virginia Company*, II. pp. 36, 37.

[2] *Vide supra*, Part I., Chapter VI.

[3] *Records of the Virginia Company*, II. p. 309.

[4] *Proceedings and Debates of the House of Commons in 1620 and 1621*, Oxford, 1766, I. p. 270.

[5] *Records of the Virginia Company*, I. p. 451.

[6] *Ibid.*, I. p. 458.   [7] *Ibid.*, I. p. 627, II. p. 13.

[8] *Ibid.*, I. p. 469.   [9] *Ibid.*, I. pp. 485, 566, 623, II. 133.

DIV. II. § 2 c] *Subsidiary Joint-Stocks* 1622   277

in it, but these anticipations were disappointed. About the same time a joint-stock for glass works in Virginia was formed, for which £1,000 was subscribed, divided into shares of £10 each[1], another for sending out shipwrights with an equal capital[2], and a third for a trade in furs for which £900 in shares of £8 each was adventured[3]. Probably to the same period the adventure of the bloomery works is to be assigned[4]. Yet another undertaking of the same kind was *the Joint-Stock for transporting* 100 *maids to be made wives*[5], and at the same time a similar venture for the Somers Islands was floated[6]. The Virginia matrimonial speculation was based on the calculation that it cost £12 for the passage of each of the young women, while the planter, who married one of them, repaid the adventurers for her expenses at the rate of 150 lbs. of tobacco. If the standard rate of 3s. per lb. was obtained, this left a gross profit on the transportation of 50 of £505, so that it is little wonder the results gave the adventurers " great contentment[7]." All the other particular joint-stocks ended in loss, except in so far as those of them, that sent out workmen, obtained a grant of land of 50 acres for each person transported.

While these joint-stocks were being brought into operation, the consideration of the proposed tobacco contract was being continued. At length on November 27th, 1622, the court of the Somers Islands company confirmed the draft as amended, after a division, in which 21 voted in favour of confirmation and 20 against[8]. On the very same day, at an extraordinary court of the Virginia company, the organization of the scheme was debated. It was proposed first that the officials, considered necessary, should be determined with their salaries. It was proposed that there should be a director receiving £500 a year, a deputy-director or treasurer who was to be paid £400, eight committees whose fees were £50 a year each (or £400 in all), and a number of minor officials, so that the whole working charges were estimated at £2,500. Sandys was to be director, and the other posts of profit were to be

[1] *Records of the Virginia Company*, I. pp. 513, 514, 566.
[2] *Ibid.*, I. p. 513, II. pp. 115, 132; Letter of the Company to the Governor and Council in Virginia, Dec. 5, 1621, in Neil, *Virginia*, p. 267.
[3] *Records of the Virginia Company*, I. pp. 515, 567, II. p. 151.
[4] *Ibid.*, II. p. 484, cf. *infra*, pp. 288–9.
[5] *Ibid.*, I. pp. 514, 566.
[6] *The Historye of the Bermudaes*, p. 271. An earlier subsidiary of the Somers Islands company was the joint-stock for sugar (1620), *Ibid.*, p. 226.
[7] Letter of the Company to the Governor and Council in Virginia, Sept. 11, 1621, in Neil, *Virginia*, p. 245; *Records of the Virginia Company*, II. pp. 15, 115.
[8] Proceedings of Quarter Court of the Somers Islands in *Records of Virginia Company*, II. p. 159. The names are given and those for the contract actually number 22, that of Sandys being interlined.

allocated amongst his supporters[1]. This proposition was first received with stupefaction and then aroused bitter opposition amongst the adventurers. The scale of payment was unprecedented. Smythe, after being governor of the East India company for five years, was offered £650 as a gratuity for the whole period, and he refused to accept more than £400[2]. For twelve years' service, as treasurer of the Virginia company, he obtained 20 shares of a nominal value of £250; Sandys received as much for his efforts in the same capacity during one year, and John Ferrar a like amount for being deputy for three years[3]. If again a comparison be made with the fees payable to officers of State out of the Exchequer the same result is reached—the Chief Justice of England received £258. 6s. 8d., the Chief Justice of Common Pleas £194. 19s. 9d., most of the other judges £188. 6s. 8d., the Master of Ceremonies £200, the Secretary of State £100, and so on[4].

The first consequence of the intense hostility, aroused on this question of salaries, was the reunion of the Smythe and Warwick parties. Since Smythe had been narrowly defeated in 1621 at the election for a governor of the Somers Islands company, and was only in a minority by one vote on the contract in November 1622 (on both of these occasions the Warwick party abstained from voting), it would seem to be certain that the joint vote would be in a considerable majority. It is possible to reconstruct a poll of this company since documents are extant, giving the names of the shareholders, the number of shares, and almost all can be assigned to the party to which they belonged[5]. It may be premised that members, who had not supplied their land, could not vote; some had gone to reside themselves in the Bermudas, and one was a woman[6]. Altogether there were 74 adventurers eligible to vote, but for various reasons four of these were unable to exercise the franchise. This left the maximum poll 70. Now, if besides the known supporters of Sandys, all those that cannot be identified as belonging to the opposite party be added, the most that he could poll on a division would be 33, leaving 37 for the Smythe-Warwick faction, or a majority of at least four votes. Probably the real superiority of the latter on a complete

[1] *Records of the Virginia Company*, II. p. 151.
[2] Court Book of the East India Company, II., July 4, 1609.
[3] *Records of the Virginia Company*, I. pp. 214, 469, II. p. 31.
[4] *An Abstract or Brief Declaration of the Present State of his Majesties Revenew*, London, 1651, pp. 39, 40, 45, 46. (This tract is reprinted in Somers, *Tracts*, x. p. I.) One of the King's physicians received £400, the rest from £50 to £100 (p. 49). Needless to say these officials had numerous perquisites.
[5] Lists of Shareholders in the Somers Islands: Manchester Papers, Nos. 257, 305; List of those that oppose the Contract: *Ibid.*, No. 310, also the voting at the Quarter Court, Nov. 27, 1622, *Records of the Virginia Company*, II. pp. 159, 160.
[6] List of those that have supplied their shares: Manchester Papers, No. 307.

poll would have been something less than ten votes. It is to be remembered that a division was taken on a show of hands; had voting been according to shares, the superiority of the Smythe-Warwick group would have been still more marked. Out of the 400 shares, approximately 287 were owned by adventurers entitled to vote, of which at least 173 were to be credited to the supporters of Smythe and Warwick, possibly 114 to Sandys, giving a majority of 59 shares. This would have been the position had every share been polled, supposing this method had been permissible, and it is noteworthy that at the contest in November 1622, when the Warwick party did not vote, Smythe had a majority in shares, the figures being approximately 72 in his favour as against 57 for Sandys[1]. The position in the Virginia company cannot be determined with the same degree of precision. At an early stage of the contest a rough list was compiled of opponents of the salaries, which contained the names of 85 adventurers[2]. If there be added those who voted against Sandys at the Somers Islands courts and who were also members of the Virginia company, as well as others who spoke against the contract at meetings of the latter body, the total would slightly exceed 100. The largest number of votes recorded in favour of Sandys at a division was 117 at the election of Southampton as treasurer against Clethero, one of the nominees of James I.[3] This was in May 1622, before the division over the salaries had occurred, and it might be expected that his self-seeking would have lost Sandys a number of supporters, so that, if the Smythe-Warwick party could muster its full strength, there would have been doubt as to the result. If the investigation be extended to the amount of capital represented in the general stock, in this case also there would probably be a balance in favour of the party which was in a minority by a mere count of heads, certainly if the leaders on each side be compared those of the Smythe and Warwick party were the largest investors. All of these were materially interested in one or other of the colonies, often in both. On the other side, though Southampton was a very large shareholder and Sandys a large one, the remainder of those who were most aggressive on this side had little more than nominal holdings. The two Ferrars, between them, had at one time only three shares in the Virginia company

---

[1] In this calculation five names in the majority cannot be identified in the lists. Those of the same number of Smythe's supporters are not given. Each of these ten persons is credited with one share each to make the totals complete. It is likely that the five supporting Smythe owned more shares than the same number voting for Sandys.

[2] List of Adventurers that dislike the present Proceedings in the Virginia and Somers Islands companies, April, 1623: Manchester Papers, No. 327.

[3] *Records of the Virginia Company*, II. p. 29.

and the same number in the Somers Islands[1]. A more flagrant instance is that of Sir Edward Sackville, who became governor of the Somers Islands company in 1623, where he only held one share, and that too is not in the list of those supplied. As for the Virginia company, though his name is in the third charter, there is no evidence that he was an adventurer in the sense of having paid any calls on shares to the cash-keeper.

It would seem certain that the Smythe-Warwick party should have regained control of the Somers Islands company. But, as against the small numerical majority, there was the risk that some of the older members, like Smythe himself, might not be able to vote, through ill-health or press of affairs. Still, when there was a distinctive superiority in their aggregate shares, it was always possible, by transferring a single share to a trusted friend, to increase the quantity of votes. There is some evidence that Warwick adopted this method, certainly at one period he "passed unto severall men" eight shares, each to a different person who was a close personal friend or supporter[2]. The method adopted by the Sandys party to maintain its ascendancy was ingenious. This consisted in "suspending" a sufficient number of their opponents to preclude the possibility of an adverse vote. According to a list, perhaps drawn up before the election of 1623, 14 adventurers were to be classed in this category. Some of them may have been disqualified for failing to supply their shares, but the majority were active followers of Warwick[3]. The management of the Virginia company was less difficult. There were powers to elect members of council, who might vote, though not shareholders; and, during the critical period, this body was largely increased in numbers. Moreover, in the past, occasionally persons of distinction had been made free of the company. From the middle of 1622 such honorary admissions became numerous. These free-men were entitled to attend meetings, and, when present, it was not unlikely that they voted[4]. Further, when a court was carried

---

[1] It may be added that John Ferrar spent capital in developing his land in the two plantations. His average for the number of persons sent to the Somers Islands is one of the highest, being eight men per share as against the usual three per share. He also promoted "a particular plantation" in Virginia.

[2] Shares of the Rich Family: Manchester Papers, No. 273. In *Rep. Royal Com. Hist. MSS.*, VIII., Part II. p. 35, this document is dated "before September 1620." If this were the true date, these names should have been included in the lists of 1622, but seven of them are wanting. Besides, in 1620, Nathaniel Butler, who is one of the eight, was in the Bermudas, cf. *Records of the Virginia Company*, II. p. 406.

[3] List indicating whose voices were suspended: Manchester Papers, No. 308.

[4] For instance Samuel Purchas was admitted in May 1622. He was a member of a court on November 19, 1623 (*Records of the Virginia Company*, II. p. 485). Purchase himself records that he "had neither lands in Virginia nor other adventure therein," being "onely a Freeman" (*Pilgrims*, XIX. p. 265).

on in the midst of great disorder, as was soon to happen, the practice of voting by ballot was subject to abuse—indeed it was alleged that, on one occasion, ladies and even serving men possessed themselves of balls and placed them in the urn or box, and that these were counted as votes[1]. Another general aspect of the controversy, which reflects little credit on either party, was that, in the heat of the strife, it would almost seem that the massacre of 1622 was ignored. The crisis in the affairs of the colony was a most serious one, and it is amazing that the minutes contain only incidental and scattered references to this great calamity. The adventurers were never told in open court of the need for sending supplies to the surviving planters until the summer of 1623, when, under pressure from the Privy Council, steps were taken to afford tardy succour. In justice to the adventurers who did not hold office, it should be added that Sandys and the Ferrars were charged with suppressing information as to the true state of the plantation and of causing misleading reports to be sent from it, which were written with the intention of making it appear that the colony was in a satisfactory condition[2]. From the admissions of the Sandys party, it can be shown that there was a considerable basis for these accusations. On one occasion, when letters had arrived from Virginia shortly before a court was held, mention was made of the fact, and it was stated that, after the officials had perused them, it would be determined whether the contents should be communicated or not. At another time it was shown that Nicholas Ferrar had withheld a petition from the colony[3]. On the other hand, the more prominent members of the opposition cannot be wholly exonerated, since they cannot have failed to have sufficient evidence of the magnitude of the disaster, through private channels of communication open to them.

These various considerations indicate the conditions under which the battle over the salaries was waged and explain the nature of the tactics pursued. The proposal had been sprung upon the court of the Virginia company held on November 27th, 1622. This was the main point made by Samuel Wrote, a member of the council, at the next meeting on December 4th. His language was forcible, and was taken as a personal insult by Southampton and Lord William Cavendish. He stated that the "busines was not fairly carried, but matters were hudled up, and some thinges were fowly and surreptitiously carried, with much art and to private endes and that the companies durst not speake because they

---

[1] *Records of the Virginia Company*, II. p. 198.
[2] Draft of Instructions for the Commissioners for Virginia, Draft of Articles of Enquiry: Manchester Papers, Nos. 330, 331.
[3] *Records of the Virginia Company*, II. p. 298.

were overawed[1]." The reply of Nicholas Ferrar to the charge of springing the question of salaries on the adventurers is not wholly convincing. He alleged that it had been propounded by himself at a meeting of the council "four or five days" before the November court[2], to which Wrote answered that no such proposition had been made in the regular course of business, that it had been impossible to follow the matters discussed through a number of those present talking together by the fire[3]. Another ground of objection was the method by which the tobacco contract was to be organized. It was proposed to form two subsidiary joint-stocks, the one for importing Spanish, the other for Virginia tobacco. The proposed capital was comparatively small, £15,000 being suggested at one time as that of the former, and further funds were to be raised as required by borrowing on the security of the tobacco purchased, backed by the credit of the seal of the company. The opponents of the salaries affected to be alarmed at the speculative character of the enterprize, and they pointed out that, in case of failure, the whole body of adventurers might be assessed, as had happened in the Russia company[4]. The debate was continued with much heat and bitterness, and finally Wrote appealed to the next Quarter Court[5]. In the meantime, however, the feud broke out in the Somers Islands court, where, on Wrote repeating that he had been overawed at the Virginia meeting by Southampton, the latter exclaimed that if any man should say "he durst not speake, it was put into his mouth by the Devill, the father of lyes, for a fowler lye himself never told"—this incident Wrote termed, giving him "the lye in the third person[6]." After several further angry and protracted meetings, Wrote was censured and suspended. But the opposition was not left without spokesmen. Sir N. Rich and Johnson were frequent speakers, openly urging conciliation, in reality, it may be guessed, endeavouring to make the scheme of the majority impracticable. On February 12th, 1623, the adversaries of the salaries refused to debate the question further in the Virginia courts, reserving their objections for the Somers Islands meeting to be held on the 17th[7]. As already shown, the Smythe-Warwick party was stronger there; and, if one of the two companies condemned the scheme, it would suffice to wreck it. This move was met shortly afterwards by both companies being forced to meet together for the transaction of such business as related to the contract. Rich, at

---

[1] *Records of the Virginia Company*, II. pp. 163–89.
[2] *Ibid.*, II. p. 164.   [3] *Ibid.*, II. p. 173.
[4] *Ibid.*, II. pp. 165, 194; with reference to this assessment of the Russia company see Division I., Section II. (B, C and D).
[5] *Ibid.*, II. p. 176; *vide supra*, p. 281.
[6] *Ibid.*, II. p. 303.   [7] *Ibid.*, II. p. 266.

this stage in his speeches, differed from Wrote in abstaining from reopening the question of the tobacco monopoly, and there was a scene between him and Southampton, through the latter describing his motion to separate the consideration of the two issues as both "impertinent and impossible[1]." The contest, which had raged so furiously at the meetings of the Somers Islands company that these assemblies were described as "cock-pits rather than courts," was now transferred to the joint-gatherings, and it was alleged that strangers, even women, were invited to be present "in a lattice-gallery" to witness the altercations[2].

Though the Smythe-Warwick party had been out-voted, in the latter half of February 1623, it had secured much for which it had contended. The Lord Treasurer told Sandys plainly that the opposition was so strong that the tobacco contract could not be given to the companies[3]. On February 19th it was announced that Sandys could by no means "any longer hold the place of director[4]." It is not without significance that at this time both the Ferrars transferred all the shares in the Virginia company save one each, and Southampton also sold some[5]. This transaction may have been with a view to qualifying additional voters, but even so it was precisely of the same nature as that condemned in the case of Warwick.

The most severe blow dealt to the Sandys administration was directed by Nathaniel Butler, who had returned from his governorship of the Somers Islands. Probably on the suggestion of the heads of the party to which he belonged, instead of coming straight home, he visited Virginia, and he arrived bringing documents attacking the dominant party in relation to both settlements. The allegations from the Somers Islands complained of unfair accounts between the owners of land and their tenants, that orphans of persons deceased were kept "in little better condition than slaves," and that the settlers "were undone by the unreasonable rates they were charged by the Magazine[6]." The reply of the company to the last accusation was that "at what rates or prices soever the goods of their Magazine was sold for there, they never received penny profitt as yet nor scarce their principall[7]"—this result it

[1] Memoriall of some thinges in the derivative preparatory Court of the Somers Islands, February 17, 1623: Manchester Papers, No. 300.
[2] Draft Statement: Manchester Papers, No. 347.
[3] *Records of the Virginia Company*, II. p. 297.   [4] *Ibid.*, II. p. 272.
[5] *Ibid.*, II. pp. 135, 243, 279, 412; State Papers, Colonial, II. 33 (printed in *Virginia Magazine*, IV. p. 299).
[6] Complaints of the Setlers in the Somers Islands, printed in *The Historye of the Bermudaes*, pp. 294, 295.
[7] Proceedings at a Court Meeting of the Somers Islands company, March 17, 1623: Ferrars Papers, Magdalene College, Cambridge.

may be noted was better than that obtained from the subsidiary joint-stocks of the other plantation. In dealing with the Bermudas, Butler had to be careful not to impugn his own government, he had no such scruples in treating of Virginia. He prepared a document containing sensational disclosures, which was entitled *the Unmasked Face of Our Colony in Virginia as it was in the Winter of the Year* 1622[1]. In all 10,000 souls had been shipped to the plantation, of whom only 2,000 remained alive, many of whom were in a sickly and desperate condition—indeed, unless a remedy were soon found, Virginia might justly be termed a slaughter house, "both odious to ourselves and contemptible to all the world." On the basis of this information, the Smythe-Warwick party determined to appeal to the Crown for a Commission of Enquiry; and, during the month of April, its leaders were busy formulating charges, and even the terms of reference of the proposed body[2]. On April 14th both parties were summoned to appear before James I., and it is reported that Sir Edward Sackville was so insolent in the royal presence that he was severely rebuked[3]. By the 17th the two factions had been summoned before the Privy Council[4], when it was decided to institute a Commission, and in the meantime the opposing leaders were to agree on general letters to the colonies and to avoid contentious subjects in the courts. At a joint-meeting of both companies on May 7th an answer to the indictment framed by Johnson was read, which not only presented the case of the other side, but concluded with a bitter attack on Warwick[5]. A number of adventurers petitioned the Privy Council, stating that the making of such accusations was a breach of the order of April 17th[6], and on May 13th the Council ordered that Cavendish, Sandys and the two Ferrars should be confined to their houses for contempt[7]. By a further order of May 20th from the King, the Somers Islands company was directed to hold separate meetings for the future[8]. The adventurers were also commanded not to elect, at the court to be held on the 21st, any of

[1] State Papers, Colonial, II. 20 (1), printed in *Records of the Virginia Company*, II. pp. 374–6.
[2] Many of these drafts are preserved amongst the Manchester Papers, Nos. 330–54.
[3] State Papers, Domestic Correspondence, James I., CXLIII. 22.
[4] State Papers, Colonial Entry Book, LXXIX. pp. 203, 204.
[5] An Answer to a Petition delivered to his Majesty by Alderman Johnson: *Records of the Virginia Company*, II. pp. 393–9.
[6] Petition of sundry adventurers in the Virginia and Somers Islands companies to the Privy Council: Manchester Papers, No. 366.
[7] State Papers, Colonial Entry Book, LXXIX. pp. 205, 206.
[8] King's Letter to the Somers Islands Company, May 20, 1623: Manchester Papers, No. 369.

those who were under restraint[1] nor such as had held office previously, the conduct of the latter being under investigation by the Commission. In the face of this letter, Sir Edward Sackville was re-elected governor, and when it was known that, according to the report of the Commission (which was in draft by June), the administration of Smythe was exonerated and that of Sandys condemned, feeling between the two parties became even more bitter than it had been, being comparable only to the violence of the feud between the Guelphs and Ghibelines[2]. At the court held on July 16th, a fracas occurred in which a number of prominent persons were involved. Sandys attacked Warwick, and Lord William Cavendish supported the former, as far as can be judged, with much heat. Warwick returned him the lie direct, with the result that a duel was arranged to take place in Flanders. The ports were watched, and Cavendish was intercepted. Warwick made the journey in disguise, returning to England in August[3].

Sackville continued as governor till November 1623. Some time between that date and January 1624 an upheaval was witnessed in the company. Numerous attacks had been made on Sackville, for instance on March 7th an order was carried touching an omission in his account of what had happened at a meeting of the Privy Council relating to the conduct of the plantations when Johnson was in office[4]. His election in May 1623 was disputed, and in December 1623 or January 1624, for some reason unknown, an extraordinary court was summoned, at which Smythe was elected governor and Edwards his deputy. It might at first sight appear that, under the King's Letter of May 20th, Smythe was ineligible, as having already held office, but in the meantime the report of the Commission had appeared, and in any case he could count on the support of James I. The re-instatement of Smythe may have been delayed until it was known whether the charter of the company would be forfeited, but it became clear that, though the Sandys administration was condemned by the Commission as to the manner in which funds had been raised towards the payment of a debt of £1,000 and on some other points[5], the company itself would be continued. In order to lessen the gravity of this reverse, the opposing party was careful to speak of Smythe as the "pretending governor," and of the courts at which he

[1] The name of Sir John Danvers is added to those given in the Order of the Privy Council.
[2] State Papers, Domestic Correspondence, James I., CXLIX. 48.
[3] *Ibid.*; Letter to Rev. Joseph Mead, July 18, 1623, printed in Brown, *Genesis of the United States*, II. p. 847.
[4] Order of a Court for Virginia and the Somers Islands, March 7, 1623: Ferrar Papers, Magdalene College, Cambridge.
[5] Draft Report of the Commissioners on the Somers Islands: Manchester Papers, No. 384.

presided as "pretended courts[1]," or as "usurpations upon the government and not lawful courts[2]"; but that the authority was in Smythe's hands is shown by the fact that his election was confirmed by the Crown[3], and that it was admitted by the opposition that the books, papers and seals were in the custody of Smythe, and that the officials took their orders from him. A "court" of the Sandys party met on February 11th, 1624, which forbade Smythe to discharge any of the functions of governor, and demanded that the officials and servants should take their directions from Sackville[4]. For some time the rivalry of the courts may have continued till events in the Virginia company extinguished the last hopes of the Sandys party. The Commission adopted the views of Smythe and his supporters as to the shortcomings of the administration during the previous four years. Out of 4,000 emigrants in that period very few remained, and those in a weak and miserable state[5]. Smythe, it was added, had resigned, leaving 1,000 persons in the plantation. Therefore the Sandys party had to account for 5,000 inhabitants. Yet according to a return, addressed to John Ferrar by the secretary of the council in Virginia, in February 1624, which would certainly not underestimate the numbers, there were at that date only 1,275 people in the colony, of whom 22 were negroes[6]. On this "census," all that the Sandys party could show for the four years it had been in office was an increase of about 275 persons, as against 4,000 transported. Even if allowance is made for the possibility of the population of Virginia being overestimated early in 1619, the result is disastrous. Sandys, moreover, in the courts of the company, was wont to say that more had been accomplished from 1619 to 1622 at an expenditure of £10,000 than had been effected by Smythe at a cost of £80,000[7]. Verbally this was true, but in reality it was most disingenuous. The outlay on account of the general stock may not have exceeded £10,000, but the great bulk of the expense was defrayed outside of this by particular adventurers. Taking this fact into account, the estimate of the capital from all sources, devoted to developing the plantation from 1619 to 1623, of between £80,000 and £90,000, becomes intelligible[8]. This would compare with £67,000 spent by

---

[1] Proceedings at a "Quarter Court of the Somers Islands" (composed of the Sandys party), Feb. 11, 1624: Manchester Papers, No. 395.

[2] *Records of the Virginia Company*, II. p. 501.

[3] Sir N. Rich's Speech to the King: Manchester Papers, No. 397.

[4] Proceedings at a "Quarter Court of the Somers Islands": Manchester Papers, No. 398.

[5] Draft Report of the Commission on Virginia: Manchester Papers, No. 382.

[6] State Papers, Colonial, III. 2. [7] *Records of the Virginia Company*, II. p. 31.

[8] Draft of An Answer to a Declaration of the Present State of Virginia: Manchester Papers, No. 362.

Smythe on account of the general stock, and, if to that sum there be added the outlay by the Magazine and on particular plantations, it is not likely that the total expenditure during Smythe's treasurership exceeded £80,000. Sandys should have been able to show very much better results, since, when he took office, many of the initial difficulties had been overcome, instead of which at approximately equal cost, under vastly more favourable conditions, he effected less[1].

On the report of the Commission it became clear that either the administration of the company or its constitution must be altered. As early as July 3rd, 1623, the Attorney-General was directed to inquire whether the company had not voided its charters, and on the 31st his investigation had been completed, when he gave his opinion that there were sufficient grounds for dissolving the corporation[2]. On October 8th the Privy Council by an order promulgated the King's resolution to change the constitution of the company by the grant of a new charter, under which the government was to be vested in a governor and twelve assistants, nominated in the first instance by the Crown. At the next election the assistants were to choose those persons out of whom the King would select the new governor. Should the adventurers not agree to surrender the existing charters, receiving a new one embodying these modifications, it was plainly indicated that steps would be taken for the recalling of all grants in favour of the company[3]. An answer acceptable to the Privy Council not being forthcoming in what was held to be a reasonable time, a *quo warranto* was instituted which began on November 3rd[4]. The suit proceeded slowly, and Sandys determined to appeal to the House of Commons, in which he had numerous political allies. A petition was drawn up and approved at the court held on April 21st, 1624[5]. Allusion was made to the danger of ruin from the factions within the company, and in the words of the document, " findinge nevertheless our selves in our body, as itt is now distempered, unable to be our owne phisicians without higher assistance," appeal for such aid was made to Parliament. This petition was received by the House of Commons and, on April 26th, was referred to the consideration of a Committee. James I. however wrote that he had already taken such steps as would rid the House of " the thorny business of

[1] The whole cost of the plantation up to 1624 is given in round numbers at £200,000 (*Short Collection of the most Remarkable passages from the Originall to the Dissolution of the Virginia Company*, 1651, p. 2). In 1622 the whole outlay on the Bermudas was said to have been 100,000 marks (*Records of the Virginia Company*, II. p. 48).

[2] State Papers, Domestic Correspondence, James I., CXLVIII. 19, CL. 31.

[3] State Papers, Colonial, II. 45, printed in *Records of the Virginia Company*, II. p. 469.

[4] *Records of the Virginia Company*, I. p. 184.   [5] *Ibid.*, II. pp. 526-8.

Virginia," so that the Committee did not meet[1]. Judgment was delivered in May against the company, and in the June following a Council was appointed by the Crown to administer the plantation[2]. The dissolution of the company was publicly announced in a proclamation dated May 13th, 1625[3].

Summary of Capital of the Virginia Company.

The General Stock.

	Subscribed.			Paid.		
	£	s.	d.	£	s.	d.
To 1619	52,624	12	9	36,624	12	9[4]
After 1619	237	10	0			
Total	£52,862	2	9			

Divisions were in land according to the rates specified, *supra*, p. 255.

Subsidiary Joint-Stocks.

The Society of Particular Adventure for Traffique with them of Virginia in a joint-stock, commonly called the Magazine, 1616–7.

Capital subscribed and paid in three equal annual instalments	£7,000
Divisions to February 1623	£4,000

Joint-Stock for Transporting of Men and Divers goods on a Fishing Voyage (1618).

Capital subscribed	£1,800

Joint-Stock for a Fishing Voyage (1620).

Capital subscribed July 7, 1620	£1,000

One-half of this amount was provided by the former adventurers, one-quarter by Southampton Hundred, one-quarter by the general stock.

A Joint-Stock for a Magazine (1620).

Capital subscribed	£1,000

A Joint-Stock for Providing Apparel and other Necessaries (1621).

On July 7, 1621, there had been subscribed	£1,800

---

[1] Chamberlain to Carleton, April 30, 1624, Domestic Correspondence, James I., CLXIII. 74, also 46. *Journals of the House of Commons,* I. pp. 775, 779.

[2] State Papers, Minute, Colonial Correspondence, 1609, p. 1.

[3] State Papers, Proclamations, Charles I., No. 10.

[4] After the list was printed in 1620 several receipts signed by Smythe or his clerks were produced, which purported to be for payments on account of shares not included in this total. *Records of the Virginia Company,* I. pp. 552, 581, 590, 618, 622, II. pp. 77, 97, 145.

A Joint-Stock for a Glass Furnace in Virginia for making Glass and Beads (1621).

On November 21, 1621, £500 had been subscribed and later there was "near £1,000 adventured" ... nearly £1,000

A Joint-Stock for Transporting 100 *Maids to Virginia to be made Wives* (1621).

On November 21, 1621, there was subscribed £800

A Joint-Stock for a Trade in Furs (1621).

The proposed capital was £900 to be paid up for three successive voyages. This was fully subscribed £900

A Joint-Stock for Transporting Ship-Wrights to Virginia (1621).

The total amount subscribed was £1,000

Proposed Joint-Stock to be known as "the Adventure for bringing home the Spanish Tobacco" (1622).

The proposed capital was £15,000
Which was later reduced to £8,000

Proposed Joint-Stock for the tobacco of the Virginia and Somers Islands Plantations (1622).

Magazines formed for Relief of the Colony (1623).

A. One formed by the Sandys Party, for which there was subscribed by July 4, 1623 ... ... £727
B. One formed by the Smythe-Warwick Party.

D. THE SOMERS ISLANDS COMPANY FROM 1625 TO 1684.

The outcome of the enquiry by the Commission of 1623, which led to the dissolution of the Virginia company, was not unfavourable to the management of the Somers Islands. Attention was drawn to the amount of the debt, which was returned at £1,400, and it was ordered that £400 of this should be paid off by a levy of 4*d.* per lb. on the tobacco brought home in 1624[1]. Otherwise the constitution and administration of the company remained unchanged, and much may be urged in favour of this decision, since a small community, such as the body of planters, required some channel by which their interests could be effectively

[1] Lefroy, *Memorials of the Bermudas,* I. pp. 324–5.

represented to the authorities in England. This was provided by the partnership which existed between the shareholders in London and the tenants on their lands in the islands, whereby the former, in their own interests, would naturally use any influence they possessed in procuring as favourable treatment as was possible for the plantation. Further, with regard to the supply of the wants of the settlers by means of the Magazine, there was a similar compensatory action, since all the shareholders of the company were not members of this subsidiary undertaking, and in this way any tendency towards an undue raising of rates for English goods would be checked. Moreover, should such enhancement have happened, even those adventurers, who were interested both in the company and in the Magazine, might not gain by it on the whole, since, though the latter enterprize would benefit, they would tend to lose by a diminution of their rents caused through the increased price paid for stores required on their properties.

The continuance of the company, as well as the result of the deliberations of the Commission, meant that the Smythe-Warwick party remained in control of the enterprize, and, on the death of Smythe, Johnson became governor, and subsequently Warwick, who frequently filled this office till the time of the Protectorate. One of the first matters to be settled, after the adventurers had emerged from the turmoil of the great struggle of the past six years, was the prevention of the manufacturing of a majority by the manipulation of voting-rights. It was determined in 1629 that shares could only be legally transferred by deed "indented under the hand and seal" of the transferror, which was to be produced in open court, "whereby it may appear that the said share or shares of land, so sett over, are really and truly, without any sinister respect, to be passed over." This method, it was expressly stated, was devised as being "a means to avoyd those inconveniences which have heretofore troubled the company by admitting tituler men, who indeed have been noe true owners of land[1]." This order may not have been unconnected with an episode which happened in 1627, which for a time threatened the better relations that were in process of being established within the company. In 1626 John Delbridge, a shareholder who resided at Barnstaple, had fitted out a vessel which had been intended to visit the islands. This action was met by an order of the court that no ship from Bristol or Barnstaple was to carry tobacco from the Bermudas, and Delbridge replied by a strongly worded "remonstrance" to the company in which he claimed that he sold the planters "a better pennyworth" than they could obtain from the London ship. To this it was replied that, by sending a small consign-

---

[1] Proceedings of a Quarter Court, June 24, 1629, MS. Rawl. D. 764, f. 23.

ment of goods, Delbridge had been able to buy the best tobacco, thereby securing the cream of the market[1]. Finally a settlement for the time being was reached by an order of November 26th, 1628, according to which " adventures of goods " might be made for the Somers Islands, provided that these were sent there in the company's ships or such other vessels as were licensed by the court, and, in any case, all tobacco sent home was to be consigned in the former only[2].

Though the "contract and salaries" proposed by Sandys in 1622 had not been completed, it was not long before a royal monopoly of tobacco was in existence, the rumour of which in 1625 was related to have caused " a wonderfull dejectedness generally " in the Bermudas[3]. The members of the company joined with owners of land in Virginia in the following year in refusing to accept the price offered by the Crown for the quantity which it was proposed to import annually from both plantations[4]. According to a calculation, made in reference to Virginia, it was impossible for the colony to maintain itself on its quota at the specified price[5]. The case of the Somers Islands was an even harder one. The population was between two and three thousand[6], being nearly equal to that of Virginia; and, with their tobacco liable to an imposition of 9d. per lb., the returns were insufficient to support the settlers. Through the detention of a great part of the crop, pending payment of this imposition, many had been reduced to great distress and some were arrested for debt[7]. The shareholders, who since 1626 had been receiving but little from their estates[8], applied to Parliament, and the House of Commons, on June 19th, 1628, petitioned Charles I., pointing out that this imposition was contrary to the charter, being six times greater than that due from the company under this instrument, nor was a drawback on exportation from England allowed. It followed that tobacco was so overcharged that many planters were in danger of "perishing utterly," and it was asked that the impost should be abated[9]. Little redress being obtainable, a bill was introduced in favour

---

[1] John Delbridge's Remonstrance to the Court of Adventurers, June 12, 1627, printed in Lefroy, *Memorials of the Bermudas*, I. p. 443.
[2] *Ibid.*, I. p. 472.
[3] *Ibid.*, I. p. 347.
[4] State Papers, Colonial, IV. 20.
[5] *Ibid.*, IV. 45.
[6] Smith, *Generall Historie*, II. p. 180.
[7] State Papers, Colonial, IV. 53.
[8] Letter of Company to the Inhabitants of the Somers Islands, Sept. 20, 1626, in Lefroy, *Memorials of the Bermudas*, I. p. 397.
[9] State Papers, Colonial, IV. 55. It is to be remembered, however, that the company itself assented to a rise in the duty on tobacco in return for the prohibition of the cultivation of it in England—cf. *supra*, p. 273.

of the company on February 10th, 1629[1]. The difficulties of cultivating tobacco were increased by an order of the Privy Council in 1631, which decreed that "only a moderate amount should be planted" and no more[2].

At this period some allowance must be made for a certain amount of exaggeration in the statement of the case of the persons interested in the islands, whether as shareholders or as planters. About 1629 both the population and the animals in the plantation were increasing, the "forts were well maintained by the merchants here and the planters there—to be briefe, this isle is an excellent bit to rule a great horse." The greatest complaint of the settlers was a want of variety of clothes, and it is noted that there were more men than women, though this phenomenon was described as "no great mischiefe, because there is so much lesse pride[3]." It is evident that by 1636 some of the colonists had been sufficiently successful to have acquired funds to purchase shares of land, and, in that year, an order was made by the Quarter Court that no transfer of land should be legal, unless the seller had first offered to sell his shares to the company[4]. It had been noticed in 1629 that the land was beginning to be over-cropped[5], and in 1639, owing to emigration from the islands, the company asked for an increase of its land-grant in Virginia so as to provide for the surplus population[6]. Meanwhile the supply of the colony by means of the Magazine had been made as little burdensome as possible. The company had to provide for the maintenance of the fortifications, the defence and internal government of the plantation. To meet the necessary expenditure it had the profit of the public land, which had been set aside for this purpose. The revenue, so obtained, did not pay all the expenses, and it had long been necessary to make a small levy of about $1d.$ per lb. on the tobacco sent to England. For convenience of collection, the whole crop that was exported was to be carried only in the ships of the company, but by 1644, there was no restriction on the trade in other products of the

---

[1] *The Proceedings and Debates of the House of Commons in the Sessions of Parliament begun the twentieth of January,* 1628, collected by Sir T. Carew, London, 1707, p. 65.

[2] Lefroy, *Memorials of the Bermudas,* I. p. 521.

[3] Smith, *Generall Historie,* II. p. 180.

[4] *Some of the Bye-Laws made by the Governour and Company of the City of London for the Plantation of the Summer Islands, humbly offered to Parliament* [Brit. Mus. $\frac{816.m.18}{35}$].

[5] Smith, *Generall Historie,* II. p. 179.

[6] Petition of the Company to the Commissioners of Trade and Plantations, July 28, 1639, in Lefroy, *Memorials of the Bermudas,* I. p. 557.

islands, and it is mentioned that the exports of cattle, hogs, fruit and provisions had been made open to all comers[1].

This little settlement did not escape the turmoil and confusion of the Civil Wars. From an early date in the history of the colony there had been religious difficulties, and in 1639 a shareholder was suspended from voting at the courts, on the ground of his having informed Laud of the nonconformity of the deputy-governor, most of the council and ministers in the Bermudas[2]. As the struggle developed in England, feeling became heated in the plantation, and the different parties, each in turn, seized the crop of tobacco[3]. In 1650 the company was ordered by the Council of State to postpone the election of officers for the coming year[4], and this command was repeated in the following year, and again in 1653[5]. At the latter date the colony was declared to be in rebellion, and the charter was superseded, seventeen persons being appointed by the Council of State to manage the company[6]. It was not long before those of the former office-bearers remaining managed to oust such as had been recently appointed[7]; and, while the administration was disorganized, the colonists complained that they had not been properly supplied with the goods they needed during a space of two years[8].

The forfeitures during the Civil Wars, the Protectorate, and after the Restoration, led to considerable changes in the composition of the body of shareholders. By 1660 the majority of the founders of the company were dead, and in many cases their representatives sold the shares. A notable instance of this tendency arose in connection with the holding of Warwick (who had died in 1658) which was disposed of by his son in 1659[9]—a transaction which resulted in litigation subsequently. Many of the purchasers were residents in the islands, and gradually the shareholders in England became fewer and fewer. The position had now grown anomalous, since membership of the company was confined to those who held shares of land, and it seems probable

---

[1] *A Declaration of the Right Honourable Robert, Earl of Warwick*, 1644 [Brit. Mus. E. 265, 6]. In 1659 it was necessary, owing to the destruction of cedar to prohibit the sale or use of this wood for any purpose, save the making of cases in which to pack the tobacco: Lefroy, *Memorials of the Bermudas*, II. p. 126.

[2] Proceedings of a Quarter Court, Nov. 27, 1639, Colonial Entry Book, III. p. 367.

[3] Lefroy, *Memorials of the Bermudas*, II. p. 23.

[4] State Papers, Interregnum, Entry Book, XCII. p. 374.

[5] *Ibid.*, XLVII. p. 106; XCVII. p. 88.

[6] State Papers, Colonial, XIII. 14.

[7] Lefroy, *Memorials of the Bermudas*, II. p. 88.

[8] State Papers, Colonial, XIII. 38 (ii.).

[9] *A True Relation of the Illegal Proceedings of the Somers Islands Company in their Courts*, 1678 [Brit. Mus. 10,470.e.12], p. 1.

that by 1660 the majority of these were owned in the islands, yet the minority in London exercised the whole government, making orders and fixing the amount of levy for the defence of the settlement. It follows that a period had been reached when it was desirable that the charter should have been surrendered, but it was decided, after the Restoration, to continue the company, and some efforts were made to infuse vigour into the administration. By 1662 a subsidiary company, in addition to the Magazine, had been formed, known as *the Adventurers in the Whale-fishing Design*. In 1663 forty shareholders in the company had agreed to subscribe £50 each, but by November 1666 only £1,000 had actually been paid. At that time £2,000 had been spent, and the "adventure" was said "of late to have taken good effect[1]." By January 1668, liabilities of £2,500 had been incurred; and, through the neglect of the officials and their irregularities, the enterprize had resulted in loss[2]. The adventurers were not prepared to continue to bear calls, and the company offered to license any group of persons (whether members or not) who would pay a royalty for the fishing. A small syndicate, composed of residents in the islands, took up this license on December 20th, 1671, which they transferred a few weeks later to Perient Trott, and in 1675 William White was the undertaker. Though oil was obtained, none of these syndicates made any considerable profit[3].

There can be little doubt that there were various sources from which friction might be expected, especially in so far as the court in London had drifted into a false position in being representative of a minority of the shareholders only. This trouble came through P. Trott, who, as early as 1656, wished to ship cedar from his plantation in ships other than those of the company. About 1667 or 1668 he had "indirectly" sent out a ship on his own account, for which the company claimed damages to the extent of £509. 2s., owing to his having forestalled the market in tobacco[4]. Trott refused to pay this fine, forgetting that under an order of August 18th, 1658, the company was entitled to seize the goods or lands of persons in default[5]. This brought up the whole question of the title to the 20 shares which Trott had bought from Warwick in 1659. It appeared on further enquiry that these shares had been entailed, and therefore the court of the company

[1] Lefroy, *Memorials of the Bermudas*, II. pp. 203, 209, 245.
[2] *Ibid.*, II. p. 256.
[3] *Ibid.*, II. pp. 302, 303, 357, 358, 437; *The Case and Grievance of Divers Merchants and Others Members of the Bermuda Company and of the Planters within the said Islands* [Brit. Mus. $\frac{816 \cdot m \cdot 13}{34}$].
[4] Lefroy, *Memorials of the Bermudas*, II. p. 325.
[5] *Some of the Bye-Laws...of...the Company*.

DIV. II. § 2 D]   *Complaints of the Colonists* 1667–79   295

ordered Trott to surrender them, on his receiving back again the same sum, namely £600, that he had paid in 1659[1]. Trott greatly resented this finding, and he published a tract attacking the administration, which the company ordered to be burnt, when found in the Bermudas[2]. The matter was not allowed to rest. Already Trott's friends in the islands had made an attack on the company in the General Assembly at St George's in 1673, accusing it of extracting from the inhabitants four times the amount of the public charges. It was said, too, that such action was due to the shares in England having fallen into the hands "of traders and mechanicks," who enhanced the goods, they sent out to the Bermudas, to an extravagant rate[3]. It was stated that the company in England only owned a small fraction of the land in the islands, and that the members were not sufficient to constitute a court according to the charter. There should have been a governor, a deputy-governor, and twenty-four assistants. Moreover, six of the latter were to retire annually, so that an attendance of thirty-two members was required, whereas, since only twenty shareholders resided in London, it was impossible to carry out these clauses, indeed it was contended that there had not been thirty-two members at a meeting of the court for the past thirty-two years. Further, the company was charged with taxing the inhabitants of the Bermudas for the benefit of the shareholders. According to one account it was out of debt in 1676, and the annual charge for government and defence was only £400[4].

To some extent the agitation against the company was a fictitious one. Trott, it is true, had some grounds for complaint, but the most energetic member of the opposition was Francis Burghill, who, as it will appear, was acting in his own interests, under pretence of assisting the colonists. By 1679 various complaints from the plantation were investigated by the Privy Council, which referred the matters in dispute to the Commissioners of Trade and Plantations, before which body the company appeared on July 15th to answer the charges against it. To the allegation that petitions from the islands had been suppressed at the instigation of the executive in London, it was replied that this was not so, but that the local governor had been directed to send such documents with his remarks upon each heading. The company was censured for depriving persons, in the occupation of land, of their holdings without

[1] *A True Relation of the Just and Unjust Proceedings of the Somers Islands Company in relation to Twenty Shares of Land*, 1676, pp. 1–5.
[2] State Papers, Colonial, XL. 62.
[3] *Ibid.*, XXX. 58, in Lefroy, *Memorials of the Bermudas*, II. pp. 382–5.
[4] *A True Relation of the Illegal Proceedings of the Somers Islands Company in the Courts at London*, 1678 [Brit. Mus. 10,470.e.12], pp. 1–22. In 1662 1*d.* per lb. on tobacco yielded £850 a year, in 1684 £1,600—State Papers, Colonial, LIII. 146.

a due process of law[1]. If, too, as had been asserted, erasures had been made in the books in connection with such proceedings, it is clear that the action of the company in this respect was blameworthy[2].

An attack was next made on Sir John Heydon, the local governor, for many acts that were said to be arbitrary, including the imposition of taxes, not authorized by the Assembly, and the imprisonment of Josiah Pitts, who had been aiding the opposition to the company in the Bermudas. The articles against Heydon were read before the Privy Council on November 21st, 1681, but "the King was pleased to remit the faults of the accused, he being an old man of fourscore years[3]."

Burghill was acute enough to take advantage of the movement for the institution of *quo warranto* proceedings in 1682–4 to prosecute his case. He obtained a promise that, in the event of the charter being recalled, he should receive the office of local governor under the Crown[4], and he was able to induce some of his supporters in London to undertake, "on behalf of the inhabitants of the Bermuda Islands," to free the Crown from all charges and to pay to the Exchequer duties of $4\frac{1}{2}$ per cent.[5] On November 22nd, 1682, a process of *quo warranto* was ordered, but Burghill soon found that he was unable to obtain the help from the colonists on which he had counted. At a very early stage the case came to a stand for want of funds, and urgent letters were sent to the planters for money—"if only £80 or £100"—"unless they intended to intail slavery on themselves and their posterity for ever[6]." Since the people, who were supposed to be primarily affected, did not think it worth while to furnish evidence nor to contribute resources to fight the case, there was a probability that the whole agitation would collapse. Proof of some of the most damaging allegations was not forthcoming, as for instance that the company had ordered the cutting down and destroying of tobacco, when more had been raised than was required. Beyond sending a further petition "against the intolerable oppressions of their Egyptian taskmasters," and a confirmation of the offer of a duty of $4\frac{1}{2}$ per cent. to the Crown, the colonists showed small interest in the proceedings. Thus Burghill complained, on July 20th, 1682, that he had not received one word of news from the islands, "and," he adds,

---

[1] State Papers, Colonial, XLIII. 58, 158 (i.); Colonial Entry Book, XVII. pp. 69–73; Lefroy, *Memorials of the Bermudas*, II. pp. 466, 467, 469, 471, 473, 476, 477.

[2] Instructions to Mr Righton, Dec. 31, 1681: MS. Rawl. D. 764.

[3] Articles and Petition of the Inhabitants of the Bermuda Islands against Sir John Heydon: MS. Rawl. D. 764, f. 30.

[4] Mr Francis Burghill's Case: MS. Rawl. D. 764, f. 50.

[5] *Ibid.*, f. 32.

[6] Letters of Francis Burghill and others: MS. Rawl. D. 764, ff. 35–49.

"tho' the company did deale with the divell, 'tis not possible they should intercept all the letters I have sent[1]."

The case at length was brought on in 1683, and, once it was pressed energetically, the result was a foregone conclusion. Not only did the Crown stand to gain about £500 from the duty offered it, but the legal position of the company was quite untenable. It was in fact, as described by its opponents, nothing more than a rump of a corporation, with too small a stake in the plantation to secure a community of interest with the colonists. Thus, once the ownership of the majority of the shares of land had been acquired by persons resident in the Bermudas, a company, consisting of only a few merchants in London, became an anachronism. Perhaps the strongest argument in favour of its continuance is to be found in the somewhat fictitious nature of the agitation against it, which was certainly not loyally supported by the majority of the inhabitants of the colony. Amongst these there were some actively hostile, some in favour of the company which they described as "our nursing father[2]," and the remainder appear to have been indifferent. Eventually, though Burghill complained of being "still put to make bricks without straw[3]," he succeeded in obtaining a verdict against the company, though not in securing his own appointment as governor, whence, in April 1685, he endeavoured to foment a new agitation to deliver the people "quite from the Hydra, for tho' the body and all its heads be dead, you are still wrapt in the tayle, where most poyson lies[4]."

[1] Burghill to Trott, July 20, 1682: MS. Rawl. D. 764, f. 40.
[2] State Papers, Colonial, XLVI. 96.
[3] Burghill to Trott, Sept. 7, 1684: MS. Rawl. D. 764, f. 48 b.
[4] Burghill to Righton, April 30, 1685: *Ibid.*, f. 50 b.

SECTION III. THE COLONIZATION OF THE NORTHERN PORTION OF THE MAINLAND OF AMERICA.

The plantation of the sea-board of America north of the territory of the first Virginia company proceeded contemporaneously, but on slightly different lines. Owing to certain circumstances, the result already achieved by the Virginia company was only accomplished, after a longer interval, by three different groups of organizations in the north. It will be remembered that the original grant of 1606 provided for the foundation of two colonies, both known as the "Virginia" plantations—the First or London colony being that the history of which has already been dealt with. The Second, Plymouth or Northern colony under this patent, though authorized to start as early as the first, did not effect any permanent settlements and confined itself to trading voyages. It so happened that by 1619 no colony had been founded and a new company, the Corporation of New England was formed. This organization went to the opposite extreme, as compared with its predecessor the "Second Virginia plantation." If the first was too little enterprizing, the second endeavoured to do too much. Enormous grants of land were made as dividends to the shareholders or in return for cash payments by non-members. Such huge estates could not be settled, unless in most cases a subordinate association were formed. Several such associations became later of great importance, as for instance the New Plymouth and Massachusetts Bay companies. Owing in part to the fact that the planters in these subordinate undertakings were animated by political ideas, differing from those of the members of the New England company, and partly to the main object of the latter body having been carried out once the land-dividends were made, it was dissolved in 1635. These three stages might be described by naming the Second Virginia company, an exploration syndicate, the New England corporation as the development or promoting organization, and the different companies and individuals, who received grants from it, as the actual colonizing agents.

A. THE SECOND "VIRGINIA" COLONY (1606-19).

The "Virginia" patent of 1606 had provided for the formation of a "second" colony, which might be planted between 38° and 45° and was to be organized by those residing in Plymouth and the other western and southern "out-ports." It is possible that this fact accounts for the slow progress made at the beginning of the undertaking, since there was difficulty in procuring capital and in securing the co-operation of persons resident in the different cities that were intended to participate in the enterprize.

The most prominent and energetic member of this company was Sir John Popham, the Chief Justice; and, largely by his efforts, a ship was sent out as early as August 1606, which was followed by a further expedition in October, bringing supplies for those who were now supposed to be established as the nucleus of a plantation. As in the case of the contemporary voyages of the southern company, there were "assured hopes," "founded on infallible reason," of finding a passage to the Pacific and of obtaining valuable minerals[1]. The first expedition was captured by the Spaniards and the second returned home. The outlay is described as having involved "no small charge" on the adventurers, and it was stated that a sum of not less than £5,000 would be required as compensation from the Spaniards to make good the loss[2]. Undeterred by this disappointment, the adventurers raised funds for another expedition, consisting of between 100 and 120 persons, which sailed in May 1607, reaching the Sagadahoc on August 16th. Here a settlement was established, a fort built and preparations made for discovery and trade[3]. The winter proved to be exceptionally cold, a part of the stores had been lost in a fire at the fort, and the settlers were depressed by the death of their leader. News was received in England by February 1608 that the situation of the plantation was desperate[4], and in the following October the last of the planters embarked for England. It is related that, while the capture of the first expedition "did much abate the rising courage of the first adventurers," the return of the settlers was "a wonderfull

---

[1] *A Brief and True Relation of the Discovery of the North Part of Virginia*, by Mr John Brereton, London, 1602, in *Collections of the Massachusetts Hist. Soc.*, 3rd Series, VIII. p. 101—cf. *supra*, pp. 248-9.

[2] Sir Fernando Gorges to Capt. Chalons, March 13, 1607, printed in Brown, *Genesis of the United States*, I. p. 96.

[3] *The Sagadahoc Colony, comprising The Relation of A Voyage into New England*, edited by Henry O. Thayer, Boston (Prince Society), 1892, pp. 13, 195.

[4] Sir F. Gorges to Sir R. Cecil, 7 Feb. 1608, *Ibid.*, p. 137.

discouragement" to the supporters of the enterprize[1]. At this stage most of the adventurers abandoned the undertaking, but a few continued to fit out ships. Sir F. Popham was the leader of one syndicate, which continued till 1611. Sir Fernando Gorges, either independently or in partnership with others, sent out expeditions till 1614, and, according to his own account, the result yielded "nothing to his private profit" for what "he gained one way he lost another[2]."

There was at this time every prospect that voyages to the northern parts of America would be discontinued. The experience of eight years seemed to show that colonizing was impracticable, and no considerable commerce had been established. There was however one consideration which operated towards the fitting out of ships for this district, namely the popular interest that had been aroused by the possibilities of the fishing-trade. Before the end of the sixteenth century, Yarmouth had reached a considerable degree of wealth and importance, altogether based on "the harvest of the sea," whence a contemporary writer sings the praises of "the puissant red-herring, the golden Hesperides red-herring, the Mæonian red-herring[3]." The success of Yarmouth was exceptional and the profits of the Dutch from fishing aroused a considerable amount of jealousy. It was said in 1601 that there was greater wealth in the British seas than in the Spanish Indies—according to one estimate 150,000 persons in the Low Countries made a living from the fisheries, according to another as many as 400,000, while it was alleged that the duties on fish in Holland in one year were more than all the customs of England in four years[4]. Again from 1612 to 1615 attention was redirected to this question, and it was frequently said that the Dutch found "their chiefest trade and principal gold mine" in fishing. It was calculated that, taking the cost of a buss at £500, it should yield a

[1] *A Brief Relation of the Discovery and Plantation of New England by the President and Council*, 1622, in *Mass. Hist. Soc. Coll.*, 2nd Series, XI. pp. 3, 4; *Sir Fernando Gorges and his Province of Maine*, by J. P. Baxter, Boston (Prince Society), 1890, I. p. 207.

[2] *A Brief Narration of the Originall Undertakings of the Advancement of Plantations into the Parts of America, especially shewing the Beginning, Progress and Continuance of that of New England*, by Sir Fernando Gorges, London, 1658, in *Collections of the Maine Historical Society*, II. (1847), pp. 23–7.

[3] *Nashe's Lenten Stuff, containing the Description and first Pro-creation of the Town of Great Yarmouth*, London, 1599, in *Harleian Miscellany*, VI. pp. 139, 162.

[4] *Policies of State Practised in Divers Kingdoms for encrease of trade and traffique beyond Seas*, by John Keymor [MSS. Edin. Univ. Lib., Laing MSS., Div. II., No. 52], ff. 3, 22–4; *Observations touching Trade and Commerce with the Hollanders*, 1601, in McCullough's *Tracts on Commerce*, 1859, p. 22; *John Keymor's Observations upon the Dutch Fishing about the Year* 1601, in *The Phoenix*, London, 1707, pp. 223, 225.

profit of about £550 when employed in this industry[1]. An estimate of the same period for the American fishery showed that the return on £2,000 might be as much as £4,000 in six months and was scarcely likely to be less than £2,000, independently of furs or other commodities obtained from the natives, whence "it may be expected in time to equalize your Hollanders gains, if not exceede them[2]." These anticipations proved somewhat optimistic, still it is recorded that a fishing voyage by Smith in 1614 gave a return of £1,500, which in all probability yielded a satisfactory profit[3]. Gradually ships began to sail for the coasts of northern Virginia for the fishing in increasing numbers. There is mention of four ships sent from London and two from Plymouth in 1615 and of eight in 1616, some of which are recorded to have met "with good success[4]." Again in 1618, 1619, and 1620 there are references to vessels returning "well fraught" and "having made good voyages" from the point of view of the owners[5].

B. THE COUNCIL ESTABLISHED AT PLYMOUTH IN THE COUNTY OF DEVON FOR THE PLANTING, RULING, ORDERING AND GOVERNING OF NEW ENGLAND IN AMERICA (1620–35).

Though the North American fisheries were beginning to yield good returns the project of planting a colony in this region had not been forgotten. John Smith advocated the re-naming of the territory, north of that assigned to the first Virginia company, as "New England," and he claimed that he succeeded in interesting Charles, Prince of Wales, in the project[6]. In 1616 there was published *a Description of New England* which urged the establishment of plantations there[7]. The following year Smith made an effort to raise capital for a new experiment in colonization, but without success[8]. For the next two years nothing was effected, capital was difficult to obtain, and suspicions were rife that

---

[1] *Of Fishing the Seas and Converting Waste into Wealth*, 1612, *England's Way to win Wealth and to Employ Ships and Marriners*, by Tobias Gentleman, 1614 (in *Harleian Miscellany*, III. p. 378), *The Trade's Increase*, by J. R., 1615 (in *Ibid.*, IV. p. 202), *Britain's Buss*, 1615, in Arber, *English Garner*, III. pp. 635-6.

[2] *The Generall Historie of Virginia, New England and the Summer Islands*, by Captaine John Smith, Glasgow, 1907, II. pp. 22–3.

[3] *Ibid.*, II. pp. 3, 4. [4] *Ibid.*, II. pp. 53, 54.
[5] *Ibid.*, II. pp. 54–6. [6] *Ibid.*, II. p. 53.

[7] *Tracts and other Papers relating principally to the Origin, Settlement, and Progress of the Colonies in North America*, edited by Peter Force, Washington, 1836, vol. II., No. 1.

[8] *Generall Historie*, II. p. 53; *Sir Fernando Gorges and his Province of Maine*, by J. P. Baxter, Boston (Prince Society), 1890, I. p. 100.

all was not well with the Virginia company. According to the statement of Gorges " men could not be drawn to adventure in actions of that kind where they were assured of loss and small hopes of gain[1]." The backwardness of support was alleged as the cause determining the constitution of a new organization which was created by a patent dated November 3rd, 1620, incorporating *the Council established at Plymouth in the County of Devon for the Planting, Ruling, Ordering and Governing of New England in America*. This body was to consist of 40 members, nominated by the Crown, who were to be " persons of honour or gentlemen of blood," with the exception of a few merchants. The limits, assigned to the council, differed to some extent from those previously granted to the second Virginia company. Instead of extending from 38° to 45°, the territory now opened to settlement lay between 40° and 48° N.[2]

It was no doubt intended, as in the earliest Virginia charter, that the influence of the council would be used to procure the subscription of capital, and negotiations were begun with a group of merchants who were to provide £100,000. By May 31st, 1622, the council decided that security should be asked as a guarantee that the financial engagements would be carried out, and on July 5th it was known that such security was unlikely to be forthcoming[3], since there was a marked opposition to the council in the western towns where it was proposed the money was to be raised[4]. Contemporaneously with this project, some capital was provided by the members of the council themselves, each of whom was to hold one share on which £110 was called up. Further, a subsidiary stock was initiated to fit out a ship and pinnace for fishing (subscription in which was optional), the shares being £50 each. It is clear that unless the members were prepared to venture large sums individually, it was unlikely that a plantation would be established through the efforts of the council once the negotiations with the merchants had been broken off. No one took up more than a single share in the general stock, and, on November 27th, 1622, less than £1,500 had been adventured in this and the fishing voyage[5]. Many refused to pay the sums due for their shares and there were frequent

---

[1] *A Brief Narration of the Originall Undertakings of the Advancement of Plantations*, in *Collections of the Maine Hist. Soc.*, II. p. 35.

[2] State Papers, Colonial Entry Book, LIX. p. 1; printed in Hazard, *Historical Collections*, I. p. 103—cf. *supra*, pp. 247, 299.

[3] The Minutes of the New England Company. The fragments of these documents were printed by Charles Deane in the *Publications of the American Antiquarian Society*. The references below are to a volume of these at the British Museum entitled *Records of the Council for New England*.

[4] *A Brief Relation of the Discovery and Plantation of New England by the President and Council*, 1622, in *Mass. Hist. Soc. Coll.*, 2nd Series, IX. pp. 13, 14.

[5] *Records of the Council for New England*, p. 27.

complaints of lack of funds from this cause. On June 28th, 1623, the fishing vessel could not sail through want of money, and it was only dispatched, after considerable delay, by the raising of a loan of 2,000 marks from six members of the council[1].

Meanwhile, quite independently of the council, a colony had been established within its territory, consisting of the settlers brought by the *Mayflower*. They had procured a grant from the Virginia company and sailed from England in August 1620. On November 19th they were in the vicinity of Cape Cod, and a landing was made at Plymouth, the place at which they decided to settle, on December 21st[2].

This plantation, though ultimately sanctioned by the New England company, had been formed upon different principles from those that governed the operations of the latter body. These took two main directions—the one in relation to fishing and the other directed towards one aspect of colonization. The American fishery had grown in popularity, and in the last years of the reign of James I. was giving excellent results. The general system on which voyages were financed was to divide the proceeds of the expedition into three equal parts. One of these was assigned to the crew, another to the owner of the ship, and the third to the undertakers and organizers of the voyage, who provided the necessary gear and materials[3]. The capital outlay for this last was returned at £800 for a ship of 200 tons, manned by 50 men, or £420 for one of 100 tons, and it was estimated that the return on the former sum would be as much as £1,340 in about nine months[4]. In practice the profit varied from 20 per cent. to 50 per cent. and even, in exceptional cases, was as much as 300 per cent.[5] It was said that "the merchants of the West country had left all other trades for this and had quickly grown rich through it[6]." As many as 35 ships were employed in the industry in 1622, and some years later the number had grown to 50[7]. The council thus found a profitable branch of commerce connected with the area over which it exercised control; and, under the plea of supervising and regulating the fishery, it was decided to impose a license of 5 per cent. (or according to another account of £5 on each 30 tons of shipping) on all vessels, not owned by members of the company[8]. Taking the number of vessels at 40 and the average tonnage

---

[1] *Records of the Council for New England*, pp. 16, 31, 32, 48², 48³.

[2] For a short account of the finances of this settlement *vide infra*, p. 311.

[3] *A Voyage into New England begun in* 1623 *and ended in* 1624, by Christopher Levett, 1628, in *Mass. Hist. Soc. Coll.*, 3rd Series, VIII. p. 186; Smith, *Generall Historie*, II. p. 81.   [4] Levett, *A Voyage into New England*, p. 186.

[5] Smith, *Generall Historie*, II. p. 82.

[6] Levett, *A Voyage into New England*, p. 185.

[7] Smith, *Generall Historie*, II. pp. 68, 76, 182.

[8] *Records of the Council for New England*, p. 18; Smith, *Generall Historie*, II. p. 182.

at 150, this would yield an annual revenue of £1,000 a year, supposing it was found possible to collect the whole amount. As against this charge on the owners of ships, the council was supposed to provide fortifications, to settle disputes and to facilitate the work of the fishermen.

As this industry progressed, there was a tendency to conjoin it with a temporary type of colony. The fishing voyages up to 1623 were limited to a season of only eight to ten weeks. It was contended that, if a vessel of 200 tons were sent with supplies, which would enable the men to remain in New England for a year, the charge on the undertakers would only be increased from £800 to £1,026. 13s. 4d., whereas fishing could be carried on for five months and the total catch would be at least doubled. Thus the third, falling to the undertakers, would realize £2,680, giving a very large clear profit, apart from the products of the labour of the planters during the months they were not engaged in fishing[1].

The formation of temporary fishing settlements was one aspect of colonization under the council. There was another which was based on the idea that this body might make a large grant of land to some person of influence, who would form a subordinate association which would provide capital for the actual planting. Thus in 1622 the province of Maine was granted to Sir Fernando Gorges and John Mason[2]. In the summer of 1623 Christopher Levett, one of the council, had formed a scheme under which he proposed to take into partnership 50 persons, who were to provide funds for transporting 50 planters to settle on 6,000 acres, granted to him, on which a city was to be built and named York[3]. Meanwhile the payments of the members of the council remained in arrear, some of them alleging that "they have nott their shares for which they are to pay[4]." To meet this complaint it was arranged that, as in other plantation companies, a dividend of land should be made. The whole area was divided into 40 lots. Since, however, the council, at this time, numbered less than 40 and more than 20 it was decided that only twenty of the members were to draw the lots. The division falling to each would thus consist of two lots of land. One of these the adventurer was entitled to retain as his own dividend. The other he held in trust with the right of nominating a suitable person; and, on the latter paying for a share in the general stock, the

[1] Levett, *A Voyage into New England*, in *Mass. Hist. Soc. Coll.*, 3rd Series, VIII. p. 186.

[2] State Papers, Colonial Entry Book, LIX. pp. 101-8.

[3] *Records of the Council for New England*, p. 46; State Papers, Colonial, II. 32.

[4] *Records of the Council for New England*, p. 48².

land was to be transferred to him. If however no such nomination was made by Michaelmas, the council reserved to itself the right of appointing an adventurer for this second lot[1]. The drawing duly took place at Greenwich, in the presence of the King, on July 29th, 1623[2], but, as far as can be judged, the adventurers were unable to establish any considerable settlements on the extensive territories allotted to them.

For nearly five years little progress was made, and it was not till 1628 that there is mention of further efforts by the council. On February 11th Charles I. ordered a contribution to be levied for the plantation of New England[3], and it would appear that there were some attempts to raise a new stock, since application was made to an adventurer for £33. 6s. 8d., "one third" of his subscription, in order that a contemplated voyage might not be prejudiced[4]. From this time onwards extensive grants of land were authorized, several of which were important, as for instance that of March 19th, 1628, of Massachusetts Bay[5], and those of November 7th, 1629, to John Mason, and of November 17th to Mason and Gorges[6]. The former was the basis of the Massachusetts Bay company and one of the latter constituted the title of the Laconia company[7]. It was formally resolved by the council in 1631 that no more small patents of land should be granted[8], and in the following year some steps were once more taken with a view of securing the co-operation of such merchants as were found to be "well-affected and willing to take pains[9]." The council however had not won the support of the mercantile classes and, as time went on, the difficulties, under which it had laboured through want of resources, became accentuated by the varying religious and political ideals of the colonies which had already been established. There was "the distressed and struggling" Puritanism of Plymouth and "the vigorous and aggressive Puritanism" of Massachusetts[10], while in other plantations there was an Anglican preponderance. Moreover, since the council had, in the main, confined itself to the promotion of independent subordinate plantations it is clear that, when the titles to these had been granted, it had divested itself of the functions for which it had existed. Accordingly, on February 3rd, 1635, the members agreed to surrender their patent on condition that the Crown would recognize the divisions of land that had

---

[1] *Records of the Council for New England*, p. 48². [2] *Ibid.*, p. 48⁴.
[3] State Papers, Sign Manual, Charles I., v. 1.
[4] State Papers, Colonial, IV. 49. [5] *Ibid.*, IV. 42, 43.
[6] Colonial Entry Book, LIX. pp. 109-14, 115-21. These and other grants of the Council are given in a convenient form in *The English in America—The Puritan Colonies*, by J. A. Doyle, London, 1887, I. pp. 430-4.
[7] *Vide infra*, pp. 312-16.
[8] *Records of the Council for New England*, pp. 50-3. [9] *Ibid.*, p. 62.
[10] *The Cambridge Modern History*, VII. p. 14.

been made[1]. The resignation of the charter was accepted by Charles I. and by May 5th the council had ceased to exist, as a corporate body. While its history had been characterized by a want both of vigour and initiative in administration, its dissolution was accompanied by no marked change in the situation. In order to complete the sketch of the joint-stock planting of New England during this period, it is necessary to glance back at the career of the active colonizing agencies, namely, the Plymouth, Massachusetts Bay, and Laconia companies.

C. (i) THE ADVENTURERS TO NEW PLYMOUTH IN NEW ENGLAND (1620).

The earliest of the settlements in New England after 1619 was that of the Puritans who landed from the *Mayflower*. Since many of these emigrants were without any considerable means, the financing of the venture presents some features of interest. For various reasons the Nonconformists, who had taken refuge in Holland under the leadership of Brewster and Robinson, desired to establish a little colony of their own in the New World. Funds were required for the transportation of the emigrants and for the starting of the plantation. The necessary sum was larger than could be expected from the donations of philanthropists, though, as has been shown[2], considerable sums had been given by such for religious and educational purposes in Virginia, therefore it was decided to procure capital by means of a joint-stock company. In the Puritans, there was a compact body of would-be settlers ready to hand and it was expected that "the gain from fishing and trading would give content to all" who provided for the transportation of the colony[3]. There being no charter from the Crown, an agreement was necessary, defining the relations of "the personal adventurers" to those who provided the greater part of the resources required for the enterprize. There were three different interests involved. First the claims of those who subscribed capital, but did not join in the expedition, secondly those who sailed as personal adventurers and were able to take with them £10 in money or a supply for the voyage which would be valued at £10, and thirdly those emigrants who needed to be provisioned at the expense of the company. It was judged equitable that all three classes should be accepted as partners in the fruits of the undertaking; and, on the basis of the experience of the Virginia

---

[1] *Records of the Council of New England*, p. 67. [2] *Vide supra*, p. 271.
[3] *Relation or Journal of the Beginning and Proceedings of the English Plantation settled at Plymouth in New England by certain English Adventurers both Merchants and Others*, by G. Mount, London, 1622, in *Mass. Hist. Soc. Coll.*, 2nd Series, IX. p. 62.

company, it was calculated that a fully equipped settler might be landed in America at a cost of £20, divided into two equal portions, representing the one the cost of his passage, and the other that of his outfit and provisions. This determined the unit of capital as being £10, at which amount the share was fixed. Every adult colonist was rated as if he had contributed this amount, while those who went with the expedition and who had money or provisions to the amount of £10 were credited with a like sum and therefore ranked as owners of two shares. Children, between 10 years of age and 16, were to be given one half-share each, those under 10 were to have no share but, when the division of land was made, these were to receive 50 acres of unmanured ground. There were protracted negotiations regarding the method of dealing with the plantation. It was agreed that for seven years there should be no division of land. The emigrants proposed however that they should be allowed to own the houses they built and any gardens adjoining them and that they should be allowed two days in each week to work on their own account. These terms were considered unfavourable to those adventurers who remained at home and one of them withdrew his subscription of £500, whereupon an agreement was signed in the form that all the land settled, as well as all profits, were to belong to the joint-stock and that, after the expiration of the specified period, "the capitall and profits, viz. the houses, lands, goods and chattels be equally divided amongst the adventurers[1]." The word "equally" in this clause is somewhat obscure and from the context it is clear that it must mean "equally amongst the shares," since otherwise the stipulations concerning double shares would be useless nor would there have been any inducement for those adventurers, who did not join the expedition, to have paid for more than a single share.

This type of constitution started from the basis of the "half-profits system"—that is the method of colonization whereby the owner of the estate received half the gain, the other half being retained by the colonists he sent out to work the land for him. It will appear below that there are grounds for believing that, at the time of the sailing of the first expedition, it was expected that the whole number of shares would be about equally divided between the emigrants and the other adventurers. But in so far as the agreement related to capital as well as income, by making the planters shareholders, it went beyond the half-profits system, and this aspect of the arrangement at once introduced a dual control of the undertaking, which tended towards friction. Those adventurers, who did not intend to join the expedition, numbered about 70 and they formed themselves into a society which elected a president

[1] *History of Plymouth Plantation*, by William Bradford, Boston, 1856, pp. 45, 47; Hazard, *Historical Collections*, I. p. 87.

and treasurer. These officials were afterwards chosen annually and they managed "ordinary business"; while, for "more weighty affairs," the assent of the whole company was required[1]. On the other hand the shareholders, who were personal adventurers, elected a governor and assistants[2], so that as soon as the colony was established, at least half the shares were represented by a president in England and the remainder by a governor in America.

Information, relating to the finances of the company, is very incomplete. In June 1620 some of the original adventurers had withdrawn their subscriptions and others were in arrear[3]. It was calculated that there were 150 persons to be transported, but there was at this time only £1,200 adventured, not counting cloth, stockings, shoes &c., so that it is added "we come £300 or £400 short[4]." It is plain that this estimate is framed on the basis of taking the cost of transporting each settler at £10. This would require £1,500, of which only £1,200 had been adventured in cash. When the whole sum was paid, there would be created on this account 150 shares, owned by the subscribers in England and, if 150 emigrants had actually sailed, approximately the same number would be assigned to them. To the shares so arrived at, there must be added those coming into existence on account of the "provision" of adventurers of their persons or for adventurers at home who subscribed commodities, instead of cash. Thus, at this time the total number of shares would be divided almost equally between those who emigrated and the others who only provided financial support.

The expenditure on the transportation of the emigrants in 1620 was not the end of the financial commitments of those shareholders in England who were not personal adventurers. Further settlers were sent in 1621 or 1622[5], while the departure from the original plan of planting under the Virginia company ultimately involved considerable expense. Between the date of the sailing of the *Mayflower* and the landing of the colonists, the district in which they established themselves had been

---

[1] Smith, *Generall Historie*, 1907, II. p. 92.

[2] *General History of New England*, in *Mass. Hist. Soc. Coll.*, 2nd Series, v. p. 90.

[3] Robinson to John Carver, in Bradford, *Hist. of Plymouth Plantation*, 1856, pp. 47, 48.

[4] Robert Cushman to John Carver, June 10, 1620 (New Style), *Ibid.*, p. 56. The cloth, &c., was the "provision" of those personal adventurers who claimed a second share, or was subscribed by other non-personal adventurers whose capital was in the form of commodities, not cash.

[5] *Records of the Colony of New Plymouth in New England*, edited by N. B. Shurtleff, Boston, XII. p. 5. The emigrants of 1623 may not have been transported at the cost of the general stock, since they were not members of the company but rented land on condition of paying half the proceeds to the joint-stock.

granted to the New England council[1], and therefore it became necessary to secure a patent from the latter body. This was obtained on June 1st, 1621, in the name of John Pierce and his associates. That deed conveyed 100 acres of land for every person transported, augmented by a like amount for every person remaining three years in the settlement or who died there, with 1,500 acres for public land[2]. A further patent was obtained by Pierce on April 20th, 1622, and he executed a deed poll to himself, to which the adventurers were not privy[3]. His action in this matter has been the subject of somewhat severe comment, but, as far as can be judged, without good reason. From all that is known of the methods of the council, no patent was obtainable from it without a consideration being paid, and since the Plymouth Adventurers, even at this time, were in want of funds, it is by no means improbable that Pierce safeguarded himself by refusing to give a complete title to the grant until he had been reimbursed. The adventurers accordingly agreed to pay him £500 for his interest[4], whereupon application was made to the council which recognized the Plymouth colony as entitled to the greater part of the patent granted to Pierce[5].

Thus by 1623 the colony was legally established and in the plantation itself considerable progress had been made. Though the first landing had been effected in mid-winter, the season had been milder than the average[6]. In 1623 a concession was made, affecting the relation of the individual planters to the joint-stock, by granting them small allotments of lands (as provided in the first form of the agreement) which became their own property, under an arrangement made in the following year[7]. Otherwise, the constitution remained unchanged and it was specially provided that the fur-trade should be carried on in the exclusive interest of the joint-stock[8]. By this time the adventurers in England had become dissatisfied. In 1622 they had, with a few exceptions, agreed to increase the amount of their adventures by one-third[9], but not long afterwards Weston had disposed of his shares, while, at the end of 1623, all pleas for further financial assistance were met by "the invincible difficulty" that no more money would be

[1] *Vide supra*, pp. 302–3.
[2] *The First Plymouth Patent*, edited by Charles Deane, Cambridge, Mass., 1854, pp. 9–12.
[3] *Records of the Council for New England*, pp. 43, 44.
[4] Deane, *The First Plymouth Patent*, p. vii.
[5] *Records of the Council for New England*, p. 45.
[6] Wood, *New England's Prospect*, 1634, in *Publications of the Prince Society*, Boston, 1865, p. 5.
[7] *Records of the Colony of New Plymouth*, xii. p. 5.
[8] *History of Plymouth Plantation*, by William Bradford, Boston, 1856, p. 144.
[9] *Ibid.*, p. 116.

subscribed. From their point of view, the investment had proved unfortunate. Though it was alleged that goods sent to the colony were invoiced at 40 per cent. advance on cost price[1], the returns from the plantation were not considerable. As yet the settlers were able to produce little that could be sent home and beyond this there were only occasional consignments of timber, the profits of trade with the Indians and the proceeds of fishing voyages[2]. The failure of the undertaking as a commercial enterprize resulted in divisions amongst the adventurers in England. "Factions" had broken out amongst them, they were described as a company "broke in pieces" and "the greatest part had wholly deserted the colony[3]." In 1625 there was no possibility of raising a new stock, which had been suggested, and the undertaking was in debt to the extent of £1,400[4]. Those of the colonists, who were shareholders, on their side also felt aggrieved. They complained that the plantation had not been supplied and that results were expected too soon. Gradually the opinion began to gain ground, both in the colony and in England, that at the expiration of the seven years, mentioned in the original agreement, the joint-stock should be dissolved. There remained the question of terms. At a meeting of the adventurers in England on October 26th, 1626, they agreed to accept £1,800 for their interest in the plantation, payable in instalments of £200 a year beginning at Michaelmas 1628. Eight of the leading colonists became personally responsible for the discharge of this obligation. They in fact purchased the shares owned in England, as trustees for the adventurers in the colony. It was agreed on January 3rd, 1628, that the division of land of 1623 should be confirmed, and each person, entitled to one share, now received a dividend of 20 acres. The cattle belonging to the late joint-stock were also made over to the settlers on certain conditions. The remainder of "the old stock" was to be kept undistributed for ten years when the original amount, with half the increase, was to be divided, the other half of the profit being reserved for the use of the poor[5].

Precise information is wanting as to how this composition compared with the sums originally adventured by the English shareholders. John Smith stated that the general stock employed in 1624 was "about £7,000[6]." From the context it is clear that this means the

[1] Bradford, *Hist. of Plymouth Plantation*, 1856, p. 201.
[2] *Ibid.*, pp. 196, 201; Smith, *Generall Historie*, II. p. 65.
[3] Bradford, *Hist. of Plymouth Plantation*, 1856, pp. 157, 196.
[4] *Ibid.*, pp. 166, 200.
[5] *Records of the Colony of New Plymouth*, XII. pp. 9–16; Hazard, *Collections*, I. pp. 179, 180; Bradford, *History of Plymouth Plantation*, p. 212; *A Chronological History of New England*, by Thomas Prince, Edin., 1887, IV. pp. 21, 22.
[6] Smith, *Generall Historie*, II. p. 91.

DIV. II. § 3 C (i)]   *The Composition of 1626*   311

sums adventured by the shareholders in England, either as payment for their shares or as loans to the company[1]. The latter item at this date amounted to £1,400, leaving £5,600[2] as the share capital according to Smith's figures. In the composition, the colony became responsible for the amount of the debt then outstanding (which was reduced to £600) so that the payment of £1,800 was available as against the share-capital. It may have been that the Massachusetts Bay company in making a similar arrangement at a later date[3] was following the precedent of the Plymouth Adventurers. Now it is known that the sum paid by the former to the English shareholders was one-third of that adventured. If the ratio was the same in the agreement of 1626–7, it would follow that the total share capital owned in England by the Plymouth Adventurers was £5,400, and on this supposition Smith's statement is, on the whole, confirmed[4]. To some extent a similar result can be reached independently. In June 1620 £1,200 in cash had been adventured besides commodities, possibly the total actually received before the expedition sailed was larger. Then there were the voyages, bringing further settlers, to be provided for and also the expenses of the patent. Probably additional subscriptions were received till the end of 1621, and then in January 1622 the capital adventured was increased by one-third. After this date, owing to the dissensions amongst the members, it seems likely that no more capital was obtained by the issue of shares and that such, as was required for trade, was raised by borrowing. The reduction of the debt from £1,400 in 1624 to £600 in 1627 shows that the produce of the colony, by the sale of which this payment was effected, had been of a nett value of £800 in three years. The joint-stock at this time may have also obtained some additional revenue from fishing voyages sent out either by members or by others under license.

[1] This account differs from that of Mr Doyle (*The English in America—The Puritan Colonies*, p. 56) who includes in the estimate of £7,000 the personal shares of each emigrant.

[2] If any profit had been made at this time which was used for the extension of the colony this sum in the text should be diminished in proportion.

[3] *Vide infra*, pp. 314–15.

[4] Estimated amount of

Shares held in England	?£5,400
Debt (1624)	£1,400
Total outlay	£6,800

This compares with the sum mentioned by Smith as furnished by the adventurers in England of "about £7,000."

C. (ii) THE GOVERNOR AND COMPANY OF THE MASSACHUSETTS BAY IN NEW ENGLAND (1628).

Very soon after the joint-stock of the Plymouth Adventurers was assigned to the trustees on behalf of the personal adventurers, another Puritan colony was in process of formation. This undertaking was itself founded on a previous partnership which had been started as a fishing settlement at Cape Ann as early as 1623. After three years' trial the venture was found to be unprofitable, but some of those interested believed that, if pursued on a larger scale, the scheme might result in the building up of a promising plantation. Accordingly, application was made to the New England council by a group of prominent Puritans, and on March 19th, 1628, a patent was granted them, covering the land from the Merrimac to three miles south of the Charles River and, like the other titles of this council, extending from sea to sea[1]. More partners were assumed and a stock raised. By this means an expedition of 60 men was dispatched, under the command of John Endicott, to take possession of the land, granted by the patent. While preparations were being made at the plantation to receive an influx of settlers, the adventurers in England were busy attracting support. Owing to the overlapping of grants by the council of New England, it was feared that the title of the company to its lands might be assailed and therefore application was made to the Crown for a charter. This instrument, which was dated February 27th, 1629, explicitly confirms the patent of the council and creates a corporation under the title of *the Governor and Company of the Massachusetts Bay in New England.* The government was committed to a governor, a deputy-governor and 18 assistants. Four general courts were to be held annually and the company was not limited to any fixed meeting-place. Other courts might be held once a month or oftener and could be summoned by the governor. The quorum consisted of seven members, of whom the governor or deputy must be one[2]. It appears that the total membership of the company was about 110[3]. The extant minute book opens in the month that the charter had been signed, and some of the earlier proceedings, during the eleven months the company had been in existence,

---

[1] State Papers, Colonial, IV. 42, 43; printed in *The History of New England*, by Daniel Neal, London, 1720, pp. 122, 123.

[2] State Papers, Sign Manual, Charles I., x. 16, printed in *Records of the Governor and Company of the Massachusetts Bay*, edited by N. B. Shurtleff, Boston, 1853, I. pp. 3–11; *Hutchinson Papers* (*Publications of the Prince Society*, 1865), I. p. 1.

[3] *Archæologia Americana*, III. p. cxxxiv.

can be gathered from it. The terms, upon which capital had been subscribed, were that the shares were to consist of £50 each; and, when the land came to be divided, each shareholder should be entitled to 200 acres upon the first distribution and in addition he was to obtain 50 acres for every servant or labourer he transported to the colony. Emigrants, who were not adventurers but who paid their own passages, were also to receive 50 acres[1]. Steps were at once taken to send a reinforcement to the colony and explicit directions were framed for the direction of the local executive, regarding religion and trade. Some disappointment was occasioned by a group of adventurers resident in Boston. They had promised to provide £400 towards the joint-stock, but, on the eve of the sailing of the ship, they communicated with the company asking that the terms of subscription should be modified. Ten of them offered to take up a half-share each by paying £250 to the joint-stock, while they undertook to "adventure in their particular" about £250 more—that is to furnish goods for trade to be sent at their own risk with the expedition. That the company, while assenting to this proposal, "thought it prejudicial to the general stock by the abatement of so much mony thereout[2]," may be readily understood when it is noted that this undertaking, like most of its contemporaries, had begun to suffer from want of capital, due at least in some measure to the failure of the adventurers to pay the instalments on their shares. After the departure of the expedition of 1629, it is noted, on June 17th, that £1,500 was needed and, to meet pressing claims, £745 was borrowed[3]. When a ship was required on July 28th, the funds of the company could not pay the amount necessary and eleven members made the purchase, taking eighth or sixteenth shares in the vessel[4]. In September attention was drawn to the large amount outstanding on instalments of the shareholders, and on October 16th mention was made of the great debt on the joint-stock[5]. When preparations were being made for the great expedition, which was to sail on March 1st, 1630, the financial stringency became accentuated—£3,000 was wanted in November 1629, and of this sum as much as £1,900 was due from adventurers who were behindhand in making the payments they had promised[6]. Two methods were adopted to facilitate the voyage. In order to minimise the delay in starting, which had been hitherto a fruitful source of expense, it was agreed that all those, who had pledged themselves to join the ships, should be subject to a penalty of £3 for each day they were late in arriving at the port of embarkation[7]. Further, many of the adventurers agreed to double the

---

[1] *Records of the Co. of Mass. Bay*, I. pp. 42, 43.   [2] *Ibid.*, I. p. 28.
[3] *Ibid.*, p. 46.   [4] *Ibid.*, p. 47.   [5] *Ibid.*, pp. 54, 57.   [6] *Ibid.*, p. 62.
[7] A true coppie of the Agreement at Cambridge, Aug. 29, 1629, in *Hutchinson Papers* (*Publications of the Prince Society*, 1865), I. p. 27.

amount of their subscriptions to the joint-stock[1]. With regard to the constitution of the company, it was thought desirable that the seat of the government should be transferred from England to the colony and counsel advised that this course would not be contrary to the provisions of the charter. But in making the change, it was important that the rights of those shareholders, who did not propose to emigrate, should be protected. On October 15th, 1629, it was proposed that the monopoly of the fur-trade should be reserved to the joint-stock for seven years and that the cost of fortifications and ministers should be borne equally by the shareholders and the planters[2]. On further consideration, it was seen that this scheme required revision. If the joint-stock were to be continued, it would need to be considerably increased and it was judged improbable that sufficient additional capital would be forthcoming[3]. On the other side, it was suggested that the joint-stock should be wound up by selling the remaining assets, but as against this plan there was the difficulty that some of the property was not of a nature for which a ready market could be found, while other parts of it (such as fortifications and landing-stages) had a value only for the colony in its corporate capacity. A third course was propounded which was borrowed, in part, from the experience of the Plymouth Adventurers, namely, that a group of "undertakers" should take over the management of the joint-stock for seven years and, at the expiration of that period, they were to be bound to repay their principal to the adventurers. Further, in order to induce men of standing to undergo the trouble and risk, it was suggested that the "undertakers" should have the monopoly of half the fur-trade, as well as the whole of that in the making of salt, the sale of goods from the magazine and the transporting of passengers, provided their rates were reasonable. When these different schemes came to be debated at the court held on November 30th, the third was received with most favour, but it was subject to the objection that it was believed that most of the original capital had been lost[4]. Accordingly a committee was appointed consisting of five adventurers and five of those, provisionally chosen as "undertakers," to value the assets belonging to the joint-stock. This body reported that, in their opinion, the joint-stock was then worth only one-third of its nominal amount[5]. This decision was received with dismay by those adventurers who had recently doubled their subscriptions. They contended that the second stock had been provided for trading and that there should not have been such a large depreciation in so short a time. The complaints of the shareholders were met by the stipulation that, besides receiving one-third of

[1] *Records of the Co. of Mass. Bay*, I. pp. 62, 66.
[2] *Ibid.*, I. p. 55.   [3] *Ibid.*, I. p. 62.
[4] *Ibid.*, I. p. 63.   [5] *Ibid.*, I. p. 64.

their capital, they should retain their right to a land-dividend and that this was to be doubled, that is that each subscriber of £50 should be entitled to receive £16. 13s. 4d. at the end of seven years and in addition 400 acres of land. Thus the cost of the division of land would have been only 20d. per acre to the shareholder. By this change in the form of the composition, the "undertakers" were not bound, during the seven years, to make good previous losses, and it was decided that, instead of the monopolies previously suggested, they were to receive 5 per cent. on the profits of the joint-stock, while it was under their management. At the expiration of the seven years, the assets belonging to this stock together with any profit remaining, after the payments due to the adventurers had been made, were to be divided amongst the colonists or, presumably in the case of property not of a divisible nature, to be transferred to the governor and assistants on behalf of the whole body of the settlers[1].

These arrangements having been made, the necessary resolutions were passed for transferring the government of the colony to America; and, on the "undertakers" taking possession of the corporate property as trustees for the colonists, the company ceased to exist as a joint-stock body. The charter, however, was utilized as the legal basis of the constitution of the plantation for the regulation of its government. The discharge of the obligations of the "undertakers" towards the adventurers was considerably delayed and for a number of years there were many financial details, under the agreement of December 1629, which remained unsettled[2].

C. (iii) The Company of Adventurers for Laconia (1629).

The only colony of any degree of importance, originating from members of the New England council, was later than either of the Puritan plantations. The leaders in this enterprize were Gorges and Mason. Both had been interested in a patent, granted in 1622, but this instrument had not been utilized for plantation purposes by the grantees. After a long experience of fishing, Gorges turned his attention to the establishing of a colony, and on November 17th, 1629, he, together with Mason, obtained a patent of all the territory on the rivers of the Iroquois, to be called Laconia. Ten days before, Mason had secured a grant of the land lying between the Merrimac and Piscataqua rivers[3].

[1] *Records of the Co. of Mass. Bay*, I. pp. 65, 68, 70. Mr Shurtleff, the editor of the Minutes, regards the charge of 5 per cent. as constituting a species of preferred stock (*vide* Index). It is clear that it was a payment for their exertions and risk as managers.   [2] *Archæologia Americana*, III. p. cxxiii.
[3] *The English in America—The Puritan Colonies*, by J. A. Doyle, London, 1887, I. p. 431.

The governing idea in this enterprize was the discovery of a route by the rivers and lakes for bringing furs to the coast, and hence the name of "Laconia[1]." Besides the two founders, there is mention of seven London merchants who were associated with them in the venture[2]. Probably there were other partners, and the whole body was known as *the Company of Adventurers for Laconia*[3]. In 1630 an expedition was sent into the interior, but it failed to discover a water-way to the fur country. Though nothing tangible had been accomplished the leader, Captain Walter Neal, sent back glowing accounts of the future prospects of the company and a settlement was effected, not on the territory to be named Laconia, but at Piscataqua on the patent of Mason. The right of the company to make this change was confirmed by a further grant from the New England council, dated November 4th, 1631[4]. Within a short period a number of schemes were either in operation or under consideration. Both planters and cattle had been sent out, fishing was being carried on for the company and had turned out profitable, while a revenue was derived from licenses for this industry to ships that visited the settlement. A manufacture of potash was being started and a considerable quantity of furs had been obtained, while the partners had good hopes of discovering mines[5]. Side by side with these various activities the search for a route to the fur country was continued, but, after three years' trial, some of the adventurers became disheartened, and at a meeting in December 1633 there had been some suggestions that the lands should be divided and the other operations of the company abandoned[6]. A few of the partners were unwilling to abandon the hope of participating in the fur-trade and Mason believed that not only could the previous losses be made good but a profit was obtainable, when the route by the lakes had been found[7]. Accordingly, it was decided that no land-division should be made for the present, but in May 1634 all the adventurers, with the exception of Mason and Gorges, refused to furnish more capital, and it was decided to pay off the servants and divide the moveable property[8]. There was a considerable stock of cattle and sheep, as well as a number of cannon and boats[9]. About the same time all the land north-east of the harbour of Piscataqua was divided amongst the shareholders[10], and it appears that at this time, or soon afterwards, the company was dissolved.

[1] *America Painted to the Life*, by Fernando Gorges, in *Coll. of the Maine Hist. Soc.* (1847), II. p. 66. [2] *Captain John Mason* (Prince Society, 1887), p. 56.
[3] State Papers, Colonial, VI. 35.
[4] *Records of the Council for New England*, Nov. 4, 1631.
[5] *Captain John Mason* (Prince Society, 1887), pp. 65, 67.
[6] *Ibid.*, p. 75.   [7] *Ibid.*, p. 74.   [8] *Ibid.*, p. 330.
[9] *New Hampshire Records*, I. p. 113.
[10] *Captain John Mason* (Prince Society, 1887), p. 329.

SECTION IV. ATTEMPTS TO COLONIZE NEW-FOUNDLAND, NOVA SCOTIA AND CANADA.

THE TREASURER AND COMPANY OF ADVENTURERS AND PLANTERS OF THE CITIES OF LONDON AND BRISTOL FOR THE COLONY OR PLANTATION IN NEWFOUNDLAND (1610).

THE UNDERTAKERS OF THE PLANTATION OF NEW SCOTLAND (NOVA SCOTIA, 1621–33).

THE COMPANY OF MERCHANT ADVENTURERS TO TRADE TO CANADA (1627).

MENTION has already been made of the early efforts of Gilbert to establish a colony in Newfoundland and of its failure[1]. It was not until 1609 that renewed attention was directed to this district. In that year John Grey, a prominent Bristol merchant, succeeded in interesting a number of those who were alive to the possibilities of plantations in his scheme and on April 27th, 1610, a charter was granted to *the Treasurer and Company of Adventurers and Planters of the Cities of London and Bristol for the Colony or Plantation in Newfoundland*[2]. This document, while granting ownership of land occupied and the usual privileges, specially excepts the fishing off the coast, which was to remain open to both English and foreigners. Grey's expedition failed to establish itself but the patent was kept in being, for, in 1615, Vaughan purchased some territory from the company, which he named Cambriol[3]. This expedition resulted in failure. Then in 1623 Sir George Calvert, afterwards Lord Baltimore, obtained a grant from the King and he began a settlement at a place he called Avalon at an expenditure of £2,500[4]. In 1629 Baltimore gave a most gloomy account of the rigours of the climate, saying that his house had been a hospital all the winter and that at one

[1] *Vide supra*, pp. 241–3.
[2] State Papers, Docquet, James I.; *Calendar, Colonial*, 1574–1660, p. 9.
[3] *A History of Newfoundland*, by L. A. Anspach (1827), p. 86.
[4] *Ibid.*, p. 87.

time 50, out of 100 persons, had been sick. He therefore petitioned the King to give him a new grant in Virginia[1]. The patent asked for was made out to his son and successor and became the foundation of the proprietary colony of Maryland. Baltimore continued to retain his plantation in Newfoundland but it was the last effort made at an organized settlement during this period.

The territory to the north of the grant of the New England company was within the sphere of French influence and Fernando Gorges formed the idea of founding another British company to settle beyond the New England grant so as to act as a buffer colony. He communicated this idea to Sir William Alexander, afterwards Lord Stirling, a Scottish nobleman, to whom he suggested that this enterprize should be undertaken by Scotsmen. Alexander replied that, as there was already a New France, a New Spain, a New England, this venture ought to be launched as a scheme for the formation of a New Scotland[2]. Accordingly on September 10th, 1621, Alexander received a charter conveying to him all lands between New England and the great river of Canada (the St Lawrence)[3]. It is noticeable, in this grant, that instead of the clause conveying lands "not in the occupation of any friendly Christian prince," Alexander describes the patent "as designing lands to him in that part which hath been questioned by the French." This charter was made out to Alexander personally and it was not until later that he assumed partners.

He started in 1622 but, being driven from land by contrary winds, was forced to winter in Newfoundland. The following year a survey of the coast of the mainland was made but no settlers were left behind, when the ships returned to Scotland[4]. The enterprize suffered from want of capital, and other means failing, Alexander applied to James I. for authorization of a rather remarkable scheme. In view of the success that had attended the plantation of Ulster, through the offer of the title of Baronet to those who contributed a certain sum, it was decided to apply the same system in the case of the Nova Scotia venture. James I. was favourably disposed to this suggestion and in 1624 a proclamation was made at Edinburgh, which stated that the planting of Nova Scotia "being ane fitt, warrandable and convenient means to disburding this his Majesties said ancient Kingdome of all such younger brether and meane gentlemen quhois moyens ar short of thair birth, worth or

[1] State Papers, Colonial, v. 27; *Calendar, Colonial*, 1574–1660, p. 101.
[2] *Royal Letters, Charters and Tracts relating to the Colonisation of New Scotland*, 1621–38 (Bannatyne Club, 1867), p. 11.
[3] *Ibid.*, p. 14, and Charter in Appendix; *Sir W. Alexander and American Colonisation*, by E. F. Slafter (Boston Prince Society, 1873), p. 127.
[4] *Royal Letters, Charters and Tracts, relating to the Colonisation of New Scotland*, p. 15.

myndis, who otherwayes most be troublesome to the houses and freindis, from whence they ar descendit (the common ruynes of most of the ancient families) or betak thameselfis to forren warke or baisser chifts to the discredite of thair ancestouris and cuntrey," such persons are recommended to join with Alexander in the enterprize[1]. The conditions were that each undertaker should pay Alexander 1,000 marks Scots for his past charges, and 2,000 marks Scots to provide capital for a new expedition as well as giving bond to bring with him six "sufficient" colonists. In return, the contributor was to receive a land-grant in New Scotland and the dignity of being a baronet of Nova Scotia—a title which still exists.

The payments made, when reduced to sterling, came to £100 for each undertaker for the furtherance of the venture (2,000 marks Scots) and, since there were 83 knights up to the end of 1632, this should have provided a capital of over £8,000. Most of the undertakers however took "seisin" of their land-grants at Edinburgh and did not join in the expeditions personally. Still the funds subscribed in the first two years were expended in the fitting out of expeditions and by 1630 a settlement had actually been effected at Port Royal (now Annapolis) in Nova Scotia[2].

Mention of this place involves a reference to two other colonizing bodies, the one French and the other English. In 1603 a French nobleman, de Mons, had been appointed Lieutenant of New France and in 1605 he had founded Port Royal[3]. In 1613 emissaries of the Virginia company had destroyed this post[4]. Then came the foundation of the *Compagnie des Cent Associés de la Nouvelle France ou du Canada* in 1628[5]. This company, or its predecessors, had the intention of fortifying Port Royal but the cannon sent from France for this purpose were intercepted by an expedition of the company of the Adventurers to Canada[6].

This left the site vacant for the Scottish undertakers, but, at the same time that the fort there was being built, Alexander had sold all his interest in the patent to Claude St Estienne, a French Huguenot, on the condition that he should hold from the Scottish Crown, for a consideration that has not been recorded[7]. On the conclusion of the French treaty of 1632, Charles I. ceded the sovereignty of Acadia,

---

[1] *Royal Letters, Charters and Tracts, relating to the Colonisation of New Scotland*, pp. 20–1. [2] *Ibid.*, p. 94.

[3] *Les Grandes Compagnies de Commerce*, by Pierre Bonnassieux, p. 347.

[4] *Cambridge Modern History*, vii. p. 72; *The Genesis of the United States, A Series of Historical Manuscripts now first printed*, edited by Alexander Brown, London, 1890, ii. pp. 698–700.

[5] *Les Grandes Compagnies, ut supra*, p. 353.   [6] *Vide infra*, p. 320.

[7] *Royal Letters, Charters and Tracts, relating to the Colonisation of New Scotland*, p. 95.

Canada and New France to Louis XIII., and the Scottish settlers received directions to give up Port Royal. In return the persons dispossessed were to receive £10,000. If this amount was ever paid, which is doubtful, the undertakers would have received their capital back, for this sum would cover both the payments they had contributed to the undertaking as well as the outlay of Stirling. In addition they retained their titles of Knights Baronets of Nova Scotia[1].

In 1627 a company, described as *the Company of Adventurers to Canada*, had been formed[2]. This may have been a subordinate branch of the Nova Scotia undertaking, but it is much more probable that it was an independent, but related venture. The Nova Scotia patent referred to the territory from the most northerly point of the New England company's lands to the St Lawrence; and the Canada company, by agreement with the patentees (Alexander was a member), was designed for trade and planting in the vicinity of the St Lawrence. The fact that the capital was found by London merchants and that the expedition started from England tends to show that, though this body was connected with the Nova Scotia plantation, it was a separate undertaking[3].

This company received a commission from Charles I. for the sole trade with the "Gulf and river of Canada" together with authority to plant there (always saving the previous grant to the New Scotland company) and to seize ships and goods of the French or Spaniards, also to "displant" the former[4]. The expedition started in 1627 under the command of Captain David Kirke. He succeeded not only in trading with the natives for furs but in conquering all Canada except Quebec. The ships returned in 1628 and in the following year a fresh venture was started and Quebec was captured[5].

These voyages occasioned considerable friction with the French merchants. They claimed that some 6,000 furs, which Kirke had brought to London, had been taken from them, while the English contended that these had been obtained by trade[6]. The Admiralty ordered that the company should not dispose of the skins till the matter was decided, but it was alleged that emissaries of the adventurers broke open the warehouse and sold some of the furs. On the conclusion of the peace of 1632 the territorial acquisitions were given back to

---

[1] *Royal Letters, Charters and Tracts, relating to the Colonisation of New Scotland*, p. 99.

[2] *The First English Conquest of Canada*, by Henry Kirke, London, 1871, p. 28.

[3] State Papers, Colonial, vi. 15; *Calendar, Colonial*, 1574–1660, p. 130.

[4] *Ibid.*, v. 1–3; *Calendar, Colonial*, 1574–1660, p. 96.

[5] *Ibid.*, vi. 15; *Calendar, Colonial*, 1574–1660, p. 130; *France and England in North America*, by Francis Packman, Boston, 1865, Part i. p. 402.

[6] State Papers, Colonial, v. 96; *Calendar, Colonial*, 1574–1660, p. 117.

France and England undertook to compensate the French traders for the losses sustained. There is mention of a sum of £14,330 paid under this head in 1632. Charles I. resented this settlement, and it is recorded that he disavowed "the transaction as not justifiable," yet required the arrangement to be carried out immediately[1]. In 1633 the Canada company counter-claimed £4,417. 2s. 6d. from the French merchants, though whether they received it is doubtful[2].

These indications, slight as they are, tend to show that, although the company obtained no direct territorial acquisition from Kirke's "conquests," it gained considerably financially. For, since the English government accepted pecuniary responsibility for the proceeds of the furs seized by the agents of the company, it follows that this undertaking was able to retain the money received for the sale of them. This was likely to have exceeded both the compensation and the original capital subscribed[3].

After the privateering expedition of 1629, several trading vessels were sent out, and in 1631 the company petitioned the Admiralty against some ships which proposed to trade within the limits assigned to it[4]. On an enquiry being made, it was found that the interlopers had already been to Canada and had prejudiced the natives against trading with the English, and that the chief persons in the venture had been warned by the company of its claims and rights[5]. In 1632 the Privy Council ordered that one of the interlopers should pay a fine to the company of £200 and another one of 400 marks, but "without expecting any of their assents[6]."

In 1633 a formal patent was granted to the adventurers (but without an incorporation clause) conferring on them the monopoly of the trade to the river and gulf of Canada, in beaver and all other skins, for 31 years[7]. Having obtained this formal acknowledgment of its position, the company hoped to prosecute its grievances against the French. On applying to the governments, the adventurers received the impression that, after the recent peace, neither was prepared to take a strong stand

---

[1] State Papers, Correspondence, France, 1632, April 19; *Calendar, Colonial*, 1574–1660, p. 142.

[2] *Ibid.*, Colonial, VI. 75; *Calendar, Colonial*, 1574–1660, p. 166.

[3] In 1660 it was stated that, by the evacuation of the Canadian territory at this time, the Kirkes and their associates had been "damnified" to the extent of £60,000. State Papers, Minutes of the Committee for America, Colonial Papers, XIV. 37; *Calendar, Colonial*, 1574–1660, p. 488; Kirke, *First English Conquest of Canada*, p. 83.

[4] State Papers, Colonial, VI. 4, 5.

[5] *Ibid.*, VI. 33; *Calendar, Colonial*, 1574–1660, p. 136.

[6] *Ibid.*, VI. 66; *Calendar, Colonial*, 1574–1660, p. 155.

[7] *Ibid.*, Minute Colonial Correspondence, 1607, Jan. 9; *Calendar, Colonial*, 1574–1660, p. 165.

in the matter, and the traders had learnt that they might "right themselves and let the strongest carry it." The English company then asked for a commission authorizing them to "right themselves," by ejecting the French settlers and holding any territory they might conquer. It is significant that it was proposed that the grant asked was to pass no further than the Privy Signet "that it may not be so publicly known[1]." There is no record of the powers applied for being accorded and it is probable that, with the growing strength of the French company, this small English body found it more and more difficult to prosecute its trade.

[1] State Papers, Colonial, IX. 1, 2; *Calendar, Colonial*, 1574–1660, p. 219.

SECTION V. COLONIZATION IN SOUTH AMERICA, CENTRAL AMERICA AND THE WEST INDIES.

A. The Governor and Company of Noblemen and Gentlemen of England for the Planting of Guiana (or the Amazon Company, 1619).

INTERACTING with the idea of English planting of the New World there were other economic motives which, to a considerable extent, determined the time at which efforts were made to effect settlements at different places. The dominant notes of enterprize at the beginning of the seventeenth century were the fishing trade and gold mining. The former stimulus was an important element in directing English adventurers to the northern part of America (as for instance to Newfoundland and New England), while the hope of gold discoveries sent ships first to the southern portion, *e.g.* to Virginia and Guiana. This was the foundation of Raleigh's expeditions to these regions, and it has already been shown how the same desire hindered the progress of the Virginia company at first[1].

Besides Raleigh's voyages to Guiana, there was another attempt to exploit this district by a small syndicate, founded by Robert Harcourt, who sailed with an expedition in 1609. Treaties of friendship were arranged with the natives, and many discoveries were made, until there came reports of certain golden mountains which, in the words of Harcourt, "filled the minds of my company so full of vain expectations and golden hopes, that their insatiable and covetous minds, being wholly set thereon, could not be satisfied with anything but only gold[2]." The prospects were considered promising by those who were interested in the scheme. They believed that, on a plantation being established, cotton, tobacco, sugar, as well as valuable dyes and drugs, could be obtained from it, in addition to which traces of gold and silver had been found[3]. The associates were confident that they would

---
[1] *Vide supra*, pp. 244, 249.
[2] *A Relation of a Voyage to Guiana*, by Robert Harcourt, 1613, in *Harleian Miscellany*, VI. pp. 455, 468.
[3] *Ibid.*, pp. 453, 468.

recover their outlay "with treble recompense[1]," and steps were taken to procure a patent from the Crown. This grant endued Harcourt and his associates with the land planted between the Amazon and Essequibo[2]. The members of the syndicate soon discovered that they could not command sufficient capital for the enterprize, and in 1613 subscriptions were invited from the general public. As in the Virginia company, persons might become interested in the plantation either as adventurers of their persons or of money, and in the latter case the share was fixed at £12. 10s. In both instances the member of the company was entitled to a division of land of 500 acres[3]. It was also provided that anyone might subscribe smaller sums, with a minimum of 10s., receiving land in proportion. For the first three years there was to be no division of the profit made, and at the expiration of that period one-quarter of the gain was to be divided amongst the adventurers and the remainder was to be utilized for the advancement of the plantation. During the next seven years the ratio was to be reversed, three-quarters being divisible and the other quarter reserved for the improvement of the settlement. When the undertaking had been in operation for ten years, it was provided that "it shall be free for everyone to make the best of his allotment at his own discretion by himself or else to trade and deal in common as he did before with others, which perhaps will be most convenient for all small adventurers." These terms applied only to those who subscribed before the second expedition sailed; such as came into the company, after that date and before the third voyage, received a land-dividend reduced by one-fifth. The penalty for late subscription continued progressively, so that the adventurer who applied for a share on the eve of the departure of the sixth expedition obtained only 100 acres for each share he took up.

Harcourt had intended to send out six supplies to Guiana, but it appears that only one of these actually started. This was in 1616–7[4]. Then came Raleigh's unfortunate venture of 1618, in which Harcourt was one of the chief adventurers.

On the failure of Raleigh's last expedition to Guiana, the hopes of an English settlement there were not allowed to languish, for in 1619 there was a "great project" for the formation of a plantation company on "the River Amazon, near Guiana." Capt. North, brother of Lord North, and many noblemen were interested in the venture[5]. This expedition aroused the hostility of Spain, and, on representations being made, James I. issued a proclamation of May 15th disavowing the

[1] Harcourt, *Relation of a Voyage to Guiana*, in *Harleian Miscellany*, vi. p. 454.
[2] *Ibid.*, p. 478.   [3] *Ibid.*, p. 479.
[4] *The Genesis of the United States*, by A. Brown, ii. p. 910.
[5] State Papers, Domestic Correspondence, James I., cviii. 85; *Calendar, Colonial, 1574–1660*, p. 21.

DIV. II. § 5 A] *The Guiana Company 1620–35*   325

company[1]. In 1620 North returned to England "well fraught[2]," but he was summoned before the King in May and the patent was suspended[3]. North was committed to the Tower in January 1621 and the goods were seized. In August of the same year the freight of the ships was released and the proceeds were subsequently divided amongst the shareholders[4]. In view of the protest of the Spanish Ambassador in 1619, no active steps were taken for some years, although in 1623 a statement was made showing that there were, at that time, English settlers in the country which was not actually occupied by the Spaniards[5]. In 1626 North and his associates succeeded in obtaining the promise of a new patent and proposals were issued inviting subscriptions which might be either £150, £100 or £50. This grant was signed on May 19th, 1627, and a company was thereby incorporated as *the Governor and Company of Noblemen and Gentlemen for the Plantation of Guiana*, with the usual powers. At this date there were 55 members; this would make the capital something over £5,000[6].

During the next three years the company was engaged in prosecuting its business, but it soon began to discover that to succeed further capital was necessary. The prominent members were deeply engaged in other colonizing ventures and the problem of raising capital presented serious difficulties. In 1629 it was proposed that Charles I. should advance £48,000 in three instalments in order to send 3,000 men and 100 pieces of ordnance. In return the company was prepared to pay the King and his successors £50,000 a year for 21 years, beginning four years after the first contingent of settlers had started[7]. It is exceedingly doubtful whether the company could have carried out its part of the bargain; but, in any case, the state of the royal resources totally precluded the advance being made. From a petition, presented by North in 1635, it appears that many of the shareholders were in arrear in paying for their shares, and, after certain changes had been made in the constitution, arrangements were concluded for a voyage to start in the following year[8]. It was also in 1635 that a group of adventurers, who were not members of the company, had prepared to trade to Guiana, and North's undertaking petitioned against this invasion of its privileges[9]. In 1638 it was

---

[1] State Papers, Proclamations, James I., 80; *Calendar, Colonial*, 1574–1660, p. 23.
[2] *Ibid.*, Colonial, IV. 3; *Calendar, Colonial*, 1574–1660, p. 77.
[3] *Ibid.*, Domestic Correspondence, James I., cxv. 51; *Calendar, Colonial*, 1574–1660, p. 24.
[4] *Ibid.*, Domestic Correspondence, James I., cxviii. 54; cxix. 10; cxxii. 31, 88; *Calendar, Colonial*, 1574–1660, pp. 77, 78.
[5] *Ibid.*, Colonial, II. 18; *Calendar, Colonial*, 1574–1660, pp. 36, 37.
[6] *Ibid.*, IV. 8, 23, 28; *Calendar, Colonial*, 1574–1660, pp. 79, 84, 85.
[7] *Ibid.*, V. 28; *Calendar, Colonial*, 1574–1660, p. 101.
[8] *Ibid.*, VIII. 51; *Calendar, Colonial*, 1574–1660, p. 200.
[9] *Ibid.*, VIII. 89; *Calendar, Colonial*, 1574–1660, p. 218.

alleged that the company was then "doing nothing" and the formation of a new one was proposed, in which adventurers were to be encouraged to underwrite[1]. Again in 1640 there was another scheme for the plantation of "the Tapoywasooze and the Towyse-yarrowes countries" upon the coast of Guiana, for which undertaking a capital of £10,000 would be required. With the usual optimism of the framers of "a preamble for subscriptions" it was added that the adventurers were certain to receive back the sums risked within a year, through the proceeds of a trade in cotton and tobacco[2].

The West India Islands.

The first English settlements in the West India Islands were fixed partly on the reports of ships touching there, when engaged in privateering expeditions towards the Spanish Main, partly by the necessity of confining occupancy to places, not already in the actual possession of Spain. St Christopher and Barbadoes dispute the claim of having been the first English plantations in the West Indies. A ship, touching at the former in 1605, endeavoured to annex it as British territory, but it appears St Kitts was occupied in 1623 and actually settled two years later, while about 1624 Courten endeavoured to plant Barbadoes.

Speaking generally, the settlement of the West Indies resembled in some respects that of Maryland, in others that of New England and, through accidental circumstances, it possessed characteristics of its own. Like Maryland, the plantation on these islands was proprietary; and, as in New England, there was much confusion through contradictory grants. Lord Carlisle obtained from Charles I. in 1627 a patent covering "the Caribbees" and including a number of islands mentioned by name[3]. Marlborough had a grant from James I., and in 1628 the Earl of Pembroke and Montgomery obtained rights in "Trinidado, Tobago, Barbudos and Fonesca[4]." There were frequent disputes, the different patentees appointed rival governors, and, while the title was in doubt, the work of development was unduly delayed. Eventually Carlisle made good his claim; but, since he soon became embarrassed, his administration of the plantation as a proprietary "province" was in difficulties from want of capital. Carlisle's success brought to an end a promising little colony in Barbadoes which had been started, as a company or co-partnership, by Sir William Courten. The title in this

---

[1] State Papers, Entry Book Petitions, 1636–8, p. 272; *Calendar, Colonial*, 1574–1660, p. 270.

[2] *Ibid.*, Colonial, x. 81; *Calendar, Colonial*, 1574–1660, p. 316.

[3] *Ibid.*, Colonial Entry Book, v. pp. 1–12; *Calendar, Colonial*, 1574–1660, pp. 85, 86.

[4] A clear account of these different grants will be found in *A Historical Geography of the British Colonies*, by C. P. Lucas, II., Chap. 5.

DIV. II. § 5 A] *West India Plantations* 1605–40 327

case was derived from Marlborough, and in 1628 the settlers, established by this company, were ejected by an agent acting for Carlisle[1]. In 1625 it was proposed to establish a West India company which was primarily intended to attack the Spanish settlements and establish a trade there[2]. Similar schemes were considered from time to time during the next twelve years, and by 1637, in view of the success of the Dutch West India company, it was suggested that an English undertaking should be established as " the most advantageous way to make war upon the King of Spain." It was estimated that a capital of £200,000 should be raised annually for five years, or £1,000,000 in all[3]. The great outlay as well as the unfavourable outlook at the time, conjoined also perhaps with the hostile influence of those who had already received West India grants, rendered this project impracticable.

B. THE GOVERNOR AND COMPANY OF ADVENTURERS FOR THE PLANTATION OF THE ISLANDS OF PROVIDENCE, HENRIETTA AND THE ADJACENT ISLANDS, BETWEEN 10° AND 20° OF NORTH LATITUDE AND 290° AND 310° OF LONGITUDE (1629–41).

In several respects the most important and progressive English settlement, in the islands off the coast of America during the reign of Charles I., was one which is no longer British territory. It was established on the Mosquito Islands, off the coast of Nicaragua. These islands had been visited by Columbus, and, during the first half of the seventeenth century, they were considered second only to Darien as a depôt for exchanging European against American commodities. Owing to the fortunate accident that the minutes of the company, which controlled this enterprize have been preserved, it is possible to trace its history[4].

The first expedition was sent out by Sir N. Rich and a group of his friends (most of whom were shareholders in the Bermuda company) and which included Lord Holland and John Pym. This syndicate subscribed £2,000 " and odd pounds " in shares of £200 each[5]. On the return of

[1] State Papers, Colonial, XIV. 37; *Calendar, Colonial*, 1574–1660, p. 488; *History Civil and Commercial of the British Colonies in the West Indies*, 1793, I. p. 333.

[2] State Papers, Domestic Correspondence, Charles I., I. 59; *Calendar, Colonial*, 1574–1660, p. 73.

[3] *Ibid.*, Colonial, IX. 61; *Calendar, Colonial*, 1574–1660, p. 257.

[4] These documents have been bound up in the Colonial Entry Books Series at the Record Office.

[5] Manchester Papers, No. 416. When the company was constituted the members of the first syndicate were credited with the amount they had contributed towards the discovery. Thus on June 19, 1632, Sir N. Rich had expended £792, of which

the first ships in 1630 it was decided to institute a company formally; and a governor, deputy-governor and treasurer were elected. At this time, or soon afterwards, the undertaking was divided into twenty-four shares, six of which were subsequently split into quarter-shares. This number remained unchanged, although the amount paid up on each share was increased from time to time. In order to provide funds for the prosecution of the enterprize, it was resolved in 1630 to call up £300 additional on each share, making them from that date £500 paid[1]. If the whole 24 shares were taken up at this time, the nominal capital would have been £12,000, but this amount was not all received since, as was usual, many of the shareholders were soon in arrear, and (in 1634), although Holland, the governor, had not made any cash payments, it was resolved to "repute him, in all dividends, an adventurer of one entire share[2]."

The company renamed one island (previously known as St Catherina) Providence and another (called Andrea) Henrietta. Explicit instructions were made out for the government and organization of the colony. It was originally intended that the land occupied should be divided amongst the shareholders, as in other plantation undertakings, and it was announced that settlers, who cultivated the estates, should receive one-half of the profits, the remainder being payable to the adventurer who obtained the land as his dividend. "Artificers" were to be paid also half the profits of their work, the other half going to the company, or alternatively they might elect to be maintained by the company with a fixed wage of £5 a year[3]. A characteristic, which shows how carefully the plan of colonization was thought out, was the provision of ministers for the settlement. They were to receive £40 a year with maintenance and to rank next in precedence to the local governor[4].

On December 4th of the same year a charter of incorporation was granted. This instrument constitutes eighteen persons named a company under the title of *the Governor and Company of the Adventurers for the Plantation of the Islands of Providence, Henrietta and the adjacent islands, between 10 and 20 degrees of North Latitude and 290 and 310 degrees of longitude.* Reducing the longitude to its

£520 was allowed against calls due on his share and the remainder was ordered to be paid to him. Colonial Entry Book, III. pp. 67, 68; *Calendar, Colonial*, 1574–1660, p. 152. It is interesting to notice that this company owned, in its corporate capacity, shares in the Somers Islands—Colonial Entry Book, III. p. 166.

[1] Minutes in Colonial Entry Book, III. pp. 1, 2; *Calendar, Colonial*, 1574–1660, pp. 121–2.

[2] *Ibid.*, p. 166; *Calendar, Colonial*, 1574–1660, p. 183.

[3] *Ibid.*, pp. 4, 5; *Calendar, Colonial*, 1574–1660, p. 122.

[4] *Ibid.*, pp. 2, 3; *Calendar, Colonial*, 1574–1660, p. 122.

DIV. II. § 5 B] *Organization of the Colony* 1629–31 329

modern equivalent[1], this area included the greater part of the Caribbean Sea, extending from Haiti on the north to the coast of Venezuela on the south and to the mainland of Central America. Besides Jamaica, then in the possession of the Spaniards, the Cayman Islands fell within these limits. Powers were granted the company to elect a governor, deputy-governor and treasurer, and to hold "the general court of the company on the last Thursday of each term," besides ordinary courts at any time. As regards the administration of the colony, very full powers were granted, such as the jurisdiction of life and death, the right of erecting forts, of repelling invaders, of declaring martial law, of establishing a mint and appointing officers and judges[2]. It appears that the fleet, sent out by the company in 1630, temporarily occupied the island of Tortuga, situated to the north of Haiti. It was just above the parallel of 20° N., and therefore in May 1631 the company petitioned the King for an addition of "only three or four degrees of northerly latitude" to its limits, so as to avoid all doubts as to rights in this island, which "had been taken above a year past and is now inhabited by more than one hundred persons[3]." This petition was granted on May 30th, 1631, and orders were given to the attorney-general to prepare a bill embodying the change. Tortuga, being situated at a considerable distance from the Mosquito Islands was developed by means of a subsidiary company, which changed the name to the Isle of Association[4]. This body was therefore described as the "Adventurers for Tortuga" or "for Association." An agreement was made with the planters, already on the island, by which the company "took them under their protection," and it was to receive in return 5 per cent. of the profits of the land already cultivated, reserving to itself half the increase of plantations to be established by settlers it brought there. Six of the planters were to be admitted into the Tortuga company. These arrangements were duly carried out, and in June 1631 a call of £70 was made from each adventurer in this subsidiary company[5]. The total number of adventurers was only eleven, making a nominal capital of £770, but in November 1634 it appears that no more than £570 had been actually paid[6]. This part of the original enterprize came to an end in 1635, when Tortuga (or Association) was taken by the Spaniards, as it was alleged, through the cowardice and negligence of the governor[7].

[1] The longitude in the charter is expressed in degrees *east*, that is (deducting 120°) equivalent to the modern notation of from 70° to 90° *west*.
[2] State Papers, Colonial Entry Book, IV. pp. 1–10; *Calendar, Colonial*, 1574–1660, p. 123.
[3] *Ibid.*, Colonial, VI. 16; *Calendar, Colonial*, 1574–1660, p. 131.
[4] *Ibid.*, Colonial Entry Book, III. pp. 33–5; *Calendar, Colonial*, 1574–1660, p. 133.
[5] *Ibid.*, pp. 21–7; *Calendar, Colonial*, 1574–1660, pp. 131–2.
[6] *Ibid.*, p. 174; *Calendar, Colonial*, 1574–1660, p. 193.
[7] *Ibid.*, p. 212; *Calendar, Colonial*, 1574–1660, p. 201.

The subordinate Tortuga company was merely an offshoot from the main undertaking, which was busily engaged in settling the Mosquito Islands. In 1631 it was decided that no divisions of the land were to be made " as yet," and it appears that, owing to the tropical climate, which made the adventurers disinclined to settle there, the islands were not divided up amongst the shareholders but were worked as a single estate on the company's account, by the employment of managers, assisted by negro labour[1]. This gradual change in the system of plantation involved the finding of larger funds by the company than in other cases where land-divisions were made and the shareholder raised the working-capital he needed to cultivate his property. Thus the Providence Island company differs from all the other important American plantation companies in this respect, and it was therefore more truly a joint-stock undertaking than the others were, since it not only provided for transportation, government and defence, but also owned and worked the properties in its corporate capacity. For this reason too, when a comparison is made of its capital with that of other colonizing companies, it appears disproportionately great. The Bermuda undertaking appears to have cost about £20,000 at the end of 1614; while in this case as much as £12,000 had been called up during the first two years. But, until this expenditure began to yield results, more capital was required, and in 1632 another £150 was called up on each share (in addition to the £500 already paid), and later on a further £100 per share was required[2]. These calls would make the shares £750 paid, and if the shareholders all responded, the capital would have been £18,000. It was recognized, however, that some members might not be willing to face the expense, and any that " shall express a desire to fall off" were granted leave to do so. In order to facilitate the making of payments, it was resolved on June 14th, 1632, that any adventurer might subdivide his share, so as to dispose of a part[3]. In pursuance of this order, up to 1635, six shares out of the twenty-four were divided into quarter-shares.

The members of the company, while satisfied as to the ultimate prospects of profit, found it difficult to raise the considerable sums required; especially since, owing to the different organization of this particular colony, the amount appeared to be unduly great. They complained of the very large amount paid up on their shares, as compared with the smaller sums of other men's adventures in other plantations. But, of course, it is to be remembered that in the other companies the number of shares was very much greater. Still the difference enabled the adventurers to quote this disparity in reply to a

[1] State Papers, Colonial Entry Book, IV. pp. 12–21; *Calendar, Colonial*, 1574–1660, pp. 126–7.

[2] *Ibid.*, III. pp. 46, 65; *Calendar, Colonial*, 1574–1660, pp. 139, 151.

[3] *Ibid.*, p. 64; *Calendar, Colonial*, 1574–1660, p. 151.

petition from the colony, in which some of the planters were reproved for forgetting their duty "to God and the company." It was urged that so far was the court in London from neglecting those engaged in improving its property that it had sent to the "furthest parts of the world to supply that, as yet, poor island with the richest commodities." Those, who were discontented, were compared to the Israelites in their murmurings, and it was threatened that they should be expelled from the colony, unless a more contented spirit was shown in the future[1]. Besides discontent there were evidences of a riotous disposition, since some of the colonists had sent for playing cards, dice and gaming tables. The local governor was ordered to burn these or "at least" send them home[2]. At this period there were at least three different tendencies in the company's operations. The seamen were tempted to capture Spanish ships, and in one case, where a frigate was taken, those involved were severely censured[3]. This unfriendly act aroused the Spaniards, who were inclined to be hostile to the company in any case, and one of its vessels was seized with a cargo valued at £30,000[4]. The commercial policy of the adventurers had two different objects, the one to cultivate diversified tropical plants on the islands and the other to build up a trade with the mainland. The former aim involved the expense of obtaining seeds from India and the latter of providing a stock-in-trade. Accordingly in 1633 it was necessary to call up another £250, bringing the shares to £1,000 paid[5]. It was made a condition that an adventurer, when paying this call, might "refuse to go further," which may be interpreted as a species of limited liability, where certain shareholders by agreement were exempt from additional calls.

In 1633 a trade was opened with the mainland and an expedition sent to Cape Gratia de Dios[6]. The profits appear to have been considerable, for application was made for an extension of the charter to cover this development of the other enterprizes[7]. The original patent included the mainland of the greater part of Central America, but at the same time it only applied to the plantation of *islands* and it was the intention of the company, not only to trade with, but to plant on the Mosquito coast.

Early in 1634 total calls of £1,025 per share had been made and it was resolved that no man should lose "his inheritance of the islands,"

[1] State Papers, Colonial Entry Book, IV. pp. 25-7; *Calendar, Colonial*, 1574-1660, p. 147.
[2] *Ibid.*, p. 40; *Calendar, Colonial*, 1574-1660, p. 150.
[3] *Ibid.*, p. 41; *Calendar, Colonial*, 1574-1660, p. 150.
[4] State Papers, Colonial, XI. 44; *Calendar, Colonial*, 1574-1660, p. 375.
[5] *Ibid.*, Colonial Entry Book, III. p. 80; *Calendar, Colonial*, 1574-1660, p. 159.
[6] *Ibid.*, IV. p. 56; *Calendar, Colonial*, 1574-1660, p. 168.
[7] *Ibid.*, III. p. 129; *Calendar, Colonial*, 1574-1660, p. 176.

without his own consent, by further assessments under penalties. At this time there were twenty of the twenty-four shares issued, the remaining four being pledged against loans, which in November 1634 amounted to £5,800[1]. Thus the total outlay at this time, under these heads, was £26,300, and there were besides outstanding liabilities, making the whole amount £28,012. 16s. 11½d.

The financial problem presented considerable difficulties. The limitation of calls must, it was resolved, be "inviolably preserved" and the policy of borrowing could not be continued indefinitely. Although further assessments could not be made, there was the alternative of issuing the remaining shares and creating new ones. Necessarily, by the former course, only the surplus, beyond the debt charged on the unissued shares, would be available for further capital expenditure, and it was evident that, when many of the shareholders would not consent to pay further calls, they were unlikely to subscribe for the new shares, unless some special inducement was offered them. To meet this difficulty, it was decided to fix the new shares as equal in nominal amount to one-quarter of the old, that is £256. 5s., and that both these and the old shares, now to be issued, should be given a certain priority. Those, who now subscribed, were to have a first charge on the profits, until they received back their capital, and thereafter they were to rank rateably for dividends as "if their last addition of adventure had remained still in stock[2]." By July 30th, 1634, out of 20 of the new quarter-shares, nine and half of another had been taken up by as many as eighteen persons, of whom three took one quarter-share each; twelve, one-half of a quarter-share each (or one-eighth of an original share); one, a quarter of a quarter, and two, one-eighth of a quarter each (the latter being one-thirty-second parts of an original share)[3]. This subscription provided less than half the funds required, and in November 1635 the sum due for principal and interest was £4,599. 9s. 8d.[4] Soon afterwards it was decided to establish a new stock of £10,000, divided into shares of £500 each. During the ensuing nine years no one was to have a voice in managing the affairs of this separate stock, unless he held a share in it, but subscribers, who owned less than £500, might join their holdings and depute one person to vote on their behalf, when the united stock was £500. The owner of two shares was entitled to two votes and so on[5]. By February 13th, 1636, £3,750 of this new stock had been applied for. One of the special inducements offered for this subscription

[1] State Papers, Colonial Entry Book, III. pp. 135, 174; *Calendar, Colonial,* 1574–1660, pp. 178, 193.
[2] *Ibid.*, p. 135; *Calendar, Colonial,* 1574–1660, p. 178.
[3] *Ibid.*, pp. 168, 169; *Calendar, Colonial,* 1574–1660, p. 185.
[4] *Ibid.*, pp. 232, 233; *Calendar, Colonial,* 1574–1660, p. 215.
[5] *Ibid.*, pp. 248, 249; *Calendar, Colonial,* 1574–1660, p. 221.

was that the adventurers in it were to be entitled to all the profits from Association during the specified nine years[1]. The attempt to regain Association was by way of reprisals against the Spaniards, whose fleet had attacked Providence in July 1635, but, after a contest lasting for five days, it had been driven off in a damaged condition[2]. At this time "the adventurers" (meaning probably settlers at Providence) had fallen off by one-half and the remaining planters were greatly discouraged. It was proposed that the whole property ought to be handed over to the State[3], and an investigation was made as to the strategic and commercial advantages of the islands. Sir John Coke reported that the able-bodied population amounted to 500 persons and that it cost on an average £30 per head to settle them in the colony. Allowing for the fact that the colonists had decreased by one-half, these figures exactly confirm the statement that up to this date £30,000 had been expended. It was calculated that 1000 men could hold Providence against any enemy, since a landing could only be made by boats. As yet there was no commerce beyond the trade just started with the natives, yet the revenue from customs was £1,000 a year. To bring the able-bodied population up to the numbers required for defence it would be necessary to send out at least 250 men the next year (1636). This would cost £7,500, and with arms, ammunition and other charges, £10,000 must be spent in 1636. The general drift of Coke's report was that this was a minimum estimate, which would apply only if the undertaking were managed by the company. If the colony were maintained at the King's expense the cost would be greater[4].

The effect of this investigation was that the company received full authority to make reprisals and it was left with the onus of raising £10,000 early in 1636[5]. Lord Brook, a leading member, at whose house the meetings were held, offered by himself to supply 200 men. The other adventurers, however, decided to subscribe to an increase of stock to the amount of £10,000 and to send out 500 men during the next two years[6]. Concurrently with this arrangement, it was felt that the settlers, who had stood by the company, should be rewarded, and in March 1636 it was ordered that "those of the better sort" should be taken as tenants for holdings of 50 acres and the others for 30 acres, both to be held on payment to the company of one-quarter profits

---

[1] State Papers, Colonial Entry Book, III. pp. 270, 271; *Calendar, Colonial,* 1574–1660, p. 233.
[2] *Ibid.,* Colonial, VIII. 81; *Calendar, Colonial,* 1574–1660, p. 216.
[3] *Ibid.,* Colonial Entry Book, III. p. 241; *Calendar, Colonial,* 1574–1660, p. 220.
[4] *Ibid.,* Colonial, VIII. 81, 83; *Calendar, Colonial,* 1574–1660, pp. 216, 217.
[5] *Ibid.,* Colonial Entry Book, III. p. 240; *Calendar, Colonial,* 1574–1660, p. 220.
[6] *Ibid.,* pp. 242–50; *Calendar, Colonial,* 1574–1660, pp. 220–1.

instead of half as previously[1]. This concession, it is recorded, gave great satisfaction in the colony.

In 1637 a proposal was made by the Dutch West India company for the purchase of the rights of the London body in the Mosquito Islands. At this period the Dutch undertaking was very prosperous, though it suffered eventually from having divided its "profits" (most of which were derived from captures of Spanish plate ships) too freely. During the period from 1623 to 1636 it had taken no less than 545 ships as prizes and the receipts exceeded the expenses by 45 million florins[2]. The English company was disposed to accept the offer, having found the islands "hitherto places of charge rather than benefit," and at first Charles I. had assented to the proposed sale, but later on he urged the adventurers to retain their settlement[3]. Once attention had been directed to this question, it was discovered that the islands were of "singular consequence" to England and the local executive was urged to maintain the forts and other defences[4]. The problem of finance had now become an urgent one and it was resolved that affairs must be so ordered "that the credit of the company stands upright[5]." After considerable deliberation it was proposed that new shares of £1,000 each should be issued to the amount of £20,000 in each of the next five years (or to a total of £100,000 in all). The owners of such new shares were to have four votes for each share so that those, who subscribed for a quarter-share, might have one vote. Adventurers in this latest stock were entitled to all the profits or prizes made by the ships they fitted out, while they participated rateably with the shares already in existence in any gains from the plantation. This proposal was subject to the condition that the creation of new shares was to cease when the profits had become sufficient to support the work "as is hoped they may be within a year or two[6]." Considering the small number of persons interested, the calling up of £100,000 of capital would have been very difficult, and by March 1638 no more than £6,000 of the shares issued the previous year, had been taken up[7].

The reason, that it was proposed to expend three times as much capital in five years as had been used in the previous seven or eight, is to be found in the new prospects that were opening out to the company.

---

[1] State Papers, Colonial Entry Book, IV. pp. 81-8; *Calendar, Colonial*, 1574-1660, p. 229.

[2] Bonnassieux, *Les Grandes Compagnies de Commerce*, p. 72.

[3] State Papers, Colonial Entry Book, III. p. 291; *Calendar, Colonial*, 1574-1660, p. 245.

[4] *Ibid.*, IV. p. 104; *Calendar, Colonial*, 1574-1660, p. 248.

[5] *Ibid.*, III. p. 295; *Calendar, Colonial*, 1574-1660, p. 252.

[6] *Ibid.*, p. 302; *Calendar, Colonial*, 1574-1660, p. 255.

[7] *Ibid.*, pp. 325-6; *Calendar, Colonial*, 1574-1660, p. 266.

DIV. II. § 5 B] *The Settlement destroyed* 1641   335

It already was cultivating cotton, tobacco, drugs and dyes at Providence. It had settled Tortuga and, after the destruction of that plantation by the Spaniards, further attempts were made to re-settle it. Then there was the trade in the vicinity of Cape de Dios and now two new ventures were being added. The adventurers were encouraged by hopes of mineral wealth, and an expert, who had tested some ore discovered in 1638, reported that it was very rich[1]. A year later it was recorded that silver ore was being shipped on behalf of the adventurers from the Bay of Darien[2], and it was ordered that the process of refining should be carried on at Providence, since the members of the company were unwilling "to subject themselves to men's scorn and derision, as others have done, when their ships brought home nothing but dirt[3]." Finally, the example of the Dutch company stimulated the adventurers to emulate their successes against the Spaniards. In spite of much provocation, it is probable this company would have continued its planting, trading and mining ventures, even after the harrying both of Tortuga and Providence, had it not suffered from one of its ships, with a cargo valued at £30,000, being captured in 1638 by a French man-of-war[4]. Reprisals were exacted from the Spaniards, and in the following year "a very rich ship was taken and safely brought to Holland[5]." There is frequent mention in the minutes of other prizes having been secured, for instance in 1640, when a ship arrived "with gold, silver, jewels and other goods of value[6]." Just at this time, when the outlook had become more favourable and the debt was being reduced, an unexpected disaster happened. A fleet of Spanish galleys, carrying 3,000 men, attacked and captured the island of Providence in July 1641, demolished the forts and securing 600 negroes, much gold and indigo, so that the value of the plunder was estimated at above half a million ducats[7]. The company was authorized to exact reprisals, and in December 1642 its agents took the *Santa Clara*, which was ransomed by the owners for £50,000[8].

On the seizure of the islands the active career of the company came

---

[1] State Papers, Colonial Entry Book, III. p. 320; *Calendar, Colonial*, 1574–1660, p. 264.

[2] *Ibid.*, p. 357; *Calendar, Colonial*, 1574–1660, p. 293.

[3] *Ibid.*, pp. 138–40; *Calendar, Colonial*, 1574–1660, p. 295. A notable case of this was the "voyages of Frobisher to the North-West," when large cargoes, supposed to be silver ore, only yielded on assay a few minute grains of the metal, cf. *supra*, p. 81.

[4] *Ibid.*, Colonial Papers, XI. 44; *Calendar, Colonial*, 1574–1660, p. 375.

[5] *Ibid.*, Colonial Entry Book, III. p. 347; *Calendar, Colonial*, 1574–1660, p. 290.

[6] *Ibid.*, p. 374; *Calendar, Colonial*, 1574–1660, p. 312.

[7] *A Letter...whereunto is added avisos from several places of the taking of the Iland of Providence by the Spaniards*, 1641 [Brit. Mus. E. 141 (10)], p. 5.

[8] State Papers, Colonial, XI. 44; *Calendar, Colonial*, 1574–1660, p. 375.

to an end, though it continued to exist in its corporate capacity for some years to wind up its affairs and to press for payment of the £50,000. It would seem from the frequent references to the debts of the undertaking during its later history that it ended in financial distress, but a closer examination of the circumstances shows that the shareholders had no reason to complain of their investment. The debts, so frequently mentioned, refer to the capital borrowed on bond, which formed a part of the total expenditure on the undertaking. Up to 1635 £30,000 had been spent, which was raised partly by issues of shares, partly by loans. Subsequently shares were created, in one case perhaps of the nominal value of £10,000, and in another £6,000 was actually subscribed. In 1639 five members of the company were indebted, either to it or on its account, to the extent of over £14,000[1]. A part of the former sum was arrears of calls on shares, so that it is unlikely that the whole expenditure, raised both by shares and loans, exceeded £40,000.

Now against this there was the payment due for the Spanish prize of 1642, which came to about the same amount. Therefore the position was that, by this payment (when made), the company received back its whole outlay. Hence any other receipts would constitute profits. These must have been considerable. As already shown, the company itself worked the plantations at Providence and received the proceeds. These were distributed as dividends to the shareholders. Some idea of the value of the shipments sent home may be gained from the fact that the ship taken was estimated at £30,000. This probably was exceptional, but there is evidence that most of the vessels were richly laden—for instance in the same year £2,000 was offered for a portion of a cargo. To this is to be added the gold, silver and jewels taken from the Spaniards from 1638 to 1641, so that altogether the amount divided to the shareholders must have been large, and it may be that it would bear comparison with the dividends of the Dutch West India company[2].

The difficulty in obtaining the indemnity of £50,000 for the release of the *Santa Clara* delayed the winding up of the company. In June 1641 the debt had been reduced to about £2,000[3], and the payment of this sum was postponed, pending the receipt of the prize-money. During the Civil Wars the adventurers were unable to collect this debt, and they met in April 1649, when it was decided to make calls on the shareholders to clear off the liability, though in one case it was urged

---

[1] State Papers, Colonial Entry Book, III. p. 352; *Calendar, Colonial*, 1574–1660, p. 290.

[2] For an account of subsequent relations of England with the Mosquito Islands, see *Hist. Geog. of the British Colonies*, II. pp. 299–302.

[3] State Papers, Colonial Entry Book, III. pp. 392, 393; *Calendar, Colonial*, 1574–1660, p. 320.

that, instead of assessing the members, it would be better to postpone these payments till the business of the Spanish ship was concluded[1]. About 1652 the company, having invoked the assistance of Parliament, was still prosecuting its claim[2].

Summary of Capital.

		£	s.	d.
Original Shares, 1629–33.	24 in number, of which 20 were issued, on each of which there was called £1,025	20,500	0	0
New Shares of 1634[3].	20 quarter shares, of which there were taken up nine and one half	2,434	7	6
,, 1635.	20 new shares of £500 each, of which up to February 1636 seven and a half had been taken up	3,750	0	0
,, 1637.	20 new shares of £1,000 each, making a new nominal capital of £20,000, the subscription for which was to be repeated in the four following years, whereby the proposed capital from 1637 to 1641 would have been £100,000. Of this issue by March 1638 there had been taken up six shares	6,000	0	0
	Total subscribed capital ...	£32,684	7	6

[1] State Papers, Colonial Entry Book, III. pp. 394, 395; *Calendar, Colonial*, 1574–1660, p. 329. The last entry in the minute book is dated, February 19, 1650, though the company continued to meet to press its claim.

[2] State Papers, Colonial, XI. 45; *Calendar, Colonial*, 1574–1660, p. 375.

[3] All the issues participated rateably in the profits of the island of Providence, but those of 1634, 1635 and 1637 possessed in addition certain privileges.

SECTION VI. PLANTING IN IRELAND.

A. The Society of the Governor and Assistants of London, of the New Plantation in Ulster within the realm of Ireland (or the Irish Society—founded in 1609).

If the strict chronological order of treating plantation undertakings, according to the priority of settlement, had been followed, the case of Ireland should have been dealt with before the American colonies. Once the idea of winning comparatively distant estates had become general, Ireland, almost inevitably, must have first attracted attention. The country was fertile, quite undeveloped commercially, within easy reach of England and Scotland, while it was under the British Crown so far as that government could make itself effective. The nomadic habits of the Celtic inhabitants, as well as the prevalence of the tribe or clan system, made it advantageous politically that English emigrants should be, if possible, established. Indeed, as early as the twelfth century Dublin was planted by emigrants from Bristol, and this connection was marked by the affiliation of the gild merchant of the Irish capital to that of the parent city[1]. The formation of the "Irish Pale" constituted a direct attempt to create a new England in the counties adjoining Dublin. From the thirteenth to the middle of the sixteenth century, the state of affairs in England prevented the development of Ireland, and it was not until 1560 that definite schemes were proposed which may be taken to mark the beginning of the plantation era. In that year Sussex proposed an English plantation in Ireland, and seven years later Humphry Gilbert undertook to settle a colony in Ulster. A proposal was made in 1569 to plant Munster, but these efforts failed to come to maturity. A fresh start was attempted in 1570, and settlers were sent to the country[2]. On the termination of Tyrone's Rebellion it was declared that the lands, he had occupied, were forfeited to the

[1] *The Gild Merchant*, by Charles Gross, 1. p. 247.
[2] *The Growth of English History and Commerce in Modern Times*, by W. Cunningham (1903), p. 123.

Crown, and early in the reign of James I. these were opened to persons who undertook to plant them. In 1608 the greater part of the counties of Armagh, Tyrone, Londonderry (then called Coleraine), Donegal, Fermanagh and Cavan was offered to planters in lots of 2,000, 1,500 and 1,000 acres, on condition that those, who accepted grants, should settle the estates and maintain places of strength[1]. Although the title of Baronet was instituted to aid this enterprize, the response was insufficient to satisfy James I., and about July 30th, 1609, he recommended the prosecution of the work of planting to the City of London, and on August 1st the Common Council agreed to undertake the enterprize[2].

Thus the London plantation in Ulster was preceded only by that of the first Virginia company, and, since it had certain complex characteristics, it is easier to understand after the more simple types of colonies have been explained. The Council might have arranged that the proposed Ulster plantation should have been carried on by means of a company of adventurers established for the purpose, but it is probable that the capital required would not have been collected sufficiently rapidly in this way. It was therefore arranged in January 1610 that the initial capital outlay should be raised by means of a rate levied on the London Livery companies, and £20,000 was immediately collected, of which £5,000 was expended " in clearing of private men's interests and things demanded," and the remaining £15,000 on the plantation[3]. In the following year it was agreed that a company should be established to manage the undertaking, and this body was in effect a joint-stock undertaking in which the capital was owned by the Livery companies, not by individuals, and was raised by assessment, not by voluntary subscription. With these important differences this organization was managed exactly like any of the other plantation companies. It was controlled by a governor, a deputy-governor and twenty-four assistants who were elected in part by the Council, in part by the other interests. Half this board retired annually. This constitution was embodied in the formal charter, which was signed March 29th, 1613, incorporating *the Society of the Governor and Assistants of London of the New Plantation in Ulster in the Realm of Ireland.* Following the precedent of the plantation company, it was proposed that a division of the lands should be made to the bodies interested, and Commissioners were sent to

[1] *A Concise View of the Origin, Constitution and Proceedings of the Honourable Society of the Governor and Assistants of London of the New Plantation in Ulster* (London, 1822), pp. 2–16; *London and the Kingdom*, by Reginald R. Sharpe (London, 1894), II. pp. 28–32.

[2] *A Concise View of the Origin…of the Honourable Society of the Governor and Assistants of London for the New Plantation in Ulster*, p. 21.

[3] *Ibid.*, p. 22.

Ireland to make a survey. They recommended that the two towns of Londonderry and Coleraine, with the fishings and lands belonging to them, should not be divided, but the rents accruing were to be allocated as profits and distributed. All the remainder was placed in lots ready for allocation[1]. At this stage a difficulty arose which was surmounted in an ingenious manner. In 1613 £40,000 had been expended and this was contributed by 54 companies. Of these twelve had paid sums varying from £2,000 to £4,000—the largest being the Merchant Tailors who had found £4,121. The others had been assessed at considerably smaller amounts—indeed four, the Musicians, Bowyers, Fletchers, and Woolmen were entered for no more than £20 each, and fifteen others for payments under £100. The analogy of the Somers Islands company throws light on the procedure adopted[2]. In the London plantation there were twelve livery companies which had contributed large amounts. It was therefore decided that the whole £40,000 should be divided into twelve equal "portions," parts or shares consisting of £3,333. 6s. 8d. each. With the exception of the two reserved towns, the whole land was also allocated into twelve equal lots. In the first instance these were assigned to the twelve chief companies and by each sub-divided, rateably, to those who held under them. In the terminology of the Somers Islands company there were thus twelve tribes (though this word is not used in the case of the London plantation) with subordinate undertakers in all, except one. The largest number of livery companies, included in a single portion, was in the Ironmongers', where there were ten different bodies interested. Further, the joining of contributions made it inevitable that the totals would not amount to the specified sum of £3,333. 6s. 8d., and in seven cases there was a small overplus which was to be paid in cash by those whose contributions were deficient. The land-dividends were made on December 13th, 1613, when the acreage was divided into twelve parts, each of which was denominated by a number. These numbers were placed in a box and were drawn by lot. The chief livery companies, having thus ascertained in what district the estates falling to their portions were situated, by a repetition of the process, discharged their obligation to the others who were subordinated to them[3].

It may be noticed that at the end of 1613 the position of the society was precisely similar to that of an American colonizing company (with the exception of the Providence Island undertaking) after the land-

[1] *A Concise View of the Origin...of the Honourable Society of the Governor and Assistants of London for the New Plantation in Ulster*, p. 34.

[2] *Vide supra*, p. 263.

[3] *A Concise View of the Origin...of the Honourable Society of the Governor and Assistants of London for the New Plantation in Ulster*, pp. 34–8. The exact amount of the £40,000 contributed by each company is given, pp. 36–8.

dividends had been made. In both the contributors had received back a division on account of their capital, and a part of the property still remained in the joint-stock, to be dealt with in the future, either to yield income or to be subsequently distributed as capital. So in this, as in other plantation companies, the results to the participants would depend to a large degree on the manner in which they developed the land that fell to their lots.

It is probable that at first the London investment was not very profitable, since in 1613 the whole rental of the undivided property was estimated at £1,800 a year[1]. This would only give a return of $4\frac{1}{2}$ per cent. on the capital outlay. But it is to be remembered that such an estimate tends to be unduly pessimistic, since not only had the property not yet recovered from the devastation of the war but much of the expenditure was as yet unremunerative. It would give a truer view of the situation to take the amount spent up to 1611 or 1612 (*i.e.* £20,000) as earning dividend, and this would yield a return of 9 per cent., with prospects of increase as the country became more settled. This was, if anything, rather less than the return on a good security at the time, so that, as yet, any profit on the investment lay in the future.

After 1613 the society was left with the reserved portions of the property, and as early as the beginning of 1615 it was able to make a "dividend of rents" to the livery companies[2]. By 1616 £1,000 a year was offered for the fishings, or more than half the whole estimated rental of the undivided property in 1613[3]. For a period of twenty years the enterprize appears to have progressed steadily until 1634 when its success excited the cupidity of the Star Chamber and the patent of James I. was revoked[4]. In spite of a vote of the House of Commons that this decree was "unlawful and unjust," the tenure of the society remained uncertain until the Restoration when a new patent was granted. From the Rebellion of 1641 to 1689 the country about Londonderry was subjected to the ravages of war and on both occasions stemmed the temporarily flowing tide of insurrection.

After the Revolution the interrupted work of development was continued and the society, which still exists, devotes the revenue of its properties to encouraging the prosperity of the districts from which they are derived[5].

From the point of view of finance, the most interesting feature in the history of the society is the ultimate outcome of the land-divisions. Were materials available for a comparison of the original contribution,

[1] *A Concise View of the Origin...of the Honourable Society of the Governor and Assistants of London for the New Plantation in Ulster*, p. 39.
[2] *Ibid.*, p. 40.   [3] *Ibid.*, p. 46.   [4] *Ibid.*, p. 56.
[5] Recently the greater part of the lands has been sold to the tenants under the Irish Land Purchase Acts.

together with subsequent capital outlay on the property obtained in this manner, it would afford considerable light on the possibility of profits ultimately being made by the shareholders in plantation companies. Unfortunately the records, both of the society and the livery companies, are imperfect and no very exact calculation can be made. All the participants, except the Mercers' company, sold their land-dividend at early periods, and it might be contended that the fact of such alienations being made is in itself evidence that the properties were not turning out very satisfactorily. But it must be recollected that the estates are to be regarded not only as business propositions but in their whole surroundings. The period from 1641 to 1652 was a very trying one to the companies which then held their land-dividends, and for the greater part of the seventeenth century the exceedingly unsettled condition of Ireland must have presented grave administrative difficulties to bodies or London merchants. There are indications that some of the companies which retained their estates into the eighteenth century found them a lucrative investment. For instance, in 1730 the Goldsmiths' company sold their manor of Goldsmiths' Hall for £14,000[1]. Now the whole original payment of this body had been £2,999, for which it received not only its portion of land but also its proportionate share of the revenue from the reserved property. Therefore for a precise result it would be necessary to know how much of the sum of £2,999 was to be allocated between the share of the reserved property, how much was to be looked on as returned in the land division. Then the history of the capital, represented by this estate, would be needed, especially as to whether it returned "economic interest" during the century and a quarter it was in the possession of the company. There is no doubt that considerable improvements were made by the executive of the Goldsmiths, which had erected a church, schools and other buildings during its ownership of the property. The rental, which had been £106 per annum in 1636, had improved to between £500 and £600 at the date of the sale[2]. These figures suggest the inference that, while there was additional capital expenditure, the appreciation was more than in proportion, but on the other hand allowance must be made for the fact that, as far as can be judged, during the early part of the company's ownership the current rate of interest was not obtained. The rental of 1636 would only yield under 5 per cent. return on the capital spent, whereas, at that time, 8 to 10 per cent. should have been obtained. Therefore, considering the capital outlay, the price obtained in 1730 would have yielded a very handsome profit, but this is curtailed by making an adjustment for

---

[1] *A Concise View of the Origin...of the Honourable Society of the Governor and Assistants of London for the New Plantation in Ulster*, p. 104.

[2] I am indebted for these interesting particulars to Sir Walter S. Prideaux, clerk of the Goldsmiths' company.

the years in which the rental gave less than the rates of interest of the period. So that it seems that the ultimate result may have been, on the latter basis of calculation, that the company obtained its capital back with arrears of interest, and that it is probable there may have been some balance of profit.

B. The Adventurers for Lands in Ireland (1642–59).

It is perhaps doubtful whether the "Adventurers for Lands in Ireland" should be included amongst the joint-stock companies. In this enterprize the plantation element is strongly marked, while the corporate one is less important and of a somewhat accidental character. The scheme came into existence as a consequence of the Irish Rebellion of 1641. Funds, to equip an army to subdue the insurgents, were urgently needed, and in 1642 "divers well affected persons" petitioned the House of Commons offering "to raise and maintain forces on their own charge," receiving in return a "recompense" out of the lands to be forfeited on the suppression of the rebellion[1]. Parliament gave effect to this arrangement in a modified form, and it was enacted that, of some two and a half million acres which were expected to be forfeited, the adventurers were to receive land rated at the following values—1,000 English acres in *Ulster* for a subscription of £200, the same amount in *Connaught* for a subscription of £300, in *Munster* for one of £450, and in *Leinster* for £600. Thus the rates per acre were in Ulster 4s., in Connaught 6s., in Munster 9s., and 12s. in Leinster. This acreage only referred to arable "or profitable" land, the unprofitable portions were added in addition, free of expense. In view of the fact that it eventually turned out that about one-third of the whole forfeited areas was unprofitable, this meant that the total acreage, on the average, assignable on these conditions would apparently be increased by one-half[2]. However an unduly large part of the unprofitable land lay in Connaught, and this province, together with the county of Clare, was withdrawn from the scheme for reasons to be explained below[3]. Allowing then for this fact, there remained in the other three provinces a large proportion of unprofitable land, to be added to the acreage specified in the act. Considering that the rate fixed by the Virginia company had been 2s. 6d. per acre thirty years before[4], the average of the rates

---

[1] Scobell, *Acts and Ordinances*, I. pp. 26–31.
[2] *On the Circumstances attending the outbreak of the Civil War in Ireland on 23rd October*, 1641, by W. H. Hardinge in *Trans. Royal Irish Academy*, XXIV. (Antiquities), Pt. VII. p. 418.   [3] *Vide infra*, p. 346.   [4] *Vide supra*, p. 255.

for the Irish adventurers of 7s. 9d., while apparently three times as much was in reality more favourable, for in the latter case it is necessary to remember the proximity of Ireland to England, that the former country had already been partially developed and that there would be a bonus of "unprofitable" land.

Thus at its inception the whole scheme was of the nature of a lottery-loan where the prizes were in kind, not money, and there were no "blanks." Even at the beginning, however, there was one feature in the conduct of the venture, that differentiates it from the subsequent state-lotteries in which there was no joint action of the persons interested. The adventurers in this case had to act in concert for the fitting out of the troops, and the capital, so used, became in effect a joint-stock. This joint-stock, under the stipulated conditions, would in the event of a successful issue become converted into land grants, made in one amount to the adventurers as a body, which were divisible amongst them individually by lot.

In the first half of 1642 several other acts were passed to encourage subscriptions, one of which offered a rebate of 8 per cent. for payment before a certain date, and another authorized companies and corporations to subscribe[1]. Then, to cut off supplies from the insurgents, it was proposed that subscriptions should be invited from the "Adventurers for additional forces by sea," and it was agreed that these should be recompensed on the same terms as the adventurers for the land service.

Some of the contributories entered upon the "adventure" from religious and patriotic motives, while others looked upon it as an investment that would eventually become profitable. A letter, written at the time by a member, shows the tendency of contemporary opinion. "I think," he writes, "the investment may be profitable and the work is a good one.... There is great hopes the war will not prove long. If you yourself or your brother at Bristol have a will to adventure monies in this kind, I conceive you will not lay it out more profitably; and, if the war should prove somewhat longer than is expected, yet the lands propounded will in all probability largely recompense the stay[2]." The same estimate evidently had been formed by persons who, later in the year, purchased adventures at par[3].

To rightly follow the changes of opinion relative to this enterprize it is necessary to remember the speculative nature of the venture. The capital subscribed was in no sense a loan to the government, for there was no promise for the repayment of the principal. In the event of

---

[1] Scobell, *Acts and Ordinances*, I. pp. 31, 32, 34.
[2] *Calendar State Papers, Ireland, Adventurers for Land* (1642–59), p. 310.
[3] *Ibid.*, p. 123.

the success of the army in Ireland, the adventurers would receive rateable grants of land at low prices. Should Ireland not be re-conquered, they had no redress. When it began to appear that the tension between King and Parliament was nearing the breaking-point, and at the same time that the insurrection in Ireland was likely to be merged in the wider struggle of the Civil War, the position of the adventurers became an unfortunate one. Not only was the time at which they might expect to obtain their lands greatly postponed, but the risk of total loss of their principal became increased. By the middle of 1643 the Parliament wanted money to continue the war in Ireland; but, owing to the position of the English forces there being unpromising, it soon became clear that the adventurers would not find additional funds without some strong inducement. By an ordinance of July 14th, 1643, it was determined that any adventurer who subscribed an additional amount, equal to one-quarter of his original subscription, should have his proportion of land doubled[1]. In other words, five-eighths of the sum, necessary to obtain a certain amount of land in 1642, would suffice in 1643, or the original subscriptions were now at an official discount of nearly 40 per cent. Subsequently, to attract more adventurers, the rate of land was "enlarged" from English measure to Irish measure, i.e. as 5 : 7. This again represented another (but a separate) discount of nearly 30 per cent. Subscribers under the later ordinances might adventure goods, which were "subscribed" at their estimated value for which credit was given. Thus, in this undertaking there was a reversion to a primitive type of business, in which capital assumed the form, both at the beginning and end, of a payment in kind. In this year (1643) sales of adventures were made at about 50 per cent. of their face value in terms of the subscription of 1642, or about 10 per cent. more than the equivalent rate of the ordinance of 1643[2].

The course of the war in Ireland up to the middle of 1649 must have been very disheartening to the adventurers, and it was not until Cromwell was able to take the field in person that they could hope for the conquest of the lands they had expected to gain. Soon the tide of battle began to turn, and, although the Confederate Forces still kept the field, they were gradually driven westwards into Connaught. On May 12th, 1652, the Irish armies laid down their arms and so, after the lapse of ten years, the adventurers were at last within sight of the confiscation and their "recompense." Where the consideration-money received on the sale of an adventure has been recorded in the assignment, it is plain that many of the owners had become wearied

---

[1] Scobell, *Acts and Ordinances*, I. pp. 23–6.
[2] *Calendar State Papers, Ireland, Adventurers for Land* (1642–59), pp. 107, 175. Both these adventures, sold in 1643, were made in the previous year.

and that they viewed the issue of their investment with considerable anxiety. In 1651, for instance, an adventure, made in 1642, for £1,200 was first sold for £400, and the purchaser parted with it within a few weeks for £500. These prices representing one-third and 41 per cent. respectively of the original subscription[1]. In another case in the same year a 1642 adventure was sold at 33⅓ per cent. of its nominal amount. During the year 1652 transfers were made at prices varying from 40 to 50 per cent.[2] In the next year, 1653, the amounts realized varied from 40 to 60 per cent. of the subscriptions of 1642, owing to different views as to how the division of the lands would be likely to work out[3].

To appreciate the position of the adventurers, it is necessary to summarize the general scheme of the forfeitures, made by the government, and the manner in which these were allocated amongst the different creditors of the State. By an ordinance of August 12th, 1642, it was enacted that persons, lately in arms against the State, should be divided into several groups according to their culpability, some losing all their estates, others two-thirds, and the rest one-third. Out of a total area of over 20 million acres, according to a contemporary survey, above 9 millions were declared unforfeited, making just 11 millions forfeited[4]. But the forfeited lands were classified as profitable and unprofitable respectively, the latter being added to the lots obtained of arable ground. Therefore the 11 millions became reduced to 7,701,972 profitable English statute acres left available for payment of the various obligations of the State. It is calculated that, at the rates of 1642, this represented a money-value of £3,390,130[5].

Several deductions had to be made before the nett land-fund could be allocated. The scheme of the government was not only one of confiscation but also a measure which aimed at the future tranquillity of the country. Originally it had been contemplated that forfeited land in Connaught should be available for the adventurers. This province was withdrawn together with the adjoining county of Clare, and it was ordained that persons, who had been subjected to forfeiture in the other three provinces, should be removed or transplanted to this area, obtaining there the acreage remaining to them, out of the escheated estates beyond the Shannon[6]. The object of this transplantation was to establish a concentration area where those, proved to be disaffected, might be isolated. The river Shannon was to be strongly held at the fords

---

[1] *Calendar State Papers, Ireland, Adventurers for Land* (1642–59), pp. 7, 8.
[2] *Ibid.*, p. 185.   [3] *Ibid.*, pp. 4, 20, 111, 117, 175, 177, 313.
[4] Hardinge, *Outbreak of Civil War, ut supra*, p. 398.   [5] *Ibid.*, p. 402.
[6] A very full account of this interesting movement is given in *The Cromwellian Settlement of Ireland*, by J. P. Prendergast (London, 1870).

and bridges, while a line of military settlers was to be established to the north to complete the cordon round the area to be segregated. Much has been written in condemnation of this transplantation, but, considered as a military measure and taking into account the treatment of "malignants" in England and Scotland, as well as the special circumstances of Ireland, it cannot be fairly characterized as unnecessarily severe in its conception, although almost unavoidably there were cases of individual hardship.

The effect then of "the transplantation" was that the province of Connaught and the county of Clare disappear from the schedules of lands available for the creditors of the State. These creditors comprised the adventurers whose subscriptions (including those written up under the ordinance of 1643) amounted to £360,000, subscribed in 1360 separate lots[1] (in which in many cases more than one person was interested). Then the army had not been paid for many years and the arrears came to £1,550,000. Lastly, there were debts for supplies, &c., amounting to £1,750,000. This gave a total of £3,660,000[2], and it was decided that the whole of it should be discharged by allotments of the forfeited lands, on terms similar to those which the adventurers had agreed to. It was further arranged that the land, payable to the adventurers, should be taken out of the following ten counties—Westmeath, Meath, Tipperary, Queen's County, King's County, Limerick, Waterford, Antrim, Down, Armagh. In view of the fact that it was supposed that it would encourage the adventurers to plant if they had soldiers settled near them, a method was adopted which provided that each of these ten counties was to be divided into two halves as nearly as possible, without dividing any barony, and that one portion should be assigned to the adventurers, the other to the other creditors by lot. The remainder of the forfeited lands in Ulster, Leinster and Munster (south of the Shannon), with certain exceptions, was to be granted in payment of the army claims amounting to £3,300,000. From the figures given in the survey, it is apparent that, at the ratio of the Adventurers' Acts, there was not enough forfeited land remaining to discharge these claims in full, and, even though some estates were allotted to the army at a higher average rate per acre, this group of creditors did not obtain an average of more than 13s. 4d. to 12s. 6d. per £.

The adventurers had a prior claim on the State and, taking the area of the profitable lands in the baronies that fell to their share, they received over 200,000 Irish acres, whereas, had all the subscriptions been

[1] Prendergast, *Cromwellian Settlement*, pp. 403–48, where the names are given and the subscriptions.
[2] Hardinge, *Outbreak of Civil War, ut supra*, p. 397; Prendergast, *Cromwellian Settlement*, p. 94.

convertible into this measure, they would only have been entitled to 181,500 acres[1]. Therefore, when allowance is made for the considerable amount of subscriptions made in 1642, which were payable in English acreage, it is obvious that the adventurers must, as a body, have obtained a very large surplus, even without taking any account of the further bonus of the unprofitable land.

In spite of the existence of this fund of surplus lands, which under the act should have been returned to make good a part of the deficiency in the share of the army, many of the adventurers were dissatisfied. It appears that those of their number, who arrived first in Ireland, either took more land than their shares or passed over that which they had drawn by lot and seized a more favourably situated estate which had fallen to another. Thus such, as were late in taking possession, were forced to accept smaller or less advantageous allotments than those that had in reality been drawn for them[2]. Accordingly, there were several petitions from the "disappointed" adventurers, and in 1658 a meeting was arranged between the committee of the adventurers and Sir William Petty, who had surveyed the forfeited lands for the soldiers. Finally, it was agreed that Petty should make a fresh survey of the estates in the ten counties allocated to the adventurers and that two lists were to be drawn up of the "redundant" and "deficient" baronies. A redundant barony was one in which there was more profitable forfeited land than the amount allotted to adventurers in that barony, and conversely. All the baronies were arranged in a certain secret order and the "unsatisfied" adventurers in the first deficient barony were to obtain their quota of land out of the first redundant barony, and so on in rotation[3]. When a portion of county Louth had been added to the ten counties already assigned for the adventurers, they, collectively, had a greater acreage than they were entitled to as a body, and in 1659 the last expedition of those, who were going to plant in Ireland, arrived in the country.

It is somewhat difficult to characterize the outcome of the adventure in Irish lands in its results as an investment. The estates, that were to be forfeited, were set out at three different rates, so that it might happen that a subscriber in 1642, who did not add to his adventure under the doubling ordinance of the following year, would lose, while another

---

[1] The area of forfeited land in each barony (both profitable and unprofitable) is given in a paper, *On Manuscript Mapped and Townland Surveys in Ireland...from 1640 to 1688*, by W. H. Hardinge in *Trans. Royal Irish Academy*, vol. xxiv. pp. 100–3. In the calculation above part of the county of Louth (which was added to the other ten counties) is included.

[2] The Humble Declaration and Petition of the Committee of Adventurers, in *The Down Survey* (ed. Larcom), p. 241.

[3] *Ibid.*, p. 253 et seq.

might gain, or neither lose nor gain. Again, the effect of recording payments, aggregating 62½ per cent., as 100 per cent. presents the appearance of a greater discount than really existed. For instance, in 1654 Robert Staunton assigned his lot of £375, doubled under the ordinance of 1643 or £700 in all, which had fallen in Armagh, for £375[1]. In this case the adventurer sold his subscription for 76 per cent. of what he had actually paid[2] and lost the interest on his capital for about eleven years besides. Further, the reference in this assignment to the county, in which the lot had fallen, introduces a fresh element of complication. In 1653 and 1654 adventures were sold specifying the district, where the land was to be laid out subsequently. It is obvious that these would be of unequal value, for the best land in a barony near an unsettled part, which was subject to the depredations of the "Tories," would sell at a lower price. An investigation of this class of assignments reveals that, where prices realized are recorded, the sales were made in certain baronies against which there was a prejudice, and secondly that, in view of the diverse nature of the security sold, the amount received varied within wide limits. The lowest being 38 per cent. (in terms of the par of 1642), and the highest over 93 per cent. with interest[3].

Besides, all these sales are to be regarded, as a rule, as those by adventurers who had been unfortunate in the drawing of lots, and therefore they cannot be taken as representative of the general result. There is indeed a case where an assignment is recorded giving the price obtained for the actual acreage drawn by lot and identified, but transferred before any improvements were made. This belonged to the London company of Wax-chandlers, which had subscribed £64. 1s. as late as 1653. The lot fell in Skeen (Meath), and therefore the company was entitled to 106 Irish acres of profitable land. In 1655, as arising out of this investment, 213 acres 2 roods were sold for £90, showing that in this case the addition of unprofitable land was above the average[4]. At this price the return was equivalent to 140 per cent., or giving back the original capital with an addition of about 25 per cent. per annum for the period the money had been invested. There can be little doubt that there were other and more advantageous cases. Where no prices are given, the names of the purchasers show that several adventurers were so well satisfied with the lots, they had drawn, that

[1] *Calendar State Papers, Ireland, Adventurers for Land* (1642–59), p. 59.
[2] That is, taking his adventure at £700 nominal for which he had paid £375+£$\frac{375}{4}$ or £468. 15s. and which he sold for £375 or half of the *nominal* amount, but 76 per cent. of the actual sum, paid in.
[3] *Ibid.*, p. 145.
[4] *Ibid.*, p. 380.

they took every opportunity of buying adjoining grants as they came on the market.

It follows then, on the whole, that the adventurers must be considered in different groups for the purposes of this enquiry. First, those who sold before 1652 suffered a loss of between two-thirds and one-half of their capital, according to the date of their subscription, with interest on the original investment. During the year 1652 and part of 1653, before the lots were drawn, sales were made at better prices. Those who had only subscribed in 1642 lost 60 to 40 per cent.; others, who came in on the later and more advantageous terms, escaped with a small shrinkage of capital, but in both cases there was nothing to make good the loss of interest. Then again persons, who disposed of allotments in a certain barony, varied in the percentage received, but it is probable that, on the average, there was some loss. There remain two very large groups who almost certainly did make considerable profits. These were the adventurers, who after subscribing, were fortunate in the drawing and who obtained the more desirable properties. Taking as typical cases two persons, who subscribed under the Act of 1642 and again in 1643 in the provinces of Ulster and Leinster respectively, it will be found that the rates per acre were very greatly reduced. Supposing that the 10 per cent. of lands, over and above the legal amount, was proportionately divided between the three provinces, the area of profitable grants would be increased accordingly. Again, adding the amount of "unprofitable" land in each case (one-quarter in Ulster and one-twelfth in Leinster[1]), the average rate for property of both kinds would be reduced to about 1*s*. 9*d*. per acre in Ulster and to about 4*s*. per acre in Leinster. The average for the three provinces would have been not very different from that in Virginia forty years before. Further, in such an average statement allowance should be made for the possibility that the more prominent adventurers, being better informed and more influential, would be likely to obtain contingent benefits from the addition of extra unprofitable land and from other sources. Finally, since it was possible for some years to purchase adventures at little more than half the most favourable terms obtained by the original subscribers, it follows that, in cases where such purchasers retained their investment and secured advantageous lots, they might hold lands at half the capital cost mentioned above, that would be at about 2*s*. per acre (profitable and unprofitable) in Leinster and under 1*s*. per acre in Ulster.

It may be concluded then on the whole that, while some of the adventurers suffered considerable losses, others obtained properties at very low rates, though it should be added that a part of the gain

---

[1] Hardinge, *Outbreak of Civil War, ut supra*, vide Appendix (H), p. 417.

was cancelled in the reign of Charles II. under the Act of Settlement. This measure may be taken to conclude the plantation of Ireland under the system of colonizing in vogue in the time of Charles I. It is true that there were subsequent forfeitures both in Ireland and Scotland, which were acquired by joint-stock companies, but these were worked as land-development undertakings and therefore, since they did not make land-dividends to the members, they are most conveniently dealt with separately[1].

[1] *Vide infra*, Division XII., Sections 2 B, 3 B—the Sword-Blade company, and the York Buildings company.

SECTION VII. THE RECLAMATION OF LAND IN ENGLAND BY DRAINAGE.

A. THE GOVERNOR, BAILIFFS AND COMMINALTY OF THE SOCIETY OF CONSERVATORS OF THE FENS IN THE COUNTIES OF CAMBRIDGE, HUNTINGDON, NORTHAMPTON, LINCOLN, NORFOLK AND SUFFOLK AND THE ISLE OF ELY.

"THE GREAT LEVEL" OR "THE BEDFORD LEVEL" (1631).

CLOSELY related in the mode of organization to the plantation companies of the early Stuart period are various undertakings for the reclamation of land in England by means of drainage works. These ventures aimed at the development of lands that had either never been cultivated or which had gone out of cultivation through inundation, and, as in the plantation undertakings, the shareholders received dividends or divisions from the properties reclaimed. In the order of time this class of enterprize began about the same period as the first efforts at planting both in America and in Ireland, but, as in the former cases, it was not until the first half of the seventeenth century that real progress was effected.

In some respects indeed the drainage of low-lying lands on a large scale was earlier than either of the other classes of land development, for, as early as the time of the Romans, efforts in this direction had been made[1]. Throughout the Middle Ages attention was given to the problem of drainage, and in the sixteenth century the Commissioners of Sewers received additional powers to levy rates on the owners of property, who benefited by the maintainance of the drainage channels. For various reasons this body failed to institute the improvements that were required, and, towards the end of the reign of Elizabeth, the problem received fresh attention and it became customary to transfer

---

[1] *The Growth of English Industry and Commerce in Modern Times*, by W. Cunningham, p. 113.

the work to an individual or a group of persons, who would find the capital and receive a proportion of the land made available for cultivation. Thus in 1592, 1593, and 1598 various schemes of this nature were instituted[1], and, towards the end of the reign of Elizabeth, Thomas Lovell was made undertaker for the drainage of Deeping Fen in Lincolnshire on the condition that he should receive one-third of the land recovered[2]. He spent £12,000 on the work but failed to realize the results he had expected, and, in the time of Charles I., he transferred his concession to others, who had been successful until the outbreak of the Civil War[3]. These and many similar undertakings had to encounter serious opposition to the compulsory powers they exercised, partly from those who made a living by various kinds of fen produce, partly from persons whose unflooded land was intersected by the drainage channels[4].

It was in 1605 that a comprehensive drainage scheme was first undertaken which afterwards became known as the "Great Level." It was proposed, by cutting new watercourses on the system in vogue in Holland, to drain a large extent of country amounting to 307,222 acres in the fens of Cambridgeshire and the adjoining counties. Sir John Popham with several others were interested. They subscribed large sums and were to receive 130,000 acres of the land recovered[5]. In 1619, it is recorded that this partnership had resulted in "much loss and disadvantage[6]." At length James I. declared that "for the honour of his kingdom he would not any longer suffer those countries to be abandoned to the will of the waters nor let them lie waste and unprofitable," and he himself became the undertaker. There is an amusing account of how he arrived at this decision. It was reported at court that there was in the vicinity a cow that could speak. The King expressed a desire to examine the prodigy. On going to the stable, he found the animal wrapped up in blankets. He insisted on removing these with his own hands and discovered a parchment scroll round one of the horns, which described the objections to the existing undertakers[7].

[1] *An Historical Account of the Great Level of the Fens, called Bedford Level and other Fens*, by W. Estobb, Lynn, 1793, p. 147; Cunningham, *English Industry in Modern Times*, p. 119; *Alien Immigrants*, p. 209.

[2] *The History of Imbanking and Draining of Divers Fens and Marshes*, by Sir William Dugdale (1732), pp. 205–6.   [3] *Ibid.*, p. 207.

[4] *Vide* a quotation from *The Anti-Projector* in Cunningham, *English Industry in Modern Times*, p. 115, note 1.

[5] Dugdale, *History, ut supra*, p. 383.

[6] Estobb, *Historical Account of the Great Level*, p. 171.

[7] *Ibid.*, p. 179; *Anti-Projector or the History of the Fen Project* [Brit. Mus. 725 . d . 35], p. 2.

About 1630 there was a widespread movement to execute drainage schemes. It was pointed out, for instance, that land, when partly drained, would be worth at least 20s. per acre, and it was calculated that as much as 400,000 acres could be recovered[1]. The Earl of Bedford, who had been interested in land reclamation at Axenholm[2] and had followed Popham's partnership, employed a Dutchman named Vermuyden and he proposed in 1631 to become undertaker, together with his associates, for the draining of the Great Level[3]. By an indenture signed on January 13th, 1631, it was agreed that the company, to be formed, was to receive 95,000 acres of the land reclaimed. Of this 12,000 acres were to be assigned to the King in return for the royal assent to the enterprize[4]. As an earnest of the King's protection he granted the adventurers a charter, incorporating them as *the Governor, Bailiffs and Comminalty of the Society of Conservators of the Fens in the Counties of Cambridge, Huntingdon, Northampton, Lincoln, Norfolk and Suffolk and the Isle of Ely* with powers to elect a governor, a deputy-governor and two bailiffs. The work was to be completed within six years from October 1st, 1631, but, when 30,000 acres had been recovered, land might then be distributed[5].

The whole undertaking was divided into twenty shares assigned to fourteen persons. Bedford owned three, Sir M. Sandys, Sir W. Russel, Sir Thomas Terrington and A. Hammond two each, and the rest one share each. It was recognized that a large capital would be required and therefore the adventurers agreed that any share, where the calls had not been paid, was subject to forfeiture. The society had the right of re-issuing such forfeited share, on the person taking it up paying "the sum imposed thereon[6]." It will be noticed that, by this type of constitution, the number of shares (as in the Mines Royal, the Mineral and Battery Works and the New River company) was fixed while the amount paid up on each share increased, so as to provide capital when required. By March 7th, 1637, when the undertaking, as far as it was carried by this company, was completed, £93,000 had been paid up or £4,650 per share[7]. This came to almost exactly £1 for every acre

---

[1] *The Humble Remonstrance of the Benefits of Draining Fenne Lands* [Brit. Mus. $\frac{816.\text{m}.8}{25}$].

[2] *The Case of the Tenants of the Manor of Epworth in the Isle of Axholm...truly stated*, by Lt.-Col. John Lilburn [1651], p. 1.

[3] Dugdale, *History, ut supra*, p. 408.

[4] State Papers, Domestic, Charles I., ccIV. 39; *Calendar*, 1631–4, p. 200.

[5] *A Collection of the Laws which form the Constitution of the Bedford Level Corporation*, by Samuel Wells (1828), I. p. 126; Dugdale, *History*, p. 408.

[6] Dugdale, *History*, p. 409.

[7] Wells, *Collection of Laws, ut supra*, I. p. 151.

to be awarded to the company, but the cost to the shareholders of their land-dividends would be more, since 12,000 acres were due to the King. Hence, while each shareholder would receive over 4,000 acres per share, he paid £4,650 for his "dividend" or nearly 22s. 6d. per acre. In an account of the payments, made by Bedford on behalf of the contributors, credit is taken for interest at 8 per cent., which made an additional charge of £34,170 or (added to the £93,000 called up) a total of £127,170. The intention of this statement is evidently to fix the total capital expenditure at the larger sum. The inclusion of interest may mean that the shareholders were in arrear in paying their calls, but in that case the claim would be from the person, who had advanced the money, against the shareholder. Or again (as seems more probable), in anticipation of modern companies which pay interest on prior charges during the period of construction out of capital, it may have been contended that, since the land-dividend was not made till 1637, the shareholders were entitled to add to the capital, actually spent, interest from the date when each instalment was paid until the land was divided. But in a case of this kind it is more accurate not to charge share-capital with interest, especially as the company had powers to divide 30,000 acres as soon as that amount had been reclaimed.

By October 12th, 1637, it was adjudged that the undertaking had been successful and the 95,000 acres specified were awarded to the company[1]. But six months later (April 14th, 1638), Charles I. decided that the work had been defective, on the ground that, while the land was freed from water in the summer, it was still subject to flooding in the winter[2]. Possibly the real basis of the censure was that the King was disappointed in not obtaining a considerable surplus of land over and above his 12,000 acres, and this suggestion is confirmed by the fact that he became undertaker himself " for the completion of the work[3]." Had it not been for the outbreak of war soon afterwards, Charles I. would probably have assigned the concession (as in so many other cases) to some nominee for a consideration.

During the Civil Wars, the Great Level drainage works, like most others elsewhere, suffered from the hostility of those who had all along been opposed to these enterprizes. In 1641, in the Remonstrance of Parliament, it was declared that drainage works were a monopoly, but this view was not maintained. Cromwell was disposed, on grounds of public policy, to encourage capitalists to repair the damage done to sluices, embankments and canals. In cases where courtiers had obtained grants for drainage and had not carried them out, the fens affected were opened to new undertakers. Where progress had been made those, who

[1] Dugdale, *History*, p. 408.
[2] *Ibid.*, p. 411.
[3] *Ibid.*, p. 412.

had obtained land-dividends, were not disturbed, unless they had fallen under the ordinances for forfeitures of their lands on other grounds. The Bedford Level was a case in point. In 1653 the then Earl of Bedford stated that the profits were not considerable in proportion to the charge and hazard. He estimated the whole expenditure, at that date, at £300,000 and the annual charge at £10,000[1]. Probably the calculation of £300,000, as the whole cost of the undertaking, is an overstatement, and it seems to have been reached by charging interest on the previous statement of an outlay of £127,170 in 1637. Some further expense may have been necessary, but this had been laid out by 1653 and the undertakers were confirmed in the possession of the 95,000 acres under the agreement of 1631[2]. Thus the Bedford Level adventurers obtained land reclaimed at about £1. 2s. 6d. per acre of original capital expenditure, or, including interest, according to the estimate of 1653, at £3. 15s. an acre. This compares with the original Irish rate of 1642 of 12s. per profitable acre in Leinster and 4s. for the same quantity in Ulster, but as shown elsewhere these prices were considerably reduced by later ordinances and other causes[3]. The colonial rate at an earlier period (*e.g.* in Virginia) was less than the first Irish rates and about the same as that on which the most fortunate adventurers secured their estates from 1643 to 1650. It was stated by Bedford that most of the adventurers had ruined themselves by the enterprize and, in comparing the cost per acre in the Great Level with that in Ireland, it is to be remembered that the latter relates to "profitable" land only, whereas the ground "reclaimed" would contain much that was only partially remunerative. Since Bedford admits in the same document that the return was not considerable in view of the "charge and hazard," it seems that the statement that some of the shareholders were ruined has reference to the difficulty of finding the capital required, the large amount of which must have been inconvenient to several of the members.

B. OTHER DRAINAGE UNDERTAKINGS IN THE TIME OF CHARLES I.

Besides the Great Level there were many other drainage undertakings, most of which worked as unincorporated partnerships, established by a patent to one or more persons. In 1626, Robert Tipper and his partners were draining lands in Lincoln, Northampton, Cambridge and Huntingdon[4]. On September 7th of the following year an extension of

[1] State Papers, Domestic, Inter., xxxix. 97; *Calendar*, 1653-4, p. 120-1.
[2] Dugdale, *History, ut supra*, p. 416.
[3] *Vide supra*, "Adventurers for Lands in Ireland," pp. 343, 350.
[4] State Papers, Domestic, Charles I., xxxii. 45; *Calendar*, 1625-6, p. 385.

time for the completion of the work was allowed[1]. The undertakers were to receive one-half the land drained for a term of years, on the enterprize being judged satisfactory; and the petition they presented in 1629, asking that their proportion should be held in fee, was described as a preposterous one[2].

In Lincolnshire there were two contemporary undertakings formed to deal with the fen-area outside the Great Level. One of these was started by a patent, dated June 1629. The undertakers in this instance were to be paid either by a tax or otherwise as the Commissioners of Sewers might decide[3]. The leading man in this partnership was Sir Arthur Thomas. It was decided that the settlement was to be through a tax on the persons who gained, though in all other cases the undertakers received land[4]. A more important venture in the same county was that known as the Lindsey Level, so called after Lord Lindsey who was most energetic in carrying it out. This scheme was encouraged by an Act of the Commissioners of Sewers dated January 13th, 1631, and by a patent on July 26th of the same year[5]. In 1638 there were eight partners who owned the eighteen shares into which the undertaking had been divided. In that year a call of £166. 13s. 4d. was made[6]. The whole expense of these works is reported to have been £45,000 or £2,500 per share[7]. The acreage divisible amongst the partners was 24,000 acres, so that, provided the whole amount had been awarded, the cost per acre would have come to £1. 17s. 6d. or 15s. an acre more than the outlay at Bedford Level on the same basis. This scheme had been carried out, but the channels were damaged during the Civil War[8]. Lindsey was also "sole undertaker" for a drainage scheme in Norfolk, on which he was engaged in 1635[9].

Besides being employed on the Great Level, Cornelius Vermuyden was interested in similar projects elsewhere. Possibly, the grant to him and his associates of the waste and surrounded lands in Nottingham in 1628 is not wholly unconnected with a loan of £10,000 he made Charles I. in the same year[10]. At the same period he, with certain partners, was carrying on drainage works in Yorkshire, and by 1633 he had reclaimed 20,738 acres, while there remained 3,767 undrained[11].

[1] State Papers, Domestic, Charles I., LXXVII. 17; *Calendar*, 1627–8, p. 336.
[2] *Ibid.*, CLII. 83; *Calendar*, 1629–31, p. 111.
[3] *Ibid.*, CXLVIII. 96; *Calendar*, 1629–31, p. 44.
[4] *Ibid.*, CLIII. 30; *Calendar*, 1629–31, p. 116.
[5] *Ibid.*, CCCLVII. 152; *Calendar*, 1637, p. 170.
[6] *Ibid.*, CCCCI. 54; *Calendar*, 1638–9, p. 98.
[7] Dugdale, *History, ut supra*, p. 418. [8] *Ibid.*, p. 419.
[9] State Papers, Domestic, Charles I., CCLXXXVII. 72; *Calendar*, 1635, p. 50.
[10] *Ibid.*, Col. Sign Manual, Charles I., VII. 26; *Calendar*, 1628–9, p. 160.
[11] *Ibid.*, Domestic, CCXXXVI. 34, COL. 7; *Calendar*, 1633–4, pp. 8, 271.

DIVISION III.

COMPANIES FOR THE DEVELOPMENT OF THE FISHING TRADE.

SECTION I. THE SOCIETY OF THE FISHERY OF GREAT BRITAIN AND IRELAND (1632–40).

In the time of Elizabeth and James I. one of the directions in which efforts were made to extend English industry was by the encouragement of the fishing trade. The progress of maritime enterprize towards the end of the sixteenth century involved a good supply of shipping, and therefore fishing was fostered as providing a school for sailors. This motive will be found blending with the colonial idea in the expeditions of Gilbert to Newfoundland from 1578 to 1583[1].

The earliest attempts to cultivate this branch of trade, by means of a considerable capital, were directed to whaling and, since these were closely connected with the Russia and East India companies, such ventures have already been dealt with under those undertakings. But at the same period attention began to be directed to the herring and deep-sea fishing off the English coasts, especially as it began to be recognized that the Dutch had found it a profitable area for similar operations. In 1603 Raleigh estimated that they made £1,759,000 a year from the sales of fish captured in British waters, and in 1615 it was calculated that 2,000 sail of Dutch busses, employing 37,000 hands, were engaged in this industry. In fact, the formation of a company for the herring fishery was strongly recommended—that industry being described as "Trades-increase," which the Dutch called their "chiefest gold-mine" and where the funds of widows and orphans were invested[2]. In 1618, according to Raleigh, the busses, owned by the Dutch, had increased to 3,000 with 50,000 hands. From these figures De Witt concluded that the trade maintained (when account was taken of the subsidiary industries) no less than 450,000 persons[3]. It was for this reason that Tobias Gentleman in 1614 urged that fishing should be encouraged[4]. On these grounds it began to be recognized that the example set by the Dutch ought to be imitated, and about 1620 John Keymor, in a memoir prepared for the King on the commercial situation,

---

[1] Cunningham, *Growth of English Industry and Commerce in Modern Times*, pp. 15, 124; vide supra, pp. 242–4.

[2] *The Trades Increase* in *Harleian Miscellany*, IV. pp. 203, 215.

[3] Anderson, *Annals of Commerce* (1790), II. p. 364.

[4] *England's way to Win Wealth*, 1614, in *Harleian Miscellany*, III. pp. 378–91.

expressly stated that the British watchword ought to be to rival the Hollanders in this trade[1]. Similar views are recorded by Thomas Mun[2] and were systematized by Misselden in 1623 in a form which eventually became the method of organization of the Society of the Fishery. He recommends that "for the encouragement of the adventurers it is fit, if so it may be brought to his Majesty's high wisdom and grace, that every county, yea every city, if it will, may have the managing and disposing of their own adventures without any general or promiscuous confusion with others and with such immunities, privileges and encouragements conferred upon them from the fountain of his Majesty's grace as may at last bring them to action and execution which we have so long had in discourse and contemplation. A brave design it is as royal as reall: as honourable as profitable. It promises renown to the King, revenue to the Crown, treasure to the kingdom, a purchase for the land, a prize from the sea, ships for navigation, navigation for ships, mariners for both, entertainment for the rich, employment for the poor, advantage for the adventurers and increase of trade for all the subjects. A mine of gold it is, the mines are deep, the veins are great, the ore is rare, the gold is pure, the extent unlimited, the wealth unknown, the worth invaluable[3]."

This quotation from Misselden may be taken as a specimen of the enthusiasm which was excited at this period by the prospects of the fishing trade. At first sight it is difficult to determine why it was that English sailors abandoned this "gold-mine" on their own coasts to the Dutch, while they sought for the precious metals in the most distant parts of the world. A little consideration will show that the Dutch were firmly established in the trade, and a small number of English fishing busses, that appeared near a fleet of Dutch boats, might count on harsh treatment. After all, such proceedings would only be a retaliation for the banishment of Dutch whalers from Spitzbergen in 1612 by the Russia company[4]. Therefore, if any serious effort was to be made to wrest even a foothold in the industry from the Dutch, it was necessary that there should be a strong unified organization with a large capital and ample powers from the State.

What might be described as the first step was made in 1630 when a commission was appointed to enquire into the fishing off the British coasts, and to establish a joint-stock company to promote it[5]. There were four main enquiries that engaged the attention of this body—the

---

[1] "Policies of State Practised in Various Kingdoms for the Encrease of Trade" (Edinburgh University Library—Laing MSS., Div. II., No. 52), ff. 22–4.
[2] *England's Treasure by Forraign Trade* (New York, 1895), pp. 81, 102, 103.
[3] *The Circle of Commerce*, p. 140.   [4] *Vide supra*, pp. 53, 54.
[5] *Foedera*, XIX. p. 211.

§ 1] *Organization proposed* 1630-1

position of Scotland in the venture and the questions of finance, organization and the privileges to be obtained. Hitherto in the whaling trade there had been considerable friction between English and Scottish interests. Indeed, since the union of the Crowns of the two countries, Scotsmen had complained that in commercial affairs they were in a disadvantageous position, for the great English regulated and joint-stock companies had been formed and there was nothing of the same kind in Scotland. The high-handed proceedings of James I., to redress the alleged grievance, failed through the want of consideration he manifested towards his own previous patents. Now that the fishing industry was to be developed, it was recognized that, for geographical and other reasons, it was desirable the scheme should apply to England, Scotland and Ireland. To induce Scotsmen to co-operate an equal number of commissioners from each country was appointed to confer as a sub-committee. This body soon discovered that there were serious difficulties to be overcome before Scotland would co-operate. In some cases noblemen were apprehensive that their rights might be jeopardized. The relation of the proposed company to the long-shore fishermen was not clear and the Scottish commissioners proposed that there should be certain excepted areas, exempt from the control of the company[1]. Then the burghs stood on their privileges. They contended that they had the sole right of fishing within "two kennings" of the shore and that they would admit no partners, either natives or strangers. Neither would they permit any persons, fishing outside this limit, to land within their jurisdiction. Subject to these exceptions they had no objection to the herring-fishing, but the tenor of their communication suggests that they were not favourably disposed towards the proposal[2].

The aloofness of the Scottish burghs brought to light another difficulty, which the commissioners had to resolve. By June 1631 it was reported that no undertakers would risk their capital until suitable fishing grounds had been chosen[3], while towards the end of the year it had been decided that there could not be a single "aggregation" of all the undertakers[4]. The scheme at last adopted was to have a general joint-stock for the Fishery society which appears to have confined itself to certain places off the English coast, while the remaining districts were assigned to prominent members, who formed subsidiary associations, in relation to the parent organization. By this device there was the possibility of considering the case made by the Scottish com-

---

[1] State Papers, Domestic, Charles I., cciii. 53, 54; *Calendar*, 1631-3, p. 185.
[2] *Ibid.*, ccvi. 45; *Calendar*, 1631-3, p. 237.
[3] *Ibid.*, cxciv. 34; *Calendar*, 1631-3, p. 83.
[4] *Ibid.*, ccvi. 50; *Calendar*, 1631-3, p. 238.

missioners, since capital might be raised locally and the employment of it controlled by persons resident near the fishing grounds or having interests there.

Meanwhile calculations had been made showing the expenses of building and equipping fishing busses and of the profits that might be expected. The cost of building and provisioning a buss, that was capable of taking 40 lasts of herring, was estimated at £835. It was expected that the value of the herring, caught on an average by each buss, would be £1,000 a year. According to one account, a fleet of 200 busses ought to make a profit of £113,000 a year, or nearly 70 per cent. of the capital expended[1]. Another estimate places the gain, in the first, second and third fishings each year with the same number of boats, at £82,707[2].

Finally, on the recommendation of the Commission, the society to be formed was to receive encouragement from the State, by a proclamation for a more strict observance of fasting in Lent, the prohibition of the import of fish caught by foreigners, and, lastly, an undertaking that all supplies of this kind required by the Navy should be purchased from the society[3].

The deliberations of the Commission had taken so much time that it was not till June 1632 that steps could be taken for the actual formation of the proposed company. At length the undertaking was incorporated by a royal charter and its operations in Scotland were confirmed by an act of the Scottish Parliament. The charter established a company, entitled *the Society of the Fishery of Great Britain and Ireland*, with the privileges recommended by the Commission. The King was its "perpetual protector" and, under him, its affairs were to be administered by a council of twelve persons, half of whom were to be English, half Scotsmen[4]. The act of the Scottish Parliament of the same year gives special prominence to the type of organization whereby, in addition to the general association, there might be several subordinate companies, and it is enacted that one of these might be established in each chief burgh or town or province. The fishing at the Island of Lewis was reserved to the King[5]. This he subsequently assigned to one of the subordinate associations.

This type of organization is explained by a comparison with the

[1] State Papers, Domestic, Charles I., ccxxix. 97, 98; *Calendar*, 1631–3, pp. 488–9.
[2] "Instructions to Captain Mason, 1630," in *Captain John Mason*, Boston (Prince Society), 1887, p. 276.
[3] Soc. Antiq. Col. Proclamations, Charles I., No. 147, dated May 24, 1631; Anderson, *Annals*, II. p. 470.
[4] State Papers, Domestic, Charles I., ccxxi. 1; *Calendar*, 1631–3, p. 384.
[5] *Acts of the Parliaments of Scotland*, v. p. 222.

New England company which had been founded in 1620[1]. In both cases the idea was to found an undertaking, confined to privileged persons, which would carry out the work of development. It would then assign portions of its property to other companies. In the case of the New England undertaking, it was some time after its formation before more than one such body had been formed, whereas in the case of the Fishery society, the work of the parent company and the establishing of subsidiary associations proceeded concurrently. Most of the local undertakings were formed to fish off different parts of the coast of Scotland; and, since each was licensed by the society, no patent or charter of incorporation was required. These bodies were described by the name of the member of the council who established any one of them, e.g. "the Earl of Pembroke and his associates in the fishing."

Postponing for the present the account of the subordinate associations, the history of the society presents several points of interest. Like many other companies of the period, it suffered from the failure of subscribers to pay the amounts they undertook to adventure. The first issue of stock was made in 1632-3, and by 1635 £22,682. 10s. had been subscribed, but only £9,914. 10s. paid[2]. All that could be collected of the adventurers of 1633 was £10,600. In 1634 an additional stock of £2,550 was taken up, making a total of £13,150 actually paid on account of the capital issued during these two years[3]. This sum had all been spent early in 1635, so that, since only £9,914. 10s. had actually been paid in, it was necessary to borrow about £3,500. By this time a considerable loss had been made, but this was disguised by inflating the value of the stores on hand and carrying forward a loss of boats (captured by "the Dunkirkers") as an asset. Thus at this time the account was made to balance as follows:

RECEIPTS.	£	s.	d.	£	s.	d.
Capital actually paid by adventurers				9,914	10	0
,, borrowed	2,600	0	0			
,, ,, from Sir W. Courten	950	7	5	3,550	7	5
				£13,464	17	5

EXPENDITURE.				£	s.	d.
Six busses *at cost*				6,000	0	0
Stock in hand, fish, salt, &c.				6,120	0	0
"Damage by Dunkirkers"				1,166	14	10
				£13,286	14	10

---

[1] *Vide supra*, pp. 301-6.
[2] State Papers, Domestic, Charles I., cccxiii. 16; *Calendar*, 1635-6, p. 208.
[3] *Ibid.*, cccxcv. 100; *Calendar*, 1637-8, p. 579.

Supposing the estimated values of stores were correct, it is plain that at least 12 per cent. of the paid up capital had been lost, unless the damages were recovered. It will be seen from figures given below that the loss was in reality much greater.

There were two causes which made it almost inevitable that the society must fail. In the first place it started with a ludicrously insufficient capital. Under the most favourable circumstances, it could not have built and manned more than twenty busses; and, owing to the delay of the stockholders in paying their calls, these could not have been sent to sea at the same time. Therefore it was likely that such a tiny fleet would be driven off the best fishing places or even captured. In the second place, any fish taken could not be salted in a suitable manner to bear the long transit. The evidence on this point is conclusive. De Witt stated that in cases when fish had been caught by the Dutch and English about the same place and time and both were offered for sale at Danzig, the former were considered good while the latter " were esteemed naught[1]." Indeed, in 1637 the society admitted this charge by implication, when, after stating that losses had been made, it was said that the trade was likely to prove beneficial "now that the true management thereof is by experience discovered[2]."

Under such unfavourable circumstances, the society could not escape from financial difficulties and fresh losses were incurred in 1635, 1636 and 1637. It had been necessary to make assessments on those who had subscribed in 1633 of 20 per cent. and again of 50 per cent. The persons liable paid the amounts due from them very slowly, fresh capital was subscribed only in small sums, so that the debt kept increasing. To encourage members to take up stock, arrangements were made whereby no stockholder's additional investment was subject to the losses incurred previously. This proposal involved an intricate system of account keeping which showed the loss incurred in each year separately, together with the capital which had to bear it. On July 30th, 1638, the whole capital subscribed had been lost, amounting to £16,975, and £6,142. 13s. 4d. in addition. According to the method of raising the deficit the subscribers of 1633 were liable to their share of the aggregate *pro rata*, while the capital adventured in 1636 and 1637 (which years were taken together) was only liable to its share of that of those years. The adventurers of 1633 lost not only their capital but also £54. 10s. 1d. per cent. more raised by assessments. The additional subscribers of 1634 also failed to save their investment and had to pay £14. 6s. 1d. per cent. as an assessment. Those of 1635 received back £47. 15s. 7d. per cent.; while others, who had come forward in the last

---

[1] Anderson, *Annals*, II. p. 504.
[2] State Papers, Domestic, Charles I., cccxlix. 58; *Calendar*, 1636–7, p. 489.

two years, were to obtain a refund of £68. 14s. 4d. per cent.[1] The following tabular statement will show more precisely the reasons for this apportionment:

Subscribed Capital and Losses of the Fishery Society.

Year	Capital subscribed	Loss	% falling on adventurers of 1633 (on capital of 1633)	% falling on adventurers of 1634 (on capital of 1634)	% falling on adventurers of 1635 (on capital of 1635)	% falling on adventurers of 1636 and 1637
	£ s. d.	£ s. d.	£ s. d.	£ s. d.	£ s. d.	£ s. d.
1633	10,600 0 0	4,261 4 8	40 4 0			
1634	2,550 0 0	8,163 19 4	62 1 8	62 1 8		
Totals	13,150 0 0	12,425 4 0	102 5 8			
1635	2,775 0 0	3,334 11 0	20 18 9	20 18 9	20 18 9	
Totals	15,925 0 0	15,759 15 0	123 4 5	83 0 5		
1636} 1637}	1,050 0 0	5,310 10 6	31 5 8	31 5 8	31 5 8	31 5 8
Totals	16,975 0 0	21,070 5 6	154 10 1	114 6 1	52 4 5	31 5 8
Deduct capital subscribed ...			100 0 0	100 0 0	100 0 0	100 0 0
Balance showing assessments to be paid on capital returned ...			−54 10 1	−14 6 1	+47 15 7	+68 14 4

In some respects the percentage returns might be misleading, and therefore the foregoing statement may be supplemented by that which follows:

	£ s. d.	£ s. d.
Total capital subscribed, 1633–7		16,975 0 0
Deduct balances returned to adventurers of 1635–7:		
i.e. £47. 15s. 7d. % of £2,775 to advs. of 1635	1,325 17 4	
£68. 14s. 4d. ,, £1,050 ,, 1636–7	721 10 6	2,047 7 10
Balance, being capital wholly lost		14,927 12 2
Add amount to be raised by assessments		6,142 13 4
Total amount of loss		£21,070 5 6

The following account shows the stage to which the liquidation had advanced by July 30th, 1638:

---

[1] State Papers, Domestic, Charles I., cccxcv. 100; *Calendar*, 1637–8, p. 579.

Liabilities and Assets, 1638.

LIABILITIES.

	£	s.	d.
Debts due to non-members	4,755	1	1
Debts due to members, being balances of capital returnable to adventurers of 1636 and 1637–8	2,047	7	10
	£6,802	8	11

ASSETS.

Adventurers of 1633.

	£	s.	d.	£	s.	d.
£54. 10s. 1d. °/₀ on £10,600 =	5,777	8	10			
Less already paid in response to assessments of 20 °/₀ and 50 °/₀	2,535	0	0			
Remaining due	3,242	8	10	3,242	8	10
Adventurers of 1634.						
£14. 6s. 1d. °/₀ on £2,550 =	364	15	2			
Less already paid	250	0	0	114	15	2
Houses, provisions, busses and debts due to the society				3,223	4	2
Various underwriting accounts				220	19	6
Cash					11	10
"Lost in fractions"					9	5
				£6,802	8	11

SECTION II. THE COMPANIES SUBSIDIARY TO THE SOCIETY OF THE FISHERY OF GREAT BRITAIN AND IRELAND.

WILLIAM NOY'S ASSOCIATION.
{LORD PORTLAND'S ASSOCIATION.}
{LORD ARUNDEL'S ASSOCIATION.}
LORD PEMBROKE'S ASSOCIATION.

THESE companies were subject to the same difficulties that beset the parent society and they had to face some of their own in addition. Hence their history is one of continued embarrassment from the beginning. Beyond this fact of financial troubles, little is known of the company founded by, or connected with the name of William Noy, the Attorney-General.

The undertaking established by Richard Lord Weston, afterwards Earl of Portland, when he was Lord Treasurer, was generally described as " the Association of the Lord Treasurer and others for the Fishing." It was proposed about 1632 that the Island of Lewis should be made the headquarters of this organization and that the members were to be naturalized Scotsmen and to be made burgesses of Stornoway, so that they might trade as well as fish[1]. In 1633 the amount of capital adventured by the members of this association amounted to £11,750, but only a very small part of that sum was paid up[2]. This body suffered considerably from the opposition of persons in Scotland and from the difficulty of escaping the payment of levies, ordered by " the Deputy Vice-Admirals of Scotland." The inhabitants of Lewis were hostile to the servants of the company and there were frequent complaints of damage sustained by the busses through attacks made on them[3].

---

[1] State Papers, Domestic, Charles I., ccxxix. 95, 96; *Calendar*, 1631-3, p. 488.
[2] *Ibid.*, ccxxxi. 15; *Calendar*, 1631-3, pp. 510, 511.
[3] *Ibid.*, cclxxxix. 62, 63; *Calendar*, 1635, p. 90.

In 1635 Lord Portland resigned his position as chief of the undertaking and he was succeeded by Lord Arundel, the Earl Marshal. Therefore from this date the company is generally described as "the adventurers in association with the Earl Marshal" or "the Earl Marshal's Association for the fishing business." Owing to various circumstances, many of the subscriptions for stock were cancelled; and, of the £11,750 proposed to be adventured, only £2,280 was actually paid, even as late as 1639[1]. It was necessary to make a leviation or assessment of 50 per cent. on the first year's stock, and in 1637 Lord Poulet was censured by the Privy Council for refusing to pay this call and for speaking of the business as "a project[2]." In the following year it was necessary to obtain an order of the Council for suing a considerable number of members who were still in arrear[3].

Like the parent society, this organization was embarrassed by want of capital, and in addition it had to contend against the hostility of the islanders as well as the depredations of the Dunkirk privateers. In the summer of 1635 two busses had been driven ashore at Stornoway and these were forcibly detained by an agent of the Scottish court of Admiralty. When other boats were fishing in the lochs of the mainland, the Highlanders had taken possession of some of the gear, on the ground that fishermen in these places must pay dues to their chiefs[4]. Although several representations were made on behalf of the company, it is doubtful whether it obtained satisfaction.

Meanwhile the number of busses had been reduced by captures made by the Dunkirkers, and the losses were estimated at £2,000 in 1635[5]. Although restitution was expected by the adventurers, none had been obtained by 1638, whereon the Lord High Admiral was ordered to make reprisals, and this command was repeated in the following year[6].

By 1639 the association had been in existence for about seven years and it had contracted debts to the extent of over £4,000[7]. The creditors could not obtain any satisfaction, and a commission was appointed to enquire into the finances of the undertaking[8]. It turned out that no more than £2,280 had been paid in by the adventurers. This was lost and, in addition to the assessment of 50 per cent. on the first year's stock, another of 33⅓ per cent. had been made on the second

---

[1] State Papers, Domestic, Charles I., ccccxxv. 43; *Calendar*, 1639, p. 381.
[2] *Ibid.*, Nicholas's *Letter-Book*, James I., ccxix. p. 164; *Calendar*, 1637-8, p. 4.
[3] *Ibid.*, Charles I., ccclxxxii. 20; *Calendar*, 1637-8, p. 260.
[4] *Ibid.*, ccxci. 4; *Calendar*, 1635, pp. 130, 131.
[5] *Ibid.*, ccxci. 25; *Calendar*, 1635, p. 136.
[6] *Ibid.*, ccccvi. 2; ccccxv. 31; *Calendar*, 1638-9, pp. 196, 602.
[7] *Ibid.*, ccccxxv. 43; *Calendar*, 1639, p. 381.
[8] *Fœdera*, xix. p. 346.

year's capital. The amount still to be paid by the members came to £2,873. 6s. 8d. and there was also in arrear £320. 19s. 6d. of the capital originally subscribed. Both together made £3,200 against a debt of £4,200, leaving a deficiency of about £1,000. Against this there was the estimated value of stores, provisions and houses at Lewis which was placed at £1,910, so that there was an apparent surplus of about £900. This, however, was subject to reduction, through the failure of members to pay their assessments; and also since the valuation of the remaining assets was subject to the comment that, although they stood in the accounts at £1,910, "little of that amount could be expected[1]."

The "Lord Chamberlain's Association," or that founded by Lord Pembroke, had a similar history. In 1633 four busses had been built, but of the subscribed capital of £2,400 only £600 was then paid, leaving £1,800 in arrear[2]. Three years later practically the same amount remained unpaid[3]. The financial position of this body resolved itself into the security for its debts being partly the calls in arrear, partly a lien on the damages to be recovered from the foreign privateers that had taken some of the busses of the association. Damages on this ground amounted in 1638 to £3,000; and, more fortunate than Arundel's company, a very rich prize was taken in that year and handed over to the members. It is to be doubted, however, whether the amount realized sufficed to discharge the debts incurred, and, if payment was made in full, an assessment on the stock would have been required.

[1] State Papers, Domestic, Charles I., cccxxv. 43; *Calendar*, 1639, p. 381.
[2] *Ibid.*, ccxliv. 49; *Calendar*, 1633–4, p. 179.
[3] *Ibid.*, cccxvii. 42; *Calendar*, 1635–6, p. 330.

SECTION III. THE GOVERNOR AND COMPANY OF THE ROYAL FISHERY OF GREAT BRITAIN AND IRELAND (1661).

AFTER the discredit of the Society of the Fishery in 1638, a spasmodic effort was made to revive it in 1640 by means of a lottery, but, even if capital had been obtained in this way, the Civil War would have interrupted any work that was being done[1]. During the Commonwealth attention was once more directed to this industry by a treatise entitled, *the Sea's Magazine Opened* (1653), and in 1654 Sir P. Andrews is said to have endeavoured to revive the trade[2]. After the Restoration renewed efforts were made towards re-establishing a herring-fleet. In 1661 John Smith published his *Trade and Fishing of Great Britain Displayed*, and the next year another pamphlet appeared named *the Royal Trade of Fishing*. About the same time "the draft preamble" of a new Royal Fishing company was prepared and subscribers were encouraged by being promised that, if they desired, they might withdraw after three years[3]. Adventurers came forward reluctantly, and in 1662 Charles II. offered to subscribe £9,000 towards the capital of the company[4]. The whole stock, taken up at this time, did not exceed £10,980, so that the public appears to have found something under £2,000 of the original capital[5]. Afterwards an additional stock of the modest amount of £1,680 was adventured. It is probable that Charles II. never intended to invest £9,000 permanently; and, "being pressed for money," he withdrew his capital[6].

[1] State Papers, Domestic, Charles I., ccccxliv. 68; *Calendar*, 1639–40, p. 440.
[2] *A Collection of Advertisements, Advices and Directions relating to the Royal Fishery*, 1695 (Brit. Mus. 1029. e. 29), p. 3, in Somers' *Tracts*, xi. pp. 309–63.
[3] State Papers, Domestic, Charles II., xli. 19, 20; *Calendar*, 1661–2, p. 83.
[4] *Ibid.*, lix. 6, 7; *Calendar*, 1661–2, p. 477.
[5] *Col. of Advices, ut supra*, p. 7; Houghton, *Collections for Husbandry and Trade*, March 19, 1703; *A General Discourse of Commerce*, by Alexander Justice, 1707, p. 39.
[6] *Universal Dictionary of Trade and Commerce*, by Malachy Postlethwaite (under Fishing).

To compensate the company, permission was given to hold lotteries as well as a formal charter of incorporation. This document, which is dated April 8th, 1664, incorporates *the Governor and Company of the Royal Fishery of Great Britain and Ireland*, and repeats the privileges and immunities granted in 1661 to the Council of the Royal Fishing. The affairs of the company were to be controlled by a governor and thirty-six assistants[1].

Thus, although incorporated under a high-sounding title, the capital available, after the King had withdrawn his £9,000, was only about £3,500, and to supplement this lotteries were instituted. For some unknown cause this lottery appears to have been less profitable than that organized previously by the Virginia company. An offer was made to the governor and assistants of £50 a year during the term they had been granted, or alternatively a single payment of £600 cash down. A later bid was as much as £200 a year rent or £1,000 for the two unexpired terms then remaining. Mr Ashton supposes that, on the determination of the original concession, the Fishery company had received some consideration not to press for a renewal of the license[2].

On the termination of the lotteries in 1667, funds were obtained by the monopoly of the issue of copper-money, which was described in the following year as "the only apparent mode of supporting the fishing[3]." In 1670 the trade was characterized as being "decayed," and the reason assigned was that the company "restrained the freedom of trade to the very few freemen." It was proposed by the author of *the Royal Fishing Revived* that a constant Council of Trade should be appointed to superintend the industry, and that a portion of the royal revenues ought to be devoted to its encouragement[4]. In *the Grand Concern of England Explained* (1673) the revival of fishing was recommended so as to give employment to the poor[5].

In spite of these and other arguments in favour of the trade, nothing was done in England for a number of years beyond throwing open the whale-fishing[6], and the development of the industry was undertaken by a separate Scottish company[7]. The English undertaking continued to exist, but it is probable that, owing to the want of capital, it manifested its activity chiefly in imposing burdens on independent adventurers who

---

[1] State Papers, Charters, Charles II., Case B, No. 1; *Calendar*, 1663-4, pp. 513, 549.

[2] *A History of English Lotteries*, by John Ashton, pp. 41-3.

[3] State Papers, Domestic, Charles II., CLXXXVIII. 24 (i), 24 (ii); CCLI. 162; *Calendar*, 1666-7, p. 439; *ibid.*, 1668-9, p. 137.

[4] *Harleian Miscellany*, III. pp. 393-5.   [5] *Ibid.*, VIII. p. 559.

[6] *Vide supra*, p. 75.   [7] *Vide infra*, p. 377.

had to purchase a license from it. As late as 1680 it was pursuing its operations, but without capital behind it[1]. In 1681, in reply to a petition of William Deane, which pointed out that since the loss of most of the busses in 1676 there had not been sufficient funds to maintain the trade, Charles II. stated that he was "desirous that all just and reasonable means should be taken for the effectual promotion of the fishing[2]." On September 17th, 1681, in spite of the fact that their predecessors "had only sustained loss" in that industry, a new group of undertakers proposed to spend £20,000 on fortifying Holy Island and furnishing boats and gear, provided they received the farm of the tobacco duties as an encouragement, promising an advance of £4,000 in this branch of the revenue[3]. In 1682–3 only £2,600 had been subscribed under this scheme, and Sir Edward Abney, in the following year, formulated a plan of raising capital by utilizing the charter for the foundation of a bank. At a meeting held on March 8th, 1683, it was determined that a stock of £20,000 to £30,000, divided into shares of £1,000 each, should be raised, and that any patentee, who did not subscribe for one share, was to be excluded. Twenty-two of the former shareholders were prepared to find more capital, and after several meetings in March (1683) an agreement with Abney was signed on April 2nd under which he had the right of introducing twenty-three persons more as proprietors of the bank, which was to be carried on as "the Royal Fishery Company of England," but under distinct management[4]. This amalgamation ended in failure, and in 1685–6 it was necessary to sell all the remaining property towards paying the outstanding liabilities[5].

After the Revolution attention was again directed towards the possibility of founding an English home fishery. It was estimated that the Dutch took fish in British waters to the value of between $4\frac{1}{2}$ and 5 million pounds annually[6]. The industrial boom of 1692–5 was considered a favourable time for starting a new company under the charter of Charles II. In 1692 the constitution was remodelled, and the governing body was composed of a governor, sub-governor, deputy-governor and twelve committees. Of the latter four were named directors and eight masters,

---

[1] *A Collection of Letters for the Improvement of Husbandry and Trade*, by John Houghton, 1681–3, II. p. 47.

[2] State Papers, Domestic, Charles II., ccccxvi. 164 a.

[3] *ibid.*, ccccxvi., "Proposals touching the Royal Fishery."

[4] *Col. of Advices*, in Somers' *Tracts*, XI. pp. 315–17; *Salt and Fishing, a Discourse*, by John Collins, Secretary of the Royal Fishery Company, London, 1682; *A General Discourse of Commerce*, by Alexander Justice, pp. 40, 41.

[5] *Col. of Advices*, in Somers' *Tracts*, XI. p. 318.

[6] *England's Safety or A Bridle to the French King*, by George St Lo, 1693 in Somers' *Tracts*, IV. p. 262; *Col. of Advices*, in Somers' *Tracts*, XI. p. 328.

in addition to which there were fifteen assistants, eight wardens and twenty-five commissioners. Any seven of the governors, committees or assistants constituted a court of assistants. The qualification for a vote was the ownership of £500 of stock. The subscription lists were opened for a capital of £300,000 or "at least £150,000," and they were not to be closed until November 30th, 1695. Calls, in order "to be made very easy," were to consist of ten equal quarterly instalments. Henceforth any loss of capital was to be made good before a dividend was paid and 10 per cent. of the funds subscribed was to be at the disposal of the court without its being called on to give any account of how the money was disbursed[1].

There were many pamphlets issued to recommend the project, which was regarded as a laudable one. The author of *Angliæ Tutamen* (1695) describes the idea "as worthy of care and application." "The Royal Fishery company," he continues, "has long been talked of, and some steps taken to make it successful; but still one accident or another has damped it and it is now again set on foot[2]." By October 1695 it was said that £50,000 had been subscribed, but, as will be shown below, only a small portion was paid in. It was resolved to "open the books" for a further issue of capital, and a discount of £3 per cent. was offered to those who would provide the first £150,000[3]. A year later the amount subscribed was described as "considerable," and fishing-boats were then being built and a further offer of stock was made[4]. Altogether £100,000 of the nominal capital was taken up, on which calls of 10 per cent. were made. Owing to the war, many difficulties were encountered, chief amongst which was the impossibility of obtaining further funds from the shareholders. The only remaining hope of the court of committees was to borrow on bottomry on the security of the busses. The company was unable to meet its liabilities and only a part of the loans was discharged by the sale of its fleet[5]. On January 30th, 1700, the company offered for sale the herring adventure at the "Three Cranes," Sommers' Quay near Billingsgate[6]. Houghton, when writing of the fishing industry, in 1703, does not mention this undertaking as being then in existence, and he adds that the reason for the failure of the

---

[1] *Somers' Tracts*, XI. pp. 319–24.
[2] P. 33. Besides the Greenland Fishing company (*vide infra*, p. 379) there was also at this time a Newfoundland company.
[3] *Postboy*, Oct. 16, 1695, a total of £300,000 was aimed at, of which it is said £100,000 was to be paid by the surviving patentees; Justice, *A General Discourse of Commerce*, p. 47.
[4] *Postboy*, Oct. 23, 1696.
[5] *Journals of the House of Commons*, XIX. p. 342.
[6] *Postman*, Jan. 30, 1700

enterprize was that "what is everybody's business is nobody's business[1]." The Commissioners of Trade add to their condemnation of "the pernicious art of stock-jobbing"; "this likewise is that which seems to us to lay a mighty obstacle in the way to the raising and recovering again of our home-fishing; which is with reason thought to require more than a private stock and the scattered endeavours of men acting separately to set it a-going and make it subsist. If therefore that part of our trade be not in so good and flourishing an estate as it could be wished, we are humbly of opinion, it is in some danger to remain so, till the hands of the poor be all brought to labour and till a common stock can be raised and a company erected upon such terms as may secure the management of it from the destructive shuffling of stock-jobbing[2]." Since, however, none of the newspapers of the time record any price for the stock of this company, it is most improbable that its failure was due to excessive speculation in the stock. The cause is rather to be sought in this case, as in that of the previous companies, in the capital having been too small to enable this undertaking to fight the Dutch. This was accentuated by the fact that many of those who took up stock during the boom of 1692–5 were unable to pay the calls and therefore the company made preparations in excess of the funds that were actually available. It appears that no more than £10,000 was paid in on the capital issued in 1694–5, and that an additional subscription made in 1701 was lost, as it was alleged, during the war. When a Grand Fishing company was proposed in 1717, some objection was raised by those who had been shareholders in the Royal company, and it was then contended that the charter of the latter was void "through neglect[3]." In 1720 another Royal Fishery company was projected with a nominal capital of no less than ten millions, and it is interesting to notice that the objection made to both this venture and the Grand company was that, without extensive powers from the State, no private undertaking could "be able to beat the Dutch out of the fishery[4]."

[1] *Collections for Husbandry and Trade*, Mar. 19, 1703.

[2] *Journals of the House of Commons*, XI. p. 595.

[3] *Special Report from the Committee appointed to enquire into the several subscriptions for Fisheries, &c.* (1720).

[4] Anderson, *Annals*, III. pp. 334, 342, 343; *Reasons Humbly offered to the House of Commons for Incorporating the Subscribers for carrying on a National Fishery* $\left[\text{Brit. Mus. } \frac{3576 \cdot \text{b} \cdot 3}{78}\right]$; cf. *infra*, Division XIII.

SECTION IV. THE ROYAL COMPANY FOR THE FISHERY IN SCOTLAND (1670-90).

FROM 1670 to 1680, although the Royal Fishery Company of Great Britain was in existence, this industry was prosecuted more actively by a company founded in Scotland. By an act passed in 1661 by the Scottish Parliament, it was arranged that a new joint-stock company should be formed as a single undertaking with extensive privileges[1]. There appears to have been considerable difficulty in arousing public interest in the matter; and, after some progress had been made, the project was in danger of failure through the jealousy of the gentry and the merchants. "Many gentlemen refused to enter, fearing that the merchants, who behoved to manage all, would cheat the other partners, and many merchants refused to enter a society wherein so many noblemen were engaged, by whom they were afraid to be overawed[2]." The King was to receive £5,000 stock, but it was represented that this capital should be earmarked to be subject to the first loss (like the royal share in the French East India company), whereupon the Commissioner objected, so that the formation of the company was considerably delayed. It would appear that there was some ground for suspicion, for Sir George MacKenzie, who was later Advocate-General, wrote, before the company was actually formed, "nor could such as bought their fishes within the country bankrupt with them, because the society might consist of the most eminent in all judicatories, whom none would hazard to prejudge, *and who would redress by their sentences any such attempts*[3]."

Eventually, on June 4th, 1670, the patent was signed, which provided that all materials, such as salt, ropes, &c. used by the company, should be free of taxes, and that it should have the sole right, exclusive of all other Scotsmen, to fish at home and off the coast of Greenland[4]. With

---

[1] *Acts of the Parliaments of Scotland*, VII. p. 259.
[2] *Memorials of the Affairs of Scotland from the Restoration of King Charles II.*, by Sir George MacKenzie, Edinburgh, 1821, p. 184.
[3] *Ibid.*, p. 183.
[4] Acts of the Privy Council, 1667-73, ff. 356, 357.

these inducements the sum of £25,000 sterling was subscribed[1], but much of the capital was soon lost and the rest "retired." Like several other companies which had obtained a monopoly, although the undertaking for which the company had been formed was no longer prosecuted, a revenue was still made by compelling all, who wished to pursue the industry, to pay a royalty to the holders of the monopoly. In the particular case of the Royal Fishery company a tax of £6 Scots was exacted on every last of herrings exported. This was felt to be an insupportable grievance, for the company gave nothing in return, either in the use of buildings or fishing requisites, the protecting or improving of navigation. Therefore the company was dissolved by act of Parliament in 1690[2].

[1] MacKenzie, *Memorials, ut supra*, p. 184.
[2] *Acts of the Parliaments of Scotland*, IX. p. 224.

SECTION V. THE COMPANY OF MERCHANTS OF LONDON TRADING INTO GREENLAND (1692).

In 1673 the whaling trade had been made free to all Englishmen. During the nineteen years from 1673 to 1692, it appears that the open trade had not been more successful than the previous privileged one, and once more the industry had to be described as decayed. In 1692 the government decided to re-establish an exclusive company. On £40,000 having been subscribed, an undertaking was incorporated by act of Parliament as *the Company of Merchants of London trading into Greenland*. The governing body consisted of a governor, deputy-governor and 16 committees. The undertaking was to last for 14 years; and, during this time, no one person might subscribe more than £2,000 of stock. The following were the voting-rights. Stock under £500 had no vote, £500 one vote, £1,000 two votes, and no stockholder could have more than two votes. It was enacted that dividends must be paid in money only, not in kind. All bargains for the sale of stock were to be void unless the transfer was completed within ten days[1]. By 1696 the nominal capital had been increased to £82,000 and, by an act of Parliament of that year, permission was given the company not to call up the additional stock until 1703 since, owing to the scarcity of seamen on account of the war with France, there was no outlet for capital in the trade. By the same measure exemption from duties on oil or whalebone, imported by the company, was granted until 1707, when its fourteen years of concession were to terminate[2]. Some time before the expiration of the concession, the subscribed capital was lost and once more the trade was laid open to any who would adventure in it[3]. Up to 1720 the non-monopolized trade still failed to yield any considerable profit, partly owing to the frequency of wars, partly to the want of skill of the commanders of the ships. These circumstances are mentioned by H. Elking as the main reasons for the failure of the Greenland company coupled with the mistake of paying the captains by a fixed salary and not by commission[4].

[1] *Statutes*, 4 Will. & Mary, c. 17.
[2] *Ibid.*, 7 & 8 Will. III., c. 33.
[3] *Ibid.*, 1 Anne, c. 16. The last voyage just failed to be a success as the company's ship was returning home, after having caught eleven whales, when she was nipped in the ice and lost.
[4] *A View of the Greenland Trade* (1725), p. 46.

DIVISION IV.

COMPANIES ENGAGED IN THE EXTRACTIVE INDUSTRIES.

SECTION I. THE GOVERNORS, ASSISTANTS AND SOCIETY OF THE MINES ROYAL (FOUNDED 1561, INCORPORATED 1568).

THE right of claiming all mines of the precious metals in England had been a part of the prerogative of the Crown from a very early period. This claim was partly based on customary law as expressed in a paragraph of the so-called laws of Edward the Confessor—"thesauri de terra domini Regis sunt"—partly "on the excellency of the metal, the necessity of it and its tendency to the public utility[1]." During the reigns of the Plantagenet Kings, it was customary to grant the privilege of discovering and working the Royal Mines within a certain district to some patentee for a limited period, reserving to the Crown either a money rent or a certain proportion of the precious metals won, frequently a tenth part. Plowden quotes several of these grants, extending over a long period[2]. A patent granted by Henry VII. in 1485 mentions a number of partners who are thereby constituted governors of the mines or, as it was expressed later, the "Masters of the mines."

[1] *The Commentaries or Reports of Edmund Plowden*, London, 1818, p. 321; cf. *Die Gesetze der Angelsachsen von Reinhold Schmid*, Leipzig, 1832; Erster Theil, p. 282; *Ancient Laws and Institutes of England*, 1840, p. 193. In the latter this passage is referred to, in the Index, under the head of "Treasure Trove," which appears to be intended by the context.

[2] Grant to Nicholas Wake, cleric, of Mines Royal in Devon, for ten years from 15 June, 8 Rich. II. (p. 316). Grant to Walter Fitzwater for England dated 10 May, 2 Henry IV. (p. 317). Grant to Francis Duke of Bedford of Mines Royal in England for ten years dated 24 Feb., 5 Henry VI. (p. 317). Grant to Richard Duke of Gloucester, Henry Earl of Northumberland and others, Mines Royal in specified places in Cumberland, Northumberland and York for fifteen years dated 23 March, 15 Ed. IV. (p. 318). Grant to Richard Duke of Gloucester and others of all Royal Mines in Northumberland, Cumberland and Westmoreland for ten years dated 11 March, 18 Ed. IV. (p. 318). Grant to Jasper Duke of Bedford, Thomas Archbishop of York and divers noblemen, soldiers and others of Mines in England and Wales...copper, lead and tin as well as gold and silver, for twenty years dated 27 Feb., 1 Henry VII. (pp. 318, 319).

In England the precious metals were always found intermixed with other ores and therefore the patentees practically controlled all mining for lead and copper, besides sometimes interfering with the tin miners.

It therefore became important that the best method should be adopted for the separation of the ores, and, for this reason, the patentees in the sixteenth century began to call in the services of miners trained abroad, who were acquainted with the latest devices for the reduction and extraction of ores. One family, named Höchstetter, was prominently connected with British mining for over a century. In 1526 there is a record of a grant of a mining lease for gold and silver in Scotland, to a company of foreigners for 43 years, and the first person named was Joachim Höchstetter[1]. In the reign of Elizabeth a Daniel Höchstetter was very prominent in mining undertakings. In 1565 he had invented a new engine for the draining of mines[2], a patent for which was granted in May 1568[3]. At the same period Thomas Thurland and John Steynbergh were also interested in mining operations. Elizabeth was anxious to increase the efficiency of mining so as to add to the royalty payable to the Crown. It was thought desirable also that a more thorough and systematic examination should be made of the different mineralized ores, with a view to the discovery of new mines. To effect this object, considerable expenditure would be required, and in 1561 steps were taken towards the formation of a " corporation for working mines in England." On July 16th of that year an indenture was signed between the Queen and John Steynbergh and Thomas Thurland with a view to accomplishing this purpose[4]. Steynbergh was soon replaced in the management by Sebastian Spydell, but it does not appear that the partners had taken any active steps under the grant up till 1563. On September 10th of the following year (1564) all the privileges under the indenture of 1561 were transferred by Spydell and Thurland to the latter and Daniel Höchstetter, on behalf of a new company, and this may be taken as the beginning of the active career of the organization which was subsequently known as "the Society of the Mines Royal." On October 10th a fresh agreement was signed by the Queen which authorized the search for gold, silver, copper, and quick-silver in the counties of York, Lancaster, Westmoreland, Cumberland, Cornwall, Devon, Gloucester, Worcester and in the Principality of Wales. The one-tenth part of all the metal won was reserved to the Crown as well as the right of pre-emption of refined gold at 18*d*. per oz. below the market price, of silver at 1*d*. per oz. below the market

---

[1] *Report of the Royal Commission on Historical MSS.*, IV. p. 517.
[2] State Papers, Domestic, Elizabeth, XXXVI. 95; *Calendar*, 1547–80, p. 255.
[3] *Ibid.*, XLVI. 69; *Calendar*, 1547–80, p. 310.
[4] *Ibid.*, XVIII. 18, 18 (1) and 18 (2); *Calendar*, 1547–80, p. 180.

DIV. IV. § 1] *Shares sold in England and Germany* 1564   385

price. Copper was purchasable at 2s. 6d. per cwt. below the current rates[1].

The method of providing the capital needed is of considerable interest. The whole undertaking was divided into 24 parts or shares, some of which were disposed of in Germany and those remaining, amounting to fourteen, were sold in England. The average price realized was £1,200 a share[2]. Since early companies did not keep a capital account, it is difficult to decide how this payment should be treated. It might be regarded either as representing the goodwill of the enterprize or else as a premium paid on the purchase of shares. It does not appear that the original grantees had any tangible assets to transfer to Thurland so that at this date it may be assumed that the payments, made by the English shareholders, were wholly for the right of participating in the monopoly. Therefore, after each of the shareholders interested in these fourteen shares had paid his £1,200, he had still to find his proportion of the assessments made to provide capital for prospecting and for the development of mineral properties. As will be seen the amount of these calls was considerable, so that very few could have afforded to pay the two kinds of liability on more than a single share and many not even on one share, and therefore it was not long before shares were divided into halves, quarters and even into eighths.

Immediately after the issue of capital in 1564, operations were prosecuted vigorously for which funds were provided by calls made upon the shareholders in England and in Germany. At first work was begun in Cumberland and Westmoreland, in which counties both copper and silver had already been found. Mention is made of "old workings" near Keswick whence "immense quantities" of copper had been obtained, and there is a reference to a find of lead ore containing 50 to 60 oz. of silver to the ton[3]. About 1566 the agents of the society had found and were working a vein of copper at Newlands near Derwentfells in Cumberland on the manor of the Earl of Northumberland. Altogether 600,000 lbs. of ore had been raised, when Northumberland prohibited the miners from removing it. This action led to a celebrated suit, the Queen *v.* the Earl of Northumberland, which was heard in the Court of Exchequer before all the judges of England and the Barons of the Exchequer. This action raised the question whether the beneficiaries under a grant of mine royal were entitled to enter on private property and remove ores, and in addition Northumberland relied on the wording of the grant of

---

[1] State Papers, Domestic, Elizabeth, xxxiv. 58–60; *Calendar,* 1547–80, p. 244.

[2] Record of George Bowes and Francis Needham, sent to take view of the Mines Royal at Keswick. MS. Lister, 17 Bodleian Library.

[3] *History and Antiquities of Westmoreland and Cumberland,* by Joseph Nicholson and Richard Burn, 1777, I. p. 50.

the lands to his predecessor in title, urging that the right of mine royal was conveyed by that grant. After exceedingly erudite arguments on both sides, all the judges and barons agreed that all mines of gold and silver within the realm, whether in the lands of the Queen or of subjects, belonged to the Crown. It was also agreed, but not unanimously, that in the case of other ores containing gold or silver these also belonged to the Queen. Three judges qualified their finding on the latter point to the effect that mines of copper, lead, &c., containing traces of the precious metals, should not be held to be royal unless the value of the latter exceeded that of the former. In spite of this minority report, the verdict against Northumberland was unanimous, the three judges, who differed from the majority, holding that, since it was admitted the Newlands ore contained silver and the quantity was not stated, the presumption was that its value exceeded that of the copper, and therefore, on their finding, the mine was royal[1]. This was a very important judgment which settled the precedent until the passing of the Mines Royal Act in the reign of William III. The difficulty contained in the decision was that it frequently happened in England that many ores contained silver and anyone mining these was subject to the interference of the society of the Mines Royal. However, it would appear that the company did not extract the uttermost under this decision, for Sir John Pettus, writing in 1670, defined a mine royal as one "that doth yield so much gold or silver that the value thereof doth exceed the charges of refining and loss of baser metal, in which it is contained[2]."

One indirect effect of this case was the realization of the original intention of uniting the members more closely as an incorporation, and on May 28th, 1568, a charter was signed which created a body therein described as *the Governors, Assistants and Comminalty of the Mines Royal*, and which confirmed the privileges of the previous indentures. The charter authorized the election of two governors, four deputy-governors and six assistants who were to be chosen from amongst the English shareholders, the number of whom was never to be less than sixteen[3].

---

[1] Plowden, *Reports, ut supra*, p. 336.   [2] *Fodinæ Regales*, London, 1670, p. 9.

[3] The voting rights were one vote for each quarter-share. *Fodinæ Regales*, p. 55. The arms of the society are blazoned on p. 23. They were...Silver with a Mount Vert. A man working within a mine with two hammers and a lamp all in their proper colours on a chief Azure. A cake of copper between a hezant and a plate on a wreath Silver. A Demiman (called in Dutch "the Schicht Master") with an escutcheon on his breast Or and Azure per bend inverted, and in one of his hands an instrument called a wedge and in the other a compass, gold-manteled Silver doubled Azure, supported with two men, the one called the hammer-man, with a hammer on his shoulder, and the other the smelter with a fork in his hand, all in proper colours; cf. *The General Armory*, by Sir Bernard Burke, London, 1878, p. 690.

In 1571 a return was made of the names of the shareholders in England and the holding of each, whence it appears that fourteen shares were divided as follows:

3 persons	held	2 shares	each	= 6 shares
2 ,,	,,	1 share	,,	= 2 ,,
1 person	,,	¾ ,,		= ¾ share
5 persons	,,	½ ,,	,,	= 2½ shares
1 person	,,	⅜ ,,		= ⅜ share
9 persons	,,	¼ ,,	,,	= 2¼ shares
1 person	,,	⅛ ,,		= ⅛ share
22				14

The remaining 10 shares were owned by Germans[1]. Therefore to have elected the twelve office bearers, authorized by the charter, would have required more than half of the whole "comminalty," and so, during the early years of the history of the company, only one governor and three assistants were chosen[2].

To defray the costs of the action against Northumberland and to provide funds for mining operations, a total amount of £850 per share was called up by 1569[3]. These assessments were paid by both the English and German shareholders, and therefore at this date the total capital was £20,400, but in 1571 three members, owning between them three whole shares, had not disbursed " such money as they ought to pay[4]," and so the actual amount received was less than £20,000 and may not have exceeded £17,850. It is to be remembered also that, in addition to the assessments, most of the English shareholders had paid £1,200 per share as a premium on joining the society.

At this period ore was being raised and smelted near Keswick. Pettus, writing in the time of Charles II., stated that "a very great profit had been made there," but contemporary statements of the officials of the society point to an opposite conclusion[5]. For instance it is recorded that the English partners, after six years' trial (i.e. at the end of 1569), *seeing no hope of profit* stayed their hands from further disbursements[6], and in a petition by some of the shareholders against the management of Höchstetter, complaint is made of the "many con-

---

[1] State Papers, Domestic, Elizabeth, LXXVII. 29 (1); *Calendar*, 1547–80, p. 408.

[2] *Fodinæ Regales, ut supra*, p. 54.

[3] MS. Lister 17, *ut supra*.

[4] State Papers, Domestic, Elizabeth, LXXVII. 29 (1); *Calendar*, 1547–80, p. 408.

[5] *Fodinæ Regales*, p. 32.

[6] MS. Lister 17.

tributions so grievous and inexpectate," while out of the great "riches" of the mines, treasure had been received by Höchstetter "and *by none else*[1]."

There is no doubt that very considerable quantities of copper had been won, but the difficulty was to obtain a market for it. At this period, the chief use for the metal was for the making of cannon and for coinage. But Elizabeth had reserved the right of receiving one-fifteenth part of the metal won or its cash equivalent. The remaining demand in England was not great and it was illegal to export copper or a number of other metals under an act of Henry VIII.[2] For this reason Höchstetter in 1570 asked permission to make exports, urging that the price at Frankfort was £3. 5s. per quintal, which compares with £3 in England for rough copper[3]. The difficulty of finding a market was accentuated in 1571 owing to the depression of trade in England during that year. Much of the capital of the society had been sunk in preliminary operations, some calls were in arrear, there was a large quantity of copper unsold and the shareholders would not subscribe more until some return on their outlay had been received. An exhaustive enquiry was made in order to ascertain the value of the tangible assets of the society, with the result that all the property was inventoried and "an Estimate of the Stock remaining at the mines and the value thereof at Christmas last" (1571) was drawn up[4]. This document is of very great importance as a very early instance of a balance sheet of a joint-stock company. The copper, silver and lead were taken in at different rates according to the labour needed to bring each to a completed state. The fuel and other stores were also entered at varying amounts and credit was taken for certain rents and other payments made in advance. In several items the arithmetic appears to be faulty, and in one instance there is a discrepancy of about £27. The following is a summary of the estimate:

		£	s.	d.	£	s.	d.	£	s.	d.
	890 quintals of copper stone at 60/- pr. q. ...				2,670	0	0			
	807 quintals of copper stone at 52/- pr. q. ...	2,098	4	0						
Deduct	53 quintals being Queen's 1/15	159	0	0						
	754				1,936	4	0[5]			

[1] Lansd. MS. 28 (6) British Museum.
[2] 33 Henry VIII. c. 7, *Statutes*, III. p. 836.
[3] *Historical MSS. Commission, Salisbury MSS.* I. p. 467.
[4] State Papers, Domestic, Elizabeth, LXXXV. 46; *Calendar*, 1547–80, p. 436.
[5] The rate here is £3 per quintal, whence the nett amount would be £1,939. 4s.

The Financial Position 1571

			£ s. d.	£ s. d.	£ s. d.
	Brought forward			4,606 4 0	
	1402 quintals of copper contained in 24,296 q. of ore				
Deduct	93 quintals being Queen's 1/15				
	1,309 at 60/- pr. q. for rough copper	3,927 0 0			
Deduct	expenses of refining[1]	2,469 12 0			
				1,457 8 0	
	1409 quintals of lead ore at 4/- pr. q.	282 0 0			
	122 quintals of lead ore at 8/- pr. q.	48 16 0			
				330 16 0	
					6,394 8 0
	Fuel, including charcoal, peat coal, wood			373 14 0	
	Horses and wagons—9 horses at 50/- each, 4 wagons at 60/- each			34 10 0	
	Furniture and bedding			90 0 0	
	Silver plate			24 0 0	
					522 4 0
	Debtors			88 18 0	
	Payments made in advance			531 9 4½	
					620 7 4½
	Brewhouse and windmill			150 0 0	
	Tools and implements			480 0 0	
					630 0 0
	"Sum total," as in MS.				£8,194 15 4½

(N.B. The sum total of the items recorded only amounts to £8,166. 19s. 4½d. There is thus an unaccounted for amount of £27.)

Buildings, e.g. melting house, coal houses, "roasting house," wheat houses, smithies, &c.			3,888 15 8
Total			£12,083 11 0½

What is most remarkable in this account is (neglecting minor errors) the sum unaccounted for. The absence of complete information, as to how the total of £8,194. 15s. 4½d. is made up, has rendered it necessary to follow the order of the original document (which has been condensed only to the extent of grouping together under one heading a number of entries given separately). But a more natural grouping of the items would be to divide the £12,055. 15s. 0½d. as between copper

[1] For the methods of smelting vide *A Discovery of Subterraneall Treasure, viz. of all Manner of Mines and Minerals, from the Gold to the Coale; with Directions and Rules for the finding of them in all Kingdoms and Countries*, London, 1639 [Lib. Trin. Coll. Dub., P. gg. 40, No. 17]; *A Collection of Scarce and Valuable Treatises upon Metals, Mines and Minerals*, London, 1740.

and lead on the one hand and buildings (including the brewhouse and windmill), tools and fuel. Thus 53 per cent. of the assets falls under the former heading and 42 per cent. under the latter, the remainder consisting of the debtors.

From another point of view, assuming that there were assets to the whole sum of £12,083. 11s. 0½d., there remains the question of the liabilities. Although considerable payments had been made in advance, there were also debts due by the society of an unknown amount[1]. In addition there was the share-capital of £20,400, so that there was a deficiency of over £8,000 or about two-fifths of the contributions from the members. To some extent this was a relative, rather than an absolute adverse balance. Against it there were the following items for which credit was not taken in the foregoing account. First 281,424 quintals of unessayed ore, which had not been valued because "it is not yet known what may be made thereof[2]." Then there was the development of the mine, and lastly the cost of the great law-suit, which must have been considerable. So that, on the whole, the balance against the subscribed capital was less than might appear at first sight and any great success, in finding a rich copper vein, would have placed the society in a sound position. But with reference to the shareholders, who had paid a premium of £1,200 per share, it is plain that only a remarkable improvement in the situation could have reimbursed them.

Once both the English and German shareholders had refused, after 1569, to pay any more calls a great difficulty was experienced in finding working capital. This was increased by the demand of Elizabeth to be paid her fifteenth in cash, and not in copper. Therefore the society had in fact not only "to carry" its own stock but also that portion of the total production, whence the royalty was to be paid. In a memorial to the governor of the company in 1571, the want of ready money is attributed to this cause, and it is added that, had the Queen been prepared "to take copper for ready money," there would have been "sufficient means to have discharged us from such need hereafter, having always the stock to maintain the work with gain[3]."

At this juncture, an ingenious method was propounded for providing further resources. The society had over 2,000 quintals of copper at various stages of extraction. This was valued at £3,383. 8s.; but, when completely smelted, it would be worth £3 a quintal or £6,000 in all, and more as finished copper. It was therefore proposed that each of the English shareholders should receive a rateable division of copper, advancing money for it at £3 per quintal[4]. The reason that this offer was confined to the English shareholders was that about this time the

---

[1] State Papers, Domestic, Elizabeth, LXXVII. 29 (1).
[2] Ibid., LXXXV. 46.   [3] Ibid., LXXVII. 29.   [4] Ibid., LXXVII. 29 (1).

German members were in difficulties themselves and, on their failure soon afterwards, their holding was acquired by a number of merchants at Augsburg[1].

The proposal of a copper division was not accepted by the members. It was in fact the provision of a loan on the security of the stock of the society. If for any reason the copper were not made, the security would be difficult to realize and, should the copper be actually delivered, the noblemen and gentlemen, who were shareholders, would find it troublesome to dispose of. The amount falling to an owner of one whole share was 83 quintals and the question would arise how a private person, not engaged in trade, could market this large quantity of about 4 tons weight. Besides, there was the financial aspect of the situation. The general feeling was that most of the shareholders, having disbursed in premium and calls £2,050 per share, were indisposed to make further payments. Each holder of one share would require, under the proposed scheme, to find £250 or to add about 12 per cent. to the existing investment. For these reasons the proposal was not adopted, and as time went on the need for working capital became greater and greater. Evidently nothing could be obtained from the shareholders and the only person, who was gaining from the venture and who was in a position to help, was Elizabeth. It was obviously to her interest that the partly refined copper should be made marketable, since her royalty would amount to nearly £430[2]. She was therefore approached by some of the prominent members of the company and consented to purchase copper to the value of £1,383, which was to be used either in the office of the Ordnance " or elles about the tombes which are meant to be edified for Kinge Henry VIIIth, Kinge Edward and Queen Marie[3]," besides lending £2,500 at 8 per cent., that being a low rate for the time[4]. The amount was partly disbursed in redeeming copper deposited as security against a loan in London and in paying a portion of the outstanding debts, leaving a sum of £201. 12s. 5d. in hand at Christmas 1575.

An account was framed at Christmas 1576 in order to show the claims then outstanding against the society. It comprises (1) the debts due in 1575; (2) the copper, silver and lead either made, partly made, or contained in ores at the same date; (3) the copper, silver and lead

[1] MS. Lister 17, *ut supra*. The Höchstetters of Augsburg were a prominent mercantile family at this time, cf. *Augsburg, Nürnberg und ihre Handelsfürsten*, von A. Kleinschmidt, Cassel, 1881, pp. 25, 41.

[2] *i.e.* Estimated total value of copper in sight £6,428
Deduct royalty of one-fifteenth 428
Balance £6,000

[3] MS. Eg. (Brit. Mus.) 2723, f. 63 b.

[4] The Extract of the Mines Royal at Christmas anno 1575. British Museum, Lansd. MS. 22 (5), cf. State Papers, Domestic, Elizabeth, cxxxi. 49.

made during the year ending December 25th, 1576; (4) "the accompte and reckoning of the premises," *i.e.* the payments made out of the loan of £2,500; (5) the balance of the loan and the sums realized by sales during the year; (6) "the estate of the mines at Christmas 1576," *i.e.* the debts then due; (7) the quantities of copper, silver and lead either made, partly made or contained in ores in 1576[1]. These various data enable a statement to be framed of the financial position of the society at this period. First of all the amount of indebtedness was decreased by nearly one-third, as will appear from the following figures:

Debts due	Christmas 1575			Christmas 1576		
	£	s.	d.	£	s.	d.
To country people for fuel and workmen's wages ...	1,458	1	8	907	3	10
"More owing diverse ways"	849	17	8	896	0	0
To Queen Elizabeth	2,500	0	0	1,300	0	0
„ „ interest at 8%				200	0	0
	£4,807	19	4	£3,303	3	10[2]

The cost of production, in relation to the quantities sold, made a favourable showing. Since the items in the account are of great intrinsic interest, it is worth giving the details.

(? Cash) Sales of copper, silver and lead, Christmas 1575 *to Christmas* 1576.

	£	s.	d.
"Sold of rough copper 437 quintalls at £3 the quintall amounting unto	1,311	0	0
Sold of wrought copper 354 quintalls, 69 lb. weight at divers prices (but most part at 10*d.* the lb.) arising one with another after the rate of £4. 7*s.* 6*d.* the quintal and better. The whole sales amounting unto	1,552	5	2
Sold of fine silver, delivered unto the mint, 87 lb. 3 oz. weight, at 4*s.* 9*d.* the oz., all duties deducted, amounting the said sales unto	334	6	10
Sold in lead 20 foulders, 12 quintall weight, part at £6 and part at £6. 10*s.* the foulder amounting to"	129	12	6
Total sales	£3,327	4	6

Expenses during the same period.

	£	s.	d.
"Paid for the whole charges of the work this year	1,878	12	8
Paid in sundry other debts owing by the mines in divers ways as by the balance and accompt appeareth[3]"	254	15	6
Total expenses	£2,133	8	2

[1] The Extract of the Mines Royal at Christmas anno 1575. Lansd. MS. 22 (5).

[2] In the account the reduction of debt is stated as £1,454. 15*s.* 6*d.*, but as a matter of fact it was £1,504. 15*s.* 6*d.* This arose from the debts, owing in 1576, being overstated by £50 apparently through an error in addition, the total being given as £3,353. 3*s.* 10*d.* instead of £3,303. 3*s.* 10*d.*

[3] The account giving these items is a purely cash account, and makes no attempt to ascertain the cost of working. It might be assumed therefore that the second

Therefore the general result is as follows:

	£	s.	d.
Proceeds of sales	3,327	4	6
Expenses	2,133	8	2
Balance	£1,193	16	4

This balance is subject to the deduction of £200 for interest on the loan, leaving a gross profit of £993. 16s. 4d. Since, moreover, £1,200 of this loan had been repaid, supposing that the results in 1577 were similar, the interest-charge would be reduced, leaving on this basis a gross profit of nearly £1,100 or about 5 per cent. on the called up capital.

Probably the shareholders accepted this estimate of the "estate of the mines" since there was a prevalent opinion amongst them that "a gain" was being made, and that all that was required was that the debts should be cleared off, so that dividends could be paid out of the surplus. There are however other facts that are not brought out in the accounts, but which may be deduced from them, which show that the apparent profit was not a real one. To obtain the amount (which was paid to Elizabeth) it was necessary to reduce to a material extent the "reserves" of copper and ore. The following are the quantities at the beginning and the end of the financial year:

Metal and ore in stock	Christmas 1575	Christmas 1576
Stock of made copper	470 quintals	212 quintals
Copper "in sundry rostes"	356 ,,	138 ,,
Ores "ready gotten above ground containing perfect copper"[1]	1,075 ,,	763 ,,
Total copper	1,901 ,,	1,113 ,,
Silver contained in lead ore	298 lbs.	264 lbs.
Lead ore	54 foulders	42 foulders

It will be noted that the reserve of copper above ground had declined by nearly 800 quintals. This was the amount sold during the year, so that it follows that absolutely no development had been done. In order to ascertain how such cessation of underground work would affect the results of the year, it is necessary to obtain some basis for

item represented a payment on account of old debts since the first is entered as "the whole charge of the work." Possibly however the first item refers to the local expenses at Keswick and the second to expenses elsewhere (except duties on silver). There is another element of uncertainty, namely the introduction amongst the *debts due by the mines* of an item of £214 *owing to the mines* for copper sold. This seems to be an old credit. The difference between these two sums may account for the discrepancy of £50 already noted.

[1] In all cases the royalty of one-fifteenth was deducted before entering these quantities.

valuing the copper in different stages of completion. Probably that adopted in 1571 would be sufficiently exact for the purpose, namely, taking the copper almost finished at 52s. per quintal and that partly made at ·37 of £3 per quintal. There would be, on this method of calculation, a deficiency in the reserve of copper and ore of about £1,260. Since the gross profit was under £1,200 it becomes evident that, under analysis, it has disappeared altogether and still some allowance should be made for the diminution in the stocks of silver and lead ore, which though smaller must also be included. Therefore the nett result was that in 1576, provided proper measures had been taken for development, the mines were working at a small loss, and that the apparent profit was realized only through suspending the winning of ore, in order to devote all the labour to smelting so as to repay a portion of the Queen's loan.

From quite a different point of view these accounts are of interest. It may be remembered that in the Northumberland case great weight was given to the presence of silver in the copper ore. It was upon this ground that the society was entitled, under the royal grant, to enter upon private property and open a mine. At Keswick in 1576 there is no record of silver being obtained from copper at that time, and during the whole future history of the company, the silver won was separated from lead ores.

After 1576 the position of the society was that it owed the balance of the sum borrowed from Elizabeth and at the same time had reduced the reserve of ore "above ground." The members, or some of them, were most unwilling to subscribe more capital and yet further resources were needed. For a short time the works were carried on, but by 1579 the want of funds became more felt and Höchstetter made two proposals, either that the shareholders should provide a further sum of £1,000 (or over £41 per share) or else that he and his partners would undertake to work the Keswick mines for a period of 15 years, guaranteeing the society against loss[1]. At the same time another German and his partners made an offer which would have provided profit to the company, and, on an assay of the ore being made, it was alleged that three times as much copper could be extracted from it as had been won by Höchstetter, while, at this rate, there were prospects of sufficient returns to discharge all the outstanding debts[2]. In 1580 it became clear that, owing to the disinclination of several shareholders to find more capital, some method of leasing the mines must be adopted[3], and

---

[1] Lansd. MS. British Museum, 28 (6).
[2] Ibid.
[3] State Papers, Domestic, Elizabeth, CXLIV. 32; *Calendar*, 1547-80, p. 688.

eventually one of the shareholders, Thomas Smythe or Smith, Collector of Customs for the Port of London, took a lease of the northern mines[1]. For some years Smith had been interested in mining ventures, and, as will be seen below, he was also engaged in working mines in Cornwall from 1583 to 1587. The society let the Keswick mines on the basis that Smith and his partners should in the first place undertake the liability of the royalty of one-fifteenth part of the copper won, due to the Queen. He bound himself moreover to pay the society one-ninth part of the produce, which royalty was estimated to amount to £166. 13s. 4d. a year, and in addition to this to make a money-rent of £433. 6s. 8d.[2] This system was the best that could have been adopted under the circumstances. It brought in some return to the shareholders and at the same time it freed those who were unable to subscribe more capital from that liability, while giving an opportunity to others desirous of undergoing further risks of reaping the reward of their enterprize. Besides, the reservation of a royalty to the society safeguarded it against parting with its property at an under-value. Should Smith's subsidiary company prove successful, a part of the profit would find its way to the parent organization and would go to providing interest on the capital which had been without any return for upwards of twenty years.

Meanwhile steps had been taken to search for silver and copper ores elsewhere within the limits of the society's charter. As early as 1579 Piers Edgecumb had written offering to form a partnership to work mines in Devon and Cornwall. In the latter county there had been a celebrated mine at Combe Martin which had yielded large quantities of silver in the time of Edward I.[3] In 1579 the mines in this district "lay unwrought and yielded no profit at all[4]." Edgecumb proposed to Lord Burghley (who owned two shares in the Mines Royal) that in the proposed partnership, Burghley should be credited with a similar proportion of the profit without any payment[5]. Edgecumb however was not at this time a member of the society, and Smith offered to lease the mines in Cornwall and Wales, taking Edgecumb into partnership. This offer was accepted, on the basis of an annual rent of £300 for the mines

[1] This Thomas Smythe was the father of Sir Thomas Smythe the governor of the East India and Russia companies and treasurer of the Virginia company. Brown, *Genesis of the United States*, II. pp. 1011, 1012.

[2] A Declaration of the yearly rents of the mineral works of England; Lansd. MS. 47 (66).

[3] Camden, *Britannia*, p. 47.

[4] Lansd. MS. 29 (1).

[5] Lansd. MS. 29 (1), *i.e.* there were 24 shares in the Mines Royal of which Burghley owned two or one-twelfth of the whole. Thus Edgecumb offered him one-twelfth of the profit of his company, which one-twelfth he estimates at £100 a year.

in Cornwall, Devon and Cardigan[1]. The society used the rent, received from Smith, to pay off the balance of the loan due to Elizabeth, and by 1586 there was only £292. 17s. 11d. outstanding. At the same date it was estimated that the "stock," or working capital at Keswick, amounted to £900 and it was proposed to devote the rent of £600 a year for the next two years to bringing the funds up to £2,100 which was calculated to be sufficient[2]. After these adjustments had been made, the society would have in royalty and rent about £900 a year as free profit. This would give nearly £38 per share; and, supposing the paid up capital remained at £850 for each share, the yield would be under $4\frac{1}{2}$ per cent. Those members, who had given a premium of £1,200, received less than 2 per cent. on the whole cost of their investment, while the loss of interest for over twenty years must be allowed for.

During the period from 1580 to 1596 the interest in the fortunes of the mines rests rather with the subsidiary, than with the parent undertaking. Reports as to the Keswick venture are contradictory. In 1586 the accountant of the society estimated that, during the five years of Smith's lease, he and his partners would gain £2,600 and it was then expected that the society would have an income from these mines in royalty and rent of £1,200 a year[3]. According to another report, also prepared for the society, it was stated that during the first seven years of Smith's farming of the works in the Keswick district he made £3,691, "so that" many of the old debts were discharged by him[4]. On the other hand it is recorded, at a later date, that Smith risked a capital of £11,000 and that he lost £500, besides receiving no interest[5]. These statements may not be so divergent as they appear, since the first two expressly relate to the Keswick mines, whereas the last may include Smith's results under the Cornwall lease, and the evidence points to the fact that, on the whole, he lost money in the south. The first mention of Smith's connection with the mines in Cornwall, Devon and Cardigan is as early as 1583, at which date his men were sinking shafts at "Treworthie" and had sunk 15 fathoms[6]. During the early part of the following year, search was made for lead mines, and by April ore had been found, through draining certain old works. The hundredweight

---

[1] Lansd. MS. 47 (66). According to another account, Lansd. MS. 47 (65), he paid £1,070. This seems to represent about $3\frac{1}{2}$ years' rent.

[2] Lansd. MS. 47 (65).

[3] Ibid.

[4] Report of George Bowes and Francis Needham, MS. Lister, 17 (Bodleian Library).

[5] State Papers, Domestic, Elizabeth, CCLXXV. 145; Calendar, 1598–1601, pp. 501–2.

[6] State Papers, Domestic, Elizabeth, CLXIV. 4; Calendar, 1581–90, p. 134.

of ore yielded on assay 50 lbs. of lead and ½ oz. of silver[1]. At this period Smith's partners refused to advance any more money[2], and the manager at the mine wrote that recent results could be of small comfort to his master, adding piously "God send him better[3]." In June it had been found impossible to overcome the water at Treworthie, but good ore in great quantities had been reached at a place called Logan[4], and it was expected that 100 tons of perfect copper a year could be made[5]. To smelt this ore, a "copper house" had been established at Neath in Wales[6]. In August, just when a good vein of lead ore had been found, "the water burst in upon the men so suddenly that they barely escaped with their lives[7]." A month later the yield at Logan had decreased and the mine at Treworthie was making a serious loss[8]. In July 1585 ores were being raised at St Ives and St Just[9], and by November of the following year the manager was able to declare that the latter mines had never been better than they were at that date[10]. In 1587 there were very favourable reports of silver at Penrose[11]; but it would appear that Smith was unable or unwilling to undertake further risks. As early as 1585 difficulty was experienced in finding £100 necessary to discharge certain debts at the mines and the wages of the men fell into arrear[12]. By 1587 the ore at St Just was seized and the workmen discharged[13], and it is probable that Smith and his partners withdrew from this district soon afterwards. His interest was bought by Piers Edgecumb, who some time afterwards restarted the Cornish mines. There is no information whether Smith prospected for silver in Wales. It is probable that, since Cardiganshire was within his lease, he made some efforts there, and indeed, according to one account, he had coins struck at the mint in London from silver he discovered in Wales[14].

It is not clear how far a remarkable discovery of silver ore, made in 1587, was related to the finances of the society. This discovery took place at Combe Martin. In a contemporary work—Stephen Atkinson's

---

[1] State Papers, Domestic, Elizabeth, CLXX. 37; *Calendar*, 1581–90, p. 172.
[2] *Ibid.*, CLXIX. 16; *Calendar*, 1581–90, p. 164.
[3] *Ibid.*, CLXX. 82; *Calendar*, 1581–90, p. 176.
[4] *Ibid.*, CLXXI. 4; *Calendar*, 1581–90, p. 179.
[5] *Ibid.*, CLXXI. 36; *Calendar*, 1581–90, p. 183.
[6] *Ibid.*, CLXXII. 16; *Calendar*, 1581–90, p. 189.
[7] *Ibid.*, CLXXII. 60; *Calendar*, 1581–90, p. 194.
[8] *Ibid.*, CLXXIII. 16; *Calendar*, 1581–90, p. 201.
[9] *Ibid.*, CLXXX. 5; *Calendar*, 1581–90, p. 250.
[10] *Ibid.*, CXCV. 39; *Calendar*, 1581–90, p. 370.
[11] *Ibid.*, CXCVIII. 68; *Calendar*, 1581–90, p. 390.
[12] *Ibid.*, CLXXXV. 6; *Calendar*, 1581–90, p. 290.
[13] *Ibid.*, CXCIX. 5, 18; *Calendar*, 1581–90, pp. 392–3.
[14] *An Historical Account of English Money*, by S. M. Leake, London, 1793, p. 287.

Discoverie of Gold Mynes—a long quotation is given from a manuscript treatise by Bevis Bulmer (who was interested in this mine), which begins by a description of the society of the Mines Royal. Since this mine was within the area of the lease of Smith, it is possible he may have derived some revenue from the discoverers of it—Adrian Gilbert and John Poppler. The ore, although rich, was "stubborn to smelt." The discovery excited so much interest, not only in England but also abroad, that foreign miners came to view it. Bevis Bulmer at this time was working lead mines in the Mendip Hills and he succeeded in obtaining a specimen of the ore and in smelting it. An agreement was made that the existing partners should have one-half of the ore won and Bulmer the other half, he paying all expenses. For the next two years the mines yielded each of the partners £10,000. From 1589 to 1590 the production of silver declined, but in the latter year the profit was £1,000. Bulmer caused the last piece of silver smelted to be made into a goblet which he presented to the City of London[1].

To return to Smith's operations, if, as suggested, he lost on his own mining in Cornwall and made a profit at Keswick, he would be more disposed to concentrate his efforts in the latter district. Accordingly, on the determination of the original lease for the northern mines, a new one was made to Smith and the German miners. This partnership was in existence between 1587 and 1596; and, during that time a capital of £1,200 had been provided, all of which was lost, with £450 in addition.

Although Smith was giving most attention to the northern mines, he retained his lease covering Cornwall, Devon and Cardigan, and on August 31st, 1594, he sub-let his rights for the two counties first named to Edgecumb who had been a shareholder since 1585[2]. In 1595 there were a number of persons interested in this lease and £2,000 had been expended, without any return as yet[3]. By 1597 the capital outlay had risen to £4,000, and the prospects appear to have been sufficiently satisfactory to induce the partnership to apply to the society for a promise of the reversion of this part of Smith's lease, which determined in 1599[4]. By that year, however, the yield was low, and it was necessary to ask for an extension of time to pay the rent, since, according to Edgecumb's statement, he and his partners had made a loss[5]. From 1599 to 1632 there is a gap in the information about the Cornish mines, which in the

---

[1] *The Discoverie and Historie of the Gold Mynes of Scotland*, by Stephen Atkinson, Edinburgh, Bannatyne Club, 1825, pp. 52, 53.

[2] *Report Royal Commission on Historical MSS.*, Cecil MSS., Part v., pp. 14, 15, 198.

[3] *Ibid.*, pp. 198–9.

[4] *Ibid.*, Part vii., p. 233.

[5] *Ibid.*, Part ix., p. 437.

latter year were leased by the society to the Earl of Suffolk and his partners for 21 years[1].

It has already been shown that the subsidiary company, constituted by Smith and the Germans, had lost money up to the end of 1596. Early in the summer of the next year the society notified Marcus Steinberg, Richard Ledes and Emanuel Höchstetter that it would hold them liable for the rent and other covenants under Smith's lease. The partners replied that, owing to the wet summers and want of peat, they had been unable to smelt their ores, and they asked time to pay the rent. It was also stated that a place called "God's Gift" was "a plentiful mine," but that the hindrance to the obtaining good returns was the want of an adequate working capital. Although for some years past a "reasonable" quantity of partly made copper had been in stock, owing to delay in obtaining payment for some of it, the wages had been unpaid and it was necessary to take up money at interest. It was estimated that the working capital required would be £2,020. 13s. 4d. calculated on the basis of 5 marks for every cwt. of copper unsold[2]. In view of these circumstances, the society decided to take again the risk of mining operations, which were now pushed forward at Caldbec and God's Gift. The "huge new water-works" at the latter place cost £301. It was reported that at Bolton there was the best coal in the country, which would be plentiful if well-wrought, but that, at this time, it was badly worked. Little hope could be expected from Caldbec. At present not more than £3 worth of silver ore was obtained annually, and the cleaning out of the old shaft and opening up the vein would require an expenditure of from £100 to £120[3]. The managers at the mines wrote that the deposits were worked out, but some of the members of the society believed that the Höchstetters had not treated the company honestly, and that very considerable profits had been made[4]. Several of the mines proved unworkable owing to the inflow of water, and when the accounts were made up to Christmas 1599 it was found that the society had lost £700 in the three years[5].

In 1600 a full enquiry was made as to the position and prospects of the undertaking. A statement was prepared showing the financial

[1] State Papers, Domestic, Charles I., ccxviii. 73; *Calendar*, 1631–3, p. 358.

[2] State Papers, Domestic, Elizabeth, cclxiv. 30 (1); *Calendar*, 1595–7, pp. 461-2. It is interesting to notice that the word directors occurs in this document, in the following connection "...as the works are now very low, four *directors or principal officers* will serve until the works increase."

[3] MS. Lister, 17 (Bodleian Library).

[4] State Papers, Domestic, Elizabeth, cclxxi. 40; *Calendar*, 1598–1601, pp. 229–30.

[5] State Papers, Domestic, Elizabeth, cclxxv. 145; *Calendar*, 1598–1601, pp. 501, 502.

history of the northern mines from 1563 to 1599. During the thirty-six years, after paying to Elizabeth £4,500 for her royalty, the account stood as follows:

Revenue and expenses of the Northern Mines, 1563 to 1599.

	£
Silver, copper and lead sold	68,103
Expenses	104,709
Deficiency	36,606
The capital outlay of the society was returned at	27,000
Leaving a balance representing losses of subsidiary undertakings and debt	9,606[1]

It may be noted that in this account the capital outlay of the society is given as £27,000. In 1569 it had been £20,400 and two years later a call of £1,000 was suggested. It is possible that, after 1569, assessments may have been made, raising the amount called up per share from £850 to the round sum of £1,000 per share. This would have provided £24,000. There is mention of the rent having been remitted as against capital outlay by the farmers and it may have been that the society provided funds out of the rents payable to it from the mines elsewhere. Altogether it would appear that after 1584 for a considerable period there was an income from rents of about £1,000 a year. The statement prepared in 1586 showed a rental of £900, derived from the mines in Cumberland, Cornwall, Devon and Cardigan, besides which the society had the privilege of mine royal in York, Lancashire, Westmoreland, Gloucester, Worcester and the remainder of Wales. Whether any revenue was drawn from these rights is doubtful, but there are indications that prospecting was being carried on, and in 1596 the governor of the society was informed by Thomas Acworth that he had good hopes of finding royal mines[2]. Whether the whole amount was divided to the shareholders does not appear. If, as suggested above, some £3,000 was spent on the Keswick mines out of revenue, it would of course have been necessary to diminish the dividend accordingly. Supposing in any year the sum, available for distribution, amounted to about £1,000, and that the paid up capital was £24,000, the return would have been only about four per cent. This view of the financial position is confirmed by a petition of Edgecumb who stated that in the seven years, ending Christmas 1594, there was due to him, as dividend on one share, 500 marks. This would represent an income for the whole undertaking for that period of £8,000[3].

[1] State Papers, Domestic, Elizabeth, CCLXXV. 145; *Calendar*, 1598–1601, pp. 501, 502.

[2] *Ibid.*, CCLVI. 61; *Calendar*, 1595–7, p. 177.

[3] *Calendar Salisbury MSS.*, Part v., pp. 198, 199, 206.

In the beginning of the seventeenth century the position of the society might be described in the following terms. The southern mines were paying some rent but not a large one, and eventually a new subsidiary company was formed by the Earl of Suffolk for this district. In Cumberland, the company had first worked copper, then had let its property there to groups of partners and had again conducted operations on behalf of the parent society. It was not long before direct working was abandoned, and these mines were leased to the Höchstetters, who appear to have carried on the industry up to the time of the Civil War. As late as 1627 Joseph and Daniel Höchstetter presented a petition asking for a release from a moiety of the royalty reserved to the Crown[1].

When matters were unfavourable to the society in Cornwall and Cumberland, it fortunately happened that silver was discovered in Wales. Smith, during the period of leases, had found some, which he brought to the Tower at London[2]. On the determination of his lease the society worked the Welsh mines for a number of years[3]. It therefore appears that Gerard Malynes was not well informed when he wrote about this time that " there is none of that company that doth advance any works that I can learn[4]." About 1620 the connection of Hugh Middleton with Welsh mining began. Pettus indeed states it was out of the profits of this undertaking that the New River was constructed, adding somewhat quaintly, had he (Middleton) not used his money in this way " he would have been master of a mass of wealth, but great wits and purses seldom know how to give bounds to their designments, and, by undertaking too many things, fail in all." Middleton paid the society £400 a year for his lease and he formed a company to work the concession, known as *the Mines Royal of Wales*, which was still in existence when he drew up his will in 1631[5]. According to Pettus, the profits of this company for some time were as much as £2,000 a month[6].

The beginning of Middleton's connection with these mines is uncertain. In 1625 it is recorded that he had, by his great industry and charges, brought certain works in Cardigan to " very good perfection." At the same time his enterprize had been frustrated to some degree by the

[1] State Papers, Domestic, Coll. Sign Manual, Charles I., III. 2; *Calendar*, 1627–8, p. 93.

[2] *An Historical Account of English Money*, by Stephen Martin Leake, London, 1793, p. 303.

[3] Pettus, *Fodinæ Regales, ut supra*, p. 33.

[4] *Consuetudo vel Lex Mercatoria*, p. 185.

[5] The Will of Sir Hugh Myddelton in *Hydraulia*, by William Matthews, London, 1835, p. 55.

[6] *Fodinæ Regales*, p. 33.

"interference" of certain persons and by want of labour. Accordingly a commission was appointed to assist him in his operations[1].

With regard to the position of the society about 1630, it was receiving £400 a year from Middleton's company, and in 1632 a new lease was made to the Earl of Suffolk and his partners of a mine at Kentwyn in Cornwall at 100 marks per annum[2]. There were in addition the northern mines and any others in Cornwall, Dorset or Wales, not included under the leases to Suffolk and Middleton. Still it is unlikely that the society was receiving as much as £700 a year from its property, which represented a slight decline as compared with the figures of 1586.

In 1636 the society granted a license to a number of persons to dig for minerals in Carmarthen, Carnarvon and Flint[3], and in the following year two of these, Thomas Bushell and Edmund Goodyere obtained a patent for the extraction of silver[4]. Bushell set to work, and he claimed to have discovered new royal mines besides "recovering the old drowned and forsaken works at Talabant." At this stage he encountered a succession of difficulties. He was unable to find sufficient fuel, "ill-disposed persons" destroyed his machinery and a local mine owner, Sir Richard Price (a predecessor of the Sir Carberry Price whose mine was acquired in the next century by the notorious Mine Adventurers company), also impeded him[5]. Moreover his title was far from clear. The license, under which he worked, did not include Cardigan, for which county the lease, now owned by Lady Middleton, was still in being. Bushell offered £1,000 a year for a lease in his own favour, but he was directed to deal with Lady Middleton, to whom he bound himself to pay £400 fine and £400 a year during the currency of her lease[6].

On this arrangement being made, Bushell proceeded to form a company, and in 1642 nine persons had undertaken to venture £3,700[7]. This company was successful in finding considerable quantities of silver, sometimes 20 lbs., sometimes 15 lbs., and sometimes 6 lbs. to the ton of lead, and the annual output was valued at about £5,000 a year[8]. To

---

[1] *Fœdera*, xviii. p. 66.
[2] State Papers, Domestic, Charles I., ccxviii. 73; *Calendar*, 1631–3, p. 358.
[3] *Ibid.*, cccxxvi. 68; *Calendar*, 1635–6, p. 369.
[4] *Ibid.*, cccxxvi. 69; *Calendar*, 1635–6, p. 569.
[5] *Journals of the House of Lords*, iv. p. 364, v. p. 78. *Reports of the Com. Hist. MSS.*, v. p. 24; *Fœdera*, xx. p. 163.
[6] *The case of Thomas Bushell truly stated*, London, 1649. British Museum, C. 27, f. 1, *A Just and true Remonstrance of His Majesties Mines Royal in Wales*, 1642.
[7] *Ibid.* Five subscribed £500 and four £300.
[8] *The Petition of Thomas Bushell* (1660) $\left[\text{Brit. Mus.} \dfrac{516 \cdot \text{m} \cdot 18}{95} \right]$.

avoid the heavy charges of sending the silver to London to be coined, a mint was established at Aberystwyth, and the coins struck there were to be marked by feathers on the obverse and reverse[1]. This mint continued its operations, in coining silver ore and plate on behalf of the Royalists, until it was seized by the Parliamentary forces. By 1647 Goodyere, one of the shareholders in Bushell's company, petitioned for its re-establishment[2].

Since most of the prominent members of the society were Royalists, its operations were suspended from 1650 to 1660[3]. After the Restoration the undertaking was revived and its organization modified in several respects. Many of the shareholders were also interested in the Mineral and Battery Works, and, partly because both had adopted the farming system, partly too since the latter had rights of mine royal elsewhere than in the counties reserved to the older society, it was decided to elect one governor (Prince Rupert), nine deputy-governors, and thirteen assistants for the two undertakings[4]. This arrangement was begun as a temporary measure in 1663, and was made permanent in 1668[5]. Another working agreement was effected with the Royal African company a few years later. The reason for this arrangement was that the latter had the right of mine royal within its chartered limits[6]. It imported considerable quantities of gold and the guineas coined from this metal were distinguished by a small elephant, copied from the arms of the company[7]. By this agreement an effort was made to control the production of the precious metals in British dominions—the Royal African company importing gold and the Society of Mines Royal supplying silver, which understanding, according to Pettus, conduced to "the better entercourse between them in such publick concerns[8]."

About 1670 an effort was made to prosecute silver mining in a vigorous manner as distinguished from the policy of depending on the proceeds of leases. In that year another subsidiary company was formed which was described as *the Undertaking for the Working of Mines*

[1] *Annals of the Coinage of Britain,* by Rogers Ruding, London, 1817, III. p. 162.

[2] *Reports of the Com. Hist. MSS.,* VI. p. 162.

[3] The revival of the society may have taken place in 1658, since Pettus speaks of his having become "a participant" "about" twelve years before 1670, *Fodinæ Regales,* dedication "to my Honoured Friends of the Societies of the Mines and Mineral Works."

[4] *Fodinæ Regales,* p. 25.

[5] *Opera Mineralia Explicata, or the Mineral Kingdom within the Dominions of Great Britain display'd, being a complete History of the Antient Corporations of the City of London, of and for the Mines, the Mineral and Battery Works,* by M[oses] S[tringer], M.D., 1713, p. ix.   [6] *Vide supra,* p. 20.

[7] State Papers, Domestic, Charles II., CXXXVI. 50; *Calendar,* 1663-4, p. 389.

[8] *Fodinæ Regales,* p. 27.

Royal in the Counties of Cardigan and Merioneth. The proposed capital was fixed at £4,200, divided into forty-two shares of £100 each. There was a clause in the "articles of subscription," which disallowed the holding of more than three shares by any member. Voting rights consisted of one vote for each share up to the maximum of three, subject to the proviso that no member might record more than a single vote, unless five shareholders were "personally present[1]." Twice a year general meetings were to be held, on which occasions the roll of shareholders was called, and those absent were fined 20s. each. At the general meetings "a standing committee" of nine persons was elected, at the deliberations of which any member might be present. A full meeting of the committee consisted of five, always provided that three at least must be members of the committee. These articles also contain full details of the salaries and duties of the subordinate officials, such as the Surveyor-General (£100 a year and $\frac{2}{40}$ths of the clear profit), the Chief Steward (the same), the Steward (£30), the Clerk of the Mines (£30), the Clerk or "Register" (£20), the Sergeant (£10)[2].

Information is wanting as to the history of this subsidiary company. It is not improbable that, after the capital had been spent, it was wound up, and the society reverted to the system of farming out the right of mine royal in certain areas. In cases where lead was found containing silver and no royalty had been paid, it endeavoured to establish its claims, and actions were said to have been frequent[3]. A somewhat remarkable instance of this happened in 1690, when Sir Carberry Price discovered a vein of lead, containing large quantities of silver, and there was considerable litigation, which resulted in the act of 1693 to prevent disputes about royal mines[4]. The society petitioned against this measure which, it was advised, "would be very prejudicial to its just rights and privileges[5]." This act, which permitted any person, owning ground containing precious metals, to work it under reservation of certain rights of pre-emption to the Crown, necessarily terminated the

---

[1] *I.e.* not represented by proxy.

[2] *Articles of Agreement and Subscription between His Highness Prince Rupert and Divers Noble and Honourable Persons and others, for the Undertakers for working of Mines Royal in the Counties of Cardigan and Merioneth*, London, 1670, British Museum, C. 27, f. 1.

[3] Lansd. MS. (British Museum), 841, ff. 161, 162.

[4] *A familiar Discourse or Dialogue concerning the Mine-Adventure*, by William Shiers, London, 1709, p. 3. According to Stringer, Price was aided by Edmund Waller, a former official of the society who was described as "a viper nourished in the Society's bosom," *Opera Mineralia Explicata*, p. 245. Waller was subsequently the manager of "the Mine Adventure."

[5] House of Lords MSS., "Corporations of London. Bill Royal Mynes reade, Jan. 26, 1693."

active existence of the society. As a corporation, in close relation to the Mineral and Battery Works, it continued to exist in as far as, it is said, meetings were held, and in 1710 a complete union was effected. Up to 1716 shares had been assigned by deed, but after that date, by-laws were made, according to which such assignments could only be effected in the transfer books of the united companies[1]. Evidently the governor and assistants were able to convince speculators that the corporate existence had been maintained, for in 1718 the charters were transferred to "Onslow's Insurance Company," by the latter purchasing the shares in the two societies from the owners of them. At this date it would appear that the shares of the Mines Royal had been increased to the same number as those of the Mineral and Battery Works, and that both were dealt with in the form of half-shares, 124 of these parts were sold for cash at £23. 6s. 8d. each, and a few of the shareholders in the societies were credited with the sums due them towards the calls on their insurance stock. On this basis the value of the Elizabethan undertakings in 1718 did not exceed £3,500. The insurance company carried on business under the very cumbrous title of the "Societies of the Mines Royal and of the Mineral and Battery Works who have undertaken to insure ships at sea." In 1720 this use of the original charters was submitted to a parliamentary committee, which decided that "the carrying on of insurance under these charters was both illegal and unwarrantable[2]." The same instruments were used during the boom of 1720 for floating a mining company[3], and from that date till the end of the century there are references which tend to show that from time to time they were still in use.

[1] MS. Rawl. (Bod. Lib.), C. 441, f. 120.
[2] *Special Report of the Committee appointed to inquire into and examine the several subscriptions for Fisheries, Insurance and Annuities for Lives*, London, 1720, p. 40. The subsequent history of the insurance company will be found below in Division XI., Section 4.
[3] *Daily Courant*, February 8, 1720.

SECTION II. THE MINES ROYAL OF SCOTLAND AND IRELAND.

GOLD.
JOACHIM HÖCHSTETTER AND PARTNERS (1526).
CORNELIUS DE VOIS AND PARTNERS (1567).
ABRAHAM PETERSON AND PARTNERS (1576).
EUSTACHIUS ROCHE AND PARTNERS (1583).
PROPOSED COMPANY OF STEPHEN ATKINSON AND PARTNERS (EARLY 17TH CENTURY).
JAMES MARQUIS OF HAMILTON AND PARTNERS (1631)

SILVER.
JOHN ACHESON AND PARTNERS (1563).
JAMES CARMICHAELL AND PARTNERS (1565).
THOMAS FOULLIS (1592).
SIR GEORGE HAMILTON AND PARTNERS (1612).
SIR WILLIAM ALEXANDER AND PARTNERS (1613).

THE mining of the precious metals in Scotland had been carried on from a very early date. As early as 1153 there is a record of a grant, by David I. to the Abbey of Dunfermline, of a tithe of all the gold, which would accrue to him[1]. In Scotland the royal right to all mines of gold and to any silver mines, where "thre half-pennys of silver may be fynit owt of the punde of leide," was established by act of Parliament in 1424[2]. Early in the sixteenth century, the gold mines at Crawfurd Muir were discovered, and these were worked at intervals until 1524.

In 1526 a group of Germans and Dutchmen, headed by Joachim Höchstetter, received a grant for forty-three years of all gold and silver mines in Scotland[3]. In the following year the partners had sustained

[1] *Early Records relating to Mining in Scotland*, by R. W. Cochran-Patrick, Edinburgh, 1878, p. xiii.
[2] *Acts of the Parliaments of Scotland*, II. p. 5.
[3] *Ibid.*, II. p. 310.

great loss, and some of them remained to coin moneys for the Crown[1]. By 1531 it was necessary to pay the passages of the miners to their homes[2].

A fresh start was made in 1539 when miners were brought from Lorraine, and it is recorded that, by 1542, 112¾ oz. of native gold had been consumed in additions to the regalia, besides a considerable quantity in coinage.

The next important effort was made by Cornelius de Vois (or de Vos), who had been engaged in searching for alum and copperas in England, and had been desirous of seeking for the precious metals there, but had been excluded by the grants to Höchstetter and Humfrey[3]. De Vois was recommended to the Scottish authorities by Queen Elizabeth and, on March 4th, 1567, a contract was signed in his favour by the Regent and Council, which set forth that the mines of gold and silver had been decayed through want of men of knowledge and judgment to work them. The council, being satisfied that De Vois possessed these qualities, and that he would "assail and enterprize" the seeking of mines without cost to the State, decreed that he and his partners might enter private property to search for minerals during a term of nineteen years. For this period, all other persons were prohibited from gold or silver mining, and also from molesting the miners under pain of death. De Vois, on his part, undertook to set labourers to work, and to pay to the Crown 8 per cent. of the gold or silver obtained by washing, and 4 per cent. of that reduced by fire[4].

On the signing of the contract, De Vois prospected the hills in Clydesdale, where "he gott a small taste of small gold—this was a whett-stone to sharpen his knife uppon, and this naturall gold tasted so sweete as the honny or honny combe[5]." These imaginative descriptions, quoted by Stephen Atkinson, appear to be the words of De Vois, who left behind him a record of his operations, which Atkinson had read. It is worth noting that these glowing expressions are less the joy of the fortunate prospector than the bait of the sixteenth-century promoter. De Vois brought to Edinburgh specimens of his finds, some the size of birds' eggs or birds' eyes—these he called the temptable or alluring gold, like "unto a woman's eye, which intiseth hir joyes into hir bosome." The joint attractions of the miner's language and of the gold itself

[1] Acts of the Lords of Council, printed in *Records of the Coinage of Scotland*, by R. Cochran-Patrick, Edinburgh, 1876, I. p. 64.

[2] R. Cochran-Patrick, *Records of Mining in Scotland*, p. xv.

[3] State Papers, Domestic, Elizabeth, xxxvi. 72; *Calendar*, 1547–80, p. 253.

[4] The Contract, Reg. Privy Council, I. p. 612, printed in *Records of Mining in Scotland*, pp. 12–15.

[5] *The Discoverie and Historie of the Gold Mynes in Scotland*, by Stephen Atkinson, written in the year 1619 (Bannatyne Club, 1825), p. 18.

sufficed to secure the formation of a syndicate to prosecute the discoveries. In the first instance, the venture was divided into fifty parts or shares, allocated amongst six different interests. De Vois and his partners in London had ten shares; another German at Edinburgh, as well as the Earl of Morton and the Secretary held the same number, and two other interests received five shares each[1]. This allocation being made, the members of the syndicate prevailed upon their friends and relatives to join in the adventure. The whole amount, subscribed, amounted to £5,000 Scots, and what is most important in the transaction is the manner in which this capital was provided. According to Atkinson's account, all the partners, "being willing, consented togeather, some bought corne, some victuals and some malt or meale, besides monies and amongst them all, £5,000 Scotts[2]." In this way, as in other contemporary undertakings, capital was furnished in the form of commodities.

Alluvial deposits were worked and 120 persons were employed, "both ladds and lasses, idle men and women, which before went a begging[3]." There were two modes of payment, either on days' wages at 4d. per day or on piece-work, when between 13s. 4d. and £1 sterling was paid for the ounce of gold. At this time the ounce was sold to the mint at Edinburgh at 60s.; so that, even the highest scale of piece-work payment left a very large profit. During one period of thirty days, no less than eight pounds of gold, valued at £450 sterling was sent to the mint[4]. In 1572 the benefits of this grant were assigned by the partners to Arnold von Bronchhorst[5].

Bronchhorst soon retired from the enterprize and Abraham Peterson, one of the partners in De Vois' company, founded a new partnership in 1576. Peterson, a German, who was also known as "Grey-beard[6]," realized his property in Edinburgh and obtained capital from some of his fellow-countrymen. Extensive store-houses were built and tools provided. For some years the operations met with considerable success, and it is related that a bowl was made of this gold, capable of containing a gallon[7].

The next grant was that in favour of Eustachius Roche in 1583, and confirmed by Parliament in the following year. It resembled that made to De Vois sixteen years before, except that the period was to be twenty-

[1] The shares mentioned by Atkinson, as divided amongst *five* persons, amount to 45. Since he says that De Vois had six partners it is likely that the other person, not named, received the remaining five shares.

[2] Atkinson, *Discoverie of Gold Mynes*, p. 20.   [3] *Ibid.*, p. 21.

[4] This single consignment exceeded the value of the capital of the company.

[5] R. Cochran-Patrick, *Records of Mining in Scotland*, p. xvii.

[6] He could tie his beard round his waist.

[7] Atkinson, *Discoverie of Gold Mynes*, p. 22.

one years and, instead of applying to gold and silver only, in this case powers were given to mine copper, tin and lead as well, with the exception of certain mines owned by the Earl of Arran, which were subsequently controlled by Roche under a separate tack. The tacksman had the sole right of searching for the metals named, of entering on private property for the purposes of such search and of taking wood, peat and coal for fuel[1].

Roche, like his predecessors, divided the concession into shares and took partners. According to his own account, the company was at "exorbitant charges" and incurred great loss[2]. Therefore it was not long before Roche and partners were in want of capital to develop the extensive concession secured. Accordingly in 1592 a number of suits were commenced against Roche for the reduction of his tack, which had still eleven years to run. He was charged with being a person of evil fame in his own country, who had neither worked the mines he had discovered nor those already known. In one case a proprietor, who had discovered a mine, could not make arrangements with Roche for the development of it. From another point of view, a more serious charge was that he had failed to pay the royalty accrued to the Crown. Roche replied to these charges, stating that he had been molested in his operations, and one of his men had been killed. Other persons became involved in the dispute, and finally the tack was reduced[3].

In connection with the proceedings against Roche, it was decided in 1592 that, owing to the failure of the tacksman to develope the mines, in future they should be controlled by a "Master of the Metalls"—an office which was established by act of Parliament[4]. The most enterprizing holder of this office was Sir Bevis Bulmer, who had been successful in silver mining in England, and who had established one of the earliest water-supply undertakings at London. Bulmer obtained some gold, which he reduced from "sapper stone" by means of a crushing-mill. James I. soon found difficulty in supplying the capital required, and devised a "plott" for carrying on the work on the same lines as the Nova Scotia undertaking[5]. Twenty-four gentlemen were to be invited to subscribe £500 sterling each, and in addition to their shares each was to obtain the title of "Knight of the Golden Mines," or "the Golden Knight[6]."

Atkinson, whose work has been frequently quoted, had found some gold, which he brought to London, and he obtained promises from

---

[1] R. Cochran-Patrick, *Records of Mining in Scotland*, pp. 16–22.
[2] *Ibid.*, p. 60.   [3] *Ibid.*, pp. 22–78.
[4] *Acts of the Parliaments of Scotland*, III. p. 555.
[5] *Vide supra*, pp. 318, 319.
[6] Atkinson, *Discoverie of Gold Mynes*, p. 45.

certain merchants to adventure with him. The specimens had been entrusted to a Groom of the Bed-chamber, from whom Atkinson was unable to recover them, so that he failed to produce the gold, when required by his partners, whereupon they withdrew their support, on the ground that the enterprize was more fitting "for princes than for subjects[1]." In 1621 a lease was granted for gold mines for 21 years and another for 7 years to James Marquis of Hamilton and his partners in 1631[2]. Dudley Dudley mentions that he saw in 1637 six men wash grains of gold, some an ounce in weight, from several barrow-loads of earth they had collected; and again in 1654 he relates how Sir James Hope showed him some bags containing gold obtained in Scotland[3].

The foregoing account of gold-mining operations shows that, in Scotland the privilege of mine royal was sought chiefly in connection with gold. At the same time efforts were made to obtain silver also. At this period copper had not been discovered in Scotland, and therefore silver was sought in lead ores. There were no means of separating it in the country, and it was necessary that the extraction should be made abroad. In 1562 John Acheson and his partners were authorized to mine and transport 20,000 stone of lead ore, paying 900 oz. of silver for the privilege. In 1565 this royalty was duly paid, and the Earl of Atholl obtained a grant to export 40,000 stone at a royalty of 50 oz. of silver per 1,000 stone of ore, as against 45 oz. paid by Acheson. These mines were situated at Glengonar and Wanloch. In the same year a similar grant was made to a partnership of Edinburgh merchants[4].

On the expiration of these leases in 1576, George Douglas of Parkhead obtained a new tack, which was transferred to Roche, who held a monopoly of all the more valuable metals. After the reduction of the lease of the latter[5], Douglas was granted a new tack of lead mines at Over-Glengonar, on a royalty of 50 oz. of silver per 1,000 stone of lead ore[6]. At the end of December 1593, Douglas sub-let his privilege to Thomas Foullis, an Edinburgh goldsmith[7]. At this time James VI. was indebted to Foullis to the extent of £14,598 Scots; and, in recognition of this loan, the goldsmith received a grant of all the mines in Lanarkshire for 21 years at a rental of 1,000 marks[8]. Foullis confined himself

[1] Atkinson, *Discoverie of Gold Mynes*, p. 33.

[2] R. Cochran-Patrick, *Records of Mining in Scotland*, p. xxi.

[3] *Dud. Dudley's Metallum Martis; or Iron made with Pit Coal, Sea Coale &c.*, 1665, reprinted in *Supplement to the Series of Letters Patent and Specifications...in the Great Seal Patent Office*, edited by Bennet Woodcroft, 1858, 1. pp. 58, 59.

[4] R. Cochran-Patrick, *Records of Mining in Scotland*, pp. 4–9.

[5] *Vide supra*, p. 409.

[6] R. Cochran-Patrick, *Records of Mining in Scotland*, p. xxxvi.

[7] *Ibid.*, p. 97.

[8] *Ibid.*, p. 99. *Edinburgh Merchants in the Olden Time*, by Robert Chambers, Edinburgh, 1859, p. 8.

to lead mining, and the property descended to his niece, who married Sir James Hope of Hopetoun, and their successors were intimately connected with Scottish lead mining during the whole of the following century.

In 1606 an important find of silver was made at Hilderston. Atkinson, who refined some of the ore sent to London, states that he obtained silver to the value of £100 sterling a day from it[1]. It was estimated that the mine would yield the King a profit of £500 a month[2], but there is good reason to believe, both from later assays and the accounts of the expenses at the mines, that the returns were much smaller[3].

In 1613 these mines were let to Sir William Alexander, Thomas Foullis, Paulo Pinto and any partners, they shall "adjeyne unto tham," at a royalty of one-tenth of the produce. It was provided in these articles that, in the event of any of the "associates" leaving no heirs, his part was to revert to the rest of the society. The King reserved a right of expropriating this company, when it had brought the mines to perfection, at a sum of £100,000 Scots[4].

Although there are isolated references to silver mining in Scotland—such as a find in Sutherland in 1620, and an improved process of extraction in 1701—it was not till 1715 that the next important discovery was made. It is stated that "14 oz. of ore produced 12 oz. of silver, and that, for a short period, the proceeds of the mine were £4,000 a week. It very soon, however, decreased in value, and eventually the workings were abandoned[5]."

The mines royal in the Pale in Ireland had been assigned to the society of the Mineral and Battery Works under the grants of Elizabeth[6]. As time went on this right was allowed to lapse, and, when in 1612 a discovery of silver was made in the parish of Kilmore in Tipperary, which yielded 3 lb. of silver to the ton, the privilege of mining was secured by a small company or syndicate in which Sir George Hamilton, Sir Basil Brook and Sir William Russel were interested[7]. In the reign of Charles I., Sir G. Hamilton procured the concession for mine royal, and he had expended "several thousand £s," especially on workings, known as the

---

[1] Atkinson, *Discoverie of Gold Mynes*, p. 47.

[2] R. Cochran-Patrick, *Records of Mining in Scotland*, p. 117.

[3] Accounts of the Silver Mines at Hilderston, MSS. General Register House, in *Records of Mining in Scotland*, pp. 141–57; *The History of England*, 1603–16, by S. R. Gardiner (1863), II. pp. 418, 419; *An Abstract or Brief Declaration of the Present State of His Majesties Revenew*, 1651, p. 13.

[4] R. Cochran-Patrick, *Records of Mining in Scotland*, p. 159.

[5] *Ibid.*, p. xliii.   [6] *Vide infra*, p. 414.

[7] *Ireland's Natural History*, by Gerard Boate, edited by Samuel Hartlib, London, 1652, p. 141.

"Silver Mine" in county Kilkenny, which gave great hopes of profit prior to the outbreak of the Civil War. Charles II. renewed the patent in favour of Sir J. Hamilton, son of the original grantee. Both he and his son, the Earl of Abercorn, appear to have found silver mining a profitable speculation, since the latter was continuing operations in 1703, when he petitioned against the Mines Royal bill then before the Irish Parliament[1].

[1] *Journals of the House of Commons of Ireland*, II. Pt. I. p. 344; *The Industrial Resources of Ireland*, by Robert Kane, Dublin, 1845, pp. 199, 209, 217, 221. Kane notes a great discovery of gold towards the end of the eighteenth century in Wicklow.

SECTION III. THE GOVERNORS, ASSISTANTS AND SOCIETY OF THE MINERAL AND BATTERY WORKS. (FOUNDED 1565, INCORPORATED 1568.)

THIS organization partook partly of the character of a mining venture, partly of the nature of a manufacture. Since however it was closely connected with the society of Mines Royal, and since moreover the two undertakings were eventually worked together, its history will be more easily followed if it is dealt with in close connection with that of the Mines Royal.

There were several lines of commercial development, apparently diverse, which converge in the establishment of the business, known as the Mineral and Battery Works, such as the smelting of iron, the drawing of iron wire and the making of a kind of brass known as "latten," as well as the searching for, and the working of a number of minerals. These various activities found a point of unity in their contact with the wool trade. One element of success lay in the carding of wool; and, before the reign of Elizabeth, the cards had been imported. It was considered desirable that there should be a reasonable quantity of these produced in England. But, to make wool cards, both iron and brass wire were needed. English iron was not sufficiently ductile to be drawn into fine wire, and therefore a manufacturer would have to produce his own iron. Then, again, the making of the mixed metal, known as "latten"—a species of brass—required, by the process used, zinc ore, which was generally spoken of as calamine stone (*lapis calaminaris*). Finally, to obtain such ores considerable prospecting and mining operations would be necessary.

On July 16th, 1565, William Humfrey petitioned for the privilege of introducing battery works into England[1]; and in September of the same year, in a fuller application, it is stated that there were at least four other persons interested, besides Humfrey[2]. This syndicate had undertaken to provide twenty foreign workmen and to draw iron wire

---

[1] State Papers, Domestic, Elizabeth, xxxvi. 81; *Calendar*, 1547-80, p. 254.
[2] *Ibid.*, xxxvii. 30; *Calendar*, 1547-80, p. 258.

by mechanical power, using a water-mill, instead of by manual labour, as had hitherto been the practice in England. In order to find the ores, required for the special iron, as well as for making latten, powers were asked for the rights of prospecting, mining, and refining a long list of various species of ores[1]. On September 17th, 1565, two grants were signed—the one authorizing Humfrey and his partners to set up battery works, and the other to possess the sole privilege of searching for calamine stone anywhere in England, and also to mine all species of minerals (except alum and copperas), in all the counties not reserved by the grant to the founders of the Mines Royal, as well as in the Pale in Ireland[2]. Furthermore, base metals might be worked in these reserved counties. The promoters were empowered to search for the specified ores, on giving compensation to the owners of property they entered, and were licensed to impress workmen, waggons and horses. It was also provided that the grant was perpetual, subject to the recalling of it by Elizabeth, who undertook that such revocation should be to control the industry herself, and in no case to re-grant these privileges to others[3].

Just as in the case of the Mines Royal, the possessors of these far-reaching concessions felt that they required the countenance of persons of influence and the assistance of capitalists. Accordingly, within a short time, shares were sold and the whole undertaking was divided into thirty-six shares, each of which was further divisible subsequently into halves or quarters.

Up to November 1565 the search for calamine had not been successful, and it was suggested that Höchstetter was impeding the investigation[4]. If this were so, such a hindrance was easily removed, since most of the prominent persons, interested in this undertaking, were shareholders in the Mines Royal. By June of the following year, Humfrey was able to announce that he had been fortunate in finding the desired ore in Somerset[5], and that he had surveyed a number of rivers with a view to fixing a site for wire works[6]. At the same date good iron ore had been

---

[1] Anderson, *Historical and Chronological Deduction of the Origin of Commerce*, Dublin, 1790, II. p. 163.   [2] *Vide supra*, p. 384.

[3] State Papers, Domestic, Elizabeth, XXXVII. 40–4; *Calendar*, 1547–80, p. 259; Sloan MS. 2483 (Brit. Mus.), ff. 4–10; *Fodinæ Regales*, by Sir J. Pettus, p. 57; *History of London*, by W. Maitland, 1774, II. p. 1269; *Opera Mineralia Explicata, or the Mineral Kingdom within the Dominions of Great Britain display'd, being a complete History of the Antient Corporations...for the Mines, the Mineral and Battery Works*, by M[oses] S[tringer], 1713, pp. 22–72.

[4] State Papers, Domestic, Elizabeth, XXXVII. 73; *Calendar*, 1547–80, p. 261.

[5] In Camden, *Britannia* (second edition, I. p. 83), it is said that calamine was found near the surface at the west end of the Mendip Hills.

[6] State Papers, Domestic, Elizabeth, XL. 9, 17; *Calendar*, 1547–80; pp. 274–5.

found in the Forest of Dean, and coal within a mile of Bristol. The Earl of Pembroke (who was a shareholder in the society of Mines Royal, and was probably interested in this undertaking) lent the castle at Bristol for temporary smelting operations[1]. It was decided to erect buildings for the making of iron and drawing of wire in Monmouthshire; and, by November of the same year, these were far advanced[2]. Towards the close of the session of Parliament, a bill was promoted to confirm the royal grant, and on December 13th, owing to "a diversity of opinion" amongst the members of the House of Lords, it was judged expedient to substitute for it two proposed measures—the one dealing with the iron works and the other with the brass manufacture[3]. The original instrument had been introduced and read a first time on December 4th, but there is no record discoverable of this or the amended proposals having been proceeded with[4]. Humfrey speaks of "exceedingly great hindrances," he had experienced, and it was not till the end of January 1568 that latten or brass was actually produced[5]. In consequence of this success and in view of the establishment of wire-drawing mills, the partners approached the Queen; and, probably through the intervention of Sir W. Cecil and the Earl of Leicester, both of whom were shareholders, a charter of incorporation was granted on May 28th, 1568. The preamble states the members had "at great charges and expense" brought the work of making iron, wire and brass "to very good effect"; and, since these manufactures were beneficial, the partners were incorporated, with perpetual succession and a common seal, so as to avoid the great inconveniences likely to be caused by deaths, as *the Governors, Assistants and Society of the Mineral and Battery Works*. The members had the right, at the annual general meeting, of choosing two governors, two deputy-governors, and eight assistants[6]. By the "constitutions, made by those that were first incorporated," it was provided that "a general, stable and set court" was to be held on the first Thursday in December annually for election of these officials, while a "full court" was to be kept on the first Tuesday of each month. At these meetings the quorum consisted of a minimum of twelve members, which must include a governor or deputy-governor, four assistants and six of the comminalty. Shareholders were subject to a fine of 40*s.* for absence from a court. It was further agreed that

[1] State Papers, Domestic, Elizabeth, XL. 63; *Calendar*, 1547–80, p. 278.
[2] *Ibid.*, XLI. 12; *Calendar*, 1547–80, p. 282.
[3] *Ibid.*, XLI. 42; *Calendar*, 1547–80, p. 283.
[4] *The Journals of all the Parliaments during the Reign of Queen Elizabeth*, by Sir Simonds D'Ewes, London, 1682, p. 110.
[5] State Papers, Domestic, Elizabeth, XLVI. 17, 18; *Calendar*, 1547–80, p. 305.
[6] Sloan MS. 2483 (Brit. Mus.), ff. 11–16; *Fodinæ Regales*, p. 60.

the governing body might borrow up to a maximum of £14. 6s. 8d. on each part or share[1].

By July 10th, 1568, Humfrey was able to complete his accounts of the expenditure incurred. The outlay was made up of the charges in bringing to England the German workmen and maintaining them, the expense of searching for calamine and other ores, as well as the cost of buildings and plant, as far as these had been established up to that date. The manner, by which capital was provided, affords an interesting example of the methods of early joint-stock finance. The whole undertaking was divided into thirty-six shares and, owing to the delay in reaching the producing stage, it was necessary to make several calls upon the shares. Humfrey seems to hint at unskilled or fraudulent management when he wrote "the thing through evill handling is presentlie of noe more estimation than at first, being also partly discredited through the great fame the Allmeignes doings had in the beginning, whereof with those great charges, noe benefit has come to any men's handes, and the like is supposed to ensue of this enterprize, yet having manifest appearance of very great commodities to induce men to an earnest opinion of much gain." It appears that Cecil and Leicester were not disposed to pay the calls required, and Humfrey sold one of three shares belonging to the latter and one of four of the former's, in order to provide funds on their behalf to satisfy the assessments on the remainder of the holding of each. In the case of Cecil, this course freed him from further liability until £200 per share had been levied. Since there were thirty-six shares, the called up capital, when this amount per share was assessed, was £7,200[2]. In a further letter, Humfrey draws attention to the delay occasioned by want of funds, and he proposes an assessment or call of £40 per share. He records a formidable list of works, still to be accomplished, such as a hammer-house for the latten-works, a foundry, a forge, "casting stones" (which are £10 per pair in Normandy) and rollers—described as "instruments of great charge at the first erecting." There were also 5 tons of copper to be paid for. To induce the shareholders to meet the call, it was shown that, in the past nine months, two miners and two labourers had raised a quantity of calamine, which had cost only £333. 6s. 8d., whereas the same amount at

---

[1] *Opera Mineralia Explicata*, pp. 84–92.

[2] State Papers, Domestic, Elizabeth, xlvii. 10; *Calendar*, 1547–80, p. 311. Humfrey's language is not very clear. He writes: "I always studied by what means your Lordship's more weighty business might not be troubled for those matters, finding no device better or safer for you than that I used for my Lord Leicester which was *to give out one of his Lordship's three parts to have the charges of the other two defrayed.*"..."I hope to get the charges of three parts borne for the fourth untill £200 be levied upon every part."

Nuremberg would have been worth four times as much[1]. It would seem that, although calls up to £200 a share were mentioned, it was not necessary to exact the whole amount proposed; since, from a document drawn up in 1597, it was stated that, for the first twenty-one years, the society had been at "charges" (*i.e.* capital outlay by assessments as distinguished from expenditure from undivided profits) of 10,000 marks or £6,666. 16*s*. 8*d*., making the sum called up per share £185[2].

The brass works were situated in Nottinghamshire and also at London. It is probable that, when iron wire was produced in Monmouthshire, it was sent thence to be made into wool-cards. Pettus records that these factories together employed 8,000 hands, and that they had been highly successful[3]. There seems little doubt that these branches of the society's operations were exceedingly lucrative, since all the "great cost" of the buildings, engines and tools for the wire works and iron mills was provided "by increase of the profits[4]." There is much important information relating to the Monmouthshire works in a series of documents drawn up by Cornelius Avenant, who had been appointed "solicitor" to the society in 1580 with a view to increasing the revenue from this part of the undertaking. In pursuance of his duties, it became necessary for him to investigate the leases made by the society to subordinate associations of its members, which farmed the wire and iron mills; and he also discovered that the Duke of Norfolk had owned one whole share, whereupon he claimed that arrears of profits on this were recoverable by Elizabeth under the forfeiture. In dealing with Avenant's statements, the special purpose he had in view must be remembered, especially when he records the past profits of the society. In his "Bill of complaint on her Majesty's behalf[5]," he begins by summarizing the privileges and constitution of the society, and shows that Norfolk held one share, which reverted to the Queen on his attainder[6]. He then states that the works in Monmouth had been erected "by increase of the profits." The document continues, "the society had been at charges in the premises to the value of 10,000 marks, and the profit for the 21 years amounted to £21,000 (£1,000 per annum).... If the mineral and battery works had been thoroughly employed, they would have yielded fifteen times as much as the wire works, amounting to £15,000 per annum[7]." The interpretation of this clause presents many difficulties. It would seem that "the premises" mean the iron and wire works, mentioned in the previous sentences, but

[1] State Papers, Domestic, Elizabeth, XLVII. 11; *Calendar*, 1547–80, p. 311.
[2] A Summary of Avenant's Bill of Complaint...against certain of the company of the Mineral and Battery Works: Brit. Mus. Lansd. MS. 56 (47).
[3] *Fodinæ Regales*, p. 33.   [4] Lansd. MS., *ut supra*, 56 (47).
[5] *Ibid.*   [6] *Ibid.*, §§ 1–3.   [7] *Ibid.*, § 4.

there is conclusive evidence that although, from about 1570, these had been let at a rent commencing at £150 a year, this rent was not paid[1]. Therefore, if the term "the premisses" refers to the Monmouthshire works, the profits, by which they were developed and which constituted the capital outlay, must have come from the other branches of the society's business. Moreover, at no time during the period ending in 1586 were the rents of the iron and wire works as much as £1,000 a year, so that it would appear certain that the capital outlay of 10,000 marks, yielding an average profit of £1,000 a year over twenty-one years, relates to the brass works and the making of wool-cards. It would therefore follow that it was out of the surplus of this profit that the Monmouthshire undertakings were established, which were leased to successive partnerships, formed by shareholders of the society at various rents. Taking all the circumstances into account, this is likely to be the true history of the early finances of the society; but, before accepting it definitely, it should be added that another interpretation of Avenant's language is possible. As "solicitor" he was prosecuting numerous suits against different associations of farmers for fraudulent or concealed profits and it may have been, that, although the works in Monmouth did not give a rent of £1,000 a year, he estimated these concealed profits at that sum. Should this be so, the outlay of 10,000 marks would relate to these undertakings, and not to the foundation of the brass and wool-card industry. This view gains some additional confirmation from the fact that Avenant's statements are concerned exclusively with the wire and iron mills, and that he nowhere expressly mentions the factories at Nottingham and London. Whatever happened as to the allocation of original outlay and profits, as between different branches of the society's manufactures, there is no doubt that it was the wool-card and brass making that was most profitable, as is shown by the fact that numerous grants were obtained during over a century to encourage these, and that there is recorded a case of a composition made by a debtor in 1593, where £1,000 was offered in satisfaction of all claims, made up of monies arising from Drake's adventure to St Domingo, a balance upon "the Barbary account," "arrears of dividends for the mineral, battery and copper works," as well as other sums from plate and some debts due to the estate[2].

The brass and wool-card industries being, as far as can be gathered, remarkably profitable during a long period, the shareholders sedulously avoided making any statements of the gains. But the accessory parts of the undertaking (namely the mills where the wire was drawn for the wool-cards and the furnaces where the special iron—described as Osmonde

---

[1] Add. MS. (Brit. Mus.) 12,503, ff. 157–64, §§ 1, 2.
[2] State Papers, Domestic, Elizabeth, ccxlvi. 12; *Calendar*, 1591–4, pp. 386, 387.

iron—suitable for making into wire, were worked) were controlled by the society, which arranged that wire should be supplied to it at a certain price.

The farming of the wire and iron works began as early as 1571, when Sir Richard Martyn[1], Richard Hanbery and a Mr Palmer took a lease for three years at £150 a year[2]. Martyn purchased additional shares and by 1574 he owned 7 or 8, which gave him a proportionate number of votes, or as they were termed "voices[3]." At the court meeting, held in December 1574, these partners exhibited an account which showed a profit per week of £3. 1s. 0d., or only a very small amount in excess of the rent they had been paying. On the basis of this showing, they offered the small sum of £24 a year for a new lease. Avenant asserted that in this account there were very grave concealments, and that the actual week's profit was £22. 18s. 4d. or £1,191. 13s. 4d. a year[4]. As against the reduced offer of Martyn and his partners, another shareholder tendered 500 marks a year, whereupon Martyn made a new bid, which was accepted for the next four years (i.e. 1575–8). He undertook to add two new hammers to those already in existence at the wire works, and to pay a rent of £200 a year[5]. At the end of 1575 the partners presented another account, according to which a profit of £600 had been made, and the lease was amended by separating the wire works from the iron furnaces. Martyn now obtained "a farm" of the former for 15 years at £250 a year and of the latter at £40 a year. Although these deeds were duly executed, according to Avenant, not only was the rent unpaid, but a quantity of stock, handed over to the "farmers," had been disposed of and not replaced. He also contended that there were concealed profits due to the society, and that altogether Martyn and his associates owed the other members a sum of £7,850[6]. At a court meeting, held in August 1580, Martyn and his partners protested against the amount of the rent due under the lease for the wire works. They now offered to buy the fee simple for 200 marks, or to take a new lease at a reduced rent of £24 a year. The rent proposed was only one-tenth of that reserved under the current lease, while the purchase price was five and a half times this new annual payment. Since the amended lease of 1575 had still about ten years to run, there was no reason to justify the acceptance of this great reduction; but it was alleged that, through Martyn's "indirect getting of voices" at the meeting, he would have carried his point, had not a motion for an adjournment been carried[7].

---

[1] Governor of the Russia company in 1582.
[2] Add. MS. 12,503, ut supra, § 1.
[3] Lansd. MS. 56 (47), § 8.
[4] Ibid., §§ 6, 7.
[5] Ibid., § 8.
[6] Add. MS. 12,503, § 2.
[7] Ibid., § 3.

The interest in these complicated transactions now shifts to some differences between Martyn and Hanbery. The former charged the latter with fraudulent concealments of profits in the partnership account, and an involved suit was commenced between the parties in the Lord Mayor's Court at London in 1582. No less than 50 "interrogatories" were filed on behalf of the plaintiff, when the case was suddenly submitted to arbitration on the basis, according to Avenant's statement, of Hanbery paying £1,900 and taking a sub-lease from Martyn at 40 marks a day or £486. 13s. 4d. a year[1]. If only a part of Avenant's account is true, it is clear that Martyn was deceiving his fellow-shareholders in the data he submitted for a reduction of his rent for the wire works from £250 to £24.

Once these facts became whispered, such information was used by Hanbery and Martyn, acting in concert, to obtain an abatement on the original lease. Hanbery now represented that he was unable to pay the amount he had agreed to Martyn, and the latter probably stated that, unless Hanbery paid him, he could not fulfil his contract with the society; and both declared that, unless an abatement were made, they would be forced to throw up the works. Hitherto there had been no competition and none was expected on this occasion, but two other members, John Challener and Thomas Fenner offered to pay annually 1,000 marks. This represented such a substantial increase that the society gladly accepted the proposal, even at the cost of paying Martyn £500 on the ground of improvements he had made[2].

Apart from the partnership dispute there was further litigation, arising out of Hanbery's management of the wire works. In 1585 Avenant found that an excessive amount of wood was being consumed by Hanbery in making common iron to the extent of 300 tons a year. The point of this charge was that, under the original concession, the society had extensive privileges for obtaining fuel, but these grants were designed to encourage the production of the special iron required for the wool-card industry. Therefore to make ordinary iron under such immunities was unfair to persons engaged in that trade, besides being a danger to the future of the Osmonde iron works. The result of these proceedings was that Hanbery was restrained, under bond of £500, from "wasting of woods[3]".

The difficulties of the farming-system were far from being ended. Challener allowed his rent to fall into arrear and then adopted methods, which by now must have become painfully familiar to the members of the society, to obtain a reduction. Before three years of his lease had elapsed, he asked for a new agreement at £400 a year, instead of £666.

---

[1] Add. MS. 12,503, § 11; Lansd. MS. 56 (47), § 11.
[2] Add. MS. 12,503, § 6.   [3] Ibid., §§ 5, 6; Lansd. MS. 56 (47), § 10.

DIV. IV. § 3] *Farm of the Wire and Iron Works* 1582–8   421

Whereupon Avenant, George and John Catchmayne proposed to take a lease of the wire works at the old rent of 1,000 marks for three years, and thereafter at £800 a year for ten or twenty-one years more. A lease was made out on this basis, but in favour of the Catchmaynes and Challener to the exclusion of Avenant. Before long the new lessees again came before the court of the society to obtain an abatement. Sir Julius Caesar, who was afterwards a governor of the society, now appeared on the scene, in partnership with others. Caesar had learned from Avenant of the profits made in the wire and iron works, which were estimated at this time at £8,000 a year. These partners made an offer for all the Monmouth works (*i.e.* for both wire and iron mills) of £1,100 a year. At this time the iron works had been let at £50 a year, so that this proposal represents an advance of about £250 on the higher rent for the second term of Avenant's proposed lease[1]. About this time it was believed that the iron works could make a profit of £1,500 a year, besides reducing the cost and increasing the wages of some 400 hands employed[2].

At this interesting point in the negotiations, Avenant's depositions end, and the whole series of transactions is of importance, as showing in a vivid manner the system of farming out subordinate parts of the industry, and still more in bringing to light an apparent want of honesty in the consequent dealings of members of the society. As to the merits of the case, it is difficult to pronounce a very decided opinion—it is a wise judge who can give an equitable verdict based on affidavits in a commercial dispute, and certainly in the sixteenth century litigants were no more truthful in their statements than in less remote periods. Consequently it would be most hazardous to decide on a purely *ex parte* statement. However, two conclusions are established on internal evidence. Martyn was acting dishonestly in endeavouring to obtain a reduction in his current lease in 1580, when he himself was able to obtain a large bonus by sub-letting. Avenant's action in the matter cannot however be described as a model of propriety, since he, by his own admission, sought to obtain a lease from a body, by which he was employed in an office of trust, at a sum greatly below the actual value.

Before passing from the history of the minor activities of the society in the sixteenth century, some notice should be taken of its connection with lead-mining. It will be remembered that the extensive concessions granted to the undertaking included the right of all kinds of mining in counties, not reserved to the society of the Mines Royal[3]. Naturally, such operations were concerned chiefly with calamine and iron, but there are indications that other metals were sought and worked. About

[1] Add. MS. 12,503, § 10.   [2] Lansd. MS. 56 (47), §§ 4, 14.
[3] *Vide supra*, p. 414.

1590, it was alleged that the "farmers" of the iron works had sent £4,000 worth of silver from Wales to the mint. This was a direct invasion of the privilege of the Mines Royal, since the whole of Wales, as far as the precious metals were concerned, was reserved to that society[1]. In connection with lead-mining, Humfrey had invented a sieve and forge for the calamine works, and this was used in Derbyshire in lead works about 1573[2]. Some twenty years afterwards Cornelius Avenant, having failed to rent the wire works at Tintern, offered to take certain lead mines in Derbyshire for twenty-one years at a rent of £500 a year. Since mention is made of an effort to gain a proclamation prohibiting the miners from working in any other manner "than they accustomably have used time out of mind," it is to be inferred that this venture contemplated smelting by improved methods[3].

After the numerous offers for the wire works and, in spite of each tenant trying to induce the society to reduce the rent, the outstanding fact, that an increased offer was always forthcoming from someone, led to the logical conclusion that the society had a very valuable property, and it was decided that it should no longer be leased but worked on behalf of the shareholders. Therefore in 1595 the society was in possession of the wire works, and Hanbery was managing the department for making iron on behalf of a partnership which had rented it. In March of that year an agreement was made that Hanbery should supply the wire works with "meete and serviceable iron" at £12 a ton. This arrangement led to fresh litigation. The iron supplied did not satisfy the managers at the works, as sufficiently ductile, and the society complained that the mills were on short time for this reason, whereby the people "weare greatlie empoversshed and unprovided of means to live." The society refused to pay Hanbery, and he brought a suit against it in the Exchequer court, claiming that he had suffered great loss, through 400 tons of iron being left on his hands. This case was pending for a considerable period; and, in the meantime, Hanbery would not supply more iron unless he was paid for that rejected. In view of the deadlock, application was made to the Privy Council, which ordered, on June 19th, 1597, that a temporary arrangement should be made and a price was fixed, at which iron up to 160 tons a year should be supplied of the quality required[4]. In the following month the

---

[1] Add. MS. 12,503, § 7.

[2] Lansd. MS. 39 (59). The "ancient custom" of the Derbyshire lead-miners as to the use of sieves is explained in "Laws of the Lead Mines of Werksworth in Derbyshire," printed by John Houghton in *Rara Avis in Terris or the Compleat Miner*, 1680, No. xv. (*A Collection of Scarce and Valuable Treatises upon Metals*, 1740, p. 254.)

[3] Add. MS. 12,503, § 12.   [4] *Ibid.*, f. 148.

company addressed a petition to the Council stating that the iron, supplied under the order, had proved bad, and asking that Hanbery and his partner should not be allowed to compel the society to purchase it[1].

It appears that the society soon gave up the control of the wire works. By 1613 they were farmed out at a rent of £300 a year. Unfortunately the old difficulties with the tenants reappeared; and an investigation of the matters in dispute was made at two special court meetings[2]. From this date there is little information as to the fate of the works in Monmouth. Judging by the experience of over 40 years, the society found itself unable to make a profit by running the works. When it had endeavoured to obtain a considerable rent, it had been met by disingenuous practices from some of its own shareholders. Of course had the whole undertaking consisted of these properties, it would have been the duty of the management to have obtained the best returns possible, either in profit or a money rent. But, in so far as the making of wire was subsidiary to the production of wool-cards, it would obviously be to the advantage of the society to accept a lower money rent, provided the agreement contained a clause that wire should be sold by the farmers to the lessors at a low rate. In conjunction with the wool-card industry, there was also the brass trade, which was a monopoly and was in addition heavily protected. Not only was brass wire used in producing wool-cards and pins, but, in the new development of foreign trade, utensils of this metal were in great demand amongst the savages, with whom exchanges were now being effected—for instance, a brass basin frequently fetched £30 in gold on the west coast of Africa.

Thus the brass and wool-card industries were the chief directions in which the activities of the society found an outlet and, through the influential position of the shareholders, very frequent grants were obtained to safeguard the monopoly of the society. It has already been shown that the undertaking started with comprehensive privileges and concessions, and that in 1566 Humfrey was seeking confirmation of these by Parliament[3]. Again in 1581 a series of arguments, in favour of an act for the encouragement of the Tintern wire works and of card-makers, were drawn up[4]; and on July 2nd, 1584, a new patent was signed confirming the exclusive grant to Humfrey to search for calamine and to mix it with other metals. It is expressly stated that these rights were in perpetuity[5]. By 1597 the society promoted a bill in Parliament,

[1] Add. MS. 12,503, f. 147. [2] Add. MS. 12,497, f. 438.
[3] *Vide supra*, pp. 413–5.
[4] State Papers, Domestic, Elizabeth, cxlviii. 7; *Calendar*, 1581–90, p. 10.
[5] *Ibid.*, ccxli. [Docquet]; *Calendar*, 1591–4, p. 186.

re-enacting an old measure[1], which prohibited the importation of wool-cards. This bill narrowly escaped rejection in the House of Commons, where the committee decided in its favour by six votes to five[2]. On the act being passed, the position of the society was made secure, as far as privileges granted by the State could safeguard it. There are few data to show whether the double monopoly of wire and brass making was a burden at this period. During the discussions of monopolies in 1597 and 1601, there is no mention of wire or wool-cards, partly because the protection of the former was statutory, not an exclusively royal grant, partly too since, although the society had a monopoly of wire-drawing, it had none for making wool-cards. Since however it was stated in 1597 that, owing to the importation of foreign cards, only one person was now employed in this industry in England where twenty had formerly made a living[3], it would appear that the price of English wire was higher than that of foreign. In the case of the brass-manufacture, one speaker mentioned calamine as a recent and presumably objectionable grant, but in the report of the Committee on Monopolies and Grants of Privilege neither calamine nor brass is included[4].

Advantage was taken of a new sovereign coming to the throne to obtain confirmation of the privileges granted by Elizabeth, and, at the same time, a fresh charter of incorporation was drawn up, which was signed on January 21st, 1604. The title in this document is *the Governors, Assistants and Society of the City of London of and for the Mineral and Battery Works*, and the members were authorized to elect two governors, two deputy-governors and eight or more assistants[5].

In 1628 the society was able to obtain a re-enactment of the statute of 39 Elizabeth prohibiting the importation of wool-cards[6]; and two years later two petitions were presented, stating that this act was then evaded by the importation of wire, which was made up into cards in England. It was urged that such wire was inferior to that produced in the mills of the society, and therefore it was desirable that, in the interests of the wool-trade, such importation should be prohibited[7].

[1] 1 Rich. III.

[2] *The Journals of all the Parliaments during the Reign of Queen Elizabeth*, by Sir Simonds D'Ewes, London, 1682, p. 571.

[3] 39 Eliz., c. 14; *Statutes*, IV., Pt. II. p. 914.

[4] D'Ewes, *Journals*, pp. 648, 650; *Journals of the House of Lords*, I. pp. 653, 658; *Parliamentary or Constitutional History of England*, 1751, IV. p. 462.

[5] State Papers, Domestic, James I., VI. [Docquet]; *Calendar*, 1603-10, p. 68; Sloan MS. (Brit. Mus.) 2483, f. 20; Pettus, *Fodinæ Regales*, p. 66. *Special Report from the Committee appointed to enquire into the several subscriptions for Fisheries, Insurance, &c.*, 1720, Brit. Mus. 375. b. 3, No. 30, p. 40.

[6] 3 Car. I., c. 4, § 22; *Statutes*, Chron. Index vol., p. 338.

[7] State Papers, Domestic, Charles I., CXLIX. 16; CLXV. 26; *Calendar*, 1629-31, pp. 50, 243

In a proclamation, dated May 7th, 1630, it was stated that this industry employed many thousands of work-people, and that, owing to the importation of foreign wire, those trained to this trade were in danger of being left destitute. Since moreover English wire was better than foreign, the importing or using of the latter was forbidden. Besides, the "translation" or trimming up of old wool-cards was prohibited, "nor shall any sell the same either at home or abroad[1]." The last clause is a striking example of the commercial policy of the time of Charles I. The monopoly of the home market, with the exclusion of competitive imports, might be expected; but, to further encourage the producer, by compelling the wool-comber to buy all the cards he needed new, was a relapse to one of the worst features of the craft-gild.

Meanwhile the brass manufacture had shown symptoms of decay; and the society, having secured the extremest form of "encouragement" for its wire business, now endeavoured to obtain similar privileges for the latten trade. Accordingly, proclamation was made on August 19th, 1638, stating that brass wire was a necessary and profitable manufacture and, to arrest the want of employment occasioned by the importation of foreign wire and latten, such importation was prohibited[2]. In spite of this proclamation, the brass works continued to decline and, when Pettus wrote in 1670, he described this part of the society's properties as being on the verge of extinction, "and those arts are almost gone with the artists[3]."

In 1639 James Lydsey had leased the wire works. He took advantage of the proclamation by raising the price from £6 per cwt. to £8, and he had been heard to express his intention of advancing it to £10 per cwt. or an increase of 66 per cent.[4] Evidently the monopoly was profitable, since in 1640 the Earl of Pembroke petitioned for a reversion of the lease which was due to expire in a few years[5].

During the confusion of the Civil Wars, work was partially or wholly suspended[6]; and, since many of the shareholders were prominent Royalists, it was not till after the Restoration that efforts were made to restart the mills. During the Commonwealth some capitalists had been attracted by the possibilities of the brass industry, and the society

---

[1] Sloan MS. 2483, f. 27; *Fœdera*, xix. p. 163.
[2] Sloan MS. 2483, f. 29; Soc. Antiq., Proclamations, Charles I., No. 231.
[3] *Fodinæ Regales*, p. 33.
[4] State Papers, Domestic, Charles I., ccccxxi. 149; *Calendar*, 1639, p. 217.
[5] *Ibid.*, Charles I., cccclxxv. 48; *Calendar*, 1640-1, p. 366. At the same time the Act of 39 Eliz. was re-enacted—*Statutes*, Chron. Index. vol., p. 338.
[6] Stringer states that even during the Rebellion the societies continued (*Opera Mineralia Explicata*, pp. 244-5); this, if true, would apply rather to the Mines Royal than to this society, cf. *supra*, p. 403.

found to its dismay that, while its works resulted in a loss, competition had sprung up. It was forced to keep the men on short time and to let out some of the furnaces. Its rivals had formed a corporation, organized by John Tripp, and operations had been begun near Bristol. It was said that this company, which had made tempting offers to some of the "chiefest" workmen, were prepared to "be loosers in their goods in order to subvert the society." Tripp was summoned before a court held on February 4th, 1662, and it was urged against him that he had paid no royalty to the Crown on the calamine, whereas the society had duly made these payments until the Rebellion. Tripp pleaded ignorance and "submitted to the society[1]."

Similar difficulties were experienced with the wire works in Monmouth, which were about to be restarted on behalf of the society[2]. About this time an iron-wire mill had been established at Sheen, near Richmond[3], and, according to the society, the price of wire was advancing. Apparently the quotation, established by Lydsey in 1640, had been maintained; for the society stated, that before the last revival of the works, the price had been £8 per cwt., and when the mills had last been running it had fallen to £5. 5s. per cwt. The list of retail prices is too incomplete either to confirm or modify this statement. In 1634 wire was 1s. 4d. per lb.; in 1645 it had fallen to 1s., and in 1697 it was again 1s.[4] Probably the first quotation might be taken as fairly typical of the result of the proclamation of 1630, while the two later ones represent less restriction of imports. In this, as in many other cases, the best arguments in favour of competition are provided by privileged manufacturers when they wished to break down the connection of a rival, and therefore it is only to be expected that the result of the contentions of the society was the passing of an act in 1662, prohibiting the importation of either cards or wire. Moreover the using of old wire with new wood was forbidden, subject to the proviso that combers might do so for their personal use or to sell abroad[5]. This act, like its predecessors in the previous fifty years, was justified by the alleged need of maintaining the standard of quality of the wool. How far the employing of cards, made of foreign or old wire, would have produced less efficient combing, it is impossible to say. That there was some ground for the contention appears possible from the many complaints of the inferiority of English manufactures, as well as from the same kind

---

[1] Sloan MS. 2483, f. 30. State Papers, Domestic, Anne, Petition Entry Book, VI., pp. 480, 481.

[2] *Fodinæ Regales*, p. 32.

[3] Anderson, *Annals of Commerce*, II. p. 628.

[4] *Agriculture and Prices*, by J. E. T. Rogers, VI. pp. 452, 453.

[5] *Statutes*, v. p. 412.

of argument adduced at later dates in the case of the Scottish Wool Card manufactory at Leith[1].

Pettus complained in 1670 that the acts for the exclusion of foreign wire were not observed[2], and in 1678 yet another proclamation was made, requiring the authorities to put in force the statutes against the importation of foreign iron wire[3].

Before this time the arrangement for close working with the Mines Royal had been effected[4]. With the enactment of the Mines Royal bill the operations of the united societies, in the direction of deriving a revenue from the production of silver, were greatly restricted. This fact seems to have made the shareholders concentrate their efforts on the working of their remaining privileges. In 1699 Moses Stringer, who was a deputy-governor, propounded an ambitious scheme, compounded of poor-relief and the development of mineral areas. He proposed that some of the funds, employed in maintaining paupers, should be granted as a subsidy for setting them to work in mines; and he promised that, if this suggestion were put in force on a sufficiently large scale, the resources of the nation would be increased by £1,000,000 annually[5]. By a later form of this plan, it was suggested that the society should be given powers to deduct 25 per cent. from the wages of those it employed, and the funds, so raised, were to be utilized in the creation and improvement of labour-colonies which were to be employed in mineral undertakings[6].

In the early years of the eighteenth century the society was manufacturing. On September 25th, 1710, it owed £20,000, against which it was claimed that it had debts due to it of "at least" £120,000 for rents and no less than £460,000 for trespass[7], both totals no doubt relating to claims mainly on account of the Mines Royal. The company was interested in a petition to Parliament in 1708 in support of the brass manufacture, when it was stated that, if the works were once closed for want of encouragement, it would require £5,000 to restart them[8]. According to another account, "the United Battery and Wire company by joining their long heads and purses together have first, after much puzzling and botching, brought the art of making brass-wire to such perfection as to undermine and almost totally exclude

---

[1] *Vide infra*, Div. IX., Section 5.
[2] *Fodinæ Regales*, p. 32.
[3] Sloan MS. 2483, f. 33.
[4] *Vide supra*, p. 403.
[5] *English and Welsh Mines and Minerals*, by Moses Stringer, 1699, pp. 11–13.
[6] *Opera Mineralia Explicata*, Appendix.
[7] *Ibid.*, p. x. At this time the office of the united societies was described as the Mineral Office in Blackfriars.
[8] *Ibid.*, p. 157.

importation thereof from Holland and Germany[1]." On July 27th, 1709, the society itself records that, "though the works were in a manner reduced, through want of able artists to carry on the same," many thousands of poor and aged people were, and still are, employed. Recently prejudice had been sustained, through Sir John Topp digging for calamine, and an injunction against him, according to the privileges of the undertaking, was asked for[2]. The appearance of Stringer's book in 1713 was doubtless intended to prepare the way for an extension of the operations of the society, but information is wanting as to how far success was attained. The united societies were acting as a corporation in 1716, but there is no record of brass-making being carried on by these bodies at that time. It is necessary however to note that very soon after the last is heard of the society in connection with the brass trade, there appears a new producer, working under a deed of co-partnership, and described as *the Proprietors of the Temple Brass Mills*[3]. Probably either the society sold its property to the later organization, or it may have been that it retired from business and, after some time, new plant was started as the Temple Mills.

The history of this later concern is obscure. The officials were described as managers, who summoned meetings of the proprietors to be held at Pewterers' Hall. A general meeting took place on August 11th, 1720, on extraordinary business[4]. This was called in all probability to sanction a further call on the shares. Originally 10*s.* per share was paid up[5], and this appears to have been increased to £10 per share[6]. On

---

[1] *A Brief Essay on the Copper and Brass Manufactures of England*, London, 1712 [Brit. Mus. $\frac{726 \cdot c \cdot 1}{3}$], p. 5.

[2] State Papers, Domestic, Anne, Petition Entry Books, VII., ff. 478–82; IX., f. 314.

[3] Nothing has been discovered to show whether this undertaking was connected with the Temple Mills founded about 1680. Defoe gives the following account of the earlier enterprize:—"About the year 1680 began the art and mystery of projecting to creep into the world. Prince Rupert, uncle to King Charles II., gave great encouragement to that part of it that respects engines and mechanical motions....The Prince has left us a metal called by his name; and the first project upon that was, as I remember, casting guns of that metal and boring them, done both by a peculiar method of his own and which died with him, to the great loss of the undertaker, who, to that purpose, with no small charge, erected a water-mill at Hackney Marsh, known by the name of the Temple-Mill: which mill very happily performed all parts of the work; and I have seen those guns on board the *Royal Charles*, a first-rate ship, being of a reddish-brown colour, different either from brass or copper."—*Essay upon Projects*, pp. 25, 26; cf. Anderson, *Annals of Commerce*, III. p. 73.

[4] *Daily Courant*, Aug. 11, 1720.

[5] The Bubbler's Mirror (Print Room Brit. Mus.).

[6] Anderson, *Annals of Commerce*, III. p. 340.

DIV. IV. § 3] *The Mineral and Battery Works* 429

August 12th it was resolved to call up £40 a share, payable on or before the 23rd, and the treasurer was to attend at the "English Brass Warehouse on Dowgate Hill" to receive payment[1]. At the height of the boom, these shares sold at £250 a share[2]. In the same month, tenders for the supply of copper and *lapis calaminaris* were advertised for[3], the inference being that, either by purchase or through lapse, there was no obstacle to anyone at this time procuring calamine.

[1] *Daily Post,* Aug. 16, 1720.
[2] The Bubbler's Mirror.
[3] *Daily Courant,* Aug. 12, 1720.

SECTION IV. THE GOVERNOR AND COMPANY OF COPPER MINERS IN ENGLAND.

(INCORPORATED 1691.)

ALTHOUGH the society of the Mines Royal had endeavoured to foster copper mining and had undoubtedly won large amounts of copper during the early years of its history, after the Civil War copper mining in England had been neglected. Matters remained in this condition until the years 1689, 1690, when several new veins of copper ore were discovered and mining operations were prosecuted with vigour[1]. Writers on the condition of trade from 1692 to 1694, such as Defoe, Houghton, and the author of *Angliæ Tutamen*, mention the large number of projects connected with the mining industry that were launched about that time. Amongst these was a scheme for the improvement of the smelting of copper ore which arose out of an invention, by John Duckett and Gabriel Wayne, of furnaces and engines for the more speedy and easy melting and refining of copper ore. Sir Joseph Herne and John Briscoe became interested in the invention and on July 3rd, 1691, these and others petitioned for a charter of incorporation[2]. The Attorney-General reported that the invention was new and that the industry would be beneficial to the country. Since, moreover, it could not be carried on without a joint-stock company to provide the capital required, he recommended the grant of a charter[3]. On July 23rd a warrant was signed for the incorporation of certain persons named as *the Governor and Company of the Copper Miners in England*, with the usual privileges of a corporation. The annual meeting was to be held on the 29th of September each year, when the shareholders were empowered to elect one governor, one deputy-governor and ten or more assistants. Members were entitled to one vote for each share, provided

---

[1] *The Present State of Mr. Wood's [Mine] Partnership* [1720] (Brit. Mus. 8223. e. 95); Report on the State of Copper Mines: *Reports from Committees of the House of Commons*, x. p. 666. State Papers, Domestic, Petition Entry Book, xi. p. 521—Pet. James Robinson and others.

[2] State Papers, Domestic, Will. and Mary, Petition Entry Book, i. p. 149.

[3] *Ibid.*, p. 155.

that such votes should be in writing. Any member, whose calls were in arrear, was subject to disfranchisement. At all meetings of the court, the quorum consisted of seven. Powers were also granted to purchase lands up to the value of £6,000 a year and to raise a joint-stock as required[1]. The charter was sealed on September 22nd. On subsequent petitions, the company was authorized to carry on its smelting operations in Ireland and America[2]. It does not appear that any application was made to the Scottish Parliament for privileges in Scotland, the reason probably being that Nicholas Dupin, deputy-governor of the King's and Queen's Corporation for the Linen Manufacture in England, was engaged in preparing the way for the formation of "the company for working Mines and Minerals in the Kingdom of Scotland[3]."

By December 1691 the company, after incurring "great expense and charges," showed that it had succeeded in refining copper from English ore, and a petition was presented, asking for the sole right to make and vend farthings, half-pence and pence made of English copper for three years, in consideration of an annual payment of £2,000[4]. It appears however that this offer was not accepted, or, if accepted, it was not renewed at the end of the three years, since it is recorded that in 1694 farthings and half-pence were coined from Swedish copper; and it was stated, as a new departure, that in 1717 many tons of English copper were used for the coinage of that year[5]. On August 6th, 1692, the company presented another petition, stating that, prior to its formation, there had been discovered a great quantity of ore which was totally unimproved. The company, after the grant of the charter, had been at great expense both in refining this ore and also in the discovery and digging of "the chiefest mines of copper ore in several counties in England," which had been successfully improved to the great advantage of the kingdom, by giving employment to many thousands of labourers and enabling copper to be produced within the country. In view of these facts, the company petitioned that the clause in the charter, authorizing the refining of copper ore, should be extended so as to permit the prospecting for and working of copper mines[6].

Frequent reference was made in the petitions, presented by the company, to the large capital outlay that had been involved in establishing its business. But, as in the case of many contemporary mining and manufacturing joint-stock undertakings, there is no precise record

[1] State Papers, Domestic, Will. and Mary, H. O. Warrant Book, vi. pp. 115–8.
[2] *Ibid.*, Petition Entry Book, i. pp. 172–3; H. O. Warrant Book, vi. p. 160.
[3] *Vide infra*, Div. ix., Section 7.
[4] State Papers, Domestic, Will. and Mary, Petition Entry Book, i. p. 219.
[5] *Reports from Committees of the House of Commons*, x. p. 666.
[6] State Papers, Domestic, Will. and Mary, Petition Entry Book, i. p. 361.

of the original share-capital. Probably the reason of this lack of information is due not so much to the loss of documents as to the manner of conducting business and the system of account keeping in vogue. Contemporary writers are unanimous in stating that the general practice, especially in mining ventures, was to divide the undertaking into a certain number of shares, which the original owners sold as required[1]. Thus the capitalization of any of the smaller businesses, towards the close of the seventeenth century, was effected not by the company itself, but through the valuation placed upon the shares in the stock-market.

It appears that the original number of shares of this company was 700, certainly there were 700 shares prior to 1720, which were then spoken of as having been long in existence[2]. The first quotation recorded by Houghton was 57 on March 30th, 1692. Supposing that the shares numbered 700, this would give a valuation by the speculative investor of £39,900 for the whole undertaking. The quotation was fairly steady till the end of April, but on May 9th it had fallen to 50, the lowest point during the part of 1692 that Houghton includes. After May 16th there was an improvement from May 23rd till June 27th (the last number issued by Houghton for 1692) the price varying from 54 to 55. During the remaining months of 1692 there must have been a considerable fall, since the next recorded quotation, on January 20th, 1693, was only 44. The price receded gradually down to 33 on February 24th, but the next week it rose abruptly to 46 (March 3rd), the highest of that year, and remained from 46 to 44 throughout the month. In April and until the middle of May any business done was at 39, and in the last fortnight of the latter month at 36. There was a recovery in June to 39, but in the first half of July the best offer was 35. During the next month, *i.e.* to the middle of August, there was an improvement to 39, but from the 18th on till September 29th the price was again 35. It was a curious coincidence that almost from the beginning of the recorded quotations, the price of English copper shares and Royal African stock had been almost the same. Both had been falling, but hitherto African stock had been a little the higher of the two. At the end of September the latter continued on the whole to decline, but on October 6th copper shares rose from 35 to 38, and this improvement was maintained till November 10th when the price declined to 36, after which it was 36, 34[3], 32, 30 in successive weeks, the

---

[1] *An Essay upon Projects* [by Daniel Defoe], London, 1697, p. 13.

[2] *Articles of Agreement between the Governor and Company of the Copper Miners in England and Thomas Chambers, Junr.*, 1725 $\left[\text{Brit. Mus. } \frac{522 \cdot \text{m} \cdot 12}{3}\right]$, p. 4.

[3] The figures 54 on Nov. 24, 1693, are evidently a misprint. There are many such.

last figure being reached on December 8th, and at this the shares remained until January 5th of the following year. The year 1694 was the culmination of the industrial and mining boom, and it was not long before English Copper shares participated in the advance in prices brought about by the general speculative activity. During the first week in January the lowest price of the previous year, 30, was repeated, the next week the quotation rose to 36 and remained at that till February 9th, the next week it was 37, then 40, and on March 2nd 41, at which it stayed till the 23rd. The following week the rise was continued, and from March 9th to 23rd the quotation was 48; which, compared with the highest recorded price of 1692, 57, shows a difference of £9 per share. In the fortnight, including March 30th to April 6th, there was a slight reaction to 45 and in the next fortnight to 43. After April 20th, although just at that time Houghton greatly extended the list of securities quoted, there are no further prices printed opposite "Herne's Copper," and the reason for this can only be a matter of conjecture. No doubt, this company shared with others the disadvantage of the sale of vendors' shares in a market that had been largely "made," and possibly the promoters having sold as many shares as they were disposed to part with, the speculation became less active. However this may have been, the company continued its operations, though there are no data for gauging its success or failure.

It is next heard of in 1709. On November 29th of that year, in a petition, it is stated that the charter of 1691 had fixed the date of the annual meeting for the election of a governor and assistants on September 29th of each year, and that 14 days' notice in writing had to be given to each member. Many of the shareholders had become "so dispersed" that the officials of the company could not discover their addresses; and therefore the Crown was asked to confirm recent elections of members of the court and to authorize the insertion of an advertisement in the *London Gazette*, instead of the personal notice required by the charter; also to make the legal date of meeting any day between September 29th and March 25th[1]. Possibly the reason for the dispersion of the members was not unconnected with the fact that, about this date, the company found it necessary to make calls on its shares, and as late as 1719 no less than 176 of the 700 shares were "detained" by the court, owing to the failure of the owners to made the necessary payments when due[2]. The petition for the alteration of the charter gave rise to a point of some interest.

The Solicitor-General reported on December 9th, 1709, that a confirmation should be granted in the terms asked, but that the old charter must be surrendered, and a warrant was accordingly granted to this

[1] State Papers, Domestic, Petition Entry Book, IX. p. 351.
[2] *Articles of Agreement, ut supra*, p. 9.

effect on May 13th, 1710. The company was unwilling to surrender its existing charter and it presented a fresh petition on September 10th, 1710, pointing out that a confirmation and a surrender of the charter were inconsistent and asking "for a confirmation leaving the surrender[1]." The second warrant, in the terms of the last petition, was signed on February 2nd, 1711, authorizing the calling of meetings by advertisement in the *London Gazette* 14 days prior to the day of meeting[2].

The court took advantage of the speculative activity of 1720 to effect an amalgamation with two important allied undertakings. At this date Thomas Chambers, junior, owned copper works at Redbrook in Gloucestershire (where the Mineral and Battery Works had established factories more than a century earlier) as well as copper mines in Cornwall. A number of other persons were interested in a copper mill at Wimbledon, which had been in existence in 1712 under the management of a partnership, in which John Essington, James Robinson, Charles Parry, John Norris and William Carpenter were interested. At that date £10,000 had been expended on procuring foreign workmen and purchasing plant, besides which the giving of credit required a constant dead stock of £20,000. Evidently the concern was considerably in debt as it was stated that new traders could not join the undertaking without becoming " liable for many dangerous consequences," to obviate which a charter was asked[3]. Essington and his partners continued to struggle on and in 1720 this enterprize was prepared to amalgamate with the English Copper company and the similar business carried on by Chambers at Redbrook. The indenture embodying the terms of union was completed on August 3rd, 1720. In this agreement it was provided that the 700 shares of the English Copper company should be increased to 21,000 of £5 each. The shareholders were to be credited with 700 new shares, without payment, and they were to receive £10,000 in cash, while a further 1,000 shares were issued, as fully paid, and were placed at the disposal of the assistants. Essington and his partners were given the right of taking up 15,000 shares at par, while Chambers had the call on 4,300 on the same terms[4]. These dispositions accounted for the whole 21,000 shares, and it is clear that the transaction was an ingenious method of bringing other copper-producers under the charter of the English company. Apparently Essington and Co., and also Chambers, were giving away their works and mines, but, had the amalgamation been successfully floated, both would have been very large gainers by reason of the premium on the shares, which rose as high as £100 per share[5]. Essington and Co., for instance, after paying for the

[1] State Papers, Domestic, Petition Entry Book, XI. p. 103.
[2] Brit. Mus. Harl. MS. 2264, f. 274.
[3] State Papers, Domestic, Petition Entry Book, XI. pp. 521, 522.
[4] *Articles of Agreement, ut supra*, pp. 4–7.
[5] Anderson, *Annals of Commerce*, III. p. 339.

DIV. IV. § 4]   *The Copper Combine of* 1720   435

shares reserved to them, would have made exactly a million and a half on the transfer of their works.

Possibilities such as these excited the envy of the court of the South Sea company, which claimed the monopoly of inflating prices. It was probably for this reason that the company found its name included in the writ of *scire facias*. Even though it was able to show that operations had been carried on since the grant of the charter and that charter was sustained at the subsequent enquiry, its credit was damaged[1]. The Prince of Wales, who had recently been elected governor, resigned[2], and the shares became almost unsaleable[3]. However the company had acted more prudently than most of its contemporaries, and it was really those who had joined on the amalgamation that suffered, by the loss of the expected premium on the shares for which they had paid in cash; so that, as against the original value of the works transferred and the sum paid on allotment, the vendors only possessed a very much depreciated security. On the other hand, the old proprietors not only received £10,000 in cash besides retaining 700 shares, but they exacted an annual payment of £100 a year for 33 years from the company[4]. If the court had succeeded in abstaining from the mania of "supporting the market," the company would have been in a position to continue business, it is true with an enlarged capital, but with additional mines and works, besides ample cash resources. However this may have been, it at least enjoyed sufficient prosperity to continue to exist until the beginning of the nineteenth century. When Maitland wrote his *History of London*, it was one of the leading joint-stock companies and had an office in Bush Lane[5]. In 1790 it joined with fourteen other smelting companies, working in Cornwall, in an agreement for regulating the price of copper ore, and as late as 1799 was still one of the leading smelting companies in that district[6].

Summary of Capital and Prices.

Capital.

Prior to 1720 ... ... 700 shares
1720 ... ... £105,000 in 21,000 shares of £5 each

Prices.

Year	Date of highest price	Highest	Lowest	Date of lowest price
1692	March 30 to April 18	57	50	May 9 to May 16
1693	March 3	46	30	December
1694	March 9 to March 23	48	30	Jan. 5
....	....	....	....	....
1720		105	—	

[1] Anderson, *Annals of Commerce*, III. p. 348.   [2] *The Historical Register*, v. p. 294.
[3] Anderson, *Annals of Commerce*, III. p. 349.
[4] *Articles of Agreement, ut supra*, p. 11.   [5] p. 1265.
[6] *Reports of Committees of the House of Commons*, x. pp. 681, 684.

SECTION V. OTHER COPPER MINING COMPANIES FOUNDED FROM 1692 TO 1694.

DOCKWRA'S COPPER COMPANY (1692).
CORNISH COPPER COMPANY (ABOUT 1694).
CUMBERLAND AND CAROLINA ROYAL MINES (ABOUT 1694).
DERBY COPPER COMPANY (ABOUT 1694).
THE GOVERNOR AND COMPANY OF THE COPPER MINES IN THE PRINCIPALITY OF WALES (1694).

BESIDES the English Copper company, other organizations were formed to develope old copper mines or to prospect for new ones, in districts where it was believed that workable deposits of ore existed. In Cornwall copper ore was discovered accidentally, when new workings were being made in connection with the tin mines, and a copper company was formed about 1694 to mine the ore[1]. The shares of this company were first quoted in September 1694, and the same price is repeated until the following May, when this company drops out of Houghton's list.

Early in the reign of William III. copper had been found in Derbyshire amongst the refuse of the lead mines at the Peak, and in 1693 a copper mine was being worked at Cotton, three miles from Derby[2]. The Derbyshire mines were held in high repute, and undoubtedly considerable profits were made by some of the small companies, which worked them. A case is recorded of some "poor tradesmen," who bought a few shares in one vein of the mine at Winster, and each of them made £2,000 clear profit[3]. In view of these expectations, the Derbyshire Copper company's shares received considerable attention in the stock market. They were first quoted in June 1694 at 23 and, from the

---

[1] *Reports of Committees of the House of Commons*, x. p. 666; Houghton, *Collections for Improvement of Husbandry and Trade*, for 1694.

[2] *Ibid.*, No. 45, April 21, 1693.

[3] *Some Account of Mines...with an Appendix relating to the Mine Adventure in Wales*, London, 1707, p. 171.

middle of July to the end of the year, the price was 20. The latter quotation was repeated early in 1695, but on March 8th it fell abruptly to 12. During 1696 the shares were steady at 12 and in 1697 they brought 10, disappearing from the list in August.

Another copper bearing district was Cumberland, where mines had been worked by the society of the Mines Royal more than a century before[1]. A company was also formed for this district and it extended its operations to Carolina, where it had the grant of mine royal. On November 9th, 1694, it advertised for miners to emigrate to Carolina; but, inasmuch as its shares were at this time selling at 9, it is probable that the venture had already lost ground.

These three companies, as well as that formed by Dockwra[2], worked without charters. Both the author of *Angliæ Tutamen* and Houghton agree in attributing the non-success of these undertakings to speculative transactions on the Stock Exchange, rather than to any defect in the mining prospects as such. The former writer says that "nothing thrives where they admit stock-jobbing, it has spoiled more good and really useful designs than all the ill accidents that have attended them beside[3]." In July 1694 Houghton considered that not only was there enough copper being produced to justify the expectation of supplying the home demand, but there was a probability of a surplus being available for export[4]. By 1697 he mentions that "a great deal of money had been spent in the search (for copper) to the prejudice not of a few, neither were they so much damaged by the search as by stock-jobbing, some men being over-cunning for the rest[5]."

There remain two other companies, which are noteworthy for different reasons. One of these was founded by William Dockwra, who had earlier established a penny post-office[6]. This company was wider in its scope than those working in Cornwall and Derby, since it carried on brass works as well as mining operations. Its mills were situated at Esher near Kingston in Surrey, where wire-drawing had been attempted by Jacob Momma about 1649. In 1697 the company had twenty-four benches for rendering brass wire malleable for drawing, which operation was performed by water power[7].

The shares of this company had been placed on the market on April 18th, 1692, at 52; and, during that year, they were slightly lower than those of the English Copper company—the mean price of

---

[1] *Vide supra*, pp. 385–94.
[2] *Vide infra*, p. 438.
[3] *Angliæ Tutamen*, p. 19.
[4] Houghton, *Collections, ut supra*, No. 103, July 20.
[5] *Ibid.*, No. 256, June 25, 1697.
[6] For an account of this undertaking, *vide* Division VII., Section 1.
[7] Houghton, *Collections, ut supra*, No. 257, July 2, 1697.

the securities of the latter being 51, that of the former 53½. In the next year the relative positions were reversed. Again, taking the mean between highest and lowest prices, that in the case of the English company was 38, while for Dockwra's it was 52. Though the quotation of the shares of the English company fell from March to December, the relapse in those of the Dockwra company was arrested in March; and, during the next six months, the price rose steadily till the last half of September, when 60 was reached. Afterwards there was a reaction to 54, which was the highest point in the subsequent year. Why Houghton should cease to print the price after September 1694 (when it was 48) is rather puzzling. The first quotation was 52, the last 48, therefore it cannot be concluded that the company was in difficulties at the end of 1694. On the contrary, three years later it was producing at that date 80 tons of copper a year. This was as much as all the other English companies together, giving a total production of 160 tons a year, which was valued at £100 a ton, or a total annual value of £16,000[1].

The subsequent history of the company is very obscure. The brass works may have been absorbed by another company which is said to have been founded in 1702, and whose chief factories were situated near Bristol[2]. The copper mines may have continued in operation long after 1697, since there was a considerable production of English copper during the earlier part of the eighteenth century, which would not be accounted for by the mines owned by the English company. Possibly, if the undertaking survived till about 1717, it may have changed its name or been absorbed by a company known as Mr Wood's mining partnership, which in 1720 had leases of all the copper ores in thirty-nine counties besides, what the promoter described as, "the best iron works in the kingdom situated near the Severn." This company expected soon to be able to make dividends of profits, which would be satisfactory to the proprietors[3].

The remaining copper company was the only one, except the English company, incorporated by charter. The grant was dated April 10th, 1694, and created *a Governor and Company of the Copper Mines in the Principality of Wales*[4]. The shares were dealt in on June 7th, 1694, but declined gradually until the quotation in 1697 was 10 nominal.

This company came into notoriety in 1720. Originally £4. 2s. 6d.

---

[1] Houghton, *Collections*, No. 256, June 25, 1697.
[2] *Reports of Committees of the House of Commons*, x. p. 666.
[3] *The Present state of Mr Wood's Partnership*, Brit. Mus. 8223. e. 95.
[4] Maitland, *History of London*, p. 1274.

had been paid up on its shares, and these rose to 90 in July 1720[1]. As it had announced a subscription for new capital, its name was included in the writ of *scire facias* and the Lords Justices found that the charter had been abandoned. In spite of this, five days after the issue of the writ, the company opened its books and made transfers and generally continued to act as a corporation[2]. In 1731 a governor and assistants were chosen[3]; and, when Maitland wrote his *History of London*, business was still carried on in Philpot Lane, and the sphere of the undertaking had been extended so as to include "the working of divers mines in England[4]."

Summary of Prices.

The Cornish Copper Company.

Year	Date of highest price	Highest	Lowest	Date of lowest price
1694		20	20	
1695		20	—	

The Cumberland and Carolina Royal Mines.

1694	June 7 to 20	12	9	Aug. 15 to Nov.

The Derby Copper Company.

1694	June 7 to 20	23	20	July 18 to Dec.
1695	Jan. 4 to March 1	20	12	March 8 to Dec.
1696		12	12	
1697		10	10	

Dockwra's Copper Company.

1692	April 18 to June 11	52	50	May to June 27
1693	Sept. 22 to 29	60	44	Feb. 24 to March 17
1694	Jan. 5 to Feb. 23, March 9	54	48	May 29 to August

The Governor and Company of the Copper Mines in the Principality of Wales.

1694	June 7 to July 11	32	15	Dec. 26
1695	Jan. to March 1	16	10	March 15 to 29
1696	Jan. to Dec. 4	15	12	Dec. 18 to 25
1697		10	10	

[1] Anderson, *Annals of Commerce*, III. p. 339.
[2] *Historical Register*, v. p. 294.   [3] *Gentleman's Magazine*, I. p. 497.
[4] p. 1274.

SECTION VI. LEAD MINING AND LEAD SMELTING COMPANIES (1692–4).

THOUGH much attention was given to the discovery of copper mines, the industry of lead mining was not neglected during the period from 1691 to 1694. The export of lead had been a source of profit to the country from a very early period, and this species of mining remained a promising speculative venture. There were in fact three distinct kinds of lead mining enterprizes. One, which had been pursued intermittently by the society of the Mines Royal[1], was most occupied in the extraction of silver from lead ore. Considerable fortunes had been made in this way; and, as late as 1697, several lead mines were yielding large percentages of silver, as for instance two in Durham where 6 to 8 oz. of silver were extracted to the cwt. of lead. A Lancashire mine yielded 4 oz. to the cwt., one in Cornwall 10 oz., and Sir Carberry Price's mines returned 19 grs. to the pound of lead, and it was anticipated that, with more careful refining, 1 dwt. to the pound might be obtained[2]. Then there were numerous attempts to utilize coal as fuel for smelting the ore, and several enterprizes were started to test certain inventions, intended to effect this object.

In view of these facts and of the facility with which capital could be obtained between 1690 and 1695, it was only to be expected that there should be considerable speculation in lead mines. Houghton mentions five companies, the shares of which were dealt in during the year 1694. He enumerates these in his list under the general heading of "Lead"—Estcourt, Evans, Derby, Price, Glover. The Estcourt and Derby companies were first quoted in April 1694, the price of shares in the former being 150 and in the latter 21. The name of the company, associated with Glover, appears in June of the same year. That, described as Price's mine, was the company formed to work the mines discovered by Sir Carberry Price, shares in which were quoted at 17 during the years 1694, 1695, 1696. This company was bought up by Sir Humphrey Mackworth, and was reorganized as the Mine Adventurers'

---

[1] *Vide supra*, pp. 389–402.
[2] Houghton, *Collections*, No. 248, May 7, 1697.

company, and its history, as far as it is known, will be found under that of the latter company[1].

The Evans, mentioned by Houghton, was Sir Stephen Evans, who joined with a number of other persons, "acquainted with the coast of New England and of Acade, lately taken from the French." They believed that royal mines were to be found there, and were prepared to prospect, and mine the minerals, paying one-tenth part of the gold or silver won, and the same proportion of all other ores to the Crown. On August 13th, 1691, they petitioned for a charter of incorporation, but apparently the matter was allowed to drop, since Houghton, when mentioning the company in 1694, does not distinguish it (as he invariably did with others) as a chartered undertaking[2].

In 1692 a company was promoted by Thomas Neale and John Tyzack (who were connected with certain enterprizes for the recovery of wrecks[3]) for the working of lead mines in England and Wales. In a petition, dated 1692, it is stated that many lead mines were unworked, partly through want of skill and partly through lack of capital, or the great risk involved. To obviate these and such other difficulties, they proposed to raise a large joint-stock and to employ skilful workmen. There was, however, an objection to such a proposal, since the society for Mines Royal was still in existence, and there was the probability that some of the new lead mines might contain silver, and they would, therefore, be claimed as Mines Royal. It was, therefore, suggested that the proposed company should undertake not to work any mines but its own; and that, before purchasing any mine containing silver, it should enter into agreements with the societies of the Mines Royal and of the Mineral and Battery Works[4]. Accordingly on June 30th, 1693, a warrant was issued for the incorporation of the petitioners and others, who would join with them, as *the Governor and Company for digging and working mines by a Joint Stock in England*, with powers to elect one governor, one deputy-governor and twenty or more assistants, to hold courts and "to raise a joint-stock to any value whatsoever." The members had one vote for each share. The company was excluded from smelting or mining copper, and all privileges conferred by this grant were to be construed as subject to the powers previously conferred on the society for the Mines Royal[5].

Finally, there was a company formed for smelting lead by means of coal in 1692. On March 12th, 1692, Constantine Vernatty and a number

---

[1] *Vide infra*, Section 7.
[2] State Papers, Domestic, Will. and Mary, Petition Entry Book, I. p. 170.
[3] *Vide infra*, Division v., Section 2.
[4] State Papers, Domestic, Petition Entry Book, I. p. 357.
[5] *Ibid.*, H. O. Warrant Book, VI. pp. 579–83.

of others showed that they had "brought to perfection a very useful invention for smelting down lead ore with pit and sea coal." They were also able to make the lead produced into sheet lead, shot, and bullets, and they asked to be incorporated as *the Governor and Company of Lead Mines in England and Wales*[1]. On July 29th an Order in Council was issued, directing the Attorney-General to prepare the heads of a charter of incorporation[2]. Apparently the name suggested in the petition was changed, for, on October 4th, a charter was signed incorporating *the Governor and Company for smelting down lead with Pit and Sea Coal*, with a court consisting of a governor, deputy-governor and twelve assistants. When Maitland wrote his *History of London*, this company was still in existence and carried on business in Ingram's Court, off Fenchurch Street[3].

[1] State Papers, Domestic, Petition Entry Book, I. p. 249.
[2] *Ibid.*, H. O. Letter Book, Secretary's, II. p. 513.
[3] p. 1268.

SECTION VII. THE GOVERNOR AND COMPANY OF THE MINE ADVENTURERS OF ENGLAND (1698).

This company was a re-organization of the undertaking connected with the name of Sir Carberry Price, which has already been mentioned[1]. About 1690 a mine had been discovered in Wales, which was yielding considerable quantities of silver. On October 22nd, 1690, the Earl of Suffolk petitioned the House of Lords, claiming a breach of privilege on the part of Lady Price in the working of a mine royal, without compounding with the society formed to develope the latter class of mines[2]. This petition was dismissed in order that the points at issue might be tried at law[3]. The cause which resulted, between the society of the Mines Royal and Sir Carberry Price, aroused considerable interest. After a lengthy hearing in 1691, Price obtained a verdict to the effect that the veins, he was working, were a lead mine not a mine royal. On the issue being re-tried this verdict was repeated, and in 1692 the Crown entered a *nolle prosequi* in this suit[4]. It was this case which is said to have occasioned the act relating to Mines Royal of 1693[5].

Price was now in a position to develope his mine. It was subject to flooding, and capital was required to deal with the influx of water[6]. He decided to divide the property into shares and in 1693 these were fixed at 4,800, and resolutions were passed for the holding of general meetings, for the keeping of a transfer-book and for voting in proportion to the shares owned by each member[7]. According to a statement submitted to

[1] *Vide supra*, p. 440.   [2] *Vide supra*, pp. 404, 405.
[3] *Reports Hist. MSS. Com.*, XIII. (6) p. 184.
[4] *A Brief Historical Relation of State Affairs*, by Narcissus Luttrell, Oxford, 1857, II. pp. 255, 256, 258, 309, III. 57.
[5] *A Familiar Discourse or Dialogue concerning the Mine Adventure*, by William Shiers, London, 1709, p. 3 [Brit. Mus. 444.a.3]. This tract was written by Mackworth, *Journals of the House of Commons*, XVI. p. 364.
[6] *A Familiar Discourse*, p. 5.
[7] *A Short State of the Case of the Company of Mine Adventurers*, 1710 [Brit. Mus. $\frac{522.m.12}{8}$], p. 2; *The Case of Sir Humphrey Mackworth—Answer to the Several particulars of the Complaint upon the Petition of Several Creditors and Proprietors of Principal Money, Annuities and Shares of the Company of Mine Adventurers* [1710], p. 1.

a meeting, held on June 1st, 1693, it was estimated that the annual profit would be £70,500 a year[1]. On the basis of this estimate, shares were sold from 1694 to 1696 at 17, and, had the prospects been realized, would have returned the purchasers 100 per cent. Several unforeseen contingencies arose, which prevented the hopes formed in 1693 from being realized. Price died in May 1694[2]; and, partly through the want of efficient control, partly through the presence of water in the workings, though the mine was rich[3], the results were not satisfactory and, in 1698, considerable debts had been incurred. At this stage, there appears upon the scene Sir Humphrey Mackworth, to whom the notoriety, which marked the subsequent history of the venture, is due.

Mackworth had bought a considerable number of the shares, owned by Price, but he found that the company was in debt to the extent of close on £15,000 for arrears of salaries and other expenses, while further working capital was needed. Under the direction of Mackworth, it was soon seen that the company was about to enter upon a career of most remarkable finance. He met the shareholders with a double option. First, though the market price was 17 or less, he stated that he was prepared, on behalf of the company, to purchase the shares of any members, who wished to sell, at £20 in cash; but, in the second place there was an alternative proposal, namely that shares might be exchanged for 6 per cent. bonds and, what was the original element in the scheme, these bonds became tickets in a lottery, in which the prizes were the shares that had been converted. At a time when lotteries were a favourite form of speculation and when even the government encouraged them, this scheme had much in it that appealed to the persons concerned. It appeared to them that, if they had average luck in the lottery, they would obtain a 6 per cent. bond and receive back the same share they originally owned, while the framers of the public announcement of the terms took care to show that the fortunate member, who drew the first prize, would obtain, against his original share of £20 nominal, a bond for the same amount and no less than 50 shares, estimated to return him an income of £2,000 a year. Every art was used to attract attention to this novel proposal. Numerous pamphlets were distributed, drawing attention to profits made in mining and other successful speculations, and it was stated that these prize-shares were "confidently expected" to go to 100. That this was no mere assertion was shown by wood-cuts of the levels of the mine, with a description of the nature of the ore, followed by affidavits testifying to its richness. Perhaps the most artistic touch in the whole glowing picture was the

---

[1] *A Familiar Discourse, ut supra*, p. 34.
[2] Luttrell, *Brief Relation*, III. p. 314.
[3] Houghton, *Collections*, No. 248, *vide supra*, p. 404.

DIV. IV. § 7] *Shares drawn as Lottery Prizes* 1699 445

plea that, from the superfluity of profits, the happy shareholder should vote considerable sums for charitable purposes[1].

To a generation, unacquainted with the wiles of the framer of a prospectus, these various inducements were very attractive and, out of 4,800 shares, 4,008 were held ready to be subscribed. The scheme was accepted by the shareholders in an indenture of August 31st, 1698[2]; and, on the following day, books were opened for the subscribing of the old shares, so that they might be converted into bonds to participate in the lottery. So eager were the shareholders not to miss the opportunity, that £26,490 was deposited at once, and by March 4th, 1699, the books were full and the drawing was announced for the 18th at Stationers' Hall[3].

The drawing was based on the following principles. There had been subscribed 4,008 shares. These were valued at £20 each; and, for every share deposited, a warrant for this sum was given which was subdivided into four bonds of £5. Such bonds had a first claim on the profits for 6 per cent. interest, until the principal was repaid. Further, these bonds became the tickets for the lottery, and therefore it required 16,032, valued at £80,160 nominal, to satisfy the claims of the shareholders, who had converted their holdings in the former company. The whole number of "tickets" was fixed at 25,000 (or £125,000) in 6 per cent. bonds, so that there remained 8,968. Of these 2,968 were offered for public subscription at par; and the proceeds, amounting to £14,840, were allocated towards the payment of salaries at the mine, which had

---

[1] *The Mine Adventure; or an Expedient for composing all differences between the partners of the Mines, late of Sir C. Pryse*, 1698 $\left[\text{Brit. Mus. } \frac{522 \cdot \text{m} \cdot 12}{6}\right]$; *The Mine Adventure; or an Undertaking advantageous to the Publick good* $\left[\frac{522 \cdot \text{m} \cdot 12}{37}\right]$; *A New Abstract of the Mine Adventure*, 1698 $\left[\frac{522 \cdot \text{m} \cdot 12}{2}\right]$; *An Answer to several objections against the Mine Adventure*, 1698; *Settlement of the Mine Adventure; A True Copy of Several Affidavits and other Proofs of the Largeness and Richness of the Mines of the late Sir Carbery Price*, 1698 $\left[\frac{726 \cdot \text{m} \cdot 25}{1}\right]$; *Value of the Mines of the late Sir C. Price*, by W. Waller, 1698 [990.c.14]; *An Account of the Cardiganshire Mines*, by W. Waller, 1699.

[2] *The Report of the Committee...to whom it was referred to consider the petitions of several Creditors and Proprietors...in the Mine Adventure*, 1710 $\left[\text{Brit. Mus. } \frac{522 \cdot \text{m} \cdot 9}{3}\right]$; *Journals of the House of Commons*, XVI. p. 311.

[3] Luttrell, *Brief Relation*, IV. pp. 434, 489; *List of the Fortunate Adventurers in the Mine Adventure* $\left[\frac{726 \cdot \text{m} \cdot 25}{3}\right]$.

fallen into arrear, and other liabilities that had been incurred. This left 6,000 tickets, valued at £30,000, of which 4,000 were issued for subscription to provide the working capital of £20,000, while the remainder were also sold and the sums realized were disbursed by Mackworth, according to his own account, in gratuities, tickets to managers, treats at the lottery and in providing liberally for his own personal expenses[1]. Unfortunately it turned out subsequently that there was an element of dishonesty in the promotion of the company. By a secret agreement between Mackworth and Waller, the manager, £2,000 in cash, £30,345 in stock, and 625 shares were to be diverted from the treasury of the company and the proceeds divided equally between the two[2]. It was characteristic of the methods of Mackworth that, under the deed of co-partnership, he had powers of disposing of the monies of the company "without account"; but, in the printed proposals of the lottery, the latter words were omitted, as it was explained afterwards, by an error of the printer[3]. The following tabular statement will make clear the somewhat complicated arrangement of the conversion of shares and the funds realized by the issue of bonds:

	Number of tickets of £5	Total value	Issued to shareholders	Issued for cash
Amount required for holders of 4,008 shares at £20 per share	16,032	£80,160	£80,160	
Amount required to discharge salaries of officials at the mine and to meet other debts ... £14,840	2,968	£14,840		14,840
Tickets reserved for the Company.				
To provide working capital ... £20,000	4,000	£20,000		20,000
Sold by Sir H. Mackworth ... £10,000	2,000	£10,000		10,000
Totals ...	25,000	£125,000		44,840

Of the £25,000 tickets 2,500 were entitled to prizes, furnished from the 4,008 shares converted, according to the following scale[4]:

---

[1] *A Short Statement of the Case of the Mine Adventurers*, 1710 $\left[\text{Brit. Mus. } \frac{522.\text{m}.12}{8}\right]$; *The Case of Sir Humphrey Mackworth, ut supra* [1710], pp. 2, 3.

[2] *The Mine Adventure laid open*, by W. Waller [Brit. Mus. 444.a.50], p. xviii. Waller complains that, though £14,000 was realized, he did not obtain his full half.

[3] *The Case of Sir Humphrey Mackworth, ut supra*, p. 2; *Journals of the House of Commons*, XVI. p. 358.

[4] *A New Abstract of the Mine Adventure*, 1698 $\left[\text{Brit. Mus. } \frac{726.\text{m}.25}{2}\right]$.

Capitalization by Lottery 1699

Number of prizes							Number of shares given as prizes
Benefit	For the first ticket drawn				...	...	10
1	First prize ...			...	...	...	50
1	Second prize			...	...	...	40
10	Third prizes of 20 shares each				...	...	200
20	Fourth	,,	10	,,	...	...	200
20	Fifth	,,	5	,,	...	...	100
40	Sixth	,,	4	,,	...	...	160
200	Seventh	,,	3	,,	...	...	600
430	Eighth	,,	2	,,	...	...	860
1,778	Ninth	,,	1 share each		...	...	1,778
Benefit	Last ticket drawn ...			...	...	...	10
2,500							4,008

When the drawing was completed, the £5 tickets or bonds were consolidated into groups of twenty (or £100 nominal) and these were generally described as "blanks," to distinguish them from the prizes or shares. The whole operation disguised a very real injustice to those shareholders who exchanged their former holdings for "tickets." The investor was in a position somewhat similar to that of the owner of some modern foreign lottery bonds. In both cases the speculator accepts a slightly lower rate of interest than he could obtain on his capital with an equal degree of risk, in the hope of obtaining more than the difference by a prize in the drawing. This comparison however is subject to the difference that, under Mackworth's scheme, the lottery was held once for all: whereas in the case of the modern bonds of the kind mentioned, there are periodic prize-drawings. In the Mine Adventure, the old shareholders, who converted, were in the position that in order to raise £35,000 they risked all their prospects of obtaining any greater return from the mines than 6 per cent. Not only so, but there were doubts as to the fairness of the drawing and suspicions that Mackworth and his friends obtained a disproportionate number of the prize-shares.

On the drawing being completed, it was found that the proprietors numbered about 700[1]. A constitution had been drawn up, which provided for the election of a governor, deputy-governor and twelve assistants or directors. The Duke of Leeds was elected to the former position and Mackworth to the latter, and it was resolved that both should hold office for life. The qualification of an assistant was the holding of twenty shares, that for a vote at general courts was the ownership of three shares. The bonds or blanks had no voting rights[2].

The dexterous advertisement, that had marked the inception of the

---

[1] *List of the Adventurers in the Mine Adventure,* 1701 $\left[\text{Brit. Mus. } \frac{726.\text{m}.25}{5}\right]$.

[2] *Journals of the House of Commons,* XVI. pp. 311, 358.

company, was continued. In the first year of its working, authorization was obtained from the Crown for the addition of the three feathers, from the arms of the Prince of Wales, to all money coined from silver produced from the mines worked by the adventurers[1]. One of the first consignments of bullion was conveyed to the Tower, to be coined, with very great ceremony. It amounted to £1,800[2]. Towards the end of 1699, there were rumours of great discoveries of valuable ore[3], and a fresh campaign was initiated to re-arouse public interest in the venture. In February 1702 advertisements were published in the papers, stating that more labour was needed, and applicants were to engage themselves at "Waller's House near the Silver Mills, Cardiganshire[4]." Two months later, it was recorded by the *Postman* that "we are credibly informed that the Mine Adventurers do now raise great quantities of ore, insomuch that Mr Waller, their steward, doubts not to entitle himself this year to his salary of £250 sterling, at the rate of £100 for every £10,000 clear gain to the company, according to his agreement, which is computed to amount to more than cent. per cent. to all the adventurers[5]." Another statement is even more emphatic, since the profit of 100 per cent. was said to be obtainable "with little or no hazard"; and it was shown that, up to December 19th, 1704, there had already been paid £42,194. 5s. 1d. to the partners[6]. To lend verisimilitude to these expectations, an elaborate series of accounts of the profit realized from silver, obtained from the lead of the company's mines, was printed in 1705, in which the nett yield was returned at from £20 to £42 from each lot of ore treated[7]. The voting of money for charitable purposes, which had been a feature of Mackworth's methods from the beginning, was continued, and every possible device was put in operation to interest the public in the undertaking. No agency was considered too mean or too remote towards contributing to this end—since even the aid of verse was called into play to advertise the mines[8].

[1] *An Historical Account of English Money*, by S. M. Leake, London, 1793, p. 399.
[2] Luttrell, *Brief Relation, ut supra*, v. p. 79.
[3] *Case of Sir Humphrey Mackworth, ut supra*, p. 4.
[4] *London Gazette*, No. 3,788.
[5] *Postman*, No. 1,073. There is an error in these figures.
[6] *Some Account of Mines...with an Appendix relating to the Mine Adventure in Wales*, London, 1707 [Advocates' Library], pp. 168, 169; [Proceedings] *At a Court of Directors*, 15 *June*, 1704 $\left[\text{Brit. Mus.} \frac{726 \cdot m \cdot 25}{8}\right]$.
[7] *An Account of the Clear Profits of Extracting silver out of Lead by the Governor and Company of the Mine Adventurers of England taken from the original Accounts*, 1705 $\left[\text{Brit. Mus.} \frac{522 \cdot m \cdot 12}{9}\right]$.
[8] *A Poem on the Mines of Sir Carbery Price*, by Thomas Yalden, Fellow of St Mary Magdalen's College, Oxford, dedicated to Sir Humphrey Mackworth, 1701.

Application was made to the Crown for a charter of incorporation by a petition, dated January 14th, 1704, which states that the company had been carried on by a settlement enrolled in Chancery, and that hitherto the members, who now numbered about 600, have "preserved a good agreement amongst themselves." In order to make further progress, in the working and manufacturing of minerals, a permanent constitution was required[1]. In accordance with this and a subsequent petition, a charter was granted, which confirmed the rules for the transaction of business, that had been adopted in 1698–9.

On the grant of a charter, new business was undertaken. For various reasons further funds were required; and, after the sale of bonds and shares belonging to the company, an engrafted stock was created and there were issued between 500 and 600 new shares, which realized £9,927. 9s.[2] Considerable sums had been borrowed; and, in 1706, it was decided to set up a bank. To provide capital, a further issue of shares was made and 2,000 new ones were created. A larger number, namely 2,020, had been taken up, but some of the subscribers afterwards withdrew. The calls were only collected with difficulty and on September 11th, 1706, there was £20,550 in arrear and a year later £12,650[3]. Then, to increase the output of the company, an agent was appointed to make purchases of ore, which was to be conveyed to Neath and smelted there. Considerable transactions were effected with another lead-mining undertaking, known as "the Quakers' company"; and it was contended that the ore, supplied by the latter, was useful for mixing with that raised from the Cardiganshire mines[4]. Little information is obtainable concerning the "Quakers' company." It had mines in Flintshire, and it appears that its operations resulted in the winning of some quantity of silver, since it was authorized to have the device of the Prince of Wales, alternately with a rose, in the quarters of the arms on the obverse of coins, made from bullion obtained from these mines[5]. The price of the securities of the Mine Adventurers' company

---

[1] State Papers, Domestic, Petition Entry Books, VI. p. 140, VII. p. 126; *An Account of the Proceedings of the Directors in relation to the Accounts, their charter and other affairs* $\left[\text{Brit. Mus. } \dfrac{522.\text{m}.12}{33}\right]$.

[2] *Journals of the House of Commons*, XVI. p. 367.

[3] *Ibid.*, XVI. p. 263; *A Short Account of the profit and Security which all persons will enjoy who advance money by way of loan to increase the stock and dividend of the Mine Adventurers* $\left[\text{Brit. Mus. } \dfrac{522.\text{m}.12}{29}\right]$.

[4] *The Case of Sir Humphrey Mackworth*, ut supra, p. 8; *An Account of the Proceedings...of the Directors with Mr D. Peck* [? 1708]; *Journals of the House of Commons*, XVI. p. 360; *A Familiar Discourse*, ut supra, p. 80.

[5] *An Historical Account of English Money*, by S. M. Leake, p. 405.

kept comparatively steady. They were first quoted in 1701; and, in this year and the next, the "blanks" fluctuated between 80 and $83\frac{1}{4}$, and the shares opened at 21, rising to 23 in November 1701 to February 1702, and closed in December from 21 to 20. The highest recorded price of the shares was reached in 1706, when, after being $15\frac{3}{4}$ in January and February, they rose to $26\frac{1}{2}$ in June. From this date onwards the tendency of the quotation is to fall.

These prices show that the Mine Adventure, up to 1707, was believed to be a successful undertaking, since the shares, for a period of seven years, stood at quotations above the nominal value, fixed at the time of the lottery. But, under the fair show of prosperity, the whole enterprize was honeycombed with fraud. Mackworth, the deputy-governor, Waller, the engineer at the mines, and perhaps Shiers, the secretary, were deeply involved and it is due to a subsequent quarrel between the two former that a series of damaging letters was produced, which shows the ingenuity of the deception of the public. As early as December 1699, Mackworth had obtained mining rights on ground adjoining that owned by the company; and Waller, finding that the workings, he was appointed to superintend, were inaccessible, owing to the inflow of water, set his men to develope Mackworth's property[1]. No information as to the change was communicated to the court, but Mackworth "demonstrated" to the shareholders that "1,000 tons of ore, raised the first year after the levels are brought home and doubled each year for five years and this added together, will raise 31,000 tons of ore, which, at £6 per ton, will amount to £186,000, which will fully pay principal and interest and £23,500 overplus[2]." When Mackworth's proceedings had formed the subject of a Parliamentary enquiry, he explained that his intention had been to make a present of this additional vein to the company. It is clear from the correspondence, however, that the design was to give the shares a fictitious value, so that those in the secret could sell their holdings to advantage[3]. It appears that ore was not obtainable in sufficient quantities from either mine; and, in the following June, Mackworth writes to Waller "You cannot imagine the cry against us in this town. All my best friends forsake us. If there is no prospect of money this June, neither blanks nor

---

[1] *The Case of Sir Humphrey Mackworth, ut supra*, p. 4; *The Mine Adventure laid open...being an Answer to a Pamphlet...by W. Shiers*, by W. Waller, 1710 [Brit. Mus. $\frac{444 \cdot a \cdot 28}{3}$].

[2] *Journals of the House of Commons*, XVI. p. 360.

[3] Thus Waller writes on Dec. 29, 1699, "I, giving an account what riches we are met with,...will raise the shares to what degree you please." *Case of Sir Humphrey Mackworth, ut supra*, p. 4.

shares will be worth picking up in the streets....I believe you had best tell us of that bargain in the north vein, without distinguishing whose ground it is on, which you may hereafter excuse, alleging you were informed that I had granted the ore to the company."..."I must beg of you to continue raising ore with pumps, engines or any thing, either in the great shaft or west level, though it cost £40 a ton. See what you can bargain for. The name of raising ore in several places will raise us money and keep our credit, till the vein is found and our interest money paid[1]." It was stated, on behalf of Mackworth, that a great vein was soon afterwards found, but it is not impossible that the ore, from which silver was extracted in 1700, had been purchased elsewhere. By means of borrowed money and sales of securities, funds were found to pay interest on the bonds and working expenses at the mines; but it became clear that the limit to this method of finance was reached and hence the excursion into banking. "If," Waller writes on June 26th, 1706, "our credit stand till this is done, we cannot doubt having £50 per share, then sell the company's shares, and sink the engrafted stock and then we may do what we please[2]." The series of indirect practices culminated in the floatation of the shares for the establishing of the "Mine Adventurers' Bank"—a project, described by Waller, as "ridiculous in the contrivance, ignorantly begun, foully carried on and scandalously ended in a labyrinth of fraud and infinite variety of sly, base designs[3]." It was arranged that the subscription might be made as to one-half either in bonds of the company or its notes for money borrowed; but, out of £1,400 taken up by Mackworth, £1,300 was paid in this way and only £100 in cash. Many names are said to have been forged to the deed of co-partnership; and subsequently some of those, who had actually subscribed, cut off portions of the deed containing their names[4].

The acceptance of paper for subscriptions to the bank brought in very little actual cash, and the effect of this operation was to transform the liability on bonds and bills into shares. The next stage in the process of manipulation of the finances was not dissimilar. In 1707 the purchases of ore from the adjoining mine owners were paid for by bills[5]. Hitherto the transformation of one species of credit instrument into another had gone on unchecked, and, though dividends were paid, the

---

[1] *Journals of the House of Commons*, XVI. p. 360.
[2] *A Familiar Discourse, ut supra*, p. 67.
[3] *The Mine Adventure laid open, ut supra*, p. 61.
[4] *Journals of the House of Commons*, XVI. p. 363.
[5] Minute Book of the Court of Directors of the Company of Mine Adventurers of England, Oct. 15, 1707—July 14, 1708 (Bod. Library Rawl. MS. C 449, ff. 49–51).

mines were not meeting their working expenses. Meanwhile money had come in, through the deposits of customers of the bank, and the company was in possession of a considerable quantity of ore, while a call was ordered on the new shares, payable on January 2nd, 1708. Accordingly, in order to support the market in the shares (the price having now fallen to about 12[1]), it was decided to declare a dividend of 5 per cent. on the shares and a like amount in repayment of principal, in addition to the usual 6 per cent. on the bonds, " all in new money to be coined from bullion to be extracted from their own lead." This resolution was passed on December 3rd, 1707, and was advertised in the *London Gazette* of the 8th[2]. At this date, the company had only £927 worth of silver, while the proposed dividend, which was payable in May, required £15,567; and the sums due, over and above the cash on hand and stock, amounted to £33,296[3]. In the face of this disastrous position, the pretence of an overflowing prosperity was maintained. On December 31st, the secretary was ordered to distribute £100 in charity, in March 1708 Waller was busy preparing maps of a new copper mine, while application was being made to the Queen for the privilege " of putting the arms of Wales on the silver to be coined at the Tower[4]."

Signs were not wanting that the career of chicanery of the management was nearing an end. On September 15th, 1707, the deed establishing the bank had been mutilated, and on January 21st, 1708, it was ordered that the door of the accountant's office was to be kept locked, and that no persons should be permitted to inspect the books, without an order from the court[5]. When, in March 1708, the Bank of England and the Sword Blade company were paying 6 per cent. on their sealed bills, it was resolved on the 17th that the payment of cash, against the notes of the company, should be suspended[6]. This proceeding (though an eventual failure was inevitable) showed the same disregard of equity that had marked previous transactions. It was said that, at the time of the suspension, the bank had funds in hand and that these were afterwards paid away to favoured depositors[7]. On some of the other members of the court mentioning to Mackworth that there were funds available, he told them curtly that "they were all fools." The reasons for the premature suspension of cash payments appears clearly from the later proceedings of the directors. It was their policy, in order to protect themselves, to attribute the financial difficulties of the company wholly to the clause in a bill, then under consideration, granting

---

[1] *Journals of the House of Commons*, xvi. p. 359.
[2] Minutes, f. 53.
[3] *Journals of the House of Commons*, xvi. p. 362.
[4] Minutes, ff. 54 et seq.   [5] *Ibid*.   [6] *Ibid*.
[7] *Journals of the House of Commons*, xvi. pp. 364, 365.

the Bank of England a monopoly in banking against any body or corporation of more than seven persons. On March 24th, 1708, the principal partners were asked to use "their utmost endeavours," against the passing of the bill in its original form. By the 29th a petition to the House of Lords had been drafted, to which were appended two alternative additional clauses, asking that the Mine Adventurers might be entitled, notwithstanding anything in the bill, to take up money on their notes or bills of credit; and the other limiting such authorization to the sum of £50,000 for "carrying on the trade for which they were incorporated"..."but not to discount any bills or in any wise deal as a bank[1]." The situation was not improved by the failure of Peck, the agent appointed in 1707 to purchase ore, and the directors reported on the position of the company to a general court on May 4th, 1708. Naturally they completely exonerated themselves, Mackworth included. They found there had been no misapplication of the moneys of the company; and that, so far from there being any defect in the mines, these were in such good circumstances that there was every prospect of "setting matters right in a short time." Therefore, in their opinion, the sole cause of the suspension was the interruption of the banking operations[2]. The number of officials in Cardiganshire and at the office at Angel Court, Snow Hill, London, was diminished from 15 to 5, and large reductions were made in the wages-bill. Some of the shareholders were induced to guarantee a further issue of shares of the nominal value of £10,000[3]; while the dividend, resolved on in December 1707, was deferred and the bullion, which had been procured towards paying it, was pledged[4].

Naturally those who were creditors of the bank pressed urgently for their money, and it became necessary to meet the allegations of fraudulent management which were now being made. Mackworth still managed to maintain the confidence of the majority of the shareholders, and it was determined that Waller, the manager, should be made the scapegoat. As a result of an enquiry, made on behalf of the directors, it was stated that the company "had been damnified under Mr Waller's management to the extent of £14,533. 16s. 2d.," consisting partly of stores unaccounted for, while his working costs were said to have been double what was

---

[1] Minutes, March 24, 29, 1708; *The Case of the Mine Adventurers on a proposed Restriction of the Issue of Notes of Credit* $\left[\text{Brit. Mus. } \frac{522 \cdot \text{m} \cdot 12}{26}\right]$.

[2] Minutes, May 4, 1708; *The Report of a Committee appointed at a General Court*, May 6, 1708 $\left[\text{Brit. Mus. } \frac{522 \cdot \text{m} \cdot 12}{13}\right]$.

[3] Minutes, May 14, 1708.

[4] *Ibid.*, May 4, June 23, 1708.

necessary[1]. Proceedings were taken against Waller and he was attacked by Mackworth and his friends in various publications[2]. A reply was soon forthcoming from Waller, in which he was able to expose some of Mackworth's devious proceedings[3]. This the directors characterized as "a throwing of dirt" at Mackworth, and reflecting upon him, by aspersing his conduct and management, "in that great pains and trouble he had taken in acting very honourably and fairly for the interest and service of the company[4]."

Meanwhile an impossible situation had resulted. The miners had "mutinied," there was no money to carry on the work, the levels underground could not be reached, owing to the "entrances into them being stopped by water and sludge[5]." Moreover, the creditors had become indignant, since the repudiation of the deed of co-partnership of the "bank" had deprived them of the security of the calls on the new shares towards the satisfaction of their debts[6]. The directors saw that some steps must be taken towards meeting the claims against the company and it was resolved that the creditors should have liberty to inspect the cash-books and all other account-books[7]. This permission was construed in a sense favourable to the directors, since not even the House of Commons could obtain the production of a certain transfer-book[8]. The first proposal for an arrangement was very unjust to the creditors, for it was suggested that all those who held bonds of the company should convert them into "blanks" at 6 per cent. interest[9]. Thus they would have had a doubtful security at a low rate of interest, without any prospect of participating in the success of the venture, should the mines yield large profits in the future. An agreement was

---

[1] Minute Book of the General Court of the Governor and Company of the Mine-Adventurers of England: July 5, 1709 to February 1, 1710 (Bod. Library Rawl. MS. C 449, ff. 90–109), July 5, 1709.

[2] e.g. in *A Familiar Discourse, ut supra*.

[3] *The Mine Adventure laid open...being an answer...to a Pamphlet by...W. Shiers*, by W. Waller, 1710 $\left[\text{Brit. Mus.} \dfrac{444.\text{a}.28}{3}\right]$. In addition to the charges of embezzlement already noticed, Waller complained of Mackworth's "extravagant management, by erecting offices and bringing in crowds of officers at his own beck and paying them large and exorbitant salaries, taking great and magnificent houses in London at high rents, sending down condemned criminals to work in the mines with a lame refiner." *Ibid.*, pp. 60, 61.

[4] *The Case of Sir Humphrey Mackworth, ut supra*, p. 14.

[5] Minutes, July 5, 1709.

[6] *Journals of the House of Commons*, xvi. p. 364.

[7] Minutes, Dec. 15, 1709.

[8] *Journals of the House of Commons*, xvi. p. 359.

[9] Minutes, July 5, 1709; [*Proceedings*] *At a General Court* $\left[\text{Brit. Mus.} \dfrac{522.\text{m}.12}{49}\right]$.

drawn up and considered early in 1710[1], but many of those affected held "separate meetings at coffee-houses" and they eventually determined to apply to Parliament[2]. Petitions were presented by the holders of the bonds or blanks on February 13th, 1710, as well as by the other creditors. Both parties agreed that the management should be taken out of the hands of the present directors, while the latter group contended that they should receive better treatment in the rearrangement than the former, who were in reality in the position of shareholders, not creditors[3]. The House of Commons ordered an enquiry, which revealed the scandals already mentioned as well as others, such as the transaction of business when there was no quorum and indeed, in one case, the entry of resolutions in the minute book when no director was present. Further, the minutes had been altered and many erasures made. Shares belonging to the company were sold without the proceeds being paid to it. Cash was entered in the books as being in the possession of the treasurer; but, on an inspection being made, after a delay of five days in obtaining the keys of the chest, it was found that there was no money in it, only bills and notes of hand of the directors[4]. Mackworth made strenuous efforts to preserve such reputation as he had left, and he produced voluminous documentary evidence to exonerate himself and to throw the blame on Waller[5]. The latter managed to justify himself and he was confirmed in the management by the creditors[6], but the House of Commons condemned Mackworth, William Shiers, the secretary, and Thomas Dykes, the accountant, as guilty of many notorious and scandalous frauds and indirect practices, and a bill was drafted (which, however, had not been passed at the end of the session) to prevent the three persons named from leaving the country or from alienating their estate[7].

In the next session of Parliament, the shareholders joined with the creditors in petitioning the House of Commons in order that a settle-

---

[1] *An abstract of the Deed or Instrument for an Union of all Parties concerned in the Mine Adventure*, 1710 $\left[\text{Brit. Mus. } \dfrac{522 \cdot m \cdot 25}{9}\right]$.

[2] *The Case of Sir Humphrey Mackworth, ut supra*, p. 14.

[3] *Journals of the House of Commons*, XVI. pp. 322, 328.

[4] *Ibid.*, XVI. pp. 359, 361.

[5] *The Case of Sir Humphrey Mackworth, ut supra*; *Book of Vouchers to prove the Case and Defence of the Deputy Governor and Directors of the Company of Mine Adventurers*, Parts I. and II. [Brit. Mus. 102. k. 37; 522. m. 12 (43)].

[6] *The Case of W. W[aller] upon the complaint of E. Vaughan* [1714] $\left[\text{Brit. Mus. } \dfrac{516 \cdot m \cdot 18}{43}\right]$.

[7] *Journals of the House of Commons*, XVI. p. 391.

ment should be effected, and a bill was drafted[1]. This produced a fresh series of leaflets in support of the different interests involved[2]. The act, which resulted in 1711, was an attempt at a compromise. In the first place, all shares beyond the 6,012, which had been created legally, were to be void, but members who had paid the whole or part of the call of February 1708 were to rank as creditors to that extent. These shares were considered to be of the nominal value of £20 each (or £120,240) and they were to be written down by one-third, that is new shares were to be issued to the old shareholders to the nominal value of £80,160, this being the exact sum at which this interest was represented in 1699. The holders of blanks were to have the nominal value of these reduced by one-fifth and new shares given for the balance, other creditors were to receive new shares to the full amount of their respective debts. These new shares were to be of the same number as the old and therefore their denomination was higher, being about £45 per share.

Reconstruction of the Mine Adventurers, 1711.

	Original values	Values after reconstruction
Creditors of the company	90,380	90,380
Bondholders for "blanks" (reduced by one-fifth) ...	125,000	100,000
Shareholders (reduced by one-third)	120,240	80,160
Total capital as rearranged, divided into 6,012 shares...		270,540

The increase in the nominal value of the shares made it desirable that the scale of qualifications and voting rights should be rearranged. Each share now entitled the owner of it to ten votes, while the qualification of the governor was ten shares, that of the deputy six, and of the remaining directors four each[3].

Either the number of creditors and the value of their claims was greater than had been calculated in 1710, or else it soon became necessary to make further calls since in 1712 the nominal amount of the share was then computed at £58[4]. During the next seven years,

---

[1] *Journals of the House of Commons*, XVI. p. 449; *A Bill for the Relief of the Creditors and Proprietors of the Mine Adventure* $\left[\text{Brit. Mus. } \frac{522 \cdot \text{m} \cdot 12}{22}\right]$.

[2] *The Advantage of the New Scheme of the Mine Adventure* $\left[\text{Brit. Mus. } \frac{522 \cdot \text{m} \cdot 12}{30}\right]$; *Reasons for passing the Mine Adventurers' Bill; Reasons against passing the Bill relating to the Mine Adventurers; Remarks on a Paper entitled Observations on a Bill relating to the Mine Adventurers* $\left[\text{Brit. Mus. } \frac{816 \cdot \text{m} \cdot 13}{79, 80 \text{ and } 81}\right]$.

[3] *Statutes*, IX. p. 485.

[4] *Case of the Creditors of the Mine Adventurers Company* $\left[\text{Brit. Mus. } \frac{522 \cdot \text{m} \cdot 12}{4}\right]$.

the company was involved in continual suits, arising out of the former management, no less than five cases being pending at the same time[1]. During the boom of 1719-20, it was not unnatural that the directors should endeavour to procure fresh capital and several proposals were under consideration[2]. Mackworth, however, reappeared upon the scene, to the great discomfiture of the directors who had replaced his nominees. He had established a new company, known as *the Mineral Manufacturers at Neath*, and he had hopes of securing the charter of the Mine Adventurers to legalize the status of his new enterprize. On "the very night" before the transfer books were closed prior to the general court, he had eighty shares transferred to his friends. These thereupon requisitioned a special court, which was held on August 16th, 1720, when a committee was appointed composed of the former directors and those of Mackworth's faction in equal numbers. The annual court for the election of officers met on November 26th, 1720, and, "in a very tumultuous manner," Mackworth was chosen governor and his nominees as directors[3]. He thereupon launched upon "many intricate, ensnaring and fraudulent schemes and fallacious computations," which caused him to be compared with John Law[4]. At the next annual meeting (1721) Sir R. Worsley was elected governor, but Mackworth persuaded him to refuse to act; and, when the election took place in the following December, a John Wallis, who was one of the turbulent majority, was selected. A shareholder had protested at the previous meeting that Mackworth had never been duly voted governor, since, "by his irregular, tumultuous, unwarrantable and illegal proceedings," the meeting had been turned into a mob. These expressions were voted false and scandalous, after which a friend of Mackworth's was elected governor and it was resolved to resume the suit formerly initiated against Waller and to sell 1197 shares for £20,000, *i.e.* at 16¾ per share[5]. Those

[1] A Representation of what has been done by the...Company of Mine Adventurers...from Nov. 26, 1720 to Nov. 28, 1721 (Bod. Lib. Rawl. MS. D 916, ff. 270–289); *The Case of the United Society for the Improvement of Mineral Works*, 1715 $\left[\text{Brit. Mus. } \frac{816 \cdot m \cdot 13}{75}\right]$.

[2] *A scheme for advancing the trading stock* $\left[\text{Brit. Mus. } \frac{522 \cdot m \cdot 13}{32}\right]$; *A Familiar Letter...containing an account of the proceedings of the Governor and Company of the Mine Adventurers of England*, 1720 $\left[\text{Brit. Mus. } \frac{726 \cdot m \cdot 12}{11}\right]$.

[3] Petition of the Proprietors of Shares in the Company of Mine Adventurers of England, on behalf of themselves and many others widows and orphans to the House of Commons 172½ (Bod. Lib. Rawl. MS. D 916, ff. 294–303).

[4] *Observations of the Scheme of Mr Law in France and of Sir Humphrey Mackworth in Great Britain* [Brit. Mus. 8223.d.7].

[5] General Court of the Governor and Company of the Mine Adventurers of England, held at Stationers' Hall, London, on Friday, December 22, 1721 (Bod. Lib. Rawl. MS. D 916, ff. 290–2).

shareholders, who had been members before the summer of 1720, handed in written protests which Mackworth refused to admit, whereupon they retired from the meeting. After holding separate meetings, they decided to appeal to Parliament and eventually regained control of the charter[1]. Officials continued to be elected[2], and late in the eighteenth century an amalgamation was effected with the undertaking, which then owned the charter of the Mineral and Battery Works, the new body being described as the " United Mines[3]."

Summary of Capital and Prices of the Shares.

Capital.

1698–9.	Blanks or bonds at 6%, giving a first charge for interest and principal	£125,000
,,	Prizes or shares—4008 with £20 reckoned as paid on each	£80,160

Prices[4].

	Bonds	Shares
1701	82½—80	23—21
1702	83—81	23—20
1703 to 1705	—	—
1706	—	26—15¾
1707	—	21—18¼
1708	—	17—12

[1] *Petition, ut supra.*

[2] *A List of the Governor and Court of Directors of the Company of Mine Adventurers*, 1727 $\left[\text{Brit. Mus. } \dfrac{522 \cdot \text{m} \cdot 12}{25}\right]$; *Gentleman's Magazine*, I. p. 497.

[3] *Reports from Committees of the House of Commons*, x. p. 681.

[4] *The New State of Europe, Post Boy,* and other Newspapers, also *Journals of the House of Commons*, XVI. pp. 359, 367.

SECTION VIII. COMPANIES FOR COAL MINING.

PARTNERSHIP FOR WORKING THE LUMLEY MINE (1606-7).
PARTNERSHIP FOR WORKING MINES AT BEDWORTH (1622).
COAL MINING AND IRON CO. IN THE FOREST OF DEAN (1653).
THE OLD BLYTHE COAL COMPANY (ABOUT 1694).
THE NEW BLYTHE COAL COMPANY (ABOUT 1694).
THE PLESSEY COAL COMPANY (ABOUT 1695).
THE DURHAM COAL AND SALT COMPANY (ABOUT 1696).

THE coal trade, like other long-established industries, did not afford much scope for joint-stock enterprize. Until the end of the sixteenth century and even later, there was a general prejudice against the use of coal as fuel. Both householders, who could afford to burn wood, as well as the more wealthy manufacturers, preferred to avoid coal. Such preference was not merely the result of conservative prejudice. The coal, which was brought to the market at this period, was procured in two ways—either by being gathered on the sea-shore where it had been cast up by the tides, having been washed out of seams which became exposed in the sea-bed or were shown in the cliffs by the action of the waves[1] (and hence known as "sea-coal") or being quarried at places where there was an "out-crop" of the seam. In following the vein, a pit was often dug into the ground and therefore the coal, so won, was known in the seventeenth century as "pit-coal." Since both "sea-coal" and "pit-coal" were at first obtained from seams near the surface, when ignited they gave off "noxious" gases; and the use of such fuel was often spoken of, in the sixteenth and seventeenth centuries, as a nuisance. During the seventeenth century the supply of wood did not suffice for the demands of domestic consumption and the growing requirements of

---

[1] This appears to have been the original meaning of the term (cf. Leland, *Itinerary*, VIII. p. 19: "the vaynes of the se coles ly sometyme upon clines of the se, as round about Coquet Island and other shores; and they, as some will, be properly called se coles"). Later the expression was used to describe sea-borne coal, in opposition to that dug inland. *The History and Description of Fossil Fuel, the Collieries and Coal Trade of Great Britain*, 1841, p. 311 (note).

certain industries, with the result that a great stimulus was given to coal mining.

When it became necessary to follow the coal veins below the surface, mining was prosecuted at first by means of what is known as the "day-hole" method, where no machinery was required, and the only capital outlay involved was that for the opening of a transverse tunnel[1]. As labour was cheap, the expenditure was seldom beyond the resources of a single proprietor or a small partnership. There was more expense involved in adopting the "pit and adit" system, which soon became necessary, since two shafts (instead of one) were required, and machinery was needed to raise the coal. With the adoption of this species of mining, we begin to hear of partnerships for the working of leases of coal-bearing properties, as for instance in 1606-7 the taking of the Lumley mines, situated on the south side of the river Wear, by a group of four persons[2].

Towards the end of the first quarter of the seventeenth century, a partnership was formed by John Briggs for farming coal mines at Bedworth, in Warwickshire. The early history of coal mining was one continuous effort after a monopoly, and Briggs and his partners followed the example of the municipality of Newcastle-on-Tyne in endeavouring to obtain control of the collieries in their district. Unfortunately for their scheme, there were rival mines, some of which were bought up but others could not be secured. Instead of cutting prices, like a modern combine, Briggs seems to have thought of the expedient, not of "crushing" competition but of *drowning* it, by turning water into the rival mines. The owners of the latter were flooded out of their pits and petitioned to the Privy Council in 1622, while the Briggs partnership replied that the miners, outside the combination, had inflicted serious loss on them by poisoning the water from which their horses drank. In 1623 it was decided that Briggs should not bore any holes that would endanger the flooding of the pits of his rivals; but in 1631 the partnership constructed a certain dam, and soon afterwards the competing mines were flooded. Whether there was any causal connection between the two events remained undetermined, and in 1632 an arrangement was sanctioned by the Privy Council for the diversion of a water-course, which it was hoped would prevent the danger of drowning any of the endangered mines[3].

In 1653 an important company with a large membership (including Oliver Cromwell) was formed to mine coal and smelt iron ore in the

---

[1] This method, as well as the "Pit and Adit" and the "Pit," is illustrated and described in *Annals of Coal Mining, and the Coal Trade*, by A. L. Galloway, 1898, p. 74.

[2] *Ibid.*, p. 166. [3] *Ibid.*, pp. 197-200.

Forest of Dean. Authority was granted the petitioners to work for 30 years, on condition of their paying the State one-eighth of the profit[1]. Possibly the foundation of this company arose more from a political than an economic need; since Newcastle, which supplied London with coal, was notoriously loyal to the monarchy, and therefore the new government would be anxious to have the supply of a commodity, which had now become so important, in the hands of "well-affected" persons.

These cases of joint-stock ownership of coal mines were comparatively isolated; and, since capital had now become necessary for the prosecution of the industry, the reason for the absence of coal mining companies is probably to be found in the monopoly of the supplying of London with coal which had been long enjoyed by the burgesses of Newcastle. The corporation owned coal mines; there was the "company of Hoastmen," with a monopoly of bringing coal from the collieries to the ships, besides various shipping rings for the conveyance of coals from the port to London. The whole trade was entangled in a net-work of privileges, and London, in particular, suffered from the "grievance of the coal trade." So much was this the case that in 1665 it was proposed to make all coal mines, mines royal; but, in the time of Charles II., the effect of the change would have probably been to transform a municipal monopoly into a royal one[2]. However, purely economic changes tended slowly to remove the grievance. The pit and adit method of mining could only be used in exceptional places towards the end of the seventeenth century, and it was necessary to win the coal by the pit system, in which both the coal and the water had to be raised to the surface by machinery. Capital was needed in larger quantities for more extensive sinking of shafts[3] and the inventor found an outlet for his powers in devising machines for draining the collieries of water[4]. In fact the new conditions of mining made the problem of freeing a mine from water one of the critical points in deciding the possibilities of profit from any given property. Coal-bearing lands were common, but, once the pit was sunk, it very often happened that it became filled with water and a pump was required to enable the work to be carried on. The author of the *Compleat Collier* says that "were it not for water, a colliery might be called a golden mine to purpose, for dry collieries would save several thousand pounds per ann., which is expended in drawing water."

[1] State Papers, Domestic, Inter., XLII. 85; *Calendar*, 1653–4, p. 322.
[2] *Ibid.*, Charles II., CXIX. 24 (1); *Calendar*, 1664–5, p. 330.
[3] *The Compleat Collier*, by J. C., London, 1708 (in Richardson's *Reprint of Rare Tracts, Miscellaneous*), p. 19.
[4] *Vide infra*, Division V., Section 1.

These and other circumstances, all pointing to the need of capital for the development of coal-mining, give the promoter of 1694 his opportunity. At that time there were in existence two coal companies, distinguished as the "Old Blythe" and the "New Blythe" companies. In 1695 Houghton mentions a third company, working collieries at Plessey, in Northumberland. The earliest records of coal mining relate to workings near the river Blythe and at Plessey[1]; and it seems that the properties were valuable ones, with a considerable capital and large number of shareholders. One of the Blythe companies found it necessary to advertise its annual meetings in the *London Gazette*[2], and the existence of a third company, owning coal mines and salt works, is shown by a similar advertisement in 1696[3].

[1] Galloway, *Annals of Coal Mining*, pp. 21, 30, 55.
[2] No. 3474, Feb. 23, 1699.   [3] *Ibid.*, No. 3258, Jan. 28, 1696.

SECTION IX. COMPANIES FOR THE SMELTING OF IRON.

A Partnership in Two Iron Works (temp. Ed. VI.).
The Company for working the Patents of Sturtevant and Rovenzon for smelting Iron with Coal (1612–13).
William Anstell's Smelting Partnership (1627).
Dudley Dudley and Partners (1638).
Dudley Dudley and Partners (1651).
An Iron Company near Belfast (1681).
The Governor and Company for Making Iron with Pit-Coal (incorporated 1693).

The deposits of iron ore in England had been worked from a very early period. It is probable that, prior to the sixteenth century, the ore was smelted on the estate where it was found—the wood, required for fuel, being provided by the landowner. The furnaces were primitive and therefore the capital, used in any given undertaking, was very small. Some of these ventures were profitable. Thus it is recorded, when a partnership was being formed to carry on iron works already in existence and to erect another plant during the reign of Edward VI., that at this time a similar smelting business on the property of Lord de Lisle was producing 138 tons of iron annually, on which a profit of £312. 7s. 4d. was earned[1].

Before the end of the sixteenth century the owners of iron-works were charged with the destruction of woods, involving a rise in the price of fuel and fears for the future of the shipping industry. Inventors had already begun to endeavour to devise methods for the utilization of coal for smelting; and it was at this point that the joint-stock system becomes connected with the iron industry, at intervals during the seventeenth century. Already in 1589 and again in 1607, patents were granted to encourage persons who claimed that they had discovered the method required, but neither of these was effectual, nor indeed does it

[1] *Report Royal Com. on Hist. MSS.*, III. pp. 120, 228.

appear that either of them was put in actual operation. In 1612 a new patent was granted to Simon Sturtevant, which became the basis of a company[1]. The privilege of this grant was divided into thirty-three parts or shares, of which eighteen were assigned to persons about the Court, James I. receiving ten, the Prince of Wales five, the Duke of York two and the Earl of Rochester one. There remained fifteen shares, by the sale of which it was intended that the capital, required for the development of the invention, should be raised. In order to demonstrate the possibilities of profit to the shareholders, Sturtevant calculated that there were at this time 800 iron-works in Great Britain and Ireland. Each of these on an average consumed annually charcoal costing £500. By means of his invention he contended that the same output could be produced, using coal as fuel, at a cost of £30, £40 or at the most £50 a year. Taking the outlay for coal at £100 a year on the average, there would be a saving of £400. Therefore, for the whole 800 iron-works, the decrease in the cost of production, under the head of fuel, would be £320,000 annually, thus giving prospects of a large royalty to the owners of the patent[2]. By reason of these expectations, Sturtevant succeeded in selling shares to investors, but he failed to smelt iron with coal. John Rovenzon, who had been an assistant of Sturtevant, undertook to continue the work, and the former patent (which had been granted for 31 years) was recalled and a new one issued in favour of Rovenzon. It was arranged that there should be thirty-three shares as before, the royal family and Rochester owning eighteen. Rovenzon was to retain one and the remaining fourteen were available for distribution "amongst the aiders, assisters, adventurers and owners of the works." It was also agreed that Rovenzon was to give recompence and satisfaction to those who had taken up shares in Sturtevant's patent[3]. Under the later revised form of the scheme, it was promised that the capital outlay on iron-works should be immensely reduced, since as large an output could be obtained under the patent by an expenditure of £100 on furnaces as was procurable by the existing methods for £1,000 or £1,500[4]. This company entered on "great undertakings" and made many trials, all of which ended in failure[5]. Further attempts by a

---

[1] *Metallica; or the Treatise of Metallica briefly comprehending the Doctrine of Diverse new Metallical Inventions*, by Simon Sturtevant, 1612; reprinted in *Supplement to the Series of Letters Patent and Specifications...recorded in the Great Seal Patent Office*, edited by Bennet Woodcroft, London, 1858, I. pp. 6–11.

[2] *Ibid.*, p. 3.

[3] *A Treatise of Metallica*, by John Rovenzon, 1613, in *Supplement to the Series of Letters Patent and Specifications*, 1858, I. pp. 44, 45.

[4] *Ibid.*, p. 50.

[5] *Dud Dudley's Metallum Martis or Iron made with Pit-Coale, Sea-Coale &c.*, 1665, in *Supplement to the Series of Letters Patent and Specifications*, I. p. 60.

DIV. IV. § 9] *Smelting Schemes of Dudley 1619–27*

servant of the Queen, named Gombleton, and subsequently by Dr Jordan were also without success.

In 1619 Dudley Dudley, then a youth of twenty years of age, was recalled from Oxford to manage a forge and two furnaces belonging to his father, Lord Dudley, which were situated in Worcestershire. He, finding wood and charcoal very scarce, endeavoured to utilize the coal which abounded near the furnace. Having already been conversant with recent efforts to solve the problem, he succeeded, according to his own account, in making iron with coal at the first trial, and that too on a profitable basis. At the second trial, the production was at the rate of three tons per week, and the inventor had great hopes of increasing the quantity obtainable by his method. On the application of his father, a patent was obtained in 1621, which was excepted from the statute of monopolies, though the monopoly of the process was thereby limited to the term of fourteen years[1].

About 1621 Dudley was able to send a consignment of iron from his furnace to the Tower, which was approved by the experts appointed by the Crown to test it. In the same year he experienced the misfortune of having his works swept away in an inundation known as "the May-Day Flood." The Dudleys, at considerable expense, re-established the works, and it was claimed that the iron then made, using coal as the fuel, was better and cheaper than any other on the market, being sold at £12 per ton[2]. Thereupon, according to Dudley's own statement, he "was outed of his works and inventions, before mentioned, by the iron-masters and others"; and he was faced by the further difficulty that, in 1627, William Anstell and his partners obtained a rival patent[3]. Dudley now removed to Staffordshire, where he succeeded by his process in making seven tons of iron a week, until his works were forcibly entered by the servants of his rivals and his bellows cut to pieces.

It will thus be seen that Dudley's production of iron was often interrupted and the prejudice against him had involved him in considerable expense. The term of his patent was drawing to a close, and he decided to obtain an extension of it, with a view to securing financial assistance. The new patent was signed on May 2nd, 1638[4], and on June 11th Dudley and four friends signed articles, under which the partnership was to repay Dudley the charges of obtaining the fresh

---

[1] *Metallum Martis, ut supra*, p. 61; *The English Patents of Monopoly*, by W. Hyde Price, Boston, 1906, pp. 192–6. Though the patent was not sealed till February 22, 1621, a warrant had been signed in March 1620.

[2] *Metallum Martis, ut supra*, p. 63: this was the price for bar-iron.

[3] *Fœdera*, xviii. p. 992.

[4] Printed in *The English Patents of Monopoly*, by W. Hyde Price, Boston, 1906, pp. 197–206.

grant, while each of the new members undertook to provide £100, making a free capital of £400[1]. This enterprize had to meet the opposition of Sir Philibert Vernatti, who had also obtained a patent, and, not long afterwards, the work of the syndicate was interrupted by the Civil Wars.

In 1651 Dudley established a new partnership near Bristol, and the three members of this body raised, between them, £700. He was unfortunate in this venture; since, having supported Charles I., he was to a considerable extent at the mercy of the dominant party. There were disputes between the other partners and Dudley, and the latter found himself involved in protracted suits in Chancery[2]. He applied in vain for an extension of his patent after the Restoration, and his secret died with him.

From 1660 to 1690 repeated efforts were made to utilize coal for the smelting of iron, of which the most promising appears to have been that of Frederick de Blewstone, who had established furnaces, burning coal, at Wednesbury in 1677[3]. This experiment at first seemed likely to be successful, but in the end it resulted in "dismal failure[4]."

In 1690 there is mention of the smelting of metals "in close and reverberatory furnaces," and John Hodges, the inventor, procured a patent for the use of this invention in Ireland[5]. The following year, Thomas Addison endeavoured to show that he had discovered a method of smelting "all sorts of iron ore, iron stone, slags, cinders and other material," using pit or sea coal, by which means good iron could be made cheaper than heretofore[6]. He obtained a warrant for a patent on February 15th, 1692[7]. Addison transferred his patent to a number of others, and he, together with his partners, petitioned on December 6th for incorporation on the ground that the undertaking required many thousands, which could only be raised by means of a joint-stock[8]. The Attorney-General reported on December 14th that the petitioners supported their request for a charter, by arguing that the requisite capital could not be raised otherwise, since "persons are unwilling to advance great sums in a way of partnership, because, in case of the bankruptcy of any of the partners, the stock in partnership would be liable to be seized," and for this and other reasons, he recommended the grant of a charter, subject to the persons proposing to be incorporated being prevented from making an ill-use of it, by the insertion of clauses providing for the determination of the patent should the undertaking prove hurtful to the public or if the works were not established and

---

[1] *Metallum Martis, ut supra*, p. 64. [2] *Ibid.*, pp. 64, 65.
[3] Plot, *Staffordshire*, p. 128.   [4] Galloway, *Annals of Coal Mining*, p. 195.
[5] State Papers, Domestic, H. O. Warrant Book, xxxv. p. 248.
[6] *Ibid.*, Petition Entry Book, I. p. 202.
[7] *Ibid.*, H. O. Warrant Book, vi. p. 257.
[8] *Ibid.*, Petition Entry Book, I. p. 423.

carried on effectually[1]. Accordingly, a charter was sealed incorporating the members as *the Governor and Company for Making Iron with Pit Coal*, with the privileges of a new invention for ever. The court consisted of a governor, deputy-governor and fourteen assistants. The shareholders had one vote for each share up to four votes, which was the maximum. Powers were given to raise a joint-stock, and the same might "increase and diminish[2]." It was agreed to raise £10,500 "on easy payments, and to make the iron, all charges included, at...per ton and to sell the same at £13 per ton, which must produce [consider]able dividends, because of the quantity that will be delivered quarterly [as] aforesaid[3]." The author of *Angliæ Tutamen* mentions, amongst other mineral companies, one dealing with iron, and it seems that the company existed at least as late as the reign of Anne, but the effectual smelting of iron with coal was established only at a later date, so that it may be concluded that this company shared the fate of the pioneers of any great invention[4]. Whatever may have been its misfortunes, it escaped the alleged evils of stock-jobbing, for its name does not appear in Houghton's list of companies, the shares of which were dealt with on the Exchange.

During the seventeenth century, the destruction of the forests in England gave a great impetus to the production of pig-iron in Ireland. In 1652 it is recorded that "whereas there was never an iron-work in Ireland before, there hath been a great number of them erected since the last peace in sundry parts of every province[5]." This industry was very profitable as long as the supply of wood lasted, as is shown by the statement that the Earl of Cork made £100,000 from his iron mines[6], and also by the statistics of certain works owned by Sir Charles Coot at Mountrath in Queen's County. The iron was shipped from Waterford, and it could be landed in London, having cost in all between £10 and £11 per ton as against a market price there of £16 to £17. 10s.[7] In at least one case, Irish iron-works were carried on by a company during the seventeenth century, since there is mention of a body whose furnaces were within two miles of Belfast, in which a Captain Lawson had "stock and interest[8]."

[1] State Papers, Domestic, Petition Entry Book, I. p. 427.

[2] *An Abstract of the Charter, granted by their late Majesties King William and Queen Mary in the fifth year of their reign, to the Governor and Company for making Iron with Pit Coal* [Brit. Mus. $\frac{816 \cdot m \cdot 13}{9}$].

[3] MS. addition to the foregoing. [4] Galloway, *Annals of Coal Mining*, p. 228.

[5] *Ireland's Natural History*, by Gerard Boate, edited by Samuel Hartlib, London, 1652, p. 120. [6] *Ibid.*, p. 137.

[7] *The Industrial Resources of Ireland*, by R. Kane, Dublin, 1845, pp. 123, 124.

[8] *A History of Belfast*, by George Benn, 1877, p. 334.

SECTION X. COMPANIES FOR THE SUPPLY OF SALT.

THE GOVERNOR, ASSISTANTS AND COMMONALTY OF THE SOCIETY OF SALT-MAKERS AT THE NORTH AND SOUTH SHIELDS IN THE COUNTIES OF DURHAM AND NORTHUMBERLAND (1635).
THE CORPORATION OF SALTERS IN THE SALT WORKS NEAR GREAT YARMOUTH (1639).
THE DROITWICH SALT WORKS COMPANY (1689).
THE ROCK-SALT COMPANY (BEFORE 1694).

In the seventeenth century salt was obtained in four different ways. First, in places where the sea-board was comparatively low-lying, during high tides water flowed into broad expanses forming shallow lakes, and, in the course of time by means of evaporation, the salt held in solution by the sea-water was deposited so that all man had to do was to collect it. Such salt was rare in Britain, being found only at the Isle of May. Unless refined, the so-called salt contained sand and sometimes mud. Even when used for pickling herrings, it was found to cause discolouration, and in 1663 its use for this purpose was prohibited. The main supply of salt was procured by evaporation either from sea-water or salt-springs. Salt-springs were utilized chiefly in Cheshire, Worcestershire, Hampshire, Northumberland and Staffordshire. The general method of procedure, towards the close of the century, was to erect a boiling-house, known as "a saltern," containing a number of shallow pans to contain the brine and fitted with furnaces beneath to hasten evaporation. During the earlier part of the century the chief source of supply was the district about North and South Shields, where the process of obtaining the salt was similar, except that sea-water was used. Reservoirs were made, whence the water was allowed to flow into wrought iron pans, eighteen or nineteen feet long, twelve feet broad and fourteen inches deep. These were heated by a "kind of crusty, drossy coal, taken from the upper part of the mine," and the process of boiling was similar to that adopted in Cheshire, except that care was needed to free the salt from sand. It was found that, when the brine was in a boiling state, the sand was precipitated sooner than the salt, and the men, who watched the operation, drew the sand by means of broad flat rakes to one side of the pan. Six or seven boilings were necessary before the salt was ready to be cleared away. The fourth source of supply of salt was from rock-salt, and until the close of the century this species was generally imported[1].

The salt-pans at Shields were celebrated from an early period. Many of the most wealthy families in the district were engaged in the trade, each proprietor working as many pans as he could afford to equip and maintain in operation[2]. The industry remained in this state of organization until it shared in the fate of the soap trade and excited the attention of persons seeking monopolies in the time of Charles I. Some of the chief operations of the society of Salt-Makers at Shields (1635-8) have been already described[3], and the chief point of interest in the organization of this monopoly is the question as to how far it was carried on by means of a joint-stock body. Under an early form of the scheme in 1631, it had been intended that the society should allow the small owners of salt-pans to produce a certain proportion or share of the output that it was intended to fix upon[4]; but when the charter had been obtained in 1635 this plan was modified and, in many cases, the society rented the salt-pans, or alternatively it licensed the makers on condition that the latter became members of the corporation and agreed to pay the duty reserved to the Crown and undertook to sell at the specified rates[5]. This mode of working suggests a type of constitution analogous to that of the Soapmakers of Westminster which is discussed elsewhere[6], and which tends to conform to the regulated, rather than to the joint-stock company. Similarly, when this society was dissolved and was succeeded by *a Corporation of Salters* in 1639, it would appear that the latter was organized on somewhat similar lines. Whatever may have been the method of working, as between themselves, of the members

---

[1] *Dictionarium Rusticum, Urbanicum, et Botanicum: or a Dictionary of Husbandry, Gardening, Trade, Commerce and all sorts of country Affairs*, London, 1717.—Article, "Salt."

[2] *A History of the Trade and Manufactures of the Tyne Wear and Tees, comprising ...papers...read at the...meeting of the British Association*, 1863, p. 135.

[3] Part I., Chapter XI.

[4] State Papers, Domestic, Notes of Secretary Coke, March 12, 1631; *Calendar*, 1629-31, p. 535.

[5] *An Answer to those printed Papers published in March last 1640 by the late Patentees of Salt in their pretended Defence against Free Trade*, composed by John Davies, 1641, p. 20.

[6] Part I., Chapter XI.

of these two bodies, it is interesting to note that it was alleged that those belonging to the second salt monopoly had succeeded, through it, in obtaining great wealth[1].

According to one account, the effect of the monopolies on the salt-making industry at Shields was disastrous. Before 1635 the annual production had been 16,000 wey, during the time of the society it fell to 10,000 wey, and in that of the corporation to 8,000 wey[2]—a decrease of one half in about six years. Unfortunately for those interested in the trade, the abrogation of the monopoly brought no relief, for it was followed by the freedom of trade with Scotland during the Protectorate, with the result that the number of pans was diminished by 80. There were many and bitter complaints of the competition of Scottish salt, it being said, for instance, that the makers in the north could always undersell English producers, because the former paid low wages which were distributed in kind, and not in money[3]. Not long after the Restoration, a further 160 pans were abandoned[4].

In the last quarter of the seventeenth century, there came discoveries which changed the localization of the main salt-producing industry from the east to the west of England. The brine-springs in Cheshire were developed, and it became customary for a number of persons to join together in providing the royalty for the working of a certain spring, which was divided into parts or shares proportioned to the subdivisions of the rent[5]. Then, in 1670, means were found for working the deposits of rock-salt. In 1689 a company had been established, which succeeded in obtaining an act of Parliament[6]. Its operations were carried on at Droitwich, and it appears to have made salt from brine. Prior to 1694 a rock-salt company had been started at Frodsham, which was well managed, and in 1695 is said to have been ready to declare a dividend. Whether this particular undertaking survived or not, the industry extended, and in 1702 it was stated that the outlay, on pits and refineries in this district, was as much as £50,000[7].

---

[1] *The Projector's Downfall or Times Changeling; Wherein the Monopolists and Patentees are unmasked to the View of the World*, 1642, p. 4.

[2] Davies, *An Answer to...the late Patentees of Salt*, p. 10.

[3] *A Narrative concerning the Salt Works in the North*, in *Reprints of Rare Tracts*, by W. A. Richardson, Newcastle, III. p. 10.

[4] *Salt and Fishing—A Discourse*, by John Collins, 1682, p. 151.

[5] *Journals of the House of Commons*, XI. p. 97.

[6] *Report Royal Com. on Hist. MSS.*, XII., Pt. VI. p. 110.

[7] *The Case of Rock-Salt* [1702] $\left[\text{Brit. Mus.} \frac{816 \cdot m \cdot 13}{108} \right]$.

SECTION XI. SALTPETRE COMPANIES.

THE UNDERTAKERS OF THE ROYAL MONOPOLY FOR SALTPETRE (TEMP. CHARLES I.).
SIR JOHN BROOKE AND THOMAS RUSSEL'S PARTNERSHIP FOR THE MAKING OF SALTPETRE (1627).
COL. OGLE AND PARTNERS (1656).
THE GOVERNOR AND COMPANY FOR MAKING SALTPETRE IN ENGLAND (1692).
A SALTPETRE COMPANY, FORMED BY THOMAS LECHMERE (1692).
A SALTPETRE COMPANY, FORMED BY HENRY LONGUEVILLE (1692).

DURING the seventeenth century the procuring of saltpetre remained an extractive industry; and the ground, whence it was obtained, was spoken of as a mine. The earth, from which saltpetre was extracted, was usually the site of deserted villages, stables or dove-houses. Having procured suitable soil, " the workmen dig two pits, flat at the bottom, like those wherein common salt is made, one of them having much more compass than the other; the latter they fill with earth so as water may run upon it for some time, and then tread it with their feet, till reduced to the consistency of pap, letting it stand for two days that the water may extract all the salt that is in the earth; that done, they pass the water into another pit, where it crystallizes into salt-petre. This they boil once or twice in a cauldron, according as they would have it whiter and purer. While the liquor is over the fire they scum it continually and fill it out into great earthenware pots, which hold twenty-five or thirty pounds. These they expose to clear nights; and, if there be any impurity remaining, it will fall to the bottom, afterwards they break the pots and dry the salt in the sun[1]."

[1] *Dictionarium Rusticum, ut supra*, Article, "Saltpetre."

On the grounds that saltpetre was essential for the making of gunpowder and that a sufficient supply of powder was necessary for the security of the State, the working of saltpetre was retained by the sovereign during the earlier part of the seventeenth century. Charles I. in 1625 issued a proclamation forbidding any person to pave the floor of any dove-house or other place, where deposits, from which saltpetre might be obtained, would be formed. Persons, deputed by the King's powder-maker, had the right of entering any premises, declared by commission to be a saltpetre mine[1]. Even with the aid of these extensive powers, the undertakers, who farmed the royal monopoly, were unable to provide more than one-third of the quantity required; and, in 1627, a patent was granted Sir John Brooke and Thomas Russel for a new invention, which consisted in artificially rendering earth saltpetre bearing[2]. Great things were expected of this method. The inventors had given demonstrative proof of the practicability of their idea and it was anticipated that they could supply the country and have a surplus remaining for export. The patentees erected a refinery at Southwark and they were encouraged by a proclamation, which was designed to foster the undertaking by certain most objectionable and insanitary methods. Apparently, in spite of demonstrative proof, the new method was too slow or altogether unsuccessful; for, in the same year, the proclamation of 1625 was repeated[3], and it was again renewed in 1634[4]. This grievance of the right of forcible entry in search of saltpetre deposits remained in force until 1656, when it was repealed by act of Parliament[5], and Colonel Ogle, who had set up powder-mills, was granted a patent in the same year[6].

By the time of Charles II. the chief source of the supply of saltpetre was through the East India company, and clauses regulating its action in this respect were inserted in many of the charters[7]. The home-supply was relatively unimportant, but it was not neglected, as is shown by the grant from Charles II. to Robert Lindsey and another for their lives.

With the outbreak of war after the Revolution a home-supply of saltpetre became of the most vital importance. The enterprizing men of that period of industrial activity were not slow to seize the opportunity, and there were many schemes for starting saltpetre companies. On December 13th, 1690, Robert Price and others presented a petition in which they stated that they had found out a new way of making saltpetre in great quantities, and that they could sell their product at a

---

[1] *Fœdera*, xviii. p. 13. [2] *Ibid.*, p. 813.
[3] *Ibid.*, p. 915. [4] *Ibid.*, p. 601.
[5] Anderson, *Annals of Commerce*, ii. p. 582.
[6] State Papers, Domestic, Inter., cxxvi. 101; *Calendar*, 1655–6, p. 292.
[7] *Charters granted to the East India Company*, i. pp. 165–6, 218, 289–90.

cheaper rate than that imported from the Indies. They had located several parcels of earth, proper for their purpose; and, since Lindsey and his partner were dead, they petitioned for a patent for making saltpetre for 31 years in England, Scotland, Ireland and Wales[1]. The patent asked for was granted on January 1st, 1691[2]. Within the next year, the original patentees sold their patent to Ralph Bucknall and others, before any saltpetre had been made[3]. Bucknall and his partners divided the benefit of the grant into twelve hundred shares, some of which had been sold by May 10th, 1692. To justify the large capitalization, a charter of incorporation was desirable and the same group applied for one on February 25th[4]. The Attorney-General reported on March 12th that the making of saltpetre in large quantities would be an advantage to the kingdom; and, inasmuch as a large capital was required, he recommended a grant of incorporation[5]. A warrant was issued for the incorporation of Bucknall and his associates, on April 21st, as *the Governor and Company for making Saltpetre in England*, with powers to elect a governor, deputy-governor and twenty-four assistants, of whom seven constituted a quorum. Members were entitled to one vote for each share. The charter was issued, subject to the proviso that the company should not dig for saltpetre in any ground, without first having obtained the consent of the owner[6].

This was the only chartered undertaking, but there were two others, which came into existence in the same year. One was organized by Thomas Lechmere and the other by Henry Longueville[7]. In Houghton's list of shares, under the heading of "Saltpetre," there is mentioned an incorporated company called "Bellamont," then as unchartered undertakings—"Dockwra, Leechmere, Long., Stapleton." "Bellamont" probably indicates "the Governor and Company for making saltpetre in England." The concerns promoted by Dockwra and Stapleton were for the manufacture of ordnance[8]. "Long." seems to be a contraction for Longueville.

With reference to the subsequent history of these undertakings, Houghton writes on July 20th, 1694, that the Saltpetre company "shut up their gates and keep all close, but they have laid out a great deal of money on buildings[9]." While this report is non-committal, that of the author of *Angliæ Tutamen* is decidedly adverse. "Great sums

[1] State Papers, Domestic, Petition Entry Book, I. p. 109.
[2] *Ibid.*, H. O. Warrant Book, VI. p. 20.
[3] *Ibid.*, Petition Entry Book, I. p. 289.
[4] *Ibid.*, p. 241.
[5] *Ibid.*, p. 254.
[6] *Ibid.*, H. O. Warrant Book, VI. pp. 308-12.
[7] *Ibid.*, Petition Entry Book, I. pp. 274, 289.
[8] *Vide infra,* Division VIII., Section 6.
[9] *Collections, ut supra,* No. 103.

have been paid in, large refining houses have been built in four or five several places in London, societies have been established and a mighty noise made for a time. Persons of a loud sounding name and quality have appeared at the head of them and abundance of gentlemen and traders were concerned, all things being seemingly disposed in a good method...Yet of all these saltpetre companies, none made any great hand of it, except the first projectors, who always are gainers and then as usual withdraw. Stockjobbing was brought in; and, thereby and by other mismanagements, they fell to nothing[1]." Defoe, also, writing a few years later, quotes saltpetre companies as instances of undertakings which started with their shares at high premium, and before long there were no buyers[2].

[1] pp. 28, 29.   [2] *An Essay upon Projects,* p. 13.

SECTION XII. COMPANIES FORMED TO WORK ALUM AND OTHER MINES.

IN addition to the companies formed after the Revolution to exploit mines for copper, silver, lead, coal, iron and salt, the author of *Angliæ Tutamen* mentions others working antimony, *lapis calaminaris* and tin[1], while Houghton notes another for developing an alum mine. No particulars of the joint-stock tin-mining company have been discovered. The undertaking for the mining of antimony was a sub-division of one of the schemes of the versatile Captain Poyntz. Since his proposals, all of which in this connection were related to the island of Tobago, assumed many forms it will be simpler to deal with these together in the last division of this part, where cases in which the same charter has been used for different purposes are considered[2]. The allusion to the mining of *lapis calaminaris* doubtless relates to the revived activities of the society of the Mineral and Battery Works[3].

There remains the alum company, and, to understand its position, it will be desirable to glance back at the conditions under which this commodity had been previously produced in England. Up to the middle of the sixteenth century, Italian producers possessed an almost complete European monopoly of the production of alum. In the reign of Elizabeth fruitless efforts were made to manufacture it, indeed these experiments tended towards the providing of a satisfactory substitute. By 1607 alum had been discovered in Yorkshire and the working of it was claimed as a royal monopoly. At first the "mines" were entrusted to a group of patentees who again were financed by others, but by 1609 the system was changed and a farmer was appointed. By 1613 it had been determined to carry on the enterprize as a royal monopoly. In two years the Crown lost considerably, and the mines were again farmed, this method being continued till 1647[4]. From this date till the Restoration, the monopoly was in abeyance. After 1660 and until the Revolution, the Crown resumed its claim to alum mines

---

[1] p. 18.   [2] Division XIII., Section 1.   [3] *Vide supra*, p. 427.
[4] The early history of the alum monopoly is very carefully worked out in *The English Patents of Monopoly*, by W. Hyde Price, Boston, 1906, pp. 82–101.

and then leased its rights to others, from whom a rent was obtained. In the time of William III. this part of the prerogative was not maintained, and a group of projectors believed that there would be no impediment placed in their way in entering on the industry. Naturally the idea of taking up a business, so long a royal monopoly, was very attractive, so that the company had been formed prior to 1694. At first it met with considerable success, indeed Houghton notices that in 1694 its stock was much increased[1]. No doubt this was one of the enterprizes which were prosperous while the war continued, but which failed to maintain themselves against foreign competition after the declaration of peace.

[1] *Collections*, No. 97, July 20, 1694.

DIVISION V.

COMPANIES OWNING OR WORKING PUMPS AND MACHINERY FOR DRAINING MINES AND LANDS AND FOR RECOVERING TREASURE FROM WRECKS.

SECTION I. COMPANIES FOR PUMPING AND OTHER ENGINES.

MR JOHN LOFTINGH AND COMPANY, PROPRIETORS OF THE SUCKING-WORM ENGINE (1689).
A COMPANY FOR CAPTAIN POYNTZ' ENGINES (1693).
A COMPANY FOR TYZACH'S NIGHT ENGINE.

As subsidiary to the extractive industries, there was a group of undertakings, during the sixteenth and seventeenth centuries, engaged in endeavouring to deal with the problem of the presence of water. As mining progressed, the difficulty of the drainage of mines soon arose[1], and inventors endeavoured to devise means of draining the underground workings by means of pumps. These inventions at first were of a very primitive nature, and the same machine was conceived capable of draining mines, or flooded lands, of forcing water into a reservoir for supplying consumers in towns and also, with trifling modifications, of being used for extinguishing fire. Thus in 1578, Sir Thomas Golding petitioned for a patent for an invention "for draining marshes and supplying towns with water[2]." The engine of Morris, erected on London Bridge, was primarily a force-pump, driven by the fall of the Thames between the arches[3]. About 1594 Bevis Bulmer had an engine, working for the raising of river-water at Broken Wharf[4]. In 1611 Edward Hayes was supplying water to houses from the Thames by means of a pumping-machine[5], and the following year a patent for a similar device was granted to Joshua Usher[6]. Sir John Hacket and Octavius de Strada obtained a patent in 1627 for draining water out of mines[7], and a similar grant was made in 1630[8].

[1] *Vide supra*, pp. 443, 461.
[2] State Papers, Domestic, Elizabeth, cxxvii. 57; *Calendar*, 1547–80, p. 611.
[3] *Vide infra*, Division vi., Section 2.
[4] *Calendar State Papers, Treasury Papers*, 1557–1696, p. 576.
[5] State Papers, Domestic, James I., lxvi. 38; *Calendar*, 1611–18, p. 78.
[6] *Calendar State Papers, Treasury Papers*, 1557–1696, p. 148.
[7] *Fœdera*, xviii. p. 870.
[8] *Ibid.*, xix. p. 239.

From 1631 the drainage of the Bedford Level was undertaken by means of a machine invented by Cornelius Vermuyden[1].

After the Civil Wars and the Great Fire, attention was again given to force-pumps for draining mines and supplying drinking water. As time went on, the obstacles to mining through flood became more marked; and, during the speculative activity of the years 1690 to 1695, an inventor, who had a promising scheme, could easily find capital to develope it. Grants of patents for such machines now become numerous. On August 4th, 1691, John Holland, clerk, stated that, "by His industry and skill in mathematics," he had discovered an engine for discharging water from drowned mines and pits and which could also supply towns with water[2], and he was granted a patent on the 14th of the same month[3]. This pump was worked by two horses, and Holland advertised on March 9th, 1693, that he had it in operation at Row Pits, in the forest of Mendip, where it was discharging 50 tons of water per hour from a depth of 100 feet[4]. Thomas Gladwin also obtained a patent for a pump which, though primarily intended for use in ships, was adapted to drain mines and quench fire. The special merits claimed for this invention were compactness and simplicity of structure[5]. In 1693 N. Barbon had discovered an idea for utilizing the flux of the tides for raising water from the Thames, without the aid of horses as in Holland's invention[6]. There were also petitions from Cornelius Losvelt, Francis Bayton and Robert Baden for force-pumps in 1693 and 1694[7]. In 1695 Samuel Cock of Wapping petitioned for a patent for a water-raising engine, by the rotation of a lanthorne and teeth, which shifting itself is continually raised and depressed and is known by the name of the "engine of the shifting motion[8]." On November 26th, 1697, Thomas Savery had discovered a steam engine, which he described as a new invention "for raising water and occasioning motion by the impellent force of fire, and which will be of great advantage for draining mines, serving towns with water, and for the working of all sorts of mills, where they have not the benefit of water or of constant winds[9]." Savery obtained his patent for 14 years on April 25th, 1699, and he succeeded in having the term extended by 21 years by an act of Parliament. His engine was not suitable for a greater depth than 30 or 35 feet and it was

[1] *Vide supra*, p. 354.
[2] State Papers, Domestic, Petition Entry Book, I. p. 167.
[3] *Ibid.*, H. O. Warrant Book, VI. p. 154.
[4] *London Gazette*, No. 2852.
[5] State Papers, Domestic, Petition Entry Book, I. p. 183; H. O. Warrant Book, VI. p. 214.
[6] *Ibid.*, Petition Entry Book, II. p. 324.
[7] *Ibid.*, Petition Entry Books, II. pp. 341, 399, III. p. 67.
[8] *Ibid.*, IV. p. 35.
[9] *Ibid.*, p. 164.

little used in mines, though several were installed at country houses, and one for supplying a small district in London from the Thames[1]. In 1698 John Yarnold obtained a patent for an engine for draining mines and for supplying towns, villages and houses with water[2]. This was confirmed by act of Parliament, 9 Will. III. c. 46[3], and the town of Newcastle-on-Tyne was supplied with water for a time by this pumping machine[4].

As a type of the nature and management of these various engines, the undertaking of John Loftingh may be selected. He, with a partner, petitioned on October 3rd, 1689, for a patent for "an engine for quenching fire, the like whereof was never seen before in this kingdom," which spouted water to a height of between 300 and 400 feet[5]; and, on December 2nd of the same year, a warrant for the usual privileges was granted[6]. The invention was developed by the capital provided through a company, which traded as *the Company for the Sucking-Worm Engines of Mr John Loftingh, merchant, at Bow Church Yard, Cheapside*[7]. Houghton, in commenting on this undertaking in 1694, says that already the usefulness of the engine for fires was past dispute and that it was likely to be a thousand times more used, when it was more known, for draining lands[8]. Even at this early period the plausibility of an advertisement, disguised as news, was known and this company availed itself of the expedient. "On December 30th [1693], a terrible fire broke out in the house of Mr William Brown, linen draper...and would have consumed the adjoining houses, and many more, had it not been for the engines of Mr John Loftingh and other merchants, commonly called the 'sucking-worm engines,' which force the water in a continued stream into alleys, yards, back-houses, staircases and other obscure places, where other engines are useless, and totally extinguished the fire[9]." A year later, the following advertisement appeared—"the sucking-worm engines of Mr John Loftingh and company have, by their experiments at the fires in Blow Bladder St., Lombard St., Leadenhall St., Thames St., etc., proved themselves the best extinguishers of fire known[10]."

Another development of the same kind of invention was the utilization of pumping machines for draining foreshores and clearing obstructions from the mouths of harbours. In 1690 Henry Ascough and a number

[1] Galloway, *Annals of Coal Mining*, pp. 196-7, where the pump is illustrated.
[2] State Papers, Domestic, Petition Entry Book, IV. p. 231.
[3] *Statutes*, VII. p. 450.
[4] *Vide infra*, Division VI., Section 5.
[5] State Papers, Domestic, Petition Entry Book, I. p. 53.
[6] *Ibid.*, H. O. Warrant Book, XXXV. p. 156.
[7] Houghton, *Collections*, No. 54, Aug. 11, 1693.
[8] *Ibid.*, No. 103, July 20, 1694.   [9] *Ibid.*, No. 75, Jan. 5, 1694.
[10] *Ibid.*, No. 155, July 19, 1695.

of others showed that they had found "instruments" for draining lands, lying between high and low water mark, whereby such land might be reclaimed[1]. On November 8th, 1692, Marmaduke Hodgeson (or Hudson) stated in a petition that he had invented an engine which could raise or discharge water from any depth to any height "without the strength of men, horses, wind, steam or current besides that of its raising." This invention was described as useful for draining fens, or mines, or freeing ships from water, also for either filling or emptying moats[2]. By November 28th a warrant was signed for the grant of a patent[3], and in the following year Hudson promoted a company in Scotland for the working of his pump[4].

An invention of this type, which excited considerable interest, was that of Captain Poyntz for raising water, whereby he could make the said water be raised (as well from standing water as from running streams) to go of itself perpetually and perform any mill-work[5]. Poyntz also had a machine for draining land and clearing obstructions from channels, and on August 8th, 1693, he petitioned for a grant of all lands recovered for 90 years, or, alternatively, for ever subject to an annual payment of £1,000 a year to the Crown[6]. At this time he had an engine working at Dublin, and in July Houghton had seen two of the machines at work. "They cleared away a great quantity of mud and almost levelled a great hill thereof, by working two hours at a time for three tides, and, I believe, in a strong stream much more may be done[7]." Immediately Poyntz had obtained his patents, he advertized that "all persons who are desirous to treat with Captain Poyntz may see him every day at Change time at Mr Blackit's, a scrivener in Finch Lane or at the Marine Coffee House in Birchin Lane[8]." The object of the interviews was the formation of a company, which was completed by the following year, and the wording of the advertisement suggests that in this, as in other small undertakings, there was no public issue of shares at a fixed price, but that the vendor sold certain fractions of his patent, as best he could, and that calls were made on the shares, so created, as capital was required. About 1697 Poyntz claimed that he could produce "diverse certificates" showing that his engine had performed considerable service in several places in the kingdom, and he stated that much more would have been effected had it not been for the obstruction

---

[1] State Papers, Domestic, Petition Entry Book, I. p. 78.
[2] *Ibid.*, p. 412.
[3] State Papers, Domestic, H. O. Warrant Book, VI. p. 447.
[4] *Vide infra*, Division IX., Section 7.
[5] State Papers, Domestic, Petition Entry Book, II. p. 349.
[6] *Ibid.*, III. p. 13.
[7] *Collections*, No. 51, July 21, 1693.   [8] *London Gazette*, No. 2895.

of trade during the war, whereby little encouragement was obtainable from any of the seaports. Accordingly, he presented a petition, asking that the term of his patent should be made fourteen years from the declaration of peace, not from the date at which it was granted[1].

Another engine, mentioned by Houghton in his list, was also managed by a company. It was known as the "night engine," and was intended, according to an advertisement, "to be set in a convenient place of any house, to prevent thieves from breaking in[2]." According to Houghton, in 1694, it had prospects of meeting with success[3].

In *Angliæ Tutamen* it is recorded that not only were engines for drainage likely to be useful in reclaiming land, but that in several cases they had, by 1694–5, actually proved successful, notably in Cornwall and Devonshire[4].

[1] *Reasons humbly offered to the House of Commons relating to the Bill for making decayed Havens, Ports &c. more navigable*, [by J. Poyntz] $\left[\text{Brit. Mus. } \dfrac{816 \cdot \text{m} \cdot 8}{62}\right]$.

[2] *London Gazette*, No. 3015, Oct. 1, 1694.

[3] *Collections*, No. 103, July 20, 1694.

[4] p. 29.

SECTION II. COMPANIES FOR THE RECOVERY OF TREASURE FROM WRECKS.

THE ADVENTURERS IN THE EXPEDITIONS OF WILLIAM PHIPPS (1687, 1688).
THE COMPANY OWNING THE DIVING-ENGINE INVENTED BY JOHN WILLIAMS (1691).
THE COMPANY OWNING THE DIVING-ENGINE INVENTED BY JOSEPH WILLIAMS (1691).
THE COMPANY OWNING THE DIVING-ENGINE INVENTED BY JOHN TYZACK (1691).
THE GOVERNOR AND COMPANY FOR RECOVERING WRECKS IN ENGLAND (1691).
THE COMPANY OWNING THE DIVING-ENGINE OF JOHN OVERING (1692).
THE COMPANY FOR RECOVERING TREASURE FROM WRECKS OFF BROADHAVEN (1691).
THE COMPANY FOR RECOVERING TREASURE FROM WRECKS OFF BERMUDA (1692).
THE COMPANY FOR RECOVERING TREASURE FROM WRECKS IN OTHER PLACES GRANTED TO THOMAS NEALE (1692).
HOUBLON AND COMPANY—FORMED TO RECOVER TREASURE OFF VIGO (1702).

THE search for treasure, either hidden on land or which had been lost at sea, is an enterprize which has always appealed to the adventurous. It is related that one of the inventions in which Prince Rupert was interested was a diving-engine, which was expected to be of material assistance in salvage operations[1]. For some years no satisfactory results were obtained, owing to the difficulty of locating wrecks which contained

[1] Anderson, *Annals of Commerce, ut supra*, III. p. 73.

treasure. It was not until William Phipps appeared upon the scene that the various elements, necessary for success, were co-ordinated. Phipps was a New England sea-captain, who had obtained information where a richly-laden Spanish plate ship had been wrecked in the vicinity of Port de la Plata, Hispaniola. He found himself unable to interest American capitalists in his scheme and he came to England, where he was fortunate in gaining an audience from Charles II. in 1683. A frigate—the *Algier Rose* of 18 guns with a crew of 95 men—was fitted out for the expedition; but, beyond verifying the report of the wreck, nothing was accomplished.

On his return, Phipps was unable to induce the Crown to proceed further in treasure-seeking. He "found himself opposed by powerful enemies that clogged his affairs with such demurrages and such disappointments as would have wholly discouraged his designs, if his patience had not bin invincible[1]." After the lapse of several years he succeeded in gaining the support of the Duke of Albemarle, and a small company was formed in 1686–7. The capital of this venture was about £2,000, and a ship and tender were hired and fitted out for the voyage. On its arrival at the scene of the wreck, the expedition encountered nothing save disappointment for a considerable period. Provisions were running out and the last boat was returning to the ship, after abandoning the search, when one of the men asked the diver to bring him up a spray of seaweed which had caught his fancy. The diver, on being drawn into the boat, reported that he had seen a number of great guns lying on the sand. The next dive resulted in the finding of an ingot of silver. Operations were prosecuted vigorously; and, altogether, 32 tons of silver, besides jewels, were recovered[2]. It was not found possible to remove all the treasure raised, but the expedition returned in 1687, bringing bullion and other valuables worth about £250,000. The result was so surprising that certain "mean men—if base, little, dirty tricks will entitle men to meanness—urged the King to seize the whole cargoe." Except by a perversion of equity, the adventurers were fairly entitled to the fruits of the expedition, since it had been authorized by a patent, under which the Crown was entitled to one-tenth. James II., however, refused to interfere, and Phipps, in recognition of his services, was knighted.

The title of the company to the treasure having been recognized, it only remained to make a division amongst the fortunate adventurers. After a bonus, promised by Phipps to the sailors, had been paid, there remained, clear of all expenses, £224,720. Out of this Phipps himself was voted £16,000. The tenth of the balance, payable to the Crown,

---

[1] *Pietas in Patriam: The Life of his Excellency Sir William Phips, Knt.* London, 1697, § 5 [Brit. Mus. 615. d. 2].

[2] *Ibid.*, § 6; State Papers, Colonial, LX. 88; *Calendar, Colonial*, 1685–8, p. 392.

came to £20,872[1], leaving £187,848. This enabled dividends to be paid of about 10,000 per cent.[2] In this connection Defoe points out how much was against this venture turning out satisfactorily. "Success," he writes, "has so sanctified some of those other sorts of projects that 'twould be a kind of blasphemy against Fortune to disallow 'em; witness Sir William Phips's voyage to the wreck; 'twas a mere project a lottery of a hundred thousand to one odds; a hazard, which if it had failed everybody would have been ashamed to have owned themselves concerned in; a voyage that would have been as much ridiculed as Don Quixot's adventure upon the windmill: Bless us! that folks should go three thousand miles to angle in the open sea for pieces of eight! Why, they would have made ballads of it, and the merchants would have said of every unlikely adventure, ''Twas like Phips his wreck-voyage'; but it had success and who reflects upon the project[3]."

Satisfactory as this distribution must have been to the members of the syndicate, some of them remembered that not only had there been treasure left in the wreck but that it had been found impossible to remove all that had been salved. Accordingly, early in 1688, a fresh company was formed and, application having been made to the King, a warrant was signed on May 31st, granting the man-of-war *Foresight* for a further expedition[4]. Phipps, however, on his arrival at La Plata discovered that the news of the find had spread and he could obtain little of value[5].

The remarkable success of the venture of 1687 directed public attention to this class of enterprize, and numerous companies began to be formed with a view of emulating the good fortune of Phipps. These may be divided in two distinct classes—the one which worked patents for "diving-engines"; and the other which, having obtained from the Crown a patent to "fish" for wrecks in a certain district, either hired the diving apparatus from the patentee or the company who worked it, or else conducted operations by means of an engine of its own.

[1] Eng. Hist. MS., Bod. Lib. b. 21.
[2] Luttrell (*Brief Relation*, I. p. 407) states that "each adventurer received £10,000 for £100 invested." Evelyn (*Diary*, May 6th, 1687, II. p. 278) mentions that some "who adventured £100 gained from £8,000 to £10,000." The treasure recovered is recorded at amounts varying from £200,000 (Luttrell, *Brief Relation*, I. p. 407, Anderson, *Annals of Commerce*, III. p. 73) to £300,000 (*Pietas in Patriam*, § 6). These differences depend on whether the figures relate to the total treasure salved or to the amount remaining after expenses were paid. The whole incident is picturesquely described in Gilbert Parker's *Trail of the Sword*.
[3] *An Essay upon Projects*, 1697, p. 16.
[4] State Papers, Domestic, H. O. Warrant Book, IV. p. 434.
[5] *The Library of American Biography*, conducted by Jared Sparks, Boston, 1837, VII.

Patents for diving machines had been granted long before this era of special interest in the seeking of treasure from wrecks—for instance in 1632, in 1634 and again in 1680[1], but after 1688 the number of grants increased greatly. On September 26th, 1689, Francis Smartfoot obtained a patent for a "sea-crab," which was designed to raise ships, guns and goods. The inventor also secured the right of working his "crab" in all seas in the King's dominions, except from the North Foreland westward by the Scilly Islands[2]. The same patent also conferred the exclusive right, for 14 years, of enabling a man to breathe under water by attaching "a pair of lungs to his back as he swims."

At the end of 1691 a group of patents was granted, all of which were transferred to companies. One was in favour of John Williams of Exeter, who had discovered a new engine for carrying four men fifteen fathoms and more under water, whereby they may work for twelve hours at a time[3]. On the same day a similar grant was made to Joseph Williams and a number of other persons[4]. On October 28th John Tyzack, one of the leading inventors of the period, petitioned for a patent for a similar contrivance, which would enable the person using it "to walk up and down by himself and work on and view any wreck in the sea and have fresh air to breathe[5]." A more important company had secured the patent of Edmund Halley and was promoted by Sir Stephen Evans and John Holland. On August 31st, 1691, they petitioned for incorporation as *the Governor and Company for raising wrecks in England*[6]; and, on September 15th, a warrant was issued for a grant of a patent[7]. Houghton had seen this apparatus at work and was of opinion that it would be "of good effect, as soon as the seas were clear[8]." As the author of *Angliæ Tutamen* puts it, "engine begat engine and project begat project." In the following year Captain Poyntz came forward with a petition, on April 20th, in which he stated that persons, who had secured patents for wrecks, sold shares at "extravagant rates and had as yet done nothing[9]." He too obtained a patent on April 29th[10]. In July John Overing specified that he had invented an engine, which seems to have been a prototype of the diving

---

[1] *Fœdera*, xix. pp. 365, 571; Anderson, *Annals of Commerce*, iii. p. 73. Anderson attributes part of the success of Phipps to the use of the engine of 1680; on the other hand, the writer of *Pietas in Patriam* credits him "with the inventing of many of the instruments necessary to the prosecution of his intended fishery."
[2] State Papers, Domestic, H. O. Warrant Book, xxxv. p. 468.
[3] *Ibid.*, Petition Entry Book, i. p. 180 (Aug. 29, 1691).
[4] *Ibid.*, H. O. Warrant Book, vi. p. 168.
[5] *Ibid.*, Petition Entry Book, i. p. 210.
[6] *Ibid.*, p. 182.
[7] *Ibid.*, H. O. Warrant Book, vi. p. 178.
[8] *Collections*, No. 103.
[9] State Papers, Domestic, Petition Entry Book, i. p. 279
[10] *Ibid.*, H. O. Warrant Book, vi. p. 317.

dress. It consisted in conveying air by pipes into new-contrived bellows, with plates covered with leather for securing the head and retaining the air about the upper part of the body, "which gives liberty for a man to see, walk and work for a considerable time many fathoms under water[1]." Having obtained his patent, Overing handed over his invention to a company. On May 29th, 1693, Samuel Wimball petitioned for encouragement for another diving engine[2], on August 3rd Captain Edward Curtis described in his petition yet another, in which men could work for a day at the bottom of the sea[3], and on October 11th John Diserote and Walter Hurst, in asking a patent for their invention, stated that little progress had been made by their rivals[4].

Besides the companies controlling diving-engines, there was the second group of undertakings that actually endeavoured to locate wrecks and to recover valuables from them. This class of enterprize required a grant from the King of the salvage recovered, which privilege was obtainable by the promise either of an immediate cash-payment or of one-tenth part of the treasure won. Thomas Neale, one of the great projectors of the time, was very prominent in securing such grants and then floating companies. Thus on March 30th, 1691, he petitioned for leave to retain any silver recovered from a ship lost off Broadhaven in Ireland, provided such treasure should be obtained before February 13th, 1694, he or his assigns paying the Crown one-tenth of the proceeds of the search[5]. Neale also obtained, in May 1692, similar grants for the Bermudas and for the district from Carthagena to Jamaica, all of which he floated as companies[6]. Finally in 1702 Wynne Houblon, and others associated with him, applied for powers to recover goods from ships sunk off Vigo[7].

None of these expeditions were successful—indeed the only "finds" consisted of a few cannon. But in 1692 these wreck-recovery projects, according to a contemporary writer, "made much noise at this time, and shares for them were presented to persons of distinction to give reputation to the affair and to draw on others....So the patentees were sure to be gainers but the sharers under them lost all they paid in, some of whom, it seems, were men of good understanding but were allured by the hopes of getting vast sudden wealth without trouble[8]." According to Defoe, there was a very marked speculation in the shares of such companies, one five-hundredth part of the undertaking being sold for

---

[1] State Papers, Domestic, Petition Entry Book, I. p. 358.
[2] Ibid., II. p. 326.
[3] Ibid., III. p. 14.
[4] Ibid., p. 35.
[5] Ibid., II. p. 247.
[6] Notes and Queries, Sixth Series, vol. x. p. 404.
[7] State Papers, Domestic, Petition Entry Book, VI. p. 40.
[8] Angliæ Tutamen, p. 20.

£100, and falling subsequently to 12, then to 10, 9, 8 and at last to nothing[1]. Probably this picture is exaggerated. Houghton records the quotations of shares in three companies of this kind, which were formed at the end of 1691. Prices are first quoted in the following April and these were very steady from that date till the middle of 1693, all three shares being sold from 20 to 16. Therefore, if there were inflation, such as is indicated by Defoe, it must have been in the last months of 1691 and the beginning of 1692. Even supposing there had been a high price, such as 100, at that period, it is difficult to understand how after a fall of 80 per cent. the quotation would remain steady during a whole year afterwards; since, as a general rule, when a slump begins, it continues, in a case of this kind, until a very low level is reached. It shows how long the expectation of success continued, that as late as May 18th, 1694, a writer as staid as John Houghton mentions that "there was great hope of gain from a Spanish wreck," and he hastened to communicate the news to his readers[2].

[1] *An Essay upon Projects*, pp. 12, 13.
[2] *Collections*, No. 94.

INDEX.

Abbot, Morris, 106
Abercorn, Earl of, his silver-mining speculations, 412
Aberdeenshire, famine in, 221
Aberystwyth, mint established at, 403
Abney, Sir Edward, association with the Fishery Company, 374
Acadia, 319
Acheson's mining partnership (1563), 406, 410
Acworth, Thomas, 400
Addison, Thomas, invention for smelting iron, 466
Adriatic, opposition to English in the, 85
Adventurers for Irish Lands (1642), 343–51
Africa, trade to, 3–35; Queen Elizabeth's partnership in African expeditions, 5; opposition of the Portuguese, 5, 7; effect of slave trade, 8, 9; importance of fortified harbours, 11; factory on the Gambia, 12; maintenance of forts, 17, 24, 25; proposed trading scheme by the East India Co., 204
African companies, 3–35
Albemarle, Duke of, assists Sir W. Phipps in his treasure search, 485
Alexander, Sir William, see Stirling, Lord
Alexander's mining partnership (1613), 406, 411
Algier Rose, frigate, 485
Allen, Sir Thomas, his whaling partnership, 75
Alum company (1694), 475, 476
Amazon company, 323–6
Ambergris, found in the Somers Islands, 260, 261
Amboyna, massacre at, 107
America, schemes for plantations, 242, 243; rise of the fishing industry, 301, 303, 304; copper smelting in, 431
— Central, colonization of, 323, 329, 331
— Northern, colonization of, 246–59, 266–89, 298–322
— South, colonization of, 323
Andalusia, seizure of the, 150
Anderson, Adam, on the Greenland trade, 69
— Thomas, 72
Andrea, island, 327
Andrews, Sir P., his endeavour to revive the fishing trade, 372

Angliæ Tutamen, quoted, 375, 437, 473, 475, 483, 487
Annapolis (Nova Scotia), 319
Anstell's smelting partnership (1627), 463, 465
Antimony mining company, 475
Antrim, county, 347
Archangel, 37, 40, 67, 68, 76
Argall, Samuel, deputy-governor of Virginia, 267
Armagh, 347; plantation of, 339
Armenia, Major, 41
— Minor, 41
Arundel's Fishing association (1635), 369, 370
Ashton, John, on lotteries in England, 373
Assada, island, 120, 121; base money coined at, 118
Association, isle of, see Tortuga
Atholl, Earl of, his mining enterprize, 410
Atkinson's proposed gold-mining company, 406, 409, 410
Augsburg, merchants of, 391
Aurangzeb, 135; East India Co.'s trouble with, 150, 151
Austria, Emperor of, 202
— treaties with, 204
Avalon, settlement at, 317
Avenant, Cornelius, on the affairs of the Mineral and Battery Works, 417–21; attempt to rent wire works at Tintern, 422
Ayscough, Henry, his drainage instrument, 481, 482

Baden, Robert, petition concerning a force-pump, 480
Baffin Land, 77
Ballot, abuse of the, 281
Ballot-box introduced by Sir E. Sandys, 106; confiscated by the Somers Islands Co., 274
Baltic Sea, 37
Baltimore, Lord, attempt to colonize Newfoundland, 317, 318
Bank of England, 210, 452; run on, 184; loan to the East India Co., 201; foundation by Paterson, 207
Bantam, the *Trade's Increase* East Indiaman burnt at, 102

492 Index

Barbadoes, its first plantation, 326
Barbon, N., invention for raising water from the Thames, 480
Barnstaple, ships from forbidden to carry tobacco from the Bermudas, 290
Baronet, title used to aid the plantation of Ulster and Nova Scotia, 318, 319, 339
Battson's whaling partnership, 74
Bayton, Francis, petition relative to a force-pump, 480
Bear Quay, fire at, 195
Beaver, trade in the skins of, 231, 232, 321
Bedford, Countess of, 263, 264
— Earl of, undertakes the draining of the Great Level, 354; estimate of expenditure on the work, 356
— Level company, 352-6
Bedfordshire, drainage of, 479
Bedworth coal mining partnership (1622), 459, 460
Belfast iron company (1681), 463, 467
Bell Sound, 70, 72, 74
Bellamont saltpetre company, 473
Bencoolen, fortification of, 155; expenditure at, 197; intemperance at, 198
Bengal, 150, 196, 197
Benin, expedition to, 10
Bermuda company, 259-97
— treasure-recovery company (1692), 484, 488
Bernardison, 150
Birchin Lane, 482
Blackit, Mr, 482
Blewstone, Frederick de, his iron furnaces at Wednesbury, 466
Bloomery works company in Virginia, 277
Blow Bladder Street, fire in, 481
Blythe coal companies, 459, 462
Board of Trade, 27
Bolton, good coal found at, 399
Bombay, fortification of, 138
Bond, William, alderman, 77; sends an expedition to Narva, 41
Bonnell, Samuel, 112, 114
Boston, 41, 42, 229, 313
Bracelets (copper), exported to Africa, 11
Brass, works in Nottinghamshire and London, 417, 418; its exchange value in Africa, 423; monopoly of its manufacture, 424; decline in production, 425; petition relating to, 427; Temple brass mills, 428, 429; mills at Esher, 437
Brazil, 3, 82
Brewster, Nonconformist leader in Holland, 306
Briggs, John, his coal-mining partnership, 460
Briscoe, John, interested in a copper mining company, 430
Bristol, 242, 466; ships from forbidden to carry tobacco from the Bermudas, 290; emigrants to Dublin from, 338; coal found near, 415
Broad Street, 230
Broadhaven treasure-recovery company (1692), 484, 488

Brocas, Mrs Mary, her loan to the Russia company, 55, 59, 60, 61
Broken Wharf, 479
Bronchorst, Arnold von, 408
Brook, Sir Basil, 411
— Lord, offer to the Mosquito Islands Co., 333
Brooke's partnership for making saltpetre (1627), 471, 472.
Brown, William, fire at his house, 481
Bucknall, Ralph, his partnership for making saltpetre, 473
Bullion, export of, 17, 135, 137, 140, 204, 205; export to India, 200, 201; to Spain, 276
Bulmer, Sir Bevis, manuscript treatise of, 398; his mining enterprize, 409; his engine for raising water, 479
Bulton, Sir Thomas & Co. (1627), 13
Burde, William, 77
Burghill, Francis, his agitation against the Somers Islands Co., 295-7
Burghley, Lord, 84; shareholder in the Mines Royal, 395
Burroughs, Stephen, reaches the river Obi, 76
Burton, Hill, on the Darien scheme, 215, 216
Bush Lane, copper company's office in, 435
Bushnell & Co., 73
Bushell, Thomas, his mining undertaking, 402
Butler, Nathaniel, 267, 269; attack on the Virginia Company, 283, 284
Butterfield, Mrs Mary, letter concerning Hudson's Bay stock, 235
Bynney company (1618), 8, 11-14, 16

Cabot, Sebastian, 36; governor of the Russia company, 38
Caesar, Sir Julius, his connection with the Mineral and Battery Works, 421
Calamine, 413, 423, 424, 475; cost in Nuremberg and England, 416, 417; search for, 428
Caldbec, mining at, 399
Calico, 120
Calvert, Sir George, *see* Baltimore, Lord
Cambridgeshire, drainage of, 352; scheme for draining the fens, 353
Cambriol, 316
Canada company (1627), 228, 317, 320-2
— (French), 228, 319
Candia, import of wine from by Venetians prohibited, 86
Canning, William, deputy-governor of the Somers Islands Co., 262; censure of, 273
Cape Ann, fishing settlement at, 312
— Blanco, 14
— Cod, *Mayflower* at, 303
— Comfort, 250
— Gratia de Dios, expedition to, 331, 335
— of Good Hope, 14, 17, 20, 82, 89, 91, 93, 95, 105
— Verde Islands, 82

Cardigan, mines and mining in, 396–8, 401, 449
Cards, see Wool-cards
Caribbean Sea, 329
Caribhes, 326
Carlile's proposed colonizing company (1583), 242, 243
Carlisle, Lord, ambassador to Russia, 67; his plantation in the West Indies, 326
Carmarthen, mining in, 402
Carmichaell's mining partnership (1565), 406
Carnarvon, mining in, 402
Carolina, copper mines in, 437
Carpenter, William, 434
Carthagena, 488
Cary, John, 161
Caspian Sea, 41, 44; expedition attacked by pirates in the, 44
Catchmayne's partnership in wire works, 421
Cathay, company of, 76, 89
Cattle, export from Somers Islands, 293
Cavan, plantation of, 339
Cavendish, Lord, 263, 281, 284, 285
Cayman Islands, 329
Cecil, Sir Robert, 245
— Sir W., interested in the Mineral and Battery Works, 415, 416
Cedar, shipped from Somers Islands, 294
Ceylon, Dutch expenditure in, 155
Challener's iron partnership, 420, 421
Chambers' Copper company at Redbrook, 434
Chancellor, Richard, his voyage to Russia, 37
Charcoal, its use in iron smelting, 464
Charles I., 70, 113–16, 118, 119, 291, 301, 305, 320, 321, 325–7, 353; holds shares in the Guinea company, 13; death of, 66; scheme for his admission to the East India Co., 109; East India Co. refuses to advance him money, 112; his association with Courten's enterprize, 113, 118; dissatisfied with the Bedford Level scheme, 355; proclamation relative to saltpetre, 472
Charles II., 17–19, 21, 130, 131, 138, 139, 143, 351, 485; grants a charter to the African Adventurers, 17; incorporates the Royal African Co., 19, 20; grants a charter to the East India Co., 131; presentation to by the East India Co., 130, 143, 157; offers a loan to the Fishery Co., 373; on the encouragement of the Fishing Trade, 374
Charles River, 312
Cherry, Sir Francis, 49–52, 68
Cherry Island, expeditions to, 49, 53
Cheshire, salt springs in, 468
Child, Sir Josia, 144, 145, 149–56, 158, 160; dividend received by, 140; defends the East India Co., 141–3
Chillis, imported from Africa, 4, 7
China, 76; north-east passage to, 36
Cinnamon, 120
Civil Wars, 15, 293, 345, 353, 355, 412, 480

Clare, county, 343, 346, 347
Clethero, nominee of James I. as treasurer of the Virginia Co., 279
Cloth, export to India, 200
Clothiers, opposition to the East India Co., 135
Clydesdale, gold found in, 407
Coal, early history and methods of mining, 459–61; companies for coal mining, 459–62
— company for making iron with coal (1693), 463, 467
— company for making lead with coal (1692) 442
Cock, Samuel, of Wapping, his engine for raising water, 480
Coke (Sir Edward) on the whalers' appeal to Parliament, 71
Coke, Sir John, report on the Mosquito Islands, 333
Coleraine, town of, 340
Colleagues for discovery of a northern passage to China (1607), 100
Colleges for discovery of north-west passage (1583), 244
Columbus, C., visit to the Mosquito Islands, 327
Combe Martin, silver mine at, 395, 397, 398
Commissioners of Trade and Plantations, 295, 376
Committee for Petitions, 59
Committee of Grievances, 13, 71
Committee of Trade, 16, 67, 72; report upon Darien, 221
Commodities, distributions made in, 99, 110
Commons, House of, 13, 14, 24, 25, 66, 75, 104, 106–8, 119, 151, 152, 155, 156, 158–60, 164, 165, 182, 184, 197, 204, 215, 268, 287, 291, 455
Compleat Collier, quoted, 461
Connaught, value of land in, 343; confederate forces driven into, 345; forfeited land in, 343, 346, 347
Consuls, officers of the Russia Co., 38
Cooke, Sir Thomas; imprisonment of, 160
Coot, Sir Charles, his iron works, 467
Copper, 248, 439; mined in Cumberland and Westmoreland, 385; its export illegal, 388; price of, 392, 394; revival of the copper-mining industry, 430; imported from Sweden, 431; works at Redbrook and Wimbledon, 434; the copper combine of 1720, 435
Copper Miners company in England (1691), 430-5
Coral, importation into Africa, 11
Cordage, trade with Russia in, 40, 41, 50
Cork, Earl of, amount made from his iron mines, 467
Cormantin, factory at, 16
Cornish copper company (1694), 436, 439
Cornwall, mining in, 384, 395–8, 400–2; copper mines in, 434–6; silver found in, 440; land reclaimed in, 483
Cossacks, losses of Russia Co. by attacks of, 43

Cotton, 323, 326, 335; imported from Africa, 11
Cotton (Derby), copper mine at, 436
Council of State, 15, 16, 120-3, 129, 130
Council of Trade, 67, 130
Court of the Exchequer, 59
Court of Wards, 14
Courten's association or East India company, 112-19
Cranfield, Sir Randall, 108
Crawfurd Muir, gold mines at, 406
Crisp & Company (1630), 14-17
Crispe's partnership in the African trade (1637), 15
Cromwell, Oliver, 66, 130; attempt to revive the Russian trade, 67; refuses to assist the East India Co., 121; grants the company a new charter, 128, 129; puts down the rebellion in Ireland, 345; attitude towards capitalists, 355; share in a coal-mining undertaking, 460
— Richard, ship licensed by, 130
Culpepper, Lord, 66
Cumberland, mining in, 384, 385, 400, 401, 437
Cumberland and Carolina copper company (?1694), 436-9
Cunningham, Sir James, 70; granted a charter and trading license by James I., 55, 104
Currants, monopoly of export from the Mediterranean, 84; importation by Venetians prohibited, 86; profitable nature of the trade, 87
Curtis, Edward, Capt., his diving engine, 488
Czar, concessions to the Russia company, 65, 66; monopoly in tobacco secured from, 162

Danes, harass the African traders, 15
Danvers, Sir John, 285 note
Danzig, Dutch and English fish sold at, 366
Darien, the Scottish company so named, 80, 203, 207-27, 327
— bay of, silver from, 335
Dartford, 80
Davenant, Charles, 22
David I., grant to the Abbey of Dunfermline, 406
Davis, John, his voyages, 49
Deane, William, petition of, 374
Deeping Fen, scheme for draining, 353
Defoe, Daniel, on the Darien Co., 219, 224; on the Temple Mills, 428 note; on saltpetre companies, 474; on Sir W. Phipps' search for treasure, 486; on schemes for recovery of treasure, 488
Delbridge, John, fits out a ship for the Somers Islands trade, 290, 291
De Mons, founder of Port Royal, 319
Derby copper company (? 1694), 436, 439
— lead company, 440
Derbyshire, lead works in, 422; copper mines in, 436

Derwentfells, 385
De Vois, Cornelius, his mining partnership, 407, 408
Devonshire, mining in, 384, 396-8, 400; land reclaimed in, 483
— Earl of, 264
De Witt, on the Dutch fishing industry, 361; comparison of English and Dutch-caught fish, 365
Digges, Sir Dudley, ambassador to Russia, 65; reply to *The Trade's Increase*, 102
Diserote, John, his invention for diving, 488
Diving machines, various machines described, 487
Dockwra's copper company (1692), 436-9
— ordnance company, 473
Dolphin, the, seized by the Spaniards, 222
Donegal, plantation of, 339
Dorsetshire, mining in, 402
Douglas, George, his mining undertaking, 410
Down, county, 347
Drainage, land drainage schemes in England, 352-7; engines used for drainage, 479
Drake, Sir Francis, 84, 245; adventure to St Domingo, 418
Droitwich salt-works company, 468, 470
Drugs, 323, 335
Dublin, planted by Bristol emigrants, 338
Ducket, John, invention for refining copper, 430
Dudley, Ambrose, Earl of Warwick, *see* Warwick
Dudley's smelting partnerships (1638 and 1651), 463, 465, 466
Dudley, Sir Robert, his expedition to India, 90
Dunfermline, abbey of, 406
Dunkirkers, capture English fishing boats, 365, 370
Dupin, Nicholas, preparing a Scottish mining company, 431
Dupps, a brewer of London, 53
Durham, silver obtained in, 440
Durham coal and salt company, 459
Dutch, harass the African traders, 15, 16; attack English ports in Africa, 17; compete for the Russian trade, 42, 43; increase of their Russian trade, 48, 50; opposition to the Russia Co.'s whaling industry, 54; they burn the warehouses of the Russia Co., 56; attack English merchants, 64; oppose the English in Russia, 66, 67; prohibited from trading with Portugal, 89; successful expedition to India, 90, 91; negotiations with the East India Co., 103; claims against, 121, 122; their expenditure in Ceylon, 155; praise of their enterprize and policy in India, 199; their success in the fishing-trade, 300, 361; fishing in English waters, 374; Dutch miners in Scotland, 406, 407
— War, 132, 134
— West India company, 327, 334
Dyes, 11, 12, 249, 323, 335

Index

Dykes, Thomas, found guilty of fraud, 455

East India company, the London or Old Company, 89-179
— the English or New Company, 179—89
— the Dutch company, 90, 143, 202
— the French company, 229
— the Scottish or Darien company, 207-27
— the United company, 189-205

Edgcumb, Piers, his mining ventures, 395, 397, 398; petition of, 400
Edinburgh, 210; illumination of, 220; English seamen executed at, 223
Edward the Confessor, laws of, 383
Edward VI., 391
Edwards, N., his whaling license, 70, 71
— Richard, his speech at a meeting of Somers Islands Co. tampered with, 274; elected deputy-governor, 285
Elizabeth, Queen, 51, 71, 86, 91, 100, 242, 352, 353, 361, 407, 424; her partnership in the African ventures, 5, 6, 7; grants a charter to the Senegal Adventurers, 10; promised alliance with Russia, 43; her investment in the Levant trade, 84; her interest in mining, 384; purchases copper of the Mines Royal, 391; claim to Duke of Norfolk's shares, 417
Ely, Isle of, drainage of, 352, 354
Endicott, John, 312
Engrafted stock, 32, 451
Esher, brass mills at, 437
Essequibo, river, 324
Essington & Company (copper miners), 434, 435
Estcourt lead-mining company, 440
Ethiopia, company of adventurers to (1553-67), 3-9, 11
Evans, Sir Stephen, his lead-mining company, 440, 441; his company for raising wrecks, 487
Excise Office, 230
Exeter, merchants of, 10
Extractive industries, 383-476

Felt, export from Russia, 40
Felt-makers, 231, 232
Feme-covert, inability to vote, 194
Fenner, Thomas, his iron-works partnership, 420, 421
Fens, schemes for draining, 352-7
Fenton, Edward, 81, 83
Fermanagh, plantation of, 339
Ferrar, John, 269, 275; the Virginia company's minutes, 273, 274; gratuity to, 278
— Nicholas, 269, 273, 281, 282, 284; petition of, 13 and note; deputy-treasurer of the Virginia Co., 275
Finch Lane, 482
Fire, Great Fire of London, 134; fire at Bear Quay, 195; engines for extinguishing fire, 479-81
Firebrace, Sir Basil, negotiates for the union of the two East India companies, 168, 169, 185

Fisheries, 323; interest awakened in the, 300, 301; progress in America, 301-4; value of the Irish Society's fisheries, 341; companies for the encouragement of, 361-78; import of foreign-caught fish prohibited, 364; English boats captured by Dunkirkers, 365, 370; value of fish taken by the Dutch in English waters, 374
Fishery company (1632-40), 361-8
— — the Royal (1661), 372-6
— — the Royal Scottish (1670), 377, 378
Fitch, Ralph, 89
Flanders, 203
Fletcher, Giles, negotiations on behalf of the Russia Co., 48
Flintshire, mining in, 402; lead mines in, 449
Flood, iron works destroyed by the May Day Flood, 465
Fonesca, 326
Foreign trade, 3-237
Foresight, man-of-war, 486
Forest of Dean coal and iron company, 459-61
Forests, destruction of in England, 467
Fort William (India), excessive expenditure at, 197
Forth, firth of, 223
Foullis, Thomas, his mining operations, 410, 411
France, peace with, 167
Frankfort, price of copper at, 388
Frobisher's voyages, company for (1576), 76-82
Frodsham rock salt company, 470
Fruit, export from Somers Islands, 293
Fur trade, 40, 228, 301, 309, 314, 316, 320

Gambia, river, 10, 12
Gambling, in the colonies, 331
Garraway, Sir H., imprisonment of, 66
Gatcombe, Richard, 72
Gates, Sir Thomas, his expedition to Virginia, 251
Gentleman, Tobias, 361
Germany, sale of Mines Royal shares in, 385, 387; German miners engaged in Scotland, 406, 407; workmen imported from, 416; brass-wire imported from, 427, 428
Gerrard, William, 83
Ghibelines, 285
Gibraltar, straits of, 85
Gilbert, Adrian, 244; discovers Combe Martin mine, 398
— Humphrey, proposes colonizing companies, 241-3
— Mr, 195
Ginger, import of, 8
Gladwin, Thomas, his pumping machine, 480
Glass, 249; beads exported to Africa, 11; company for glass works in Virginia, 277
Glengonar, lead mines at, 410

Gloucestershire, mining in, 384, 400
Glover lead-mining company, 440
Goa company (1637), 104; convention of, 112
God's Gift, a mine, water-works at, 399
Godfrey, Mr, dispute with the East India Co., 153
Godolphin, Lord, arbitrates between the two East India companies, 174
Godolphin's Award, 187
Gold, 23, 248, 323, 335, 336; import of, 4, 5, 9, 15, 17; gold found by Frobisher, 77, 78
Gold mining, 323; in Scotland, 384, 406
"Golden Knight," origin of, 409
Golding, Sir Thomas, his invention for draining marshes, 479
Goldsmiths' Hall, manor of, 342
Gombleton, his attempt to smelt iron, 465
Goodyere, Edmund, his mining undertaking, 402, 403
Gorges, Sir Fernando, 300, 302, 315, 316; grants to, 304, 305; proposes the foundation of Novia Scotia, 318
Gosnold, Capt. Bartholomew, his voyage to America, 246
Graines, *see* Chillis
Grand Committee for Trade, 142
Grand Concern of England Explained, 373
Granville, Sir Richard, voyage of, 244
Great Level, drainage scheme, 352
"Greenland" (*i.e.* Spitzbergen), 55, 58, 59, 104; trade of, 69-75; fishing rights off the coast of, 377
Greenland company of Adventurers (1622), 58-61
— — (1692), 379
Greenwich, 305
Gregory, Thomas, of Taunton, 11
Gresham, Sir Thos., 77
Grey, John, his expedition to Newfoundland, 316
"Grey-beard," *see* Peterson, Abraham
Groseilliers, a pioneer of the Hudson's Bay Co., 229
Guelphs, 285
Guerchy, Sieur de, 3
Guiana company, 323-6
Guinea company (1553-67), 3-9, 11
— — (1630), 14-17
— — (1662-72), 17-20, 230
— — (1672), 20-35, 68, 222, 432
— — of Scotland, 16
Gunpowder, supply of saltpetre for, 472
Gynney and Bynney company (1618), 8, 11-14, 16

Hacket, Sir John, patent for draining mines, 479
Hackney Marsh, brass mill at, 428
Haiti, 329
Hakluyt, 10; on the Levant trade, 83
Halley, Edmund, patent for a diving apparatus, 487
Hambleton, Marquis of, *see* Hamilton
Hamburgh, memorial presented to the senate, 222

Hamilton, Sir George, his mining partnership, 411
— James, Marquis of, 264; his mining partnership, 406, 410
Hammersly, Alderman, governor of the Russia Co., 59, 63
Hammond, A., 354
Hampshire, salt springs in, 468
Hampton Court, 202
Hanbery, Richard, 422; his partnership in wire and iron works, 419, 420
Harbye, Clement, his account, 62, 63
Harcourt, Robert, his expedition to Guiana, 323, 324
Harrington Tribe, 265
Hart, Sir John, 49
Hawkins, Sir John, 3, 11; voyages of, 8, 9; begins to trade in slaves, 8, 9; his slave traffic resented by the Spaniards, 9
Hawkins, William, voyages of, 3
Hawkins' voyages, company for (1562-67), 3, 9
Hayes, Edward, his pumping machine, 479
Hayward, Rowland, 83
Heathcote, Gilbert, 161
Hemp, export from Russia, 40
Henrietta Island, 327
Henry VII., patent granted by relating to mines, 383
Herne's copper company, 430, 433
Herring fishery, 361, 372; tax on export of, 378
Heydon, Sir John, attack on, 296
Hides, import of, 8, 12
Hilderston, silver found at, 411
Hispaniola, 8
Hoastmen, company of, 461
Höchstetter, family engaged in the British mining industry, 384; Cumberland mines leased to, 401
— Daniel, his mining enterprize and invention, 384; complaints against, 387, 388; petition of, 401
— Emanuel, 399
— Joachim, 384; grant to for mining in Scotland, 406
— Joseph, petition of, 401
Hodges, John, invention for smelting metals, 466
Hodgeson, Marmaduke, *see* Hudson
Hogs, export from the Somers Islands, 293
Holder, Richard, his allegations against the Royal African Co., 22
Holland, an East India company to be financed in, 115; importation of brass wire from, 427, 428
Holland, John, engine for draining mines, etc., 480; his company for raising wrecks, 487
— Lord, 327, 328
Holy Island, 374
Hope, Sir James, 410, 411
Hopkins, John, 193
Horn Sound, 71-4
Horsley, Jerome, negotiations on behalf of the Russia Co., 48

Index

Horth, John, 230
Horth's whaling partnership, 74
Houblon & Company, a salvage scheme (1702), 484, 488
Houghton, John, on the Guinea Co., 26; the fishing industry, 375; quotations by, 432; on copper companies, 437; on lead mining companies, 440; colliery companies, 462; saltpetre companies, 473; alum mining, 475, 476; on Loftingh's fire engine, 481; on Captain Poyntz's engines, 482; on diving machines, 487; on companies for recovery of treasure, 489
Hudson, Henry, 228; expedition to find the N. West Passage, 100
— Marmaduke, his pumping engine, 482
Hudson Straits, 77
Hudson's Bay company, 228–37
Hull, 41, 42, 73; merchants compete with the Russia Co., 49, 53; activity of shipowners in the whaling industry, 70
Hull and York whaling company, 74
Humfrey, William, founds the Mineral and Battery Works, 413–16; his inventions for the calamine works, 422; his grant to search for calamine, 423
Huntingdonshire, drainage of fens in, 352
Hurst, Walter, his invention for diving, 488
Hyrcania, 41

Inch of Candle, sale by, 22
Indenture Tripartite, 169–73, 185, 186, 189
India, 17, 114, 149, 159, 160; Portuguese in, 89; first expedition to, 90; advantages of commerce with, 138; trouble with East India Co.'s servants in, 190, 197, 198; increase of duty on Indian goods, 192; value of trade with, 196; seeds from to plant in the West Indies, 331
Indian Ocean, 148
Indigo, 120, 335
Inventions and Patents—refining copper, 430; smelting metals, 465, 466; making saltpetre, 472, 473; fire extinguishing, 479–81; prevention of thieves, 479, 483; engines for diving, 484, 487, 488; pumping, draining, raising water, 479–82; raising wrecks, 487
Ireland, plantations in, 338; early attempts to plant, 338; City of London undertake the plantation of Ulster, 339; the rebellion, 341, 343, 344; result of the undertaking, 342; new company of adventurers formed, 343; rebellion put down by Cromwell, 345; gains and losses of adventurers, 350, 351; mining of silver in, 411, 412; copper smelting in, 431; production of pig-iron, 467
Irish Pale, 338
— Society, 338–43
— Lands company (1642), 343–51
Iron, 249; ore found in the Forest of Dean, 414, 415; price of, 422
Iron smelting, 413, 415; companies employed in, 463–7

Iron wire, manufactured in Monmouthshire, 417
Iron work, export to Africa, 11
Iron Works, farming of by the Mineral and Battery Works, 419, 420
Iroquois, 315
Isle of Ely, drainages of, 352, 354
Italy, trade with, 83; production of alum in, 475
Ivory, import of, 3, 4, 7, 11, 12; levy on, 15

Jamaica, 329, 488; proclamation against the Darien settlement, 220, 222
James I., 98, 100, 104, 209, 271, 279, 284, 285, 287, 318, 324, 326, 339, 341, 361, 364; grants a charter to the Guinea Co., 11; grants a monopoly for whale-fishing, 53; incorporates the Scottish East India and Greenland Co., 55; his offer of partnership, 107; antagonism to Sir E. Sandys, 272; on the drainage of the Fens, 353; scheme for financing a Scottish mining company, 409; shares assigned to, 464
James II., 209, 231; acquires East India stock, 149; knights William Phipps, 485
Jeffrey, an East India merchant, his losses, 150
Jeffries, Judge, sums up in the Sandys case, 149
Jewels, 335, 336
John Baptist, ship, 7, 8
Johnson, Alderman, 269, 270, 282, 285, 290; argument with the Earl of Southampton, 274
Joint-stock company, first English, 36
Jordan, Dr, attempt to smelt iron, 465

Kathai, company of (1576), 75–82
Katharine, ship, 12
Kentwyn, Cornwall, mine at, 402
Keswick, 394; mining at, 385, 387, 396, 398, 400
Keymor, John, on the fishing trade, 361, 362
Kilmore, Tipperary, silver found at, 411
King's and Queen's corporation for the linen manufacture, 431
King's County, 347
Kirke, Capt. David, his successful expedition to Canada, 320, 321
Knight of the Golden Mines, origin of, 409
Kynaston, Thomas, 112–14

Labrador, 228
Laconia company, 305, 306, 315, 316
Lanarkshire, lead mining in, 410, 411
Lancashire, mining in, 384, 400; silver found in, 440
Lancaster, Capt. James, commands the first expedition to India, 90
Land, division of in Virginia, 255, 256; in Somers Islands, 263; in Ireland, 341, 343, 347; transfer of in the Somers Islands, 292; dividends in, 324; comparative values in Ireland and Virginia, 343; purchase values, 356

S. C. II. 32

Lapis calaminaris, 413; mining of, 573, *see also* Calamine
Latten, manufacture of, 413, 425, *see also* Brass
Laud, Archbishop, 293
Law, John, 457
Law's Mississippi scheme, 217
Lawson, Capt., his interest in iron works, 467
Lead, 385; price of, 392
Lead mining, companies for, 440-2
Leadenhall St, fire in, 481
Lechmere's saltpetre company (1692), 471, 473
Ledes, Richard, 399
Leeds, Duke of, impeachment of, 160; elected governor of the Mine Adventurers, 447
Leicester, Earl of, interested in the Mineral and Battery Works, 415, 416
Leinster, value of land in, 343, 350; forfeited lands in, 347
Leith, wool-card factory at, 427
Lemos, Conde de, 9 note
Lent, stricter fasting enjoined to encourage the Fishery society, 364
Levant company, 83-8, 105, 135, 139, 140, 148
Levett, Christopher, his colonization proposals, 304
Lewis, island of, fishery reserved to the King, 364; inhabitants hostile to the Fishing Association, 369, 370
Limerick, county, 347
Lincolnshire, drainage of fens in, 352, 357
Lindsey, Lord, his drainage schemes, 357
— Robert, grant for making saltpetre, 472
Lindsey Level, 357
Linen, export to Africa, 11; King's and Queen's corporation for manufacture of, 431
Linschoten, his experience of India, 90
Lisbon, 89
Lisle, Lord de, iron smelting on his property, 463
Livonia, 37
Lodge, Sir Thomas, 8
Loftingh, John, his fire engine, 481
Logan, copper mine at, 397
Lok, John, 11
— Michael, 77-9, 81
Lombard St, fire in, 481
London, merchants of, 3, 10; financial crisis in 1697, 233; the Common Council undertake the planting of Ulster, 339; coal supply of, 461
London Bridge, pump erected on, 479
Londonderry, plantation of, 339
— town of, 340
Long Parliament, 119
Longueville's saltpetre company (1692), 471, 473
Lords, House of, 21, 25, 57, 60, 65, 72, 119, 161, 165, 215, 415, 443
Lorraine, miners imported from, 407

Losvelt, Cornelius, petition relating to a force-pump, 480
Lotteries, money raised for colonization by, 252-5; companies financed by, 272, 372, 373, 444-7; John Ashton on lotteries in England, 373
Louis XIII., 320
— XIV., 231
Louth, county, 348
Lovell, Thomas, undertakes the drainage of Deeping Fen, 353
Lumley mine partnership, 459, 460
Luttrell, Narcissus, 183
Lydsey, James, lease of wire works, 425
Lyon, ship, 12

Mackenzie, Sir George, on the Scottish Fishery Co., 377
Mackworth, Sir Humphrey, 440; his association with the Mine Adventurers, 444; doubtful character of his proceedings, 450-2; attempt to inculpate Waller, 453-5; condemned by the House of Commons, 455; gets into power again, 457
Madagascar, 118
Madre de Dios, capture of, 90
Magazine, 248, 270, 273, 287, 289, 290, 292, 294; account of, 256; its relation to the early plantations, 264, 269, 279; effect of the tobacco monopoly, 273; unfair rates charged by, 283
Magazine company for Somers Islands, 264, 290, 292
— — — Virginia (1616-17), 256, 270, 287-90
— — — (1620), 270, 289
Magellan, straits of, 82, 93
Maids, company for the transport of, 277
Maine, province of, granted to Sir F. Gorges and John Mason, 304
Maitland's *History of London*, referred to, 435, 439, 442
Malynes, Gerard, defends the East India Co., 105, 106; on the Mines Royal, 401
Mann, Joseph, 266
Mansefield, Sir William, 264
Marine Coffee House, 482
Marlborough, Earl of, 326, 327
Martin, Captain, rewarded by the East India Co. for bravery, 194
Martyn, Sir Richard, his wire and iron venture, 419-21
Mary, Queen, 71, 391
Maryland, 326; foundation of the colony, 318
Mason, John, 315, 316; grants to, 304, 305
Massachusetts Bay company, 298, 305, 306, 311-15
Master of the Metalls, office of, 409
Masts, import from Russia, 40
May, isle of, salt found at, 468
May Day Flood, iron works destroyed by, 465
Mayflower, 306, 308; reaches Plymouth (Mass.), 303

Index 499

Meath, county, 347
Media, 41
Mediterranean, 43, 83, 84, 97, 105, 148
Mellinge, Thomas, 109
Mendip Forest, 480
Mendip Hills, lead mines in the, 398
Mendoza, Spanish Ambassador, 83; on the Levant trade, 84, 85
Merlin, ship, 7
Merrick, Sir John, ambassador to Russia, 63, 65
Merrimac, river, 312, 318
Meta Incognita, 77
Michelborne, Sir Edward, 112; his expedition to the East, 98, 99
Middleton, Sir Hugh, his connection with Welsh mining, 401
— Lady, 402
Mine Adventurers' company (1698), 443–58
— — banking company, 451
Mine Royal, right of given to the African Co., 20; definition, 386
Mineral and Battery Works company, 413–29
Mines Royal society or company, 384–405
— company of Wales (? 1620), 401
— — — Cardigan (1670), 403, 404
Mines and minerals, scheme for the employment of paupers in mines, 427; companies dealing with, 383–476
Mines Royal Bill, 427
— company for digging and working, (1693), 441
Mining, progress in England, 384; engines used for draining mines, 479, 480
Minion, ship, 6, 7, 8
Misselden, Edward, 105; defends the East India Co., 185; on the fishing industry, 362
Mississippi Scheme (Law's), 217
Moluccas, 103
Momma, Jacob, wire drawing at Esher, 437
Monmouthshire, iron works established in, 415; production of iron wire in, 417, 418, 421, 423, 426
Monopolies, their advantage and disadvantage in foreign trade, 9; agitation against, 50, 51; report of committee on, 424
Moore, Richard, governor of the Somers Islands, 260, 263
Morris, Peter, his pump on London Bridge, 479
Morton, Earl of, 408
Moscow, 67
Mosquito Islands, settlement of, 327
Mountrath (Queen's Co.), iron works at, 467
Mun, Thomas, 105; his defence of the East India Co., 112; on the fishing trade, 362
Munster, proposal to plant, 338; value of land in, 343; forfeited lands in, 347
Muscovia company (*i.e.* Russia company), 36–69

Muscovia House, 48
Muscovy, *see* Russia
Muslin, 201

Narva, 68; taken by the Russians, 41; sea fight near, 42
Navigation Act, 41
Navy, supply of fish to be purchased from the Fishery society, 364
— Committee, 72; East India Co's loan to, 119
Neal, Capt. Walter, 316
Neale, Thomas, his lead-mining company, 441; scheme for recovering treasure, 488
Neath, smelting at, 397, 449
Negroes, 12, 23
New Caledonia, colony at, 222
Newcastle-on-Tyne, 41, 42; control of local collieries by the municipality 460; held the monopoly of the London supply, 461; its water supply, 481
New England, 301, 318, 326; plantation of, 301; settled by the Puritans, 306–11; fishing trade of, 323
— company, 301–5
Newfoundland company, 317, 318
New France, 318, 320
Newlands, copper found at, 385, 386
New Plymouth company, 298–311
New River, constructed out of the profits of Welsh mining, 401
— company, 231, 254
New Scotland, *see* Nova Scotia
New Scotland company, 317–20
New Spain, 318
New Trades, company of (*i.e.* Russia company), 36–69
Nicaragua, 327
Night Engine company, 479, 483
Nightingale, Luke, 66.
Nonconformists in Holland, 306
Norfolk, drainage of fens in, 352
— Duke of, his shares claimed by Queen Elizabeth, 417
Norris, John, 434
— Sir William, harsh treatment of Old East India Co's council at Surat, 190
North, Captain, expedition to Guiana, 324; committed to the Tower, 325
— Lord, 324
North Foreland, 487
North Pole, 244
North West Passage, company for the discovery of (1576), 76–82
— company for (1612), 100
Northamptonshire, drainage of fens in, 352
Northumberland, salt springs in, 468
— Earl of, his action against the Mines Royal, 385, 386
Nottingham, Earl of, trading monopoly granted to, 10
Nottinghamshire, grant of lands in, 357
Nova Britannia, prospectus of the first Virginia company, 251
Nova Scotia company, 317–20

Noy's fishery association, 369
Nuremberg, cost of calamine at, 416, 417

Obi, river, 76
Ogle's partnership for making saltpetre, 472
Oil, 294
Orange, Prince of, 143
Ordnance, undertakings for the manufacture of, 473
Osborne, Sir Edward, 83, 84
Osmonde iron works, 420
Ostend, interloping expeditions from, 202, 203, 205
Overing's diving-engine company (1692), 484, 487, 488
Overton, Mrs, her loan to the Russia Co., 55, 59

Pagett, Lord, 264
Palm oil, import of, 11
Palmer, Mr, 419
Panama, commercial importance of, 207, 208
Papillon, Thomas, 144, 146, 150, 154, 167
Paris, 229
Parliament, petitions to, 22, 23, 24, 26, 29, 41, 44
Parry, Charles, 434
Patents, abuses of, 13, see also Inventions
Paterson, William, founder of the Bank of England and the Darien company, 207, 208, 209; much esteemed in Scotland, 215; loss of influence, 218, 219
Patna, 197
Paupers, scheme for their employment in mining, 427
Peak, copper found in the, 436
Pearls, import of, 8, 9
Peck, D., agent of the Mine Adventurers, his failure, 453
Pembroke, 2nd Earl of, 415
— 3rd Earl of, 264, 326
— 4th Earl of, his fishery association, 365, 369, 371; petition of, 425
Penkevell, Richard, his expedition, 100
Penrose, silver found at, 397
Pepper, 120; imported from Africa, 4, 11, 12; price raised by the Dutch, 91; export of, 102, 103; heavy duty on, 114; East India Co's. stock bought by Charles I., 116
Pernambuco, taken by Capt. Lancaster, 90
Persia, 41; trade with, 43–6, 49, 51, 54
Persian Voyages, 109, 110, 114
Peterson's mining partnership (1576), 406, 408
Pettus, Sir John, definition of Mine Royal, 386; on the profits of the Welsh mining industry, 401; on the Mines Royal, 403; on the success of the wool-card manufacture, 417; on the decline of the brass manufacture, 425; on the exclusion of foreign wire, 427
Petty, Sir William, surveyor of the forfeited lands in Ireland, 348

Pewterers' Hall, 428
Philip II. of Spain, 89
Philpot Lane, 439
Phipps, Sir William, company for his treasure-seeking expeditions, 484–6
Pierce, John, patents granted to, 309
Pinto, Paulo, 411
Pirates, in the Levant, 85
Piscataqua, river, 315
Pitch, 249
Pitts, Josiah, imprisonment of, 296
Plague, its effect on trade, 97
Plantations, companies for, 241–351
Plate, export of, 93
Plessey coal company, 452, 462
Plymouth, 243, 247, 299, 305
Poland, 40, 83
Pollexfen, on companies, 161
Popham, Sir F., 300
— Sir John, one of the undertakers of the Great Level, 299, 353, 354
Poppler, John, discoverer (with Adrian Gilbert) of the Combs Martin mine, 398
Port de la Plata, treasure found near, 485
Port Nelson River, 232
Port Royal, 319, 320
Porter, Endymion, his privateering enterprize, 112, 113, 119
Portland, Earl of, his fishery association, 369
Portuguese, harass the English traders to Africa, 5, 7, 8; their advantageous position in Africa, 11; their wealth obtained by trading, 36
Post Office, penny post office established by William Dockwra, 437
Potash, manufacture of, 316
Poulet, Lord, censured by the Privy Council, 370
Powell, John, quarrel with the East India Co., 191, 196, 197
Poyntz, Captain, his antimony mining scheme, 475; invention for raising water, 482; patent for raising wrecks, 487
— engine company (1693), 479, 482
Praslin, Duc de, 3
Price, Sir Carbery, 402; his discovery of silver, 404; his silver mines, 440, 443; lawsuit against the Mines Royal, 443; his death, 444
— Charles, and the *Andalusia* seizure, 150
— Lady, petition against, 443
— Sir Richard, 402
— Robert, patent for making saltpetre, 472, 473
Price's lead company, 440
Prideaux, William, ambassador to Russia, 67
Primrose, ship, 4, 5, 6
Privy Council, 10, 15, 44, 57, 70, 71, 76, 87, 88, 91, 92, 94, 96, 115, 139, 152–4, 271, 281, 285, 287, 292, 295, 296, 321, 341, 343, 370, 422, 460
Privy Signet, 322
Providence Island company, 327–38
Pulo Run, 121

Index 501

Pumping engines, 479
Puritans, their settlement in New England, 306-16
Pym, John, 327
Pyndar, Sir Paul, his share in Sir W. Courten's East India association, 113

Quakers, in the East India Co. permitted to affirm, 180
Quakers' lead-mining company, 449
Quebec, capture of, 320
Queen's County, 347

Radisson, a pioneer of the Hudson's Bay Co., 229 and note
Raleigh, city of, 244
— Sir Walter, companies for his voyages to Virginia and Guiana, 244-5, 323, 324
Rats, threatened destruction of crops by, 263, 265
Red Sea, 112, 114
Redbrook (Glos.), copper works at, 434
Red-wood, levy on, 15; rise in price of, 22
Regulated companies, 36, 148
Rent, fluctuation of, 136
Revel, 40
Rich, Sir N., 266, 282; expedition to the Mosquito Islands, 327
— Robert, afterward Earl of Warwick, *see* Warwick
Richmond, wire mill near, 426
Rie, 40
Roberts, Lewes, on the East India trade, 117
Robinson, John, leader of Nonconformists in Holland, 306
— James, 434
Roche's mining partnership (1583), 406, 408, 409
Rochester, Earl of, share assigned to, 464
Rock Salt company (1689), 468, 470
Rovenzon's iron-smelting company, 463, 464
Row Pits (Mendip), pumping engine at, 480
Royal Fishery Revived, 373
Royal Trade of Fishing, 372
Rupert, Prince, seizes vessels of the Guinea company, 16; governor of an African company, 17; association with the Hudson's Bay Co., 229, 230; governor of the Mines Royal, 403; account of, 428 note; interest in a diving engine, 484
Russel, Thomas, invention for making saltpetre, 472
— Sir William, 354, 411
Russia, 104; trade to, 36; trade affected by its unsettled condition, 65
Russia, company for importing tobacco into (1898), 162
Russia company, 36-69
Rycaut, Sir Peter, 222
Ryswick, treaty of, 233

Sackville, Sir Edward, 284, 285; governor of the Somers Islands Co., 280

Sagadahoc, river, settlement established at the, 299
St Catherina, island, *see* Providence
St Christopher, the planting of, 326
St Domingo, Drake's adventure to, 418
St Estienne, Claude, 319
St George's, 295
St Ives, mining at, 397
St John, ship, 12
St John and Company (1618), 8, 11-14, 16
St John's, Newfoundland, 243
St Just, mining at, 397
St Kitts, its plantation, 326
St Lawrence, river, 318, 320
St Nicholas Bay, 41
St Thomas, governor of, 16
Sales by inch of candle, 22
Sallee, 17, 20
Salt, monopoly of the manufacture, 314; companies for the supply of, 468-70; how and where produced, 468, 469; salt pans at Shields, 469; effect of monopoly on production, 470; Scottish competition, 470
Salt Makers, society of, 468, 469
Salters, corporation of, 468, 469
Saltpetre, 160; companies for producing, 471-4; how made, 471, 472; chiefly supplied by the East India Co., 472
San Filipe, capture of, 20
Sandys, Sir Edwin, 110, 164, 275, 281; opposition to Sir Thos. Smythe, 106, 107; succeeds him as treasurer of the Virginia Co., 257; quarrel with Sir Thos. Smythe, 267-9, 271, 273; antagonism of James I., 272; his blow at the Somers Islands Co., 274, 275; secures control of both companies, 275; gratuity paid to, 278; confined to his house for contempt, 284
— George, 267
— Sir M., 354
— Thomas, sued by the East India Co., 148, 149
Santa Clara, Spanish vessel taken by the Mosquito Islands Co., 335, 336
Sassafras, 248
Savery, Thomas, his steam-engine for raising water, 480, 481
Scilly Isles, 487
Scotland, enthusiasm for the Darien scheme in, 207, 216; failure of harvests in, 221; union with England, 222, 223; land forfeitures in, 351; its share in the Fishery society, 363-5; gold and silver mining in, 384, 406; copper mining in, 431; salt production in, 470
Scottish African company, 207-27
— East India company, 207-27
— East India and Greenland company, 55, 104
— Guinea company, 16
— Parliament, 211, 223, 364, 377, 431
Sea-coal, definition, 459
Sea's Magazine Opened, treatise on the fisheries, 372
Sebastian, King of Portugal, 6

Secret service money, outlay by East India Co., 160
Seething Lane, 195
Senegal, 10, 11, 13, 14
Senegal company (1588), 10
Seymour, Edward, 21
Shaftesbury, Earl of, 231
Shannon, river, 346
"Shares" of New East India Co., 171; origin of, 182, 185-7; difficulties in settling the claims of holders, 187, 195, 196
Sheen, iron-wire mill at, 426
Shepherd, Samuel, a large subscriber to the East India Co., 180; suspends payment, 185
Shields, production of salt at, 468, 469; effect of salt monopoly on, 470
Shiers, William, secretary of the Mine Adventurers, 450; condemned by the House of Commons, 455
Shrewsbury, Earl of, his adventure in Courten's syndicate, 113
Sierra Leone, 16, 82
Silk industry, opposed to the East India Co., 135
Silver, 23, 323, 335, 336; import of, 9; for private trade shipped in East India Co.'s vessels, 192, 193; mined in Scotland, 384, 406; in Cumberland and Westmoreland, 385; price of, 392; mine at Combe Martin, 395; mining in Wales, 401-4, 442; in Ireland, 411, 412; production of, 427; obtained from lead ore, 440; salved by Sir W. Phipps, 485
"Silver Mine," in County Kilkenny, 412
Skeen (Meath), 349
Skinner incident, 150
Slave trade, 10, 15; first mention of, 4; its commencement and effect on ordinary trade, 8, 9; increased price of slaves, 24
Smartfoot, Francis, invention for raising ships, 487
Smerthwicke, Thomas, his opposition to the East India Co., 109, 110, 115
Smith, Fabian, ambassador to Russia, 65
— John, treatise on fisheries, 372
— Capt. John, 268, 301; on the New Plymouth Adventurers, 310, 311
— Thomas, see Smythe
Smuggling, India goods taken to Ostend, 203, 204
Smythe, Sir Richard, suit against Hammersly, 59, 60
— Thomas, collector of customs, his mining undertaking, 395
— Sir Thomas, 52, 57-60, 91, 92, 250, 251, 263, 275, 286, 287; his quarrel with Sandys, 106, 107, 273; resigns the treasurership, 257, 258; governor of the Somers Islands Co., 262; quarrel with the Earl of Warwick, 266-9, 278, 279; gratuities paid to, 278; elected governor, 285, 216; his death, 290
Smythe's Hundred, 257

Soap, manufacture of, 53; relation to the Greenland trade, 71
Soap-ashes, 249
Soapmakers of Westminster, 469
Society for Christian Knowledge in Foreign Parts, 194
Solemn League and Covenant, 216
Somers, Sir George, shipwrecked in the Bermudas, 259, 260
Somers Islands company, 259-97
— Magazine company, 264, 290, 292
— whale fishing company, 294
Somersetshire, calamine found in, 414
Sommer's Quay, 375
South Sea company, 194, 204, 205, 217, 435
Southampton, merchants of in the African trade, 3
— Earl of, 264, 279, 281; his Virginia expedition, 246; chosen treasurer of the Virginia Co., 272; at the court meeting of the Somers Islands Co., 274; returned governor of the Somers Islands Co., 275
Southwell, Captain, 267
Spain, 8; jealous of the West Indian slave trade, 9; wealth acquired by trading, 36; opposition to English trade, 83, 85; war with, 85; Portugal absorbed by, 89; opposition to the Darien Co., 219, 221; claims territory occupied by the company, 219, 221; hostility to the Guiana expedition, 324; Spanish ships taken by the Dutch, 334
Spanish Armada, 90
Spice Islands, 103
Spices, import of, 12; brought from Lisbon, 89; fall in prices, 103
Spitzbergen, 71; Dutch whalers driven from, 362; see also Greenland
Spruson —, a supporter of Sandys in the Virginia Co., 109
Spydell, Sebastian, 384
Staffordshire, salt springs in, 468
Stapleton —, his undertaking for manufacture of ordnance, 473
Star Chamber, 341
Stationers' Hall, lottery drawn at, 445
Staunton, Robert, loss on his Irish land investment, 349
Steinberg, Marcus, 399
Stephens, Thomas, his communication from India, 89
Steynbergh, John, his mining operations, 384
Stirling, Lord, expedition to Nova Scotia, 318; his mining partnership, 406, 411
Stornoway, 369; fishing vessels driven ashore at, 370
Strada, Octavius de, patent for draining mines, 479
Stringer, Moses, scheme for employing paupers in mining, 427
Sturtevant's iron-smelting undertaking, 463, 464
Sucking-worm Engine company (1689), 479, 481

Suffolk, drainage of fens in, 352
Suffolk, Earl of, his mining ventures, 399, 401, 402; petition of, 443
Sugar, 323; import of, 3; plantations in the West Indies, 15
Sultan, concession from, 83
Summer Islands, *see* Somers Islands
Surat, 119; factory at, 103; factors imprisoned at, 114; rivalry of the two companies at, 190; officials censured, 197
Sussex, Earl of, proposes a plantation in Ireland, 338
Sutherlandshire, silver found in, 411
Swally, 119
Sweden, African traders harassed by Swedes, 16; copper from, 431
Swift, Richard, 52 note, 63
Sword Blade company, 452

Talabant, disused mine at, 402
Tallow, export from Russia, 40
Tapoywasooze, in Guiana, 326
Tar, 249
Taunton, 11
Temple Brass Mills company, 428 note
Terentius Varro, 155
Terminable stocks, 96, 97
Terrington, Sir Thomas, 354
Thames, river, 223
Thames Street, 195; fire in, 481
Thieves, engine for the prevention of, 483
Thomas, Sir Arthur, his Lincolnshire draining scheme, 357
Three Cranes, Billingsgate, herring adventure sold at, 375
Thurland, Thomas, his mining operations, 384, 385
Timber, 248, 249
Tin, production of, 475
Tintern, wire works at, 422, 423
Tipper, Robert, his drainage scheme, 356, 357
Tipperary, 347
Tobacco, 323, 326, 335; experimental consignment from Virginia, 255; shipped from the Somers Islands, 262, 263, 265; planting forbidden in England, 273; amount imported from Spain and Virginia, 276, 282; companies for the trade in, 282; the tobacco monopoly, 13, 274, 276, 282, 283, 291
Tobago, island of, 326, 475
Topp, Sir John, search for calamine, 428
Tortuga company (1631), 329, 333, 335
Tower of London, 448
Tower Street, 195
Towyse-yarrowes, in Guiana, 326
Trade and Fishing of Great Britain Displayed, 372
Trade's Increase, tract opposed to East India Co., 102, 103
Trade's Increase, East Indiaman burnt at Bantam, 102
Train oil, import of, 40, 49, 53; threatened famine of, 74
Treasure, recovery of, from wrecks, 484-9

Treasurer, ship, incident concerning, 271
Treworthie, mine at, 396; flooded, 397
Trinidad, 70, 326
Tripp, John, brass undertaking by, 426
Trott, Perient, conflict with the Somers Islands Co., 294, 295
Tucker, Daniel, governor of the Somers Islands, 263, 265-7
Turkey, 85, 86
Tyrone, planting of, 339
Tyrone's Rebellion, 338
Tyzack, John, his lead-mining Co., 441; Co. for his diving apparatus, 487

Ulster, plantation in, 338; value of land in, 343, 350; forfeited lands in, 347
United Mines company, 458
Usher, Joshua, his pumping engine, 479
Utrecht, treaty of, 234

Varro, Terentius, 155
Vasilowich, Ivan, favourable to the Russian Co., 37
Vassell & Company (1849), African traders, 15
Vaughan, Dr, failure of his Newfoundland expedition, 316
Venezuela, 329
Venice, difficulties of English merchants at, 83, 85; jealousy of English traders, 85
Venner, Capt., 90
Vermuyden, Cornelius, employed in drainage works, 354; loan to Charles I., 357; his drainage invention, 480
Vernatti, Sir Philibert, his patent for smelting iron, 466
Vernatty, Constantine, smelting invention, 441, 442
Vernon, Sir William, on the Darien settlement, 220
Victory, ship, an interloper from Ostend, 202
Virginia, the "First" company, 246-59, 267-89
— the "Second" company, 299-301
— Old Magazine company, 256, 270, 287-90
— New Magazine company, 270, 289
— Magazine company for apparel, 276, 288
— other subsidiary companies, 288, 289
Virginiola, proposed name for the Bermudas, 260
Vois, *see* De Vois

Wales, mining in, 384, 395, 400-4, 422, 443
— Henry, Prince of, shares assigned to, 464
— George Augustus, Prince of (afterwards George II.), petition to, 202
Waller, William, manager of the Mine Adventurers, 446, 448; his quarrel with Mackworth leads to exposure, 450, 451; blamed for mismanagement, 453, 454
Wallis, John, selected as governor of the Mine Adventurers, 457

Walrus, its trade value, 49
Wanloch, lead mines at, 410
Warr, Lord de la, his expedition to Virginia, 251
Warwick, Ambrose Dudley, Earl of, 76
— Robert Richard, afterwards Earl of, 264, 266; quarrel with Sir Thomas Smythe, 266-9, 278, 279; his method of securing votes, 280; governor of the Somers Islands Co., 290; his death, 293
Water supply, engines for, 479, 480
Waterford, county, 347
— town, iron shipped from, 467
Watts, John, his privateering expedition, 90, 97
Wax, import of, 12; export from Russia, 40, 41
Wayne, Gabriel, invention for refining copper, 430
Wear, river, 460
Wednesbury, iron furnaces at, 466
Welsh copper company (1694), 436-9
West Indies, sale of slaves in, 8, 9; development of sugar plantations, 15; increased price of slaves, 24; colonization of, 323; success of the Dutch in, 327
Westmeath, 347
Westmoreland, mining in, 384, 385, 400
Weston, Thomas, 309
— Richard, Lord, afterwards Earl of Portland, see Portland
Weymouth, Capt. George, his voyage to America, 246
Whaling, 69-75, 104, 294, 361, 373; the Russia Co. commences whaling, 53, 54; expedition dispersed by the Dutch, 56; a new company formed, 58; Somers Islands Co. begin whaling, 263; Dutch whalers driven from Spitzbergen, 362; Greenland company formed, 379
White, Samuel, his losses, 150
— William, 294
Whitwell's whaling partnership, 74
William III., 75, 167, 168, 209; his association with the East India Co., 152, 155, 156; presentation to by the company, 157; discouragement of the Darien company, 220, 221
Williams, John, diving-engine company, 484, 487
— Joseph, diving-engine company, 484, 487
Willson, Beccles, on the Hudson's Bay company, 230

Wimball, Samuel, his diving engine, 488
Wimbledon, copper mill at, 434
Windebank, his share in Sir W. Courten's syndicate, 113
Wine, import from Candia, 86
Winster, copper mine at, 436
Wire, manufacture of, 413-15, 419; works at Tintern, 422; monopoly of its manufacture, 424; importation prohibited, 425-7; mill at Sheen, 426; price of, 425, 426
Wolstenholme, Sir John, 269
Woodall, —, censure of, 273
Wood's mining partnership, 438
Wool-cards, importation of, 413; manufacture of, 417, 418, 423; factory at Leith, 427; importation prohibited, 423, 424, 426
Woollen industry, 161; export of woollen goods, 11, 136, 137; opposition to the East India company, 135; lack of prosperity, 136
Worcestershire, mining in, 384, 400; salt springs in, 468
Worsley, Sir R., elected governor of the Mine Adventurers, 457
Wrecks, recovery of treasure from, 484-9
Wright, N., 71
Wriothesley, see Southampton, Earl of
Wrote, Samuel, on the salaries of the officials of the Virginia Co., 281-3
Wroth, Sir Thomas, challenges the accuracy of the minutes of the Virginia company, 273

Yarmouth, 71; its early importance in the fishing industry, 300
Yarnold, John, his engine for draining mines, 481
Yeardley, Sir George, 270
York and Hull whaling company, 74
York, merchants of, 70
— proposed city in America, 304
— Charles, Duke of, afterwards Charles I., shares assigned to, 464
— James, Duke of, afterwards James II., governor of the African Co., 21; presentation to, 130; his share in the East India company, 148
Yorkshire, drainage works in, 357; mining in, 384, 400; alum found in, 475

Zealanders, attack on whalers, 56
Zinc ore, 413, see also Calamine

Milton Keynes UK
Ingram Content Group UK Ltd.
UKHW010152040424
440506UK00019B/1063